Thinking in Writing

W9-BQS-912

Thinking in Writing

Third Edition

Donald McQuade
University of California, Berkeley

Robert Atwan
Seton Hall University

McGraw-Hill, Inc.
New York St. Louis San Francisco Auckland Bogotá
Caracas Lisbon London Madrid Mexico City Milan
Montreal New Delhi San Juan Singapore
Sydney Tokyo Toronto

This book is printed on acid-free paper.

Photo credits (in-text, black and white):

p. 70 The Louvre Museum, Paris
p. 73: (top) Courtesy, New York Historical Society, New York City. (bottom) Library of Congress
p. 117: (top) Newark Public Library, Newark, New Jersey. (bottom) Library of Congress

Other copyright acknowledgments appear on pages 579–583

THINKING IN WRITING

Third Edition
5 6 7 8 9 0 DOC/DOC 9 9 8 7 6 5

Copyright © 1988, 1983, 1980 by McGraw-Hill, Inc. All rights reserved. Printed in the United States of America. Except as permitted under the United States Copyright Act of 1976, no part of this publication may be reproduced or distributed in any form or by any means, or stored in a data base or retrieval system, without the prior written permission of the publisher.

Library of Congress Cataloging-in-Publication Data
Thinking in writing.

Includes index.
1. College readers. I. McQuade, Donald
II. Atwan, Robert. III. title.
PE1417.T478 1988 808′.042 87-23348
ISBN 0-07-554637-X

Cover painting: Milton Avery, "Two Figures at Desk," 1944. Collection of Neuberger Museum, State University of New York at Purchase, gift of Roy R. Neuberger.

Cover design by: Sandra Josephson

FOR

Max Anthony Maxwell

Preface

Thinking in Writing, Third Edition, is designed to help students overcome two of the most frustrating obstacles to effective and productive writing: getting ideas and developing them. Writing instructors have long noted that a major part of their students' difficulties with composition derives from these two problems. Students often complain that it takes them an unendurably long time to think of "something to say" so that they can begin writing and that once they've finally begun they discouragingly "run out of things to say" very quickly. For many students, then, the act of writing becomes a physically and mentally exhausting cycle of getting started and getting stuck.

This book—through its methods and models—offers a practical approach to the ever-difficult task of finding ideas and developing them in composition. A large part of the problem we all face in trying to write fluently and intelligently is not how we think or how we write but rather how we handle the continuous interplay between both activities while composing. If our tendency is to wait patiently for ideas to come to us fully expressed and "paper ready," we will sooner or later come to view composition as a kind of mental torture. We may never get started. On the other hand, if our tendency is to slap down whatever ideas come into our heads without paying attention to the structural patterns that can be generated from them, our compositions will always remain haphazard and undeveloped—a mental torture to our readers.

Clearly, if we're the type of person who likes to see solid results after spending a reasonable amount of time at our desk writing, we need to become conscious of how the interaction of thinking and writing can remarkably improve our motivation and momentum. We need to learn how we can extend and develop our ideas by seeing how small segments of writing contain the germ of larger organizational units. We need to see how a thought pattern can lead to an essay structure, how single words and metaphors can sometimes shape an entire piece of writing. And, most importantly, we need to trust our own intelligence; we need to relax into our own eloquence.

The main instructional principle of this book can be stated quite simply: we think most rigorously and productively when we make the effort to put our thoughts down in writing, and we write most fluently and maturely when we recognize the underlying patterns of our thinking. In the chapters that follow, thinking and writing will be considered as interrelated mental processes that stimulate and reinforce each other. So closely intertwined are these two indispensable human activities that the writer and educator Carlos Baker claims quite simply: "Learning to write is learning to think."

In one respect, this book runs counter to a deeply rooted idea about the relationship between thought and language. We are accustomed to consider thinking as a kind of internalized, preparatory activity and writing as its external, finished expression. Our very language constantly reinforces this venerable notion; we speak quite casually of "expressing an idea" or "putting our thoughts into words." The assumption, of course, is that our thoughts and ideas truly exist in some formidable fashion *before* they exist in words. This may be so. But the question we should be in the habit of asking ourselves when we write is: Do we really know what we want to say before we actually say it? That is one of the tough, basic questions that pertains to the contemporary study of rhetoric and it is one that has fairly recently begun to occupy the attention of psycholinguists and other theorists whose concern is primarily with the deep connections between mental and verbal behavior. For the purposes of this book, however, we want to encourage writers to consider this question from a practical point of view. What are the benefits of working as though thinking were not a preparatory activity but rather one that can and does proceed *simultaneously* with writing? In other words, what are the benefits of learning to do our thinking *in* writing? In this respect, consider the wisdom of Gertrude Stein's advice on trying to make meaning in composition: "You will write if you will write without thinking of the results in terms of a result, but think of the writing in terms of discovery, which is to say that creation must take place between the pen and the paper, not before in a thought or afterwards in a recasting. Yes, before in a thought, but not in careful thinking." The instructional design of *Thinking in Writing,* especially in the early sections, will help students explore both the potential of thinking in writing as well as the practical benefits to be gained by focusing their attention on the interaction between what is going on in their heads and what is happening on paper.

Obviously, anyone who tries to think about thinking is on shaky ground. Though human beings have been having thoughts for presumably well over two million years, no one really knows for certain exactly what thinking is. This book does not intend to come up with a solution to that ultimate philosophical problem. But just as we can ride a bicycle without being able to say exactly how we do it, so too we can think—and sometimes do so incessantly—without knowing precisely how it happens. Throughout this book, thinking will be considered not in an abstract, theoretical fashion but in a concrete, operational way. It will also be regarded as a wide-ranging mental activity that includes far more than the power of logical reasoning. To be sure, reasoning is one of the principal types of thinking (it will be treated at some length in the section entitled "Argument") and is usually what we first think of when we think about thinking. Yet cognitive behavior encompasses a broad spectrum of activities. Surely we are thinking when we discover interrelations between dissimilar ideas; when we find resemblances in seemingly disparate things; when we perceive sequential arrangements; when we move back and forth between our observations and inferences or between the abstract and the concrete, the general and the specific; when we recognize similar ideas within different contexts; when we sift relevant points from extraneous material, and so on. Quite clearly, our capacity to think involves many different operations, just as does our ability to walk, see, or feel.

Thinking in Writing responds to both the growing concern for the mental development of college students and the professional need to combine a systematic introduction to rhetoric with the actualities of the writing process. The book demonstrates in accessible language how familiar rhetorical structures can stimulate the production of thoughts to the point where they will do us the most good—as words on paper. From there, once we can see, read, and rethink our thoughts, we will find ourselves in a position to use the structures and strategies that will help us shape and extend those thoughts into coherent essays. The book's organization represents a traditional approach to rhetoric, placed within the context of some of the most distinguished theoretical and practical work done in the fields of composition and cognitive studies. In this respect, the particular arrangement of material in *Thinking in Writing* continuously highlights the interconnectedness—in fact, the simultaneity—of thinking and writing. This overriding interest in the relation of rhetoric to the overlapping processes of thinking and writing is apparent in the scope of the book and helps determine the distinctive order of the following sections.

Generating Ideas. This section tackles the fundamental problems of getting our thinking and writing started and reminds writers of the opportunities various types of informal and fragmentary prose can offer. While all the selections in the book are meant to activate thinking and writing, those in the first two chapters, on *"Exploring Key Words"* and *"Making Metaphors,"* focus on words as the center of composition. Working with the denotations and connotations of individual key words and trying out metaphors represent two practical procedures for generating ideas and getting preliminary thoughts about a subject down on paper where they can start working for us.

Shaping Ideas. This section features two basic patterns of thinking that help shape ideas and make writing possible—the intellectual rhythms of *observation and inference, abstract and concrete.* An understanding of these primary mental operations can help writers establish a controlling idea about a subject and prepare the way for more extended compositions.

Developing Sequences. Writers frequently develop ideas by tracking our familiar patterns of thinking that depend on spatial, temporal, and causal sequences. What follows what, Where? When? How? and Why? These are instinctive human concerns that appear to have an underlying basis in thinking and language. This section shows how *description, narration, process analysis,* and *cause and effect* function in the production and arrangement of our thoughts and compositions.

Clarifying Ideas. Clarity and distinctness—these are two rock-bottom criteria by which people have always judged the effectiveness of thought. In this section, we examine the mental and rhetorical workings of *definition, classification,* and *illustration.* Mastery of these mental processes will help us avoid vagueness and confusion; their skillful rhetorical management will help us refine our ideas and arrange them into the larger structures of paragraphs and essays.

Discovering Resemblances. According to Jacob Bronowski, "the discoveries of science, the works of art are explorations—more, are explosions—of a hidden likeness." This section concentrates on how mapping our resemblances through *comparison and contrast* as well as *analogy* can stimulate our thinking and immeasurably extend the context of our ideas. These two procedures can help us move beyond the initially perceived limits of our thinking and supply us with larger structures in and through which we can make unexpected connections, uncover differences, and explore similarities.

Making Claims. As speakers and writers, we are continually making claims, some of which we back up with inductive and deductive reasoning and some of which we support with ethical, emotional, or authoritative appeals. In this section, the rhetorical procedures of *argument* and *persuasion* are examined separately in order to show the different types of logical reasoning involved in each and the organizational strategies commonly used to gain an audience's assent and consent.

The organization of *Thinking in Writing* has been designed to allow composition classes to cover traditional rhetorical territory, to concentrate on the interaction of thinking and writing, and to try out some well-tested methods for getting thoughts started and essays launched. Yet, because instruction necessarily proceeds sequentially, it is difficult to reflect the simultaneous, overlapping nature of various cognitive and rhetorical skills. Obviously, each category and procedure included in the following sections deserves to be studied and practiced both in isolation and in conjunction with other categories and procedures—most especially with a good deal of healthy attention to rethinking and rewriting what we want to say. Aside from the first two sections, the book's organization is not intended to reflect any *necessary* sequence of rhetorical modes and strategies. The book's organization does offer, however, a reasonable instructional order based on expected difficulty, the level of cognitive ability required, and the syllabi of many introductory composition courses.

To accomplish its instructional purposes, *Thinking in Writing* contains the following main features:

- An accessible blend of classic and contemporary selections that represent an appealing cross-disciplinary spread and that are arranged within each section according to length and increasing complexity
- Fifteen detailed, "how-to" introductions that provide thorough coverage of basic rhetorical and compositional procedures
- Sets of discussion questions for each selection that build in increasing difficulty and place specific reading skills and responses in the context of thinking and writing
- A set of "Additional Rhetorical Strategies" for nearly every selection—designed to highlight the realistic mixture of rhetorical forms that marks most good writing
- A convenient glossary that defines the critical terms most commonly used to discuss writing styles and strategies

In addition, prior to each selection, an informative headnote supplies significant biographical details and directs attention to relevant compositional elements.

To underscore the practical, realistic purposes of *Thinking in Writing,* we have added another rhetorical feature to this new edition. Each rhetorical section is introduced by a selection from Lewis Thomas, the celebrated American physician and essayist. Our intention is to show students that writers are not characterized by a single dominant rhetorical mode but are able to adopt different organizational strategies from essay to essay. Since such rhetorical changes are expected of students in most writing courses, we thought it only fair that they have an opportunity to observe a single writer moving from one form to another. To make the selections more useful, each Lewis Thomas essay is preceded by a brief consideration of his rhetorical goals and is followed by a longer, paragraph-by-paragraph discussion of how those goals are achieved. We trust that such "hands on" coverage of one writer's methods will help bridge the instructional gap that usually exists between a section introduction's discussion of a rhetorical form and the several readings that illustrate it.

This book will have succeeded if students view clear-headed thinking and effective writing as far more manageable, more "doable" activities than they may now be inclined to consider them. Thinking, after all, is a basic need—"reason's need," the philosopher Hannah Arendt calls it. And writing, too, is a need—a powerful social and professional one. Neither activity should feel particularly strange to anyone; we use practically all of the rhetorical procedures discussed and demonstrated in this book in our "off-duty" language every day. To be sure, learning to write well requires the conscious mastery of these time-honored rules and procedures. That is an educational fact that nearly everyone who wants to learn how to write must face up to. But the act of writing doesn't begin with the mastery of basic compositional skills. It begins, quite simply, with something far more fundamental and broadly human: the stubborn itch to think for ourselves and the corresponding urge to say something that means something.

Donald McQuade

Robert Atwan

Acknowledgments

As was the case with the previous editions of *Thinking in Writing,* our work on this revision has benefited greatly from the solid advice and generous encouragement of our colleagues across the country. We would especially like to acknowledge the extensive, incisive, and judicious reviews of Bonnie Barthold of Western Washington University, John Brereton of the University of Massachusetts, Boston, Santi Buscemi of Middlesex County College, Robert Dunn of St. Joseph's University, George Kennedy of Washington State University, Elizabeth Metzger of the University of South Florida, Carol Reeves of Norwalk Community College, and Margaret Urie of the University of Nevada, Reno.

We would also like to thank the following colleagues for their careful readings and useful suggestions: David Bartholomae, University of Pittsburgh; Joseph Boles, Northern Arizona University; Terry Engebretsen, Iowa State University; Lester Faigley, University of Texas at Austin; John Fleming, West Valley College; Stephen Gurney, Bemidji State University; Robert Keefe, University of Massachusetts, Amherst; D.G. Kehl, Arizona State University; George Miller, University of Delaware; William Miller, Diablo Valley College; and Betty Park, Bucks County Community College.

Many friends and colleagues have had—and continue to have—considerable influence on the shape of *Thinking in Writing,* and we are grateful to them as well. Among them are: Trudy Baltz, William Berry, Janet Brown, Ken Bruffee, Frank D'Angelo, Rosemary

Deen, David Follmer, Richard Garretson, Lynn Goldberg, the late Betsy Kaufman, Richard Larson, Robert Lyons, Elaine Maimon, Gerard McCauley, Christine Pellicano, Marie Ponsot, David Rothberg, Sharon Shaloo, Sandra Schor, the late Mina Shaughnessy, Nancy Sommers, David Spiedel, Rockwell Stensrud, Liz Stern, Ruth Stern, Judith Summerfield, William Vesterman, Harvey Wiener, as well as John Jameson and John Walker.

We would also like to acknowledge the many people at Alfred A. Knopf who have contributed to the success of *Thinking in Writing,* especially Seibert Adams, June Smith, the people in production, and the many college representatives. Steve Pensinger has been an exemplary editor in every respect, and we are grateful for his many thoughtful contributions to the project as well as his resolute confidence. Beena Kamlani has managed the revision with great skill and intelligence. An outstanding copyeditor, she has skillfully and variously strengthened *Thinking in Writing* with her fine judgment and quiet efficiency.

David Elderbrock, Richard Mikita and Christopher Motley brought inestimable intelligence, imagination, and energy to this project. Sarah Hubbard, Frank Lortscher, Jane Jubilee, and Jack Roberts contributed first-rate research and editorial assistance. We believe that *Resources for Thinking in Writing,* prepared by Christopher Motley and Marlene Mollinoff in earlier editions and by David Elderbrock in this edition, is itself an outstanding piece of criticism and an invaluable pedagogical aid for helping students to think in writing more effectively.

Susanne McQuade and Helene Atwan have continued most generously to take time from their own busy lives to help us out. Thanks, too, to Christine and Marc McQuade as well as Gregory Atwan for their patience. Finally, though it may seem odd, we would like to thank each other—for helping to maintain the strength of friendship throughout yet another collaboration.

Contents

An insert of color photographs can be found between pages 74 and 75.

Preface *vii*

Acknowledgments *xv*

Part 1 Generating Ideas 1

EXPLORING KEY WORDS *1*

Simone de Beauvoir Woman *6*

Langston Hughes That Word *Black* *8*

Russell Baker Life Can Be Hard *11*

Betty Edwards Left and Right *15*

Terence McLaughlin Dirt *17*

MAKING METAPHORS *21*

George Lakoff and Mark Johnson Metaphors We Live By *29*

D. H. Lawrence The Emotional Mind *35*

Calvin Trillin Rural Literalism 36

Edward Hoagland Gramercy Gym 40

Michael Anania Starting 43

Part 2 Shaping Ideas 47

OBSERVATION AND INFERENCE 47

Annie Dillard Dumbstruck 52

Mary Gordon More Than Just a Shrine: Paying Homage to the Ghosts of Ellis Island 55

Mary Leakey Footprints in the Ashes of Time 62

John Canaday The Bellelli Family 68

ABSTRACT AND CONCRETE 75

Joan Didion On Morality 80

Nikki Giovanni Knoxville Revisited 83

Helen Keller A World of Impressions 86

Ellen Goodman The "Sixties Kid" 89

Irene Oppenheim On Waitressing 93

Part 3 Developing Sequences 103

DESCRIPTION 103

❧ *Lewis Thomas* Ponds 109

Nathaniel Hawthorne and Edward Dicey On Abraham Lincoln 113

Sir Frederick Treves The Elephant Man 118

John Muir Yosemite Falls 122

Virginia Woolf The Death of the Moth *125*

E. B. White The Ring of Time *129*

Gretel Ehrlich The Solace of Open Spaces *135*

NARRATION *149*

❧ *Lewis Thomas* Amity Street *156*

Maxine Hong Kingston The Wild Man of the Green Swamp *164*

Marsha Rabe Passages *167*

Neil Bell In the Dark *170*

Frederick Douglass How a Slave Was Made a Man *174*

George Orwell A Hanging *181*

PROCESS ANALYSIS *188*

❧ *Lewis Thomas* On Transcendental Metaworry *193*

Kurt Vonnegut How to Write with Style *197*

Ernest Hemingway When You Camp Out, Do It Right *202*

John McPhee The Birch-Bark Canoe *208*

Alan Devoe The Hibernation of the Woodchuck *217*

Rachel Carson The Grey Beginnings *220*

CAUSE AND EFFECT *231*

❧ *Lewis Thomas* On Magic in Medicine *236*

Barry Commoner Three Mile Island *241*

Anne Hollander Why It's Fashionable to Be Thin *245*

Sheila Tobias Who's Afraid of Math, and Why? *249*

Sir Frederick Hoyle The Next Ice Age *256*

Part 4 Clarifying Ideas 265

DEFINITION *265*

❧ *Lewis Thomas* Alchemy *270*

Charles Dickens What Is a Horse? *275*

Thomas Sowell We're Not Really "Equal" *279*

Bruno Bettelheim The Holocaust *283*

Karen Horney Fear and Anxiety *288*

Peter Homans The Western: The Legend and the Cardboard Hero *291*

Ralph Ellison Hidden Name and Complex Fate *298*

CLASSIFICATION *305*

❧ *Lewis Thomas* Notes on Punctuation *310*

Larry McMurtry Drinking in Houston *313*

Susan Allen Toth Cinematypes *316*

Donald Hall Four Kinds of Reading *321*

Sissela Bok The Need for Secrecy *326*

ILLUSTRATION *335*

❧ *Lewis Thomas* Death in the Open *339*

Ralph Linton One Hundred Per Cent American *342*

Roy Blount, Jr. Winning: Why We Keep Score *346*

Joyce Maynard I Remember . . . *354*

Ruth Schwartz Cowan Less Work for Mother? *360*

Part 5 Discovering Resemblances 375

COMPARISON AND CONTRAST *375*

❧ *Lewis Thomas* The Tucson Zoo *382*

Aristotle Youth and Old Age *385*

Tom Wolfe Columbus and the Moon *389*

Jack Newfield Stallone vs. Springsteen *394*

Marie Winn Television and Reading *404*

John Mack Faragher Pioneer Diaries of Women and Men *412*

Susan Sontag A Rhetoric of Disease *419*

ANALOGY *428*

❧ *Lewis Thomas* The Attic of the Brain *432*

Plato Allegory of the Cave *436*

Mark Twain Reading the River *443*

William Humphrey The Salmon Instinct *447*

Michael Arlen Prufrock Aloft; Prufrock Before the Television Set *451*

Part 6 Making Claims 459

ARGUMENT *459*

❧ *Lewis Thomas* The Hazards of Science *468*

Jeffrey L. Pasley The Idiocy of Rural Life *476*

Henry Fairlie The Idiocy of Urban Life *485*

Adam Smith Fifty Million Handguns *495*

Henry A. Selib The Case Against More Laws *503*

PERSUASION *509*

Lewis Thomas Late Night Thoughts on Listening to Mahler's Ninth Symphony *515*

Advertisement "Stop Handguns Before They Stop You" *520*

Advertisement "In the U.S., Crime Pays Because Criminals Don't!" *521*

Mike Royko A Faceless Man's Plea *523*

H. L. Mencken Why Nobody Loves a Politician *527*

Barry Lopez The Passing Wisdom of Birds *534*

Frances D. Gage Sojourner Truth: And A'n't I a Woman? *546*

Adrienne Rich Claiming an Education *551*

Glossary *558*
An Alternate Table of Contents *567*
Contents, Alphabetical by Author *576*
Copyright Acknowledgments *579*

1. GENERATING IDEAS

Exploring Key Words

1 No matter what we are going to write about—whether our subject is required or inspired—we begin with words. Though this may sound fairly obvious, we often forget just how important a part words play in the way we perceive a subject, in the way we generate ideas about a subject, and in the way we continue to think about that subject throughout each stage of composition. Words are not simply handy building-blocks to be fitted into their proper places. They are, rather, powerful activators that continuously shape and reshape our thinking and writing.

2 In any composition, certain terms will be worked harder than others. These are the ones that help carry our composition from the exploratory phase, through to its starting point, and on to revision and completion. They are the words—simple or complex, idiomatic or formal—that trigger our thoughts about a subject and help give our initial ideas solidity and purpose. As we begin to consider a subject, any subject, we necessarily start to encounter all sorts of words. These may be, as they frequently are, the given words of an assigned topic ("Discuss your attitude toward capital punishment"); or words that form in our minds as we randomly imagine various subjects we might write about ("the neighborhood I grew up in," "a teacher who has meant a great deal to me"); or words that spontaneously pop up as we jot down notes in a diary or journal ("Why did I find the film tonight so depressing?"). Whatever we want to write about, no matter how visual or nonverbal it seems at first, words will

automatically attach themselves to our subject and become inseparable from our thinking about it.

3 Thinking carefully about words can be especially helpful in the difficult, formative stages of composition—getting a line on our subject and getting started. The subjects that come to us at first, even those we're assigned, are usually too general and unwieldy for the practical purposes of composition. Before we can start writing about them, we need to bring them down to manageable proportions and find some point or points of entry. Though many of the rhetorical strategies discussed in the following chapters can help us isolate a subject and start writing about it, a more fundamental way to begin is simply to identify certain words and take our lead from their definitions and associations. We can do this by paying attention to two types of meaning—**denotative** and **connotative**.

4 The denotative value of a word is its primary dictionary definition—what Fowler's *Dictionary of Modern English Usage* calls "its barest adequate definition." Its connotative value, on the other hand, includes the word's entire range of public and private associations. Imagine words as tiny solar systems with concentric circles of meaning that radiate out from basic definitions, through middle spheres of publicly accepted connotations, to outer orbits of private associations. Thus, a word like *work* would have at its core the denotative sense *exertion or effort directed to produce or accomplish something,* but its meaning would spread outward through cultural connotations suggesting the value of work in our civilization (*work* as *job;* as a category opposed to *unemployment;* as *a work of art;* and so on), to our own private associations (*work* as *a series of meaningless tasks* or as *rewarding career,* and so on). Generally speaking, the wider the range of a word's denotations and connotations, the more complex and powerful the word. (This, of course, has nothing to do with the word's surface difficulty; *healthy,* for example, is a far more powerful word than *salubrious.*) Even words we often use interchangeably can exist within different systems of denotation and connotation: *home* suggests more than *house; modern* has a wider range of associations than *recent.*

5 Suppose we have been asked to write a short paper explaining our attitude toward capital punishment. The assignment, naturally, requires that we do more than say whether we are for it or against it. We are not being asked to vote on the subject, but to articulate as persuasively as we can what we think about the issue and why we think the way we do. It is possible that we have very strong feelings about the subject yet have never really thought our ideas out past the slogan stage of "It's wrong to take a life" or "An eye

for an eye and a tooth for a tooth." Like most vital terms, *capital punishment* comes to us embedded in a web of meanings, many of which are strongly connected to various religious beliefs and social philosophies. Making a list of some of the words suggested by the subject and some of their associations may not alter our feelings about capital punishment, but it will set up for us an intricate circuitry of related ideas that can spark our thinking throughout all phases of our writing.

6 For many writers, the compilation of a word list is an essential first step in the writing process. Though such a list will usually contain some degree of private and random associations (a few of which may lead to something promising), we should be concerned mainly with setting down as many of the principal terms related to our subject as possible. Many words will suggest themselves almost automatically; others will come to mind as we notice the relationships between various words in the list. Once assembled, our list will provide us with much more than a catalog of inert terms. It will give us a special vocabulary of terms that will take an active role in our composition, the words we will be working with.

7 For example, if we begin by looking up *capital punishment* in a dictionary in order to fix the term's rock-bottom meaning, we will find something like the following: "punishment by death for a crime; death penalty." That seems pretty straightforward—but is it? People often use *capital punishment* and *death penalty* interchangeably, but what about the connotations of these terms? *Capital punishment* sounds legal, emotionally detached; *death penalty* sounds harsher, more violent. We might speculate whether advocates for one or another favor one or another term. We might want to consider the differences between a punishment and a penalty—that one (a punishment) is something we *receive,* whereas the other (a penalty) is something we *pay.* But this is just a start. As we think (on paper) about the terms *capital punishment* and *death penalty,* the following train of associations might easily be jotted down:

prisons
crime
retribution/revenge
judgment
jury system
Is the death penalty a deterrent to crime?
Life sentences—are they any better?

parole
rehabilitation
"cruel and unusual punishment"
death row
electric chair/gas chamber/firing squad
social classes/minorities treated unequally

Plenty of other words, phrases, and questions may suggest themselves, but this list gives an adequate illustration of how a pool of related words can be formed.

8 Within this pool, some terms will spark more connections and ideas than others: they will become our *working words.* For example, we might think about the associations (and misassociations) of such complex words as *revenge* or *retribution* in the same way that Betty Edwards investigates the terms *left* and *right* (see p. 15) or Langston Hughes examines the term *black* (see p. 8). Thinking carefully about a word like *deterrence* may lead us to consider whether capital punishment can actually prevent crime—a process of thinking that may in turn lead to the type of cause-and-effect analysis outlined later in this book (see pp. 231–236). Or, we might want to take such a closely linked pair of terms as *penalty* and *punishment* and see what makes them tick by applying the kind of comparative analysis that the psychiatrist Karen Horney uses to distinguish between *fear* and *anxiety* (see p. 288). But whatever words we select to work with and whatever writing strategy they may help lead us to, our complete list will come in handy throughout the process of composition. It will provide us with a tangible cluster of closely related terms and concepts—a working vocabulary for thinking about our subject—that we can draw on for incentive at any time.

9 Our word list in itself, moreover, represents a preliminary exercise in *thinking in writing,* one that helps us get our composition flowing. We jot down a word, and that makes us think of a closely related word; that process, in turn, suggests an interesting connection (call it an "idea") that we may not have made if we hadn't set the two words down in writing. And as we quickly jot down the connection, we may think of another closely associated word or phrase. Our word list expands; it grows into a work sheet that is actually a verbal picture of our thinking. Surely this is a better method for getting started than scratching our head, sipping coffee, sharpening pencils, and staring at a blank page. Not only have we begun to think actively about our subject, but we have also started to write about it—perhaps not in complete sentences and paragraphs, but at least in words, phrases, and fragments. Not all of these, of course, will be useful finally, but some will carry us into the more consecutive writing we'll do later on. What is most important is that we now have something working for us on paper: a special set of related terms to think with and to think about, to write with and to write about.

10 Not only can mapping out the interplay of our working words

help us find something valuable to say about our subject but the process itself can become the very subject of our writing. Writers often investigate the associations among a set of related terms either in the form of an essay in itself (see Russell Baker's "Life Can Be Hard" on p. 11) or as a way of vivifying larger concepts (see Simone de Beauvoir's "Woman" on p. 6). For example, in the following paragraph, Mark Twain isn't as interested in attempting a formal definition of "repentance" as he is in examining one of the most common associations people bring to the word:

> It is curious—the misassociation of certain words. For instance, the word Repentance. Through want of reflection we associate it exclusively with Sin. We get the notion early, and keep it always, that we repent of bad deeds only; whereas we do a formidably large business in repenting of good deeds which we have done. Often when we repent of a sin, we do it perfunctorily, from principle, coldly and from the head; but when we repent of a good deed the repentance comes hot and bitter and straight from the heart. Often when we repent of a sin, we can forgive ourselves and drop the matter out of mind; but when we repent of a good deed, we seldom get peace—we go on repenting to the end. And the repentance is so perennially young and strong and vivid and vigorous! A great benefaction conferred with your whole heart upon an ungrateful man—with what immortal persistence and never-cooling energy do you repent of that! Repentance of a sin is a pale, poor, perishable thing compared with it.

Though Twain's subject is more about life than language, his witty insight into human behavior clearly grew out of his thinking closely about the range of associations and misassociations of a familiar word.

11 Throughout the earliest stages of composition, writing is primarily an intellectual process of extension. We put a little bit down on paper, and we attempt to go on from there to say more. Only after we get enough written do we need to begin worrying about such matters as style, sequence of points, clarity, logical consistency, persuasiveness, and so on. As we try to get started, however, it helps to view writing as a kind of mental stretching. Experienced writers know from countless pages of practice how a few key points can be expanded intelligently into a well-formulated and fluent composition. Less experienced writers produce work frequently marked by choppiness, abrupt stops, dead ends, and premature conclusions mainly because they quickly "run out of things to say." One of the

most important lessons to learn about composition is that ideas don't engender writing as readily as writing engenders ideas. To write productively we don't need to keep coming up with new ideas so much as we need to get the most mileage out of the ideas we already have on paper. That is why starting out with a work sheet of key words makes sense: by enlarging the scope of our working vocabulary, we gain insights and make connections that will help us generate more writing about our subject than we may at first have thought possible.

12 As we explore our subject, then, it pays to consider carefully the words that first come to mind, checking their denotative meanings and listing their range of connotations. Words on paper seem to be more constructive, or conducive to composition, than the same words in our heads. Hence, many experienced writers, even if they already have a clear idea of what they want to say, still perform these preliminary verbal operations either in rough phrase-outline or in such lists as the preceding one. We can also discover working words in diaries or journals and through prewriting exercises in which we spontaneously jot down whatever enters our minds as we think about a subject. In the brief selections that follow, we will see how a few writers find their working words and put them to use at various stages of composition. We will begin by showing how key words can activate a writer's thinking at the start of composition and even become the principal subject of an essay.

Woman

Simone de Beauvoir

"When I use the words woman *or* feminine,*" Simone de Beauvoir (1908–1986) wrote in the introduction to* The Second Sex *(1949, tr. 1953), her classic study of what it means to be a woman, "I evidently refer to no archetype, no changeless essence whatever. . . . It is not our concern here to proclaim eternal verities, but rather to describe the common basis that underlies every individual feminine existence."*

Born in Paris and educated at the Sorbonne, Simone de Beauvoir lived at the heart of the French Existentialist movement. She taught philosophy at several colleges before devoting herself full time to writing in 1943. Her many novels examine aspects of life from a philosophical perspective. Her other books include a celebrated study, The Marquis de Sade *(tr. 1953), and* The Coming of Age *(tr. 1972), a historical-cultural examination of the treatment of the elderly.* The Second Sex, *her most widely acclaimed book, opens with the following paragraph, in which de Beauvoir explores a range of meanings associated with the word* woman.

1 Woman? Very simple, say the fanciers of simple formulas: she is a womb, an ovary; she is a female—this word is sufficient to define her. In the mouth of a man the epithet *female* has the sound of an insult, yet he is not ashamed of his animal nature; on the contrary, he is proud if someone says of him: "He is a male!" The term "female" is derogatory not because it emphasizes woman's animality, but because it imprisons her in her sex; and if this sex seems to man to be contemptible and inimical even in harmless dumb animals, it is evidently because of the uneasy hostility stirred up in him by woman. Nevertheless he wishes to find in biology a justification for this sentiment. The word *female* brings up in his mind a saraband of imagery—a vast, round ovum engulfs and castrates the agile spermatozoon; the monstrous and swollen termite queen rules over the enslaved males; the female praying mantis and the spider, satiated with love, crush and devour their partners; the bitch in heat runs through the alleys, trailing behind her a wake of depraved odors; the she-monkey presents her posterior immodestly and then steals away with hypocritical coquetry; and the most superb wild beasts—the tigress, the lioness, the panther—bed down slavishly under the imperial embrace of the male. Females sluggish, eager, artful, stupid, callous, lustful, ferocious, abased—man projects them all at once upon woman. And the fact is that she is a female. But if we are willing to stop thinking in platitudes, two questions are immediately posed: what does the female denote in the animal kingdom? And what particular kind of female is manifest in woman?

Exercises for Reading, Thinking, and Writing

1. What is the word for *woman* that de Beauvoir is most concerned with here? What are the differences between men's attitude toward this

word and their attitude toward the comparable word for their own sex? How do men justify this attitude? What does de Beauvoir think of it?

2. Look up these words in a dictionary, if necessary: epithet, inimical, saraband, spermatozoon, satiated, coquetry, callous, abased, platitudes.

3. Why do you think that de Beauvoir decided to focus on the word *female,* rather than on, say, *woman* or *lady*? What insights does her doing so give rise to? Suppose, for example, that she had chosen *lady.* Could she have still made the same point and used the same examples from the animal kingdom? Why, or why not?

4. Write a paragraph in which you explore the implications of another word used to denote a woman: lady, girl, old lady, or some other. What attitude toward women does the word imply? What associations does the word have that can help you to discover this attitude? Do you think that the word should or should not be used to describe women?

That Word Black

Langston Hughes

Woman *and* black *have been two of the most volatile words of recent history. Over the last two decades, women and blacks have worked extraordinarily hard to give positive social and political value to these key identifying words, which they feel have been long used inadequately or disparagingly. Because of their efforts, few people any longer refer to a college woman as a "girl" or a black person as a "Negro."*

When Langston Hughes (1902–1967) wrote the following essay, the word black *was usually used in a negative sense. The acceptable word at the time—the word Hughes himself would have used—was Negro. His essay, written in the 1940s, is one of the earliest explorations of the linguistic side of racism, something which would be studied in far more detail in the 1960s. That the analysis appears in such a casual, colloquial form only adds to its social and verbal significance.*

Hughes, a prolific writer of varied talents, was a prominent figure of the Harlem Renaissance of the 1920s. Among his most popular works are the series of essays and tales which feature the doings and musings of Jesse B. Semple ("Simple"), a character based on a "character" Hughes met at a Harlem bar in 1942. In "That Word Black,*" Simple shows himself to be a master of connotation.*

1 "This evening," said Simple, "I feel like talking about the word *black.*"

2 "Nobody's stopping you, so go ahead. But what you really ought to have is a soap-box out on the corner of 126th and Lenox where the rest of the orators hang out."

3 "They expresses some good ideas on that corner," said Simple, "but for my ideas I do not need a crowd. Now, as I were saying, the word *black,* white folks have done used that word to mean something bad so often until now when the N.A.A.C.P. asks for civil rights for the black man, they think they must be bad. Looking back into history, I reckon it all started with a *black* cat meaning bad luck. Don't let one cross your path!

4 "Next, somebody got up a *black-list* on which you get if you don't vote right. Then when lodges come into being, the folks they didn't want in them got *black-balled.* If you kept a skeleton in your closet, you might get *black-mailed.* And everything bad was *black.* When it came down to the unlucky ball on the pool table, the eight-rock, they made it the *black* ball. So no wonder there ain't no equal rights for the *black* man."

5 "All you say is true about the odium attached to the word *black,*" I said. "You've even forgotten a few. For example, during the war if you bought something under the table, illegally, they said you were trading on the *black* market. In Chicago, if you're a gangster, the *Black Hand Society* may take you for a ride. And certainly if you don't behave yourself, your family will say you're a *black* sheep. Then if your mama burns a *black* candle to change the family luck, they call it *black* magic."

6 "My mama never did believe in voodoo so she did not burn no black candles," said Simple.

7 "If she had, that would have been a *black* mark against her."

8 "Stop talking about my mama. What I want to know is, where do white folks get off calling everything bad *black*? If it is a dark night, they say it's *black* as hell. If you are mean and evil, they say you got a *black* heart. I would like to change all that around and say that the

people who Jim Crow me have got a *white* heart. People who sell dope to children have got a *white* mark against them. And all the white gamblers who were behind the basketball fix are the *white* sheep of the sports world. God knows there was few, if any, Negroes selling stuff on the black market during the war, so why didn't they call it the *white* market? No, they got to take me and my color and turn it into everything *bad.* According to white folks, black is bad.

9 "Wait till my day comes! In my language, bad will be *white.* Blackmail will be *white* mail. Black cats will be good luck, and *white* cats will be bad. If a *white* cat crosses your path, look out! I will take the black ball for the cue ball and let the *white* ball be the unlucky eight-rock. And on my blacklist—which will be a *white* list then—I will put everybody who ever Jim Crowed me from Rankin to Hitler, Talmadge to Malan, South Carolina to South Africa.

10 "I am black. When I look in the mirror, I see myself, daddy-o, but I am not ashamed. God made me. He did not make us no badder than the rest of the folks. The earth is black and all kinds of good things comes out of the earth. Trees and flowers and fruit and sweet potatoes and corn and all that keeps mens alive comes right up out of the earth—good old black earth. Coal is black and it warms your house and cooks your food. The night is black, which has a moon, and a million stars, and is beautiful. Sleep is black which gives you rest, so you wake up feeling good. I am black. I feel very good this evening.

11 "What is wrong with black?"

Exercises for Reading, Thinking, and Writing

1. According to Simple, what connotations does the word *black* have in modern English? Who is responsible for these connotations? How would the language he imagines reflect the fact that he is black?

2. Why do you think Hughes chose dialogue to explore the connotations of *black* here? Suppose that he had, instead, given us a long monologue by Simple. Would the passage feel more exploratory to you, or less? Why?

3. Think of a word with connotations that interest you: *masculine, feminine, romantic,* or the like. After thinking of the ways in which the

word is used, write a brief composition in which you explore the connotations you have discovered. In what ways do they influence our thinking? You may use dialogue, if you wish, or expository prose.

Life Can Be Hard

Russell Baker

Awarded his first Pulitzer Prize in 1979 for his columns on the foibles of the contemporary American political and social scenes as well as a second in 1982 for his bittersweet autobiography, Growing Up, *Russell Baker (1925–) remains one of America's most widely read humorists and political satirists. "I didn't set out in life to be a humorist," he once observed, "I set out in life to be a novelist, and I look like a novelist. Art Buchwald looks like a humorist. . . . I don't look like him and most of the time I don't even look like myself." His column, "Observer," is currently syndicated in nearly 500 newspapers. His collected columns have appeared as* No Cause for Panic *(1964),* Baker's Dozen *(1964),* All Things Considered *(1965),* Poor Russell's Almanac *(1972),* So This Is Depravity *(1980), and* The Rescue of Miss Yaskell and Other Ripe Dreams *(1983).*

As he reports in Growing Up, *Baker "was issued uneventfully into the governance of Calvin Coolidge" at a time, he notes, "when World War I was seven years past, the Russian Revolution was eight years old, and the music on my grandfather's wind-up Victrola was 'Yes, We Have No Bananas'." After earning a B.A. at Johns Hopkins in 1947, Baker worked as a reporter for the* Baltimore Sun. *In 1953, he served as head of that paper's London office and wrote a weekly series entitled "From a Window on Fleet Street." He joined the Washington bureau of* The New York Times *in 1954 and covered the White House and Congress for eight years, until, as he reports, he tired of sitting in hallways hoping that people would announce news. "I began to wonder why, at age 37, I was wearing out my hams waiting for somebody to come out and lie to me." As an incentive to stay on at the* Times, *Baker was offered the "Observer" column in 1962, which he has written ever since. This national forum enables him, in the words of a* Time *profile, to walk "the high wire between light humor and substantive comment," a skill that is gracefully evident in the following essay.*

1 Hard-liners are hard-nosed and play hardball. Inevitably, they lead hard lives because they spend so much time between a rock and a hard place.

2 They work hard and they play hard.

3 They are hard-talking, too, but only because they have to be, just as they have to be hardheaded realists.

4 The reason: Life is hard.

5 It is full of hard rows to hoe.

6 They are always telling children, "I'm not going to soft-soap you, kid. I'm going to hard-soap you: Life is not a rose garden. No sirree. Life is a place where you're going to meet not only hardened criminals, but also hardened veterans who know from hard experience that there are only two kinds of people in the world—those who give others a hard time, and those who are given a hard time."

7 Whereupon they counsel the young to take a hard-eyed view of the world.

8 Children appalled by the granite message often ask, "But won't I meet any softened veterans at all?"

9 Oh yes, the hard-nosed hardball players of Hardworld are human, too, but they know there are times when the best thing you can do for a child is to be hardhearted.

10 And so when a child begs to be told that, yes, he might meet one or two softened veterans as he pursues his hard destiny, the citizen of Hardworld must tell the child some hard truths.

11 "I'm going to give you the hard facts, youngster, so listen carefully."

12 At which the child often says, "You mean you want me to be hard-eared?"

13 Hard is the task of the Hardworld philosopher.

14 "No, child. As you go through life you must be hardheaded, hard-nosed, hard-eyed and hardhearted, but hard-eared is not an authorized condition, maybe because it could be too easily confused with hard of hearing."

15 Softened veterans? What could be more absurd. Sure, veterans

come in many varieties. There are grizzled veterans and grizzled old veterans. Wise old veterans. Canny veterans of many a campaign. Make that many a hard-fought campaign.

16 But softened veterans? Never. And softened criminals? Impossible. Does anybody think we make judges sentence criminals to hard labor to soften them?

17 Can women also be hard-liners, have hard noses, play hardball and all the rest, just like men?

18 They can now, thanks to the women's liberation movement. In the old days, women could be hard-liners, but could not be hard-nosed or play hardball.

19 They could work hard, but not play hard.

20 They could be hardheaded, but not hardhearted.

21 Now, thanks to the feminist movement, no woman can be forced any longer to go through life with a soft heart and soft nose. Now, women can share in the once strictly male joy of being hit in the head playing hardball.

22 Life in Hardworld has become more delightfully savage than ever since its full range of opportunity has been opened to women.

23 Hardworld has some extremely bizarre geography. Reference was made above to that terrifying peninsula known as "between a rock and a hard place," but is it any more dreadful than "the cutting edge"?

24 Inhabitants of Hardworld think of "the cutting edge" as mountain climbers think of Everest. It is the ultimate test.

25 Think of Hardworld's greatest achievers. What will be said of them in their obituaries?

26 To be sure, their hard-nosed hardball skills will be praised, as will their hardheaded realism, their hard-earned experience and their hard-eyed view of the world, as well as the way hard-fought campaigns turned them into wise, grizzled, old, hardened veterans.

27 Anecdotes will be retold about how their hardhearted resolution enabled them to turn hard faces to sentimental softness. In obituaries, such stories make nice preludes to little tales of secret kindnesses done to stray kittens, which reveal that within that hard shell, unbeknownst to a world that trembled at his frown, cringed just another old softy.

28 But the obituary's lead will say that he was "at the cutting edge." That is the dream of every inhabitant of Hardworld: to stand some day at the awesome "cutting edge."

29 If he gets there, the hacks whose praise he seeks will say of him in their newspapers, "He stands at the cutting edge of. . . ."

30 Of what? The cutting edge cuts and, having cut, slashes on to cut again. One hears of the cutting edge of events, of history, of the struggle for the President's mind.

31 This last was said recently of a notorious citizen of Hardworld: He was at the cutting edge of the struggle for President Reagan's mind.

32 This was the ultimate accolade, for to be at the cutting edge of that particular struggle, he obviously had to know the whereabouts of the President's mind. Knowledge this remarkable makes him an extraordinary man. Later, it will gain him an obituary of at least six paragraphs.

Exercises for Reading, Thinking, and Writing

1. Russell Baker violates two standard rules of effective writing in this essay: avoid cliché and minimize repetition. Toward what end does Baker ignore these rules? With what effect?
2. List the various ways in which Baker defines the word "hard" in this essay. Given Baker's repetition of the word, what happens to our sense of the word's meaning? What is the effect of Baker's repeating other terms? Consider, for example, his use of "softened" and "the cutting edge." How do the associations of these terms contribute to the point he is trying to make about "Life is hard"?
3. How would you define the beliefs of the "Hardworld philosopher"? (In formulating your response, resist the temptation to resort to cliché.) What does Baker's use of cliché suggest about the nature of "Hardworld" philosophy? In what sense might his essay be regarded as an antidote to the "hard life"?
4. How would you describe the inhabitants of "Hardworld"? What are their distinctive characteristics? What, according to Baker, is the most important sign of success in "Hardworld"?
5. What is the effect of Baker's emphasis on the obituaries of "Hardworld's greatest achievers"? What is the relation of Baker's interest in these obituaries to his remark: "The cutting edge cuts and, having cut, slashes on to cut again"? What does he mean by this?

6. Baker's essay is obviously intended to be taken humorously. Yet in what ways, if any, do you think Baker is using the essay to make a more serious or perhaps even satiric point? What specific moments in the essay do you think are meant to be taken seriously or satirically?

Left and Right

Betty Edwards

Several years ago, Betty Edwards (1926–) became aware of the "split-brain" studies carried out during the 1950s and 1960s at the California Institute of Technology by Nobel Prize winner Roger W. Sperry and his associates. Briefly stated, the Cal Tech group found that both *hemispheres of the human brain are involved in thinking, but that the two hemispheres employ different methods or modes of processing information. (The right hemisphere also controls the movements of the left side of the body, while the left hemisphere controls the right side.) For Edwards, these studies led to the "sudden illumination that an individual's ability to draw was perhaps mainly controlled by the ability to shift to a different-from-ordinary way of processing visual information"—to shift, that is, from verbal, analytic processing (left mode) to spatial, global processing (right mode). Among her current works is* Drawing on the Artist Within *(1986).*

In the following selection from Drawing on the Right Side of the Brain *(1979), Betty Edwards, who teaches drawing at California State University, Long Beach, explores our responses to the basic words* right *and* left *by tracing their etymologies and associations.*

1 Words and phrases concerning concepts of left and right permeate our language and thinking. The right hand (meaning also the left hemisphere) is strongly connected with what is good, just, moral, proper. The left hand (therefore the right hemisphere) is strongly linked with concepts of anarchy and feelings that are out of conscious control—somehow bad, immoral, dangerous.

2 Until very recently, the ancient bias against the left-hand/right hemisphere sometimes even led parents and teachers of left-handed

children to try to force the children to use their right hands for writing, eating, and so on—a practice that often caused problems lasting into adulthood.

3 Throughout human history, terms with connotations of *good* for the right-hand/left hemisphere and connotations of *bad* for the left-hand/right hemisphere appear in most languages around the world. The Latin word for left is *sinister,* meaning "bad," "ominous," "sinister." The Latin word for right is *dexter* from which comes our word "dexterity," meaning "skill" or "adroitness."

4 The French word for "left"—remember that the left hand is connected to the right hemisphere—is *gauche,* meaning "awkward" from which comes our word "gawky." The French word for right is *droit,* meaning "good," "just," or "proper."

5 In English, "left" comes from the Anglo-Saxon *lyft,* meaning "weak" or "worthless." The left hand of most right-handed people is in fact weaker than the right, but the original word also implied lack of moral strength. The derogatory meaning of "left" may reflect a prejudice of the right-handed majority against a minority of people, who were different, that is, left-handed. Reinforcing this bias, the Anglo-Saxon word for "right," *reht* (or *riht*) meant "straight" or "just." From *reht* and its Latin cognate *rectus* we derived our words "correct" and "rectitude."

6 These ideas also affect our political thinking. The political right, for instance, admires national power, is conservative, resists change. The political left, conversely, admires individual autonomy and promotes change, even radical change. At their extremes, the political right is fascist, the political left is anarchist.

7 In the context of cultural customs, the place of honor at a formal dinner is on the host's right-hand side. The groom stands on the right in the marriage ceremony, the bride on the left—a nonverbal message of the relative status of the two participants. We shake hands with our right hands; it seems somehow wrong to shake hands with our left hands.

8 Under "left handed," the dictionary lists as synonyms "clumsy," "awkward," "insincere," "malicious." Synonyms for "right handed," however, are "correct," "indispensable," and "reliable." Now, it's important to remember that these terms were all made up, when languages began, by some persons' left hemispheres—the left brain calling the right bad names! And the right brain—labeled, pinpointed, and buttonholed—was without a language of its own to defend itself.

Exercises for Reading, Thinking, and Writing

1. How does Edwards attempt to convince us of the seriousness of the right-left bias? Which of her examples do you think have the most serious consequences and which the least? Explain why you think so.

2. Reread the selection carefully, this time paying attention to the various kinds of associations Edwards uses. Besides synonyms and etymologies, what other associations with right and left does she build into her essay? How does she use the associations to widen the cultural and social significance of the right-left bias?

3. Use this short essay as an introduction to important reference tools. A half-hour trip to the library will acquaint you with some of the most important reference books designed for readers and writers. Most students know about the handy desk dictionary, but few know about special dictionaries for etymology, synonyms, slang, and so forth. Ask the reference librarian where you can find the following books and take a few minutes to browse through them:

   The Oxford English Dictionary
   Roget's International Thesaurus
   Eric Partridge's *Origins: A Short Etymological Dictionary of Modern English*
   Dictionary of American Slang (compiled by Harold Wentworth and Stuart Berg Flexner)

4. In this section, we have seen how common words like *woman, black, right,* and *left* can have powerful prejudicial associations. Think of another common term that can affect us in similar ways. Then, using the above-mentioned reference books for information, write a brief essay on how the associations of that word can "permeate our language and thinking."

Dirt

Terence McLaughlin

Some of the most powerful words in our vocabulary are those we are least likely to examine. Take, for example, the simple-sounding, ordinary word dirt, *a word that has been in our possession since earliest childhood.*

Most of us use the word so frequently and confidently in our everyday speech—think how often the word comes up in advertising—that we have little incentive to consider it as a complex concept in itself. Like many other apparently simple terms, however, the more we think about it, the more intricate its meaning becomes. And like many other basic words, the more attention we pay to the range of things we refer to when we say it, the more we will find to say about it. Tracking down such a range of associations can, as we have seen, be the stimulus for an absorbing essay.

When Terence McLaughlin (1928–   ) decided to investigate the word dirt, *he deliberately didn't take his opening cue from the dictionary, where he would have found a definition like "any foul or filthy substance, as mud, grime, dust, excrement, etc." Instead, he started by considering some of the things we associate with* dirt *in order to show how much our use of the word depends upon context and situation. McLaughlin's examination of the word plays an integral part in his full-length study of pollution,* Dirt: A Social History as Seen Through the Uses and Abuses of Dirt *(1971). The opening passage is reprinted here to provide a working model of how an inquiry into a basic word and its associations can lead directly to an interesting essay.*

Terence McLaughlin is a member of the Royal Institute of Chemistry and an authority on pollution.

1 Dirt is evidence of the imperfections of life, a constant reminder of change and decay. It is the dark side of all human activities—human, because it is only in our judgements that things are dirty: there is no such material as *absolute* dirt. Earth, in the garden, is a valuable support and nourishment for plants, and gardeners often run it through their fingers lovingly; earth on the carpet is dirt. A pile of dung, to the dung-beetle, is food and shelter for a large family; a pile of dung, to the Public Health Inspector, is a Nuisance. Soup in a plate, before we eat it, is food; the traces that we leave on the plate imperceptibly become dirt. Lipstick on a girl's lips may make her boy-friend more anxious to touch them with his own lips; lipstick on a cup will probably make him refuse to touch it.

2 Because of this relativity, because dirt can be almost anything that we choose to call dirt, it has often been defined as 'matter out of place.' This fits the 'earth (garden)/earth (carpet)' difference quite well, but it is not really very useful as a definition. A sock on the grand piano or a book in a pile of plates may be untidy, and they are certainly out of place, but they are not necessarily dirty.

To be dirt, the material also has to be hard to remove and unpleasant. If you sit on the beach, particularly if you bathe, sand will stick to you, but not many people would classify this as *dirt,* mainly because it brushes off so easily. However, if, as often happens the sand is covered with oil, tar, or sewage, and this sticks to you, it is definitely dirt.

3 Sartre, in his major philosophical work on Existentialism, *L'Être et le Néant*[1] presents a long discussion on the nature of *sliminess* or stickiness which has quite a lot to do with our ideas of dirt. He points out that quite small children, who presumably have not yet learned any notions of cleanliness, and cannot yet be worried by germs, still tend to recognize that slimy things are unpleasant. It is because slimy things are clinging that we dislike them—they hold on to us even when we should like to let them go, and, like an unpleasant travelling companion or an obscene telephone caller, seem to be trying to involve us in themselves.

4 'If an object which I hold in my hands is solid,' says Sartre, 'I can let go when I please. . . . Yet here is the slimy reversing the terms . . . I open my hands, I want to let go of the slimy material and it sticks to me, it draws me, it sucks at me. Its mode of being is neither the reassuring inertia of the solid nor a dynamism like that in water which is exhausted in fleeing from me. It is a soft yielding action, a moist and feminine sucking, it *lives* obscurely under my fingers. . . .'

5 This is the feeling of *pollution,* the kind of experience where something dirty has attached itself to us and we cannot get rid of the traces, however hard we try. Ritual defilement is one aspect of this feeling, and one which provides an enormous field of study for anthropologists (when they are not engaged in their favourite activity of reviling one another), but powerful irrational feelings of defilement exist in the most sophisticated societies. Try serving soup in a chamber-pot. However clean it may be, and however much a certain type of guest may find it 'amusing,' there will be a very real uneasiness about the juxtaposition. There are some kinds of dirt that we treat, in practice, as irremovable—as in the case of the old lady who was unlucky enough to drop her false teeth down the lavatory, where they were flushed into the sewer. When a search failed to find them,

[1]*L'Être et le Néant* (1943), trans. as *Being and Nothingness,* written by Jean-Paul Sartre (1905–1980). [Eds.]

she heaved a sigh of relief. 'I would never have fancied them again,' she said, and most people would agree.

Exercises for Reading, Thinking, and Writing

1. Look up the word *dirt* in at least three different dictionaries. How similar or different are the definitions? Which definition gives you the most promising start for an essay on the subject? Why?
2. You sometimes hear it said that so-and-so is a "dirty player." In what sense is the word *dirt* used in that expression? List other common expressions in which the word *dirt* or its variations are used. Use that list to construct a brief essay on the meaning of the word *dirt* in our *personal* lives (e.g., the way the word is used as an insult, etc.).
3. How does McLaughlin build up a set of associations for the term? How important is the dictionary definition to his opening? What is the most important source of his associations?
4. Use McLaughlin's opening as a model for a two-paragraph discussion of the word *clean.* Build your discussion upon the associations we bring to the word, not upon a dictionary definition. But before you begin writing, draw up a word list of all the associations the word *clean* suggests to you. Write down whatever comes to mind. Then use that list as the basis for your discussion of the term.

Making Metaphors

1 In the previous chapter, we saw how a little preliminary work with the denotative and connotative meanings of words can help us get a fix on a subject. In this section, we'll look at another procedure for exploring a subject and bridging that always difficult gap between having an idea and getting a paper started—the making of metaphors. Like our key words, our metaphors perform at the most fundamental level of the writing process, supplying us with sets of associated terms and concepts that we can draw on throughout our composition.

2 *Metaphor* comes from a Greek word meaning *transfer* and is the classical term for the rhetorical process by which we find resemblances between different kinds of things or ideas. When we see or think of something as though it were like something else, when we discover the similar in the dissimilar, we are using metaphor. We use metaphors all the time: for some students, school may seem to be *a factory,* their courses *a grind,* their social life *a bad joke;* years later, they consider their college days to have been *a picnic,* courses *a breeze,* their social life *a continuous riot.* Our everyday speech is packed with metaphors, many of which we use unconsciously—we don't, for example, realize that we are using a metaphor when we speak of someone's death as "a tragedy." We also tend in our everyday conversations to make up metaphors on the spot: we may say of a clumsy dancer that he moves with all the grace of "a drunken left tackle." Metaphor is sometimes distinguished from simile, in that metaphor works by

implicit comparison ("Her mind is a computer"), whereas simile works by the explicit connection of *like* or *as* ("Her mind is like a computer"). Though at times the difference between the two rhetorical figures can be significant, simile, as Aristotle said, usually differs from metaphor "only in the way it is put." (For convenience, metaphor will be used in this book to cover both kinds of rhetorical procedures.)

3 It is common to think of metaphor as merely stylistic decoration. When we complain of "flowery language," we are usually referring to a highly metaphorical style. However, as we work closely with metaphor, we should remember that it is not simply a cosmetic device, but a potentially powerful mental act that underlies all discourse and pervades all rhetorical strategies and structures. Metaphor does, of course, play a vital part in enlivening and vivifying the surface of our prose, but it can also function structurally at much deeper levels of thinking and writing. By allowing us to form images and concepts of one thing in terms of another, metaphor helps us to see new connections that can frequently lead to unexpected insights. Far from being merely a special kind of stylistic ornament or a poetic addition to prose, it is rather an irreducible part of language itself. We can neither write nor think without it.

4 Making metaphors—perceiving similarity in dissimilar things—represents one of the supreme activities of human intelligence. Aristotle regarded metaphor as a "sign of genius" and "the greatest thing by far." Certainly the ability to make metaphors proficiently is a sure sign of a verbally creative person. But metaphors play an important role in less individually creative areas of thought as well. We are frequently relying on metaphor to express key ideas or concepts even when we think we're being quite literal. Nearly all of the abstract terms we use every day had their origins in metaphor (*idea* comes from an ancient Greek term meaning "the shape or blueprint a craftsman uses to begin work with"), and many of these terms still carry with them some vestiges of their figurative roots. The word *idea,* for example, still *conveys* the sense of something being in its planning stage, something not yet implemented ("That looks like a good idea, but will it work?").

5 Everyday speech abounds with metaphorical expressions. In the opening selection of this chapter, George Lakoff and Mark Johnson convincingly demonstrate how ordinary figurative expressions structure many of our everyday concepts and thus affect not only

how we think about something but also how we may even experience it. For example, much of our ordinary use of the word *argument* refers explicitly to war, a verbal habit that can easily be observed by considering a few common expressions:

> Your claims are *indefensible.*
> He *attacked* every weak point in my argument.
> His criticism was *right on target.*
> I *demolished* his argument.
> I've never *won* an argument with her.
> You disagree? Okay, *shoot!*
> If you use that *strategy,* he'll *wipe you out.*
> He *shot down* all of my arguments.

And these are merely a few. What Lakoff and Johnson want us to see is not just that we talk about arguments *in terms of* war or violent contests, but that many of the things we *do* in arguing are partially structured by the concept of war. So pervasive are such figurative expressions in our language that we could take practically any abstract concept and list a cluster of commonly related metaphors that give it shape and substance. Such clusters will conveniently show how important a role metaphor plays (note the theatrical metaphor) in our everyday thinking.

6 Entire books have been devoted to the philosophical, literary, and linguistic significance of metaphor. Here, for simplicity, we will divide metaphor into two basic types, according to how they are commonly used in writing:

Stylistic Metaphors. One of the values of metaphor, Aristotle claimed, is that it "gives style clearness, charm, and distinction as nothing else can." It is difficult to find examples of good writing that are not interlaced with perceptive and well-chosen metaphors. When N. Scott Momaday wants to describe what the Oklahoma landscape is like in the dry heat of summer, he writes that "the prairie is an anvil's edge." Or when John Updike wants to show how perfect the beer can was before our technology "improved" it, he writes that it was "as beautiful as the clothespin, as inevitable as the wine bottle, as dignified and reassuring as the fire hydrant." Such metaphors ripple across the surface of sentences like well-toned muscle, giving the writing strength and vigor. But good metaphors do more than perk our attention and make us sensitive to a writer's style. They also make us *see* things in new ways—the unfamiliar in the familiar, the familiar in the strange. To see the summer prairie as an "anvil's edge" is to see it with a freshness and immediacy not soon forgotten.

Structural Metaphors. These are extended expressions of resemblance around which paragraphs and entire compositions can be constructed. A structural metaphor can therefore be a strategic element for expository writing: it allows us to find a structure and to extend the context for a subject in ways otherwise closed to us.

7 Metaphors can be particularly useful in helping us to explore a subject and discover an angle of approach. As we compile a list of words and phrases associated with our subject or jot down sentences spontaneously in a notebook, we will undoubtedly turn up metaphors—some commonplace, some original, some flashy, some with structural possibilities. Pursuing the implications of promising metaphors may provide us with a point of entry into our composition and, possibly, if the metaphor is rich enough, an organizational pattern for our entire essay.

8 For example, in the process of exploring an assignment on advertising's influence on American life, we compile a set of working words and associations. Our list includes some of the goods and services promoted through advertising—foods, clothes, drugs, appliances, transportation, cigarettes, cosmetics, household products, and so on. We decide to confine our attention to transportation, and then compile another list of closely related words and phrases. We know more about cars, say, than other types of transportation, so we choose to focus on automobile advertising. As we think hard about what cars mean in our lives, we come up with additional terms, such as *independence, expense, fun, mobility, driving, status, commuting, pollution.* In this cluster of terms, we notice a word that suggests a promising range of meaning—*mobility.* Americans, we know, are considered a highly mobile people, and American society depends enormously on automobiles. We observe that the *-mobile* part of *automobile* itself suggests mobility and recall that there is even a gasoline called "Mobil." But *mobile,* we realize as we reflect on the word, also suggests status: sociologists often talk of "upward mobility." In this word, then, there is a metaphor that might offer an entry into our subject. We think of the vast quantity of automobile advertising that appeals to the consumer's desire for both types of mobility—physical (travel) and social (status). If we pursue it further, we may find that the metaphor associates

itself closely with a popular expression, "going places," which also conveys both physical and social mobility. The implications of this metaphor could lead us to an opening paragraph such as this:

> Americans like to think of themselves as a highly mobile people—both on the road and in society—and no popular art confirms this national characteristic more emphatically than advertisements for automobiles. In common speech, "going places" has long implied a social as well as a geographic destination.

The rest of the paper might demonstrate how advertisements for cars try to influence consumers to buy something that is both an object of luxury and a practical source of transportation.

9 Metaphors can also exert a continuing presence in our composition by actively guiding our thoughts while we write. Some of the resemblances we come across in the preliminary sketching out of our ideas will take us further than merely an opening paragraph. Should we then decide to stick to one of these key resemblances and organize our entire composition around it, we would be using a structural metaphor.

10 For example, suppose we want to write an essay on the subject of television and American society. What can we say about it? How would we begin to shape this vast subject into an interesting idea that will be manageable within a short essay? We try to think about the overall subject actively—that is, not just in our heads but by putting words, phrases, sentences, just as they occur, down on paper, where we can actually see what we are thinking. Let us suppose one of the thoughts we put down goes something like this: "Some people—my parents?!—seem to watch television all the time. The TV is always on. Why? Are they lonely? Are they all talked out? Who knows? Maybe they're just TV addicts." Now, embedded in this spontaneous combination of observation, generalization, criticism, perplexity, and concern lurks a metaphor: watching TV much of the time is similar to being addicted to drugs. It is not a startlingly new metaphor; the fact that it came up idiomatically suggests that it is part of everyday speech. But suppose we decide to push the metaphor a bit further than its easy idiomatic use seems at first to justify. (In everyday speech we automatically pass over words and idioms all the time without thinking about their enormous potential.) As we "unpack" the metaphor that television resembles a drug, we may begin to think

of some of the ideas associated with drug addiction. We may think of types of drugs, reasons for addiction, psychological consequences, social solutions, and so on. But, at the same time, we are still thinking about television—the shows people watch, sports, commercials. The metaphor may begin to suggest questions that can help us shape an appropriate subject: "Are some shows more addictive than others? Why does so much drug advertising appear on the nightly news?"

11 Notice that what we have done (and with a fairly ordinary metaphor) is set two vocabularies in motion at the same time: one vocabulary derived from television, the other from drugs. Since our principal subject is television, however, we will use the drug terminology as a way of commenting on television and not the other way around. In other words, our primary transfer of terms will be from drugs to television, not vice versa. As we examine some of the terms that suggest themselves in our notes *(turn-on, junk, sedation, compulsive viewer),* we may start to obtain an overall, clear idea for structuring our composition. We may decide to stay with the notion of addiction and try to demonstrate vividly how long hours of television watching produce altered states of consciousness. We may think that drug dependency is basically an escapist route and speculate about some of the ways television programming serves that psychological need. We may start to wonder whether the sedative effects of television help create pliant audiences for commercials. But no matter which direction we move in, our original comparison between television and drugs will govern the production and organization of our thoughts and sentences.

12 Here is how a professional writer, Marie Winn (see p. 404), puts this metaphor to good use in a paragraph on "television addiction" from her book *The Plug-in Drug:*

> Let us consider television viewing in the light of the conditions that define serious addictions.
>
> Not unlike drugs or alcohol, the television experience allows the participant to blot out the real world and enter into a pleasurable and passive mental state. The worries and anxieties of reality are as effectively deferred by becoming absorbed in a television program as by going on a "trip" induced by drugs or alcohol. And just as many alcoholics are only inchoately aware of their addiction, feeling that they control their drinking more than they really do ("I can cut it out any time I want—I just like to have three or four drinks before din-

> ner"), people similarly overestimate their control over television watching. Even as they put off other activities to spend hour after hour watching television, they feel they could easily resume living in a different, less passive style. But somehow or other while the television set is present in their homes, the click doesn't sound. With television pleasures available, those other experiences seem less attractive, more difficult somehow.

Notice how the writer's use of the addiction metaphor allows her to make a convincing case about how people delude themselves into thinking they have more control over their television habit than they actually do. Had she simply registered this fact without the support of metaphor, it would have been far less persuasive.

13 Once we sense its possibilities, a key metaphor like the television-addiction resemblance above can play a vital part in helping us start and structure a composition. It will work for us throughout the writing process. Such a key metaphor stimulates and directs our preparatory efforts, helps guide our selection of material, controls our particular emphases, and, in general, furnishes us with a uniform frame of reference within which our separate ideas, observations, and snippets of information about the principal subject can be enhanced and consolidated. For all its expository utility, however, a structural metaphor need never be stated explicitly. Many writers introduce structural metaphors inconspicuously, allowing the separate vocabularies to intersect at appropriate junctures without ever spelling out the basic comparison that underpins the composition.

THE MISUSE OF METAPHOR

14 Metaphors must be properly handled. For all their stylistic and structural utility, they are a potential source of awkwardness and absurdity. Here are five common forms of misused and abused metaphors:

1. *Broken metaphors:* When starting a metaphor or using a word with a strong metaphorical sense, we should make sure we sustain the imagery or points of resemblance. Otherwise, we leave a picture dangling in midsentence and it looks as though we either chose the wrong word or did not know how to extend the metaphor. In the following sentence, notice that the comparison is abandoned, leaving the reader with a sense of incompleteness: "Cooking spaghetti is an

art form not unlike painting; we need to mix our ingredients carefully—a dash of oil, a pinch of garlic, and a sprinkling of parsley."

2. *Mixed metaphors:* When using two or more metaphors in the same sentence, we should make sure they are consistent in their imagery. Mixed metaphors thrive on clichéd idioms and are a delightful source of absurdity. The famous novelist Vladimir Nabokov found the following example in an old *Life* magazine: Peter the Great "singlehanded, booted Russia into progress."

3. *Far-fetched metaphors:* Our metaphors should bear a fitting proportion to our subject matter and not be drawn out to an unnecessary extent. The journalist Jessica Mitford cites the following example of a particularly ridiculous and unruly metaphor from a mortuary advertisement:

> Deep sea fishing off Mexico can't be beat! When you feel that old tug on your pole and that line goes whistling into the deep, that's it brother! And, there's nothing quite like the way I feel about Wilbert burial vaults either. The combination of a ⅜" pre-cast asphalt inner liner plus extra thick, reinforced concrete provides the essential qualities for proper burial. My advice to you is, don't get into "deep water" with burial vaults made of the new lightweight synthetic substitutes. Just keep "reeling in" extra profits by continuing to recommend Wilbert burial vaults. . . .

4. *Dead metaphors:* These are expressions of resemblance that have been around for so long we no longer respond to them as metaphors—the arms of a chair, the eye of a needle, a blade of grass, the face of a clock, a bright or dull person. Since such expressions are nearly unavoidable (and therefore not clichés), there is nothing wrong with using them. We need only make sure we don't set them against each other in such a way that the reader is presented with an absurdity. The poet Robert Graves gives as an example of the misuse of metaphor the following sentence from a novel: "Kay Rimmer sat with her head in her hands and her eyes on the floor."

5. *Clichéd metaphors:* Like dead metaphors, these make up a large part of common parlance, but unlike them they are avoidable. In fact, we should always try to avoid such expressions as *dog-tired, pretty as a picture, feeling down in the dumps, mad as a hornet, lightning fast.* Such metaphors have long lost whatever vitality or descriptive power they may have once had. And what is worse for composition, they come so automatically that it appears to the reader that language is control-

ling the writer. Clichéd metaphors are incessantly deployed by the mass media—in advertising copy, newspaper headlines, book titles, and so on. Thus, an advertisement for frozen foods tries to convince housewives that a particular brand won't get them "icy stares" from cranky husbands; a review of a book about boomerangs is entitled *Many Happy Returns;* a serious report on arson is headlined "Playing with Fire." Making such clichés literal can be fun (see Calvin Trillin's "Rural Literalism," p. 36); it can also trigger verbal and conceptual associations that can lead to new ways of thinking about our subject. But clichéd metaphors are very difficult to revitalize, and in careful expository writing we should use them either not at all or most judiciously.

15 In the selections that follow, we will examine some of the productive ways writers make metaphors to enliven their compositions and discover organizational patterns for their ideas.

Metaphors We Live By

George Lakoff and Mark Johnson

Our metaphors allow us to understand and experience one kind of thing in terms of another. This essential characteristic of metaphor is also an essential activity of the human mind. Metaphorical constructions are not special literary devices favored by poets and writers but are a principal feature of our ordinary thinking. Try thinking about anything and in no time a metaphor will surface (just like this one). Much of what we do and say every day is powerfully inspired and influenced by the metaphor-making disposition of our minds.

In the following selection from George Lakoff and Mark Johnson's provocative study, Metaphors We Live By *(1980), we can see how our ordinary, casual expressions reflect the essentially metaphorical way in which we think about some of the most fundamental things in life. So ingrained are these expressions in our thought, speech, and writing that we seldom pay any conscious attention to them. But to do so—as Lakoff and Johnson have done—is to discover how persistently we express ourselves in metaphor and how surprisingly figurative we are even when we think we are being most literal.*

George Lakoff teaches linguistics at the University of California, Berkeley. Mark Johnson teaches philosophy at Southern Illinois University.

1 We have been claiming that metaphors partially structure our everyday concepts and that this structure is reflected in our literal language. Before we can get an overall picture of the philosophical implications of these claims, we need a few more examples. In each of the ones that follow we give a metaphor and a list of ordinary expressions that are special cases of the metaphor. The English expressions are of two sorts: simple literal expressions and idioms that fit the metaphor and are part of the normal everyday way of talking about the subject.

2 THEORIES (AND ARGUMENTS) ARE BUILDINGS

Is that the *foundation* for your theory? The theory needs more *support.* The argument is *shaky.* We need some more facts or the argument will *fall apart.* We need to *construct* a *strong* argument for that. I haven't figured out yet what the *form* of the argument will be. Here are some more facts to *shore up* the theory. We need to *buttress* the theory with *solid* arguments. The theory will *stand* or *fall* on the *strength* of that argument. The argument *collapsed.* They *exploded* his latest theory. We will show that theory to be without *foundation.* So far we have put together only the *framework* of the theory.

3 IDEAS ARE FOOD

What he said *left a bad taste in my mouth.* All this paper has in it are *raw facts, half-baked ideas, and warmed-over theories.* There are too many facts here for me to *digest* them all. I just can't *swallow* that claim. That argument *smells fishy.* Let me *stew* over that for a while. Now there's a theory you can really *sink your teeth into.* We need to let that idea *percolate* for a while. That's *food for thought.* He's a *voracious* reader. We don't need to *spoon-feed* our students. He *devoured* the book. Let's let that idea *simmer on the back burner* for a while. This is the *meaty* part of the paper. Let that idea *jell* for a while. That idea has been *fermenting* for years.

4 With respect to life and death IDEAS ARE ORGANISMS, either PEOPLE OR PLANTS.

5 IDEAS ARE PEOPLE

The theory of relativity *gave birth to* an enormous number of ideas in physics. He is the *father* of modern biology. Whose *brainchild* was that?

Look at what his ideas have *spawned.* Those ideas *died off* in the Middle Ages. His ideas will *live on* forever. Cognitive psychology is still in its *infancy.* That's an idea that ought to be *resurrected.* Where'd you *dig up* that idea? He *breathed new life into* that idea.

6 IDEAS ARE PLANTS

His ideas have finally come to *fruition.* That idea *died on the vine.* That's a *budding* theory. It will take years for that idea to *come to full flower.* He views chemistry as a mere *offshoot* of physics. Mathematics has many *branches.* The *seeds* of his great ideas were *planted* in his youth. She has a *fertile* imagination. Here's an idea that I'd like to *plant* in your mind. He has a *barren* mind.

7 IDEAS ARE PRODUCTS

We're really *turning (churning, cranking, grinding) out* new ideas. We've *generated* a lot of ideas this week. He *produces* new ideas at an astounding rate. His *intellectual productivity* has decreased in recent years. We need to *take the rough edges off* that idea, *hone it down, smooth it out.* It's a rough idea; it needs to be *refined.*

8 IDEAS ARE COMMODITIES

It's important how you *package* your ideas. He won't *buy* that. That idea just won't *sell.* There is always a *market* for good ideas. That's a *worthless* idea. He's been a source of *valuable* ideas. I wouldn't *give a plugged nickel for* that idea. Your ideas don't have a chance in the *intellectual marketplace.*

9 IDEAS ARE RESOURCES

He *ran out of* ideas. Don't *waste* your thoughts on small projects. Let's *pool* our ideas. He's a *resourceful* man. We've *used up* all our ideas. That's a *useless* idea. That idea will *go a long way.*

10 IDEAS ARE MONEY

Let me put in my *two cents' worth.* He's *rich* in ideas. That book is a *treasure trove* of ideas. He has a *wealth* of ideas.

11 IDEAS ARE CUTTING INSTRUMENTS

That's an *incisive* idea. That *cuts right to the heart of* the matter. That was a *cutting* remark. He's *sharp.* He has a *razor* wit. He has a *keen* mind. She *cut* his argument *to ribbons.*

12 IDEAS ARE FASHIONS

That idea went *out of style* years ago. I hear sociobiology *is in* these days. Marxism is currently *fashionable* in western Europe. That idea is *old hat!* That's an *outdated* idea. What are the new *trends* in English criticism? *Old-fashioned* notions have no place in today's society. He keeps *up-to-*

date by reading the New York Review of Books. Berkeley is a center of *avant-garde* thought. Semiotics has become quite *chic.* The idea of revolution is no longer *in vogue* in the United States. The transformational grammar *craze* hit the United States in the mid-sixties and has just made it to Europe.

13 UNDERSTANDING IS SEEING; IDEAS ARE LIGHT-SOURCES; DISCOURSE IS A LIGHT-MEDIUM

I *see* what you're saying. It *looks* different from my *point of view.* What is your *outlook* on that? I *view* it differently. Now I've got the *whole picture.* Let me *point something out* to you. That's an *insightful* idea. That was a *brilliant* remark. The argument is *clear.* It was a *murky* discussion. Could you *elucidate* your remarks? It's a *transparent* argument. The discussion was *opaque.*

14 LOVE IS A PHYSICAL FORCE (ELECTROMAGNETIC, GRAVITATIONAL, ETC.)

I could feel the *electricity* between us. There were *sparks.* I was *magnetically drawn* to her. They are uncontrollably *attracted* to each other. They *gravitated* to each other immediately. His whole life *revolves* around her. The *atmosphere* around them is always *charged.* There is incredible *energy* in their relationship. They lost their *momentum.*

15 LOVE IS A PATIENT

This is a *sick* relationship. They have a *strong, healthy* marriage. The marriage is *dead*—it can't be *revived.* Their marriage is *on the mend.* We're getting *back on our feet.* Their relationship is *in really good shape.* They've got a *listless* marriage. Their marriage is *on its last legs.* It's a *tired* affair.

16 LOVE IS MADNESS

I'm *crazy* about her. She *drives me out of my mind.* He constantly *raves* about her. He's gone *mad* over her. I'm just *wild* about Harry. I'm *insane* about her.

17 LOVE IS MAGIC

She *cast her spell* over me. The *magic* is gone. I was *spellbound.* She had me *hypnotized.* He has me *in a trance.* I was *entranced* by him. I'm *charmed* by her. She is *bewitching.*

18 LOVE IS WAR

He is known for his many rapid *conquests.* She *fought for* him, but his mistress *won out.* He *fled from* her *advances.* She *pursued* him *relentlessly.* He is slowly *gaining ground* with her. He *won* her hand in marriage. He *overpowered* her. She is *besieged* by suitors. He has to *fend* them *off.* He *enlisted the aid* of her friends. He *made an ally* of her mother. Theirs is a *misalliance* if I've ever seen one.

19 WEALTH IS A HIDDEN OBJECT

He's *seeking* his fortune. He's flaunting his *new-found* wealth. He's a *fortune-hunter.* She's a *gold-digger.* He *lost* his fortune. He's *searching for* wealth.

20 SIGNIFICANT IS BIG

He's a *big* man in the garment industry. He's a *giant* among writers. That's the *biggest* idea to hit advertising in years. He's *head and shoulders above* everyone in the industry. It was only a *small* crime. That was only a *little* white lie. I was astounded at the *enormity* of the crime. That was one of the *greatest* moments in World Series history. His accomplishments *tower over* those of *lesser* men.

21 SEEING IS TOUCHING; EYES ARE LIMBS

I can't *take* my eyes *off* her. He sits with his eyes *glued to* the TV. Her eyes *picked out* every detail of the pattern. Their eyes *met.* She never *moves* her eyes *from* his face. She *ran* her eyes *over* everything in the room. He wants everything *within reach of* his eyes.

22 THE EYES ARE CONTAINERS FOR THE EMOTIONS

I could see the fear *in* his eyes. His eyes were *filled* with anger. There was passion *in* her eyes. His eyes *displayed* his compassion. She couldn't *get* the fear *out* of her eyes. Love *showed in* his eyes. Her eyes *welled* with emotion.

23 EMOTIONAL EFFECT IS PHYSICAL CONTACT

His mother's death *hit* him *hard.* That idea *bowled me over.* She's a *knockout.* I was *struck* by his sincerity. That really *made an impression* on me. He *made his mark on* the world. I was *touched* by his remark. That *blew me away.*

24 PHYSICAL AND EMOTIONAL STATES ARE ENTITIES WITHIN A PERSON

He has a pain *in* his shoulder. Don't *give* me the flu. My cold has *gone from my head to my chest.* His pains *went away.* His depression *returned.* Hot tea and honey will *get rid of* your cough. He could barely *contain* his joy. The smile *left* his face. *Wipe* that sneer *off* your face, private! His fears *keep coming back.* I've got to *shake off* this depression—it keeps *hanging on.* If you've got a cold, drinking lots of tea will *flush it out* of your system. There isn't a *trace* of cowardice *in* him. He hasn't got *an honest bone in his body.*

25 VITALITY IS A SUBSTANCE

She's *brimming* with vim and vigor. She's *overflowing* with vitality. He's *devoid* of energy. I don't *have* any energy *left* at the end of the day. I'm *drained.* That *took a lot out of* me.

26 LIFE IS A CONTAINER

I've had a *full* life. Life is *empty* for him. There's *not much left* for him *in* life. Her life is *crammed* with activities. *Get the most out of* life. His life *contained* a great deal of sorrow. Live your life *to the fullest.*

27 LIFE IS A GAMBLING GAME

I'll *take my chances.* The *odds are against me.* I've got an *ace up my sleeve.* He's *holding all the aces.* It's a *toss-up.* If you *play your cards right,* you can do it. He *won big.* He's a real *loser.* Where is he when the *chips are down?* That's my *ace in the hole.* He's *bluffing.* The president is *playing it close to his vest.* Let's *up the ante.* Maybe we need to *sweeten the pot.* I think we should *stand pat.* That's *the luck of the draw.* Those are *high stakes.*

28 In this last group of examples we have a collection of what are called "speech formulas," or "fixed-form expressions," or "phrasal lexical items." These function in many ways like single words, and the language has thousands of them. In the examples given, a set of such phrasal lexical items is coherently structured by a single metaphorical concept. Although each of them is an instance of the LIFE IS A GAMBLING GAME metaphor, they are typically used to speak of life, not of gambling situations. They are normal ways of talking about life situations, just as using the word "construct" is a normal way of talking about theories. It is in this sense that we include them in what we have called literal expressions structured by metaphorical concepts. If you say "The odds are against us" or "We'll have to take our chances," you would not be viewed as speaking metaphorically but as using the normal everyday language appropriate to the situation. Nevertheless, your way of talking about, conceiving, and even experiencing your situation would be metaphorically structured.

Exercises for Reading, Thinking, and Writing

1. Read over the "argument as war" example in the introduction. Make another list of ordinary expressions to fit this concept. Your list should include both simple, literal expressions as well as idioms that fit the metaphor.

2. Try to imagine a place where arguments are *not* viewed in terms of war, where no one wins or loses, where there is no sense of attacking or defending, gaining or losing ground. Now try to imagine how arguments would be conceived in this place. Consider some other ways to think about arguments: as dance, as play, as musical

expression, and so forth. How would your replacement of the war metaphor with a different metaphor affect the ways in which people perceive arguments? What would be gained and what lost?

3. Think of a key concept of everyday life that Lakoff and Johnson don't discuss, and make a list of the metaphorical expressions that support it. Then use your list as the basis for a brief essay in which you show how our grasp of this concept is partially determined by the metaphors we use when we think about it. Conclude your essay with a discussion of the particular consequences these metaphorical expressions have on our thinking about that concept.

The Emotional Mind

D. H. Lawrence

One of the most powerful writers of our century, D. H. Lawrence (1885–1930) courageously explored the far reaches of human passion and emotion in such now classic novels as Sons and Lovers *(1912),* The Rainbow *(1915),* Women in Love *(1921),* Lady Chatterley's Lover *(1928), and such idiosyncratic studies as* Psychoanalysis of the Unconscious *(1921) and* Phantasia of the Unconscious *(1922). So vigorously and graphically did Lawrence pursue the range of relations between men and women that some of his books were subjected to extensive expurgation. The trial that preceded publication of* Lady Chatterley's Lover *represents a landmark in the history of contemporary censorship. Lawrence's determination to record vividly the delicate equilibrium of our inner life led him in his fiction and essays to examine closely the dynamics of human consciousness. Such concerns are clearly evident in the following brief passage in which Lawrence uses a striking metaphor to depict the movements of a mind working its way toward a decision.*

1 Now the emotional mind, if we may be allowed to say so, is not logical. It is a psychological fact, that when we are thinking emotionally or passionately, thinking and feeling at the same time, we do not think rationally: and therefore, and therefore, and therefore. Instead, the mind makes curious swoops and circles. It touches the point of pain or interest, then sweeps away again in a cycle, coils round and

approaches again the point of pain or interest. There is a curious spiral rhythm, and the mind approaches again and again the point of concern, repeats itself, goes back, destroys the time-sequence entirely, so that time ceases to exist, as the mind stoops to the quarry, then leaves it without striking, soars, hovers, turns, swoops, stoops again, still does not strike, yet is nearer, nearer, reels away again, wheels off into the air, even forgets, quite forgets, yet again turns, bends, circles slowly, swoops and stoops again, until at last there is the closing-in, and the clutch of a decision or a resolve.

2 This activity of the mind is strictly timeless, and illogical. Afterwards you can deduce the logical sequence and the time sequence, as historians do from the past. But in the happening, the logical and the time sequence do not exist.

Exercises for Reading, Thinking, and Writing

1. What metaphor dominates this passage? How explicit does Lawrence make it? What, for example, can be said to "swoop," "circle," "sweep away in a cycle," and so on?
2. How is the "curious spiral rhythm" Lawrence talks about evident in the passage itself? Point to the operations of particular sentences to support your response.
3. Lawrence's paragraph encourages us to reconsider the ways in which the mind actually works. Write a paragraph in which you create a different metaphor to describe the mind at work. Try to make your sentences as vivid and detailed as Lawrence's.

Rural Literalism

Calvin Trillin

When economists talk about "pump priming," we don't usually visualize an old-fashioned pump handle atop a dry well. Or when they mention "windfalls," we are not expected to picture a pile of apples beneath a tree. Obviously, the expressions are metaphorical and are intended to be taken as such. Yet the literal sense of these and similar metaphorical expressions should not escape the attention of alert readers and writers. At times, as the Lakoff and Johnson selection (p. 29) shows, it can be intellectually useful to look closely at metaphors whose literal meanings have become invisible through habitual use. At other times, as Calvin Trillin entertainingly shows, it can be downright amusing to take common metaphorical language literally. There is a point to Trillin's amusement, however: What would ordinary communication be like if we were so well versed in country things that we took everything literally? Would we then always miss the forest for the trees?

A reporter, essayist, novelist, and humorist, Calvin Trillin has crisscrossed this country since the late 1960s writing a regular column for The New Yorker *magazine entitled "U.S. Journal." His amusing adventures and his relentless struggle "to get something decent to eat" are chronicled in* American Fried *(1974), an extremely witty and incisive study of eating out in America. He has also published two novels—*Rune Struck *(1977) and* Floater *(1980)—and several collections of essays, the most recent of which are* Uncivil Liberties *(1982) and* Killings *(1984). In addition, he served as a contributing editor to* The Nation, *where the following essay originally appeared.*

1 My problem with country living began innocently enough when our well ran dry and a neighbor said some pump priming would be necessary.

2 "I didn't come up here to discuss economics," I said. Actually, I don't discuss economics in the city either. As it happens, I don't understand economics. There's no use revealing that, though, to every Tom, Dick and Harry who interrupts his dinner to try to get your water running, so I said, "I come up here to get away from that sort of thing." My neighbor gave me a puzzled look.

3 "He's talking about the water pump," my wife told me. "It needs priming."

4 I thought that experience might have been just a fluke—until, on a fishing trip with the same neighbor, I proudly pulled in a fish with what I thought was a major display of deep-sea angling skill, only to hear a voice behind me say, "It's just a fluke."

5 "This is dangerous," I said to my wife, while helping her weed the vegetable garden the next day. I had thought our problem was limited to the pump-priming ichthyologist down the road, but that morning at the post office I had overheard a farmer say that since we

seemed to be in for a few days of good weather he intended to make his hay while the sun was shining. "These people are robbing me of aphorisms," I said, taking advantage of the discussion to rest for a while on my hoe. "How can I encourage the children to take advantage of opportunities by telling them to make hay while the sun shines if they think that means making hay while the sun shines?"

6 "Could you please keep weeding those peas while you talk," she said. "You've got a long row to hoe."

7 I began to look at my wife with new eyes. By that, of course, I don't mean that I actually went to a discount eye outlet, acquired two new eyes (20/20 this time), replaced my old eyes with the new ones and looked at my wife. Having to make that explanation is just the sort of thing I found troubling. What I mean is that I was worried about the possibility of my wife falling into the habit of rural literalism herself. My concern was deepened a few days later by a conversation that took place while I was in one of our apple trees, looking for an apple that was not used as a *dacha* by the local worms. "I just talked to the Murrays, and they say that the secret is picking up windfalls," my wife said.

8 "Windfalls?" I said. "Could it be that Jim Murray has taken over Exxon since last time I saw him? Or do the Murrays have a natural-gas operation in the back forty I didn't know about?"

9 "Not those kinds of windfalls," my wife said. "The apples that fall from the tree because of the wind. They're a breeding place for worms."

10 "There's nothing wrong with our apples," I said, reaching for a particularly plump one.

11 "Be careful," she said. "You may be getting yourself too far out on a limb."

12 "You may be getting yourself out on a limb yourself," I said to my wife at breakfast the next morning.

13 She looked around the room. "I'm sitting at the kitchen table," she said.

14 "I meant it symbolically," I said. "The way it was meant to be meant. This has got to stop. I won't have you coming in from the garden with small potatoes in your basket and saying that what you found was just small potatoes. 'Small potatoes' doesn't mean small potatoes."

15 "Small potatoes doesn't mean small potatoes?"

16 "I refuse to discuss it," I said. "The tide's in, so I'm going

fishing, and I don't want to hear any encouraging talk about that fluke not being the only fish in the ocean."

17 "I was just going to ask why you have to leave before you finish your breakfast," she said.

18 "Because time and tide wait for no man," I said. "And I mean it."

19 Had she trapped me into saying that? Or was it possible that I was falling into the habit myself? Was I, as I waited for a bite, thinking that there were plenty of other fish in the sea? Then I had a bite—then another. I forgot about the problem until after I had returned to the dock and done my most skillful job of filleting.

20 "Look!" I said, holding up the carcass of one fish proudly, as my wife approached the dock. "It's nothing but skin and bones."

21 The shock of realizing what I had said caused me to stumble against my fish-cleaning table and knock the fillets off the dock. "Now we won't have anything for dinner," I said.

22 "Don't worry," my wife said. "I have other fish to fry."

23 "That's not right!" I shouted. "That's not what that means. It means you have something better to do."

24 "It can also mean that I have other fish to fry," she said. "And I do. I'll just get that other fish you caught out of the freezer. Even though it was just a fluke."

25 I tried to calm myself. I apologized to my wife for shouting and offered to help her pick vegetables from the garden for dinner.

26 "I'll try to watch my language," she said, as we stood among the peas.

27 "It's all right, really," I said.

28 "I was just going to say that tonight it seems rather slim pickings," she said. "Just about everything has gone to seed."

29 "Perfectly all right," I said, wandering over toward the garden shed, where some mud seemed to be caked in the eaves. I pushed at the mud with a rake, and a swarm of wasps burst out at me. I ran for the house, swatting at wasps with my hat. Inside, I suddenly had the feeling that some of them had managed to crawl up the legs of my jeans, and I tore the jeans off. My wife found me there in the kitchen, standing quietly in what the English call their smalls.

30 "That does it," I said. "We're going back to the city."

31 "Just because of a few stings?"

32 "Can't you see what happened?" I said. "They scared the pants off me."

Exercises for Reading, Thinking, and Writing

1. Reread the essay, this time underlining all the metaphorical expressions. How does Trillin use these expressions? How do his neighbor and his wife use them? What does Trillin mean by "rural literalism"?
2. Whose approach toward language do you prefer—Trillin's or his wife's? Why? What are the advantages and disadvantages of each approach? Which do you think can lead to the greatest amount of confusion?
3. Literalism, of course, can occur in any area. Cities, too, have their special expressions. Why do you think Trillin used rural expressions to make his point? What connection can you find between the rural language and the economic theme of the essay?
4. After rereading carefully the introduction to this section, try letting the metaphorical possibilities in our everyday language help you to develop a paragraph about some subject. After quickly writing out a series of statements about the subject, check them for metaphors. For example, how might you develop a statement that your little brother is a pest, or that your high school was a zoo? Let the metaphor help you think of your subject in new ways.

Gramercy Gym

Edward Hoagland

In our camera-dominated age, readers frequently skip over descriptive writing in the belief that "a picture is worth a thousand words." But no photograph can compete with the descriptive power of a fresh and appropriate metaphor. A camera, for example, can supply us with excellent pictures of a boxing match, but no photograph could show us what Edward Hoagland (1932–) shows us in the following selection—fighters "whose heavy arms flip out of a clinch like a thick tunafish." When writing comes at us so vividly, we can honestly say that a few well-chosen words can be worth a thousand pictures.

Edward Hoagland is a writer who seems to take visceral delight in physical description. A Harvard-educated novelist, essayist, and travel writer, Hoagland frequently writes about men, women, and animals living on the primitive edges of survival; his essay "The Courage of Turtles" is a contemporary classic. His most recent books include African Calliope: A Journey to the Sudan *(1979) and* The Tugman's Passage *(1982). A collection of his writings was published under the title* The Edward Hoagland Reader *(1979).*

1 The Gramercy Gym is two flights up some littered, lightless stairs that look like a mugger's paradise, though undoubtedly they are the safest stairs in New York. Inside, two dozen bodies are chopping up and down, self-clocked, each fellow cottoned in his dreams. Some are skipping rope, turbaned in towels, wrapped in robes in order to sweat. These are white-looking figures, whereas the men who are about to spar have on dark headguards that close grimly around the face like an executioner's hood. There are floor-length mirrors and mattresses for exercising and rubdowns, and two speedbags banging like drums, and three heavy bags swinging even between the rounds with the momentum of more than a decade of punches. The bell is loud, the fighters jerk like eating and walking birds, hissing through their teeth as they punch, their feet sneakering the floor with shuffly sounds. They wear red shoelaces in white shoes, and peanut-colored gloves, or if they're Irish they're in green. They are learning to move their feet to the left and right, to move in and out, punching over, then under an opponent's guard, and other repetitive skills without which a man in the ring becomes a man of straw. The speedbags teach head-punching, the heavy bags teach body work, and one bag pinned to the wall has both a head and torso diagrammed, complete with numbers, so that the trainer can shout out what punches his fighter should throw. "Bounce, bounce!" the trainers yell.

2 There are mongooses and poleaxes, men who hog the floor with an aggressive stance, men whose heavy arms flip out of a clinch like a thick tunafish. The room is L-shaped with a rickety ring set in the L, and so crowded that one might infer that the sport is thriving, though most of the young fighters speak Spanish now. Chu-Chu Malave, a promising welterweight of twenty-one with hard fists and a 15–3 record, has girl-length hair that he ties in a rubber band when he is fighting; and he trains in a shirt with Bach's head on it. He is an acting student, lives in the East Village, and seems touching and young. Another boy wears an "Alaska Hiway" shirt and lizard-green

shoes. He sucks in a mouthful of water and spurts it out grandly. Everybody is trying to sock his way upwards through life, but they are divided between those who prefer to fight while moving forward and those who like to fight as they move back. Naturally, the arena matchmakers will try to pair a man from group A with one from group B.

3 In the ring the spittle flies when the punches connect and the real rumbles start. Gym fighters sometimes don't look quite as good under the klieg lights, and sometimes are never given much chance to fight anywhere else—the "animals" down in Philadelphia, who are left to rot in their gyms and fight their hearts out where nobody can see them, are still joked about—so everybody likes to look good at least here.

4 The Gramercy Gym's king is Carlos Ortiz, a blocky lightweight who has been fighting professionally for seventeen years. He was the champ in 1962–65 and 1965–68, retiring the next year, but in 1971 began a comeback. He has fought four or five tune-up appearances in the same number of months, and the word is that although he may have lost his legs, he has not lost his punch. He sports a red head-guard, baggy blue sweatpants and an NMU shirt, has a nose that looks bobbed because of all the violence wreaked upon it, and fights as watchfully as a lathe operator bending to a machine. It is perhaps this attentiveness that's so overwhelming. But with the youngsters he is gentle, pulling every punch even as he shovels their resistance aside and swarms over them. (I thought of the legendary way wolf cubs take on their lupine form, licked into shape by the tongues of their mothers.) Then he leaves for the day with a gorgeous redhead with a million curls.

Exercises for Reading, Thinking, and Writing

1. Go back over the selection and circle all the examples of metaphor. Do you notice anything that the metaphors have in common? What central resemblance do most of the metaphors cluster around? How does this resemblance affect your response to the world Hoagland describes?

2. To what extent are Hoagland's metaphors successful? How do they help you visualize the fighters? Does his figurative language convey more positive or negative connotations about prize fighters? What attitude toward the fighters do you think Hoagland wants to convey?

3. Think of a metaphor for a group of athletes, and try to develop that metaphor into a paragraph or more. For example, how might you develop the statement that a professional football team is like a small army?

Starting

Michael Anania

Michael Anania (1938–) is a poet and critic who lives in Chicago and teaches at the University of Illinois at Chicago. Born in Omaha, Nebraska, Anania earned a B.A. from the University of Nebraska and a Ph.D. in literature from the State University of New York at Buffalo. In addition to teaching, Anania worked first as the poetry and then as the literary editor of the Swallow Press. Besides his numerous essays on contemporary American culture and reviews of literature, Anania has published three volumes of poetry (The Color of Dust *[1970],* Riversongs *[1978], and most recently* The Sky at Ashland *[1986]*) *and a novel entitled* The Red Menace, *a portrait of American culture in the 1950s. In addition to serving as a contributing editor of* Tri-Quarterly, *Anania writes frequently for* Chicago *magazine, where the following essay first appeared.*

Michael Anania reports that the most challenging and satisfying aspect of writing lies in the process of discovering—and making—relationships between and among our ideas. Engaged in the work of establishing connections in an essay, Anania usually reserves questions of technique for revision. When asked to explain the origins of "Starting," Anania notes, "I enjoy any excuse to write about cars." In the process, Anania turns the delicate ritual of starting a car into a delightfully engaging metaphor for a good deal of contemporary experience.

1 "First of all, I pat the gas, just once, with the key off. Then I turn the key on, push it all the way to the floor, and let up slowly. Halfway up and I start it."

2 "With mine, you gotta hold the pedal all the way down to the floor, crank it till it catches, and when it does, let it up about two-thirds of the way."

3 Five or six of us are stamping around the outer lobby of my apartment building in down parkas and ski gloves. It is January in

Chicago, one of the mornings of the car. Outside, the bright sun gives the air a blue sheen like finely worked carbon steel. It scrapes against the glass front wall of the lobby and hones itself along the three-week mounds of snow layered like limestone beside the walk.

4 "Four times." It's Eddie leaning against the heater vents behind the mailboxes. His tone is canonical. "Four times. Just pump it four times, and it starts right up."

5 "I try to go out at night, you know, and start her up. And after the engine's hot, I rev it up real high, turn the key off, and push the gas all the way down. You can just hear her sucking gas up to the engine."

6 "Well, with my diesel, you have to wait for this light on the dash to go off. That means the glow plug's hot enough to start it, but by then on a day like today, you've used up too much of the battery, and it won't start anyway."

7 Diesel? Light on the dash? No wonder his car doesn't start. Cars that start have a system, a private ritual worked out by their owners on days like this one, sitting shivering and hopeful in their machines. They have, these devices, the force of private truth—how and when and how many times the pedal is pushed, how far the choke is pulled out and when, whether the key is turned on before or after the pedal is pushed. Some of this lore comes from tow-truck jump starters who bob up from under the hood and shout, "Keep it all the way to the floor," or "Get your foot off the gas," or "Pump it." How much of this really matters is impossible to know. It matters, obviously, to the way we live with cars, and standing around the lobby with the guys it has a curiously familiar and disquieting ring to it, a touch of early high-school locker-room sex education—vain, improbable, idiosyncratic, and just as indispensable.

8 There is something intimate, however painful, about trying to start your car on a bitter cold morning. After the little rituals of pedal pushing and precision choke pulling, the deepening, sad song of a slowing starter motor, the inside of the windshield hazed over with your own quickening breath, a haze eventually webbed with threads of self-propelled crystal that run at loony angles across the glass. Bits of advice, a lifetime of pseudo-mechanic's lore carols up out of the collective technological unconscious—to avoid flooding the engine put the gas pedal to the floor, or to avoid flooding the engine keep your foot off the pedal entirely, pump it, never pump it, add heat, crank it, don't crank it you'll wear down the battery, try it again, call the motor club.

9 The engine is nearing death, and the starter's grind reaches a slow, trembling note that is as much attuned to sadness and despair as the loneliest of Big Walter Horton's quavering train-whistle obbligatos or the most mournful of B. B. King's spine-quivering chords. By now you're bowing into the steering wheel, your stomach tightening as the engine slows, the edge of the cold key cutting into your finger and your thumb. You try each contradictory piece of advice in turn—first slowly, punctuating each separate attempt with a moment of silence, then rapidly, in quick succession, until the dashboard warning lights darken and the last bit of energy from the overburdened battery clicks like ice on glass against the failing solenoid.

10 This is the zero point of your love of your car, your love of cars in general, the moral retribution for every sin it has suffered on your account, punishment for a long string of specific failures beginning with the profligacies of the show room and ending with last night's lack of concern for a full gas tank and for an even longer misguided faith in the efficacy of cars, all the way back to the first moment in late childhood when you knew, watching a Pontiac Catalina drift by like a cream-and-turquoise Beatrice, that wheels were the way to freedom, love, and happiness. Neighbors slip by on the way to work. Old Chevys clamor to life, rust-bitten Fords, the painfully modest compact in the next parking stall, all of them kicking up white plumes of exhaust above the blackening snow. Just one rebuke after another.

11 *Mea culpa, mea culpa, mea maxima culpa . . .* or hit the steering wheel in disgust . . . or stand outside in the cold, the hood up and your battery cables raised like a begging bowl. At 26 below help comes from all sides. Everyone's tragedy is no one's tragedy. But at a mere ten below, you are alone, a very special and conspicuous failure, leprous, unclean.

12 Nothing, except love and America, promises more than a car, so there are few disappointments more bitter. Remember when you saw it on television, swooning like a dancer through the curves of a mountain road as lushly green as any of the emerald visions of the Hudson River school or skimming the surface of Pacific Ocean water along the California coast or conquering the Baja or lasering toward the vanishing point of a crayon-colored Mojave sunset, irresistibly lustrous and fluid? They don't sell us cars with tires whitened with salt and salt streaks trailing like tears from the lash tips of their windshield wipers, this Lot's wife of a car, immovable, dead.

Exercises for Reading, Thinking, and Writing

1. This essay contains a number of figurative comparisons. Reread the essay carefully and locate as many as possible. What other kinds of activities are related to starting a car? In what ways, then, does this essay describe more than a single event?

2. Characterize the nature of the figurative language used in this essay. What are the principal sources of Anania's metaphors and similes? How does his choice of these metaphors and similes affect the tone of the piece?

3. How would you describe the author's relationship with his car? What, in effect, is his attitude, his feeling toward his car? What words and phrases help you to identify this relationship? How does Anania react to his car's failure to start? Whom does he blame? What other "failures" does this specific failure evoke?

4. How many different kinds of advice does the essay feature? Why does Anania include so many contradictory "bits of advice"? What, for example, is the effect of starting the essay with two paragraphs of advice in the form of first-person narration? Trace Anania's use of first-person accounts of starting cars. What pattern, if any, do you notice? How does this pattern reflect the overall structure of the essay? What is the effect of Anania's moving back and forth between general "meditations" on car-starting and specific, physical description?

5. Consider the ending of Anania's essay. What is the effect of the long sentence in the final paragraph, beginning "Remember when you saw it on television . . ."? What is the point of introducing the biblical metaphor in the essay's last sentence?

6. Beginnings (startings) and endings are often marked by highly conventional rituals. What other activities can you think of which make use of such "lore"?

7. This essay is also about "private ritual." Why are these rituals so important to the author? Describe in detail a "private ritual" that you engage in, one that, as Anania says, has "the force of private truth." Explain why this ritual is so important to you.

2. SHAPING IDEAS

Observation and Inference

1 Effective writing invariably develops out of thinking carefully about a subject—preparing something intelligent and interesting to say about it. Neither thinking nor writing is by any means restricted to a rigid and unalterable sequence of activities. The precise nature of either process can vary widely, depending on the writer's subject, purpose, audience, and experience.

2 In this chapter, we will examine one basic and very practical procedure writers can use to form an idea about a subject—namely, moving from observation to inference, from paying close attention to what exists around us to making judgments based on those observations. Making an *observation* involves more than simply perceiving an object or event; it requires us to notice something distinctive about it. For example, seeing a sofa in a room does not qualify as an observation, though noticing dog hair on the sofa does. Drawing an *inference* from an observation involves discovering something about what we can't immediately see from what we can see. If we were to assume that the owners of the sofa also have a dog, we would be drawing an inference.

3 There are at least three advantages to be gained from learning how to make the leap from observation to inference, from one level of thinking to another. Basing our inferences upon solid observations helps us, first, to progress from what we are sure we know to what we do not yet know; second, to acquire lively, yet disciplined, habits

of thinking and writing; and, third, to strengthen our confidence that what we finally decide to say about a subject will be both incisive and distinctively our own.

4 We write best when we know what we are talking about. Perhaps the surest way to increase our knowledge of a subject is to make observations about it. Nearly all forceful thinking and writing are grounded in observing—in regarding something attentively, considering it carefully, or inspecting it systematically. Observation is basic to all inquiry, from the scientist's analysis of the data gathered during an experiment to the poet's expression of the insights emerging from an intense personal experience. Yet most of us do not pause long enough to observe closely. Consider, for example, the most prominent building on campus. How carefully have we ever observed it? How much, finally, do we really know about it? How specific could we be if asked to describe it to someone who's never seen it? To know the world around us is to observe it carefully. Observation begins with first-hand acquaintance, with using our senses to extend the limits of what we know.

5 Observation, as we alluded to before, is not simply passive awareness of something perceived before ("That is a sofa"). It is, rather, a deliberate mental activity; we probe a subject in order to discover as much as possible about it. For example, observing a football game can be much more satisfying than simply following the ball. So, too, reading a novel can involve a good deal more than merely keeping an eye on the plot. Practice in observation gradually educates us to be more selective—to know what to look for, to find the most meaningful aspects of what is being observed, and to note the relationships that bind the parts into a whole.

6 Just as important as observation to our intellectual lives is inference. Most talk, whether private or public, is regularly informed by these two processes. We also encounter patterns of observation and inference constantly in our reading. For example, we routinely infer from newspaper reports on what politicians have said how they are likely to vote on a particular issue. So, too, as readers of literature, we regularly draw inferences about, say, the main character's values and prejudices from the novel's dialogue and action.

7 Our observations provide us with the facts from which we draw inferences. There are different kinds of facts. *Private facts* are those that can be experienced only by the individual involved (the fact of a backache, of enjoyment in the taste of fruit, and the like).

There are also *public facts,* those that the world at large has agreed to (the meaning of hour, meter, kilogram). Then there are *scientific facts,* the principles of physics, mathematics, biology, and so on—theories that are regarded as facts but are always subject to modification. Finally, there are *primary facts,* those about which there can be no disagreement (for example, the number of fingers on a hand, the number of cars parked in our driveway). Primary facts are indisputable. If a primary fact is something known with certainty, then it must finally have a demonstrable, observable existence.

8 Any writer considering any subject has a responsibility to provide convincing, factual evidence to support each assertion. And all writers, whatever their purpose or point of view, rely on essentially three sources of knowledge: *direct observation,* the data gathered from first-hand experience; *recollection,* the remembrance of what was once observed; and *testimony,* the reports of what others have observed or recalled. The quality of each observation depends on how familiar we are with the subject at hand. First-semester biology students, for example, may well have some initial difficulty deciding exactly what to focus on and what inferences to draw as they watch a classmate dissect a frog. But in the end, careful observation should provide us with a good deal of manageable information: perceptions that are concrete, limited, and verifiable. If, for example, we apply these criteria to the observations we make while conducting a laboratory experiment, reading a textbook, or even walking down the street, we will discover that observation suggests a pattern in our thinking, a movement toward greater lucidity and eventually toward converting that understanding into an idea about a subject.

9 Our thinking normally follows a pattern of observation and inference—moving from what we perceive of an experience through our senses to what is suggested by that experience. Based on our observations, we draw inferences about a subject. As noted earlier, to draw an inference is to make a statement about what is still uncertain on the basis of what is certain. To take one example, let us suppose that we are driving through a small coastal community in Florida. We observe extensive damage to the roads, homes, and shops in the town. From its location, as well as from the lingering signs of rain and diminishing winds, we infer, reasonably enough, that the community has been hit by a hurricane. We generalize on the basis of our observations (the weather conditions, the damage done) and then we infer what we have not observed directly (the hurricane). In

this, and in all other instances, inference takes us beyond what is present, beyond what can be immediately seen.

10 Inference is speculative, adventurous thinking. It involves making statements about what is absent based on what is present. For example, nearly all detective work depends on moving from observation to inference. By carefully examining the evidence in a case, the police can infer a great deal about, for example, the date and time of a crime, the criminal's motive, and perhaps even the culprit's identity. The pattern of our own thinking in writing, when we are deliberate about it, is quite similar to the investigative procedures of a detective. We, too, combine numerous fragmentary observations into some sort of generalized whole from which we draw inferences in order to arrive at an idea about the problem or subject in question. And we should remember that the accuracy of our inferences depends on the thoroughness of our observations.

11 We always run the risk of making mistakes in our thinking when we move from observable facts to inferences drawn from these facts; that is, from the certain to the uncertain. Accordingly, we ought to be aware of how our own background, temperament, interests, prejudices, and special training may influence the inferences we draw. Consider, for example, how our political beliefs might affect the way we think about what we've seen while driving through a torn-down district of an inner city. So, too, we should be sure to base our inferences on a sufficient number of careful observations. In effect, we should train ourselves to draw inferences that can be tested for accuracy and thoroughness. To do so will both broaden and strengthen the core of information created by our observations.

12 But how does working with observation and inferences help us to write better? Moving from observation to inference is one fundamental method writers can use to form an idea about a subject. But what do we mean when we talk about having an idea about a subject? And how, exactly, can observation and inference help us form that idea? To have an idea about a subject is to come to a conclusion about it, however tentative. Like a hypothesis, an idea about a subject is a proposition—a provisional conclusion—that must be proven. Raising the question of how we form an idea is equivalent to asking how we reach a particular conclusion, no matter how tentative it might be.

13 An expository essay introduces our tentative conclusion about a subject and then proceeds to clarify and verify—to explain and offer evidence to support—the point we want to make. If, for example, we were writing about the end of the energy crisis, our principal

tasks would be to explain and prove our idea about this subject: say, that natural gas offers America its most abundant source of energy for the decades ahead. Ultimately, expository writing does not explain a subject as much as it *explains our idea about a subject.*

14 Suppose that we have been asked to write an essay on the popularity of running in America. Using the procedure outlined in the chapter "Exploring Key Words" (see pp. 1–6), we jot down a list of the words we associate with the subject: *exercise, health, satisfaction, getting in shape, James Fixx, marathon, Bill Rodgers, sneakers, shorts, sweatsuits, expenses.* Thinking of the *expenses* of running may well lead us to consider the extent to which big business is involved in the sport: advertising, retail chains of specialty jogging shops, and so on. The phrase *big business,* though rather vague, might make us pause and consider how such a simple recreational activity has been transformed into an enormous commercial enterprise: newsletters, magazines, books, documentaries, heavily promoted marathons, clothing, and a bagful of special equipment. These observations may lead us to think about running in a new way. While we all have heard a great deal about the benefits of running, perhaps few of us have ever considered its full costs. We gradually are settling on a subject: the escalating costs of running. We might even come up with a title: "The Complete Cost of Running."

15 But before we can form a precise idea about the cost of running, we must learn enough about the subject. We do this by combining direct observations of joggers with some basic research on what has been written about the physical, psychological, and economic advantages and disadvantages of the activity. We compile testimony on the common injuries (shin splints, torn tendons, broken ankles, and so on) as well as the rising number of accidents involving runners (hit by cars on poorly lit roads, attacked by dogs, and so on). We piece together this basic information and infer that there are greater risks to jogging than most devotees would suspect. Our own observations and the inferences we draw from them carry us closer to our idea—our tentative conclusion. From watching so many people actually waddle around a track in European-designer outfits and day-glo sneakers, we infer, among other things, that jogging is steadily becoming more enterprise than exercise. It would now be reasonable to shape an idea: that such factors as higher prices for more "required" equipment, as well as greater risk of accident, have raised the *personal cost* of running to an unprecedented level.

16 Our work—our responsibilities to our audience—does not stop

once we have put together an idea. We are further obligated to test the idea with additional observation. In this instance, we would need to follow through by analyzing and validating each of our inferences. We can measure the quality of our inferences by placing them on a scale ranging from solid *judgment* (the ability to make reasonable decisions and to perceive relationships among even incomplete observations) to mere *opinion* (the kind of inference we have invested with nothing more than emotion or will). Inferences based on judgment aid us not only in getting hold of an idea but also in evaluating its soundness. As soon as we've worked out our idea and tested it thoroughly, we'll be in a much stronger position to convince our audience of its validity.

17 Observation and inference are an elementary, and therefore invaluable, means to extend and enrich our knowledge. Understanding how the mind moves between observation and inference is essential for cultivating lively, productive habits of thinking in writing. Awareness of this process also helps develop a disciplined mind, one that can suspend judgment while inquiry continues. Finally, knowing something more about the workings of our own minds may well be one of the most significant and enduring satisfactions of our lives.

Dumbstruck

Annie Dillard

The author of intense, almost religious meditations on the beauty and suffering in nature, Annie Dillard (1945–   ) describes her excursions into the natural world in these terms: "I am an explorer, and I am also a stalker . . . the instrument of the hunt itself." The observations of nature recorded in Pilgrim at Tinker Creek *earned her a Pulitzer Prize for nonfiction in 1974. In the following selection, drawn from that book, she watches the terrifying death of a frog and infers that the creature is the victim of a giant water beetle. Annie Dillard is also the author of* Holy the Firm *(1978),* Living by Fiction *(1982), and* Teaching a Stone to Talk *(1982).*

1 A couple of summers ago I was walking along the edge of the island to see what I could see in the water, and mainly to scare frogs. Frogs have an inelegant way of taking off from invisible positions on the bank just ahead of your feet, in dire panic, emitting a froggy "Yike!" and splashing into the water. Incredibly, this amused me, and, incredibly, it amuses me still. As I walked along the grassy edge of the island, I got better and better at seeing frogs both in and out of the water. I learned to recognize, slowing down, the difference in texture of the light reflected from mudbank, water, grass, or frog. Frogs were flying all around me. At the end of the island I noticed a small green frog. He was exactly half in and half out of the water, looking like a schematic diagram of an amphibian, and he didn't jump.

2 He didn't jump; I crept closer. At last I knelt on the island's winter-killed grass, lost, dumbstruck, staring at the frog in the creek just four feet away. He was a very small frog with wide, dull eyes. And just as I looked at him, he slowly crumpled and began to sag. The spirit vanished from his eyes as if snuffed. His skin emptied and drooped; his very skull seemed to collapse and settle like a kicked tent. He was shrinking before my eyes like a deflating football. I watched the taut, glistening skin on his shoulders ruck, and rumple, and fall. Soon, part of his skin, formless as a pricked balloon, lay in floating folds like bright scum on top of the water: it was a monstrous and terrifying thing. I gaped bewildered, appalled. An oval shadow hung in the water behind the drained frog; then the shadow glided away. The frog skin bag started to sink.

3 I had read about the giant water bug, but never seen one. "Giant water bug" is really the name of the creature, which is an enormous, heavy-bodied brown beetle. It eats insects, tadpoles, fish, and frogs. Its grasping forelegs are mighty and hooked inward. It seizes a victim with these legs, hugs it tight, and paralyzes it with enzymes injected during a vicious bite. That one bite is the only bite it ever takes. Through the puncture shoot the poisons that dissolve the victim's muscles and bones and organs—all but the skin—and through it the giant water bug sucks out the victim's body, reduced to a juice. This event is quite common in warm fresh water. The frog I saw was being sucked by a giant water bug. I had been kneeling on the island grass; when the unrecognizable flap of frog skin settled on the creek bottom, swaying, I stood up and brushed the knees of my pants. I couldn't catch my breath.

Additional Rhetorical Strategies

Narration (throughout); Description (paragraph 2); Process Analysis (paragraph 3).

Examining Words and Meaning

1. Why is the simile "like a kicked tent" (paragraph 2) so effective? What other similes in the paragraph have a similar effect for you?
2. Check these words in a dictionary, if necessary: dire (paragraph 1); schematic (paragraph 1); dumbstruck (paragraph 2); ruck (paragraph 2); enzymes (paragraph 3).

Focusing on Structures and Strategies

1. Why does Dillard repeat "he didn't jump" at the beginning of paragraph 2? How does the repetition bring us closer to her experience as she watched the events she describes here?
2. At what point in this passage does she explicitly say that the frog has been killed by a giant water bug? Why does she wait so long to do so? Suppose that she had started the passage by saying, "One day I saw a frog killed by a giant water bug"? How might her account be less effective?

Suggestions for Further Discussion and Writing

1. Compare this account of the frog's death with the selection by Neil Bell (p. 170). How does Dillard's description of an animal's death differ from his? Does she seem more or less detached than he is from the scene she describes?
2. Observe carefully some sequence of events in nature: a dog making the rounds of the neighborhood, a bee in the garden, a pigeon in the park. Write an account of what you see, using what you have read

or learned to draw conclusions about your observations. Try structuring your account as Dillard has structured hers, withholding your conclusions until the end of the essay.

More Than Just a Shrine: Paying Homage to the Ghosts of Ellis Island

Mary Gordon

Mary Gordon (1949–) reports that she doesn't compose on a typewriter. She drafts her short stories, novels, and essays in longhand, on narrow lines in bound notebooks imported from England. "I have a fetish about my writing tools," she observes, "I cannot work without those notebooks and my special fine-point, felt-tipped pens." Her attention to detail and to nuances in thinking and writing is amply evident in the following essay, "More Than Just a Shrine."

Born on Long Island, New York, Mary Gordon attended Catholic elementary and secondary schools before graduating with a B.A. from Barnard College in 1971. She has taught writing at community colleges and at Amherst College. "I think you teach tricks," she reports. "You cannot teach people to have an interesting mind. You cannot give them an ear. You can tell them craftsmanly tricks and give them some kind of self-criticism. You can make them see that writers are real people, too."

Her Roman Catholic background is everywhere present in her fiction. Her novels, Final Payments *(1978),* The Company of Women *(1981) and* Men and Angels *(1985), have earned her a wide readership as well as an exceptional amount of critical attention and acclaim. Judged "one of the most gifted writers of her generation" and a writer whose work "combines the high moral seriousness of Doris Lessing and the stylistic elegance of Flannery O'Connor," Gordon crafts sentences with the precision and metaphorical authority of one dedicated to exploring language's potential to render the richness and complex textures of experience. "I don't think I write about things that are trivial. I had a fortunate background in that I was exposed in a real sense to the 'complicatedness' of people's lives. On the other hand, the working-class people around me in my Long Island community led seemingly straightforward lives, yet they had a rich inner religious life." Their lives, she says, "taught me to look a little below the surface."*

In "More Than Just a Shrine," first published in the New York Times Magazine, *Gordon uses her skills as an observer to draw inferences from the visible remnants of the "complicatedness" that so many immigrants brought with them as they entered the New World through the dismal halls of Ellis Island.*

1 I once sat in a hotel in Bloomsbury trying to have breakfast alone. A Russian with a habit of compulsively licking his lips asked if he could join me. I was afraid to say no; I thought it might be bad for détente. He explained to me that he was a linguist, and that he always liked to talk to Americans to see if he could make any connection between their speech and their ethnic background. When I told him about my mixed ancestry—my mother is Irish and Italian, my father a Lithuanian Jew—he began jumping up and down in his seat, rubbing his hands together and licking his lips even more frantically.

2 "Ah," he said, "so you are really somebody who comes from what is called the boiling pot of America." Yes, I told him, yes I was, but I quickly rose to leave. I thought it would be too hard to explain to him the relation of the boiling potters to the main course, and I wanted to get to the British Museum. I told him that the only thing I could think of that united people whose backgrounds, histories and points of view were utterly diverse was that their people had landed at a place called Ellis Island.

3 I didn't tell him that Ellis Island was the only American landmark I'd ever visited. How could I describe to him the estrangement I'd always felt from the kind of traveler who visits shrines to America's past greatness, those rebuilt forts with muskets behind glass and sabers mounted on the walls and gift shops selling maple sugar candy in the shape of Indian headdresses, those reconstructed villages with tables set for 50 and the Paul Revere silver gleaming? All that Americana—Plymouth Rock, Gettysburg, Mount Vernon, Valley Forge—it all inhabits for me a zone of blurred abstraction with far less hold on my imagination than the Bastille or Hampton Court. I suppose I've always known that my uninterest in it contains a large component of the willed: I am American, and those places purport to be my history. But they are not mine.

4 Ellis Island is, though; it's the one place I can be sure my people

are connected to. And so I made a journey there to find my history, like any Rotarian traveling in his Winnebago to Antietam to find his. I had become part of that humbling democracy of people looking in some site for a past that has grown unreal. The monument I traveled to was not, however, a tribute to some old glory. The minute I set foot upon the island I could feel all that it stood for: insecurity, obedience, anxiety, dehumanization, the terrified and careful deference of the displaced. I hadn't traveled to the Battery and boarded a ferry across from the Statue of Liberty to raise flags or breathe a richer, more triumphant air. I wanted to do homage to the ghosts.

5 I felt them everywhere, from the moment I disembarked and saw the building with its high-minded brick, its hopeful little lawn, its ornamental cornices. The place was derelict when I arrived; it had not functioned for more than 30 years—almost as long as the time it had operated at full capacity as a major immigration center. I was surprised to learn what a small part of history Ellis Island had occupied. The main building was constructed in 1892, then rebuilt between 1898 and 1900 after a fire. Most of the immigrants who arrived during the latter half of the 19th century, mainly northern and western Europeans, landed not at Ellis Island but on the western tip of the Battery at Castle Garden, which had opened as a receiving center for immigrants in 1855.

6 By the 1880's the facilities at Castle Garden had grown scandalously inadequate. Officials looked for an island on which to build a new immigration center because they thought that on an island immigrants could be more easily protected from swindlers and quickly transported to railroad terminals in New Jersey. Bedloe's Island was considered, but New Yorkers were aghast at the idea of a "Babel" ruining their beautiful new treasure, "Liberty Enlightening the World." The statue's sculptor, Frédéric Auguste Bartholdi, reacted to the prospect of immigrants landing near his masterpiece in horror; he called it a "monstrous plan." So much for Emma Lazarus.

7 Ellis Island was finally chosen because the citizens of New Jersey petitioned the Federal Government to remove from the island an old naval powder magazine that they thought dangerously close to the Jersey shore. The explosives were removed; no one wanted the island for anything. It was the perfect place to build an immigration center.

8 I thought about the island's history as I walked into the building and made my way to the room that was the center in my imagina-

tion of the Ellis Island experience: the Great Hall. It had been made real for me in the stark, accusing photographs of Louis Hine and others who took those pictures to make a point. It was in the Great Hall that everyone had waited—waiting, always, the great vocation of the dispossessed. The room was empty, except for me and a handful of other visitors and the Park Ranger who showed us around. I felt myself grow insignificant in that room, with its huge semicircular windows, its air, even in dereliction, of solid and official probity.

9 I walked in the deathlike expansiveness of the room's disuse and tried to think of what it might have been like, filled and swarming. More than 16 million immigrants came through that room; approximately 250,000 were rejected. Not really a large proportion, but the implications for the rejected were dreadful. For some, there was nothing to go back to, or there was certain death; for others, who left as adventurers, to return would be to adopt in local memory the fool's role, and the failure's. No wonder that the island's history includes reports of 3,000 suicides.

10 Sometimes immigrants could pass through Ellis Island in mere hours, though for some the process took days. The particulars of the experience in the Great Hall were often influenced by the political events and attitudes on the mainland. In the 1890's and the first years of the new century, when cheap labor was needed, the newly built receiving center took in its immigrants with comparatively little question. But as the century progressed, the economy worsened, eugenics became both scientifically respectable and popular and World War I made American xenophobia seem rooted in fact.

11 Immigration acts were passed; newcomers had to prove, besides moral correctness and financial solvency, their ability to read. Quota laws came into effect, limiting the number of immigrants from southern and eastern Europe to less than 14 percent of the total quota. Intelligence tests were biased against all non-English-speaking persons and medical examinations became increasingly strict, until the machinery of immigration nearly collapsed under its own weight. The Second Quota Law of 1924 provided that all immigrants be inspected and issued visas at American consular offices in Europe, rendering the center almost obsolete.

12 On the day of my visit, my mind fastened upon the medical inspections, which had always seemed to me most emblematic of the ignominy and terror the immigrants endured. The medical inspectors, sometimes dressed in uniforms like soldiers, were particularly obsessed with a disease of the eyes called trachoma, which they checked

for by flipping back the immigrants' top eyelids with a hook used for buttoning gloves—a method that sometimes resulted in the transmission of the disease to healthy people. Mothers feared that if their children cried too much, their red eyes would be mistaken for a symptom of the disease and the whole family would be sent home. Those immigrants suspected of some physical disability had initials chalked on their coats. I remembered the photographs I'd seen of people standing, dumbstruck and innocent as cattle, with their manifest numbers hung around their necks and initials marked in chalk upon their coats: "E" for eye trouble, "K" for hernia, "L" for lameness, "X" for mental defects, "H" for heart disease.

13 I thought of my grandparents as I stood in the room; my 17-year-old grandmother, coming alone from Ireland in 1896, vouched for by a stranger who had found her a place as a domestic servant to some Irish who had done well. I tried to imagine the assault it all must have been for her; I've been to her hometown, a collection of farms with a main street—smaller than the athletic field of my local public school. She must have watched the New York skyline as the first- and second-class passengers were whisked off the gangplank with the most cursory of inspections while she was made to board a ferry to the new immigration center.

14 What could she have made of it—this buff-painted wooden structure with its towers and its blue slate roof, a place Harper's Weekly described as "a latter-day watering place hotel"? It would have been the first time she'd have heard people speaking something other than English. She would have mingled with people carrying baskets on their heads and eating foods unlike any she had ever seen—dark-eyed people, like the Sicilian she would marry 10 years later, who came over with his family, responsible even then for his mother and sister. I don't know what they thought, my grandparents, for they were not expansive people, nor romantic; they didn't like to think of what they called "the hard times," and their trip across the ocean was the single adventurous act of lives devoted after landing to security, respectability and fitting in.

15 What is the potency of Ellis Island for someone like me—an American, obviously, but one who has always felt that the country really belonged to the early settlers, that, as J. F. Powers wrote in "Morte D'Urban," it had been "handed down to them by the Pilgrims, George Washington and others, and that they were taking a risk in letting you live in it." I have never been the victim of overt discrimination; nothing I have wanted has been denied me because

of the accidents of blood. But I suppose it is part of being an American to be engaged in a somewhat tiresome but always self-absorbing process of national definition. And in this process, I have found in traveling to Ellis Island an important piece of evidence that could remind me I was right to feel my differentness. Something had happened to my people on that island, a result of the eternal wrongheadedness of American protectionism and the predictabilities of simple greed. I came to the island, too, so I could tell the ghosts that I was one of them, and that I honored them—their stoicism, and their innocence, the fear that turned them inward, and their pride. I wanted to tell them that I liked them better than the Americans who made them pass through the Great Hall and stole their names and chalked their weaknesses in public on their clothing. And to tell the ghosts what I have always thought: that American history was a very classy party that was not much fun until they arrived, brought the good food, turned up the music, and taught everyone to dance.

Additional Rhetorical Strategies

Narration (throughout); Cause and Effect (paragraphs 7, 10–11); Description (paragraph 8).

Examining Words and Meaning

1. Why, in general, is Mary Gordon not drawn to American "shrines"? What does she mean when she notes that "it all inhabits for me a zone of blurred abstraction" (paragraph 3)? Despite this—and other—reservations, why does she feel "connected" to Ellis Island? What does the island represent for her?
2. Gordon writes, "I suppose it is part of being an American to be engaged in a somewhat tiresome but always self-absorbing process of national definition" (paragraph 15). What does she mean by this? How would you define what it means to be an American? How does what Gordon says here relate to the way in which she develops her essay?

Focusing on Structures and Strategies

1. What is the dominant impression Gordon gives of the island? What specific observations does she work from in order to "reconstruct" the island's past? What inferences does she draw from these observations?

2. How does Gordon characterize the "Americans" who screened the immigrants on Ellis Island? How did they treat the immigrants? Historically, she describes a shift in the American attitude toward immigrants. What caused that change? How did it affect immigration laws?

3. How does she characterize the immigrants? In what ways does she identify with these "ghosts"? Consider the structure and purpose of the final sentence in this essay. What is the effect of ending her essay on a fragment? What does the last sentence suggest about her attitude toward immigrants?

4. Why does she begin the essay by describing her encounter with the Russian linguist? What issues connected with her account of Ellis Island are raised by the encounter? In what specific ways is the setting in which she meets the Russian linguist important? Why is she so unreceptive to the Russian's interest in her?

5. Why does she describe in such detail the process of choosing a place to process immigrants? What does her explanation reveal about the American attitude toward immigrants? What other details in her account add to this impression?

Suggestions for Further Discussion and Writing

1. Gordon seems to identify particularly with her maternal grandmother. What observations prompt this identification? How does she imagine her grandmother's reaction to America? Consider your own identification with special members of your family. Do you identify with any particular ancestor more than others? Why?

2. Consider the history of your own family. Choose an object (a family photograph, a set of dishes, a piece of jewelry, and the like) and observe its distinctive features carefully. What inferences about your family's history can you draw from these observations? Write an essay in which you use your detailed description of this object as the basis for drawing reasonable inferences about your identification with this family member.

Footprints in the Ashes of Time

Mary Leakey

British anthropologist Mary Leakey (1913–) has spent most of her life excavating stretches of the African landscape in search of man's earliest ancestors. She and her husband, Dr. Louis Leakey, first searched a section of northern Tanzania called Laetoli in 1959 but found little of interest there. They moved on to Olduvai Gorge, where they discovered fossil remains of a humanlike creature called Zinjanthropus—over a million years older than any found previously. In 1975, Mary Leakey and her co-workers returned to Laetoli and found evidence that the human race's past began much earlier than their previous discoveries had suggested: they uncovered footprints of two humanlike creatures made between 3.6 and 3.8 million years ago. Among her recent writings are Olduvai Gorge: My Search for Early Man *(1979) and* Disclosing the Past *(1984), her autobiography. In the following selection, Mary Leakey makes both scientific and imaginative inferences that communicate her sense of who might have made those prints so many years ago.*

1 It happened some 3,600,000 years ago, at the onset of a rainy season. The East African landscape stretched then, much as it does now, in a series of savannas punctuated by wind-sculptured acacia trees. To the east the volcano now called Sadiman heaved restlessly, spewing ash over the flat expanse known as Laetoli.

2 The creatures that inhabited the region, and they were plentiful, showed no panic. They continued to drift on their random errands. Several times Sadiman blanketed the plain with a thin layer of ash. Tentative showers, precursors of the heavy seasonal rains, moistened the ash. Each layer hardened, preserving in remarkable detail the footprints left by the ancient fauna. The Laetolil Beds, as geologists designate the oldest deposits at Laetoli, captured a frozen moment of time from the remote past—a pageant unique in prehistory.

3 Our serious survey of the beds, which lie in northern Tanzania 30 miles by road south of Olduvai Gorge, began in 1975 and gained intensity last summer after the discovery of some startling footprints. This article must stand as a preliminary report; further findings will almost certainly modify early interpretations.

4 Still, what we have discovered to date at Laetoli will cause yet another upheaval in the study of human origins. For in the gray, petrified ash of the beds—among the spoor of the extinct predecessors of today's elephants, hyenas, hares—we have found hominid[1] footprints that are remarkably similar to those of modern man. Prints that, in my opinion, could only have been left by an ancestor of man. Prints that were laid down an incredible 3,600,000 years ago . . . !

5 In 1976 Peter Jones, my assistant and a specialist in stone tools, and my youngest son, Philip, noticed what they believed to be a trail of hominid footprints. After considerable analysis I agreed and announced the discovery the following year. Of the five prints, three were obscured by overlying sediment impossible to remove. The two clear examples, broad and rather curiously shaped, offered few clues to the primate that had trudged across the plain so long ago.

6 Nonetheless, the implications of this find were enormous. Dr. Garniss Curtis of the University of California at Berkeley undertook to date the footprint strata. These deposits possess relatively large crystals of biotite, or black mica. Biotite from ash overlying the prints, when subjected to potassium-argon testing, showed an age of about 3.6 million years; that from below tested at about 3.8 million years. The footprints had been preserved sometime within this span. Dr. Richard L. Hay, also of Berkeley, showed that the ash forming the layers fell within a month's time.

7 The hominid footprints attested, in my considered opinion, to the existence of a direct ancestor of man half a million years before the earliest previous evidence—fossils unearthed by Dr. Donald C. Johanson and his party in the Afar triangle of Ethiopia beginning in 1973.

8 Faced with this, we largely abandoned our hunt for fossils and focused our three-month campaign of 1978 on the footprints—plotting and photographing them, making plaster and latex casts, and even removing certain specimens. While Dr. Paul Abell of the University of Rhode Island was attempting—delicately and successfully—to quarry out a block of rhinoceros tracks, he noticed a barely exposed, hominidlike heel print.

9 When we removed the surrounding overburden, we found a trail some 23 meters long; only the end of the excavation season in

[1]In anthropology, a member of the human family and its ancestors. One of the toughest problems in such excavations as Leakey describes here is to distinguish between the prints of primates (see paragraphs 25–26) and those that are definitely human. [Eds.]

September prevented our following it still farther. Two individuals, one larger, one smaller, had passed this way 3,600,000 years ago.

10 The footsteps come from the south, progress northward in a fairly straight line, and end abruptly where seasonal streams have eroded a small, chaotic canyon through the beds. The nature of the terrain leads us to believe that the footprints, though now covered, remain largely intact to the south. And that is where we will continue our effort.

11 The closeness of the two sets of prints indicates that their owners were not walking abreast. Other clues suggest that the hominids may have passed at different times. For example, the imprints of the smaller individual stand out clearly. The crispness of definition and sharp outlines convince me that they were left on a damp surface that retained the form of the foot.

12 On the other hand, the prints of the larger are blurred, as if he had shuffled or dragged his feet. In fact, I think that the surface when he passed was loose and dusty, hence the collapsed appearance of his prints. Nonetheless, luck favored us again; the bigger hominid left one absolutely clear print, probably on a patch of once damp ash.

13 What do these footprints tell us? First, they demonstrate once and for all that at least 3,600,000 years ago, in Pliocene times, what I believe to be man's direct ancestor walked fully upright with a bipedal, free-striding gait. Second, that the form of his foot was exactly the same as ours.

14 One cannot overemphasize the role of bipedalism in hominid development. It stands as perhaps the salient point that differentiated the forebears of man from other primates. This unique ability freed the hands for myriad possibilities—carrying, tool-making, intricate manipulation. From this single development, in fact, stems all modern technology.

15 Somewhat oversimplified, the formula holds that this new freedom of forelimbs posed a challenge. The brain expanded to meet it. And mankind was formed.

16 Even today, millions of years beyond that unchronicled Rubicon, *Homo sapiens* is the only primate to walk upright as a matter of course. And, for better or for worse, *Homo sapiens* dominates the world.

17 But what of those two hominids who crossed the Laetolil Beds so long ago? We have measured their footprints and the length of their stride. Was the larger one a male, the smaller a female? Or was one mature, the other young? It is unlikely that we will ever know

with certainty. For convenience, let us postulate a case of sexual dimorphism and consider the smaller one a female.

18 Incidentally, following her path produces, at least for me, a kind of poignant time wrench. At one point, and you need not be an expert tracker to discern this, she stops, pauses, turns to the left to glance at some possible threat or irregularity, and then continues to the north. This motion, so intensely human, transcends time. Three million six hundred thousand years ago, a remote ancestor—just as you or I—experienced a moment of doubt.

19 The French have a proverb: *Plus ça change, plus c'est la même chose*—"The more it changes, the more it is the same." In short, nothing really alters. Least of all, the human condition.

20 Measurements show the length of the smaller prints to be 18.5 centimeters (slightly more than 7 inches) and 21.5 centimeters for the larger. Stride length averages 38.7 centimeters for the smaller hominid, 47.2 centimeters for the larger. Clearly we are dealing with two small creatures.

21 An anthropological rule of thumb holds that the length of the foot represents about 15 percent of an individual's height. On this basis—and it is far from exact—we can estimate the height of the male as perhaps four feet eight inches (1.4 meters); the female would have stood about four feet.

22 Leg structure must have been very similar to our own. It seems clear to me that the Laetoli hominid, although much older, relates very closely to the remains found by Dr. Johanson in Ethiopia. Dr. Owen Lovejoy of Kent State University in Ohio studied a knee joint from Ethiopia—the bottom of the femur and the top of the tibia—and concluded that the Afar hominid had walked upright, with a free, bipedal gait.

23 Our footprints confirm this. Furthermore, Dr. Louise Robbins of the University of North Carolina, Greensboro, an anthropologist who specializes in the analysis of footprints, visited Laetoli and concluded: "The movement pattern of the individual is a bipedal walking gait, actually a stride—and quite long relative to the creature's small size. Weight-bearing pressure patterns in the prints resemble human ones. . . ."

24 I can only assume that the prints were left by the hominids whose fossils we also found in the beds. In addition to part of a child's skeleton, we uncovered adult remains—two lower jaws, a section of upper jaw, and a number of teeth.

25 Where can we place the Laetoli hominids and their Afar cousins in the incomplete mosaic of the rise of man? This question, quite honestly, is a subject of some contention among paleontologists. One school, including Dr. Johanson, classifies them as australopithecines.[2]

26 But the two forms of *Australopithecus,* gracile and robust, represent, in my opinion, evolutionary dead ends. These man apes flourished for their season, and perished—unsuccessful twigs on the branch that produced mankind. Of course, the Laetoli hominid resembles the gracile *Australopithecus,* but I believe that, so far back in time, all the hominids shared certain characteristics. However, the simple evidence of the footprints, so very much like our own, indicates to me that the Laetoli hominid stands in the direct line of man's ancestry.

27 We have encountered one anomaly. Despite three years of painstaking search by Peter Jones, no stone tools have been found in the Laetolil Beds. With their hands free, one would have expected this species to have developed tools or weapons of some kind. But, except for the ejecta of erupting volcanoes, we haven't found a single stone introduced into the beds. So we can only conclude, at least for the moment, that the hominids we discovered had not yet attained the toolmaking stage. . . .

28 But in the end one cannot escape the supreme importance of the presence of hominids at Laetoli. Sometimes, during the excavating season, I go out and watch the dusk settle over the gray tuff with its eerie record of time long past. The slanting light of evening throws the hominid prints into sharp relief, so sharp that they could have been left this morning.

29 I cannot help but think about the distant creatures who made them. Where did they come from? Where were they going? We simply do not know. It has been suggested that they were merely crossing this scorched plain toward the greener ridges to the north. Perhaps so.

30 In any case, those footprints out of the deep past, left by the oldest known hominids, haunt the imagination. Across the gulf of time I can only wish them well on that prehistoric trek. It was, I believe, part of a greater and more perilous journey, one that—through millions of years of evolutionary trial and error, fortune and misfortune—culminated in the emergence of modern man.

[2]Primates of an extinct genus of the Pleistocene epoch, found mainly in Southern Africa. [Eds.]

Additional Rhetorical Strategies

Process Analysis (paragraph 2); Cause and Effect (paragraphs 14–15).

Examining Words and Meaning

1. Why does Leakey think that the creatures who made the footprints she discusses were not walking abreast? What else about these creatures does she infer from observing and measuring their footprints? Does she explain the reasoning process behind all these inferences? Does she react to the prints emotionally? Use specific passages from the text to support your answer.
2. In paragraph 4 Leakey says that her discoveries will bring about an "upheaval" in the study of our origins. Why, given her subject, is the word appropriate here? In what other contexts have you seen the word used?
3. What does Leakey mean by "the incomplete mosaic of the rise of man"? What does "mosaic" convey to us that "jigsaw puzzle" would not?
4. To what historical event is Leakey referring in the phrase "unchronicled Rubicon" (paragraph 16)? Why is the allusion appropriate here?
5. Look up these words in a dictionary, if necessary: savannas (paragraph 1); precursors (paragraph 2); fauna (paragraph 2); spoor (paragraph 4); mica (paragraph 6); latex (paragraph 8); bipedal (paragraph 13); salient (paragraph 14); myriad (paragraph 14); dimorphism (paragraph 17); poignant (paragraph 18); femur (paragraph 22); tibia (paragraph 22); tuff (paragraph 28).

Focusing on Structures and Strategies

1. What paragraphs in this selection would you classify as the introduction? Why? What do you think Leakey's purpose is in this introductory section? What words and phrases could you cite to show that she intends to give more than an informative, objective set of background facts?

2. Why does Leakey tell us how the prints were found? Does this add anything to the scientific usefulness of the article? Where else does she apparently digress from reporting on her subject? What effect do these sections have on the tone of the article?
3. Quickly review the selection, marking those passages that you consider observation and those that you consider inference. How does Leakey arrange these sections? Are all the observations and all the inferences grouped together? What are the advantages of this approach?

Suggestions for Further Discussion and Writing

1. "Nothing really alters," says Leakey (paragraph 19). Do you agree? When you read books written a hundred or a thousand years ago, when you see old buildings, when you see old movies, when you read of the ways people acted in generations past, are you struck by the similarities or by the differences between our ancestors and us? Do our societies define our human nature, or does our human nature exist independently of particular cultures?
2. Probably few of us will make scientific discoveries of the magnitude of Leakey's, but that need not keep us from writing clearly about the inferences that people have made from observations. Choose a scientific discovery that interests you—the discovery that the earth is round, that lightning is electricity, that gravity is a function of mass and distance—and write a brief account of how people proceeded from observation to inference to make the discovery. This should not be a major research paper. Instead, it should be a clear tracing of a reasoning process.

The Bellelli Family

John Canaday

One of the requirements for being an outstanding art critic is to be able to observe carefully—to be able to detect the significance of details and nuances. John Canaday's (1907–   ) art criticism consistently shows him to be a first-rate observer. His description of Edgar Degas's famous portrait, The Bellelli Family, *is an instructive example of how careful observation can yield the most reasonable inferences—in this instance, about each figure's temperament and the nature of their relationships.*

John Canaday had accumulated a great deal of experience in art before he joined The New York Times *in 1959 as its leading art critic. Canaday began as a painter and later taught art history for more than a decade at the University of Virginia and at Tulane before serving as the director of the education division at the Philadelphia Museum of Art from 1952 to 1959. He left* The New York Times *in 1976 to concentrate on freelance magazine writing and book-length art criticism. He is the author of more than twelve studies of art, most notably the award-winning* Mainstreams of Modern Art: David to Picasso *(1959) and* What Is Art? *(1980), from which the following selection is taken.*

1 Superlatives [in writing art criticism] are dangerous, but there is less danger than usual in describing *The Bellelli Family* [Edgar Degas] as the finest psychological group portrait ever painted. The temperament of each of the four members is individualized for us, and, beyond that, their interrelationship is analyzed. Before you read the following paragraphs, you may want to ask yourself on the evidence of the picture what these people were like. In that case try to decide what the relationship of the father to the rest of the family might be, what the emotional tie of each of the little girls is to each of the parents, and what the difference is, temperamentally, between these two children. The chances are that you will learn as much from the picture itself as you will know when you have read the following summary, with the exception of specific historical facts.

2 From references in family letters we gather that the Baron was a man of uneven temperament, given to moods and, at least during the time Degas visited the family, conscious of frustrations and discouragements both in his personal life and in his career. His only son had died (the family is still in mourning in the portrait) and the Baron was marking time as a political exile from his native Naples. His disturbed life made him half a stranger in his own household, a condition aggravated by an increasing rift with his wife. Social conventions of respectability in the mid-nineteenth century placed limitations on a woman in the Baroness's situation. A reserved, intelligent, and patient woman—if we can accept the judgment of her young nephew—she seems to have shouldered even more of the responsibility for the home and the children than did the average

wife of her time. Of the two little girls, the elder, Giovanna, was placid and closely attached to her mother, whereas the younger, Giuliana, was more energetic and restless, temperamentally sympathetic to her father but, by force of circumstance, more securely bound within the lives of her mother and sister.

3 The most casual observer must notice that in Degas's portrait the father is separated from the rest of the family by a series of vertical lines, which, violating normal compositional rules, separate a generous third of the picture from the rest. In addition, he sits unconventionally, with his back toward us and his profile in shadow. His features are painted less decisively than those of the other figures. He is the only one of the family who is not completely revealed to us as a person; we are left with the feeling that we do not know him as we know the mother and daughters. He has a life beyond this room; perhaps he leads a life more important to him than the life we are seeing here; he is an outsider.

4 But this vagueness, incompleteness, and isolation are reversed in the figure of the wife. She stands with decision, dignity, and

The Bellelli Family (Edward Degas, 1859)

forbearance, dominating the room by her quietness. Of all the figures, hers is the simplest and strongest in silhouette; that is why we return to her always, no matter how interesting the rest of the picture may be in its greater detail and variety.

5 Her right hand rests on the shoulder of Giovanna, the more placid daughter, who was like her and closest to her. This little girl is held within the larger silhouette of the mother's figure; her way of standing echoes her mother's, as does her general silhouette—and she stands quietly. She is the only one of the family who looks at us, although the others are aware of our presence. She looks at us unquestioningly, content to stay within her mother's support and protection.

6 But the other child, Giuliana, partially breaks away from the pair. She occupies the side of the picture separated from the father, yet we feel strongly her connection with him. She is the only one whose glance could, and in a moment might, meet her father's. She sits restlessly, one leg tucked up under her, as if impatient with sitting for her artist-cousin, unable to remain still, the volatile member of the group. Just as she is divided in her loyalty to her mother and her father, so she does not belong wholly to either in the composition of the painting.

7 It is apparent, then, that Degas set about expressing a specific set of circumstances with the help of appropriate compositional means. When we know the circumstances, the picture takes on some peripheral interest; but it is a great picture because it is expressive of the interrelationships of four people, whether or not we know the specific circumstances. The picture has a life of its own beyond the immediate reasons for its creation. If the identity of the painter and the family were unknown to us, any meaning *The Bellelli Family* might lose would be of little consequence.

8 The Bellellis are not important to us as individuals. It makes no difference how they looked. Their troubles were never of any significance except to themselves. The relationships so brilliantly revealed were neither unique nor on the grand scale. The picture's greatness lies in its ability to stir us to thought beyond the limited considerations of a single family's not unusual circumstances. And it does so because Degas has crystallized his material into forms of perfect order, rid of all confusions, incidentals, vagaries, and distractions. In the resultant clarity our sensibilities and understanding may expand.

9 Degas was one of the greatest of all pictorial composers, and *The Bellelli Family,* an early painting, is only one (though one of the best) of a succession of startlingly original compositions. Degas is

preeminent in this unconventionality without freakishness. Other great masters of pictorial composition time and again demonstrate their ability to use conventional devices more skillfully than their contemporaries. But Degas invents compositions without direct precedent, and each of these compositions is so special to its subject that none is directly useful to followers hunting a formula.

Additional Rhetorical Strategies

Illustration (throughout); Narration (paragraph 2); Description (paragraphs 2–6).

Examining Words and Meaning

1. In the opening paragraph, Canaday advises his readers: "The chances are that you will learn as much from the picture itself as you will know when you have read the following summary, with the exception of specific historical facts." Having read his "summary," what specifically has it added to your understanding of Degas's painting and its historical significance?
2. How reasonable are the inferences Canaday draws from Degas's painting? Can you think of any that he has omitted? Consider, for example, Canaday's statement that the father "has a life beyond this room; perhaps he leads a life more important to him than the life we are seeing here; he is an outsider" (paragraph 3). Does your "reading" of the painting lead you to a similar conclusion? Explain.
3. What does Canaday mean when he claims that the figures in this painting "are aware of our presence" (paragraph 5)? In paragraph 8, he says, "The Bellellis are not important to us as individuals." What point is he making here, and do you agree with him? Explain.

Focusing on Structures and Strategies

1. In paragraph 2, Canaday talks of the "limitations on a woman in the Baroness's situation." What, exactly, is the nature of her

The Peale Family (Charles Wilson Peale, 1773 and 1809)

Farm family, St. Charles County, Missouri (Arthur Rothstein, 1939)

predicament? How thoroughly does Canaday tell us about it? How important is such knowledge to our understanding and appreciation of the painting?

2. Canaday claims that Degas's painting is "a great picture . . . whether or not we know the specific circumstances" (paragraph 7). If such is the case, why do you think that Canaday presents these circumstances in such detail, and why so early? Do you think Canaday's essay would have been more effective if he had delayed the revelation of these particular circumstances? Explain. In this respect, compare Canaday's strategy with Annie Dillard's description of the death of a frog (p. 52).

3. What does Canaday mean by "forms of perfect order" (paragraph 8)? How does this idea connect with his discussion of the unconventional nature of Degas's forms, as spoken of in paragraph 9?

Suggestions for Further Discussion and Writing

1. Canaday suggests that Degas's paintings depart from the norm, that they are unconventional. In what ways are such norms established? Are Degas's techniques considered part of the current norms in art? Explain. Consider your own field of special interest. How are norms established there? What are the conventions of your discipline? Can you think of some examples of what would be considered "unconventional" by the current leaders in your field?

2. Examine the painting and photograph on p. 73 carefully, several times. Based on your observations of these family portraits, what can you infer about the relationships among the individuals in each? Make notes on your observations, select either the painting or photograph to write about, and work up your notes into a draft of an essay, modeled on Canaday's.

3. Locate a family portrait—a photograph of your family or that of a friend or relative. Study the photograph carefully, and then write an essay in which you use the principles of observation and inference as the basis for an analysis of the relationships depicted in that family photograph.

Abstract and Concrete

1 The words *abstract* and *concrete* are conventionally used to describe a writer's style. On the simplest level, the terms refer to word choices. *Concrete words* denote what can be perceived by the senses, what is practical and tangible in our experience. *Abstract words* point to ideas, to the theoretical, to whatever is removed from sense experience. For nearly all of us, thinking swings naturally between the abstract and the concrete, between ideas and their confirmation in sense experience. This movement is such a basic mental activity that we often pay little attention to it and neglect to practice it in our writing. All of us would agree, however, that effective writing ought to balance the abstract and the concrete, that we ought to support each abstract statement with enough concrete details for our readers to hold on to as they follow the course of our thinking in an essay. To trace how writing moves back and forth between the concrete and the abstract is to chart one of the basic patterns of thinking that leads to ideas and makes writing possible.

2 Much of our thinking consists of partially formed abstractions, of loosely formed ideas about subjects that would require further thinking and an accumulation of evidence to make our ideas at all convincing. Rarely, however, are we pressed to push our thinking beyond this point. The media help make this so, supplying much of what we need to know in order to talk casually about the subjects that are in the public eye. Suppose, for example, that we were asked to write an essay on some aspect of the Chernobyl nuclear disaster. How easy would it be to write a first-rate essay on such a subject?

3 Nearly all of us carry around some vague, media-sponsored version of the harrowing events that occurred in a place that to most of us is no more than a name. But, despite the saturation coverage of the political and legal issues involved, our thinking about the victims of the disaster probably would not be very specific at all. To think in *specific* terms is to be explicit, to be definite in what we say about a subject. Few of us, for example, would ever need to know the actual dimensions of the nuclear plant or the exact floor plans of the plant. Nonetheless, we undoubtedly could write about the Chernobyl disaster in *general* terms—that is, we could make broad statements about the events there as indicative of the potentially hazardous environments we live in, comparing the disaster with other similar disasters or discussing it in terms of the increasing threats to individuals in contemporary life. Yet little, if any, of our thinking about the disaster in Chernobyl would be *concrete*—tied directly to immediate sense experience. After all, few outsiders—other than a few officials and observers as well as media representatives—ever entered the nuclear power plant. Our knowledge of the tragedy is restricted, then, to what we watched, read, or heard about it through the media. Our knowledge of such events remains indistinct and abstract, far removed from the stark reality of what occurred.

4 What we know about an event like the catastrophe in Chernobyl demonstrates how much our thinking consists of hazy abstractions and indirect experience—of how much ours is a mediated world. To come to know something in such an imprecise way may explain why we so often seem uncomfortable thinking in abstractions and why we have so much difficulty making our writing more concrete. (For an example of how a writer converts an abstraction into concrete terms, see Joan Didion's essay, "On Morality," p. 80.) But exactly what do we mean by abstract and concrete writing, and how does moving from one to the other help us to form ideas?

5 Our writing may be described as concrete when we record our observations of objects and behavior in the world around us. Anything that can be perceived immediately by the senses is *concrete:* a pear, a truck, a pizza, a shoe. Most often, concrete words are learned in the presence of the object or behavior described. We first understood the meaning of *giraffe,* for example, by seeing a picture of it in a book or observing one at a zoo. We need not reflect on concrete words to understand them; they are confirmed immediately through the senses. As we have seen in the previous chapter, to form an idea

about a subject is to come to a conclusion about it—however tentative that conclusion might be. To write concretely about an idea is to use sense experience to explain and prove what we want to say.

6 Concrete writing is strengthened by specificity. To be *specific* is to state something explicitly, to be particular and definite. Suppose we had witnessed a robbery in our local supermarket and had been asked by the police to write a report on what had taken place. In this case, our writing would most likely be concrete: we saw this; we heard that. It would also be specific as soon as our description was more exact: "The thief was a young man, approximately twenty years old and about six feet tall. He wore faded blue jeans, a light-green sweatshirt, and blue, high-top sneakers. He was slim and frail-looking, with a lean face and a large, crescent-shaped scar on his left cheek. He had a ginger handlebar mustache and short, curly hair. He nervously fingered his rimless glasses each time he ordered the manager to do something. . . ." All of the discernible features of the thief's appearance and behavior—taken together—make this passage concrete.

7 The origin of the word *abstract* tells us a great deal about its meaning and the role it plays in our thinking and writing. *Abstract* can be traced to the Latin word meaning "to remove, to draw out, to pull away." As an adjective, *abstract* refers to whatever is removed from immediate sense experience, to whatever is not subject to direct observation and therefore not instantly understood. Such words as *dignity, honesty,* and *love* can be described as abstract because they cannot be understood directly through the senses. Instead, we rely primarily on our past experiences and social conditioning—on the associations abstract words carry—to grasp what they mean. As a verb, *abstract* extends the Latin definition by including also "to consider theoretically"—that is, to think of a quality or an attribute without reference to a particular object or example. In this sense, such words as *motion, dryness,* and *cold* may be considered to be abstractions—thoughts apart from things.

8 Abstractions refer to whatever we cannot apprehend with our senses. Such words as *hatred, freedom, justice,* and *peace* express states of mind or concepts. For example, we cannot see, hear, or smell freedom. Because abstractions do not point to objects or actions, we should try to be as concrete and specific as possible whenever we use them. Our meaning will be much clearer if we place abstractions in a context of sense experience. Consider the alternatives: popular and sentimental definitions ("Happiness is . . . ," "Friendship is . . .") or the flabby

and ineffectual sentences swelling so many recent self-help books. The following passage shows how dangerously easy it is to trade on abstractions:

> Love means giving and sharing as well as accepting, and not being stand-offish, defensive, and defiant. In evaluating your capacity to develop relationships, to endure frustration, and to give, consider whether you can admit to biases, prejudices, and weaknesses. Can you accept the loss of a relationship and still persevere, entering into other mutually rewarding relationships?
>
> Openness, honesty, and integrity create strong relationships. Unwillingness to admit to failings or unpleasant emotions generates problems. Fearing rejection, people sometimes hesitate to express the most powerful of emotions—love.

Piling up so many unsupported abstractions obviously limits the impact of this and any similar piece of writing. We should remember that our abstractions must always be able to withstand the test of concrete illustration. When we return our thinking about a subject from the abstract to the concrete, we increase the likelihood that our abstractions will gain expressive power both for ourselves and for those who read or listen to us.

9 It also helps us to consider abstraction as a process. To abstract is really to engage in a method of selection. When we abstract from something, we single out some part of our experience, some quality or attribute of it. We experience the world around us, to quote the philosopher William James, as a "blooming, buzzing confusion." To identify one element out of the whole is to abstract it from the whole. In many ways the process of abstraction in thinking is similar to that of lens focusing in photography. From the vast concrete scene in front of them, photographers focus on someone or something and try to highlight their subject's essential characteristics. In doing so, they relegate whatever else remains in their field of vision to the fringe of the photograph. Our minds work in much the same way. As we shape an idea in our thinking, our words move through a similar pattern of field and focus, of concrete and abstract.

10 When we write, we come close to reversing the natural order of thinking (concrete→abstract→concrete). An essay starts with the abstract. We take our idea, our tentative conclusion, about our subject and put it up front. What follows is a gradual unfolding of our

concrete explanation of that idea. Writing an essay is, in effect, a process of "unpacking" an idea, of moving from an abstraction to a series of concrete statements explaining the idea.

11 For example, suppose that we've been asked to write an essay in which we assess how our conception of heroism has been affected by films about Vietnam. We might well begin by identifying and exploring the key words in this writing exercise: *films, Vietnam,* and *heroism.* (For more on key words, see pp. 1–6.) Since *heroism* is also an abstraction, we would want to examine the traditional associations of the term: World War I "aces" dueling in the sky, John Wayne striding across the screen, an anonymous G.I. single-handedly destroying an enemy stronghold. As we continue to press harder in our thinking about *heroism,* we recognize that the connotations of the word arise largely from literature and the media—especially those films produced before the Vietnam War and now regularly featured on late-night television. We might decide to select, to focus on, the contrasts between those late-night television reruns and the most recent releases from Hollywood. We gradually come to a tentative conclusion about our subject. We form an idea about it—that the heroism depicted in war movies on late-night television differs markedly from the gallantry evident in the numbing and grotesquely realistic film reconstructions of battlefield scenes in Vietnam. In this sense, our idea can be described as abstract; that is, it can maintain an existence independent of any proof. Yet should we want or need to express this idea, we would have to return once again to concrete and specific observations for evidence. We might, for example, contrast the image of an edgy squad out on patrol searching for an almost invisible enemy in a Southeast Asian jungle with the spectacular feats of the celluloid warriors of World War II. We might also contrast the faceless precision of B-52 raids to the charismatic daring of old-time dogfights, or the reactions of different generations of American prisoners of war to threats of torture and death. As this example suggests, the movement of our thinking as we form an idea about a subject gets progressively more selective—more abstract at first and then more concrete.

12 Since we can arrive at an idea about a subject by following various paths of thinking, we ought to distinguish between abstraction and generalization. To *generalize* is to make broad statements about a subject. We could easily generalize about heroism: that it belongs to rural worlds, embodies national ideals, involves personal fantasy, and so on. Generalizing is a process of accumulation, of

gathering up enough evidence from individual instances so that we can draw inferences about what has happened in the past and what to expect in the future. (See also "Observation and Inference," pp. 47–52.) Generalization builds upon comparisons in which we discover common elements among various objects or events. As such, it builds more slowly toward forming an idea about a subject than does abstraction. Abstraction isolates a subject and examines it more painstakingly. Abstraction is finally more intellectually demanding and does more for our thinking and writing than generalization. Abstraction enables us to take in the world around us, to separate it into parts, to examine each carefully, and eventually to map out what may well be the complex terrain of an experience. The process of abstraction helps us to adjust, to adapt to the relentless flow of everyday concrete experience. Abstraction also provides the framework within which we can select, explore, and control the concrete.

13 The essays that follow highlight the interdependence of the abstract and the concrete. As these selections demonstrate, the movement of our thinking and writing between the abstract and the concrete often works like a pendulum—a steady, dependable motion between two equally irresistible extremes.

On Morality

Joan Didion

Not only students but also professional writers may find themselves struggling with assigned topics. In the opening section of her essay "On Morality," novelist and culture critic Joan Didion (1934–) describes the process of her thinking as she tries to tackle the difficult concept of morality. "My mind veers inflexibly toward the particular," she notes, and with characteristic attention to specific details, Didion pursues the private associations that lurk behind her interpretation of this complex abstraction.

Born and raised in Sacramento and educated at Berkeley, Joan Didion worked briefly in New York for Vogue *magazine before returning to California and making it the focus for most of her writing.*

*Her novels—*Run River *(1963),* Play It As It Lays *(1970), and* A Book of Common Prayer *(1977)—and her collected essays—*Slouching Toward Bethlehem *(1968),* The White Album *(1980),* Salvador *(1983), and* Democracy *(1985)—have consistently revealed a reporter's eye for the telling particulars that give texture to a story. Also a highly successful screenwriter, Didion has been heralded as "the finest woman prose stylist writing in English today."*

The spare, flinty prose of the following selection also demonstrates Didion's special ability to discover in her own experience concrete parallels to an issue seemingly as abstract as the state of contemporary American values.

1 As it happens I am in Death Valley, in a room at the Enterprise Motel and Trailer Park, and it is July, and it is hot. In fact it is 119°. I cannot seem to make the air conditioner work, but there is a small refrigerator, and I can wrap ice cubes in a towel and hold them against the small of my back. With the help of the ice cubes I have been trying to think, because *The American Scholar* asked me to, in some abstract way about "morality," a word I distrust more every day, but my mind veers inflexibly toward the particular.

2 Here are some particulars. At midnight last night, on the road in from Las Vegas to Death Valley Junction, a car hit a shoulder and turned over. The driver, very young and apparently drunk, was killed instantly. His girl was found alive but bleeding internally, deep in shock. I talked this afternoon to the nurse who had driven the girl to the nearest doctor, 185 miles across the floor of the Valley and three ranges of lethal mountain road. The nurse explained that her husband, a talc miner, had stayed on the highway with the boy's body until the coroner could get over the mountains from Bishop, at dawn today. "You can't just leave a body on the highway," she said. "It's immoral."

3 It was one instance in which I did not distrust the word, because she meant something quite specific. She meant that if a body is left alone for even a few minutes on the desert, the coyotes close in and eat the flesh. Whether or not a corpse is torn apart by coyotes may seem only a sentimental consideration, but of course it is more: one of the promises we make to one another is that we will try to retrieve our casualties, try not to abandon our dead to the coyotes. If we have been taught to keep our promises—if, in the simplest terms, our upbringing is good enough—we stay with the body, or have bad dreams.

4 I am talking, of course, about the kind of social code that is sometimes called, usually pejoratively, "wagon-train morality." In fact that is precisely what it is. For better or worse, we are what we learned as children: my own childhood was illuminated by graphic litanies of the grief awaiting those who failed in their loyalties to each other. The Donner-Reed Party, starving in the Sierra snows, all the ephemera of civilization gone save that one vestigial taboo, the provision that no one should eat his own blood kin. The Jayhawkers, who quarreled and separated not far from where I am tonight. Some of them died in the Funerals and some of them died down near Badwater and most of the rest of them died in the Panamints. A woman who got through gave the Valley its name. Some might say that the Jayhawkers were killed by the desert summer, and the Donner Party by the mountain winter, by circumstances beyond control; we were taught instead that they had somewhere abdicated their responsibilities, somehow breached their primary loyalties, or they would not have found themselves helpless in the mountain winter or the desert summer, would not have given way to acrimony, would not have deserted one another, would not have *failed.* In brief, we heard such stories as cautionary tales, and they still suggest the only kind of "morality" that seems to me to have any but the most potentially mendacious meaning.

Additional Rhetorical Strategies

Narration (paragraph 1); Illustration (paragraphs 2, 3, 4).

Examining Words and Meaning

1. Why does Didion "distrust" the word *morality?* How does she illustrate this statement? What abstract point does she make with her examples?

2. What does Didion say the consequence would be if we were to abandon a dead body? Does she mean this consequence to be taken literally? Explain. What does she mean by the "wagon-train morality" (paragraph 4)?

Focusing on Structures and Strategies

1. Explain how Didion's thinking in this selection gravitates toward her own personal experience. Why does she allow it to? How personal, actually, are her examples?

2. If you were to outline the sequence of Didion's thoughts on morality, what percentage would be abstract? What percentage concrete? Explain precisely how this selection is an example of the tendency of her mind to veer "inflexibly toward the particular" (paragraph 1). When does her essay return to the abstract? Why does she allow it to do so? What is the effect on the reader?

Suggestion for Further Discussion and Writing

1. Reread the essay carefully, this time paying special attention to the ways the author uses the word *morality* to order her thinking. Then write an essay in which you work with an abstraction—*justice, truth,* or *happiness,* for example—as the basis of an essay that "veers inflexibly toward the particular."

Knoxville Revisited

Nikki Giovanni

Poet, essayist, and lecturer, Nikki Giovanni (1943–) was born in Knoxville, Tennessee, and attended Fisk College and the University of Pennsylvania. She is the author of many books and volumes of poetry, including Black Judgment *(1968) and* Those Who Ride the Night Winds *(1983), and has been an editor of* Black Dialogue *as well as editorial consultant to* Encore *magazine.*

The following selection is taken from the first chapter of Gemini *(1971), which Nikki Giovanni describes as "an extended autobiographical statement on my first twenty-five years of being a black poet." The passage recalls her Knoxville childhood from the perspective of her return there as a celebrity in the early 1970s. Giovanni's series of concrete, intensely personal associations culminates in a final, abstract statement: "Linden Avenue was pretty but it had no life."*

1 Gay Street is to Knoxville what Fifth Avenue is to New York. Something special, yes? And it looked the same. But Vine Street, where I would sneak to the drugstore to buy *Screen Stories* and watch the men drink wine and play pool—all gone. A wide, clean military-looking highway has taken its place. Austin Homes is cordoned off. It looked like a big prison. The Gem Theatre is now some sort of nightclub and Mulvaney Street is gone. Completely wiped out. Assassinated along with the old people who made it live. I looked over and saw that the lady who used to cry "HOT FISH! GOOD HOT FISH!" no longer had a Cal Johnson Park to come to and set up her stove in. Grandmother would not say, "Edith White! I think I'll send Gary for a sandwich. You want one?" Mrs. Abrum and her reverend husband from rural Tennessee wouldn't bring us any more goose eggs from across the street. And Leroy wouldn't chase his mother's boyfriend on Saturday night down the back alley anymore. All gone, not even to a major highway but to a cutoff of a cutoff. All the old people who died from lack of adjustment died from a cutoff of a cutoff.

2 And I remember our finding Grandmother the house on Linden Avenue and constantly reminding her it was every bit as good as if not better than the little ole house. A bigger back yard and no steps to climb. But I knew what Grandmother knew, what we all knew. There was no familiar smell in that house. No coal ashes from the fireplaces. Nowhere that you could touch and say, "Yolande threw her doll against this wall," or "Agnes fell down these steps." No smell or taste of biscuits Grandpapa had eaten with the Alaga syrup he loved so much. No Sunday chicken. No sound of "Lord, you children don't care a thing 'bout me after all I done for you," because Grandmother always had the need to feel mistreated. No spot in the back hall weighted down with lodge books and no corner where the old record player sat playing Billy Eckstine crooning, "What's My Name?" till Grandmother said, "Lord! Any fool know his name!" No breeze on dreamy nights when Mommy would listen over and over again to "I Don't See Me in Your Eyes Anymore." No pain in my knuckles where Grandmother had rapped them because she was determined I would play the piano, and when that absolutely failed, no effort on Linden for us to learn the flowers. No echo of me being the only person in the history of the family to curse Grandmother out

and no Grandpapa saying, "Oh, my," which was serious from him, "we can't have this." Linden Avenue was pretty but it had no life.

Additional Rhetorical Strategies

Illustration (paragraphs 1, 2); Description (paragraphs 1, 2).

Examining Words and Meaning

1. Why does Giovanni specify in paragraph 1 that "a wide, clean military-looking highway" has taken the place of her old neighborhood? How do the details she gives us about life in that neighborhood make the contrast between the past and the present so effective? How does the repetition of "gone" and "all gone" in this paragraph help to convey Giovanni's feelings about this contrast?

Focusing on Structures and Strategies

1. Notice that much of paragraph 2 consists of a series of phrases all starting with "no" or "nowhere." What is the effect of this repetition? Why might complete sentences be less effective here?
2. Giovanni says at the end of paragraph 2 that "Linden Avenue was pretty but it had no life." How do the concrete details leading up to this statement help to make its meaning more clear? Why is the statement at the end, rather than at the beginning, of the paragraph?

Suggestion for Further Discussion and Writing

1. Giovanni suggests in this selection that what is often thought of as progress can cut people off from their pasts. Write an essay in which you consider some other ways that the rapid rate of change in our culture has a similar effect. For example, Americans move from place to place more than almost any other people. What is the effect of

this mobility on our sense of home or neighborhood? Use as much concrete detail as possible to make your meaning clear.

A World of Impressions

Helen Keller

Blind and deaf since the age of eighteen months, Helen Keller (1880–1968) was extraordinarily sensitive to the palpable qualities of her world. In the following passage, she eloquently describes the act of abstraction that enabled her to move from "touch-sensations" to intangible ideas.

After graduating with honors from Radcliffe in 1904, Helen Keller lectured widely in America, Europe, and Asia to raise money to train the sightless. The passage below is from the second of her six books, The World I Live In *(1908).*

1 Ideas make the world we live in, but impressions furnish ideas.

2 My world is built of touch-sensations, devoid of physical color and sound; but without color and sound it breathes and throbs with life. Every object is associated in my mind with tactual qualities which, combined in countless ways, give me a sense of power, of beauty, or of incongruity: for with my hands I can feel the comic as well as the beautiful in the outward appearance of things. Remember that you, dependent on your sight, do not realize how many things are tangible. All palpable things are mobile or rigid, solid or liquid, big or small, warm or cold, and these qualities are variously modified. The coolness of a water-lily rounding into bloom is different again from the coolness of the rain that soaks into the hearts of growing things and gives them life and body. The velvet of the rose is not that of a ripe peach or of a baby's dimpled cheek. The hardness of the rock is to the hardness of wood what a man's deep bass is to a woman's voice when it is low. What I call beauty I can find in certain combinations of all these qualities, and is largely derived from the flow of curved and straight lines which is over all things.

3 "What does the straight line mean to you?" I think you will ask.

4 It *means* several things. It symbolizes duty. It seems to have the quality of inexorableness that duty has. When I have something to do that must not be set aside, I feel as if I were going forward in a straight line, bound to arrive somewhere, or go on forever without swerving to the right or to the left.

5 That is what it means. To escape this moralizing you should ask, "How does the straight line feel?" It feels, as I suppose it looks, straight—a dull thought drawn out endlessly. Eloquence to the touch resides not in straight lines, but in unstraight lines, or in many curved and straight lines together. They appear and disappear, are now deep, now shallow, now broken off or lengthened or swelling. They rise and sink beneath my fingers, they are full of sudden starts and pauses, and their variety is inexhaustible and wonderful. So you see I am not shut out from the region of the beautiful, though my hand cannot perceive the brilliant colors in the sunset or on the mountain, or reach into the blue depths of the sky.

6 Physics tells me that I am well off in a world which, I am told, knows neither color nor sound, but is made in terms of size, shape, and inherent qualities; for at least every object appears to my fingers standing solidly right side up, and is not an inverted image on the retina which, I understand, your brain is at infinite though unconscious labor to set back on its feet. A tangible object passes complete into my brain with the warmth of life upon it, and occupies the same place that it does in space; for, without egotism, the mind is as large as the universe. When I think of hills, I think of the upward strength I tread upon. When water is the object of my thought, I feel the cool shock of the plunge and the quick yielding of the waves that crisp and curl and ripple about my body. The pleasing changes of rough and smooth, pliant and rigid, curved and straight in the bark and branches of a tree give the truth to my hand. The immovable rock, with its juts and warped surface, bends beneath my fingers into all manner of grooves and hollows. The bulge of a watermelon and the puffed-up rotundities of squashes that sprout, bud, and ripen in that strange garden planted somewhere behind my finger-tips are the ludicrous in my tactual memory and imagination. My fingers are tickled to delight by the soft ripple of a baby's laugh, and find amusement in the lusty crow of the barnyard autocrat. Once I had a pet rooster that used to perch on my knee and stretch his neck and crow. A bird in my hand was then worth two in the—barnyard.

7 My fingers cannot, of course, get the impression of a large whole at a glance; but I feel the parts, and my mind puts them

together. I move around my house, touching object after object in order, before I can form an idea of the entire house. In other people's houses I can touch only what is shown me—the chief objects of interest, carvings on the wall, or a curious architectural feature, exhibited like the family album. Therefore a house with which I am not familiar has for me, at first, no general effect or harmony of detail. It is not a complete conception, but a collection of object-impressions which, as they come to me, are disconnected and isolated. But my mind is full of associations, sensations, theories, and with them it constructs the house. The process reminds me of the building of Solomon's temple, where was neither saw, nor hammer, nor any tool heard while the stones were being laid one upon another. The silent worker is imagination which decrees reality out of chaos.

8 Without imagination what a poor thing my world would be! My garden would be a silent patch of earth strewn with sticks of a variety of shapes and smells. But when the eye of my mind is opened to its beauty, the bare ground brightens beneath my feet, and the hedge-row bursts into leaf, and the rose-tree shakes its fragrance everywhere. I know how budding trees look, and I enter into the amorous joy of the mating birds, and this is the miracle of imagination.

Additional Rhetorical Strategies

Illustration (paragraphs 2, 4, 6, 7); Analogy (paragraph 2); Definition (paragraph 2); Process Analysis (paragraph 7).

Examining Words and Meaning

1. What senses is Helen Keller deprived of? Does she therefore feel that her world is poorer than ours? What qualities does she perceive in the world that we tend not to notice?

2. What is the difference, for her, between a familiar and an unfamiliar house? What part of her mind does she use to synthesize the separate sensations of a strange house into a sense of the whole? What else does this power of mind allow her to do?

3. What are some of the words that Helen Keller uses to describe, in paragraph 5, the beauty of lines? How does she use these words to make us understand what her perceptions of the world must be?

Focusing on Structures and Strategies

1. What is the abstract idea that Helen Keller is conveying to us here? Why would a direct statement of this idea be inadequate for her purposes? What does she do to make her world accessible to us? Point to specific words and phrases that put us in touch with it.
2. Consider the ending of this selection (paragraph 8). What sense is Keller speaking of when she says "the bare ground brightens beneath my feet"? What other senses does she appeal to in this last paragraph? What is the effect of her doing so at this point in the selection?

Suggestion for Further Discussion and Writing

1. Go with a friend to someplace secluded and quiet. Close your eyes or blindfold yourself, stop your ears, and for half an hour or so explore the tactile qualities of your surroundings. Have your companion lead you around. What do you notice that you have never noticed before? How do objects feel? What is it like to go up stairs or other inclines? Write an account of this experience, choosing your words so that someone who has not had the experience can understand how it felt to be blind and deaf for half an hour.

The "Sixties Kid"

Ellen Goodman

Ellen Goodman is a Pulitzer Prize-winning columnist whose intelligent and wry observations on contemporary American life have earned her a large and loyal audience in more than 200 newspapers across the country. A graduate of Radcliffe and the winner of a prestigious Nieman Fellowship in journalism at Harvard, Ellen Goodman is a self-described critic-at-large whose columns have been collected in Close to Home *(1980),* At Large *(1981), and* Keeping in Touch *(1985). Her original, clear-eyed, entertaining, and thoughtful essays range freely among public issues and private lives, the latest fads and the most venerable traditions.*

As the following essay reveals, Goodman also has a special knack for recognizing quintessential characters, people for whom life remains more abstract than concrete—in this case, a burnt-out remnant of the 1960s, a person whose brittle clichés signal "a permanent loss of will."

1 She spied him right away as he jaywalked across Harvard Square. It was 26 degrees out and he was only wearing an old green army jacket and jeans. His shoes were soaked by the snow and his hands were stuffed into pockets instead of gloves.

2 That was Jack. He was thirty years old, six feet tall, skinny, scruffy, and he refused to dress for the weather. He looked like a boy who still had to be told to put on his boots. Perhaps he was afraid that if he wore a hat, he'd be mistaken as a serious applicant for adulthood.

3 She ran into him like this when he came into town occasionally to make some money or have his car fixed. Once or twice a year they ended up having coffee together.

4 The two had met briefly in the late sixties on some story about campus unrest. He was involved; she was reporting. At the time Jack had been a sophomore and she was already a mother. Then he dropped out—not only from college but from growing up—and the gap between their ages had widened.

5 Now it occurred to her, as they slid into the restaurant booth and ordered coffee, that somebody was always writing about the Sixties Kids. They wrote about the former radicals who were running things like government bureaucracies or businesses—the ones wearing ties and paying Social Security. They wrote about the ones who had moved to communes and stayed on to raise kids, who lived in country towns where the natives regarded them as neighbors now rather than hippies. But very few wrote about the burn-outs. Very few wrote about those who had suffered some psychic disease, a permanent loss of will. Like Jack.

6 Slowly, Jack told her about the past year. He talked as if he

were reading a shopping list of events in no particular order of importance: His car was still working. He still had no furniture, no wife, and no children. He'd had a dog for a while, but no more. He was still painting houses for bread money—outside in the summer, inside in the winter.

7 Then, from the pockets of his green jacket, he emptied the more serious lint of his life. There was the quarterly letter from his parents pleading with him to go back to school. His unfinished childhood seemed to keep them in a state of painfully incomplete parenting. Behind the letter was a picture of the woman he had lived with last summer, and under that were some fuzzy directions to the house where he planned to spend the winter with friends. Only he couldn't remember whether the house was in Vermont or New Hampshire.

8 For some reason he irritated her. Thirty years old and he didn't know whether he was headed for Vermont or New Hampshire? States, statistics, plans, slipped through his mind as if through a sieve. She began badgering him. What were his goals now? "I'd like to keep my car running through the winter." Why are you still drifting? "I'm not drifting, I'm living my life."

9 The woman sipped her coffee. He wasn't the only Sixties Kid she knew. Others, like Jack, had lost the conviction that "it" made any difference; that "they" could make a difference. The distinctions between friends, ideals, politics, jobs, seemed no more important to them at this point than the choice of drinking black coffee or regular.

10 They did not seem to regard *anomie* as a disease of the spirit, but as a truth. They embraced their lack of purpose as if it were a benign response to a harsh world. They regarded struggle as foolish, differences as illusions. She knew this.

11 But suddenly she wanted to shake this Jack hard until something rattled out of him, a piece of engagement or anger. She wanted to squeeze his passivity out until it oozed through his damp shoes.

12 Why was she so mad? Because he had committed the sin of *accidie*—not becoming what he might have? Or because she felt in her gut that it was cowardly of him to quit in this way?

13 She had never been especially impressed by the heroics of the people convinced that they are about to change the world. She was more awed by the heroism of those who are willing to struggle to make one small difference after another. And he had attacked her heroes.

14 The two walked back out of the restaurant, onto the brick sidewalk. It had started snowing again. There were windchill factors

being read on radios in the cars that drove by them. She wanted to say something important to Jack. As he turned to say goodbye, he stuffed his bare hands in his pockets, and she blurted out, "For Gawd's sakes, get some mittens!"

Additional Rhetorical Strategies

Description (paragraphs 1, 2); Classification (paragraph 5); Narration (paragraph 6); Illustration (paragraphs 6, 7); Cause and Effect (paragraphs 8, 12).

Examining Words and Meaning

1. What is the purpose of this essay? What central point does Goodman try to make in her portrait of the "Sixties Kid"?
2. How does the author illustrate her contention in paragraph 5 that Jack has suffered "a permanent loss of will"? Characterize the woman's attitude toward Jack. Is she, for example, hostile toward him? Sympathetic? Indifferent? Point to specific words and phrases to support your response.
3. Comment on the effects of Goodman's use of such words as *anomie* (paragraph 10) and *accidie* (paragraph 12). Do these terms add to or detract from the particular response she is trying to elicit from her readers? Explain.

Focusing on Structures and Strategies

1. Trace precisely how the notion of being a parent orders Goodman's thoughts about Jack and her response to him.
2. Why do you think Goodman has chosen *not* to write this essay in the first person? What does she gain or lose as a result? Be as specific as possible.
3. How does the essay end? Does the last sentence strike you as consistent or inconsistent with the woman's attitude toward Jack? Explain.

Suggestion for Further Discussion and Writing

1. Most of us have encountered someone who seemed to typify a particular group, period, or life style. Choose one such person from your own experience and write an essay in which you create an incident that allows you to give concrete dramatic expression to what is finally a historical or cultural abstraction.

On Waitressing

Irene Oppenheim

Irene Oppenheim began her career as a writer shortly after graduating with a B.A. in English from San Francisco State University in 1971: "I wrote a rather lengthy letter to the San Francisco Bay Guardian *challenging the competence of one of their ballet reviews. A few days later, a* Guardian *editor called, offering me a position as a dance critic." Within a short period, her responsibilities included writing theater as well as dance reviews. She remained the dance/theater critic at the* Bay Guardian *for the next eight years, during which time she also served as a correspondent for* Dance Magazine, *received a fellowship in criticism from the O'Neill Theater Center, and wrote essays for such periodicals as* City Magazine, New West, *and the* Village Voice.

More recently, Oppenheim has devoted her time to writing drama. Her plays have been produced both in this country and in Europe. She has been awarded a National Endowment for the Arts grant for radio drama and has won several national playwriting competitions. She continues to write essays on aesthetic issues, individual artists, and on her own intellectual adventures in what she describes as the "checkered episodes of employment [that] continue to provide me with material." At various times, Oppenheim has worked as an interviewer in a mental health survey and as a secretary for "Breakdown Services," which supplies Hollywood agents "with lists of character types needed in upcoming TV shows and films . . . a job that offered at least one memorable pleasure; each of the early day's phone calls could be answered with the heartfelt salutation 'Good morning, Breakdown'."

"Among the glories of writing is that life's more dismal episodes can sometimes be put to good use." Yet, as Oppenheim explains, "This doesn't always work, and I've had to abandon pieces on traumatic

hospital stays and on ungrateful stray cats." However, "Waitressing," published in The Threepenny Review, *offers a strikingly concrete example of writing an essay in which the "right elements seemed to come together, allowing me to act as a guide into a world which, for many of my readers, was as unfamiliar as a foreign country."*

1 In September of 1985 I needed a job that would give me a regular income for a few months. I hadn't worked as a waitress for more than a decade, and at first didn't consider that a possibility. But as I searched for more demure employment, I found that one after another of my interviewers would glance at my resume, sadly mumble something about "all that writing," and proceed, making as much eye-contact as I'd permit, to ask "sincerely" about my intentions, naming anything less than full commitment a form of deceit. Unable to assuage their concern with a convincingly forthright response, I soon found myself applying for work at Canter's, a sprawling twenty-four-hour-a-day Jewish (though non-kosher) bakery, delicatessen, and restaurant which for the past forty-five years has been dishing up kishka and knishes in the Fairfax district of Los Angeles. I knew that neither of my most recent waitress references would check out—Herb of Herb's Hamburgers in San Francisco had thrown down his spatula some years ago and gone to work in a hardware store, while the Sand Dollar Cafe in Stinson Beach had changed owners, so no one there would remember just how deftly I could sling hash. I told all this to Jackie Canter who, in her early twenties, is among a number of Canter relations working in the family business. She hesitated, but I was hired anyway.

2 While I don't wish to discredit my powers of persuasion, getting hired at Canter's was hardly a difficult affair. The "Help Wanted" sign in Canter's front window was a faded, permanent fixture. And in the two months I ultimately worked at the restaurant, the volume of employee comings and goings was never less than impressive. There were, however, exceptions to this transitoriness, and some among the large Canter crew had been with the restaurant for ten, twenty, or even thirty years. These were mostly older women who remained through a combination of loyalty, age, narrow skills, and inertia. The younger people tended to find the work too demanding and the income increasingly unreliable. Canter's heyday had been in the pre-McDonalds, pre-cholesterol days of the 1950s and 60s. And while the erosion was gradual, it was clear that the combination

of fast food and *nouvelle cuisine* was steadily reducing Canter's corned beef/pastrami/chopped liver clientele. Despite trendy additions to the menu, such as an avocado melt sandwich (not bad) and the steamed vegetable plate (not good), there were now many quiet afternoons when the older waitresses, wiping off ketchup bottles and filling napkin holders to pass the time, would tell you about the days when the lines for Canter's stretched right down from the door to the corner of Beverly Boulevard.

3 Canter's could still get enormously busy—on holidays, for instance, or weekend nights. Sometimes for no reason at all the place would suddenly be mobbed. But it all had become unpredictable. And while this unpredictability made the owners niggardly and anxious, its more immediate toll was on the waiters and waitresses, who were almost totally dependent on customer tips. Canter's is a "union house," which means that for sixteen dollars a month the workers are covered by a not-too-respected grievance procedure and a well-loved medical/dental plan. The pay for waiting on tables, however, remains $3.37 per hour (two cents above minimum wage), so at Canter's, as with most restaurants, any real money has to come from tips.

4 Until a few years ago these tips were untaxed, which made waitressing a tough but reasonably lucrative profession. Now tips have to be regularly declared, and through a complicated process that involves the IRS taking eight percent of a restaurant's gross meal receipts and dividing that amount up among the number of food servers, a per-employee tip figure is arrived at, and any waiter who declares less than that may very well be challenged. In some restaurants the management automatically deducts the estimated amount from the paychecks. At Canter's each individual makes a weekly declaration. But in either case there's great bitterness among the table waiters about the way the tax is estimated. In every restaurant, for instance, some shifts are far more profitable than others, a subtlety the IRS doesn't take into account. There's also a built-in bias toward "class" operations where the bills are high and the tips generally run fifteen to twenty percent, while at Canter's with its soup and sandwich fare, ten percent or less is the norm. Also, waitresses and waiters volubly and resentfully claim that others in service professions, such as porters, cab drivers, or hairdressers, are left to make simple declarations, without the income of the business being involved.

5 Where it is possible, most restaurant workers under-declare their tips and simply hope they can get away with it. But a few of

them at Canter's had been called in each year, and the more canny of the waitresses told me I should keep a daily tally of all my checks in case the IRS claimed I'd made not just more than I'd declared, but more than I really took in. What all this meant in terms of an actual paycheck was that, after meal deductions, regular taxes, and taxes declared on my tips, my average check for a forty-hour week was $74.93 or, in the first week of the month, when union fees were due, $58.93. Whatever else I took home was in the form of tips, and if business wasn't good these could become an unnervingly scarce commodity.

6 Still, most waitresses at Canter's made more than they would as bank tellers, store clerks, or non-managerial office workers. And even for those whose options were somewhat less grim, waitressing was not without its alluring aspects. The range of tips—which, depending on how many customers of what kind you got on a shift, might be as low as twelve dollars or as high as eighty—gave the job a gambling flavor which appealed to some. (Gambling, in fact, was rather a big item at Canter's. More than a few of the waitresses played as much bingo as paying their rent allowed, while the kitchen help would, almost every day, pool their money and purchase long strings of lottery tickets, with any winnings divided among the buyers.) Others among the waitresses worked there because they preferred the restaurant's physical demands to the boredom of paper work, and several were performers or students who took advantage of the night hours and flexible scheduling. But no one was really happy to be at Canter's. It simply wasn't a very happy place.

7 I've never worked anywhere that had more rules than Canter's. The staff bulletin board was so crammed with admonitions that the overflow had to be taped to the adjacent wall. The topics of these missives varied. One sign, for example, warned that bags and purses might be checked on the way out for purloined food; another that those who didn't turn up for their shifts on holidays such as Christmas (Canter's is open every day of the year except Rosh Hashanah and Yom Kippur) would be automatically dismissed; a third firmly stated that no food substitutions were permitted, which meant that it was against regulations to give a customer who requested it a slice of tomato instead of a pickle. When working on the floor, one encountered even more elaborate rules. All ice cream, juice, or bakery items, for instance, had to be initialed on your check by that shift's hostess, lest you serve something without writing it down. To further complicate matters, orders for deli sandwiches had to be written on

a slip of paper along with your waitress number (mine was #35), and these slips were then matched against your checks to make sure, for example, that if you ordered two pastrami sandwiches the customer had paid for two. I was castigated by Jackie one day for—along with the more major infraction of not charging fifty cents extra for a slice of cheese—charging ten cents too little for a cup of potato salad. It seems like a small thing, said Jackie (I concurred), but then she added grimly that little mistakes like mine with the potato salad cost the restaurant many thousands of dollars each year. I was tempted to point out that undoubtedly an equal number of errors were made in the restaurant's favor. But I held my tongue, knowing by then that, in the face of a documented Canter's money loss, anything that could be construed as less than acute remorse would only serve to bring my checks under even closer scrutiny.

8 The waitresses were generally good to each other, though such camaraderie didn't often run deep and rarely extended to any auxiliary personnel such as the bus boys. These were constantly (and mostly unjustly) suspected of stealing tips from the tables and thereby adding to their required tips from the waitresses (I'm not sure exactly what this came to per individual bus boy, but every waitress contributed about twenty dollars a week which was divided up among the bus boys). At one time Canter's bus boy positions had been filled by strapping immigrant Jewish boys from places such as Bulgaria and Lithuania. But now the bus boys were almost all Mexican, as were the cooks, and a troublesome plate of blintzes or latkes would be garnished by a storm of Spanish curses. In the back kitchen, too, where they made the soups and mixed together enormous vats of tuna salad, the workers were mostly Spanish-speaking. Things in the back kitchen were usually less frantic than in the front, and the back kitchen guys would smile and try to make conversation as you negotiated your way over the wooden floor slats to the bathroom or the time clock. From the deli and kitchen men, however, surliness was a virtual constant, with their black moods frequently exacerbated into anger by such things as the restaurant's awkward design and organization. It was required, for example, that a waitress serving a cheddar cheese omelette first write a slip for the cheese, which had to be sliced and picked up at the front deli counter, and then, after writing another slip for the kitchen, hand-carry the cheese back to the grill. When the place got busy, tempers also ran short among the waitresses themselves, who would swear at the always recalcitrant toasters, at the bagels (or lack of them), or at each other, as fast movers stumbled into slower ones. But in the arena of churlishness

the waitresses never came close to competing with the hardworking deli men. Brandishing knives and hunks of meat with a rhythmic skill and an admirable—even graceful—economy of movement, they set the tone at Canter's. And I remember a time when, having made a mistake, I said to one of the deli men, by way of apology, that I'd try to improve. "Don't try," he snarled back. "Do."

9 One of the more graphic symbols of Canter's changing times was the uniform closet. The male waiters—a relative novelty at Canter's—were allowed to work in a black-pants/white-shirt combo, with some of them opting to appear in the "I Love Canter's" T-shirt available for eight dollars (*their* eight dollars) at the front cash register.

10 The women could get "I Love Canter's" stenciled free on the off-work shirt of their choice, but their on-the-job dress code was more severe. No one's memory reached back to a time when Canter's waitresses had worn anything other than cream-colored outfits with a single brown stripe running down from each shoulder. There were many of these lined up in the uniform closet. In most cases the uniforms were well-worn, with underarms stained an irreparable gray and hems which had been let up or down more than once. But their dominant characteristic was size. Most of the available uniforms could have doubled as small tents. And no matter how many pins or tucks you employed, material would billow out over your tightly pulled apron strings, an irrepressible tribute to the amplitude of your predecessors.

11 Although there was a locker room at Canter's it was deemed dangerous for reasons I never explored, and I always arrived with my uniform already on. At first I'd worked various shifts—twelve P.M. to eight P.M., eight P.M. to four A.M.—but finally was assigned to days, primarily because I was considered easy-going and the day shift had a contentious reputation. My first task was to relieve Pauline at the counter. She went on duty at six A.M., and technically I was to relieve her at nine A.M. when my shift began. Though the management preferred you didn't clock it in, the rules at Canter's required you to be on the floor fifteen minutes before your shift time, and I'd generally show up around 8:40, which would give Pauline a chance to finish off her checks and put together her own breakfast—usually a mixture of Frosted Flakes and Wheaties put together from the little boxes kept on display right near the coffee machine.

12 There was nothing contentious about Pauline. She was a slow, heavy woman in her early sixties. She was having tooth problems

during the time I knew her. But her feet were also troublesome, and she'd made long knife cuts in the front of her white shoes so that, defying the beige of her nylons, the flesh of each foot pushed out rosy-pink between the slits. Pauline had been working at Canter's for twenty-five years, and was the only one of the waitresses left who had her name machine-embroidered onto her uniform. The rest of us were given pins with our first names punched out on a black dymo label. But Pauline's was sewn right in, so you knew she represented a different, less transient era at the restaurant. You could tell by watching her, too, by the deliberate way she moved, that this was a place she was intimately familiar with.

13 Only one part of the counter was open in the morning. It sat around fourteen people and included, as part of the station, three adjacent two-person booths as well as any take-out coffee orders. Almost everyone hated working the counter because the turnover could be impossibly fast and the tips were always small. On the other hand, the counter didn't involve as much running around as the other stations, and Pauline preferred it. She'd move as though she were doing a little dance, reaching toward the coffee machine, and then the toaster, and then scooping up packets of strawberry jam (strawberry was the only jam flavor Canter's served), with a steady elegance that belied her girth—a factor substantial enough to make it virtually unfeasible for both of us to work behind the counter at once.

14 Pauline was always glad to see me, for the half-hour's rest I represented would be the longest break she'd have until getting off work at two P.M. I liked Pauline too, and we got along well, but the counter was another matter. Generally two kinds of people showed up at the counter: those who were alone and in a hurry to get somewhere else, and a group of "regulars" for whom time was not a consideration. This latter group was dominated by retired men who met at Canter's punctually each day to have windy discussions which would begin focused on a single topic—such as how people on welfare should be prevented from buying lottery tickets—that would gradually merge into a broader lament about the disintegration of the neighborhood, the city, the nation, and onward. From my standpoint, both these counter groups meant trouble: those who were alone tended to be impatient, while those who came in every day expected special treatment which included remembering details about their preferences (water without ice, or a cherry danish heated with soft butter on the side), and they'd become belligerent if these idiosyncrasies were forgotten or if they felt some mere counter itinerant were getting better service. But there were other regulars too, lonely souls who were not

part of the clique. As you stopped for a moment to write out their check, they'd start to tell you about painful cataracts or distant children. I remember one woman who liked her single piece of rye toast burnt almost black. She'd occasionally whisper, so that I had to bend down to hear her, that she was short of cash, and would ask to borrow a dollar from me to pay the bill. I'd always do it. And next day the loan would be stealthily but triumphantly repaid, the dollar slipped into my hand or pocket with a conspiratorial smile as though this act of trust and complicity had secretly bonded us together.

15 My Canter's career was to come to an unfortunately abrupt end. A restaurant as large as Canter's was bound to have "walk-outs" who'd leave without paying their checks, and I'd had a few. There was one obese woman who asked me a couple of times if she could pay with a credit card (Canter's didn't accept them) and then left me a tip before managing to get away without paying for her hamburger and coke. Another man had me take his bacon and eggs back to the kitchen twice for repairs; he left me a tip too, but the eggs and bacon went unpaid for. Though there was an element of disgrace in having a walk-out, these small incidents were too common for much of a fuss to be made. But one busy Saturday I had a party of seven who each ordered around ten dollars worth of food and then made a calculated escape while I was in the back adding up their check. Jackie sat me down at the staff table and grimly said that while she didn't blame me for what happened, she did want me to know that it was the largest walk-out loss in the history of Canter's. Nothing was mentioned about my leaving, though Jackie did say that from this point on she wanted me immediately to report to her or the hostess any of my customers who seemed suspicious. I worked the rest of my shift, but everyone I served began to look vaguely suspicious. And with my reputation securely if infamously etched into Canter's history, it seemed time to move on.

Additional Rhetorical Strategies

Comparison and Contrast (paragraph 2); Description (paragraphs 2, 8, 9); Illustration (throughout); Definition (paragraph 3); Process Analysis (paragraphs 4, 7, 8); Analogy (paragraph 6); Cause and Effect (paragraph 6).

Examining Words and Meaning

1. What is the dominant impression of Canter's restaurant conveyed by this essay? Identify the concrete language in Oppenheim's account which helps form your impression. What reasons does she give for why people work at Canter's? How do the employees relate to one another? To the management? To the customers? What suggestions does Oppenheim present that would help you to explain why the people at Canter's behave as they do?
2. Oppenheim finally quits her job because she begins to distrust all her customers. In what other ways is the issue of trusting people raised in this essay? How would you describe Oppenheim's attitude toward trust? How does it affect the quality of her job at Canter's?

Focusing on Structures and Strategies

1. This essay is an account of Oppenheim's personal experience, yet it contains very few generalizations—or abstract language—about her experience. Instead, it provides a wealth of detail, both descriptive and explanatory. Identify some of the specific information provided in the essay and comment on its contribution to the essay's overall account of waitressing at Canter's.
2. How does Oppenheim portray herself in this essay? How would you describe her personality? What elements of the essay contribute to your impression of her? Why doesn't she seem to fit in at Canter's?
3. What is the effect of Oppenheim's decision to write this essay in the first person? What does she gain/lose by adopting this point of view? She applied for work at Canter's because, she declares, "I needed a job that would give me a regular income for a few months." Oppenheim reports that the reaction of her interviewers, when they recognized on her resume her interest in writing, was to "sadly mumble something about 'all that writing,' and proceed . . . to ask 'sincerely' about my intentions, naming anything less than full commitment a form of deceit." In what specific ways does Oppenheim's experience as a writer become evident in what she notices—and reports on—at Canter's?
4. What is the point of Oppenheim's detailed explanation in paragraph 4 of the process of calculating the tax due on an employee's tips?

What does this paragraph contribute to the overall effect of the essay?

Suggestions for Further Discussion and Writing

1. In paragraph 2, Oppenheim sets up a series of comparisons and contrasts between, for example, young and old waitresses, traditional restaurants and fast-food chains. Characterize the nature of each comparison/contrast and comment on the effectiveness of each. In what specific ways does Oppenheim express her reservations about the decision of Canter's management to have the restaurant compete more effectively with more recent additions to Los Angeles's restaurant scene?

2. Write a detailed account of a job that you took in order to "give [yourself] a regular income for a few months" rather than because you were especially attracted to that kind of work. Use the concrete details of your account (your description of the setting, your portraits of the people with whom you worked, etc.) to *suggest* your attitude toward that experience—rather than to state that attitude explicitly. For example, if you wished to imply that working at a local supermarket was boring, you might write a description in which you focused on how easily you were distracted by the appearances of the customers—or by the overheard fragments of their conversations. How might such an account be more effective than an essay in which one argues that working in a supermarket is boring?

3. DEVELOPING SEQUENCES

Description

1 Nearly all of the writing we will ever want or be asked to do—whether for college courses, personal, or professional reasons—will include some description. Writers use description to create a picture in words of a person, place, object, or state of mind. In our media-oriented society, descriptive writing invariably competes with painting, film, and especially photography as a means of transmitting a mental image or impression of the world around or inside us. Yet description in writing also allows for metaphor, for using words in distinctive combinations to create images that we could never see in a painting, film, or photograph. Words provide us, in effect, with an open-ended opportunity to think about thinking and to recreate the world in our own terms. Descriptive writing also helps develop our thoughts into clear sequences and invariably adds liveliness and specificity to our prose.

2 Description appears frequently in expository writing—primarily to reinforce the effects created by other rhetorical techniques. It may be used, for example, to create a setting for narration, to make a definition livelier, to strengthen an account of cause and effect, to make an illustration more specific, to flesh out an explanation of a process, to make a classification clearer, or to deepen the impact of a particularly striking comparison or analogy. But as we'll see in the selections that follow, description can also serve as the dominant rhetorical strategy in an entire essay.

3 The nature and purpose of an essay determine how central or

subordinate a role description will play in our thinking and writing. Suppose that we've been asked to write an essay in which we discuss the one room we regard as the center of our lives at home. From among several possibilities, we choose to focus on the kitchen. Although we may well want to tell our readers about the important events that happen there (that is, to use narration), we might first want to create an accurate picture of what the kitchen looks like. Describing in detail the physical appearance of the room, its contents, and perhaps even some of the people who regularly use it would help our audience recreate the special liveliness we associate with the kitchen. We could, for example, lead our readers around the room, describing each of its features in enough detail and in clear enough sequence for them to capture a vivid sense of the distinctive sights, sounds, smells, and activities identified with it. To do so would be to rely on description as the key rhetorical element in the success of such an essay.

4 In addition to portraying verbally the physical characteristics of a person, place, or object, description can also be used to recreate an idea, an emotion, a quality, or a mood. In the case of the kitchen, our description might include attention to the ways in which the mood in the kitchen changes at various times of the day and the year. Think of the extended description we could write focusing on the kitchen in the midst of the daily routines that distinguish, say, breakfast from lunch and dinner or of the richness of detail associated with such special occasions as a birthday, Thanksgiving, and the New Year. Our efforts to describe an abstraction like the "holiday spirit" of a room depend finally on our ability to gather concrete illustrations of it. In this instance, we could undoubtedly point to the number of visitors at the house, the variety of food served, the smell of special cooking, the pile of dishes in the sink, and so on. (For a thorough discussion of this procedure for thinking and writing, see "Abstract and Concrete," p. 75.) In all such instances—whether we are picturing something concrete (the furniture or appliances in the kitchen) or something abstract (the spirit in the room during a holiday)—the process of writing an effective description remains essentially the same. We should start with an overview of whatever we want to describe. We should then proceed to select the most striking and significant details and develop them in an intelligible sequence that produces the effect we intended to create.

5 Basically, there are two kinds of description: objective and subjective. Although descriptive prose falls somewhere between

these extremes, combining both in some distinctive proportion, it is useful to keep the following general distinctions in mind. *Objective description* is primarily factual, omitting any attention to the writer. *Subjective description* includes attention to both the subject described and the writer's reactions to it. For example, we could objectively describe the cost of traveling air coach from Los Angeles to New York as $149; writing subjectively, we might say that the price of the trip was "a great bargain." The focus in the first is on the fact, in the second on the way the writer responds to the fact. Or, we might objectively describe a particular automobile as a 1956 cream and gold DeSoto with a push-button transmission and long fins for rear fenders. A more subjective description might add that the car is an "enormous chunk of nostalgia." (For a masterly blending of objective and subjective description, see Virginia Woolf's "The Death of the Moth," p. 125.) Purpose and audience determine whether we ought to use primarily objective or primarily subjective description. Before deciding which form is the more appropriate for an essay, we should ask ourselves, "What is this description being used for?" and "Who is going to read it?"

6 Writers use *objective description* whenever they want to make an impartial presentation of observable facts. Objective description is impersonal prose, as literal and matter-of-fact as possible. The following passage exemplifies the essential features of an objective description:

> The kitchen table is rectangular, seventy-two inches long and thirty inches wide. Made of a two-inch-thick piece of oak, its top is covered with a waxy oilcloth patterned in dark red and blue squares against a white background. In the right corner, close to the wall, a square blue ceramic tile serves as the protective base for a brown earthenware tea pot. A single white place mat has been set to the left of the tile, with a knife and fork on either side of a white dinner plate. On the plate are two thick pieces of chicken.

The emphasis here is quite clearly on the presentation of information. Observable facts are conveyed in a detached tone of voice and in simple, relatively short sentences. The focus in the passage is on the objects, not on the writer's responses to them. Accordingly, the sentences rely on nouns and adjectives, rather than verbs, to carry the description. Equal attention is paid to each item in the description. Also, the writer concentrates on the *denotative meaning* of words—that is, on their dictionary meanings. While the passage involves several sense impressions (the objects have particular shapes and tactile properties, and a few even convey odors), the sense of sight dominates this objective description—and most others as well. Objective description reminds us of the need for the visual element in writing. Yet there is a static quality to this kind of description. The objects are described as simply "being there"—as though they were reflected in a mirror.

7 Besides being the substance of most scientific and technical writing, objective description is also a distinguishing feature of professional brochures, catalogs, and reports. In college life, objective description appears most frequently in textbooks, encyclopedias, reference books, science papers, departmental course guides, and in the classified ads that crowd the back pages of student newspapers and the walls of campus bookstores.

8 Writers use *subjective description* whenever they want to convey their personal interpretations of an object, place, person, or state of mind. In subjective description, there is as much emphasis on the writer's feelings as there is on what is being described. Since subjective description is impressionistic, it is likely to depend on strong verbs, forceful modifiers, and graphic figures of speech—language that signals the writer's feelings about what is being described. Though it may lack some of the technical precision of objective description, it usually makes a more immediate and dramatic appeal to our senses. Here is a subjective description of that same kitchen table:

> Our lives at home converged around the kitchen table. It was a magnet that drew our family together. Cut from the toughest oak, the table was sturdy, smooth, and long enough for my mother, my two sisters, and me to work or play on at the same time. Our favorite light-blue ceramic tile, stationed in the right corner, was the table's sole defense against the ravages of everything from a steaming tea pot to the latest red-hot gadget from the Sears catalogue. More often than not, however, the heat would spread quickly beyond the small tile and onto the checkered oilcloth, which just as quickly exuded a rank odor. Yet no matter how intensely the four of us competed for elbow room at the table, none dared venture near the lone dinner place arranged securely to the left of the tile. There was no telling when HE would get home from work, but, when he did, he expected things to be ready. He liked to eat right away—chicken mostly—two thick pieces in the middle of his plate for openers.

The description in this passage is relational—that is, the objects described are controlled by the significance the writer attaches to them. Each object is described as being more than simply "out there." Unlike the previous illustration, in which a neutral tone of voice prevails, this sample of subjective description projects a real sense of a speaker in each sentence, a personal voice that mixes facts and feelings. Accordingly, the language used is more evocative, richer in suggestion than in precision. No numbers, for example, are mentioned. The verbs, nouns, adjectives, and figures of speech depend on *connotation*—the range of associations and implications extending far beyond dictionary meanings—for their effect. Hence, it is not unusual to see a greater variety of sentence structure in subjective than in objective description. The writer invariably works with fewer details but tries to do much more with each of them. Subjective description is a staple of autobiography, drama, fiction, and poetry. It also marks certain types of expository writing, especially the informal or personal essays featured in magazines and newspapers. (E. B. White's essay "The Ring of Time," p. 129, offers an outstanding example.)

9 We can increase the likelihood that we will write successful description, whether objective or subjective, if we keep in mind a fairly simple sequence for our thinking and writing. First, we must observe the object, person, or scene carefully. The fundamental role of descriptive writing is to make our readers *see.* Yet while description is primarily visual—we create word pictures—we should not ignore the power of language to make readers hear, taste, smell, and even touch our subject as well. Moreover, when we set out to recreate our sense impressions, we invariably will help move our thinking and writing from that level to the point where we can draw inferences. (See "Observation and Inference," p. 47.)

10 Our second task—once we have observed our subject carefully—is to choose the most appropriate and evocative details. This is perhaps our most important decision when writing description. More often than not, we will have far more details to select from than we can possibly use. By focusing on the uniqueness of our subject, we should be able to decide which significant details are needed to make the subject as vivid as possible for our audience. If, for example, we wanted to drop off our car at the garage and leave a note for the mechanic explaining what is wrong with it, we would obviously need to be more specific than writing simply, "It doesn't start easily." So, too, we need not describe the car's exterior if we are concerned about

the motor's not running. It is the quality, not the quantity, of details that counts. Keeping our purpose and audience in mind will undoubtedly help us decide which details will have the greatest impact in our sentences.

11 Having selected the most appropriate details, we then need to make sure, especially in a subjective description, that what we say about one detail will be clear enough so that when we move on to the next our readers will not forget those already discussed. The way to avoid this potential problem is to begin the description with a brief overview. (In our earlier case, the kitchen table "was a magnet that drew our family together.") Each detail will then contribute to what may be called the essay's *dominant impression*—the most important point we intend to convey. In the essay describing the kitchen, the dominant impression might be summarized in the family's locating "stability" in the objects and activities identified with the kitchen table. Or, to take another example, suppose we were walking in a thick woods early on a May morning. The scene may have been so pleasant that we wished to write to a friend to report what it was like. Having observed the scene carefully, we would make each of the details selected work toward establishing the dominant impression: the freshness of the morning. (John Muir's sketch of the awesome spectacle of Yosemite Falls—p. 122—is an excellent example of creating a dominant impression in description.)

12 In writing description, we need to pay close attention not only to the details of what is being described but also to the sequence—the movement of thought—in the description itself. The simplest way to secure the most memorable sequence of details is to present them as the eye discovers them arranged in space. This *spatial order* might progress, for example, from top to bottom or left to right (or vice versa) when describing a person or an object, respectively. When picturing a scene, however, an order of near to far (or vice versa) may prove most effective. There are several standard alternative sequences for developing description: from general to specific, from small to large, and from most common to most unusual feature, or vice versa. We could also begin with an overview of the subject to be described and then gradually focus on its outstanding feature. Whichever sequence we choose to develop, we ought to remember to work with an order natural enough to be followed easily by our audience.

13 Our point of view—where we stand literally and figuratively in relation to our subject—plays a large role in determining the extent and intensity of a description. Consider, for example, how different a description of a police station could be, depending on the writer's

point of view: that of the victim, the accused, the arresting officer, the desk sergeant, the lawyer, or the parents. Generally speaking, the closer we bring our audience to the person, place, object, or state of mind, the greater the number of precise details needed to portray the subject adequately. Whether our point of view is *fixed* (for example, standing in one spot to describe a room) or *moving* (describing, say, what we see as we raft down the Colorado), we should either maintain a consistent point of view throughout the essay or alert readers to any shifts in perspective (for example, moving a description of a house from the outside to the inside). A consistent point of view helps unify descriptive writing.

14 Description stabilizes and enriches our thinking and writing. It not only places our ideas in a clearer context but also adds specificity to our sentences. It thickens our writing. When it works well, description strengthens our thinking by converting random sense impressions into a coherent series of interrelated details. Descriptive writing falters when we simply pile up loosely connected details. When we do this, we invariably run the risk of boring, if not confusing, our readers. We ought, instead, to manage the details of our descriptions with care, choosing those that are best suited to our purpose and audience. Writing effective description is challenging work, but when we succeed at it, we make our prose more precise, realistic, immediate, and engaging.

Ponds

Lewis Thomas

"We have language and can build metaphors as skillfully and precisely as ribosomes make proteins," writes Lewis Thomas (1913–), a man who moves through language and the laboratory with energy and eloquence. In addition to being a doctor, researcher, professor, and director of the Memorial Sloan-Kettering Cancer Center in New York City, Thomas is a National Book Award winner in Arts and Letters whom Time *magazine has called "quite possibly the best essayist on science now working anywhere in the world." His first book,* The Lives of a Cell *(1974), has sold well over 300,000 copies, making it one of the*

most popular works of its kind. Although he began writing poetry during his college days at Princeton and has published over 200 scientific papers, Thomas did not begin his career as an essayist until 1970, when he was fifty-seven years old. Since then he has continued to write his monthly column for the New England Journal of Medicine. *A second collection of essays,* The Medusa and the Snail, *from which this selection was taken, was published in 1979 and quickly joined the best-seller list. Thomas has also published* Late Night Thoughts on Listening to Mahler's Ninth Symphony *(1982) and* The Youngest Science: Notes of a Medicine-Watcher *(1983).*

Clear, vivid descriptive prose usually contains two important stylistic ingredients: the abundance of concrete details and the use of precise terminology. In other words, good descriptive writing makes us see, *and see* accurately. *In "Ponds," Lewis Thomas invites us to see the strange, artificial urban bodies of water that form in the block-long holes dug during the first stages of construction for new buildings. These "ponds" may even begin to fill up with fish, in a parody of evolution that Thomas believes city dwellers find quite disturbing. Note how Thomas's language—characteristically concrete and precise—keeps our sights focused on particular details so that we will not only see what he sees, but see it with the same feeling and fascination.*

1 Large areas of Manhattan are afloat. I remember when the new Bellevue Hospital was being built, fifteen years ago; the first stage was the most spectacular and satisfying, an enormous square lake. It was there for the two years, named Lake Bellevue, while the disconsolate Budget Bureau went looking for cash to build the next stage. It was fenced about and visible only from the upper windows of the old hospital, but pretty to look at, cool and blue in midsummer, frozen gleaming as Vermont in January. The fence, like all city fences, was always broken, and we could have gone down to the lake and used it, but it was known to be an upwelling of the East River. At Bellevue there were printed rules about the East River: if anyone fell in, it was an emergency for the Infectious-Disease Service, and the first measures, after resuscitation, were massive doses of whatever antibiotics the hospital pharmacy could provide.

2 But if you cleaned the East River you could have ponds all over town, up and down the East Side of Manhattan anyway. If you lifted out the Empire State Building and the high structures nearby, you would have, instantly, an inland sea. A few holes bored in the right places would let water into the subways, and you'd have lovely underground canals all across to the Hudson, uptown to the Harlem

River, downtown to the Battery, a Venice underground, without pigeons.

3 It wouldn't work, though, unless you could find a way to keep out the fish. New Yorkers cannot put up with live fish out in the open. I cannot explain this, but it is so.

4 There is a new pond, much smaller than Lake Bellevue, on First Avenue between Seventieth and Seventy-first, on the east side of the street. It emerged sometime last year, soon after a row of old flats had been torn down and the hole dug for a new apartment building. By now it is about average size for Manhattan, a city block long and about forty feet across, maybe eight feet deep at the center, more or less kidney-shaped, rather like an outsized suburban swimming pool except for the things floating, and now the goldfish.

5 With the goldfish, it is almost detestable. There are, clearly visible from the sidewalk, hundreds of them. The neighborhood people do not walk by and stare into it through the broken fence, as would be normal for any other Manhattan pond. They tend to cross the street, looking away.

6 Now there are complaints against the pond, really against the goldfish. How could people do such a thing? Bad enough for pet dogs and cats to be abandoned, but who could be so unfeeling as to abandon goldfish? They must have come down late at night, carrying their bowls, and simply dumped them in. How could they?

7 The ASPCA was called, and came one afternoon with a rowboat. Nets were used, and fish taken away in new custodial bowls, some to Central Park, others to ASPCA headquarters, to the fish pound. But the goldfish have multiplied, or maybe those people with their bowls keep coming down late at night for their furtive, unfeeling dumping. Anyway, there are too many fish for the ASPCA, for which this seems to be a new kind of problem. An official stated for the press that the owners of the property would be asked to drain the pond by pumping, and then the ASPCA would come back with nets to catch them all.

8 You'd think they were rats or roaches, the way people began to talk. Get those goldfish out of that pond, I don't care how you do it. Dynamite, if necessary. But get rid of them. Winter is coming, someone said, and it is deep enough so that they'll be swimming around underneath the ice. Get them out.

9 It is this knowledge of the East River, deep in the minds of all Manhattan residents, more than the goldfish themselves, I think. Goldfish in a glass bowl are harmless to the human mind, maybe even helpful to minds casting about for something, anything, to think

about. But goldfish let loose, propagating themselves, worst of all *surviving* in what has to be a sessile eddy of the East River, somehow threaten us all. We do not like to think that life is possible under some conditions, especially the conditions of a Manhattan pond. There are four abandoned tires, any number of broken beer bottles, fourteen shoes and a single sneaker, and a visible layer, all over the surface, of that grayish-green film that settles on all New York surfaces. The mud at the banks of the pond is not proper country mud but reconstituted Manhattan landfill, ancient garbage, fossilized coffee grounds and grapefruit rind, the defecation of a city. For goldfish to be swimming in such water, streaking back and forth mysteriously in small schools, feeding, obviously feeding, looking as healthy and well-off as goldfish in the costliest kind of window-box aquarium, means something is wrong with our standards. It is, in some deep sense beyond words, insulting.

10 I thought I noticed a peculiar sort of fin on the undersurface of two of the fish. Perhaps, it occurs to me now in a rush of exultation, in such a pond as this, with all its chemical possibilities, there are contained some mutagens, and soon there will be schools of mutant goldfish. Give them just a little more time, I thought. And then, with the most typically Manhattan thought I've ever thought, I thought: The ASPCA will come again, next month, with their rowboat and their nets. The proprietor will begin pumping out the pond. The nets will flail, the rowboat will settle, and then the ASPCA officials will give a sudden shout of great dismay. And with a certain amount of splashing and grayish-greenish spray, at all the edges of the pond, up all the banks of ancient New York landfill mud, crawling on their new little feet, out onto the sidewalks, up and down and across the street, into doorways and up the fire escapes, some of them with little suckers on their little feet, up the sides of buildings and into open windows, looking for something, will come the goldfish.

11 It won't last, of course. Nothing like this ever does. The mayor will come and condemn it in person. The Health Department will come and recommend the purchase of cats from out of town because of the constitutional boredom of city cats. The NIH will send up teams of professionals from Washington with a new kind of antifish spray, which will be recalled four days later because of toxicity to cats.

12 After a few weeks it will be finished anyway, like a lot of New York events. The goldfish will dive deep and vanish, the pond will fill up with sneakers, workmen will come and pour concrete over

everything, and by next year the new building will be up and occupied by people all unaware of their special environmental impact. But what a time it was.

Reading for Rhetorical Strategy

Lewis Thomas sets the scene by first offering a charming picture of the former "Lake Bellevue" ("cool and blue in midsummer, frozen gleaming as Vermont in January"). In paragraph 4, he introduces the latest Manhattan pond, locates it precisely, and gives us a clear sense of its size and shape ("more or less kidney-shaped, rather like an outsized suburban swimming pool"). Note in paragraph 9, Thomas's use of precise terminology—"sessile" is a technical term in biology referring to the way parts of a plant are attached to the base. In the same paragraph Thomas offers an especially concrete depiction of the pond's filthy condition, right down to the number of abandoned tires and discarded shoes. Note in paragraph 10, how his use of detail allows us to form a vivid picture of the ambulatory goldfish of his imagination.

On Abraham Lincoln

Nathaniel Hawthorne and Edward Dicey

Few images are so deeply imprinted on the collective American mind as that of Abraham Lincoln. Though his contemplative profile (as seen on a penny) and his countless portraits (like the one on a five-dollar bill) may seem timeless to us now, Lincoln struck his contemporaries as the epitome of the nineteenth-century Yankee: tall, lanky, sallow, and permanently disheveled.

The following nineteenth-century "word portraits"—the first (I) by Nathaniel Hawthorne (1804–1864), one of America's great novelists, and the second (II) by Edward Dicey, an English journalist—give us some idea of what Lincoln looked like as well as the impression his appearance made on observers. These descriptions are followed by two photographs of our sixteenth President.

I

1 Unquestionably, Western man though he be, and Kentuckian by birth, President Lincoln is the essential representative of all Yankees, and the veritable specimen, physically, of what the world seems determined to regard as our characteristic qualities. It is the strangest and yet the fittest thing in the jumble of human vicissitudes, that he, out of so many millions, unlooked for, unselected by any intelligible process that could be based upon his genuine qualities, unknown to those who chose him, and unsuspected of what endowments may adapt him for his tremendous responsibility, should have found the way open for him to fling his lank personality into the chair of state—where, I presume, it was his first impulse to throw his legs on the council-table, and tell the Cabinet Ministers a story. There is no describing his lengthy awkwardness, nor the uncouthness of his movement; and yet it seemed as if I had been in the habit of seeing him daily, and had shaken hands with him a thousand times in some village street; so true was he to the aspect of the pattern American, though with a certain extravagance which, possibly, I exaggerated still further by the delighted eagerness with which I took it in. If put to guess his calling and livelihood, I should have taken him for a country school-master as soon as anything else. He was dressed in a rusty black frock coat and pantaloons, unbrushed, and worn so faithfully that the suit had adapted itself to the curves and angularities of his figure, and had grown to be an outer skin of the man. His hair was black, still unmixed with gray, stiff, somewhat bushy, and had apparently been acquainted with neither brush nor comb that morning, after the disarrangement of the pillow; and as to a nightcap, Uncle Abe probably knows nothing of such effeminacies. His complexion is dark and sallow, betokening, I fear, an insalubrious atmosphere around the White House; he has thick black eyebrows and an impending brow; his nose is large, and the lines about his mouth are very strongly defined.

2 The whole physiognomy is as coarse a one as you would meet anywhere in the length and breadth of the States; but, withal, it is redeemed, illuminated, softened, and brightened by a kindly though serious look out of his eyes, and an expression of homely sagacity, that seems weighted with rich results of village experience. A great deal of native sense; no bookish cultivation, no refinement; honest at heart, and thoroughly so, and yet, in some sort, sly—at least, endowed with a sort of tact and wisdom that are akin to craft, and

would impel him, I think, to take an antagonist in flank, rather than to make a bull-run at him right in front. But, on the whole, I like this sallow, queer, sagacious visage, with the homely human sympathies that warmed it; and, for my small share in the matter, would as lief have Uncle Abe for a ruler as any man whom it would have been practicable to put in his place.

II

1 Personally, his aspect is one which, once seen, cannot easily be forgotten. If you take the stock English caricature of the typical Yankee, you have the likeness of the President. To say that he is ugly is nothing: to add that his figure is grotesque is to convey no adequate impression. Fancy a man six-foot high, and thin *out of* proportion, with long bony arms and legs, which, somehow, seem to be always in the way, with large rugged hands, which grasp you like a vice when shaking yours, with a long scraggy neck, and a chest too narrow for the great arms hanging by its side; add to this figure, a head cocoa-nut shaped and somewhat too small for such a stature, covered with rough, uncombed and uncombable lank dark hair, that stands out in every direction at once; a face furrowed, wrinkled, and indented, as though it had been scarred by vitriol; a high narrow forehead; and, sunk deep beneath bushy eyebrows, two bright, somewhat dreamy eyes, that seemed to gaze through you without looking at you; a few irregular blotches of black bristly hair in the place where beard and whiskers ought to grow; a close-set, thin-lipped, stern mouth, with two rows of large white teeth; and a nose and ears, which have been taken by mistake from a head of twice the size. Clothe this figure, then, in a long, tight, badly-fitting suit of black, creased, soiled, and puckered up at every salient point of the figure—and every point of this figure is salient—put on large, ill-fitting boots, gloves too long for the long bony fingers, and a fluffy hat, covered to the top with dusty, puffy crape; and then add to all this an air of strength, physical as well as moral, and a strange look of dignity coupled with all this grotesqueness, and you will have the impression left upon me by Abraham Lincoln. You would never say he was a gentleman: you would still less say he was not one. There are some women about whom no one ever thinks in connexion with beauty, one way or the other—and there are men to whom the epithet of "gentlemanlike" or "ungentlemanlike" appears utterly incongruous, and of such the President is one. Still there is about him

a complete absence of pretension, and an evident desire to be courteous to everybody, which is the essence, if not the outward form, of high-breeding. There is a softness, too, about his smile, and a sparkle of dry humour about his eye which redeem the expression on his face. . . .

Examining Words and Meaning

1. What details of Lincoln's appearance does each writer focus on? What do the differences in the descriptions tell you about the attitude of each writer toward the President?
2. What is the effect of Dicey's phrase "a head cocoa-nut shaped and somewhat too small for such a stature"? What other words and phrases in Dicey's description have a similar effect? Does Hawthorne include any words or phrases that strike you in the same way? Considering the word choices of each writer, would you call these descriptions subjective or objective?

Focusing on Structures and Strategies

1. Which writer, Hawthorne or Dicey, makes you more aware of *his* reaction to being with Lincoln? Which seems to concentrate more on Lincoln's physical appearance? Compare the effects of these strategies. Which account seems to you more intimate?
2. At what point in his description does Dicey seem most favorably disposed toward the President? What is the effect of his being more admiring here? Does he weaken or reinforce the effect of his description of Lincoln's appearance? How does his rhetorical strategy differ from Hawthorne's in this respect?

Suggestions for Further Discussion and Writing

1. Try writing a description of someone you know and respect for an audience that might not be immediately appreciative of that person. Keep your description objectively accurate as well as conducive to

Abraham Lincoln, 1860 (probably Preston Butler)

Abraham Lincoln, 1864 (Anthony Berger)

the effect you intend to make. You might try describing someone whom you suspect your parents would not approve of, or you might show the worth of someone whom most people might look down on.

2. As an in-class experiment, write a description of the president of your college. You and your classmates might then read some of the descriptions aloud and compare them. What differences in perception do you find? What details does each writer focus on? How do different writers organize their descriptions? Does everyone seem to be seeing the same person?

3. Compare and contrast the descriptions of Lincoln by Hawthorne and Dicey with the photographs of him on p. 117. How is point of view indicated in each of these four documents? What do you suspect is the purpose of each? Which do you find most effective? Why?

The Elephant Man

Sir Frederick Treves

Descriptions of persons, places, and things largely reflect a writer's professional point of view. Much of what we see depends on what we are looking for. When Sir Frederick Treves first saw John Merrick, the "Elephant Man," Treves was the lecturer on anatomy at the London Hospital's Medical College. In the following passage from Treves's The Elephant Man and Other Reminiscences *(1923), we can clearly watch the anatomist's meticulous habit of close physical observation. But though we are indebted to Treves for leaving us his vivid scientific description of the Elephant Man, we are even more indebted to him for his rare capacity to see that beyond his grotesque description was a genuine man named John Merrick.*

The Elephant Man *has been the subject of an award-winning Broadway play and a motion picture.*

1 In the Mile End Road, opposite to the London Hospital, there was (and possibly still is) a line of small shops. Among them was a vacant greengrocer's which was to let. The whole of the front of the

shop, with the exception of the door, was hidden by a hanging sheet of canvas on which was the announcement that the Elephant Man was to be seen within and that the price of admission was twopence. Painted on the canvas in primitive colours was a life-size portrait of the Elephant Man. This very crude production depicted a frightful creature that could only have been possible in a nightmare. It was the figure of a man with the characteristics of an elephant. The transfiguration was not far advanced. There was still more of the man than of the beast. This fact—that it was still human—was the most repellent attribute of the creature. There was nothing about it of the pitiableness of the misshapened or the deformed, nothing of the grotesqueness of the freak, but merely the loathing insinuation of a man being changed into an animal. Some palm trees in the background of the picture suggested a jungle and might have led the imaginative to assume that it was in this wild that the perverted object had roamed.

2 When I first became aware of this phenomenon the exhibition was closed, but a well-informed boy sought the proprietor in a public house and I was granted a private view on payment of a shilling. The shop was empty and grey with dust. Some old tins and a few shrivelled potatoes occupied a shelf and some vague, vegetable refuse the window. The light in the place was dim, being obscured by the painted placard outside. The far end of the shop—where I expect the late proprietor sat at a desk—was cut off by a curtain or rather by a red tablecloth suspended from a cord by a few rings. The room was cold and dank, for it was the month of November. The year, I might say, was 1884.

3 The showman pulled back the curtain and revealed a bent figure crouching on a stool and covered by a brown blanket. In front of it, on a tripod, was a large brick heated by a Bunsen burner. Over this the creature was huddled to warm itself. It never moved when the curtain was drawn back. Locked up in an empty shop and lit by the faint blue light of the gas jet, this hunched-up figure was the embodiment of loneliness. It might have been a captive in a cavern or a wizard watching for unholy manifestations in the ghostly flame. Outside the sun was shining and one could hear the footsteps of the passers-by, a tune whistled by a boy and the commonplace hum of traffic in the road.

4 The showman—speaking as if to a dog—called out harshly: "Stand up!" The thing arose slowly and let the blanket that covered its head and back fall to the ground. There stood revealed the most

disgusting specimen of humanity that I have ever seen. In the course of my profession I had come upon lamentable deformities of the face due to injury or disease, as well as mutilations and contortions of the body depending upon like causes; but at no time had I met with such a degraded or perverted version of a human being as this lone figure displayed. He was naked to the waist, his feet were bare, he wore a pair of threadbare trousers that had once belonged to some fat gentleman's dress suit.

5 From the intensified painting in the street I had imagined the Elephant Man to be of gigantic size. This, however, was a little man below the average height and made to look shorter by the bowing of his back. The most striking feature about him was the enormous and misshapened head. From the brow there projected a huge bony mass like a loaf, while from the back of the head hung a bag of spongy, fungous-looking skin, the surface of which was comparable to brown cauliflower. On the top of the skull were a few long lank hairs. The osseous growth on the forehead almost occluded one eye. The circumference of the head was no less than that of the man's waist. From the upper jaw there projected another mass of bone. It protruded from the mouth like a pink stump, turning the upper lip inside out and making the mouth a mere slobbering aperture. This growth from the jaw had been so exaggerated in the painting as to appear to be a rudimentary trunk or tusk. The nose was merely a lump of flesh, only recognizable as a nose from its position. The face was no more capable of expression than a block of gnarled wood. The back was horrible, because from it hung, as far down as the middle of the thigh, huge, sack-like masses of flesh covered by the same loathsome cauliflower skin.

6 The right arm was of enormous size and shapeless. It suggested the limb of the subject of elephantiasis. It was overgrown also with pendent masses of the same cauliflower-like skin. The hand was large and clumsy—a fin or paddle rather than a hand. There was no distinction between the palm and the back. The thumb had the appearance of a radish, while the fingers might have been thick, tuberous roots. As a limb it was almost useless. The other arm was remarkable by contrast. It was not only normal but was, moreover, a delicately shaped limb covered with fine skin and provided with a beautiful hand which any woman might have envied. From the chest hung a bag of the same repulsive flesh. It was like a dewlap suspended from the neck of a lizard. The lower limbs had the characters of the deformed arm. They were unwieldy, dropsical looking and grossly misshapened.

7 To add a further burden to his trouble the wretched man, when a boy, developed hip disease, which had left him permanently lame, so that he could only walk with a stick. He was thus denied all means of escape from his tormentors. As he told me later, he could never run away. One other feature must be mentioned to emphasize his isolation from his kind. Although he was already repellent enough, there arose from the fungous skin-growth with which he was almost covered a very sickening stench which was hard to tolerate. From the showman I learnt nothing about the Elephant Man, except that he was English, that his name was John Merrick and that he was twenty-one years of age.

Additional Rhetorical Strategy

Narration (paragraphs 2, 3).

Examining Words and Meaning

1. Why does Treves begin with a description of the setting rather than of the Elephant Man himself? What effect does this tactic have on the reader?
2. What does Treves find most repellent about the Elephant Man, and how does he convey this? What particular words does he use to achieve the effect of a horrifying experience?
3. What is the effect of the following terms: *osseous* (paragraph 5), *occluded* (paragraph 5), *aperture* (paragraph 5), *tuberous* (paragraph 6)? Look these words up in a dictionary, if necessary. What area of experience are the terms drawn from? Do they enhance or lessen the repulsiveness of the scene? Explain your answer.

Focusing on Structures and Strategies

1. Why do you think Treves first describes his encounter with an "intensified painting" of the Elephant Man? How does this prepare the reader for the encounter with the Elephant Man?

2. Underline words and phrases that you think represent objective and subjective description (as explained in the introduction to this section). Which do you think predominates in the passage? What is the cumulative effect of the shifts between objective and subjective description?

Suggestions for Further Discussion and Writing

1. *The Elephant Man* is one among many movies successfully portraying grotesque characters. (Recent science-fiction movies, for example, have specialized in this.) Select a grotesque character from a movie or television show that you've seen recently, and describe that character from both an objective, impersonal viewpoint and a subjective, personal one.
2. Much of how we describe something or someone depends on our point of view. Pretend you are the Elephant Man, and write a description of Sir Frederick Treves as he might be seen from your point of view.

Yosemite Falls

John Muir

Explorer and naturalist John Muir (1838–1941) was born in Scotland but moved with his family to America while still quite young. His autobiography, The Story of My Boyhood and Youth *(1913), is an account of his years spent on a Wisconsin farm. During his extensive hiking trips through the Midwest, the West, and Canada, Muir kept a daily journal of his observations and reflections. He wrote impassioned articles arguing for the preservation of wilderness areas and is generally considered the leader of the forest conservation movement.*

The following passage is an excellent example of the use of description to create a dominant impression—in this case, of the awesome spectacle of Yosemite Falls.

1 During the time of the spring floods the best near view of the fall is obtained from Fern Ledge on the east side above the blinding

spray at a height of about 400 feet above the base of the fall. A climb of about 1400 feet from the Valley has to be made, and there is no trail, but to any one fond of climbing this will make the ascent all the more delightful. A narrow part of the ledge extends to the side of the fall and back of it, enabling us to approach it as closely as we wish. When the afternoon sunshine is streaming through the throng of comets, ever wasting, ever renewed, the marvelous fineness, firmness, and variety of their forms are beautifully revealed.

2 At the top of the fall they seem to burst forth in irregular spurts from some grand, throbbing mountain heart. Now and then one mighty throb sends forth a mass of solid water into the free air far beyond the others, which rushes alone to the bottom of the fall with long streaming tail, like combed silk, while the others, descending in clusters, gradually mingle and lose their identity. But they all rush past us with amazing velocity and display of power, though apparently drowsy and deliberate in their movements when observed from a distance of a mile or two. The heads of these comet-like masses are composed of nearly solid water, and are dense white in color like pressed snow, from the friction they suffer in rushing through the air, the portion worn off forming the tail, between the white lustrous threads and films of which faint, grayish pencilings appear, while the outer, finer sprays of waterdust, whirling in sunny eddies, are pearly gray throughout.

3 At the bottom of the fall there is but little distinction of form visible. It is mostly a hissing, flashing, seething, upwhirling mass of scud and spray, through which the light sifts in gray and purple tones, while at times, when the sun strikes at the required angle, the whole wild and apparently lawless, stormy, striving mass is changed to brilliant rainbow hues, manifesting finest harmony.

4 The middle portion of the fall is the most openly beautiful; lower, the various forms into which the waters are wrought are more closely and voluminously veiled, while higher, towards the head, the current is comparatively simple and undivided. But even at the bottom, in the boiling clouds of spray, there is no confusion, while the rainbow light makes all divine, adding glorious beauty and peace to glorious power.

5 This noble fall has [by] far the richest, as well as the most powerful, voice of all the falls of the Valley, its tones varying from the sharp hiss and rustle of the wind in the glossy leaves of the live oaks and the soft, sifting, hushing tones of the pines, to the loudest rush and roar of storm winds and thunder among the crags of the summit peaks. The low bass, booming, reverberating tones, heard

under favorable circumstances five or six miles away, are formed by the dashing and exploding of heavy masses mixed with air upon two projecting ledges on the face of the cliff, the one on which we are standing and another about 200 feet above it. The torrent of massive comets is continuous at time of high water, while the explosive, booming notes are wildly intermittent, because, unless influenced by the wind, most of the heavier masses shoot out from the face of the precipice, and pass the ledges upon which at other times they are exploded.

6 Occasionally the whole fall is swayed away from the front of the cliff, then suddenly dashed flat against it, or vibrated from side to side like a pendulum, giving rise to endless variety of forms and sounds.

Additional Rhetorical Strategy

Structural Metaphor ("throng of comets," paragraph 1).

Examining Words and Meaning

1. What is the point of view in this description? Is it the one that most viewers of the falls would have? What advantage does such a point of view give Muir in writing his description?
2. What are some of the words Muir uses to describe movement in this selection? Looking back over these words, would you say that his description is objective or subjective?

Focusing on Structures and Strategies

1. In what order does Muir describe the three parts of the falls? Why does he elect to arrange his description in this way?
2. Consider the second sentence of paragraph 3. Does it seem likely that a sentence structured in this way would fit easily into an objective description? Why or why not? How would the effect of

this sentence be different if, say, we eliminated all adjectives but *hissing* from the first phrase?

Suggestion for Further Discussion and Writing

1. Observe some object or scene in nature—a waterfall, a tree, a wheatfield, a lawn, or the like—from an unusual point of view. You might want to describe a lawn from eye level, for example. Then write a *subjective* description of what you are observing, paying close attention to the order in which you arrange your details. Try to use similes, metaphors, and striking verbs, as Muir does, to make the object come alive for your reader.

The Death of the Moth

Virginia Woolf

"Somehow or other," wrote Virginia Woolf (1882–1941), "by dint of labour or bounty of nature, or both combined, the essay must be pure—pure like water or pure like wine, but pure from dullness, deadness, and deposits of extraneous matter." Continually concerned with achieving that ideal, Virginia Woolf noted in her diary for 1929 that she "must learn to write more succinctly. Especially in the general interest essays. . . . I am horrified by my own looseness. This is partly that I don't think things out first; partly that I stretch my style to take in crumbs of meaning."

An important force in twentieth-century fiction, Virginia Woolf experimented with and succeeded in developing the "stream of consciousness" technique, which she used to explore the problem of personal identity in her later novels: Mrs. Dalloway *(1925),* To the Lighthouse *(1927), and* The Waves *(1931). In the following essay, she describes in stunning detail the death of a moth.*

1 Moths that fly by day are not properly to be called moths; they do not excite that pleasant sense of dark autumn nights and ivy-

blossom which the commonest yellow-underwing asleep in the shadow of the curtain never fails to rouse in us. They are hybrid creatures, neither gay like butterflies nor sombre like their own species. Nevertheless the present specimen, with his narrow hay-coloured wings, fringed with a tassel of the same colour, seemed to be content with life. It was a pleasant morning, mid-September, mild, benignant, yet with a keener breath than that of the summer months. The plough was already scoring the field opposite the window, and where the share had been, the earth was pressed flat and gleamed with moisture. Such vigour came rolling in from the fields and then down beyond that it was difficult to keep the eyes strictly turned upon the book. The rooks too were keeping one of their annual festivities; soaring round the tree tops until it looked as if a vast net with thousands of black knots in it had been cast up into the air; which, after a few moments sank slowly down upon the trees until every twig seemed to have a knot at the end of it. Then, suddenly, the net would be thrown into the air again in a wider circle this time, with the utmost clamour and vociferation, as though to be thrown into the air and settle slowly down upon the tree tops were a tremendously exciting experience.

2 The same energy which inspired the rooks, the ploughmen, the horses, and even, it seemed, the lean bare-backed downs, sent the moth fluttering from side to side of his square of the windowpane. One could not help watching him. One was, indeed, conscious of a queer feeling of pity for him. The possibilities of pleasure seemed that morning so enormous and so various that to have only a moth's part in life, and a day moth's at that, appeared a hard fate, and his zest in enjoying his meagre opportunities to the full, pathetic. He flew vigorously to one corner of his compartment, and, after waiting there a second, flew across to the other. What remained for him but to fly to a third corner and then to a fourth? That was all he could do, in spite of the size of the downs, the width of the sky, the far-off smoke of houses, and the romantic voice, now and then, of a steamer out at sea. What he could do he did. Watching him, it seemed as if a fibre, very thin but pure, of the enormous energy of the world had been thrust into his frail and diminutive body. As often as he crossed the pane, I could fancy that a thread of vital light became visible. He was little or nothing but life.

3 Yet, because he was so small, and so simple a form of the energy that was rolling in at the open window and driving its way through

so many narrow and intricate corridors in my own brain and in those of other human beings, there was something marvelous as well as pathetic about him. It was as if someone had taken a tiny bead of pure life and decking it as lightly as possible with down and feathers, had set it dancing and zigzagging to show us the true nature of life. Thus displayed one could not get over the strangeness of it. One is apt to forget all about life, seeing it humped and bossed and garnished and cumbered so that it has to move with the greatest circumspection and dignity. Again, the thought of all that life might have been had he been born in any other shape caused one to view his simple activities with a kind of pity.

4 After a time, tired by his dancing apparently, he settled on the window ledge in the sun, and, the queer spectacle being at an end, I forgot about him. Then, looking up, my eye was caught by him. He was trying to resume his dancing, but seemed either so stiff or so awkward that he could only flutter to the bottom of the window-pane; and when he tried to fly across it he failed. Being intent on other matters I watched these futile attempts for a time without thinking, unconsciously waiting for him to resume his flight, as one waits for a machine, that has stopped momentarily, to start again without considering the reason of its failure. After perhaps a seventh attempt he slipped from the wooden ledge and fell, fluttering his wings, on to his back on the window sill. The helplessness of his attitude roused me. It flashed upon me that he was in difficulties; he could no longer raise himself; his legs struggled vainly. But, as I stretched out a pencil, meaning to help him to right himself, it came over me that the failure and awkwardness were the approach of death. I laid the pencil down again.

5 The legs agitated themselves once more. I looked as if for the enemy against which he struggled. I looked out of doors. What had happened there? Presumably it was midday, and work in the fields had stopped. Stillness and quiet had replaced the previous animation. The birds had taken themselves off to feed in the brooks. The horses stood still. Yet the power was there all the same, massed outside indifferent, impersonal, not attending to anything in particular. Somehow it was opposed to the little hay-coloured moth. It was useless to try to do anything. One could only watch the extraordinary efforts made by those tiny legs against an oncoming doom which could, had it chosen, have submerged an entire city, not merely a city, but masses of human beings; nothing, I knew, had any chance against

death. Nevertheless after a pause of exhaustion the legs fluttered again. It was superb this last protest, and so frantic that he succeeded at last in righting himself. One's sympathies, of course, were all on the side of life. Also, when there was nobody to care or to know, this gigantic effort on the part of an insignificant little moth, against a power of such magnitude, to retain what no one else valued or desired to keep, moved one strangely. Again, somehow, one saw life, a pure bead. I lifted the pencil again, useless though I knew it to be. But even as I did so, the unmistakable tokens of death showed themselves. The body relaxed, and instantly grew stiff. The struggle was over. The insignificant little creature now knew death. As I looked at the dead moth, this minute wayside triumph of so great a force over so mean an antagonist filled me with wonder. Just as life had been strange a few minutes before, so death was now as strange. The moth having righted himself now lay most decently and uncomplainingly composed. O yes, he seemed to say, death is stronger than I am.

Additional Rhetorical Strategy

Narration (paragraphs 2, 4, 5).

Examining Words and Meaning

1. Woolf first refers to the moth as "the present specimen." What does this word choice suggest about her attitude at this point? Does her attitude remain the same throughout the selection?
2. Does Woolf use the word *I* in the first two paragraphs? If not, what word does she use to indicate her point of view? Does she use *I* in paragraphs 3 and 4? What is the effect of her word choice in this respect? What point might she be trying to suggest?
3. How has the scene beyond the window changed as the moth starts to die? Does Woolf *explicitly* attach any significance to these changes? If not, what is her purpose for including them at all?
4. Look up these words in the dictionary if they are unfamiliar to you: hybrid (paragraph 1); benignant (paragraph 1); share (paragraph 1);

vociferation (paragraph 1); downs (paragraph 2); diminutive (paragraph 2); bossed (paragraph 3).

Focusing on Structures and Strategies

1. Why does Woolf go to such lengths in paragraph 1 to describe the scene beyond the window, since the essay is about the death of the moth? What keeps the fields and the birds from being irrelevant?
2. What details does Woolf give us about the moth's appearance? What details doesn't she give us? Why might she choose to omit so much?

Suggestions for Further Discussion and Writing

1. Suppose that Woolf had written a purely objective description of the moth and its death. In what respects would it differ from this description?
2. It often happens that an insignificant event such as the death of a moth can become part of a whole network of reflection. Think back on your own experience, and choose one such incident that caused you to think about the far-reaching questions we sometimes ask ourselves: our commitment to our jobs or schoolwork, our relationship with another person, our mortality, what our lives mean. Write an essay describing the incident, making its significance clear to your reader.

The Ring of Time

E. B. White

"There are as many kinds of essays," wrote E. B. White (1899–1985), "as there are human attitudes or poses, as many essay flavors as there are Howard Johnson ice creams." The essayist "can be any sort of

person, according to his mood or his subject matter—philosopher, scold, jester, raconteur, confidant, pundit, devil's advocate, enthusiast." Author of over twenty books and the recipient of many awards, E. B. White at one time or another in his long career was all of those persons in his essays.

In "The Ring of Time," despite his protestation of failure, White—a master of blending description and narration for the purposes of exposition—succeeds brilliantly in making vivid the unforgettable moment he once experienced while watching a young performer practice her horse-riding act for a traveling circus.

Fiddler Bayou, March 22, 1956

1 After the lions had returned to their cages, creeping angrily through the chutes, a little bunch of us drifted away and into an open doorway nearby, where we stood for a while in semidarkness, watching a big brown circus horse go harumphing around the practice ring. His trainer was a woman of about forty, and the two of them, horse and woman, seemed caught up in one of those desultory treadmills of afternoon from which there is no apparent escape. The day was hot, and we kibitzers were grateful to be briefly out of the sun's glare. The long rein, or tape, by which the woman guided her charge counterclockwise in his dull career formed the radius of their private circle, of which she was the revolving center; and she, too, stepped a tiny circumference of her own, in order to accommodate the horse and allow him his maximum scope. She had on a short-skirted costume and a conical straw hat. Her legs were bare and she wore high heels, which probed deep into the loose tanbark and kept her ankles in a state of constant turmoil. The great size and meekness of the horse, the repetitious exercise, the heat of the afternoon, all exerted a hypnotic charm that invited boredom; we spectators were experiencing a languor—we neither expected relief nor felt entitled to any. We had paid a dollar to get into the grounds, to be sure, but we had got our dollar's worth a few minutes before, when the lion trainer's whiplash had got caught around a toe of one of the lions. What more did we want for a dollar?

2 Behind me I heard someone say, "Excuse me, please," in a low voice. She was halfway into the building when I turned and saw her—a girl of sixteen or seventeen, politely threading her way through us onlookers who blocked the entrance. As she emerged in front of us, I saw that she was barefoot, her dirty little feet fighting the uneven ground. In most respects she was like any of two or three

dozen showgirls you encounter if you wander about the winter quarters of Mr. John Ringling North's circus, in Sarasota—cleverly proportioned, deeply browned by the sun, dusty, eager, and almost naked. But her grave face and the naturalness of her manner gave her a sort of quick distinction and brought a new note into the gloomy octagonal building where we had all cast our lot for a few moments. As soon as she had squeezed through the crowd, she spoke a word or two to the older woman, whom I took to be her mother, stepped to the ring, and waited while the horse coasted to a stop in front of her. She gave the animal a couple of affectionate swipes on his enormous neck and then swung herself aboard. The horse immediately resumed his rocking canter, the woman goading him on, chanting something that sounded like "Hop! Hop!"

3 In attempting to recapture this mild spectacle, I am merely acting as recording secretary for one of the oldest of societies—the society of those who, at one time or another, have surrendered, without even a show of resistance, to the bedazzlement of a circus rider. As a writing man, or secretary, I have always felt charged with the safekeeping of all unexpected items of worldly or unworldly enchantment, as though I might be held personally responsible if even a small one were to be lost. But it is not easy to communicate anything of this nature. The circus comes as close to being the world in microcosm as anything I know; in a way, it puts all the rest of show business in the shade. Its magic is universal and complex. Out of its wild disorder comes order; from its rank smell rises the good aroma of courage and daring; out of its preliminary shabbiness comes the final splendor. And buried in the familiar boasts of its advance agents lies the modesty of most of its people. For me the circus is at its best before it has been put together. It is at its best at certain moments when it comes to a point, as through a burning glass, in the activity and destiny of a single performer out of so many. One ring is always bigger than three. One rider, one aerialist, is always greater than six. In short, a man has to catch the circus unawares to experience its full impact and share its gaudy dream.

4 The ten-minute ride the girl took achieved—as far as I was concerned, who wasn't looking for it, and quite unbeknownst to her, who wasn't even striving for it—the thing that is sought by performers everywhere, on whatever stage, whether struggling in the tidal currents of Shakespeare or bucking the difficult motion of a horse. I somehow got the idea she was just cadging a ride, improving a shining ten minutes in the diligent way all serious artists seize free mo-

ments to hone the blade of their talent and keep themselves in trim. Her brief tour included only elementary postures and tricks, perhaps because they were all she was capable of, perhaps because her warmup at this hour was unscheduled and the ring was not rigged for a real practice session. She swung herself off and on the horse several times, gripping his mane. She did a few knee-stands—or whatever they are called—dropping to her knees and quickly bouncing back up on her feet again. Most of the time she simply rode in a standing position, well aft on the beast, her hands hanging easily at her sides, her head erect, her straw-colored ponytail lightly brushing her shoulders, the blood of exertion showing faintly through the tan of her skin. Twice she managed a one-foot stance—a sort of ballet pose, with arms outstretched. At one point the neck strap of her bathing suit broke and she went twice around the ring in the classic attitude of a woman making minor repairs to a garment. The fact that she was standing on the back of a moving horse while doing this invested the matter with a clownish significance that perfectly fitted the spirit of the circus—jocund, yet charming. She just rolled the strap into a neat ball and stowed it inside her bodice while the horse rocked and rolled beneath her in dutiful innocence. The bathing suit proved as self-reliant as its owner and stood up well enough without benefit of strap.

5 The richness of the scene was in its plainness, its natural condition—of horse, of ring; of girl, even to the girl's bare feet that gripped the bare back of her proud and ridiculous mount. The enchantment grew not out of anything that happened or was performed but out of something that seemed to go round and around and around with the girl, attending her, a steady gleam in the shape of a circle—a ring of ambition, of happiness, of youth. (And the positive pleasures of equilibrium under difficulties.) In a week or two, all would be changed, all (or almost all) lost: the girl would wear makeup, the horse would wear gold, the ring would be painted, the bark would be clean for the feet of the horse, the girl's feet would be clean for the slippers that she'd wear. All, all would be lost.

6 As I watched with the others, our jaws adroop, our eyes alight, I became painfully conscious of the element of time. Everything in the hideous old building seemed to take the shape of a circle, conforming to the course of the horse. The rider's gaze, as she peered straight ahead, seemed to be circular, as though bent by force of circumstance; then time itself began running in circles, and

so the beginning was where the end was, and the two were the same, and one thing ran into the next and time went round and around and got nowhere. The girl wasn't so young that she did not know the delicious satisfaction of having a perfectly behaved body and the fun of using it to do a trick most people can't do, but she was too young to know that time does not really move in a circle at all. I thought: "She will never be as beautiful as this again"—a thought that made me acutely unhappy—and in a flash my mind (which is too much of a busybody to suit me) had projected twenty-five years ahead, and she was now in the center of the ring, on foot, wearing a conical hat and high-heeled shoes, the image of the older woman, holding the long rein, caught in the treadmill of an afternoon long in the future. "She is at that enviable moment in life [I thought] when she believes she can go once around the ring, make one complete circuit, and at the end be exactly the same age as at the start." Everything in her movements, her expression, told you that for her the ring of time was perfectly formed, changeless, predictable, without beginning or end, like the ring in which she was traveling at this moment with the horse that wallowed under her. And then I slipped back into my trance, and time was circular again—time, pausing quietly with the rest of us, so as not to disturb the balance of a performer.

7 Her ride ended as casually as it had begun. The older woman stopped the horse, and the girl slid to the ground. As she walked toward us to leave, there was a quick, small burst of applause. She smiled broadly, in surprise and pleasure; then her face suddenly regained its gravity and she disappeared through the door.

8 It has been ambitious and plucky of me to attempt to describe what is indescribable, and I have failed, as I knew I would. But I have discharged my duty to my society; and besides, a writer, like an acrobat, must occasionally try a stunt that is too much for him. At any rate, it is worth reporting that long before the circus comes to town, its most notable performances have already been given. Under the bright lights of the finished show, a performer need only reflect the electric candle power that is directed upon him; but in the dark and dirty old training rings and in the makeshift cages, whatever light is generated, whatever excitement, whatever beauty, must come from original sources—from internal fires of professional hunger and delight, from the exuberance and gravity of youth. It is the difference between planetary light and the combustion of stars.

Additional Rhetorical Strategy

Narration (paragraphs 1, 2, 4, 7).

Examining Words and Meaning

1. In your own words, describe what fascinates White about the girl on the horse. What does he think the girl's sense of time is? Why is the moment so poignant to him?
2. How would you characterize the tone of the phrase "gaudy dream" (paragraph 3)? Is White simply being critical? In considering your answer, keep in mind what he says about the circus in the preceding sentences.
3. Look up these words in a dictionary, if necessary: desultory (paragraph 1); career (paragraph 1); languor (paragraph 1); goading (paragraph 2); microcosm (paragraph 3); cadging (paragraph 4); hone (paragraph 4); jocund (paragraph 4); gravity (paragraph 7).

Focusing on Structures and Strategies

1. Where does White first seem to step back and make general observations on the experience? What is the effect of his *not* doing so in an introduction? After this point, does White return to description for the rest of the essay? Does he continue making general statements? Or does he alternate description and generalization? What are the advantages of this structure?
2. What is your reaction to White's last paragraph? Is it necessary? Could this selection have concluded just as well at the end of paragraph 7? What is the effect of his being so self-effacing, so apologetic here?

Suggestions for Further Discussion and Writing

1. Discuss what experiences you have had that have been, like White's, rich in their plainness. Have you ever had a feeling similar to

White's from watching ballplayers practice? From hearing a band going over its songs in a basement? From watching a rehearsal of a play? What other everyday moments have taken on a similar significance for you?

2. After you have discussed the ways in which we all have experiences somewhat like White's, pick one such experience you have had and write about it. It may be similar to White's—watching someone practice—or it may be something even more commonplace: watching children playing in a schoolyard, seeing someone you have known for a long time and suddenly realizing how much you like the person. In any case, it should be an experience that, momentarily at least, made you look at the world in a slightly different way. Describe the experience, leading into it with a narrative opening and making sure to say what the experience meant to you.

The Solace of Open Spaces

Gretel Ehrlich

Gretel Ehrlich (1946–) describes writing as "a meditation on experience." "From the moment of first intention," she explains, "writing is an act of surrender, of losing myself in what is around me." And in "The Solace of Open Spaces," Ehrlich becomes absorbed in what she has recently described as "the constantly unrolling scroll of nature."

In the Preface to The Solace of Open Spaces *(1985), her chronological arrangement of essays on her life on the open range of Wyoming, Gretel Ehrlich recounts the personal circumstances that led her to abandon her life as a filmmaker and urbanite in favor of settling in the remote stretches of the American West:*

> *Beginning in 1976, when I went to Wyoming to make a film, I had the experience of waking up not knowing where I was, whether I was a man or a woman, or which toothbrush was mine. I had suffered a tragedy and made a drastic geographical and cultural move fairly baggageless, but I wasn't losing my grip. . . . What I* had *lost (at least for a while) was my appetite for the life I had left: city surroundings, old friends, familiar comforts. It had occurred to me that comfort was only a disguise for discomfort; reference points, a disguise for what will always change.*

> *Friends asked when I was going to stop "hiding out" in Wyoming. What appeared to them as a landscape of lunar desolation and intellectual backwardness was luxurious to me. For the first time I was able to take up residence on earth with no alibis, no self-promoting schemes. . . .*

Born and raised in southern California, Gretel Ehrlich attended Bennington College in Vermont, UCLA Film School, and the New School for Social Research before she discovered what she calls "the geography of possibility" in the vast openness of Wyoming. Work on a documentary film first led her to the state in 1976. She soon took up ranching and eventually began creating memorable images of both the Wyoming landscape and the resolute people who work its "open country."

Writing full-time since 1979, Ehrlich has earned numerous awards for her work, including fellowships from the National Endowment for the Arts as well as the Wyoming Council for the Arts. Her essays have appeared in such publications as The Atlantic, Harpers, New Age Journal, *the* New York Times, *and the* Casper Star Journal. *She has also published two collections of poems and coedited with Edward Hoagland a volume of stories entitled* City Tales, Wyoming Stories *(1986).*

"The Solace of Open Spaces" demonstrates Ehrlich's ability to satisfy her own standards of excellence in writing: "The truest art I would strive for in any work would be to give the page the same qualities as earth: weather would land on it harshly; light would elucidate the most difficult truths; wind would sweep away obtuse padding. . . ." The result is a refreshingly detailed view of the majestic beauty and unrelenting harshness of nature in the American West and of the sturdy people who contend with what Ehrlich calls the "theater of weather in Wyoming."

1 It's May and I've just awakened from a nap, curled against sagebrush the way my dog taught me to sleep—sheltered from wind. A front is pulling the huge sky over me, and from the dark a hailstone has hit me on the head. I'm trailing a band of two thousand sheep across a stretch of Wyoming badlands, a fifty-mile trip that takes five days because sheep shade up in hot sun and won't budge until it's cool. Bunched together now, and excited into a run by the storm, they drift across dry land, tumbling into draws like water and surge out again onto the rugged, choppy plateaus that are the building blocks of this state.

2 The name Wyoming comes from an Indian word meaning "at the great plains," but the plains are really valleys, great arid valleys,

sixteen hundred square miles, with the horizon bending up on all sides into mountain ranges. This gives the vastness a sheltering look.

3 Winter lasts six months here. Prevailing winds spill snowdrifts to the east, and new storms from the northwest replenish them. This white bulk is sometimes dizzying, even nauseating, to look at. At twenty, thirty, and forty degrees below zero, not only does your car not work, but neither do your mind and body. The landscape hardens into a dungeon of space. During the winter, while I was riding to find a new calf, my jeans froze to the saddle, and in the silence that such cold creates I felt like the first person on earth, or the last.

4 Today the sun is out—only a few clouds billowing. In the east, where the sheep have started off without me, the benchland tilts up in a series of eroded red-earthed mesas, planed flat on top by a million years of water; behind them, a bold line of muscular scarps rears up ten thousand feet to become the Big Horn Mountains. A tidal pattern is engraved into the ground, as if left by the sea that once covered this state. Canyons curve down like galaxies to meet the oncoming rush of flat land.

5 To live and work in this kind of open country, with its hundred-mile views, is to lose the distinction between background and foreground. When I asked an older ranch hand to describe Wyoming's openness, he said, "It's all a bunch of nothing—wind and rattlesnakes—and so much of it you can't tell where you're going or where you've been and it don't make much difference." John, a sheepman I know, is tall and handsome and has an explosive temperament. He has a perfect intuition about people and sheep. They call him "Highpockets," because he's so long-legged; his graceful stride matches the distances he has to cover. He says, "Open space hasn't affected me at all. It's all the people moving in on it." The huge ranch he was born on takes up much of one county and spreads into another state; to put 100,000 miles on his pickup in three years and never leave home is not unusual. A friend of mine has an aunt who ranched on Powder River and didn't go off her place for eleven years. When her husband died, she quickly moved to town, bought a car, and drove around the States to see what she'd been missing.

6 Most people tell me they've simply driven through Wyoming, as if there were nothing to stop for. Or else they've skied in Jackson Hole, a place Wyomingites acknowledge uncomfortably because its green beauty and chic affluence are mismatched with the rest of the state. Most of Wyoming has a "lean-to" look. Instead of big, roomy

barns and Victorian houses, there are dugouts, low sheds, log cabins, sheep camps, and fence lines that look like driftwood blown haphazardly into place. People here still feel pride because they live in such a harsh place, part of the glamorous cowboy past, and they are determined not to be the victims of a mining-dominated future.

7 Most characteristic of the state's landscape is what a developer euphemistically describes as "indigenous growth right up to your front door"—a reference to waterless stands of salt sage, snakes, jack rabbits, deerflies, red dust, a brief respite of wildflowers, dry washes, and no trees. In the Great Plains the vistas look like music, like Kyries of grass, but Wyoming seems to be the doing of a mad architect—tumbled and twisted, ribboned with faded, deathbed colors, thrust up and pulled down as if the place had been startled out of a deep sleep and thrown into a pure light.

8 I came here four years ago. I had not planned to stay, but I couldn't make myself leave. John, the sheepman, put me to work immediately. It was spring, and shearing time. For fourteen days of fourteen hours each, we moved thousands of sheep through sorting corrals to be sheared, branded, and deloused. I suspect that my original motive for coming here was to "lose myself" in new and unpopulated territory. Instead of producing the numbness I thought I wanted, life on the sheep ranch woke me up. The vitality of the people I was working with flushed out what had become a hallucinatory rawness inside me. I threw away my clothes and bought new ones; I cut my hair. The arid country was a clean slate. Its absolute indifference steadied me.

9 Sagebrush covers 58,000 square miles of Wyoming. The biggest city has a population of fifty thousand, and there are only five settlements that could be called cities in the whole state. The rest are towns, scattered across the expanse with as much as sixty miles between them, their populations two thousand, fifty, or ten. They are fugitive-looking, perched on a barren, windblown bench, or tagged onto a river or a railroad, or laid out straight in a farming valley with implement stores and a block-long Mormon church. In the eastern part of the state, which slides down into the Great Plains, the new mining settlements are boomtowns, trailer cities, metal knots on flat land.

10 Despite the desolate look, there's a coziness to living in this state. There are so few people (only 470,000) that ranchers who buy and sell cattle know one another statewide; the kids who choose to

go to college usually go to the state's one university, in Laramie; hired hands work their way around Wyoming in a lifetime of hirings and firings. And despite the physical separation, people stay in touch, often driving two or three hours to another ranch for dinner.

11 Seventy-five years ago, when travel was by buckboard or horseback, cowboys who were temporarily out of work rode the grub line—drifting from ranch to ranch, mending fences or milking cows, and receiving in exchange a bed and meals. Gossip and messages traveled this slow circuit with them, creating an intimacy between ranchers who were three and four weeks' ride apart. One old-time couple I know, whose turn-of-the-century homestead was used by an outlaw gang as a relay station for stolen horses, recall that if you were traveling, desperado or not, any lighted ranch house was a welcome sign. Even now, for someone who lives in a remote spot, arriving at a ranch or coming to town for supplies is cause for celebration. To emerge from isolation can be disorienting. Everything looks bright, new, vivid. After I had been herding sheep for only three days, the sound of the camp tender's pickup flustered me. Longing for human company, I felt a foolish grin take over my face; yet I had to resist an urgent temptation to run and hide.

12 Things happen suddenly in Wyoming, the change of seasons and weather; for people, the violent swings in and out of isolation. But good-naturedness is concomitant with severity. Friendliness is a tradition. Strangers passing on the road wave hello. A common sight is two pickups stopped side by side far out on a range, on a dirt track winding through the sage. The drivers will share a cigarette, uncap their thermos bottles, and pass a battered cup, steaming with coffee, between windows. These meetings summon up the details of several generations, because, in Wyoming, private histories are largely public knowledge.

13 Because ranch work is a physical and, these days, economic strain, being "at home on the range" is a matter of vigor, self-reliance, and common sense. A person's life is not a series of dramatic events for which he or she is applauded or exiled but a slow accumulation of days, seasons, years, fleshed out by the generational weight of one's family and anchored by a land-bound sense of place.

14 In most parts of Wyoming, the human population is visibly outnumbered by the animal. Not far from my town of fifty, I rode into a narrow valley and startled a herd of two hundred elk. Eagles look like small people as they eat car-killed deer by the road. Ante-

lope, moving in small, graceful bands, travel at sixty miles an hour, their mouths open as if drinking in the space.

15 The solitude in which westerners live makes them quiet. They telegraph thoughts and feelings by the way they tilt their heads and listen; pulling their Stetsons into a steep dive over their eyes, or pigeon-toeing one boot over the other, they lean against a fence with a fat wedge of Copenhagen beneath their lower lips and take in the whole scene. These detached looks of quiet amusement are sometimes cynical, but they can also come from a dry-eyed humility as lucid as the air is clear.

16 Conversation goes on in what sounds like a private code; a few phrases imply a complex of meanings. Asking directions, you get a curious list of details. While trailing sheep I was told to "ride up to that kinda upturned rock, follow the pink wash, turn left at the dump, and then you'll see the water hole." One friend told his wife on roundup to "turn at the salt lick and the dead cow," which turned out to be a scattering of bones and no salt lick at all.

17 Sentence structure is shortened to the skin and bones of a thought. Descriptive words are dropped, even verbs; a cowboy looking over a corral full of horses will say to a wrangler, "Which one needs rode?" People hold back their thoughts in what seems to be a dumbfounded silence, then erupt with an excoriating perceptive remark. Language, so compressed, becomes metaphorical. A rancher ended a relationship with one remark: "You're a bad check," meaning bouncing in and out was intolerable, and even coming back would be no good.

18 What's behind this laconic style is shyness. There is no vocabulary for the subject of feelings. It's not a hangdog shyness, or anything coy—always there's a robust spirit in evidence behind the restraint, as if the earth-dredging wind that pulls across Wyoming had carried its people's voices away but everything else in them had shouldered confidently into the breeze.

19 I've spent hours riding to sheep camp at dawn in a pickup when nothing was said; eaten meals in the cookhouse when the only words spoken were a mumbled "Thank you, ma'am" at the end of dinner. The silence is profound. Instead of talking, we seem to share one eye. Keenly observed, the world is transformed. The landscape is engorged with detail, every movement on it chillingly sharp. The air between people is charged. Days unfold, bathed in their own music. Nights become hallucinatory; dreams, prescient.

20 Spring weather is capricious and mean. It snows, then blisters with heat. There have been tornadoes. They lay their elephant trunks out in the sage until they find houses, then slurp everything up and leave. I've noticed that melting snowbanks hiss and rot, viperous, then drip into calm pools where ducklings hatch and livestock, being trailed to summer range, drink. With the ice cover gone, rivers churn a milkshake brown, taking culverts and small bridges with them. Water in such an arid place (the average annual rainfall where I live is less than eight inches) is like blood. It festoons drab land with green veins; a line of cottonwoods following a stream; a strip of alfalfa; and, on ditch banks, wild asparagus growing.

21 I've moved to a small cattle ranch owned by friends. It's at the foot of the Big Horn Mountains. A few weeks ago, I helped them deliver a calf who was stuck halfway out of his mother's body. By the time he was freed, we could see a heartbeat, but he was straining against a swollen tongue for air. Mary and I held him upside down by his back feet, while Stan, on his hands and knees in the blood, gave the calf mouth-to-mouth resuscitation. I have a vague memory of being pneumonia-choked as a child, my mother giving me her air, which may account for my romance with this windswept state.

22 If anything is endemic to Wyoming, it is wind. This big room of space is swept out daily, leaving a bone yard of fossils, agates, and carcasses in every stage of decay. Though it was water that initially shaped the state, wind is the meticulous gardener, raising dust and pruning the sage.

23 I try to imagine a world in which I could ride my horse across uncharted land. There is no wilderness left; wildness, yes, but true wilderness has been gone on this continent since the time of Lewis and Clark's overland journey.

24 Two hundred years ago, the Crow, Shoshone, Arapaho, Cheyenne, and Sioux roamed the intermountain West, orchestrating their movements according to hunger, season, and warfare. Once they acquired horses, they traversed the spines of all the big Wyoming ranges—the Absarokas, the Wind Rivers, the Tetons, the Big Horns—and wintered on the unprotected plains that fan out from them. Space was life. The world was their home.

25 What was life-giving to Native Americans was often nightmarish to sodbusters who had arrived encumbered with families and ethnic pasts to be transplanted in nearly uninhabitable land. The

great distances, the shortage of water and trees, and the loneliness created unexpected hardships for them. In her book *O Pioneers!,* Willa Cather gives a settler's version of the bleak landscape:

> 26 The little town behind them had vanished as if it had never been, had fallen behind the swell of the prairie, and the stern frozen country received them into its bosom. The homesteads were few and far apart; here and there a windmill gaunt against the sky, a sod house crouching in a hollow.

27 The emptiness of the West was for others a geography of possibility. Men and women who amassed great chunks of land and struggled to preserve unfenced empires were, despite their self-serving motives, unwitting geographers. They understood the lay of the land. But by the 1850s the Oregon and Mormon trails sported bumper-to-bumper traffic. Wealthy landowners, many of them aristocratic absentee landlords, known as remittance men because they were paid to come West and get out of their families' hair, overstocked the range with more than a million head of cattle. By 1885 the feed and water were desperately short, and the winter of 1886 laid out the gaunt bodies of dead animals so closely together that when the thaw came, one rancher from Kaycee claimed to have walked on cowhide all the way to Crazy Woman Creek, twenty miles away.

28 Territorial Wyoming was a boy's world. The land was generous with everything but water. At first there was room enough, food enough, for everyone. And, as with all beginnings, an expansive mood set in. The young cowboys, drifters, shopkeepers, schoolteachers, were heroic, lawless, generous, rowdy, and tenacious. The individualism and optimism generated during those times have endured.

29 John Tisdale rode north with the trail herds from Texas. He was a college-educated man with enough money to buy a small outfit near the Powder River. While driving home from the town of Buffalo with a buckboard full of Christmas toys for his family and a winter's supply of food, he was shot in the back by an agent of the cattle barons who resented the encroachment of small-time stockmen like him. The wealthy cattlemen tried to control all the public grazing land by restricting membership in the Wyoming Stock Growers Association, as if it were a country club. They ostracized from roundups and brandings cowboys and ranchers who were not members, then denounced them as rustlers. Tisdale's death, the second such cold-

blooded murder, kicked off the Johnson County cattle war, which was no simple good-guy-bad-guy shoot-out but a complicated class struggle between landed gentry and less affluent settlers—a shocking reminder that the West was not an egalitarian sanctuary after all.

30 Fencing ultimately enforced boundaries, but barbed wire abrogated space. It was stretched across the beautiful valleys, into the mountains, over desert badlands, through buffalo grass. The "anything is possible" fever—the lure of any new place—was constricted. The integrity of the land as a geographical body, and the freedom to ride anywhere on it, were lost.

31 I punched cows with a young man named Martin, who is the great-grandson of John Tisdale. His inheritance is not the open land that Tisdale knew and prematurely lost but a rage against restraint.

32 Wyoming tips down as you head northeast; the highest ground—the Laramie Plains—is on the Colorado border. Up where I live, the Big Horn River leaks into difficult, arid terrain. In the basin where it's dammed, sandhill cranes gather and, with delicate legwork, slice through the stilled water. I was driving by with a rancher one morning when he commented that cranes are "old-fashioned." When I asked why, he said, "Because they mate for life." Then he looked at me with a twinkle in his eyes, as if to say he really did believe in such things but also understood why we break our own rules.

33 In all this open space, values crystalize quickly. People are strong on scruples but tenderhearted about quirky behavior. A friend and I found one ranch hand, who's "not quite right in the head," sitting in front of the badly decayed carcass of a cow, shaking his finger and saying, "Now, I don't want you to do this ever again!" When I asked what was wrong with him, I was told, "He's goofier than hell, just like the rest of us." Perhaps because the West is historically new, conventional morality is still felt to be less important than rock-bottom truths. Though there's always a lot of teasing and sparring, people are blunt with one another, sometimes even cruel, believing honesty is stronger medicine than sympathy, which may console but often conceals.

34 The formality that goes hand in hand with the rowdiness is known as the Western Code. It's a list of practical do's and don'ts, faithfully observed. A friend, Cliff, who runs a trapline in the winter, cut off half his foot while chopping a hole in the ice. Alone, he dragged himself to his pickup and headed for town, stopping to open the ranch gate as he left, and getting out to close it again, thus losing,

in his observance of rules, precious time and blood. Later, he commented, "How would it look, them having to come to the hospital to tell me their cows had gotten out?"

35 Accustomed to emergencies, my friends doctor each other from the vet's bag with relish. When one old-timer suffered a heart attack in hunting camp, his partner quickly stirred up a brew of red horse liniment and hot water and made the half-conscious victim drink it, then tied him onto a horse and led him twenty miles to town. He regained consciousness and lived.

36 The roominess of the state has affected political attitudes as well. Ranchers keep up with world politics and the convulsions of the economy but are basically isolationists. Being used to running their own small empires of land and livestock, they're suspicious of big government. It's a "don't fence me in" holdover from a century ago. They still want the elbow room their grandfathers had, so they're strongly conservative, but with a populist twist.

37 Summer is the season when we get our "cowboy tans"—on the lower parts of our faces and on three fourths of our arms. Excessive heat, in the nineties and higher, sends us outside with the mosquitoes. In winter we're tucked inside our houses, and the white wasteland outside appears to be expanding, but in summer all the greenery abridges space. Summer is a go-ahead season. Every living thing is off the block and in the race: battalions of bugs in flight and biting; bats swinging around my log cabin as if the bases were loaded and someone had hit a home run. Some of summer's high-speed growth is ominous: larkspur, death camas, and green greasewood can kill sheep—an ironic idea, dying in this desert from eating what is too verdant. With sixteen hours of daylight, farmers and ranchers irrigate feverishly. There are first, second, and third cuttings of hay, some crews averaging only four hours of sleep a night for weeks. And, like the cowboys who in summer ride the night rodeo circuit, nighthawks make daredevil dives at dusk with an eerie whirring sound like a plane going down on the shimmering horizon.

38 In the town where I live, they've had to board up the dancehall windows because there have been so many fights. There's so little to do except work that people wind up in a state of idle agitation that becomes fatalistic, as if there were nothing to be done about all this untapped energy. So the dark side to the grandeur of these spaces is the small-mindedness that seals people in. Men be-

come hermits; women go mad. Cabin fever explodes into suicides, or into grudges and lifelong family feuds. Two sisters in my area inherited a ranch but found they couldn't get along. They fenced the place in half. When one's cows got out and mixed with the other's, the women went at each other with shovels. They ended up in the same hospital room but never spoke a word to each other for the rest of their lives.

39 After the brief lushness of summer, the sun moves south. The range grass is brown. Livestock is trailed back down from the mountains. Water holes begin to frost over at night. Last fall Martin asked me to accompany him on a pack trip. With five horses, we followed a river into the mountains behind the tiny Wyoming town of Meeteetse. Groves of aspen, red and orange, gave off a light that made us look toasted. Our hunting camp was so high that clouds skidded across our foreheads, then slowed to sail out across the warm valleys. Except for a bull moose who wandered into our camp and mistook our black gelding for a rival, we shot at nothing.

40 One of our evening entertainments was to watch the night sky. My dog, a dingo bred to herd sheep, also came on the trip. He is so used to the silence and empty skies that when an airplane flies over he always looks up and eyes the distant intruder quizzically. The sky, lately, seems to be much more crowded than it used to be. Satellites make their silent passes in the dark with great regularity. We counted eighteen in one hour's viewing. How odd to think that while they circumnavigated the planet, Martin and I had moved only six miles into our local wilderness and had seen no other human for the two weeks we stayed there.

41 At night, by moonlight, the land is whittled to slivers—a ridge, a river, a strip of grassland stretching to the mountains, then the huge sky. One morning a full moon was setting in the west just as the sun was rising. I felt precariously balanced between the two as I loped across a meadow. For a moment, I could believe that the stars, which were still visible, work like cooper's bands, holding together everything above Wyoming.

42 Space has a spiritual equivalent and can heal what is divided and burdensome in us. My grandchildren will probably use space shuttles for a honeymoon trip or to recover from heart attacks, but closer to home we might also learn how to carry space inside our-

selves in the effortless way we carry our skins. Space represents sanity, not a life purified, dull, or "spaced out" but one that might accommodate intelligently any idea or situation.

43 From the clayey soil of northern Wyoming is mined bentonite, which is used as a filler in candy, gum, and lipstick. We Americans are great on fillers, as if what we have, what we are, is not enough. We have a cultural tendency toward denial, but, being affluent, we strangle ourselves with what we can buy. We have only to look at the houses we build to see how we build *against* space, the way we drink against pain and loneliness. We fill up space as if it were a pie shell, with things whose opacity further obstructs our ability to see what is already there.

Additional Rhetorical Strategies

Illustration (throughout); Definition (paragraphs 2, 33); Comparison and Contrast (paragraph 6); Narration (throughout); Cause and Effect (paragraphs 32, 37).

Examining Words and Meaning

1. Ehrlich's essay focuses on the encounter between place and its inhabitants. What are the major characteristics of Wyoming in her description? How have the state's residents adapted to their environment? In what ways do they "reflect" characteristics of the place they inhabit?

2. Ehrlich also devotes a great deal of time in this essay to developing her own, more personal, response to Wyoming. What reasons does she offer for having gone there in the first place? What did she expect to find? How did she respond instead? In what sense does "open space" provide "solace"?

3. What does Ehrlich mean when she says "we might also learn how to carry space inside ourselves in the effortless way we carry our skins" (paragraph 42)? Reread carefully Ehrlich's final paragraph. What does she mean when she says "we build *against* space"? How appropriately does this notion characterize the residents of Wyoming and their relation to "open spaces"?

Focusing on Structures and Strategies

1. Consider Ehrlich's skills as a writer of description. What accounts for her success in creating a clear sense of place in this essay? How does her description of several people reinforce the effects she seeks to evoke in her readers?
2. This essay appears to move "randomly" from one topic to another. What principles of organization does Ehrlich rely on to help her lend unity and coherence to her paragraphs and to the essay as a whole? Explain how, for example, Ehrlich uses particular themes to link various parts of the essay. Consider also her use of time. How does this factor help to order her essay?
3. Reread carefully the opening paragraph of the essay. What is the effect of Ehrlich's beginning as she does? What is the significance of her awakening? What importance does she attach to her position, "sheltered from wind"? Of the scene she awakens to? How does she develop each of these elements as the essay proceeds?
4. At the end of paragraph 1, Ehrlich creates a strikingly effective image of sheep who "drift across dry land, tumbling into draws like water and surge out again onto the rugged, choppy plateaus that are the building blocks of this state." At many other moments in the essay, Ehrlich builds her sentences and paragraphs toward a culminating metaphor or simile. Reread her essay carefully, and note as many of her uses of metaphor and simile as possible. What are the individual—and cumulative—effects of Ehrlich's use of figurative language?
5. How does Ehrlich demonstrate that "in Wyoming, private histories are largely public knowledge"? Discuss the role that Ehrlich assigns to history in the formation of Wyoming and in the attitudes of its residents.

Suggestions for Further Discussion and Writing

1. What does Ehrlich mean by the phrase "Western Code"? What are some of its rules? What other, similar "unwritten" laws can you think of in your own social environment? What are the distinctive features—and consequences—of each?
2. In paragraph 6, Ehrlich observes that "people here still feel pride because they live in such a harsh place, part of the glamorous

cowboy past. . . ." In what specific ways does Ehrlich follow up on this point? How, and with what effect, does she demonstrate that residents of Wyoming take pleasure in identifying themselves with "the glamorous cowboy past"?

3. Consider a particular place to which you have a special sense of attachment, a place that evokes a string of descriptive memories: the particular street or area in which you used to live, the house in which you grew up, the place where you and your family used to go for vacations, etc. Focus on one such place and write about it, letting all of your associations come to mind. Write an essay in which you describe this place in detail, using your description to convey a clear, strong sense of what this place means, and has meant, to you.

Narration

1 We want to tell someone what happened to us as we waited hours in line to register for classes. We try to explain to our roommate exactly how the Astros scored thirteen runs in the fifth inning. A friend who left the party just before the police arrived wants us to tell her everything she missed. All of these situations call for a basic thought process we use every day—narration.

2 Narration is a way of telling what happened. We use it for a wide variety of practical and creative purposes: to tell a joke, to provide autobiographical information, to write history, to record a laboratory experiment, to make a journal entry, to put the details of an accident on an insurance form, to tell a story (either true or fictional), to report a news event, and so on. But no matter how many different ways we may use narration, we are generally performing a single operation: linking a succession of events together into a meaningful sequence.

3 The most elementary type of narration merely relates a series of events: "and then . . . and then . . . and then." Though this may work well for children's stories, accident reports, and some banal movies—where all that matters is "what happens next"—a simple string of loosely related events narrated in a strict chronological sequence can be monotonous and uninformative. When using narration in expository writing, we should try to avoid the formula "*A* happened, then *B* happened, then *C* happened. . . ." Instead of merely relating one event followed by another, we should try constructing

a sequence of interdependent events in which one thing *leads* to another. To do this effectively requires, first, a skillful selection of *details;* second, control of the time sequence, or *duration;* third, a clear sense of *direction;* and fourth, a logical *development.*

4 Paying close attention to these four elements can bring clarity and coherence to most narratives. Let's take a fairly ordinary, though complex, writing occasion. Suppose we are composing a letter to a close friend and want to report how we are getting along at school. We have a lot to say on the subject—some of it optimistic, some of it pessimistic; some of it about our courses, some of it about our social life—and we feel the need to put our thoughts across clearly, effectively, succinctly. Since most of our account will be rooted in personal experience, cover a fairly long stretch of time, and involve a relatively complex succession of events, we'll probably find ourselves instinctively choosing a narrative format to convey our autobiographical message. We have a rough idea of what we want to say but before we begin to write, we may want to think about some of our options. We can do this conveniently by considering *detail, duration, direction,* and *development.*

Detail. Most subjects, especially those based on personal experiences, are made up of innumerable details, ranging from the highly memorable and unique to the trivial and easily forgotten. From the mass of details that cluster around and form our subject, we must *select* those most appropriate to our general purpose. If we want to say in our letter how surprised we were to find we really do have mathematical ability, we can do this by relating the sequence of anxieties we experienced while waiting for our grade and the amazement we felt when it turned out to be an A. Or, if we want to convey how tiresome the freshman orientation lecture series was, we might give a blow-by-blow account of how we got ourselves through it: toying with a pencil, doodling, gazing out the window, glancing at our watch—details that may seem insignificant in themselves, yet will unmistakably convey our intended effect. The choice of details is crucial. We can never recount everything that happened (which is one reason why life and art are two different things), so we must carefully select only those events and actions which matter, either because of their intrinsic importance or because of what they represent. A good rule in narration is to try to make every detail relevant, to make each one contribute in some way to the overall narrative effect. (In George Orwell's "A Hanging," p. 181, notice how the horror of an execution is enhanced by the observation of an almost insignificant detail—the condemned man's stepping aside to avoid a puddle moments before his death.)

Duration. In narration, no matter what sort of subject we are considering, we will be handling the passage of time. Since we usually have a limited time to tell our story in, we must find ways of scheduling narrative events so that we can cover our subject in a much shorter time than the events we are writing about actually occupied. In other words, we have to make chronological time fit comfortably into narrative time. We do this, of course, by eliminating a large number of details, by compressing others, and by subordinating some parts of the action to others more relevant to our purpose. Narrative, however, is flexible and allows us to work with different rates of time in different ways. In some instances (relating the precise movements of an acrobat's stunt or the play of expressions on a lover's face), we may want to prolong a split-second phenomenon for many pages. Our narrative durations will generally depend on our expository purpose or the dramatic effect we want to achieve.

5 In our letter to a friend we may be able in five or six pages to tell about events that occurred over a period of two to three months. To do this adequately requires a careful management of time. If our subject involves a long succession of complex events, we can divide our narrative into a series of related episodes. We can, for example, talk about our anxieties on the first day of school, move from there to the pleasure we felt in running into an old high-school friend in the cafeteria, and then proceed to an account of a class we particularly enjoy. Or we may compress time in another way. We may choose to narrate one continuous episode and focus on it in such a way that it alone conveys the impression we want to give of our life at college. A few pages on getting up in the morning and getting to biology class can be done in a narrative fashion that lucidly portrays in miniature everything we want to say about life at school.

6 Strict chronological order may at first suggest itself as the most natural way to proceed with narration. But there are other ways to construct a narrative. We can begin at the end, then move to the beginning and proceed from there (as do many news reports), simply reversing the normal sequence. Or we can begin *in medias res* ("in the middle of things") in the fashion of much literature. (Stephen Crane's *The Red Badge of Courage,* for example, begins on the eve of a battle and flashes back to the days before the hero's enlistment.) Or we can

begin at the beginning, move quickly to the end, and then supply the middle portions. In short, our narrative chronology—the time scheme we devise for the purposes of our composition—can take whatever sequence we wish to give it. We can begin at any time we want to. We can start our letter by recalling how we felt on the eve of an examination, flash back to our decision to apply to college, and then return to a straightforward chronological order that takes us up to the day of our letter. We should be careful, however, not to put too heavy a strain on our narrative (as well as our reader) by moving back and forth in time unnecessarily or by constructing a more elaborate narrative sequence than our subject and purpose actually call for.

7 Regulating our time scheme involves more than carving out and reordering selected episodes from whatever stretch of time we are considering. It means controlling smaller elements of composition as well—especially those having to do with tense sequence and words related to time. Most narrative is organized around the past tense ("When Ms. Long passed out the math midterm and I saw the first question, I thought *I* would pass out."), though we may occasionally mix in the present tense, as do many storytellers, to create dramatic immediacy (see Marsha Rabe's "Passages," p. 167). Because verbs play such a vital part in all types of narration, we should be particularly attentive to the consistency and coordination of tenses. We need to make sure that tenses follow each other in a logical sequence and are not shifted indiscriminately: "As I *walked* into the classroom and *saw* the questions on the board, I suddenly *realized* that I *had studied* all the wrong chapters last night and I thought: 'I *will* flunk this test for sure.' "

8 In well-regulated narration, we need to rely on many familiar words having to do with time: *now, then, when, no sooner had . . ., previously, meanwhile, afterward, just, since,* and so on. These words can be thought of as the glue which holds narrative together. They help keep our narrative from getting into a monotonous "and then . . . and then" rhythm. They also allow for the proper subordination of events, as in the following:

> *No sooner* had I sat down than I looked at all the questions on the board *again* and *this time* realized that they were intended for another section. *When* the instructor handed out our test questions, I saw *at once* that I had studied not only the right material but the exactly right material. I got an A on the test and *since then* have had more confidence in statistics than I ever thought I'd have. *Now,* when I think about how

> much I worried all those weeks *before* the test, I want to laugh at myself for being so intimidated by mere numbers. *During* the last few weeks of classes, I've been something of an ace on the subject. In fact, *after* the last class yesterday, our instructor asked me if I'd be interested in attending a special workshop to study the election returns. The workshop doesn't start *until* next week, so in the *meantime* I'm brushing up on sampling methods.

As this example shows, organizing the relation of events syntactically by means of time words can add strength and purpose to our narratives.

Direction. One of the effects of well-articulated narrative is a sense of forward movement. We normally say of a well-told story that it "flowed," that it "carried us right along." One of the best means of achieving this "flow" or forward movement when composing narrative is to begin with and maintain a clear sense of direction. (In "How a Slave Was Made a Man," p. 174, for example, Frederick Douglass sustains a forceful steady movement by always keeping his narrative purpose clear: to recount how he rose from slavery to manhood.) So that our audience will feel our narrative is definitely going somewhere, we should avoid clogging it with extraneous details and unnecessary digressions. Our direction need not be explicitly stated. In our letter, for example, the narrative may move step by step toward a single event—the A on the math exam—which dramatically shows (rather than tells) that we think our decision to attend Silas Marner University was the right one after all. A clear sense of direction will help us maintain the steady forward movement through a succession of events that is one of the strengths of narrative.

Development. Effective narrative moves along not just sequentially but *consequentially.* In other words, it develops: *A* leads to *B,* which leads to *C,* which leads to *D,* and so on in a closely linked chain. When constructing a narrative, we should aim to make each step in our sequence follow necessarily (or, as Neil Bell does in "In the Dark," p. 170, at least with a high degree of probability) out of the preceding step. Suppose we want to tell our friend how we have grown more independent since we started school. The *direction* of our narrative would point toward this new sense of independence, while the *development* of our narrative would show how that independence was cumulative, built up out of a succession of connected experiences—living away from home, managing our own affairs, arranging our own schedules, and so on. If narrative direction is concerned with where we are going, narrative development is concerned with how we are getting there. Development gives the forward movement of our narrative orderly progression and logical connectedness. Two common mistakes in composing narratives involve development: one is overlooking or misplacing a critical step in our sequence, thus disrupting the entire chain; the other is inserting a totally arbitrary item into the narrative sequence, thus rendering the entire series improbable.

9 We should remember that this introduction covers only the rudiments of narration. Touched on here have been a few significant elements pertaining to the kind of narratives we are most likely to use in constructing sequential explanations or in rendering the upshot of a succession of events. But narration is also a highly complex area of literary study. Novels, short stories, and many types of poetry depend enormously on narrative creativity. For students interested in finding out more about literary narration, there are a number of useful books on the subject, ranging from Percy Lubbock's influential early study, *The Craft of Fiction* (1921), to Scholes and Kellogg's *The Nature of Narrative* (1966). Three fundamentals of literary narrative are relevant to expository writing and deserve attention here:

1. *Point of view:* Narration implies a narrator, someone who relates the narrative, who tells the story. Our choice of narrator often determines the point of view from which events will be perceived. In our letter about school, we would most likely narrate events in the first-person singular—the "I" would be ourselves. But we could also—in playfulness, irony, or satire—invent an "I" that was not identical to ourselves and then tell our own story from the invented point of view. Either way, the "I" would still occupy a central position in the narrative. But it is possible, too, to create an "I" who relates a story in which he or she plays merely a peripheral role. (In F. Scott Fitzgerald's *The Great Gatsby,* for example, the narrative "I" belongs to Nick Carraway, a young man who presents himself as someone not central to the main action of the novel.)

The third-person singular provides us with another point of view, a relatively objective one common to many forms of expository narration. It is even possible to use it in autobiography; we may, for example, write an essay in which we look at ourselves from a distance ("Three months ago, Sheila was a timid, dependent young woman with no clear sense of what she wanted to do in life. Now . . ."). Though expository writing generally works within a much narrower range of narrative viewpoints than does fiction or poetry, we should think clearly about our narrative vantage point before we begin to write. The first-person narrative "I" comes to mind almost automatically, but it may not always be the most effective way to proceed.

2. *Voice:* Once we decide who will narrate our composition, we then have to create a voice that will characterize the narrator and establish the dominant *sound* of our narrative. The narrative voice is what our audience literally hears, and in some cases it can exert a more powerful influence than our message or logic. (Consider how many advertisers identify their product with a warm, intimate voice rather than with the coaxing pitch of a salesperson.) A narrative voice is not always a simple thing to put down on paper; it is not enough merely to sound "natural." When we try to create a narrative voice, we should remember that our own speaking voice is largely a complex interweaving of word choice, tone, speech cadences, dialect, and idioms. If we want to create a voice in writing—even our own—we need to listen carefully to how both our voice and other voices sound. In most expository narration, however, the voice we use will not be a mimicry of a "real" individual voice, but a carefully regulated educated voice that retains enough personality to sound authentic and sheds just enough of its idiosyncrasy to be broadly communicative.

3. *Dialogue:* We frequently need to incorporate conversation and dialogue into expository narration. News reports, for example, often include quotations and dialogue to enhance the on-the-spot quality of the account and, more important, to record significant comments. In our narrative writing, we should introduce dialogue economically and judiciously, taking special care that it sounds authentic, relates to our main action, and advances the narrative. Dialogue can either be direct ("I think you have a pretty solid chance of getting accepted to medical school four years from now if you keep up your work," she said) or indirect (She told me that she thought I had a pretty solid chance of getting accepted to medical school four years from now if I keep up my work). If we want to write factual narrative, we should be sure we are reporting quotations and dialogue accurately.

There is a tendency in writing to make dialogue sound artificial and stiff. Paying close attention to *how* people talk, not just to what they are talking about, can help us—with practice, of course—write natural-sounding dialogue. The more authentic our dialogue sounds, the more we can rely on quotations alone to characterize speakers, and the less we have to depend upon the monotony of "he said . . . she said," or, worse, such strained variations as "he replied . . . she retorted."

The following selections illustrate a number of ways we can work with narrative structures in our compositions. Some further characteristics of expository narration will be covered in the next section, "Process Analysis."

Amity Street

Lewis Thomas

One of the most familiar forms of narrative occurs in autobiography, when a writer sets out to relate in chronological sequence the personal experiences that have made up his or her life. Anyone who has attempted to write even a few episodes of autobiography soon realizes the difficulties of keeping to a strict chronological order. We often need to go backward in time to explain something, or we need to lump together months or sometimes years of recurring activities in order to give our reader a general impression of our everyday lives. As you read the following autobiographical essay, taken from The Youngest Science, *observe how Lewis Thomas manages to deal with a compositional problem that affects most personal narratives: as he drifts back and forth in time to explain or to convey general impressions, he still succeeds in constructing a forward-moving story with a purposeful sense of direction.*

For biographical information on Lewis Thomas, see page 109.

1 I have always had a bad memory, as far back as I can remember. It isn't so much that I forget things outright, I forget where I stored them. I need reminders, and when the reminders change, as most of them have changed from my childhood, there goes my memory as well.

2 The town I was born and raised in disappeared. The only trace left behind to mark the location of the old clapboard house we lived in is the Long Island Rail Road, which still penetrates and crosses the town through a deep ditch, and somewhere alongside that ditch, behind a cement wall, is the back yard of my family's house. All the

rest is gone. The yard is now covered by an immense apartment house. The whole block, and the other blocks around where our neighbors' clapboard houses and back-yard gardens were, are covered by apartment houses, all built fixed to each other as though they were a single syncytial structure. The trees, mostly maples and elms, are gone. The church my family went to, most Sunday mornings, is still there, looking old and beat-up, with a sign in the front indicating that it is no longer the Dutch Reformed Church and now is Korean Protestant. I drove down this block, darkened now like a tunnel by the apartment buildings set close to the curb on each side, and saw nothing to remind me of any part of my life.

3 Lacking landmarks, I cannot be sure that the snatches of memory still lodged in my brain have any reliability at all; I could have made them up, or they could be the memories of dreams. I do dream about Flushing from time to time, finding myself on a bicycle on Boerum Avenue between Amity Street and Madison Street (all of these street names are gone, replaced now by numbers), and there is the town garbage wagon, horse-drawn, driven by a wild-eyed and red-haired youngish man named Crazy Willie, racing along the block on his high seat, talking to himself. I'm pretty sure of that memory; there was such a garbage wagon, driven by Crazy Willie, but why do I still have the image taped in my temporal lobe ready for replaying so many late nights, and so little else? I remember, now that I think of it, the late Sunday afternoon when the Lawnmower family arrived for a visit, friends of my family from somewhere far away, Ohio maybe, whose name turned out years later to be Lorrimer. It must have been around the same time that I discovered what the maid told me was copper beneath the sandbox, great soggy sheets of friable copper, enough to secure the family's fortune, which I already knew needed securing, and then, a couple of years later, I lost the fortune on learning that she must have been saying carpet. There was a huge cherry tree at the back of the yard, close to the cement fence, and something went wrong with it, death I suppose, it was cut down and chopped up there in the yard, and what remains stored in my brain now, sixty years later, is the marvelous smell of that wood, the smell of the whole earth itself, all over the yard and, for a few days until it was carted away, in all the rooms of our house.

4 My earliest clear memory of my mother is her tall figure standing alone in the center of the lawn behind the house, looking down at the grass, turning in a slow circle, scanning the ground. From the time of my earliest childhood I knew this to be a mild signal of

trouble for my mother, trouble for the family. Sometimes she stood there for only a few moments, sometimes for as long as five minutes. Then, in the quickest of movements, she would reach down to pluck the four-leaf clover she was hunting and come back to the house. If I was there on the back porch, watching as she came, she would laugh at me and say, always the same sentence, "The Lord will provide."

5 So far as I know, this was her only superstition, or anyway, the only one she ever acted on. And it was always used for the same purpose, which was to get my father's patients to pay their bills.

6 Very few of the patients paid promptly, and a good many never paid at all. Some sent in small checks, once every few months. A few remarkable and probably well-off patients paid immediately, the whole bill at once, and when this happened my father came upstairs after office hours greatly cheered.

7 There was never an end to worrying about money, although nobody talked much about it. The family took it for granted that my father had to worry about his income at the end of every month, and we knew that he was absolutely determined to pay all his bills on the first of each month, without fail. He believed that being in debt was the worst of fates, and he paid everyone—the grocer and the butcher, the coal man, taxes, and the instrument and drug houses that supplied his office—as soon as he could after the bills arrived, depending on how much cash he had in the bank. But it was not the style of the time to pay the doctor quickly.

8 These were the years everyone thinks of as the good times for the country, the ten years before the Great Depression. The town was prosperous, but the practice of medicine was accepted to be a chancy way to make a living, and nobody expected a doctor to get rich, least of all the doctors themselves. In the town where I grew up, there were two or three physicians whose families seemed rich, but the money was old family money, not income from practice; the rest of my father's colleagues lived from month to month on whatever cash their patients provided and did a lot of their work free, not that they wanted to or felt any conscious sense of charity, but because that was the way it was.

9 My father kept his own books, in a desk calendar that recorded in his fine Spencerian handwriting the names of the patients he had seen each day, each name followed by the amount he charged, and that number followed by the amount received. It was the last column that mattered. My mother kept a careful eye on those numbers, and it was always toward the end of the month that she went back to the lawn to find her four-leaf clovers.

10 I'll never understand how she did it. As I grew older, seven or eight years old, I liked to go along while she sought the family fortune, to help out if I could, but I never spotted a single one, even though my eyes were a lot closer to the ground. We would stand side by side, and I would try to scan the same patches of lawn, staring hard, but even as she swooped down to pick one, I was never able to see it until it was in her fingers.

11 Much later, when I was a fourth-year medical student at Harvard, I learned more objectively some of the facts of medical economics. The yearbook for the class of 1937 was edited by Albert Coons, my closest friend in the class, and I was invited to be on the editorial staff because I'd written a rather long and disrespectful poem about medicine and death, called "Allen Street." Coons prepared a questionnaire for the book and sent it out late in 1936, to the Harvard graduates from the years 1927, 1917, and 1907. The questions dealt mainly with the kinds of internship and residency training experiences most highly regarded by Harvard doctors ten, twenty, and thirty years out of school, but there were also a couple of lines asking, delicately and promising anonymity, for the respondent's estimated income for 1937, and then a generous empty space at the bottom of the page requesting comments in general, advice to the class of 1937.

12 Surprisingly, 60 percent of the questionnaires were filled in and returned, and they made interesting reading for Coons and me and all our classmates. Most of the papers neglected the business about postgraduate training and concentrated on the money questions. The average income of the ten-year graduates was around $3500; $7500 for the twenty-year people. One man, a urologist, reported an income of $50,000, but he was an anomaly; all the rest made, by the standards of 1937, respectable but very modest sums of money.

13 The space at the bottom of the page had comments on this matter, mostly giving the same sort of advice: medicine is the best of professions was the general drift, but not a good way to make money. If you could manage to do so, you should marry a rich wife.

14 It was very hard work, being a doctor. All the men (there were only men in those Harvard classes) had a line or two about the work: long hours, no time off, brief holidays. Prepare to work very hard was their advice to the class of 1937, and don't expect to be prosperous.

15 Watching my father's work was the most everyday part of my childhood. He had his office at home, like all the doctors in Flushing. The house was a large Victorian structure with a waiting room and office in the ground-floor area that would have been the parlor and drawing room for other houses of the period. My family had their

sitting room on the second floor, but the dining room was downstairs, a door away from the patients' waiting room, so we grew up eating more quietly and quickly than most families.

16 In the best of times, right up until the start of the Depression, we had a live-in maid who had her room on the third floor and a laundress who worked in the basement; then a part-time maid during the first years of the Depression; finally nobody. My mother always did the cooking, even when there was a maid; later, she did all the cleaning and everything else in the house, and in her free time she worked the garden around the edges of the back yard. We had had a gardener once, I remember, in the early 1920s, an Italian named Jimmy who came up from Grove Street. Jimmy and my mother would discuss the progress of the garden every day, he in rapid torrents of passionate, arm-waving Italian, she in slow, careful, but firmly put English, and they got along fine. Later on, in the Depression years, she gardened the whole place herself, while the children mowed the lawn.

17 Two streets scared the children away by their strangeness: Grove Street, just beneath the Long Island Rail Road Station, where the Italians lived, several dozen families, all poor, all speaking Italian at home and broken English elsewhere; and Lincoln Street, where the black people lived. Lincoln Street was not a ghetto, it was right in the center of Flushing, the best part of town, but two blocks of Lincoln Street were entirely black. I used to wonder how that happened, why all the Negroes lived together on those two blocks, but it was never explained; it had always been like that.

18 Memorial Day and the Fourth of July were the town's major events. Both involved parades, the first down Northern Boulevard to Town Hall and the Civil War Monument, where a Boy Scout was required to recite Lincoln's Gettysburg Address (one year I had to do it), the second up from Main Street along Sanford Avenue. The people lined the streets waiting for the open cars containing the Civil War veterans, old, grizzled, confused-looking men in their eighties, wearing Union uniforms, then the World War I veterans (it was called the Great War then, nobody thought of giving it a number), young and fresh, in khaki uniforms and puttees. Brass bands, flags, the Masons and the Knights of Columbus, the village police and firemen, streams of children in Boy Scout, Girl Scout, Girl Pioneer, Sea Scout uniforms, and smaller children from the parochial school in everyday clothes, faces flushed pink with pleasure.

19 The two most important people in town, known and respected by everyone, were Miss Guy, who taught first grade at P.S. 20, and

Mr. Pierce, the principal. Miss Guy was the great eminence, having taught several generations of Flushing people. Mr. Pierce owed his social distinction to the loftiness of his position alone, having arrived from out of town only ten years earlier.

20 All the children in Flushing were juvenile delinquents. We roamed the town in the evening, ringing doorbells and running around the side of the house to hide, scrawling on the sidewalks with colored chalk, practicing for Halloween, when we turned into vandals outright, breaking windows, throwing garbage cans into front yards, twisting the street signs to point in the wrong direction. We shoplifted at Woolworth's, broke open the nickel-candy machines fixed on the backs of the seats in the Janice Cinema, bought Piedmont cigarettes and smoked them sitting on the curb on Main Street, at the age of ten. A bad lot.

21 In the time of my childhood, nothing but the worst was expected of children. We were expected to be bad, there was no appealing to our better selves because it was assumed that we had no better selves. Therefore, to be contrary, as is the habit of children, we turned out rather well.

22 My father never had an office nurse or a secretary. The door bell was answered by my mother or by whatever child was near at hand, or by my father if he was not involved with a patient. The office hours were one to two in the afternoon and seven to eight in the evening. I remember those numbers the way I remember old songs, from hearing my mother answering the telephone and, over and over again, repeating those hours to the callers: there was a comforting cadence in her voice, and it sounded like a song—one to two in the after*noon,* seven to eight in the *eve*ning.

23 The waiting room began to fill up an hour before the official office hours, and on busy days some of the patients had to wait in their cars outside or stand on the front porch. Most days, my father saw ten patients in each hour; I suppose half of these were new patients, the other half people coming back to be checked from earlier visits.

24 Except for the office hours and quick meals, my father spent his hours on the road. In the early morning he made rounds at the local hospital, where, as chief of surgery, he would see the patients in the surgical wards as well as his own private patients. Later in the morning, and through the afternoon, he made his house calls. In his first years of practice, when he and my mother moved out from New York City to Flushing, which they picked because it was a small country town with good trees and gardens but with the city still accessible

by train, he had a bicycle, then a year later a horse and buggy, each of which he detested. A year or so before I was born, he had prospered enough to buy an automobile. First it was a Maxwell, which broke down a lot and kept him in a continual temper, then a snub-nosed Franklin sedan, finally a quite expensive Franklin coupé with a "modern" conventional front.

25 He spent the major part of his life in these cars, driving to the hospital and then around Flushing and through the neighboring towns, seeing one patient after another. He came home around nine or ten most evenings.

26 But it was at night, long after the family had gone to sleep, that my father's hardest work began. The telephone started ringing after midnight. I could hear it from my bedroom down the hall, and I could hear his voice, tired and muffled by sleep, asking for details, and then I could hear him hang up the phone in the dark; usually he would swear "Damnation," sometimes he was distressed enough to use flat-out "Damn it," or worse, "Damn"; rarely did I hear him say, in total fury, "God damn it." Then I could hear him heave out of bed, the sounds of dressing, lights on in the hall, and then his steps down the back stairs, out in the yard and into the car, and off on a house call. This happened every night at least once, sometimes three or four times.

27 I never learned, listening in the dark, what the calls were about. They always sounded urgent, and sometimes there were long conversations in which I could hear my father giving advice and saying he'd be in the next morning. More often he spoke briefly and then hung up and dressed. Some were for the delivery of babies. I remember that because of my mother's voice answering the phone even later at night, when he was off on his calls, saying that the doctor was out on a "confinement." But it was not all babies. Some were calls from the hospital, emergencies turning up late at night. Some were new patients in their homes, frightened by one or another sudden illness. Some were people dying in their beds, or already dead in their beds. My father must have been called out for patients who were dying or dead a great many of his late nights.

28 Twenty years later, when I was on the faculty at Tulane Medical School and totally involved in the science of medicine, I had another close look at this side of doctoring. I had been asked to come to the annual meeting of a county medical society in the center of Mississippi, to deliver an address on antibiotics. The meeting was at the local hotel, and my host was the newly elected president of the society, a general practitioner in his forties, a successful physician

whose career was to be capped that evening, after the banquet, by his inauguration; to be the president of the county medical society was a major honor in that part of the world. During the dinner he was called to the telephone and came back to the head table a few minutes later to apologize; he had an emergency call to make. The dinner progressed, the ceremony of his induction as president was conducted awkwardly in his absence, I made my speech, the evening ended, and just as the people were going out the door he reappeared, looking harassed and tired. I asked him what the call had been. It was an old woman, he said, a patient he'd looked after for years; early that evening she had died, that was the telephone call. He knew the family was in distress and needed him, he said, so he had to go. He was sorry to have missed the evening, he had looked forward to it all year, but some things can't be helped, he said.

29 This was in the early 1950s, when medicine was turning into a science, but the old art was still in place.

Reading for Rhetorical Strategy

Lewis Thomas begins the essay in the present: he has driven back to his old neighborhood looking for landmarks, traces of his childhood. Finding none, he must depend on his memories, which he believes are not always reliable. Still, they are all he has. In paragraph 3, he summons up a series of earliest childhood memories, most of them associated with physical objects. In paragraphs 5–7, he begins to narrate recurring activities, events that occurred habitually, not at any specific time. We often use the auxiliary verb "would" to describe these moments (paragraph 4: "she would reach down to pluck the four-leaf clover she was hunting"). In paragraph 8, Thomas's recollections move forward into the 1920s, but he still (see paragraphs 9–10) narrates habitual activities—the customary anxiety over money—within that period. Recalling this anxiety leads Thomas to jump forward in time to his medical-student days when he worked on a questionnaire about medical incomes. In paragraph 15, Thomas returns to his childhood of the 1920s and 1930s, still lumping events together in habitual time. In paragraph 28, Thomas concludes by jumping ahead to the early 1950s to relate an episode that occurred while he was a professor of medicine. Note that though the essay moves back and forth in time and though it deals with large stretches of recurring activities, Thomas never loses sight of the underlying movement of his narrative as he unfolds a story that takes us through some sixty years of interrelated memories.

The Wild Man of the Green Swamp

Maxine Hong Kingston

Narration is the art of arranging events in time. That sounds disarmingly simple until we realize that even in our most ordinary thinking, time does not proceed in a straight line, step-by-step. Anyone who has ever tried to relate a simple story knows this. No sooner do we say "Then Al left college to take a job in his father's restaurant" than we need to circle backward momentarily to say something like "Well, Al hadn't been doing very well in school anyway." Narratives twist and turn, and the best storytellers allow time to shuttle back and forth while keeping a sense of forward movement. Narration is the art of thinking along a continuum of tenses.

It is an art Maxine Hong Kingston (1940–) has mastered. The logic of time shifts clearly dominates the way she thinks about a subject. In "The Wild Man of the Green Swamp," her understanding of a recent event is inseparable from her narration of it. Her prose constantly shifts through levels of time as she attempts to find a connection between a recent public event and a childhood memory.

Retrospection is at the center of her writing. Her first book, The Woman Warrior: Memoirs of a Girlhood Among Ghosts *(1976), which won the prestigious National Book Critics Circle Award for nonfiction, was followed by* China Men *(1980). Maxine Hong Kingston was born in Stockton, California, and now lives in Hawaii, where she teaches creative writing. So closely does she associate the act of writing with autobiographical understanding that she can say, "I have no idea how people who don't write endure their lives."*

1 For eight months in 1975, residents on the edge of Green Swamp, Florida, had been reporting to the police that they had seen a Wild Man. When they stepped toward him, he made strange noises as in a foreign language and ran back into the saw grass. At first, authorities said the Wild Man was a mass hallucination. Man-eating animals lived in the swamp, and a human being could hardly find a place to rest without sinking. Perhaps it was some kind of a bear the children had seen.

2 In October, a game officer saw a man crouched over a small fire, but as he approached, the figure ran away. It couldn't have been a bear because the Wild Man dragged a burlap bag after him. Also, the fire was obviously man-made.

3 The fish-and-game wardens and the sheriff's deputies entered the swamp with dogs but did not search for long; no one could live in the swamp. The mosquitoes alone would drive him out.

4 The Wild Man made forays out of the swamp. Farmers encountered him taking fruit and corn from the turkeys. He broke into a house trailer, but the occupant came back, and the Wild Man escaped out a window. The occupant said that a bad smell came off the Wild Man. Usually, the only evidence of him were his abandoned campsites. At one he left the remains of a four-foot-long alligator, of which he had eaten the feet and tail.

5 In May a posse made an air and land search; the plane signaled down to the hunters on the ground, who circled the Wild Man. A fish-and-game warden "brought him down with a tackle," according to the news. The Wild Man fought, but they took him to jail. He looked Chinese, so they found a Chinese in town to come translate.

6 The Wild Man talked a lot to the translator. He told him his name. He said he was thirty-nine years old, the father of seven children, who were in Taiwan. To support them, he had shipped out on a Liberian freighter. He had gotten very homesick and asked everyone if he could leave the ship and go home. But the officers would not let him off. They sent messages to China to find out about him. When the ship landed, they took him to the airport and tried to put him on an airplane to some foreign place. Then, he said, the white demons took him to Tampa Hospital, which is for insane people, but he escaped, just walked out and went into the swamp.

7 The interpreter asked how he lived in the swamp. He said he ate snakes, turtles, armadillos, and alligators. The captors could tell how he lived when they opened up his bag, which was not burlap but a pair of pants with the legs knotted. Inside, he had carried a pot, a piece of sharpened tin, and a small club, which he had made by sticking a railroad spike into a section of aluminum tubing.

8 The sheriff found the Liberian freighter that the Wild Man had been on. The ship's officers said that they had not tried to stop him from going home. His shipmates had decided that there was something wrong with his mind. They had bought him a plane ticket and arranged his passport to send him back to China. They had driven him to the airport, but there he began screaming and weeping and

would not get on the plane. So they had found him a doctor, who sent him to Tampa Hospital.

9 Now the doctors at the jail gave him medicine for the mosquito bites, which covered his entire body, and medicine for his stomachache. He was getting better, but after he'd been in jail for three days, the U.S. Border Patrol told him they were sending him back. He became hysterical. That night, he fastened his belt to the bars, wrapped it around his neck, and hung himself.

10 In the newspaper picture he did not look very wild, being led by the posse out of the swamp. He did not look dirty, either. He wore a checkered shirt unbuttoned at the neck, where his white undershirt showed; his shirt was tucked into his pants; his hair was short. He was surrounded by men in cowboy hats. His fingers stretching open, his wrists pulling apart to the extent of the handcuffs, he lifted his head, his eyes screwed shut, and cried out.

11 There was a Wild Man in our slough too, only he was a black man. He wore a shirt and no pants, and some mornings when we walked to school, we saw him asleep under the bridge. The police came and took him away. The newspaper said he was crazy; it said the police had been on the lookout for him for a long time, but we had seen him every day.

Additional Rhetorical Strategy

Description (paragraph 10).

Examining Words and Meaning

1. Reread Kingston's short essay, this time paying close attention to the details of the verb tenses. Which event is farthest off in time? Which closest? Why does she arrange her chronology the way she does?
2. What is the direction of Kingston's narrative? What event does it lead to? Why doesn't she begin with that event? What effect does she gain by starting where she starts?
3. Why does she continually refer to the figure as a "Wild Man" when, according to her sources, his name is known? What is it about the man's life she is most interested in?

Focusing on Structures and Strategies

1. In chronological time, where do the events described in paragraph 10 fit into the story? If you were reordering the story in a strict chronological sequence, where would you place paragraph 10? Why does Kingston end the Wild Man's story with this event and these details?
2. Of what importance to Kingston's essay is the final paragraph? If she had reversed the entire sequence of events and begun her essay with her childhood memory, do you think the impact would still be the same? Why or why not? Base your answer on the sequence of events alone.

Suggestions for Further Writing and Discussion

1. Kingston's essay dramatically juxtaposes an event she has only read about with one she personally experienced. Think of a similar moment in your own life, when something you read about in the papers or saw on television triggered a childhood memory. Use the structure of Kingston's essay to write your own narrative account of these two events.
2. Do you think Kingston believes in the existence of Wild Men? What details in her essay make you feel that she does or does not believe that the man in the swamp and the man she recalls from childhood are actually Wild Men?

Passages

Marsha Rabe

A freelance writer for newspapers and magazines, Marsha Rabe brings a bit of the flatland of the Midwest and a special evening in 1915 into the here and now with her evocative rendition of an event from her father's boyhood. Subtly switching tenses to control the tracks of time, Rabe shows us how much the power of nostalgia owes to the power of narrative.

1 There is land in central Illinois that is as flat as the floor. It does not roll and ripple into hills, nor does it fill, lift, and erupt like sails into mountains the way some land does. The most it grants, and this begrudgingly, is to warp and buckle where rare and subtle sorts of lumps appear; but these lumps are not hills and this land is very flat.

2 It happens more frequently of late that when I imagine my father, I see him not as the large, soft, hazy man I have always known, but as a boy of nine, standing on a dark spot in this flat Illinois land, standing near a railroad crossing. It is night and it is hot. Summer here is dreadful, windless. The air clots and settles close to the ground, while the sky, smeared thick with stars, floats farther away than at other times of the year. It is cricket season, baseball season.

3 My father's father was a passenger conductor on the Chicago and Alton Railroad. He had the best and fastest run from Chicago to St. Louis. It was 1915 when on Friday afternoon my grandfather, who had gone to Chicago on a morning train, phoned Walt Hempfing, the dispatcher in my father's hometown, and asked him to call my grandmother and tell her to pack an overnight bag and have Louis, my father, at the crossing that night at 11 o'clock so he could pick him up as his train swept through town. "The Cubs are in St. Louis tomorrow, Walt. Jim Lavender is pitching. It's time Louis sees a big league game. It's time he sees the Cubs."

4 The signal switch near where my father stands lights and begins to swing back and forth. In the clockwork flashing back and forth, back and forth like a pendulum, I see that my father is a little boy. He is wearing baggy knickers that billow around his thick, straight legs like a cloud. Long, thin socks pucker at his knees and tuck into high-button shoes cut just above his ankles. He also wears a loose, wrinkled white shirt, a long, thin tie, and a cloth-banded straw hat. From his left hand hangs a small suitcase, and in his right he holds a pocket watch. His head is bent—I cannot see his face for the flashing shadows and the brim of his hat—but I *can* see that he is looking into the palm of his right hand to check the time.

5 As I watch, the signal switch begins to clang and my father looks to his left. A train is coming. First to arrive is its whistle, a metallic honk like an elephant's call. Then its threading lights appear, bright across the cow pastures and corn fields, blinking on and off behind the trees and barns, scintillating, seeming to shatter and then, miraculously, to heal and reappear, whole. My father watches, then notes the time. 10:58. It's on time.

6 So there he is and I see him, a little boy on a hot night, waiting on flat, adamant land, while a huge, punctual monster uncoils toward him, rushing and rising up out of the dark, hurtling across the still fields, frightening small animals and birds, shocking the earth itself. The train is the only thing with lights for miles around, and his father is bringing it to him. For a long time he watches, because the land is so flat and he can see so far, and all the time I watch him watching I try to imagine how grand he must feel, the object of all this roaring commotion, of this hissing power.

7 Here it comes, closer, larger, louder. Brakes grind, out pours steam like a wet sigh. The engine chokes, jolts, and gently stops in front of him. Directly, deliberately in front of him. His father lowers a large hand and whisks him aboard. Sweaty smiles and grave excitement all around, and they are off, off to St. Louis, off to Jim Lavender, and off to the Cubs, who lost that game, my father tells me, 3 to 2.

Additional Rhetorical Strategy

Description (paragraphs 2, 4).

Examining Words and Meaning

1. What is the focus of Rabe's essay: the land in central Illinois? her father? the narrative sequence of her own recollections?

2. Where are Rabe's liveliest verbs to be found? Why has she concentrated so much of her energy in these sentences?

Focusing on Structures and Strategies

1. Trace the shift in the tenses of the verbs. Why does the author move back and forth between the present and the past? How does she avoid confusing her audience with such shifts in tense?

2. Why does Rabe wait until paragraph 4 to describe her father in any detail? From what point of view does she describe him? How closely does she identify herself with her father in paragraph 6? What do we learn about his reactions to going off to St. Louis to watch a baseball game?

Suggestion for Further Discussion and Writing

1. Think of one or two anecdotes that center on each of your parents' lives. Discuss the incidents with each of them in some detail. Choose one and write an essay in which you narrate the anecdote from a point of view similar to Marsha Rabe's; that is, try to create the sense that you identify yourself closely with your parent's experience.

In the Dark

Neil Bell

Neil Bell (1887-1964), an English novelist, was a prolific writer of picaresque, fantasy and mystery novels, and children's books. Bredon & Sons *(1934) was one of his best-known novels. He also published extensively under the name Stephen Southwold.*

The drake "got away," says a hunter to his wife upon returning home, but for Neil Bell that is only the beginning of the story. Moving from the circumstances of the hunter to the sequence of events that began after the drake got away, Bell imagines in telling detail the effect of that hunter's gunshot.

1 Darkness had long since fallen over the November landscape. The air of the marshes was still and frosty and faintly odorous of

rotting vegetation and of the smoke drifting over from a village three miles away at the edge of the moor.

2 The man stood still, cursing slowly and monotonously and without zest; he kicked his toes against his heels to stir the blood in his numbed and sodden feet. He shifted his gun and blew upon his fingers, and at the sound the mongrel bitch behind him lifted her muzzle and whined softly. He bent to cuff her, felt her nose against his knee and the excited tension of her body. And then overhead he heard the whir of wings and, taking but the most random aim, fired both barrels.

3 The mallard duck, fifty feet up and invisible in the blackness, folded its wings jerkily, lowered its head, tipped its stern, and fell like a stooping hawk. The drake swerved, dipped, rose again, and then went on in a laboring switchback flight, its left eye sheared away.

4 The mongrel retrieved the duck, and the man thrust it into his bag, stood hesitating a few moments, and then, shaking his head, he tucked the gun under his arm, mumbled something to the bitch, and set off at a brisk walk, squelching heedlessly through ankle-deep slush, his head down, his shoulders hunched, his hands deep in his pockets.

5 It was nearly an hour before he reached his cottage. He stamped his feet on the concrete slab outside the kitchen door and then, opening the door, entered. A woman looked up from her ironing. "Any luck?" she said.

6 The man shook his head. "Nothing much; a duck, that's all." He tossed his bag on to a chair. "Drake got away. Too perishin' cold, so I turned it in. My boots leak like a sieve. Grub ready?"

7 "It's in the oven. Take your boots and socks off, and I'll lay the table's soon as I've done these shirts."

8 The drake continued its stumbling flight toward the moors; it did not fly in a straight line but in long straggling arcs as if it unconsciously corrected its veer to the left. Presently it came round in a wide sweeping curve and flew back the way it had come, only to return an hour later as if it were pursuing a search or were bewildered or lost. At last, toward morning, it came down on to the still, weedy water of a dyke, some twenty miles from where its mate had been shot down.

9 All the next day and night it quartered the countryside, its flight more and more erratic as the sight of its other eye began to fail and the world slowly darkened. At the end of the fourth night it woke just before dawn and took wing in a strange blackness which

did not lift with the coming of the sun. It flew now in great circles of three or four miles in diameter, plunging ever and again on to the surface of water, resting awhile, and then flapping up again in panic flight.

10 Toward evening that day it circled about the sedgy reach of a great river, nearly two hundred miles from the place where darkness had shut down upon it. The twisted skeletons of alders and willows overhung the banks of the river. The drake shot down toward the water, flying clumsily, its brain confused, the swift play of its nerves and muscles dulled and leaden. An outstretched wing struck an alder branch, and the bird, with a squawk of terror, dropped heavily into the water, trailing a broken wing.

11 It slept and woke and swam round in small circles endlessly throughout three nights and days, its sleep lengthening as hunger and the pain of its broken wing weakened it.

12 Late in the afternoon of the third day some boys coming home from school saw it, tried to reach it with long sticks, and failing, began to pelt it with mud and turf and bits of stick, none of them being lucky enough to find anything more lethal. At each impact of a missile on the water near it the drake fluttered its sound wing desperately, attempting to rise from the water, but succeeding only in driving its body round and round in panic circles.

13 Presently it drifted into a current and was borne out of the boys' range, and with a final volley and a chorus of hallooing they abandoned the sport and went off in search of other excitement.

14 The drake drifted on in the current, its broken wing trailing, its head drooped. It was bedraggled and thin; all the bright beauty of its plumage was faded; all its colors, the greenish black of the head and neck, the white collar, the chestnut breast and gray-brown back, seemed to have merged into a mired dinginess. It might have been a bundle of dirty feathers floating on the tideway.

15 An eddy took it and swept it round and brought it toward the riverbank. Ambushed under a submerged root two bright, beadlike eyes watched it. An eel, five feet in length and as thick at the shoulders as a man's calf, slid out of the rooty blackness and shot swiftly upward. Its jaws closed about the drake's feet. The bird squawked on a note that was almost a scream and beat a frantic wing upon the water. The eel, retaining its grip, sounded, and the waters sucked over the drake as it went under. Presently, a few feathers rose slowly to the surface and drifted away on the tide.

Additional Rhetorical Strategies

Description (paragraphs 1, 14); Process Analysis (paragraphs 8–15).

Examining Words and Meaning

1. What is the significance of the title here? What sorts of darkness appear in this story? Why does Bell include the detail that the hunter's aim was "most random"? What might this detail suggest about the role of chance in the workings of the world?
2. Does the hunter consider killing the mallard an important event? If not, why has Bell included his reaction in the narrative? Do you feel that the drake dies with dignity or not? Point to specific words and phrases to support your answer.

Focusing on Structures and Strategies

1. What is the point of view in the first seven paragraphs of the story? What is the point of view after this point? What is the effect of this shift? Why doesn't Bell simply maintain one point of view throughout?
2. Does the *mood* of the first seven paragraphs of the story bear any resemblance to the mood of the second part? What words and phrases can you point to in order to support your answer? How would you describe the mood of the piece as a whole?
3. What, in the terms of the introduction to this chapter, is the *direction* of this narrative? Where is the story headed? How does Bell *develop* toward this goal? Which seems to you to be emphasized here—the goal or the process of getting there?

Suggestions for Further Discussion and Writing

1. Compare this story to Virginia Woolf's "The Death of the Moth" (see p. 125). Both writers describe the death of animals, but do the two pieces have anything else in common? Which writer makes more

overt statements about the significance of the events? Which simply narrates? Which writer seems more sentimental? Which, finally, do you prefer?

2. Write a narrative in which you recount an incident involving an animal. For at least part of the narrative, adopt the point of view of the animal.

How a Slave Was Made a Man

Frederick Douglass

Born into slavery in Maryland, Frederick Douglass (1817–1895) worked as a field hand and house servant until, disguised as a servant, he escaped to New York City in 1838. A leading figure in the abolitionist movement, Douglass recruited black troops for the North during the Civil War and held various federal appointments thereafter. His commanding presence as a civil-rights champion served as a model for such future black leaders as Booker T. Washington and W. E. B. Du Bois.

Thousands of slave narratives were written during the nineteenth century and many of them still provide readers with a powerfully detailed account of what it was like to live in slavery. The great theme—the geographical and spiritual movement from slavery to freedom—lent itself naturally to an episodic narrative structure that had deep roots in African storytelling traditions. In the following episode from one of the most famous of all slave narratives, the Narrative of the Life of Frederick Douglass, an American Slave *(1845), Douglass recounts the incident that helped him to stop thinking of himself as a slave and allowed him to start thinking of himself as a man.*

1 I have already intimated that my condition was much worse, during the first six months of my stay at Mr. Covey's, than in the last six. The circumstances leading to the change in Mr. Covey's course toward me form an epoch in my humble history. You have seen how

a man was made a slave; you shall see how a slave was made a man. On one of the hottest days of the month of August, 1833, Bill Smith, William Hughes, a slave named Eli, and myself, were engaged in fanning wheat. Hughes was clearing the fanned wheat from before the fan. Eli was turning, Smith was feeding, and I was carrying wheat to the fan. The work was simple, requiring strength rather than intellect; yet, to one entirely unused to such work, it came very hard. About three o'clock of that day, I broke down; my strength failed me; I was seized with a violent aching of the head, attended with extreme dizziness; I trembled in every limb. Finding what was coming, I nerved myself up, feeling it would never do to stop work. I stood as long as I could stagger to the hopper with grain. When I could stand no longer, I fell, and felt as if held down by an immense weight. The fan of course stopped; every one had his own work to do; and no one could do the work of the other, and have his own go on at the same time.

2 Mr. Covey was at the house, about one hundred yards from the treading-yard where we were fanning. On hearing the fan stop, he left immediately, and came to the spot where we were. He hastily inquired what the matter was. Bill answered that I was sick, and there was no one to bring wheat to the fan. I had by this time crawled away under the side of the post and rail-fence by which the yard was enclosed, hoping to find relief by getting out of the sun. He then asked where I was. He was told by one of the hands. He came to the spot, and, after looking at me awhile, asked me what was the matter. I told him as well as I could, for I scarce had strength to speak. He then gave me a savage kick in the side, and told me to get up. I tried to do so, but fell back in the attempt. He gave me another kick, and again told me to rise. I again tried, and succeeded in gaining my feet; but, stooping to get the tub with which I was feeding the fan, I again staggered and fell. While down in this situation, Mr. Covey took up the hickory slat with which Hughes had been striking off the half-bushel measure, and with it gave me a heavy blow upon the head, making a large wound, and the blood ran freely; and with this again told me to get up. I made no effort to comply, having now made up my mind to let him do his worst. In a short time after receiving this blow, my head grew better. Mr. Covey had now left me to my fate. At this moment I resolved, for the first time, to go to my master, enter a complaint, and ask his protection. In order to do this, I must that afternoon

walk seven miles; and this, under the circumstances, was truly a severe undertaking. I was exceedingly feeble; made so as much by the kicks and blows which I received, as by the severe fit of sickness to which I had been subjected. I, however, watched my chance, while Covey was looking in an opposite direction, and started for St. Michael's: I succeeded in getting a considerable distance on my way to the woods, when Covey discovered me, and called after me to come back, threatening what he would do if I did not come. I disregarded both his calls and his threats, and made my way to the woods as fast as my feeble state would allow, and thinking I might be overhauled by him if I kept the road, I walked through the woods, keeping far enough from the road to avoid detection, and near enough to prevent losing my way. I had not gone far before my little strength again failed me. I could go no farther. I fell down, and lay for a considerable time. The blood was yet oozing from the wound on my head. For a time I thought I should bleed to death; and think now that I should have done so, but that the blood so matted my hair as to stop the wound. After lying there about three quarters of an hour, I nerved myself up again, and started on my way, through bogs and briers, barefooted and bareheaded, tearing my feet sometimes at nearly every step; and after a journey of about seven miles, occupying some five hours to perform it, I arrived at my master's store. I then presented an appearance enough to affect any but a heart of iron. From the crown of my head to my feet, I was covered with blood. My hair was all clotted with dust and blood; my shirt was stiff with blood. My legs and feet were torn in sundry places with briers and thorns, and were also covered with blood. I suppose I looked like a man who had escaped a den of wild beasts, and barely escaped them. In this state I appeared before my master, humbly entreating him to interpose his authority for my protection. I told him all the circumstances as well as I could, and it seemed, as I spoke, at times to affect him. He would then walk the floor, and seek to justify Covey by saying he expected I deserved it. He asked me what I wanted. I told him, to let me get a new home; that as sure as I lived with Mr. Covey again, I should live with but to die with him; that Covey would surely kill me; he was in a fair way for it. Master Thomas ridiculed the idea that there was any danger of Mr. Covey's killing me, and said that he knew Mr. Covey, that he was a good man, and that he could not think of taking me from him; that, should he do so, he would lose the whole year's wages; that I belonged to Mr. Covey for one year, and that I must go back to him, come what might; and that I must not trouble him with any more stories, or that he would himself *get hold of me.* After threatening me thus, he gave me a very large dose of salts, telling me that I might remain in St. Michael's that night, (it being quite late) but that I must be off back to Mr. Covey's early in the morning; and that if I did not, he would *get hold of me,* which meant that he would whip me. I remained all night, and, according to his orders, I started off to Covey's in the morning, (Saturday morning,) wearied in body and broken in spirit. I got no supper that night, or breakfast that morning. I reached Covey's about nine o'clock; and just as I was getting over the fence that divided Mrs. Kemp's fields from ours, out ran Covey with his cowskin, to give me another whipping. Before he could reach me, I succeeded in getting to the cornfield; and as the corn was very high, it afforded me the means of hiding. He seemed very angry, and searched for me a long time. My behavior was altogether unaccountable. He finally gave up the chase, thinking, I suppose, that I must come home for something to eat; he would give himself no further trouble in looking for me. I spent that day mostly in the woods, having the alternative before me—to go home and be whipped to death, or stay in the woods and be starved to death. That night, I fell in with Sandy Jenkins, a slave with whom I was somewhat acquainted. Sandy had a free wife who lived about four miles from Mr. Covey's; and it being Saturday, he was on his way to see her. I told him my circumstances, and he very kindly invited me to go home with him. I went home with him, and talked this whole matter over, and got his advice as to what course it was best for me to pursue. I found Sandy an odd adviser. He told me, with great solemnity, I must go back to Covey; but that before I went, I must go with him into another part of the woods, where there was a certain *root,* which, if I would take some of it with me, carrying it *always on my right side,* would render it impossible for Mr. Covey, or any other white man, to whip me. He said he had carried it for years; and since he had done so, he had never received a blow, and never expected to while he carried it. I at first rejected the idea, that the simple carrying of a root in my pocket would have any such effect as he had said, and was not disposed to take it; but Sandy impressed the necessity with much earnestness, telling me it could do no harm, if it did no good. To please him, I at length took the root, and, according to his direction, carried it upon my right side. This was Sunday morning. I immediately started for home; and upon entering the yard gate, out came Mr. Covey on his way to meeting. He spoke to me very kindly, bade me drive the pigs from a lot near by, and passed on towards the church. Now, this singular conduct of Mr. Covey really made me begin to think that there was something in the *root* which Sandy had given me; and had it been on any other day than Sunday, I could have attributed the conduct to no other cause than the influence of that root; and as it was, I was half inclined to think the *root* to be something more than I at first had taken it to be. All went well till Monday morning. On this morning, the virtue of the *root* was fully tested. Long before daylight, I was called to go and rub, curry, and feed, the horses. I obeyed, and was glad to obey. But whilst thus engaged, whilst in the act of throwing down some blades from the loft, Mr. Covey entered the stable with a long rope; and just as I was half out of the loft, he caught hold of my legs, and was about tying me. As soon as I found what he was up to, I gave a sudden spring, and as I did so, he holding to my legs, I was brought sprawling on the stable floor. Mr. Covey seemed now to think he had me, and could do what he pleased; but at this moment—from whence came the spirit I don't know—I resolved to fight; and, suiting my action to the resolution, I seized Covey hard by the throat; and as I did so, I rose. He held on to me, and I to him. My resistance was so entirely unexpected, that Covey seemed all taken aback. He trembled like a leaf. This gave me assurance, and I held him uneasy, causing the blood to run where I touched him with the ends of my fingers. Mr. Covey soon called out to Hughes for help. Hughes came, and, while Covey held me, attempted to tie my right hand. While he was in the act of doing so, I watched my chance, and gave him a heavy kick close under the ribs. This kick fairly sickened Hughes, so that he left me in the hands of Mr. Covey. This kick had the effect of not only weakening Hughes, but Covey also. When he saw Hughes bending over with pain, his courage quailed. He asked me if I meant to persist in my resistance. I told him I did, come what might; that he had used me like a brute for six months, and that I was determined to be used so no longer. With that, he strove to drag me to a stick that was lying just out of the stable door. He meant to knock me down. But just as he was leaning over to get the stick, I seized him with both hands by his collar, and brought him by a sudden snatch to the ground. By this time, Bill came. Covey called upon him for assistance. Bill wanted to know what he could do. Covey said, "Take hold of him, take hold of him!" Bill said his master hired him out to work, and not to help to whip me; so he left Covey and myself to fight our own battle out. We were at it for nearly two hours. Covey at length let me go, puffing and blowing at a great rate, saying that if I had not resisted, he would not have whipped me half so much. The truth was that he had not whipped me at all. I considered him as getting entirely the worst end of the bargain; for he had drawn no blood from me, but I had from him. The whole six months afterwards, that I spent with Mr. Covey, he never laid the weight of his finger upon me in anger. He would occasionally say he didn't want to get hold of me again. "No," thought I, "you need not; for you will come off worse than you did before."

3 This battle with Mr. Covey was the turning-point in my career as a slave. It rekindled the few expiring embers of freedom, and revived within me a sense of my own manhood. It recalled the departed self-confidence, and inspired me again with a determination to be free. The gratification afforded by the triumph was a full compensation for whatever else might follow, even death itself. He only can understand the deep satisfaction which I experienced, who has himself repelled by force the bloody arm of slavery. I felt as I never felt before. It was a glorious resurrection, from the tomb of slavery, to the heaven of freedom. My long-crushed spirit rose, cowardice departed, bold defiance took its place; and I now resolved that, however long I might remain a slave in form, the day had passed forever when I could be a slave in fact. I did not hesitate to let it be known of me, that the white man who expected to succeed in whipping, must also succeed in killing me.

4 From this time I was never again what might be called fairly whipped, though I remained a slave four years afterwards. I had several fights, but was never whipped.

5 It was for a long time a matter of surprise to me why Mr. Covey did not immediately have me taken by the constable to the whipping-post, and there regularly whipped for the crime of raising my hand against a white man in defence of myself. And the only explanation I can now think of does not entirely satisfy me; but such as it is, I will give it. Mr. Covey enjoyed the most unbounded reputation for being a first-rate overseer and negro-breaker. It was of considera-

ble importance to him. That reputation was at stake; and had he sent me—a boy about sixteen years old—to the public whipping-post, his reputation would have been lost; so, to save his reputation, he suffered me to go unpunished.

Additional Rhetorical Strategy

Cause and Effect (paragraph 2; the anecdote of the root).

Examining Words and Meaning

1. Why is Douglass working for Mr. Covey, if he is owned by someone else? What does this suggest about the master's attitude toward his slave?
2. Why doesn't Covey strike Douglass the morning after he has hidden in the cornfield? Does Douglass suggest that it has anything to do with the root Sandy Jenkins has given him?
3. Check the dictionary for these words, if necessary: fanning (paragraph 1); sundry (paragraph 2); curry (paragraph 2); quailed (paragraph 2).

Focusing on Structures and Strategies

1. Douglass's narrative starts on Friday afternoon and ends on Monday morning, but he doesn't account for every hour in that period. What periods of time does he skip over quickly or de-emphasize? Why, then, does he choose to emphasize the periods that he does?
2. Does Douglass describe Covey's appearance? Does he give a detailed description of his master's store? What, in other words, does his selection of details tell us about his purpose in writing this section of his autobiography?
3. How would you describe Douglass's voice here? As chatty? Formal? Enraged? How might the fact that his audience was for the most part composed of white Northern abolitionists influence his voice here?

Might Douglass have written differently had he been writing for Southern blacks?

Suggestions for Further Discussion and Writing

1. Vivid narrative often features dialogue, but Douglass introduces very little. What might his reasons be for including so little speech? Would too much dialogue have thwarted his purpose in writing?

2. Fortunately none of us has literally been a slave, as Douglass was, but we have all experienced moments when our conception of ourselves changed, if only slightly. Write a narrative in which you talk of one such moment. Be sure to lead up to the moment so that your reader will know how it happened and what its significance was to you. Here are some suggestions: making a varsity athletic team; asking someone out for the first time; standing up for your rights as a woman; deciding to call your relatives by their first names. Try to choose a moment of significant transition in your life.

A Hanging

George Orwell

"A man may take to drink because he feels himself to be a failure, and then fail all the more completely because he drinks," wrote George Orwell (1903–1950), who went on to note that it "is rather the same thing that is happening to the English language. It becomes ugly and inaccurate because our thoughts are foolish, but the slovenliness of our language makes it easier for us to have foolish thoughts."

One of the leading British novelists and essayists of the twentieth century, George Orwell (pen name for Eric Arthur Blair) was deeply affected by the social and political conditions of his time. His works are particularly responsive to questions of human freedom, and his best-known novels, Animal Farm *(1946) and* Nineteen Eighty-four *(1949), are both terrifying excursions into the world of totalitarianism.*

1 It was in Burma, a sodden morning of the rains. A sickly light, like yellow tinfoil, was slanting over the high walls into the jail yard. We were waiting outside the condemned cells, a row of sheds fronted with double bars, like small animal cages. Each cell measured about ten feet by ten and was quite bare within except for a plank bed and a pot for drinking water. In some of them brown, silent men were squatting at the inner bars, with their blankets draped round them. These were the condemned men, due to be hanged within the next week or two.

2 One prisoner had been brought out of his cell. He was a Hindu, a puny wisp of a man, with a shaven head and vague liquid eyes. He had a thick, sprouting moustache, absurdly too big for his body, rather like the moustache of a comic man on the films. Six tall Indian warders were guarding him and getting him ready for the gallows. Two of them stood by with rifles and fixed bayonets, while the others handcuffed him, passed a chain through his handcuffs and fixed it to their belts, and lashed his arms tight to his sides. They crowded very close about him, with their hands always on him in a careful, caressing grip, as though all the while feeling him to make sure he was there. It was like men handling a fish which is still alive and may jump back into the water. But he stood quite unresisting, yielding his arms limply to the ropes, as though he hardly noticed what was happening.

3 Eight o'clock struck and a bugle call, desolately thin in the wet air, floated from the distant barracks. The superintendent of the jail, who was standing apart from the rest of us, moodily prodding the gravel with his stick, raised his head at the sound. He was an army doctor, with a grey toothbrush moustache and a gruff voice. "For God's sake hurry up, Francis," he said irritably. "The man ought to have been dead by this time. Aren't you ready yet?"

4 Francis, the head jailer, a fat Dravidian in a white drill suit and gold spectacles, waved his black hand. "Yes sir, yes sir," he bubbled. "All iss satisfactorily prepared. The hangman iss waiting. We shall proceed."

5 "Well, quick march, then. The prisoners can't get their breakfast till this job's over."

6 We set out for the gallows. Two warders marched on either side of the prisoner, with their rifles at the slope; two others marched close against him, gripping him by arm and shoulder, as though at once pushing and supporting him. The rest of us, magistrates and the like

followed behind. Suddenly, when we had gone ten yards, the procession stopped short without any order or warning. A dreadful thing had happened—a dog, come goodness knows whence, had appeared in the yard. It came bounding among us with a loud volley of barks, and leapt round us wagging its whole body, wild with glee at finding so many human beings together. It was a large woolly dog, half Airedale, half pariah. For a moment it pranced round us, and then, before anyone could stop it, it had made a dash for the prisoner, jumping up tried to lick his face. Everyone stood aghast, too taken aback even to grab at the dog.

7 "Who let that bloody brute in here?" said the superintendent angrily. "Catch it, someone!"

8 A warder detached from the escort, charged clumsily after the dog, but it danced and gambolled just out of his reach, taking everything as part of the game. A young Eurasian jailer picked up a handful of gravel and tried to stone the dog away, but it dodged the stones and came after us again. Its yaps echoed from the jail walls. The prisoner, in the grasp of the two warders, looked on incuriously, as though this was another formality of the hanging. It was several minutes before someone managed to catch the dog. Then we put my handkerchief through its collar and moved off once more, with the dog still straining and whimpering.

9 It was about forty yards to the gallows. I watched the bare brown back of the prisoner marching in front of me. He walked clumsily with his bound arms, but quite steadily, with that bobbing gait of the Indian who never straightens his knees. At each step his muscles slid neatly into place, the lock of hair on his scalp danced up and down, his feet printed themselves on the wet gravel. And once, in spite of the men who gripped him by each shoulder, he stepped slightly aside to avoid a puddle on the path.

10 It is curious, but till that moment I had never realized what it means to destroy a healthy, conscious man. When I saw the prisoner step aside to avoid the puddle I saw the mystery, the unspeakable wrongness, of cutting a life short when it is in full tide. This man was not dying, he was alive just as we are alive. All the organs of his body were working—bowels digesting food, skin renewing itself, nails growing, tissues forming—all toiling away in solemn foolery. His nails would still be growing when he stood on the drop, when he was falling through the air with a tenth-of-a-second to live. His eyes saw the yellow gravel and the grey walls, and his brain still remembered,

foresaw, reasoned—reasoned even about puddles. He and we were a party of men walking together, seeing, hearing, feeling, understanding the same world; and in two minutes, with a sudden snap, one of us would be gone—one mind less, one world less.

11 The gallows stood in a small yard, separate from the main grounds of the prison, and overgrown with tall prickly weeds. It was a brick erection like three sides of a shed, with planking on top, and above that two beams and a crossbar with the rope dangling. The hangman, a grey-haired convict in the white uniform of the prison, was waiting beside his machine. He greeted us with a servile crouch as we entered. At a word from Francis the two warders, gripping the prisoner more closely than ever, half led half pushed him to the gallows and helped him clumsily up the ladder. Then the hangman climbed up and fixed the rope round the prisoner's neck.

12 We stood waiting, five yards away. The warders had formed in a rough circle round the gallows. And then, when the noose was fixed, the prisoner began crying out to his god. It was a high, reiterated cry of "Ram! Ram! Ram! Ram!" not urgent and fearful like a prayer or cry for help, but steady, rhythmical, almost like the tolling of a bell. The dog answered the sound with a whine. The hangman, still standing on the gallows, produced a small cotton bag like a flour bag and drew it down over the prisoner's face. But the sound, muffled by the cloth, still persisted, over and over again: "Ram! Ram! Ram! Ram! Ram!"

13 The hangman climbed down and stood ready, holding the lever. Minutes seemed to pass. The steady, muffled crying from the prisoner went on and on, "Ram! Ram! Ram!" never faltering for an instant. The superintendent, his head on his chest, was slowly poking the ground with his stick; perhaps he was counting the cries, allowing the prisoner a fixed number—fifty, perhaps, or a hundred. Everyone had changed colour. The Indians had gone grey like bad coffee, and one or two of the bayonets were wavering. We looked at the lashed, hooded man on the drop, and listened to his cries—each cry another second of life; the same thought was in all our minds: oh, kill him quickly, get it over, stop that abominable noise!

14 Suddenly the superintendent made up his mind. Throwing up his head he made a swift motion with his stick. "Chalo!" he shouted almost fiercely.

15 There was a clanking noise, and then dead silence. The prisoner had vanished, and the rope was twisting on itself. I let go of the dog, and it galloped immediately to the back of the gallows; but when it

got there it stopped short, barked, and then retreated into a corner of the yard, where it stood among the weeds, looking timorously out at us. We went round the gallows to inspect the prisoner's body. He was dangling with his toes pointed straight downwards, very slowly revolving, as dead as a stone.

16 The superintendent reached out with his stick and poked the bare brown body; it oscillated slightly. "*He's* all right," said the superintendent. He backed out from under the gallows, and blew out a deep breath. The moody look had gone out of his face quite suddenly. He glanced at his wrist-watch. "Eight minutes past eight. Well, that's all for this morning, thank God."

17 The warders unfixed bayonets and marched away. The dog, sobered and conscious of having misbehaved itself, slipped after them. We walked out of the gallows yard, past the condemned cells with their waiting prisoners, into the big central yard of the prison. The convicts, under the command of warders and armed with lathis, were already receiving their breakfast. They squatted in long rows, each man holding a tin pannikin, while two warders with buckets marched round ladling out rice; it seemed quite a homely, jolly scene, after the hanging. An enormous relief had come upon us now that the job was done. One felt an impulse to sing, to break into a run, to snigger. All at once everyone began chattering gaily.

18 The Eurasian boy walking beside me nodded towards the way we had come, with a knowing smile: "Do you know, sir, our friend (he meant the dead man) when he heard his appeal had been dismissed, he pissed on the floor of his cell. From fright. Kindly take one of my cigarettes, sir. Do you not admire my new silver case, sir? From the boxwallah, two rupees eight annas. Classy European style."

19 Several people laughed—at what, nobody seemed certain.

20 Francis was walking by the superintendent, talking garrulously: "Well, sir, all hass passed off with the utmost satisfactoriness. It was all finished—flick! like that. It iss not always so—oah, no! I have known cases where the doctor wass obliged to go beneath the gallows and pull the prisoner's legs to ensure decease. Most disagreeable!"

21 "Wriggling about, eh? That's bad," said the superintendent.

22 "Ach, sir, it iss worse when they become refractory! One man, I recall, clung to the bars of hiss cage when we went to take him out. You will scarcely credit, sir, that it took six warders to dislodge him, three pulling at each leg. We reasoned with him. 'My dear fellow,'

we said, 'think of all the pain and trouble you are causing to us!' But no, he would not listen! Ach, he wass very troublesome!"

23 I found that I was laughing quite loudly. Everyone was laughing. Even the superintendent grinned in a tolerant way. "You'd better all come out and have a drink," he said quite genially. "I've got a bottle of whiskey in the car. We could do with it."

24 We went through the big double gates of the prison into the road. "Pulling at his legs!" exclaimed a Burmese magistrate suddenly, and burst into a loud chuckling. We all began laughing again. At that moment Francis' anecdote seemed extraordinarily funny. We all had a drink together, native and European alike, quite amicably. The dead man was a hundred yards away.

Additional Rhetorical Strategies

Description (paragraphs 1, 2, 11); Comparison and Contrast (implied throughout; the prisoner and the jail officials).

Examining Words and Meaning

1. How does the prisoner's avoiding a puddle help Orwell to see the entire situation in a new light? Does he maintain this changed attitude throughout the experience? Use specific words and phrases to support your answer.

2. How does the mood of those present change once they leave the scene of the hanging? What impulse does Orwell feel? What do you think his attitude toward that impulse is when he is writing this essay?

3. What is the effect of Orwell's describing the prisoner's moustache as "absurdly too big for his body" (paragraph 2)? Why does Orwell say that the result of hanging the man would be "one mind less, one world less" (paragraph 10)? What does he mean by "one world less"?

4. Check these words in a dictionary: pariah (paragraph 6); aghast (paragraph 6); gambolled (paragraph 8); servile (paragraph 11); timorously (paragraph 15); oscillated (paragraph 16); lathis (paragraph 17); garrulously (paragraph 20); refractory (paragraph 22).

Focusing on Structures and Strategies

1. What purpose does the first paragraph serve? The second? What necessary information do they give us? What information do they not give us? Do we know, for example, why the prisoner is to be executed? Do we know what Orwell is doing there? What do Orwell's omissions suggest about his purpose in writing this essay?
2. Look carefully at the way Orwell describes his laughing after the hanging. Does he say precisely when he started to laugh? What is the effect of his presenting things in this way?
3. How does the essay end? What does the last sentence do? Why does this simple statement of fact make such an effective ending?

Suggestions for Further Discussion and Writing

1. Compare Orwell's essay to E. B. White's "The Ring of Time" (see p. 129). In both essays we find a speaker observing an event and later writing about it. What other similarities can you find? Would you think it accurate to say that description can sometimes be narration, and narration description?
2. Choose an incident from your experience in which you were confronted with something painful, terrifying, or deeply moving: an accident, a dying animal, a birth, and so forth. Write a narrative about it, trying to record not only your reactions but also the responses of those around you. Use dialogue, if possible.

Process Analysis

1 Process analysis explains how to do something, how something works, or how something happened. As a procedure for developing sequences in thinking and writing, process analysis resembles narration and causal analysis in its attention to a series of related events. But its purpose and method distinguish it from these other rhetorical forms. Narration tells *what* happened. Cause and effect accounts for *why.* Process analysis explains *how.* If, for example, we wanted to write about automobiles, we could define, classify, illustrate, or compare them. We could also describe one in detail, narrate a story about it, and discuss it, say, as a factor in the increasing death rate on holiday weekends. But as soon as we consider how an automobile works, how it is made, how it can be repaired, or how it can be driven, we are engaged in process analysis. Process analysis examines a series of actions that bring about a particular result.

2 There are two basic kinds of process analysis: specified and informative. *Specified* process analysis explains how to do something (for example, how to get from one place to another, how to play lacrosse, how to prepare for a job interview, or how to build a skyscraper). *Informative* process analysis explains how something works or happened—that is, how something is or was done (for example, how a computer works, how oil is refined, how calculators are manufactured, or how a dictatorship was overthrown). In both forms of process analysis, the writer presents a brief overview of the subject to be covered, then divides the part of the whole operation into steps

or stages, and proceeds to consider each in precise enough detail for readers either to perform the actions indicated or to understand them fully. The writer of a successful process analysis relies on simple language, accurate verbs, distinct transitions, and, most important, on a clear chronological sequence to explain or make a *single point:* say, how to take better notes in class or how a small group of citizens rallied to defeat a giant utility's proposal to build a nuclear reactor in their community.

3 We are all familiar with the many forms of *specified* process analysis. We commonly encounter it in cookbooks, instruction manuals, handbooks, rule books, and textbooks of various sorts. Specified process analysis is frequently written in the second person; the writer leads an audience through a series of moves to a predetermined end. The success of a specified process analysis depends on the clarity and completeness of our directions. Let's suppose, for example, that our neighbor wanted to know how we prepared an especially tasty spaghetti sauce. We might well begin our recipe with a brief general statement about how it saves time and money. We would then list the necessary ingredients and equipment, and follow up with a precise set of directions for preparing and serving it. But specified process analysis may be applied to *any* subject that calls for how-to-do-it guidance: writing an essay, putting an end to procrastination, managing personal finances, achieving success in business, or coping with gadgets. In each case, we examine the situation carefully, clarify our purpose, and identify our audience. We also need to consider the kind and amount of information required to complete the process, being careful not to overestimate what our audience knows about our subject. We would then move on to establish as simple a sequence as possible for the process. In effect, we must present information complete enough for anyone in our established audience to go through the process, carry out all the procedures, and produce the intended results. To that end, we may supplement our written instructions with graphics—especially when they simplify, clarify, or condense our words, thereby heightening reader responsiveness and comprehension.

4 *Informative* process analysis provides readers with a thorough understanding of a process that they would like to know something (or know more) about: how a friend saved several hundred dollars each year when shopping for clothes, how earthquakes get started, how a "gasahol" engine works. (For a distinctive account of how the world began, see p. 220.) The process may also be one that readers

are unlikely or unable to perform themselves: how hang gliders stay aloft, how lasers are used in surgery, how a photographer shoots an underwater scene in shark-infested waters. In informative process, the emphasis shifts from how-to-do-it instruction to how-it-is-done explanation. Readers should come away from informative process writing with a general understanding of the principles involved in how something works or happened—whether it is a simple household appliance or a complex political crisis.

5 In order to understand how something works, we frequently need to understand how it is put together. For example, describing the interrelation of parts in a television set may be necessary before showing how the set functions. Informative process analysis may be classified as *mechanical* (how an instant camera works), *scientific* (how molecules are formed), *historical* (how the United States came to suffer in Vietnam what has been called its first defeat in war), *natural* (how rain clouds form), *social* (how women's roles in society are changing), *creative* (how novels are written), or *psychological* (how dreams can be interpreted).

6 Examine for a moment the opening paragraphs of a newspaper report on how helicopters fly:

> It is in the very nature of the helicopter that its great versatility is found. To begin with, the helicopter is the fulfillment of one of man's earliest and most fantastic dreams, the dream of flying—not just like a bird—but of flying as nothing else flies or has ever flown. To be able to fly straight up and straight down—to fly forward or back or sidewise, or to hover over one spot till the fuel supply is exhausted.
>
> To see how the helicopter can do things that are not possible for the conventional fixed-wing plane, let us first examine how a conventional plane "works." It works by its shape—by the shape of its wing, which deflects air when the plane is in motion. That is possible because air has density and resistance. It reacts to force. The wing is curved and set at an angle to catch the air and push it down; the air, resisting, pushes against the under surface of the wing, giving it some of its lift. At the same time the curved upper surface of the wing exerts suction, tending to create a lack of air at the top of the wing. The air, again resisting, sucks back, and this gives the wing about twice as much lift as the air pressure below the wing. This is what takes place when the wing is pulled forward by propellers or pushed forward by jet blasts. Without the motion the wing has no lift.
>
> Now the helicopter combines in its whirling rotor blades—

> which are merely long, thin wings—both the function of the conventional wing, which is lift, and the function of the propeller, which is thrust. As the blades whirl around the top of the helicopter fuselage the air passes over and under them, giving enough lift to hoist the plane up. By changing the angle of pitch of the whirling rotors, the pilot gives the plane direction. If he tilts the blades forward, the plane goes ahead; if he hauls them back, the craft flies backward. By tilting them to one side or the other he moves to his right or left, and when the angle of pitch is flattened the craft hovers over one spot. This tilting is accomplished by the most important part of the helicopter's moving mechanism—called the rotor head—which is mounted at or near the top of the drive shaft from the power plant.

This passage is an excellent example of informative process analysis because the writer tells us virtually everything we need to know in order to understand how helicopters fly. By comparing a helicopter with a conventional fixed-wing plane in nontechnical, easily understood language, the writer allows even those with no scientific training to understand a helicopter's basic operations. After reading this passage, many of us may not have completely overcome our fear of flying in such machines, but all of us should have an extremely clear sense of the aerodynamic principles that govern its flight. So, too, we should have a much better sense of how to organize a process analysis essay in which we might be asked to explain a seemingly complicated, highly technical operation.

7 The writer of any process analysis essay typically follows a sequence of moves. First, he or she presents a general description of the process and its purpose. This makes the writer's next move more readily accessible to the audience: breaking the process down into its chief stages and then further down into particular steps. Each step in the process is then described in detail. In doing so, the writer needs to maintain a balance between presuming too little knowledge on the part of the audience (thus risking boredom) and presuming too much (thus nearly guaranteeing confusion). Along the way, the writer defines any unavoidable special terms and identifies any ingredients crucial to completing the process—as Alan Devoe does when writing about the hibernation of a woodchuck (p. 217). Finally, the writer may choose to conclude the essay by summarizing the main stages of the process and perhaps offering a general comment on it.

8 The most important factor in the success of a process analysis essay is a clear and systematic chronological sequence. Establishing a precise order for a series of actions or functions may be complicated

by the fact that several things may happen at once. For example, explaining how a washing machine works would be more difficult than advising someone on how to assemble a model airplane: when a washing machine is in operation, several actions take place simultaneously. Perhaps the best way to deal with this predicament is to organize the process into several general operations (in this case, washing, rinsing, and spin-drying the laundry) and then to consider each in detail and in the clearest chronological sequence.

9 Writing is another process marked by simultaneous activities. For the sake of clarity, writing is usually divided into three general chronological stages: pre-writing, writing, and rewriting. Yet most writers rarely follow such neat, discrete steps while composing. To be more precise, we literally think before, during, and after we put our pens to paper. Most of us, for example, are hardly even conscious of how much we rewrite as our hand moves across a page. We are writing to find out what it is we think. And as soon as we have discovered that, we are apt to make changes. Breaking down writing—and many other complicated processes—into separate stages is done primarily for pedagogical reasons: we want to unravel the process, to make it specific and simple enough to be understood, at least basically. We are thereby sacrificing precision for general understanding. (For an example of one writer's instructions on writing well, see Kurt Vonnegut's "How to Write with Style," p. 197.) But whether we are trying to convey a basic or an exact sense of how either a sentence or a washing machine works, we must be confident that we know enough about our subject to determine which operation should be described first and to arrange the most easily understood sequence for our audience. So, too, we must create a sense of closure—a satisfying sense of completeness—for the process analyzed.

10 Process analysis can be applied to any number of actions, operations, functions, or changes—and each will require that a distinctive sequence be developed. The decision whether to use specified or informative process analysis depends, of course, on the subject: the process of repairing a motorcycle would necessitate specified; the process of explaining how a roommate passed math for the first time, informative. In each instance, there is a different set of principles underlying the sequence. But no matter whether it appears as one of several rhetorical features of an essay or as the dominant rhetorical strategy, process analysis is one of the most methodical—and instructive—ways to develop and order our compositions.

On Transcendental Metaworry (TMW)

Lewis Thomas

Giving instructions is one of the most common uses of process analysis. When we give someone instructions, we usually break down procedures into their various steps or stages in order to narrate an activity from start to finish—whether it's a laboratory experiment, a recipe, or the composition of an essay. In the essay below, from The Medusa and the Snail, *Lewis Thomas relies on process analysis to parody the popular technique of "Transcendental Meditation" (TM). Thomas, however, recommends an alternative to relaxation and provides step-by-step instructions for reaching the essence of Western Wisdom—"pure worry about pure worry."*

For biographical information on Lewis Thomas, see page 109.

1 It is said that modern, industrialized, civilized human beings are uniquely nervous and jumpy, unprecedentedly disturbed by the future, despaired by the present, sleepless at memories of the recent past, all because of the technological complexity and noisiness of the machinery by which we are surrounded, and the rigidified apparatus of cold steel and plastic which we have constructed between ourselves and the earth. Incessant worry, according to this view, is a modern invention. To turn it off, all we need do is turn off the engines and climb down into the countryside. Primitive man, rose-garlanded, slept well.

2 I doubt this. Man has always been a specifically anxious creature with an almost untapped capacity for worry; it is a gift that distinguishes him from other forms of life. There is undoubtedly a neural center deep in the human brain for mediating this function, like the centers for hunger or sleep.

3 Prehistoric man, without tools or fire to be thinking about, must have been the most anxious of us all. Fumbling about in dimly lit caves, trying to figure out what he ought really to be doing, sensing the awesome responsibilities for toolmaking just ahead, he must have spent a lot of time contemplating his thumbs and fretting about

them. I can imagine him staring at his hands, apposing thumbtips to each fingertip in amazement, thinking, By God, that's something to set us apart from the animals—and then the grinding thought, What on earth are they for? There must have been many long, sleepless nights, his mind all thumbs.

4 It would not surprise me to learn that there were ancient prefire committees, convened to argue that thumbs might be taking us too far, that we'd have been better off with simply another finger of the usual sort.

5 Worrying is the most natural and spontaneous of all human functions. It is time to acknowledge this, perhaps even to learn to do it better. Man is the Worrying Animal. It is a trait needing further development, awaiting perfection. Most of us tend to neglect the activity, living precariously out on the thin edge of anxiety but never plunging in.

6 For total immersion in the experience of pure, illuminating harassment, I can recommend a modification of the technique of Transcendental Meditation, which I stumbled across after reading an article on the practice in a scholarly magazine and then trying it on myself, sitting on an overturned, stove-in canoe under a beech tree in my backyard. Following closely the instructions, I relaxed, eyes closed, breathing regularly, repeating a recommended mantra, in this instance the word "om," over and over. The conditions were suitable for withdrawal and detachment; my consciousness, which normally spends its time clutching for any possible handhold, was prepared to cut adrift. Then, suddenly, the telephone began to ring inside the house, rang several times between breathed "om"s, and stopped. In the instant, I discovered Transcendental Worry.

7 Transcendental Worry can be engaged in at any time, by anyone, regardless of age, sex, or occupation, and in almost any circumstance. For beginners, I advise twenty-minute sessions, in the morning before work and late in the evening just before insomnia.

8 What you do is sit down someplace, preferably by yourself, and tense all muscles. If you make yourself reasonably uncomfortable at the outset, by sitting on a canoe bottom, say, the tension will come naturally. Now close the eyes, concentrate on this until the effort causes a slight tremor of the eyelids. Now breathe, thinking analytically about the muscular effort involved; it is useful to attempt breathing through one nostril at a time, alternating sides.

9 Now, the mantra. The word "worry," repeated quite rapidly, is itself effective, because of the allusive cognates in its history. Thus,

intruding into the recitation of the mantra comes the recollection that it derives from the Indo-European root *wer,* meaning to turn or bend in the sense of evading, which became *wyrgan* in Old English, meaning to kill by strangling, with close relatives "weird," "writhe," "wriggle," "wrestle," and "wrong." "Wrong" is an equally useful mantra, for symmetrical reasons.

10 Next, try to float your consciousness free. You will feel something like this happening after about three minutes, and, almost simultaneously with the floating, yawing and sinking will begin. This complex of conjoined sensations becomes an awareness of concentrated, irreversible trouble.

11 Finally you will begin to hear the *zing,* if you are successful. This is a distant, rhythmic sound, not timed with either the breathing or the mantra. After several minutes, you will discover by taking your pulse that the *zing* is synchronous, and originates somewhere in the lower part of the head or perhaps high up in the neck, presumably due to turbulence at the bend of an artery, maybe even the vibration of a small plaque. Now you are In Touch.

12 Nothing remains but to allow the intensification of Transcendental Worry to proceed spontaneously to the next stage, termed the Primal Wince. En route, you pass through an almost confluent series of pictures, random and transient, jerky and running at overspeed like an old movie, many of them seemingly trivial but each associated with a sense of dropping abruptly through space (it is useful, here, to recall that "vertigo" also derives from *wer*). You may suddenly see, darting across the mind like a shrieking plumed bird, a current electric-light bill, or the vision of numbers whirring too fast to read on a gasoline pump, or the last surviving humpback whale, singing a final song into empty underseas, or simply the television newscast announcing that détente now signifies a Soviet-American Artificial-Heart Project. Or late bulletins from science concerning the pulsing showers of neutrino particles, aimed personally by collapsing stars, which cannot be escaped from even at the bottom of salt mines in South Dakota. Watergate, of course. The music of John Cage. The ascending slopes of chalked curves on academic blackboards, interchangeably predicting the future population of pet dogs in America, rats in Harlem, nuclear explosions overhead and down in salt mines, suicides in Norway, crop failures in India, the number of people at large. The thought of moon gravity as a cause of baldness. The unpreventability of continental drift. The electronic guitar. The slipping away of things, the feel of rugs sliding out from under every-

where. These images become confluent and then amorphous, melting together into a solid, gelatinous thought of skewness. When this happens, you will be entering the last stage, which is pure worry about pure worry. This is the essence of the Wisdom of the West, and I shall call it Transcendental Metaworry (TMW).

13 Now, as to the usefulness of TMW. First of all, it tends to fill the mind completely at times when it would otherwise be empty. Instead of worrying at random, continually and subliminally, wondering always what it is that you've forgotten and ought to be worrying about, you get the full experience, all in a rush, on a schedule which you arrange for yourself.

14 Secondly, it makes the times of the day when there is really nothing to worry about intensely pleasurable, because of the contrast.

15 Thirdly, I have forgotten the third advantage, which is itself one less thing to worry about.

16 There are, of course, certain disadvantages, which must be faced up to. TMW is, admittedly, a surrogate experience, a substitute for the real thing, and in this sense there is always the danger of overdoing it. Another obvious danger is the likely entry of technology into the field. I have no doubt that there will soon be advertisements in the back pages of small literary magazines, offering for sale, money back if dissatisfied (or satisfied), electronic devices encased in black plastic boxes with dials, cathode screens, earphones with simulated sonic booms, and terminals to be affixed at various areas of the scalp so that brain waves associated with pure TMW can be identified and volitionally selected. These will be marketed under attractive trade names, like the Angst Amplifier or the Artificial Heartsink. The thought of such things is something else to worry about, but perhaps not much worse than the average car radio.

Reading for Rhetorical Strategy

Lewis Thomas sets the stage for his Metaworry techniques by first reminding us, in paragraph 5, that to worry is "the most natural and spontaneous of all human functions." In paragraph 6, he introduces the main topic, his accidental discovery of "Transcendental Worry" while he was attempting to engage in a practice that promised a more relaxed state of mind. The instructions begin in paragraph 7 and are described in step-by-step detail from paragraph 8 through paragraph 12. Narrating a process usually means maintaining a clear, continuous sequence of steps through time. Note the terms that help conduct the reader through these stages: "Now close the eyes . . . Now breathe . . . Now, the mantra . . . Next, try to float . . . Finally you will begin to hear . . . After several minutes, you will discover . . . Now you are In Touch," etc. Though Thomas's intentions are clearly humorous and parodic, the steps in the process are described so convincingly that achieving the tormented state of TMW actually seems possible.

How to Write with Style

Kurt Vonnegut

*In 1979, the International Paper Company began sponsoring a series of advertisements on the "Power of the Printed Word." Designed to help young people "*read *better,* write *better, and* communicate *better," this advertising campaign has featured such celebrities and writers as Steve Allen, Bill Cosby, James Michener, and George Plimpton, discussing topics like how to use a library and how to enjoy the classics. International Paper reports that the series has been an enormous success; at one point, the company received nearly 1000 letters a day requesting reprints. International Paper also obviously recognizes that the more readers there are of books, magazines, and newspapers, the more paper it will sell.*

Kurt Vonnegut (1922–   ) is one of America's most popular contemporary novelists. The author of such campus favorites as Cat's Cradle *(1963),* Slaughterhouse Five *(1969),* Breakfast of Champions *(1973),* Jailbird *(1976),* Deadeye Dick *(1982),* Galapagos *(1985), and* Between Time & Timbuktu *(1986), Vonnegut has also written several plays and contributed short fiction to periodicals ranging from the* Saturday Evening Post *and* Ladies' Home Journal *to* Cosmopolitan *and* Playboy. *In the following advertisement from the series sponsored by International Paper, Vonnegut offers some practical tips on how to write well.*

1 Newspaper reporters and technical writers are trained to reveal almost nothing about themselves in their writings. This makes them freaks in the world of writers, since almost all of the other ink-stained wretches in that world reveal a lot about themselves to read-

ers. We call these revelations, accidental and intentional, elements of style.

2 These revelations tell us as readers what sort of person it is with whom we are spending time. Does the writer sound ignorant or informed, stupid or bright, crooked or honest, humorless or playful—? And on and on.

3 Why should you examine your writing style with the idea of improving it? Do so as a mark of respect for your readers, whatever you're writing. If you scribble your thoughts any which way, your readers will surely feel that you care nothing about them. They will mark you down as an egomaniac or a chowderhead—or worse, they will stop reading you.

4 The most damning revelation you can make about yourself is that you do not know what is interesting and what is not. Don't you yourself like or dislike writers mainly for what they choose to show you or make you think about? Did you ever admire an empty-headed writer for his or her mastery of the language? No.

5 So your own winning style must begin with ideas in your head.

1. FIND A SUBJECT YOU CARE ABOUT

6 Find a subject you care about and which you in your heart feel others should care about. It is this genuine caring, and not your games with language, which will be the most compelling and seductive element in your style.

7 I am not urging you to write a novel, by the way—although I would not be sorry if you wrote one, provided you genuinely cared about something. A petition to the mayor about a pothole in front of your house or a love letter to the girl next door will do.

2. DO NOT RAMBLE, THOUGH

8 I won't ramble on about that.

3. KEEP IT SIMPLE

9 As for your use of language: Remember that two great masters of language, William Shakespeare and James Joyce, wrote sentences which were almost childlike when their subjects were most profound. "To be or not to be?" asks Shakespeare's Hamlet. The longest word is three letters long. Joyce, when he was frisky, could put together a sentence as intricate and as glittering as a necklace for Cleopatra, but my favorite sentence in his short story "Eveline" is this one: "She was tired." At that point in the story, no other words could break the heart of a reader as those three words do.

10 Simplicity of language is not only reputable, but perhaps even sacred. The *Bible* opens with a sentence well within the writing skills of a lively fourteen-year-old: "In the beginning God created the heaven and the earth."

4. HAVE THE GUTS TO CUT

11 It may be that you, too, are capable of making necklaces for Cleopatra, so to speak. But your eloquence should be the servant of the ideas in your head. Your rule might be this: If a sentence, no matter how excellent, does not illuminate your subject in some new and useful way, scratch it out.

5. SOUND LIKE YOURSELF

12 The writing style which is most natural for you is bound to echo the speech you heard when a child. English was the novelist Joseph Conrad's third language, and much that seems piquant in his use of English was no doubt colored by his first language, which was Polish. And lucky indeed is the writer who has grown up in Ireland, for the English spoken there is so amusing and musical. I myself grew up in Indianapolis, where common speech sounds like a band saw cutting galvanized tin, and employs a vocabulary as unornamental as a monkey wrench.

13 In some of the more remote hollows of Appalachia, children still grow up hearing songs and locutions of Elizabethan times. Yes, and many Americans grow up hearing a language other than English, or an English dialect a majority of Americans cannot understand.

14 All these varieties of speech are beautiful, just as the varieties of butterflies are beautiful. No matter what your first language, you should treasure it all your life. If it happens not to be standard English, and if it shows itself when you write standard English, the result is usually delightful, like a very pretty girl with one eye that is green and one that is blue.

15 I myself find that I trust my own writing most, and others seem to trust it most, too, when I sound most like a person from Indianapolis, which is what I am. What alternatives do I have? The one most vehemently recommended by teachers has no doubt been pressed on you, as well: to write like cultivated Englishmen of a century or more ago.

6. SAY WHAT YOU MEAN TO SAY

16 I used to be exasperated by such teachers, but am no more. I understand now that all those antique essays and stories with which

I was to compare my own work were not magnificent for their datedness or foreignness, but for saying precisely what their authors meant them to say. My teachers wished me to write accurately, always selecting the most effective words, and relating the words to one another unambiguously, rigidly, like parts of a machine. The teachers did not want to turn me into an Englishman after all. They hoped that I would become understandable—and therefore understood. And there went my dream of doing with words what Pablo Picasso did with paint or what any number of jazz idols did with music. If I broke all the rules of punctuation, had words mean whatever I wanted them to mean, and strung them together higgledy-piggledy, I would simply not be understood. So you, too, had better avoid Picasso-style or jazz-style writing, if you have something worth saying and wish to be understood.

17 Readers want our pages to look very much like pages they have seen before. Why? This is because they themselves have a tough job to do, and they need all the help they can get from us.

7. PITY THE READERS

18 They have to identify thousands of little marks on paper, and make sense of them immediately. They have to *read,* an art so difficult that most people don't really master it even after having studied it all through grade school and high school—twelve long years.

19 So this discussion must finally acknowledge that our stylistic options as writers are neither numerous nor glamorous, since our readers are bound to be such imperfect artists. Our audience requires us to be sympathetic and patient teachers, ever willing to simplify and clarify—whereas we would rather soar high above the crowd, singing like nightingales.

20 That is the bad news. The good news is that we Americans are governed under a unique Constitution, which allows us to write whatever we please without fear of punishment. So the most meaningful aspect of our styles, which is what we choose to write about, is utterly unlimited.

8. FOR REALLY DETAILED ADVICE

21 For a discussion of literary style in a narrower sense, in a more technical sense, I commend to your attention *The Elements of Style,* by William Strunk, Jr., and E. B. White (Macmillan, 1979). E. B. White is, of course, one of the most admirable literary stylists this country has so far produced.

22 You should realize, too, that no one would care how well or badly Mr. White expressed himself, if he did not have perfectly enchanting things to say.

Additional Rhetorical Strategies

Definition (paragraph 1); Cause and Effect (paragraphs 3, 16); Illustration (paragraphs 7, 9, 10, 12, 13, 16).

Examining Words and Meanings

1. What response(s) does this ad hope to elicit? Based on what he has said here, what do you think Vonnegut would list as the chief characteristics of a first-rate style? Be as specific as possible.
2. How would you characterize Vonnegut's diction in this advertisement? Is it formal or informal? Is the language of the ad primarily abstract or concrete? Cite specific words and phrases to support your response.
3. What advice does Vonnegut offer as aids to revision and editing?

Focusing on Structures and Strategies

1. Reread the section of the introduction to this section which focuses on specified process analysis. How thoroughly does Vonnegut follow the model outlined there? Does he use informative process analysis at all?
2. Vonnegut implicitly makes audience a paramount concern for writers. How would you characterize Vonnegut's attitude toward *his* audience? Does he treat them, for example, as though they were ignorant or informed? Point to specific words and phrases to support your answer.
3. Comment on the effectiveness of Vonnegut's use of metaphor here. What are the primary sources of his metaphors? How effectively does he use analogy? Again, be as specific as possible.

4. How does Vonnegut make his subject interesting? How does he make you think of style in new ways?

Suggestions for Further Discussion and Writing

1. The poet Robert Frost once defined style in these terms: "I am not satisfied to let it go with the aphorism that style is the man. The man's ideas would be some element then of the man's style. So would his deeds. But I would narrow the definition. His deeds are his deeds; his ideas are his ideas. His style is the way he carries himself toward his ideas and deeds." How compatible is Frost's definition with the one Vonnegut offers here? Be as specific as possible.
2. Look through the Table of Contents for *Thinking in Writing.* Choose an essay that you particularly enjoyed reading. Review it carefully, this time emphasizing how well the writer's style is consistent with Vonnegut's advice.
3. Think of an activity which you are reasonably confident you do well. Using specified process analysis as your basic structure, write an essay in which you explain to someone less experienced how best to perform this activity. Remember to be, as Vonnegut says, a "sympathetic and patient" teacher, "ever willing to simplify and clarify."

When You Camp Out, Do It Right

Ernest Hemingway

"No matter how good a phrase or a simile a writer may have," wrote Ernest Hemingway (1899–1961) in Death in the Afternoon, *"if he puts it where it is not absolutely necessary and irreplaceable he is spoiling his work for egotism." In his own distinctly terse prose style,*

Hemingway most frequently wrote about men leading dangerous or adventuresome lives—soldiers, bullfighters, hunters, and fishermen. With the publication of The Sun Also Rises *in 1926, Hemingway became the leading public voice of a group of disillusioned postwar expatriates living in Paris that Gertrude Stein named the "lost generation."*

In the following selection, published originally in the Toronto Star *newspaper, Hemingway draws generously on his own experience in the wilderness and provides detailed advice on the process of not only how others might talk about "roughing it in the woods" but also of how they "can be really comfortable in the bush."*

1 Thousands of people will go into the bush this summer to cut the high cost of living. A man who gets his two weeks' salary while he is on vacation should be able to put those two weeks in fishing and camping and be able to save one week's salary clear. He ought to be able to sleep comfortably every night, to eat well every day and to return to the city rested and in good condition.

2 But if he goes into the woods with a frying pan, an ignorance of black flies and mosquitoes, and a great and abiding lack of knowledge about cookery the chances are that his return will be very different. He will come back with enough mosquito bites to make the back of his neck look like a relief map of the Caucasus. His digestion will be wrecked after a valiant battle to assimilate half-cooked or charred grub. And he won't have had a decent night's sleep while he has been gone.

3 He will solemnly raise his right hand and inform you that he has joined the grand army of never-agains. The call of the wild may be all right, but it's a dog's life. He's heard the call of the tame with both ears. Waiter, bring him an order of milk toast.

4 In the first place he overlooked the insects. Black flies, no-see-ums, deer flies, gnats and mosquitoes were instituted by the devil to force people to live in cities where he could get at them better. If it weren't for them everybody would live in the bush and he would be out of work. It was a rather successful invention.

5 But there are lots of dopes that will counteract the pests. The simplest perhaps is oil of citronella. Two bits' worth of this purchased at any pharmacist's will be enough to last for two weeks in the worst fly and mosquito-ridden country.

6 Rub a little on the back of your neck, your forehead and your wrists before you start fishing, and the blacks and skeeters will shun

you. The odor of citronella is not offensive to people. It smells like gun oil. But the bugs do hate it.

7 Oil of pennyroyal and eucalyptol are also much hated by mosquitoes, and with citronella they form the basis for many proprietary preparations. But it is cheaper and better to buy the straight citronella. Put a little on the mosquito netting that covers the front of your pup tent or canoe tent at night, and you won't be bothered.

8 To be really rested and get any benefit out of a vacation a man must get a good night's sleep every night. The first requisite for this is to have plenty of cover. It is twice as cold as you expect it will be in the bush, four nights out of five, and a good plan is to take just double the bedding that you think you will need. An old quilt that you can wrap up in is as warm as two blankets.

9 Nearly all outdoor writers rhapsodize over the browse bed. It is all right for the man who knows how to make one and has plenty of time. But in a succession of one-night camps on a canoe trip all you need is level ground for your tent floor and you will sleep all right if you have plenty of covers under you. Take twice as much cover as you think that you will need, and then put two-thirds of it under you. You will sleep warm and get your rest.

10 When it is clear weather you don't need to pitch your tent if you are only stopping for the night. Drive four stakes at the head of your made-up bed and drape your mosquito bar over that, then you can sleep like a log and laugh at the mosquitoes.

11 Outside of insects and bum sleeping the rock that wrecks most camping trips is cooking. The average tyro's idea of cooking is to fry everything and fry it good and plenty. Now, a frying pan is a most necessary thing to any trip, but you also need the old stew kettle and the folding reflector baker.

12 A pan of fried trout can't be bettered and they don't cost any more than ever. But there is a good and bad way of frying them.

13 The beginner puts his trout and his bacon in and over a brightly burning fire the bacon curls up and dries into a dry tasteless cinder and the trout is burned outside while it is still raw inside. He eats them and it is all right if he is only out for the day and going home to a good meal at night. But if he is going to face more trout and bacon the next morning and other equally well-cooked dishes for the remainder of two weeks he is on the pathway to nervous dyspepsia.

14 The proper way is to cook over coals. Have several cans of Crisco or Cotosuet or one of the vegetable shortenings along that are as good as lard and excellent for all kinds of shortening. Put the bacon

in and when it is about half cooked lay the trout in the hot grease, dipping them in corn meal first. Then put the bacon on top of the trout and it will baste them as it slowly cooks.

15 The coffee can be boiling at the same time and in a smaller skillet pancakes being made that are satisfying the other campers while they are waiting for the trout.

16 With the prepared pancake flours you take a cupful of pancake flour and add a cup of water. Mix the water and flour and as soon as the lumps are out it is ready for cooking. Have the skillet hot and keep it well greased. Drop the batter in and as soon as it is done on one side loosen it in the skillet and flip it over. Apple butter, syrup or cinnamon and sugar go well with the cakes.

17 While the crowd have taken the edge from their appetites with flapjacks the trout have been cooked and they and the bacon are ready to serve. The trout are crisp outside and firm and pink inside and the bacon is well done—but not too done. If there is anything better than that combination the writer has yet to taste it in a lifetime devoted largely and studiously to eating.

18 The stew kettle will cook your dried apricots when they have resumed their predried plumpness after a night of soaking, it will serve to concoct a mulligan in, and it will cook macaroni. When you are not using it, it should be boiling water for the dishes.

19 In the baker, mere man comes into his own, for he can make a pie that to his bush appetite will have it all over the product that mother used to make, like a tent. Men have always believed that there was something mysterious and difficult about making a pie. Here is a great secret. There is nothing to it. We've been kidded for years. Any man of average office intelligence can make at least as good a pie as his wife.

20 All there is to a pie is a cup and a half of flour, one-half teaspoonful of salt, one-half cup of lard and cold water. That will make pie crust that will bring tears of joy into your camping partner's eyes.

21 Mix the salt with the flour, work the lard into the flour, make it up into a good workmanlike dough with cold water. Spread some flour on the back of a box or something flat, and pat the dough around a while. Then roll it out with whatever kind of round bottle you prefer. Put a little more lard on the surface of the sheet of dough and then slosh a little flour on and roll it up and then roll it out again with the bottle.

22 Cut out a piece of the rolled out dough big enough to line a pie

tin. I like the kind with holes in the bottom. Then put in your dried apples that have soaked all night and been sweetened, or your apricots, or your blueberries, and then take another sheet of the dough and drape it gracefully over the top, soldering it down at the edges with your fingers. Cut a couple of slits in the top dough sheet and prick it a few times with a fork in an artistic manner.

23 Put it in the baker with a good slow fire for forty-five minutes and then take it out and if your pals are Frenchmen they will kiss you. The penalty for knowing how to cook is that the others will make you do all the cooking.

24 It is all right to talk about roughing it in the woods. But the real woodsman is the man who can be really comfortable in the bush.

Additional Rhetorical Strategies

Cause and Effect (paragraphs 1, 2, 4).

Examining Words and Meaning

1. What is Hemingway's purpose in writing this essay? Where does he announce that purpose? What relationship does this purpose establish between Hemingway and his readers? Define the kind of response that Hemingway attempts to evoke in the reader and show by what compositional means this attempt is made.
2. In Hemingway's view, what motivation seems to prompt most people's interest in camping? Given what he says in this essay, why do the "thousands of people" who "go into the bush" each summer *not* satisfy their expectations about camping? What might they do to increase that sense of satisfaction?

Focusing on Structures and Strategies

1. Outline each of the processes Hemingway describes in this essay. Describe the priorities that seem to inform the order in which Hemingway presents these processes.

2. To whom is the essay addressed? Whom does Hemingway *not* include among the readers he imagines for his essay? Why are these people excluded? What is the effect of not including some readers?

3. How would you characterize the sound of Hemingway's voice in this essay? Which of the following terms accurately describe the speaker's voice in this essay: tough-minded; strident; impetuous; experienced; worldly? Would some other term be a more accurate characterization of the speaker's relation with his readers? Point to specific words and phrases to verify your response. Does the speaker maintain the same tone throughout the essay? What changes, if any, do you notice in the sound of the speaker's voice as the essay proceeds? If you notice any changes, when and how do these changes occur? With what effect?

4. Characterize the speaker's relationship with his audience. Does he consider himself essentially different from his readers or similar to them? What can you infer about the speaker's view of the audience's knowledge about camping? Does the speaker appear to expect, for example, his readers to be familiar with the information he is providing? Point to the use of specific words and phrases to validate your answer.

Suggestions for Further Discussion and Writing

1. What sentence in this essay best summarizes Hemingway's feelings about camping? How would you describe the structure of that sentence? In what specific ways is that sentence's structure similar to/different from the structure of other sentences in this essay? How does Hemingway use that structure to reinforce the effects of the process he is describing?

2. Write a rough draft of an essay in which you present a specified process analysis of some knowledge (or creative ability) that you have. Use Hemingway's essay as a model of your relationship with your readers, and especially their knowledgeability. Then prepare another rough draft of an essay in which you present the same information to a group of readers who are equally knowledgeable of the subject as you are. Compare and contrast the differences in your word choices and sentence structures in the two drafts.

The Birch-Bark Canoe

John McPhee

Born in 1931, John McPhee, distinguished author of well over a dozen books of non-fiction and scores of magazine articles, was raised and educated in Princeton, New Jersey, where he has now permanently settled. His writing career began in a high-school English course that required three compositions (plus outlines) per week, a regimen which prepared him excellently for the carefully documented "fact pieces"—to use The New Yorker*'s term—he would write and which would create a unique identity for McPhee among contemporary American writers. He currently teaches a writing course ("The Literature of Fact") at Princeton and is a staff writer for* The New Yorker.

John McPhee declared to an interviewer, "A few years ago people looked to factual articles only for information. But now factual characters can live as much on the page as any fictional character. . . . It all starts with seeing that a piece of writing is more than just the delivery of information per se." The "factual" character in the following selection is Henri Vaillancourt, a young man living in New Hampshire who was making birch-bark canoes by hand, in the Indian fashion. McPhee visited Vaillancourt and carefully observed the process of making these canoes. McPhee's report on the process is, in the terms of William Howarth, the editor of The John McPhee Reader, *much like Vaillancourt's canoes, "tight and seamless, lashed together with precise descriptions and fluctuating moods. . . ."*

The origins of this account of the birch-bark canoe might well be traced to McPhee's youth, when he often spent summers at a camp in Vermont called "Keewaydin." According to Howarth, McPhee was fascinated by a "venerable bark canoe" that was suspended from the rafters of the camp's dining hall. The canoe had "grown dusty and brittle from its long years of dry dock. At mealtimes McPhee studied that canoe diligently, and one year he finally determined to rebaptize it afloat. The task required a dark night, fellow conspirators, and liquid fortification. But the old canoe sank dismally, and the party struggled for several predawn hours to return it to the rafters. All went undetected until breakfast, when water dripped from the boat onto the plates of diners below." McPhee's report on Vaillancourt's artistry enabled him to reaffirm his long-standing interest in birch-bark canoes.

1 In the middle of one morning, Vaillancourt left the shop, got into his car, drove two or three miles down the road, and went into the woods to cut a birch. The weather was sharp, and he was wearing a heavy red Hudson's Bay coat. His sandy-brown hair, curling out in back, rested on the collar. He carried a sheathed Hudson's Bay axe and a long wooden wedge and a wooden club (he called it a mallet) of the type seen in cartoons about cave societies. His eyes—they were pale blue, around an aquiline nose over a trapper's mustache—searched the woodlot for a proper tree. It need not be a giant. There were no giants around Greenville anyway. He wanted it for its sapwood, not its bark—for thwarts (also called crosspieces and crossbars) in a future canoe. After walking several hundred feet in from the road, he found a birch about eight inches in diameter, and with the axe he notched it in the direction of a free fall. He removed his coat and carefully set it aside. Beneath it was a blue oxford-cloth button-down shirt, tucked into his blue-jeans. He chopped the tree, and it fell into a young beech. "Jesus Christ!" he said. "It is so frustrating when Nature has you beat." The birch was hung up in the beech. He heaved at it and hauled it until it at last came free.

2 What he wanted of the tree was about six feet of its trunk, which he cut away from the rest. Then he sank the axe into one end of the piece, removed the axe, placed the wedge in the cut, and tapped the wedge with the mallet. He tapped twice more, and the entire log fell apart in two even halves. He said, "You get some birch, it's a bastard to split out, I'll tell you. But, Christ, this is nice. That's good and straight grain. Very often you get them twisted." Satisfied, he shouldered the tools and the wood, went back to the road, and drove home.

3 In the yard, he split the birch again, and he now had four pieces, quarter-round. One of these he cut off to a length of about forty inches. He took that into the shed. He built a fire, and in minutes the room was warm. He sat in his rocking chair and addressed the axe to the quarter-round log—the dark heartwood, the white sapwood. Holding the piece vertically, one end resting on the floor, he cut the heartwood away. He removed the bark and then went rapidly down the sapwood making angled indentations that caused the wood to curve out like petals. He cut them off, and they fell as big chips to the floor. A pile began to grow there as the axe head moved up and down, and what had been by appearance firewood was in a short time

converted to lumber—a two-by-three, knotless board that might almost have been sawn in a mill.

4 He then picked up his crooked knife and held its grip in his upturned right hand, the blade poking out to the left. The blade was bent near its outer end (enabling it to move in grooves and hollows where the straight part could not). Both blade and grip were shaped like nothing I had ever seen. The grip, fashioned for the convenience of a hand closing over it, was bulbous. The blade had no hinge and protruded rigidly—but not straight out. It formed a shallow V with the grip.

5 Vaillancourt held the piece of birch like a violin, sighting along it from his shoulder, and began to carve, bringing the knife upward, toward his chest. Of all the pieces of a canoe, the center thwart is the most complicated in the carving. Looked at from above, it should be broad at the midway point, then taper gradually as it reaches toward the sides of the canoe. Near its ends, it flares out in shoulders that are penetrated by holes, for lashings that will help secure it to the gunwales. The long taper, moreover, is interrupted by two grooved protrusions, where a tumpline can be tied before a portage. The whole upper surface should be flat, but the underside of the thwart rises slightly from the middle outward, then drops again at the ends, the result being that the thwart is thickest in the middle, gradually thinning as it extends outward and thickening again at the gunwales. All of this comes, in the end, to an adroit ratio between strength and weight, not to mention the incidental grace of the thing, each of its features being a mirror image of another. The canoe's central structural element, it is among the first parts set in place. Its long dimension establishes the canoe's width, and therefore many of the essentials of the canoe's design. In portage, nearly all of the weight of the canoe bears upon it.

6 So to me the making of a center thwart seemed a job for a jigsaw, a band saw, a set of chisels, a hammer, a block plane, a grooving plane, calipers, templates, and—most of all—mechanical drawings. One would have thought that anyone assertive enough to try it with a knife alone would at least begin slowly, moving into the wood with caution. Vaillancourt, to the contrary, tore his way in. He brought the knife toward him with such strong, fast, heavy strokes that long splinters flew off the board. "Birch is good stuff to work with," he said. "It's almost as easy to work as cedar. This feels like a hot knife going through butter. I used to use a drawknife. That God-damned thing. You've got to use a vise to hold the work. With

the crooked knife, I can work in the woods if I want. I saw an Indian on TV in Canada using one. I got one, and I worked and worked with it to get the knack. Now it almost feels as if it's part of me. If anybody ever comes out with a tool that will rival a crooked knife, I'd like to hear about it." He sighted along the wood, turned it over, and began whipping splinters off the other side. He said that steel tools had come with the white man, of course, and that most people seemed to imagine that Indian workmanship had improved with steel tools. "But I doubt it," he continued. "With bone and stone tools, it just took longer. The early Indians relied more on abrasion. With the exception of the center thwart, there is no fancy carving in a canoe. It's all flatwork. In fact, I'm doing experiments with bone tools." He stopped carving, reached to a shelf, and picked up a bone awl. "Make two holes with a bone awl in a piece of cedar, take out the wood between the holes with a bone chisel, and you have a mortise for a thwart to fit into." He reached for a piece of cedar (wood debris was all over the shop), made two holes, picked up a wooden mallet and a bone chisel, and made a mortise in the cedar. Then he picked up the long, curving incisor of a beaver. "I made a knife last winter out of a beaver's tooth," he said. "The original crooked knife was made out of a beaver's tooth." He sat down and continued to carve. The strokes were lighter now as he studied the wood, carved a bit, studied the wood, and carved some more. The piece was beginning to look roughly like a thwart, and the gentler motions of the knife were yielding thin, curling shavings that settled down on the bed of chips and splinters around his feet.

7 "Where the crooked knife was, the bark canoe was," he said. "People from Maine recognize the crooked knife. People from New Hampshire do not. All they knew was the drawknife. The God-damned drawknife—what a bummer."

8 The bark canoe was also where the big white birches were, and that excluded a good part of New Hampshire, including Greenville. Vaillancourt goes north to find his bark. The range of the tree—*Betula papyrifera,* variously called the white birch, the silver birch, the paper birch, the canoe birch—forms a swath more than a thousand miles wide (more or less from New York City to Hudson Bay) and reaches westward and northwestward to the Pacific. Far in from the boundaries of this enormous area, though, the trees are unlikely and always have been unlikely to grow large enough for the building of good canoes, and this exclusion includes most of the West, and even the Middle West. The biggest trees and the best of Indian canoes were

in what are now New Brunswick, Nova Scotia, Maine, Quebec, and parts of Ontario. Even within this region, the most accomplished craftsmen were concentrated in the east. Of these, the best were the Malecites. So Henri Vaillancourt builds Malecite canoes. Before all other design factors, he cares most about the artistic appearance of the canoes he builds, and he thinks the best-looking were the canoes of the Malecites. The Malecites lived in New Brunswick and parts of Maine. Vaillancourt builds the Malecite St. John River Canoe and the Malecite St. Lawrence River Canoe. He builds them with modifications, though. Toward the end of the nineteenth century, tribes started copying one another and gave up some of the distinctiveness of their tribal styles, and to varying extents, he said, he has done the same.

9 His carving became even slower now, and he studied the piece carefully before making his moves, but he measured nothing. "There's really no need for feet and inches," he said. "I know more or less what's strong and what isn't. If I want to find the middle of this crosspiece, I can put a piece of bark across it from end to end, and then fold it in half to find the center." He had measured the length—thirty-five inches—and had cut to it exactly. In the spring, when the time came to make the gunwales, he would measure them as well. But that is all he would measure in the entire canoe. According to the prescript passed on by Adney and Chapelle, the center thwart he was working on should taper

> slightly in thickness each way from its center to within 5 inches of the shoulders, which are 30 inches apart. The thickness at a point 5 inches from the shoulder is ¾ inch; from there the taper is quick to the shoulder, which is 5⁄16 inch thick, with a drop to ¼ inch in the tenon. The width, 3 inches at the center, decreases in a graceful curve to within 5 inches of the shoulder, where it is 2 inches, then increases to about 3 inches at the shoulder. The width of the tenon is, of course, 2 inches, to fit the mortise hole in the gunwale.

10 Yet the only instruments Vaillancourt was using to meet these specifications were his eyes.

11 He finished off the tumpline grooves. The thwart appeared to be perfect, but he picked up a piece of broken glass and scraped it gently all over. Fine excelsior came away, and the surface became shiningly smooth. It was noon. He had cut the birch in the woods at

half past nine. Now he held the thwart in his hand, turning it this way and that. It was a lovely thing in itself, I thought, for it had so many blendings of symmetry. He said he could have done it in an hour if he had not been talking so much. And he was glad the tree in the woods had turned into this thwart instead of "all the chintzy two-bit things they make out of birch—clothespins, dowels, toothpicks, Popsicle sticks." As he worked, he had from time to time scooped up handfuls of chips and shavings and fed them into the stove. Even so, the pile was still high around him, and he appeared to be sitting in a cone of snow.

12 He soon added more to the pile. From the rafters he took down a piece of cedar and, with the knife, sent great strips of it flying to the floor. He was now making a stempiece, the canoe part that establishes the profile of the bow or the stern. "Sometimes, when there are, you know, contortions in the grain, you can get into a real rat's nest," he said. "Around a knot, there will be waves in the grain. You cut to the knot from one side, then the other, to get a straight edge. At times like that, I'm tempted just to throw the thing out."

13 The wood he was working now, though, was clear and without complications, and after a short while, in which most of it went to the floor, he had made something that looked very much like a yardstick—albeit a heavy one—a half inch thick. Its corners were all sharp, and it seemed to have been machine-planed. Then he pressed the blade of the crooked knife into one end of the stick and kept pressing just hard enough to split the stick down fifty percent of its length. He pressed the knife into the end again, near the first cut, and made another split, also stopping halfway. Again and again he split the wood, going far beyond the moment when I, watching him, thought that further splitting would be impossible, would ruin the whole. He split the board thirty-one times—into laminations each a half inch wide and a sixteenth of an inch thick. And all the laminations stopped in the middle, still attached there; from there on, the wood remained solid. "You split cedar parallel to the bark," he commented. "Hickory you can split both ways. There are very few woods you can do that with."

14 He plunged the laminated end of the piece into a bucket of water and left it there for a while, and then he built up the fire with scraps from the floor. In a coffee can he brought water to a boil. He poured it slowly over the laminations, bathing them, bathing them again. Then he lifted the steaming cedar in two hands and bent it.

The laminations slid upon one another and formed a curve. He pondered the curve. It was not enough of a curve, he decided. So he bent the piece a little more. "There's an awful lot of it that's just whim," he said. "You vary the stempiece by whim." He liked what he saw now, so he reached for a strip of basswood bark, tightly wound it around the curve in the cedar, and tied it off. The basswood bark was not temporary. It would stay there, and go into the canoe. Bow or stern, the straight and solid part of the stempiece would run downward from the tip, then the laminated curve would sweep inward, establishing the character of the end—and thus, in large part, of the canoe itself.

15 The canoe-end profile was the principal feature that distinguished the styles of the tribes. The Ojibway Long-Nose Canoe, for example, had in its bow (and stern) an outreaching curve of considerable tumblehome (an arc—like a parenthesis—that turns more than ninety degrees and begins to come back on itself). The end profiles of the Algonquin Hunter's Canoe were straight and almost vertical, with a small-radius ninety-degree curve at the waterline. The departure from the vertical was inward, toward the paddler. The end profiles of certain Malecite canoes were similar, but the departure from vertical was outward. Other Malecite canoes had long-radius, "compass sweep" bows and sterns.

16 I mentioned to Vaillancourt that, before and during college years, I had spent a lot of time around a place in Vermont that still specializes in sending out canoe trips, and a birch-bark canoe hangs in the dining hall there.

17 "Near Salisbury," he said. "Lake Dunmore—am I right?" He took down a worn, filled notebook and began to whip the pages. "Let's see. Yeah. Here. Keewaydin. Is that it?"

18 That was it. He had not been there, but he would stop by someday. He hoped to see every bark canoe in existence. There were, for example, sixteen bark canoes in Haliburton, Ontario; one in Upper Canada Village, near Morrisburg, Ontario; a couple at Old Jesuit House, in Sillery, Quebec. In his notebook he had the names and addresses of museums, historical societies, and individuals from Maine to Minnesota, Nova Scotia to Alberta, and as far south as Virginia. Peter Paul, a Malecite in Woodstock, New Brunswick, had one. Vaillancourt had been to see him. The most skillfully built birch-bark canoe he had ever seen was made in Old Town, Maine, and was signed "Louis P. Sock." "I've seen only two or three canoes that were near perfect," he said. "But I've never seen a bark canoe

that wasn't graceful. I've never seen an Eastern Cree canoe or a Montagnais. Most of the canoes I've seen did not have a definite tribal style. There's a bark canoe on Prince Edward Island. A sign says it's a Micmac canoe. It isn't."

19 I told him I'd long ago been told that the bark canoe at Keewaydin was an Iroquois.

20 He said he doubted that very much, because the Iroquois, except in early times, had had limited access to good birch, and had made their canoes—when they made canoes at all—out of elm or hickory bark. Various tribes had also used the bark of the spruce, the basswood, the chestnut. But all were crude compared to birch. If they wanted to get across a river, they might—in one day—build an elm-bark canoe, and then forget it, leave it in the woods. "You couldn't, by any stretch of the imagination, compare an elm-bark or a hickory-bark canoe to a birch canoe," he said. "Barks other than birch bark will absorb water the way wood will. Canoes made from them—even well made—got waterlogged and heavy. Most were just, you know, rough shells. Good for nothing, like automobiles. Automobiles last, you know, five or six years. A birch-bark canoe lasted the Indians ten."

21 I asked him how much experience he had had by now in more modern canoes. He said he had been in an aluminum canoe twice and in wood-and-canvas canoes only a few times in his life. Otherwise, he had never paddled anything but a birch-bark canoe. He did not paddle much around home, he said, because when he went canoeing he wanted to go to Maine.

22 "Where in Maine?"

23 "Oh, up north of Moosehead Lake. The Penobscot River. Chesuncook Lake. Caucomgomoc Lake. It's not just to get out in the canoe—it's to get out and see wildlife. A moose, you know, thirty feet away. Next time I go, I'm going down the Penobscot and on to the Allagash lakes."

24 I said, "Next time you go, I'd like to go with you."

25 He said, "Bring your own food."

26 I had been yearning to make a trip into that region for what was now most of my life. Keewaydin had run trips there, but one circumstance or another had always prevented me from going. Just the thought of making a journey there in a birch-bark canoe was enough to make me sway like a drunk. I thought of little else through the winter and the spring.

Additional Rhetorical Strategies

Narration (throughout); Description (paragraphs 1, 5, 6, 16); Cause and Effect (paragraphs 7, 9, 24).

Examining Words and Meaning

1. What is McPhee's purpose in providing such a detailed description of the making of a birch-bark canoe? What response is he trying to evoke from his readers—toward the object being made? toward the maker of that object? What other, perhaps larger, purpose seems to be implied in McPhee's account of the making of a birch-bark canoe?
2. Consider McPhee's use of such technical terms as "thwarts" (paragraph 1) and "*Betula papyrifera*" (paragraph 8). Locate other examples of such technical terms, and especially those associated with building canoes. What effect does McPhee create in introducing such terms? What purpose do they serve?

Focusing on Structures and Strategies

1. What do you sense is the relationship between the narrator and Vaillancourt? Is it, for example, intimate? friendly? respectful? distant? What has McPhee done as a writer to create this impression?
2. What is your impression of Vaillancourt? What details does McPhee use to give his readers a sense of Vaillancourt's character? Consider, for example, the way in which Vaillancourt splits the birch. Consider, too, the way in which he responds to the narrator's questions.
3. How would this selection be different had McPhee chosen not to include dialogue? What does the dialogue add to his account? What does the use of dialogue suggest to you about McPhee's purpose in writing about building a birch-bark canoe?
4. Describe McPhee's use of figurative language in this selection. What is his primary source for creating his metaphors and similes? Explain how McPhee uses figurative language to reinforce—or to contrast—the overall effect he is trying to create.

Suggestions for Further Discussion and Writing

1. Think back to the last time you witnessed someone engaged in a process with which you were unfamiliar. What details of that process might you focus on in order to give your readers a sense of not only how that process worked but also how you felt as you watched this person perform his/her work with great skill? Choose one such process and write an essay in which you recount those processes—of both how something is made and how you reacted to the experience of watching it be made. If possible, use dialogue.
2. Process analysis is frequently thought of as a functional—and noncreative—form of writing. Write a specified process analysis in which you describe any process in creative terms, attempting to embody a personal spirit or philosophy in the activity, as Vaillancourt does in creating the birch-bark canoe. The process you describe may be anything you choose—from putting on makeup to preparing a violin concerto for public performance.

The Hibernation of the Woodchuck

Alan Devoe

From about the middle of September through the middle of March the woodchuck hibernates, withdrawing from a winter world that cannot afford it a means of survival. Tracing the stages of that remarkable process, naturalist Alan Devoe (1909–1955) takes the reader through the hibernation's gradual beginnings, into its half-year holding pattern (what Robert Frost called its "long sleep"), and on to the animal's rather abrupt awakening. The following passage is taken from Devoe's study of animal behavior, Lives Around Us *(1942).*

1 The woodchuck's hibernation usually starts about the middle of September. For weeks he has been foraging with increased appetite among the clover blossoms and has grown heavy and slow-moving. Now, with the coming of mid-September, apples and corn and yarrow tops have become less plentiful, and the nights are cool. The

woodchuck moves with slower gait, and emerges less and less frequently for feeding trips. Layers of fat have accumulated around his chest and shoulders, and there is thick fat in the axils of his legs. He has extended his summer burrow to a length of nearly thirty feet, and has fashioned a deep nest-chamber at the end of it, far below the level of the frost. He has carried in, usually, a little hay. He is ready for the Long Sleep.

2 When the temperature of the September days falls below 50 degrees or so, the woodchuck becomes too drowsy to come forth from his burrow in the chilly dusk to forage. He remains in the deep nest-chamber, lethargic, hardly moving. Gradually, with the passing of hours or days, his coarse-furred body curls into a semicircle, like a foetus, nose-tip touching tail. The small legs are tucked in, the handlike clawed forefeet folded. The woodchuck has become a compact ball. Presently the temperature of his body begins to fall.

3 In normal life the woodchuck's temperature, though fluctuant, averages about 97 degrees. Now, as he lies tight-curled in a ball with the winter sleep stealing over him, his body heat drops ten degrees, twenty degrees, thirty. Finally, by the time the snow is on the ground and the woodchuck's winter dormancy has become complete, his temperature is only 38 or 40. With the falling of the body heat there is a slowing of his heartbeat and his respiration. In normal life he breathes thirty or forty times each minute; when he is excited, as many as a hundred times. Now he breathes slow and slower—ten times a minute, five times a minute, once a minute, and at last only ten or twelve times in an hour. His heartbeat is a twentieth of normal. He has entered fully into the oblivion of hibernation.

4 The Long Sleep lasts, on an average, about six months. For half a year the woodchuck remains unmoving, hardly breathing. His pituitary gland is inactive; his blood is so sluggishly circulated that there is an unequal distribution in the chilled body; his sensory awareness has wholly ceased. It is almost true to say that he has altered from a warm-blooded to a cold-blooded animal.

5 Then, in the middle of March, he wakes. The waking is not a slow and gradual thing, as was the drifting into sleep, but takes place quickly, often in an hour. The body temperature ascends to normal, or rather higher for a while; glandular functions instantly resume: the respiration quickens and steadies at a normal rate. The woodchuck has become himself again, save only that he is a little thinner, and is ready at once to fare forth into the pale spring sunlight and look for grass and berries.

6 Such is the performance each fall and winter, with varying detail, of bats and worms and bears, and a hundred other kinds of creatures. It is a marvel less spectacular than the migration flight of hummingbirds or the flash of shooting stars, but it is not much less remarkable.

Additional Rhetorical Strategy

Cause and Effect (paragraphs 2–5).

Examining Words and Meaning

1. What reasons does Devoe give for the woodchuck's changing behavior? What, in other words, is the physiological process being described here?
2. Look up the following words in a dictionary, if necessary: foraging (paragraph 1); yarrow (paragraph 1); axils (paragraph 1); lethargic (paragraph 2); foetus (paragraph 2); fluctuant (paragraph 3); dormancy (paragraph 3).

Focusing on Structures and Strategies

1. At what point in Devoe's account of the hibernation cycle does process analysis begin? In what way does he include information about what has been happening to the woodchuck up to this point?
2. Consider the description of the fall of the woodchuck's body temperature (paragraph 3). Why doesn't Devoe simply say the body temperature falls from 97 to 38? What words does he use to signal the transitions in this process?
3. What is the topic of each paragraph here? Why does Devoe, in other words, start each paragraph where he does? How does he move from one paragraph to another?

Suggestion for Further Discussion and Writing

1. Following Devoe's lead, write a short process analysis of the operations of some natural law. Some possibilities include the life cycle of a butterfly; the maturing of a dog; the yearly life cycle of a tree or plant; the decaying of an orange; the sprouting of a seed. Pay close attention to paragraphing, and include transitional words (*now, then, finally,* and *so forth*) to make the stages of the process clear to your reader.

The Grey Beginnings

Rachel Carson

In all of her books, American writer and marine biologist Rachel Carson (1907–1964) brought a strong poetic sensibility to bear upon scientific observations. In the following passage from The Sea Around Us *(1951), she takes the reader from the beginning of the world and the forming of the seas to the quickening of the first single-celled speck of life and on to man's dominion over the land. Her evocative description traces one of the possible evolutionary lines that we and our world may have traveled in order to reach our present condition.*

And the earth was without form, and void; and darkness was upon the face of the deep.

Genesis

1 Beginnings are apt to be shadowy, and so it is with the beginnings of that great mother of life the sea. Many people have debated how and when the earth got its ocean, and it is not surprising that their explanations do not always agree. For the plain and inescapable truth is that no one was there to see, and in the absence of eyewitness accounts there is bound to be a certain amount of disagreement. So if I tell here the story of how the young planet Earth acquired an ocean, it must be a story pieced together from many sources and containing whole chapters the details of which we can only imagine.

The story is founded on the testimony of the earth's most ancient rocks, which were young when the earth was young; on other evidence written on the face of the earth's satellite, the moon; and on hints contained in the history of the sun and the whole universe of star-filled space. For although no man was there to witness this cosmic birth, the stars and the moon and the rocks were there, and, indeed, had much to do with the fact that there is an ocean.

2 The events of which I write must have occurred somewhat more than 2 billion years ago. As nearly as science can tell that is the approximate age of the earth, and the ocean must be very nearly as old. It is possible now to discover the age of the rocks that compose the crust of the earth by measuring the rate of decay of the radioactive materials they contain. The oldest rocks found anywhere on earth—in Manitoba—are about 2.3 billion years old. Allowing 100 million years or so for the cooling of the earth's materials to form a rocky crust, we arrive at the supposition that the tempestuous and violent events connected with our planet's birth occurred nearly 2½ billion years ago. But this is only a minimum estimate, for rocks indicating an even greater age may be found at any time.

3 The new earth, freshly torn from its parent sun, was a ball of whirling gases, intensely hot, rushing through the black spaces of the universe on a path and at a speed controlled by immense forces. Gradually the ball of flaming gases cooled. The gases began to liquefy, and Earth became a molten mass. The materials of this mass eventually became sorted out in a definite pattern: the heaviest in the center, the less heavy surrounding them, and the least heavy forming the outer rim. This is the pattern which persists today—a central sphere of molten iron, very nearly as hot as it was 2 billion years ago, an intermediate sphere of semiplastic basalt, and a hard outer shell, relatively quite thin and composed of solid basalt and granite.

4 The outer shell of the young earth must have been a good many millions of years changing from the liquid to the solid state, and it is believed that, before this change was completed, an event of the greatest importance took place—the formation of the moon. The next time you stand on a beach at night, watching the moon's bright path across the water, and conscious of the moon-drawn tides, remember that the moon itself may have been born of a great tidal wave of earthly substance, torn off into space. And remember that if the moon was formed in this fashion, the event may have had much to do with shaping the ocean basins and the continents as we know them.

5 There were tides in the new earth, long before there was an ocean. In response to the pull of the sun the molten liquids of the earth's whole surface rose in tides that rolled unhindered around the globe and only gradually slackened and diminished as the earthly shell cooled, congealed, and hardened. Those who believe that the moon is a child of earth say that during an early stage of the earth's development something happened that caused this rolling, viscid tide to gather speed and momentum and to rise to unimaginable heights. Apparently the force that created these greatest tides the earth has ever known was the force of resonance, for at this time the period of the solar tides had come to approach, then equal, the period of the free oscillation of the liquid earth. And so every sun tide was given increased momentum by the push of the earth's oscillation, and each of the twice-daily tides was larger than the one before it. Physicists have calculated that, after 500 years of such monstrous, steadily increasing tides, those on the side toward the sun became too high for stability, and a great wave was torn away and hurled into space. But immediately, of course, the newly created satellite became subject to physical laws that sent it spinning in an orbit of its own about the earth. This is what we call the moon.

6 There are reasons for believing that this event took place after the earth's crust had become slightly hardened, instead of during its partly liquid state. There is to this day a great scar on the surface of the globe. This scar or depression holds the Pacific Ocean. According to some geophysicists, the floor of the Pacific is composed of basalt, the substance of the earth's middle layer, while all other oceans are floored with a thin layer of granite, which makes up most of the earth's outer layer. We immediately wonder what became of the Pacific's granite covering and the most convenient assumption is that it was torn away when the moon was formed. There is supporting evidence. The mean density of the moon is much less than that of the earth (3.3 compared with 5.5), suggesting that the moon took away none of the earth's heavy iron core, but that it is composed only of the granite and some of the basalt of the outer layers.

7 The birth of the moon probably helped shape other regions of the world ocean besides the Pacific. When part of the crust was torn away, strains must have been set up in the remaining granite envelope. Perhaps the granite mass cracked open on the side opposite the moon scar. Perhaps, as the earth spun on its axis and rushed on its orbit through space, the cracks widened and the masses of granite began to drift apart, moving over a tarry, slowly hardening layer of

basalt. Gradually the outer portions of the basalt layer became solid and the wandering continents came to rest, frozen into place with oceans between them. In spite of theories to the contrary, the weight of geologic evidence seems to be that the locations of the major ocean basins and the major continental land masses are today much the same as they have been since a very early period of the earth's history.

8 But this is to anticipate the story, for when the moon was born there was no ocean. The gradually cooling earth was enveloped in heavy layers of cloud, which contained much of the water of the new planet. For a long time its surface was so hot that no moisture could fall without immediately being reconverted to steam. This dense, perpetually renewed cloud covering must have been thick enough that no rays of sunlight could penetrate it. And so the rough outlines of the continents and the empty ocean basins were sculptured out of the surface of the earth in darkness, in a Stygian world of heated rock and swirling clouds and gloom.

9 As soon as the earth's crust cooled enough, the rains began to fall. Never have there been such rains since that time. They fell continuously, day and night, days passing into months, into years, into centuries. They poured into the waiting ocean basins, or, falling upon the continental masses, drained away to become sea.

10 That primeval ocean, growing in bulk as the rains slowly filled its basins, must have been only faintly salt. But the falling rains were the symbol of the dissolution of the continents. From the moment the rains began to fall, the lands began to be worn away and carried to the sea. It is an endless, inexorable process that has never stopped—the dissolving of the rocks, the leaching out of their contained minerals, the carrying of the rock fragments and dissolved minerals to the ocean. And over the eons of time, the sea has grown ever more bitter with the salt of the continents.

11 In what manner the sea produced the mysterious and wonderful stuff called protoplasm we cannot say. In its warm, dimly lit waters the unknown conditions of temperature and pressure and saltiness must have been the critical ones for the creation of life from nonlife. At any rate they produced the result that neither the alchemists with their crucibles nor modern scientists in their laboratories have been able to achieve.

12 Before the first living cell was created, there may have been many trials and failures. It seems probable that, within the warm saltiness of the primeval sea, certain organic substances were fash-

ioned from carbon dioxide, sulphur, nitrogen, phosphorus, potassium, and calcium. Perhaps these were transition steps from which the complex molecules of protoplasm arose—molecules that somehow acquired the ability to reproduce themselves and begin the endless stream of life. But at present no one is wise enough to be sure.

13 Those first living things may have been simple microorganisms rather like some of the bacteria we know today—mysterious borderline forms that were not quite plants, not quite animals, barely over the intangible line that separates the non-living from the living. It is doubtful that this first life possessed the substance chlorophyll, with which plants in sunlight transform lifeless chemicals into the living stuff of their tissues. Little sunshine could enter their dim world, penetrating the cloud banks from which fell the endless rains. Probably the sea's first children lived on the organic substances then present in the ocean waters, or, like the iron and sulphur bacteria that exist today, lived directly on inorganic food.

14 All the while the cloud cover was thinning, the darkness of the nights alternated with palely illumined days, and finally the sun for the first time shone through upon the sea. By this time some of the living things that floated in the sea must have developed the magic of chlorophyll. Now they were able to take the carbon dioxide of the air and the water of the sea and of these elements, in sunlight, build the organic substances they needed. So the first true plants came into being.

15 Another group of organisms, lacking the chlorophyll but needing organic food, found they could make a way of life for themselves by devouring the plants. So the first animals arose, and from that day to this, every animal in the world has followed the habit it learned in the ancient seas and depends, directly or through complex food chains, on the plants for food and life.

16 As the years passed, and the centuries, and the millions of years, the stream of life grew more and more complex. From simple, one-celled creatures, others that were aggregations of specialized cells arose, and then creatures with organs for feeding, digesting, breathing, reproducing. Sponges grew on the rocky bottom of the sea's edge and coral animals built their habitations in warm, clear waters. Jellyfish swam and drifted in the sea. Worms evolved, and starfish, and hard-shelled creatures with many-jointed legs, the arthropods. The plants, too, progressed, from the microscopic algae to branched and curiously fruiting seaweeds that swayed with the tides and were plucked from the coastal rocks by the surf and cast adrift.

17 During all this time the continents had no life. There was little to induce living things to come ashore, forsaking their all-providing, all-embracing mother sea. The lands must have been bleak and hostile beyond the power of words to describe. Imagine a whole continent of naked rock, across which no covering mantle of green had been drawn—a continent without soil, for there were no land plants to aid in its formation and bind it to the rocks with their roots. Imagine a land of stone, a silent land, except for the sound of the rains and winds that swept across it. For there was no living voice, and no living thing moved over the surface of the rocks.

18 Meanwhile, the gradual cooling of the planet, which had first given the earth its hard granite crust, was progressing into its deeper layers; and as the interior slowly cooled and contracted, it drew away from the outer shell. This shell, accommodating itself to the shrinking sphere within it, fell into folds and wrinkles—the earth's first mountain ranges.

19 Geologists tell us that there must have been at least two periods of mountain building (often called "revolutions") in that dim period, so long ago that the rocks have no record of it, so long ago that the mountains themselves have long since been worn away. Then there came a third great period of upheaval and readjustment of the earth's crust, about a billion years ago, but of all its majestic mountains the only reminders today are the Laurentian hills of eastern Canada, and a great shield of granite over the flat country around Hudson Bay.

20 The epochs of mountain building only served to speed up the processes of erosion by which the continents were worn down and their crumbling rock and contained minerals returned to the sea. The uplifted masses of the mountains were prey to the bitter cold of the upper atmosphere and under the attacks of frost and snow and ice the rocks cracked and crumbled away. The rains beat with greater violence upon the slopes of the hills and carried away the substance of the mountains in torrential streams. There was still no plant covering to modify and resist the power of the rains.

21 And in the sea, life continued to evolve. The earliest forms have left no fossils by which we can identify them. Probably they were soft-bodied, with no hard parts that could be preserved. Then, too, the rock layers formed in those early days have since been so altered by enormous heat and pressure, under the foldings of the earth's crust, that any fossils they might have contained would have been destroyed.

22 For the past 500 million years, however, the rocks have pre-

served the fossil record. By the dawn of the Cambrian period, when the history of living things was first inscribed on rock pages, life in the sea had progressed so far that all the main groups of backboneless or invertebrate animals had been developed. But there were no animals with backbones, no insects or spiders, and still no plant or animal had been evolved that was capable of venturing onto the forbidding land. So for more than three-fourths of geologic time the continents were desolate and uninhabited, while the sea prepared the life that was later to invade them and make them habitable. Meanwhile, with violent tremblings of the earth and with the fire and smoke of roaring volcanoes, mountains rose and wore away, glaciers moved to and fro over the earth, and the sea crept over the continents and again receded.

23 It was not until Silurian time, some 350 million years ago, that the first pioneer of land life crept out on the shore. It was an arthropod, one of the great tribe that later produced crabs and lobsters and insects. It must have been something like a modern scorpion, but, unlike some of its descendants, it never wholly severed the ties that united it to the sea. It lived a strange life, half-terrestrial, half-aquatic, something like that of the ghost crabs that speed along the beaches today, now and then dashing into the surf to moisten their gills.

24 Fish, tapered of body and stream-molded by the press of running waters, were evolving in Silurian rivers. In times of drought, in the drying pools and lagoons, the shortage of oxygen forced them to develop swim bladders for the storage of air. One form that possessed an air-breathing lung was able to survive the dry period by burying itself in mud, leaving a passage to the surface through which it breathed.

25 It is very doubtful that the animals alone would have succeeded in colonizing the land, for only the plants had the power to bring about the first amelioration of its harsh conditions. They helped make soil of the crumbling rocks, they held back the soil from the rains that would have swept it away, and little by little they softened and subdued the bare rock, the lifeless desert. We know very little about the first land plants, but they must have been closely related to some of the larger seaweeds that had learned to live in the coastal shallows, developing strengthened stems and grasping, rootlike holdfasts to resist the drag and pull of the waves. Perhaps it was in some coastal lowlands, periodically drained and flooded, that some such plants found it possible to survive, though separated from the sea. This also seems to have taken place in the Silurian period.

26 The mountains that had been thrown up by the Laurentian

revolution gradually wore away, and as the sediments were washed from their summits and deposited on the lowlands, great areas of the continents sank under the load. The seas crept out of their basins and spread over the lands. Life fared well and was exceedingly abundant in those shallow, sunlit seas. But with the later retreat of the ocean water into the deeper basins, many creatures must have been left stranded in shallow, landlocked bays. Some of these animals found means to survive on land. The lakes, the shores of the rivers, and the coastal swamps of those days were the testing grounds in which plants and animals either became adapted to the new conditions or perished.

27 As the lands rose and the seas receded, a strange fishlike creature emerged on the land, and over the thousands of years its fins became legs, and instead of gills it developed lungs. In the Devonian sandstone this first amphibian left its footprint.

28 On land and sea the stream of life poured on. New forms evolved; some old ones declined and disappeared. On land the mosses and the ferns and the seed plants developed. The reptiles for a time dominated the earth, gigantic, grotesque, and terrifying. Birds learned to live and move in the ocean of air. The first small mammals lurked inconspicuously in hidden crannies of the earth as though in fear of the reptiles.

29 When they went ashore the animals that took up a land life carried with them a part of the sea in their bodies, a heritage which they passed on to their children and which even today links each land animal with its origin in the ancient sea. Fish, amphibian, and reptile, warm-blooded bird and mammal—each of us carries in our veins a salty stream in which the elements sodium, potassium, and calcium are combined in almost the same proportions as in sea water. This is our inheritance from the day untold millions of years ago, when a remote ancestor, having progressed from the one-celled to the many-celled stage, first developed a circulatory system in which the fluid was merely the water of the sea. In the same way, our lime-hardened skeletons are a heritage from the calcium-rich ocean of Cambrian time. Even the protoplasm that streams within each cell of our bodies has the chemical structure impressed upon all living matter when the first simple creatures were brought forth in the ancient sea. And as life itself began in the sea, so each of us begins his individual life in a miniature ocean within his mother's womb, and in the stages of his embryonic development repeats the steps by which his race evolved, from gill-breathing inhabitants of a water world to creatures able to live on land.

30 Some of the land animals later returned to the ocean. After perhaps 50 million years of land life, a number of reptiles entered the sea about 170 million years ago, in the Triassic period. They were huge and formidable creatures. Some had oarlike limbs by which they rowed through the water; some were web-footed, with long, serpentine necks. These grotesque monsters disappeared millions of years ago, but we remember them when we come upon a large sea turtle swimming many miles at sea, its barnacle-encrusted shell eloquent of its marine life. Much later, perhaps no more than 50 million years ago, some of the mammals, too, abandoned a land life for the ocean. Their descendants are the sea lions, seals, sea elephants, and whales of today.

31 Among the land mammals there was a race of creatures that took to an arboreal existence. Their hands underwent remarkable development, becoming skilled in manipulating and examining objects, and along with this skill came a superior brain power that compensated for what these comparatively small mammals lacked in strength. At last, perhaps somewhere in the vast interior of Asia, they descended from the trees and became again terrestrial. The past million years have seen their transformation into beings with the body and brain of man.

32 Eventually man, too, found his way back to the sea. Standing on its shores, he must have looked out upon it with wonder and curiosity, compounded with an unconscious recognition of his lineage. He could not physically re-enter the ocean as the seals and whales had done. But over the centuries, with all the skill and ingenuity and reasoning powers of his mind, he has sought to explore and investigate even its most remote parts, so that he might re-enter it mentally and imaginatively.

33 He built boats to venture out on its surface. Later he found ways to descend to the shallow parts of its floor, carrying with him the air that, as a land mammal long unaccustomed to aquatic life, he needed to breathe. Moving in fascination over the deep sea he could not enter, he found ways to probe its depths, he let down nets to capture its life, he invented mechanical eyes and ears that could re-create for his senses a world long lost, but a world that, in the deepest part of his subconscious mind, he had never wholly forgotten.

34 And yet he has returned to his mother sea only on her own terms. He cannot control or change the ocean as, in his brief tenancy of earth, he has subdued and plundered the continents. In the artifi-

cial world of his cities and towns, he often forgets the true nature of his planet and the long vistas of its history, in which the existence of the race of men has occupied a mere moment of time. The sense of all these things comes to him most clearly in the course of a long ocean voyage, when he watches day after day the receding rim of the horizon, ridged and furrowed by waves; when at night he becomes aware of the earth's rotation as the stars pass overhead; or when, alone in this world of water and sky, he feels the loneliness of his earth in space. And then, as never on land, he knows the truth that his world is a water world, a planet dominated by its covering mantle of ocean, in which the continents are but transient intrusions of land above the surface of the all-encircling sea.

Additional Rhetorical Strategies

Classification (paragraphs 14–16); Illustration (paragraphs 28, 29); Analogy (paragraph 29).

Examining Words and Meaning

1. In what ways, according to Carson, are we still creatures of the sea? What evidence do we carry around with us? How does Carson use this evidence to explain our feelings for the sea?
2. What is the effect of calling the first animal to crawl onto land a "pioneer" (paragraph 23)? What other words in this part of the selection reinforce her metaphor?
3. Check the following words in the dictionary, if necessary: semiplastic (paragraph 3); viscid (paragraph 5); oscillation (paragraph 5); leaching (paragraph 10); aggregations (paragraph 16); amelioration (paragraph 25); arboreal (paragraph 31).

Focusing on Structures and Strategies

1. How does Carson first describe the sea? What does her word choice suggest to you about her attitude toward her subject? To what use

does she put her metaphor later in this chapter, when she discusses the reverence men have for the sea?

2. Review paragraphs 4 through 18. Do the events Carson describes there follow each other in strict chronological sequence, or are some of them simultaneous? What transitional words and phrases does Carson use to clarify the temporal relationships of the events in this section?

Suggestions for Further Discussion and Writing

1. In the thirty-seven years that have elapsed since Carson wrote *The Sea Around Us,* geologists have come around to thinking that the continents and oceans probably *have* moved a great deal. It is possible, then, that Carson's writing may be considered less factually accurate than it seemed when it was published. Does this make it less valuable, or can we consider it, like the Indian creation myth, an interesting narrative despite its inaccuracies?

2. Try doing what Carson does here, but on a smaller scale. Take some everyday development—the growth of a garden, the construction of a building, the maturing of a younger brother or sister—and describe it in an informative process analysis. Be sure to make your subject accessible to someone not familiar with its intricacies.

Cause and Effect

1 Something happens and we want to find out *why.* In many ordinary situations we do not have to look very far to find an answer: the record sounds fuzzy because the phonograph needle is worn down; the parking lot is full because of a rock concert. But understanding why something happens in other situations can be far more complicated: Is the baby crying because he is tired, uncomfortable, or sick? Did we fail to make the interview on time because of heavy traffic or an unconscious desire to miss it? Did the nuclear reactor shut down because of instrument failure or human error? In all of these examples we are dealing with a phenomenon that is at the heart of much of our empirical knowledge: the relation of cause and effect.

2 Because it seems so basic to human perception and reason, causal explanation is usually thought of as a fairly obvious mental procedure. We believe that every effect must have a cause; that the cause can be discovered by retracing the sequence of events that led to it; that similar causes will produce similar effects. But such beliefs, though they play an influential role in everyday life, have long been discredited in many areas of physics, philosophy, and psychology, where belief in causation is considered, as British philosopher Bertrand Russell put it, "a relic of a bygone era." It would be, of course, wholly impractical to adopt the same attitude toward causation in our daily affairs as physicists adopt in their investigation of subatomic particles, but it is, nevertheless, a good rule of thinking and writing to interpret and construct causal explanations cautiously.

3 When working with causal explanations in our compositions, we may proceed by moving either backward, from effect to cause, or forward, from cause to effect. We observe event or phenomenon *B* and show what caused it; or we observe event or phenomenon *A* and show what effect it will have. Whether we progress from *A* to *B* or from *B* to *A* will depend on our evidence and the kind of case we want to make—for example, do we want to explain or to predict? But whichever direction we decide to go in, it is important to remember that nothing becomes a cause or an effect merely by our calling it one. We must establish solid grounds for a causal sequence. If we can determine no causal explanation for event *B,* we have no valid reason to think of it as an "effect," nor should we think of *A* as a "cause" if we can calculate no possible consequences that would result from it. To call something an effect presupposes the existence of a cause, and vice versa.

4 In our casual thinking we tend to consider mainly single causes and single effects. But seldom are events so simple. When thinking hard about cause-and-effect relationships, we would do best to outline an entire set of causal possibilities (some immediate, some remote, some coexistent with effects, and some merely contributory), all of which are in some way connected with the effect or effects we are examining. Then, once we have systematically assembled a set of possible causes, we may proceed to select and isolate a few of the most significant and examine in detail their relation to the effect(s). The very selection of causes and effects can reveal much about our methods and predispositions. What a drug company, for example, may see as the harmless side-effects of one of its products, a government regulatory agency may find deadly. Whereas one historian would base a causal analysis of the American involvement in Vietnam almost exclusively upon world economic factors, another might lean toward an explanation based upon the power drives of high-level political figures. In fact, cause-and-effect reasoning—whether explicit or implicit, valid or invalid—occurs quite frequently as a strategy in many forms of persuasion—from political propaganda to toothpaste commercials.

5 The complexity of our subject and our purpose, the depth of our information, and the angle of our interpretation will usually determine our method of causal exposition. Suppose we are reporters analyzing the crash of a jetliner. The following four rhetorical patterns will suggest possible ways to organize a cause-and-effect essay.

A Single Cause Leading to a Single Effect. This is quite clearly the easiest pattern to work with, though it is often open to the charge of oversimplification. We determine that the crash was caused by the fracture of a pylon bolt that holds the engine in place. The single-cause-single-effect procedure is commonly used to establish blame: "Who or what caused *X*?" can usually be rephrased as "Who or what is to blame for *X*?" It can be represented thus:

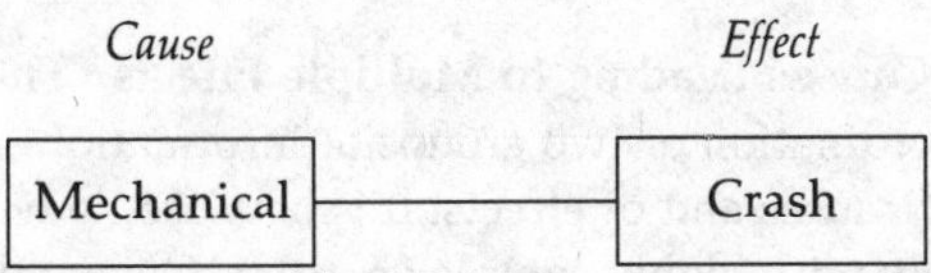

A Single Cause Leading to Multiple Effects. We pinpoint the fractured bolt as being responsible for the crash and then show how the crash was not a single event but a spectrum of interrelated tragedies and losses—all the consequence of a tiny bit of metal. This pattern frequently is used dramatically to show how small events can have enormous consequences. It can be shown figuratively in this way:

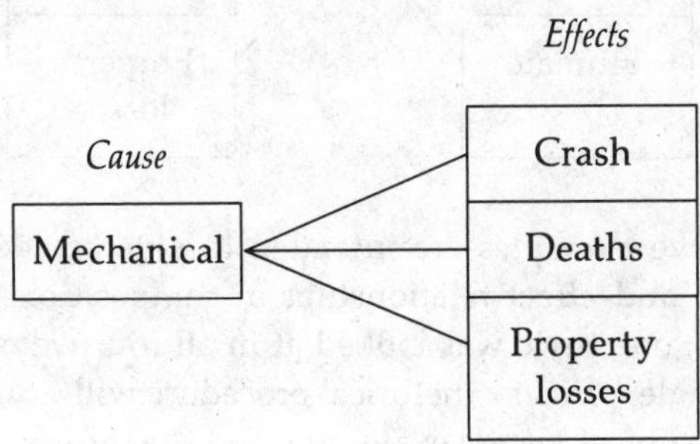

Multiple Causes Leading to a Single Effect. Since we usually perceive effects singly and since most significant effects can be traced to a number of causes, this is perhaps the most common cause-and-effect pattern. We see the crash as the consequence of many interlocking factors: the fractured bolt, unexpected damage to the plane's hydraulic system, inadequate maintenance standards, poor aerodynamic design, an inattentive ground crew, and so on. That pattern of cause and effect would look like this:

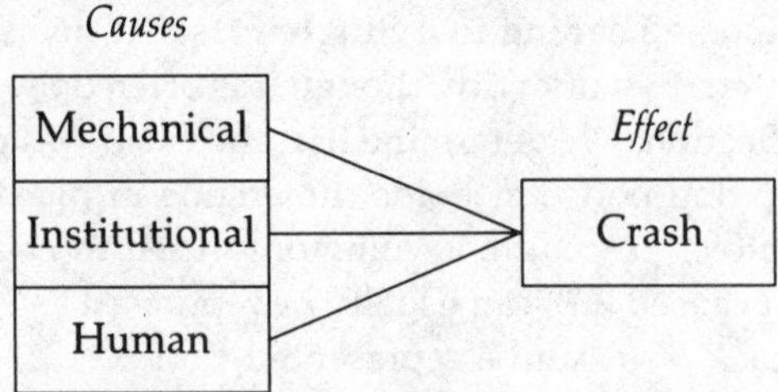

Multiple Causes Leading to Multiple Effects. This pattern demands the coordination of two groups of information—an analytical breakdown of causes and of effects. It is best used when we want to deal judiciously with highly complex matters. We would analyze the crash as a number of separate effects (deaths, property loss, recriminations, disruptions), produced by a number of causes, as in the following representation:

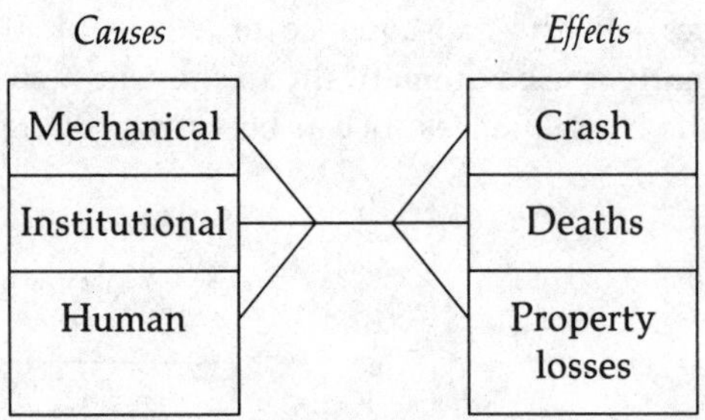

6 The above examples are intended to give an idea of how to manage cause-and-effect relationships in composition. For the sake of illustration, one topic was looked at in all four ways. In practice, however, a single, primary rhetorical procedure will usually be determined by the subject we are examining and the information we have at our disposal. In the case of the plane crash, the most satisfactory explanation would probably result from retracing a single effect back to its multiple causes. But in cases which have more far-reaching or lasting effects, such as wars, cultural movements, or political revolutions, we might do better to examine the subject with respect to multiple causes leading to multiple effects.

7 Cause-and-effect explanations are particularly susceptible to erroneous reasoning. We can easily fall into traps when constructing

causal explanations because of confusions stemming from the similarity of cause-and-effect relationships to other types of relationships.

8 What follows are seven common sources of confusion:

1. *Confusing a cause with an effect:* One of the first things we need to do in a causal analysis is make sure we distinguish between causes and effects—was the cracked steering column the principal cause of the accident or was it simply one of the effects of the crash?

2. *Confusing a cause with an antecedent:* That *A* occurs *before B* is no reason to think *A* causes *B.* A sore throat may precede a fever, but it does not produce the fever. This is one of the most prevalent fallacies (it goes by the name *post hoc, ergo propter hoc*—"after this, therefore because of this") and is often used as the basis for commercial and political propaganda: President *X* is elected, the economy improves, and President *X* promotes himself as the *cause* of that improvement.

3. *Confusing a cause with a necessary condition:* A necessary condition is a condition without which something could not have occurred. It is closely connected to causal sequences, but should not be mistaken for a cause. The jetliner didn't crash *because* it took off, but its having taken off was a necessary condition of the crash. A boy struck by a car while crossing a street was not hit *because* he crossed the street (to think so would be superstitious), but his crossing was a necessary condition for the accident.

4. *Confusing a cause with a sign or symptom:* An ache or pain is not in itself the cause of our illness, but rather a symptom of it; sexual impotence may be a sign of marital problems, not necessarily a cause. Signs and symptoms are often closely associated with causal sequences and need to be examined carefully to make sure we do not mistake a peripheral event for a pivotal one.

5. *Confusing cause with correlation:* Statistics may show that 99 percent of the people who use Sparkle toothpaste have no cavities; but that figure may not signify any causal connection, for those who use Sparkle may rely on any number of dental aids, all of which may be causal factors in helping to eliminate decay. When examining statistical information, we should investigate all the relevant facts surrounding a case or claim. A high degree of correlation between two sets of data (for example, cigarette smoking and the incidence of lung cancer) may strongly suggest a causal relationship, but it alone does not conclusively demonstrate that relationship.

6. *Confusing a cause with the whole of which it is but a part:* Sometimes an important causal factor may be only one element of a larger

aggregate of elements. We may loosely speak of candy (a whole) as causing acne, but to establish precisely a cause-and-effect relationship between the two, we would need to specify which ingredient (which part) of a particular type of candy produces the physiological reaction that gives rise to pimples.

7. *Confusing a cause with a purpose:* A purpose may sometimes be similar to a cause ("Upton Sinclair wrote *The Jungle* to expose the evils of the meat-packing industry"), but not always. We have eyes to see with—that is their purpose—but seeing did not cause us to have eyes. Whenever we are tracing a chain of causes back to a first cause, we need to be clear about our use of *purpose* and *cause.* In general, it is convenient to think of a purpose as connected with the future, a cause as connected with the past.

9 Tightly linked cause-and-effect sequences are not easily established. Causal analysis is one of the toughest and most challenging types of thinking required in composition. In the following selections, we'll see how different writers with different purposes construct causal connections to help explain why things happen (or have happened) in many different areas of study: technology, art, sociology, education, and science.

On Magic in Medicine

Lewis Thomas

"People have always wanted causes that are simple and easy to comprehend," claims Lewis Thomas in this essay from The Medusa and the Snail. *In "On Magic in Medicine," he examines causal explanations and at the same time pokes fun at a few recent "scientific" methods for avoiding illness and living longer. The control of disease, of course, depends seriously on causal explanations, whether the disease has "a single, dominant, central cause" or whether it is "multifactorial." But a preoccupation with simplistic causal explanations can lead to such popular delusions as the list of "Seven Healthy Life Habits" with its emphasis on good breakfasts and regular exercise, an emphasis Lewis Thomas thinks is somewhat misleading.*

For biographical information on Lewis Thomas, see page 109.

1 Medicine has always been under pressure to provide public explanations for the diseases with which it deals, and the formulation of comprehensive, unifying theories has been the most ancient and willing preoccupation of the profession. In the earliest days, hostile spirits needing exorcism were the principal pathogens, and the shaman's duty was simply the development of improved techniques for incantation. Later on, especially in the Western world, the idea that the distribution of body fluids among various organs determined the course of all illnesses took hold, and we were in for centuries of bleeding, cupping, sweating, and purging in efforts to intervene. Early in this century the theory of autointoxication evolved, and a large part of therapy was directed at emptying the large intestine and keeping it empty. Then the global concept of focal infection became popular, accompanied by the linked notion of allergy to the presumed microbial pathogens, and no one knows the resulting toll of extracted teeth, tonsils, gallbladders, and appendixes: the idea of psychosomatic influences on disease emerged in the 1930s and, for a while, seemed to sweep the field.

2 Gradually, one by one, some of our worst diseases have been edited out of such systems by having their causes indisputably identified and dealt with. Tuberculosis was the paradigm. This was the most chronic and inexorably progressive of common human maladies, capable of affecting virtually every organ in the body and obviously influenced by crowding, nutrition, housing, and poverty; theories involving the climate in general, and night air and insufficient sunlight in particular, gave rise to the spa as a therapeutic institution. It was not until the development of today's effective chemotherapy that it became clear to everyone that the disease had a single, dominant, central cause. If you got rid of the tubercle bacillus you were rid of the disease.

3 But that was some time ago, and today the idea that complicated diseases can have single causes is again out of fashion. The microbial infections that can be neatly coped with by antibiotics are regarded as lucky anomalies. The new theory is that most of today's human illnesses, the infections aside, are multifactorial in nature, caused by two great arrays of causative mechanisms: 1) the influence of things in the environment and 2) one's personal life-style. For medicine to become effective in dealing with such diseases, it has become common belief that the environment will have to be changed, and personal ways of living will also have to be transformed, and radically.

4 These things may turn out to be true, for all I know, but it will

take a long time to get the necessary proofs. Meanwhile, the field is wide open for magic.

5 One great difficulty in getting straightforward answers is that so many of the diseases in question have unpredictable courses, and some of them have a substantial tendency toward spontaneous remission. In rheumatoid arthritis, for instance, when such widely disparate therapeutic measures as copper bracelets, a move to Arizona, diets low in sugar or salt or meat or whatever, and even an inspirational book have been accepted by patients as useful, the trouble in evaluation is that approximately 35 percent of patients with this diagnosis are bound to recover no matter what they do. But if you actually have rheumatoid arthritis or, for that matter, schizophrenia, and then get over it, or if you are a doctor and observe this to happen, it is hard to be persuaded that it wasn't *something* you did that was responsible. Hence you need very large numbers of patients and lots of time, and a cool head.

6 Magic is back again, and in full force. Laetrile cures cancer, acupuncture is useful for deafness and low-back pain, vitamins are good for anything, and meditation, yoga, dancing, biofeedback, and shouting one another down in crowded rooms over weekends are specifics for the human condition. Running, a good thing to be doing for its own sake, has acquired the medicinal value formerly attributed to rare herbs from Indonesia.

7 There is a recurring advertisement, placed by Blue Cross on the op-ed page of *The New York Times,* which urges you to take advantage of science by changing your life habits, with the suggestion that if you do so, by adopting seven easy-to-follow items of life-style, you can achieve eleven added years beyond what you'll get if you don't. Since today's average figure is around seventy-two for all parties in both sexes, this might mean going on until at least the age of eighty-three. You can do this formidable thing, it is claimed, by simply eating breakfast, exercising regularly, maintaining normal weight, not smoking cigarettes, not drinking excessively, sleeping eight hours each night, and not eating between meals.

8 The science which produced this illumination was a careful study by California epidemiologists, based on a questionnaire given to about seven thousand people. Five years after the questionnaire, a body count was made by sorting through the county death certificates, and the 371 people who had died were matched up with their answers to the questions. To be sure, there were more deaths among the heavy smokers and drinkers, as you might expect from the

known incidence of lung cancer in smokers and cirrhosis and auto accidents among drinkers. But there was also a higher mortality among those who said they didn't eat breakfast, and even higher in those who took no exercise, no exercise at all, not even going off in the family car for weekend picnics. Being up to 20 percent overweight was not so bad, surprisingly, but being *underweight* was clearly associated with a higher death rate.

9 The paper describing these observations has been widely quoted, and not just by Blue Cross. References to the Seven Healthy Life Habits keep turning up in popular magazines and in the health columns of newspapers, always with that promise of eleven more years.

10 The findings fit nicely with what is becoming folk doctrine about disease. You become ill because of not living right. If you get cancer it is, somehow or other, your own fault. If you didn't cause it by smoking or drinking or eating the wrong things, it came from allowing yourself to persist with the wrong kind of personality, in the wrong environment. If you have a coronary occlusion, you didn't run enough. Or you were too tense, or you *wished* too much, and didn't get a good enough sleep. Or you got fat. Your fault.

11 But eating breakfast? It is a kind of enchantment, pure magic.

12 You have to read the report carefully to discover that there is another, more banal way of explaining the findings. Leave aside the higher deaths in heavy smokers and drinkers, for there is no puzzle in either case; these are dangerous things to do. But it is hard to imagine any good reason for dying within five years from not eating a good breakfast, or any sort of breakfast.

13 The other explanation turns cause and effect around. Among the people in that group of seven thousand who answered that they don't eat breakfast, don't go off on picnics, are underweight, and can't sleep properly, there were surely some who were already ill when the questionnaire arrived. They didn't eat breakfast because they couldn't stand the sight of food. They had lost their appetites, were losing weight, didn't feel up to moving around much, and had trouble sleeping. They didn't play tennis or go off on family picnics because they didn't *feel* good. Some of these people probably had an undetected cancer, perhaps of the pancreas; others may have had hypertension or early kidney failure or some other organic disease which the questionnaire had no way of picking up. The study did not ascertain the causes of death in the 371, but just a few deaths from such undiscerned disorders would have made a significant statistical

impact. The author of the paper was careful to note these possible interpretations, although the point was not made strongly, and the general sense you have in reading it is that you can live on and on if only you will eat breakfast and play tennis.

14 The popular acceptance of the notion of Seven Healthy Life Habits, as a way of staying alive, says something important about today's public attitudes, or at least the attitudes in the public mind, about disease and dying. People have always wanted causes that are simple and easy to comprehend, and about which the individual can *do* something. If you believe that you can ward off the common causes of premature death—cancer, heart disease, and stroke, diseases whose pathogenesis we really do not understand—by jogging, hoping, and eating and sleeping regularly, these are good things to believe even if not necessarily true. Medicine has survived other periods of unifying theory, constructed to explain all of human disease, not always as benign in their effects as this one is likely to be. After all, if people can be induced to give up smoking, stop overdrinking and overeating, and take some sort of regular exercise, most of them are bound to feel the better for leading more orderly, regular lives, and many of them are surely going to look better.

15 Nobody can say an unfriendly word against the sheer goodness of keeping fit, but we should go carefully with the promises.

16 There is also a bifurcated ideological appeal contained in the seven-life-habits doctrine, quite apart from the subliminal notion of good luck in the numbers involved (7 come 11). Both ends of the political spectrum can find congenial items. At the further right, it is attractive to hear that the individual, the good old freestanding, free-enterprising American citizen, is responsible for his own health and when things go wrong it is his own damn fault for smoking and drinking and living wrong (and he can jolly well pay for it). On the other hand, at the left, it is nice to be told that all our health problems, including dying, are caused by failure of the community to bring up its members to live properly, and if you really want to improve the health of the people, research is not the answer; you should upheave the present society and invent a better one. At either end, you can't lose.

17 In between, the skeptics in medicine have a hard time of it. It is much more difficult to be convincing about ignorance concerning disease mechanisms than it is to make claims for full comprehension, especially when the comprehension leads, logically or not, to some sort of action. When it comes to serious illness, the public tends,

understandably, to be more skeptical about the skeptics, more willing to believe the true believers. It is medicine's oldest dilemma, not to be settled by candor or by any kind of rhetoric; what it needs is a lot of time and patience, waiting for science to come in, as it has in the past, with the solid facts.

Reading for Rhetorical Strategy

Note in the essay that Lewis Thomas both comments on and uses causal analysis. In paragraphs 1–3 he gives us a brief history of medicine that illustrates single-cause and multiple-cause theories. In paragraphs 4–6 he touches on the connections between magic and various causal explanations in medicine, and then in paragraph 7 he introduces the statistical study of healthy life habits that forms his central example of medicine and magic. Thus far, Thomas has mainly commented on causal explanations. In paragraph 11, however, he begins his own causal analysis, suggesting in paragraph 13 that the California statistical report may have turned "cause and effect around": people may not be getting sick because they've skipped breakfast, but they may be skipping breakfast because they're already sick. From paragraph 14 on, Thomas pushes his causal analysis even further by attempting to explain some of the reasons why such notions as the "Seven Healthy Life Habits" manage to attain such enormous popularity.

Three Mile Island

Barry Commoner

In March 1979 the eastern part of the nation came close to catastrophe when a series of mechanical and human failures at the Three Mile Island nuclear plant in Harrisburg, Pennsylvania, nearly resulted in a meltdown. Barry Commoner, a renowned authority on energy policy, here talks about what happened in that accident. His analysis, a model of clarity, shows that a single incident—in this case the failure of a pump—can set off a whole chain of causes and effects.

Currently teaching at Queens College, C.U.N.Y., where he is the director of the Center for Biology of Natural Systems, Barry Commoner is also an active member of numerous committees and professional associations. He has contributed more than 200 articles to journals in his field and was awarded the first International Humanist Award by the International Humanist and Ethical Union in 1970. The following selection is taken from The Politics of Energy *(1979).*

1 The high and growing cost of nuclear power plants is due not so much to the difficulties associated with the technology that it has in common with non-nuclear plants—that is, the conversion of energy of steam into electricity—but rather to its unique feature, the use of fission to supply the heat needed to produce steam. The accident at Harrisburg showed that a failure in the steam-to-electricity section of the plant that would have caused very little trouble in a conventional power plant came close to producing a catastrophic disaster in the nuclear one and has shut down the plant for a long time, and possibly permanently.

2 The Three Mile Island Power Plant produced the steam needed to drive its electric turbines in a pressurized-water reactor. In such a reactor, water is circulated through the reactor's fuel core, where—because it is under pressure—it is heated far above its normal boiling point by the heat generated by the fission reaction. The superheated water flows through the reactor's "primary loop" into a heat exchanger where it brings water, which circulates in a "secondary loop," to the boiling point, and the resulting steam flows into the turbine to generate electricity. The spent steam is recondensed and pumped back to the heat exchanger, where it is again converted to steam, and so on. A third loop of cooling water is used to condense the steam, carrying off the excess heat to a cooling tower where it is finally released into the air. This arrangement is much more complex than the design of a conventional power system, where the steam generated in the boiler passes directly into the turbine. In this type of nuclear plant the water that circulates through the reactor (which is equivalent to the boiler in a conventional plant) becomes intensely radioactive, and the complex successive circulation loops are essential to keep that radioactivity from leaving the reactor.

3 On March 28, 1979, at 3:53 A.M., a pump at the Harrisburg plant failed. Because the pump failed, the reactor's heat was not drawn off in the heat exchanger and the very hot water in the primary loop overheated. The pressure in the loop increased, opening a release

valve that was supposed to counteract such an event. But the valve stuck open and the primary loop system lost so much water (which ended up as a highly radioactive pool, six feet deep, on the floor of the reactor building) that it was unable to carry off all the heat generated within the reactor core. Under these circumstances, the intense heat held within the reactor could, in theory, melt its fuel rods, and the resulting "meltdown" could then carry a hugely radioactive mass through the floor of the reactor. The reactor's emergency cooling system, which is designed to prevent this disaster, was then automatically activated; but when it was, apparently, turned off too soon, some of the fuel rods overheated. This produced a bubble of hydrogen gas at the top of the reactor. (The hydrogen is dissolved in the water in order to react with oxygen that is produced when the intense reactor radiation splits water molecules into their atomic constituents. When heated, the dissolved hydrogen bubbles out of the solution.) This bubble blocked the flow of cooling water so that despite the action of the emergency cooling system the reactor core was again in danger of melting down. Another danger was that the gas might contain enough oxygen to cause an explosion that could rupture the huge containers that surround the reactor and release a deadly cloud of radioactive material into the surrounding countryside. Working desperately, technicians were able to gradually reduce the size of the gas bubble using a special apparatus brought in from the atomic laboratory at Oak Ridge, Tennessee, and the danger of a catastrophic release of radioactive materials subsided. But the sealed-off plant was now so radioactive that no one could enter it for many months—or, according to some observers, for years—without being exposed to a lethal dose of radiation.

4 Some radioactive gases did escape from the plant, prompting the Governor of Pennsylvania, Richard Thornburgh, to ask that pregnant women and children leave the area five miles around the plant. Many other people decided to leave as well, and within a week 60,000 or more residents had left the area, drawing money from their banks and leaving state offices and a local hospital shorthanded.

5 Like the horseshoe nail that lost a kingdom, the failure of a pump at the Three Mile Island Nuclear Power Plant may have lost the entire industry. It dramatized the vulnerability of the complex system that is embodied in the elaborate technology of nuclear power. In that design, the normally benign and easily controlled process of producing steam to drive an electric generator turned into a trigger for a radioactive catastrophe. . . .

Additional Rhetorical Strategies

Process Analysis (paragraphs 2, 3); Comparison and Contrast (paragraphs 2, 5).

Examining Words and Meaning

1. It is in paragraph 3 that Commoner gives us most of the cause-and-effect analysis in this selection. Review the paragraph, underlining those words and phrases that establish relationships of cause and effect. Suppose that Commoner had substituted *and* and *then* for these words and phrases. Why would his analysis have been less clear?
2. Why did the Three Mile Island plant twice run the danger of a meltdown? At what stages in the events was the danger of a meltdown greatest? What other dangers were apparent during the incident?

Focusing on Structures and Strategies

1. Why is it necessary for Commoner's analysis of what happened at Three Mile Island that he describe in paragraph 2 how a nuclear power plant works? Why would his analysis of the incident be more confusing if he had included this matter in paragraph 3?
2. Did the near-disaster at Three Mile Island result from a single cause or from multiple causes? If you think that the causes were multiple, is there a cause-and-effect relationship among those causes? How might the incident have been averted?
3. List some of the effects that resulted from the failure of the pump at the plant. What is the relation of these effects to each other? In what sense might what Commoner discusses in his last paragraph be considered an effect?

Suggestion for Further Discussion and Writing

1. Commoner presents a cause-and-effect analysis of the accident at Three Mile Island. Think of another accident which had disastrous or

near-disastrous consequences: the wreck of a supertanker, a mid-air collision, a raging fire in a skyscraper. Write an account of the incident, analyzing as many causes and effects as possible.

Why It's Fashionable to Be Thin

Anne Hollander

An art historian with a special interest in the history of costume and design, Anne Hollander has also written extensively on a variety of cultural subjects for such periodicals as The New Republic, Commentary, *and* The New York Times Magazine. *In* Seeing Through Clothes *(1978), her comprehensive assessment of the changing significance of dress in Western civilization, Hollander suggests that clothes "stand for knowledge and language, art and love, time and death—the creative, struggling state of man."*

The connection between what we wear and how we look at our bodies is central to Hollander's study of clothing. In the following selection from Seeing Through Clothes, *she examines the social, cultural, and aesthetic causes that led to the modern ideal of thinness.*

1 The strong appeal of female slimness in the twentieth century is usually accounted for by social and economic changes rather than through a purely aesthetic development of style. Feminine emancipation from many physical and moral restraints, the increasing popularity of sport for women, together with new possibilities for gainful employment and political power, all eventually contributed to the new physical ideal. Good sense and good health, mental and physical, were seen to be properly served by freedom and activity, and feminine clothing evolved so as to allow for these and (more importantly) for the look of these. What is meant by "modern" looks developed after the First World War with the aid of clothing that expressed (although it did not always provide) an ideal of comfort and the possibility of action.

2 The most important expressive element in this new visual conception of female dress was not the uncorseted torso but the short-

ened skirt. After women's skirts had risen off the ground, any given clothed woman was perceptibly smaller in scale than formerly. Hair was shortened, as well as skirts, and worn close to the head. Hats shrank. During most of the nineteenth century a fashionable woman's dress, including coiffure, headgear, and a possible muff, handbag, and parasol, had consisted of an extensive, complicated system with many different sections (sleeves, bodice, skirt, collar, train). These were all separately conceived and embellished and all tended to enlarge the total volume of the clothed body, partly by being difficult to perceive all at once. After the First World War a woman's dress came more and more to present a compact and unified visual image. This is what men's clothes had already succeeded in doing a century before. The new simplified and reduced clothes for women, although they were designed and made absolutely differently from men's clothes and out of different fabrics, nevertheless expressed the new sense of the equality of the sexes—an equality, that is, with respect to the new character of their important differences.

3 Female sexual submissiveness, either meek or wanton, was no longer modish and no longer avowed by elements of dress. Feminine sexuality had to abandon the suggestion of plump, hidden softness and find expression in exposed, lean hardness. Women strove for the erotic appeal inherent in the racehorse and the sports car, which might be summed up as a mettlesome challenge: a vibrant, somewhat unaccountable readiness for action but only under expert guidance. This was naturally best offered in a self-contained, sleekly composed physical format: a thin body, with few layers of covering. Immanent sexuality, best expressed in a condition of stasis, was no longer the foundation of female allure. The look of possible movement became a necessary element in fashionable female beauty, and all women's clothing, whatever other messages it offered, consistently incorporated visible legs and feet into the total female image. Women, once thought to glide, were seen to walk. Even vain or fruitless or nervous activity, authorized by fashionable morbid aestheticism, came to seem preferable to immobility, idleness, passivity. The various dance crazes of the first quarter of the century undoubtedly were an expression of this restless spirit, but its most important vehicle was the movies.

4 The rapid advance of the movies as the chief popular art made the public increasingly aware of style in feminine physical movement. Movies taught everyone how ways of walking and dancing, of

using the hands and moving the head and shoulders, could be incorporated into the conscious ways of wearing clothes. After about 1920 the fact that women's clothes showed such a reduction in overall volume was undoubtedly partly due to the visual need for the completely clothed body to be satisfactorily seen *in motion.* Perfect feminine beauty no longer formed a still image, ideally wrought by a Leonardo da Vinci or a Titian into an eternal icon. It had become transmuted into a photograph, a single instant that represented a sequence of instants—an ideally moving picture, even if it were momentarily still. For this kind of mobile beauty, thinness was a necessary condition.

5 The still body that is nevertheless perceived as ideally in motion seems to present a blurred image—a perpetual suggestion of all the other possible moments at which it might be seen. It seems to have a dynamic, expanding outline. The actual physical size of a human body is made apparently larger by its movements, and if its movements are what constitute its essential visual reality, they must be what gives it its visual substance. Even if a body is perceived at a motionless instant, the possibility of enlargement by movement is implicit in the image. Before consciousness had been so much affected by photography, a body perceived as ideally still could be visually enlarged by layers of fat or clothing with aesthetic success, but a body that is perceived to be about to move must apparently replace those layers with layers of possible space to move in. The camera eye seems to fatten the figure; human eyes, trained by camera vision, demand that it be thin to start with, to allow for the same effect in direct perception. The thin female body, once considered visually meager and unsatisfying without the suggestive expansions of elaborate clothing (or of flesh, which artists sometimes had to provide), has become substantial, freighted with potential action.

6 It came about that all the varieties of female desirability conceived by the twentieth century seemed ideally housed in a thin, resilient, and bony body. Healthy innocence, sexual restlessness, creative zest, practical competence, even morbid but poetic obsessiveness and intelligence—all seemed appropriate in size ten. During the six decades following the First World War, styles in gesture, posture, and erotic emphasis have undergone many changes, but the basically slim female ideal has been maintained. Throughout all the shifting levels of bust and waist and the fluctuating taste in gluteal and mammary thrust, the bodies of women have been conceived as ideally slender, and clearly supported by bones. . . .

Additional Rhetorical Strategy

Comparison and Contrast (paragraphs 2, 5).

Examining Words and Meaning

1. Hollander says that the "modern" look in clothing developed after the First World War. How would you describe this new look? What specific changes in American social and cultural values in the 1920s does Hollander associate with the fashion to be thin? How did the new clothing alter attitudes toward female sexuality?
2. Characterize the nature of Hollander's diction in the opening paragraph. Is it primarily abstract or concrete? Does the diction remain consistent throughout the essay?
3. If necessary, consult a dictionary for the meaning of the following terms: immanent (paragraph 3); stasis (paragraph 3); morbid aestheticism (paragraph 3); icon (paragraph 4); gluteal (paragraph 6).

Focusing on Structures and Strategies

1. Hollander is writing an explanation of the causes of something that finally seems rather unscientific. How does this affect her word choices? How does she develop and control her essay? What, in effect, is the principle of organization for the sequence of thoughts presented here?
2. Hollander sees the movies as an extremely important factor in increasing the public's awareness of style. How does this attention to the movies carry over into the metaphors she creates?

Suggestion for Further Discussion and Writing

1. Hollander's essay suggests that movies have been important factors in determining what the latest American ideal in fashion will be. Consider for a few moments the movies you have seen in the past year or two. Which stand out in your mind? Have any of these set a

new direction for American fashion? For behavior? Write an essay in which you analyze fully the nature and extent of this particular movie's influence on American taste.

Who's Afraid of Math, and Why?

Sheila Tobias

"How does it happen there are people who do not understand mathematics?" asked Henri Poincaré, one of the great mathematicians of the nineteenth century. He thought that the ability to intuit relationships was the key to mathematical comprehension: "We know that this feeling, this intuition of mathematical order, that makes us divine hidden harmonies and relations, can not be possessed by everyone." But many who might possess that intuition are dissuaded from ever discovering it, according to Sheila Tobias, author of Overcoming Math Anxiety *(1978). One of the founding members of the National Organization for Women (NOW), Tobias became interested in the fears people have of math while she was studying the tracking of women into traditionally female occupations. In the following selection from* Overcoming Math Anxiety, *she attempts to trace the causes of those fears.*

1 The first thing people remember about failing at math is that it felt like sudden death. Whether the incident occurred while learning "word problems" in sixth grade, coping with equations in high school, or first confronting calculus and statistics in college, failure came suddenly and in a very frightening way. An idea or a new operation was not just difficult, it was impossible! And, instead of asking questions or taking the lesson slowly, most people remember having had the feeling that they would never go any further in mathematics. If we assume that the curriculum was reasonable, and that the new idea was but the next in a series of learnable concepts, the feeling of utter defeat was simply not rational; yet "math anxious" college students and adults have revealed that no matter how much the teacher reassured them, they could not overcome that feeling.

2 A common myth about the nature of mathematical ability holds that one either has or does not have a mathematical mind. Mathematical imagination and an intuitive grasp of mathematical principles may well be needed to do advanced research, but why should people who can do college-level work in other subjects not be able to do college-level math as well? Rates of learning may vary. Competency under time pressure may differ. Certainly low self-esteem will get in the way. But where is the evidence that a student needs a "mathematical mind" in order to succeed at learning math?

3 Consider the effects of this mythology. Since only a few people are supposed to have this mathematical mind, part of what makes us so passive in the face of our difficulties in learning mathematics is that we suspect all the while we may not be one of "them," and we spend our time waiting to find out when our nonmathematical minds will be exposed. Since our limit will eventually be reached, we see no point in being methodical or in attending to detail. We are grateful when we survive fractions, word problems, or geometry. If that certain moment of failure hasn't struck yet, it is only temporarily postponed.

4 Parents, especially parents of girls, often expect their children to be nonmathematical. Parents are either poor at math and had their own sudden-death experiences, or, if math came easily for them, they do not know how it feels to be slow. In either case, they unwittingly foster the idea that a mathematical mind is something one either has or does not have.

MATHEMATICS AND SEX

5 Although fear of math is not a purely female phenomenon, girls tend to drop out of math sooner than boys, and adult women experience an aversion to math and math-related activities that is akin to anxiety. A 1972 survey of the amount of high school mathematics taken by incoming freshmen at Berkeley revealed that while 57 percent of the boys had taken four years of high school math, only 8 percent of the girls had had the same amount of preparation. Without four years of high school math, students at Berkeley, and at most other colleges and universities, are ineligible for the calculus sequence, unlikely to attempt chemistry or physics, and inadequately prepared for statistics and economics.

6 Unable to elect these entry-level courses, the remaining 92

percent of the girls will be limited, presumably, to the career choices that are considered feminine: the humanities, guidance and counseling, elementary school teaching, foreign languages, and the fine arts.

7 Boys and girls may be born alike with respect to math, but certain sex differences in performance emerge early according to several respected studies, and these differences remain through adulthood. They are:

1. Girls compute better than boys (elementary school and on).
2. Boys solve word problems better than girls (from age thirteen on).
3. Boys take more math than girls (from age sixteen on).
4. Girls learn to hate math sooner and possibly for different reasons.

8 Why the differences in performance? One reason is the amount of math learned and used at play. Another may be the difference in male-female maturation. If girls do better than boys at all elementary school tasks, then they may compute better for no other reason than that arithmetic is part of the elementary school curriculum. As boys and girls grow older, girls become, under pressure, academically less competitive. Thus, the falling off of girls' math performance between ages ten and fifteen may be because:

1. Math gets harder in each successive year and requires more work and commitment.
2. Both boys and girls are pressured, beginning at age ten, not to excel in areas designated by society to be outside their sex-role domains.
3. Thus girls have a good excuse to avoid the painful struggle with math; boys don't.

9 Such a model may explain girls' lower achievement in math overall, but why should girls even younger than ten have difficulty in problem-solving? In her review of the research on sex differences, psychologist Eleanor Maccoby noted that girls are generally more conforming, more suggestible, and more dependent upon the opinion of others than boys (all learned, not innate, behaviors). Being so, they may not be as willing to take risks or to think for themselves, two behaviors that are necessary in solving problems. Indeed, in one test of third-graders, girls were found to be not nearly as willing to

estimate, to make judgments about "possible right answers," or to work with systems they had never seen before. Their very success at doing what is expected of them up to that time seems to get in the way of their doing something new.

10 If readiness to do word problems, to take one example, is as much a function of readiness to take risks as it is of "reasoning ability," then mathematics performance certainly requires more than memory, computation, and reasoning. The differences in math performance between boys and girls—no matter how consistently those differences show up—cannot be attributed simply to differences in innate ability.

11 Still, if one were to ask the victims themselves, they would probably disagree: they would say their problems with math have to do with the way they are "wired." They feel they are somehow missing something—one ability or several—that other people have. Although women want to believe they are not mentally inferior to men, many fear that, where math is concerned, they really are. Thus, we have to consider seriously whether mathematical ability has a biological basis, not only because a number of researchers believe this to be so, but because a number of victims agree with them.

THE ARGUMENTS FROM BIOLOGY

12 The search for some biological basis for math ability or disability is fraught with logical and experimental difficulties. Since not all math underachievers are women, and not all women are mathematics-avoidant, poor performance in math is unlikely to be due to some genetic or hormonal difference between the sexes. Moreover, no amount of research so far has unearthed a "mathematical competency" in some tangible, measurable substance in the body. Since "masculinity" cannot be injected into women to test whether or not it improves their mathematics, the theories that attribute such ability to genes or hormones must depend for their proof on circumstantial evidence. So long as about 7 percent of the Ph.D.'s in mathematics are earned by women, we have to conclude either that these women have genes, hormones, and brain organization different from those of the rest of us, or that certain positive experiences in their lives have largely undone the negative fact that they are female, or both.

13 Genetically, the only difference between males and females

(albeit a significant and pervasive one) is the presence of two chromosomes designated X in every female cell. Normal males exhibit an X-Y combination. Because some kinds of mental retardation are associated with sex-chromosomal anomalies, a number of researchers have sought a converse linkage between specific abilities and the presence or absence of the second X. But the linkage between genetics and mathematics is not supported by conclusive evidence.

14 Since intensified hormonal activity commences at adolescence, a time during which girls seem to lose interest in mathematics, much more has been made of the unequal amounts in females and males of the sex-linked hormones androgen and estrogen. Biological researchers have linked estrogen—the female hormone—with "simple repetitive tasks," and androgen—the male hormone—with "complex restructuring tasks." The assumption here is not only that such specific talents are biologically based (probably undemonstrable) but also that one cannot be good at *both* repetitive and restructuring kinds of assignments.

SEX ROLES AND MATHEMATICS COMPETENCE

15 The fact that many girls tend to lose interest in math at the age they reach puberty (junior high school) suggests that puberty might in some sense cause girls to fall behind in math. Several explanations come to mind: the influence of hormones, more intensified sex-role socialization, or some extracurricular learning experience exclusive to boys of that age.

16 One group of seventh-graders in a private school in New England gave a clue as to what children themselves think about all of this. When asked why girls do as well as boys in math until the sixth grade, while sixth-grade boys do better from that point on, the girls responded: "Oh, that's easy. After sixth grade, we have to do real math." The answer to why "real math" should be considered to be "for boys" and not "for girls" can be found not in the realm of biology but only in the realm of ideology of sex differences.

17 Parents, peers, and teachers forgive a girl when she does badly in math at school, encouraging her to do well in other subjects instead. " 'There, there,' my mother used to say when I failed at math," one woman says. "But I got a talking-to when I did badly in French." Lynn Fox, who directs a program for mathematically gifted junior high boys and girls on the campus of Johns Hopkins University, has

trouble recruiting girls and keeping them in her program. Some parents prevent their daughters from participating altogether for fear that excellence in math will make them too different. The girls themselves are often reluctant to continue with mathematics, Fox reports, because they fear social ostracism.

18 Where do these associations come from?

19 The association of masculinity with mathematics sometimes extends from the discipline to those who practice it. Students, asked on a questionnaire what characteristics they associate with a mathematician (as contrasted with a "writer"), selected terms such as rational, cautious, wise, and responsible. The writer, on the other hand, in addition to being seen as individualistic and independent, was also described as warm, interested in people, and altogether more compatible with a feminine ideal.

20 As a result of this psychological conditioning, a young woman may consider math and math-related fields to be inimical to femininity. In an interesting study of West German teenagers, Erika Schildkamp-Kuendiger found that girls who identified themselves with the feminine ideal underachieved in mathematics, that is, did less well than would have been expected of them based on general intelligence and performance in other subjects.

STREET MATHEMATICS: THINGS, MOTION, SCORES

21 Not all the skills that are necessary for learning mathematics are learned in school. Measuring, computing, and manipulating objects that have dimensions and dynamic properties of their own are part of the everyday life of children. Children who miss out on these experiences may not be well primed for math in school.

22 Feminists have complained for a long time that playing with dolls is one way of convincing impressionable little girls that they may only be mothers or housewives—or, as in the case of the Barbie doll, "pinup girls"—when they grow up. But doll-playing may have even more serious consequences for little girls than that. Do girls find out about gravity and distance and shapes and sizes playing with dolls? Probably not.

23 A curious boy, if his parents are tolerant, will have taken apart a number of household and play objects by the time he is ten, and, if his parents are lucky, he may even have put them back together again. In all of this he is learning things that will be useful in physics

and math. Taking parts out that have to go back in requires some examination of form. Building something that stays up or at least stays put for some time involves working with structure.

24 Sports is another source of math-related concepts for children which tends to favor boys. Getting to first base on a not very well hit grounder is a lesson in time, speed, and distance. Intercepting a football thrown through the air requires some rapid intuitive eye calculations based on the ball's direction, speed, and trajectory. Since physics is partly concerned with velocities, trajectories, and collisions of objects, much of the math taught to prepare a student for physics deals with relationships and formulas that can be used to express motion and acceleration.

25 What, then, can we conclude about mathematics and sex? If math anxiety is in part the result of math avoidance, why not require girls to take as much math as they can possibly master? If being the only girl in "trig" is the reason so many women drop math at the end of high school, why not provide psychological counseling and support for those young women who wish to go on? Since ability in mathematics is considered by many to be unfeminine, perhaps fear of success, more than any bodily or mental dysfunction, may interfere with girls' ability to learn math.

Additional Rhetorical Strategies

Illustration (paragraph 4); Comparison and Contrast (throughout); Definition (paragraph 15).

Examining Words and Meaning

1. According to Tobias, when do boys and girls generally start performing differently in math? What are some of the reasons such differences may first appear? Why might they become more pronounced as the boys and girls become older?

2. If you are unfamiliar with any of the following words, look them up in the dictionary: fraught (paragraph 12); albeit (paragraph 13); ideology (paragraph 16); ostracism (paragraph 17); inimical (paragraph 20); dysfunction (paragraph 25).

Focusing on Structures and Strategies

1. Of the four categories of cause-and-effect essays described in the introduction to this section, which best fits this essay? Does Tobias seem to focus more on effects or on causes?
2. Would you say that Tobias emphasizes causes or effects in the first three paragraphs of the article? In the last three paragraphs? What does this tell you about her rhetorical strategy?
3. How does Tobias introduce her discussion of the biological explanations for differences in math ability? How does this introduction affect our reading of the evidence?

Suggestions for Further Discussion and Writing

1. Tobias cites a 1972 study of the mathematical backgrounds of first-year students at Berkeley. It is meant to be representative of a national trend. Exactly how have things changed since 1972? In a group discussion, consider the math backgrounds of men and women in your class. Do any differences emerge? If so, do the factors that Tobias offers as causes seem to you an adequate explanation of the difference?
2. What other myths about an aspect of behavior, of intelligence, or of talent can you think of? Do you disagree, for example, with the idea that women are naturally more emotional than men? Is it false to say that some people are just born with the ability to write, and some are not? Take one such myth and explode it, taking care to include a thorough assessment of the causes of the myth, and some discussion of its effects.

The Next Ice Age

Sir Frederick Hoyle

Analyzing chains of causality is essential to both the methods and aims of science, but while most scientists are content to pursue cause and effect in highly specialized areas, Sir Frederick Hoyle has never shrunk from great schemes and ultimate questions. In 1950, he published The Nature of the Universe, *a book which advanced the now unfashionable steady-state hypothesis of an infinitely expanding universe. As ambitious as its title, the book was both attacked as an oversimplification and celebrated as "one of the finest pieces of scientific exposition for the layman which has appeared in recent years." Similar controversy has followed his other publications, which include* Frontiers of Astronomy *(1955),* Man and Materialism *(1956),* Of Men and Galaxies *(1966), and a large number of essays and science-fiction novels.*

Although he is both reviled and praised as a "popularizer" of science, Hoyle's academic and professional credentials are impressive. Born in Yorkshire in 1915, he graduated from Cambridge with distinction in mathematics and later became the first director of that university's Institute of Theoretical Astronomy. Since then he has received countless other honors and appointments, including knighthood in 1972. The following essay finds him investigating, with characteristic meticulousness, a causal chain that leads to a vast possibility: the strong likelihood of another ice age.

1 More than three-quarters of all the ice in the world is in the southern polar continent of Antarctica, a conveniently distant place. Most of the rest of the world's ice lies in Greenland, also a remote place. So we are accustomed to thinking of the heavily populated lands of the Earth as being ice-free, except for the minute smears of the stuff we encounter in winter.

2 The Stone Age people who executed the magnificent cave paintings to be seen in southwest France and Spain did not enjoy such a pleasant situation. Twenty thousand years ago an ice sheet comparable to the one now in Greenland lay across Scandinavia. It had extensions reaching into Russia, Germany, and Britain. Another ice sheet of polar dimensions lay across the heartland of Canada, and its extensions reached beyond Chicago.

3 Nor was the grim situation of 20,000 years ago confined to the northern temperate latitudes. That ice age extended fingers even into the tropics. Substantial glaciers appeared on high tropical mountains such as those in Hawaii.

4 In the luxury of our present ice-free state we are apt to think that the ice age is over. But all the evidence is that the piling of vast quantities of ice onto the northern temperate latitudes (a belt of land running from the U.S.S.R. through Western Europe to Canada and the U.S.) has scarcely begun. To understand the overwhelming threat

the future has in store for mankind, let us go back several tens of millions of years.

5 It is well known that the continents of the Earth are not in fixed positions; they drift about slowly in characteristic periods of 50 to 100 million years. About 40 million years ago the continent of Antarctica moved toward the South Pole. This caused the first glaciers there, and about 20 million years ago Antarctica was substantially ice covered.

6 A sinister process then set in, with its origin in the remarkable inability of the direct rays of the sun to melt either snow or ice. Most sunshine is reflected by snow, while it penetrates ice so deeply and diffusely that it has little melting effect at its surface. The sun does nothing directly to Antarctic ice, which would accumulate indefinitely from repeated snowfalls if icebergs did not break away into the sea at the outer edges of the ice sheet.

7 By about 20 million years ago a balance between the gain of new ice and the loss of old ice had been set up. The icebergs chilled the surrounding salty water. If this cooled water had remained at the ocean surface no harm would have been done. Despite its inability to melt ice and snow, sunlight is highly effective at warming the surface layers of the ocean, and would soon have resupplied the heat lost to the icebergs. This did not happen, however, because the dense, cool water sank from the surface to the ocean depths and the deep basins began to fill with water that was literally ice-cold.

8 This process eventually changed the warm world ocean of 50 million years ago into today's overwhelmingly ice-cold world ocean—with a thin skin of warmer water at its surface. Only this thin warm skin protects us from the next ice age.

9 As the chilling of the deep ocean occurred slowly and inexorably the Earth's climate worsened. By about 10 million years ago glaciers had appeared in Alaska. The first major intrusion of ice onto the lands of the northern temperate belt occurred about two million years ago. From time to time the ice would melt and for a while the land would be ice-free. Then the ice would come, again and again.

10 The ice-age periods became progressively longer than the intervening interglacials. In the past million years the situation has worsened, until the average interglacial period has now shrunk to no more than 10,000 years. Since this is just the length of time since the present warm interglacial period began, our ration of ice-free conditions is over. The next ice age is already due.

11 A sequence of ice ages continues for as long as the continent in question resides at the pole in question. Our present sequence of ice ages will therefore continue for as long as the continent of Antarctica remains at the South Pole, which will probably be for several more tens of millions of years. The conclusion is that the present sequence of ice ages has scarcely begun. There are hundreds of ice ages still to come.

12 Why should there be an alternating sequence of ice ages and interglacials? At present snow lies during the winter over most of the northern temperate region. Instead of accumulating year by year into continental ice sheets, it melts each spring and summer. This is the essence of the interglacial condition. We are ice-free now, not because of a lack of snowfall but because of the spring thaw.

13 Melting comes from warmth in the air. Unlike the sun's direct rays, the longer-wave heat radiation generated by warm air is absorbed in snow or ice, which therefore melts almost immediately, thin surface layer after thin surface layer. The process is highly efficient and, given a sufficient supply of warm air, a whole winter's snow melts in a few days. Thus winter snow stays until warm air comes, and almost in a flash it is gone.

14 Where does the warm air get its heat? Mostly from the surface layer of warm ocean water that overlies the mass of ice-cold deeper water. Remove the surface layer of warm ocean water and there would then be no warm air. The snows of winter would not melt, ice sheets would begin to build, and the next ice age would have arrived.

15 The important surface layer of warm ocean water stores about ten times more heat than is required by the air and the land each year, a ten-to-one margin of safety. That is enough to have prevented the next ice age for 10,000 years, but not sufficient to withstand every kind of accident. The finest particles of ash thrown into the air by the recent eruption of the Mount St. Helens volcano will take about ten years to settle down to ground level. Fine particles of any electrically insulating material reflect sunlight back into space and so reduce the amount available to heat the ocean surface. The Mount St. Helens volcanic eruption was not remotely big enough to have produced such a reflecting layer around the Earth.

16 In 1815 Mount Tambora in the Dutch East Indies produced an explosion that threw a sufficient quantity of fine ash into the high atmosphere to have a noticeable effect on the Northern Hemisphere summer of 1816. It was a summer of agricultural disaster in New

England, the coldest on record at places as widely separated as New Haven and Geneva.

17 As an astronomer, I prefer to consider the possibility of a similar but much more violent effect triggered from outside the Earth: the impact of a giant meteorite. There is no question that giant meteorites, half a mile long or more, must hit the Earth from time to time, and such collisions must throw a vast quantity of debris into the atmosphere.

18 The most notable meteoritic event of modern times occurred in July, 1908. Miss K. Stephens wrote to *The Times* from Godmanchester about a strange light she had seen in the midnight sky, commenting that "it would be interesting if anyone could explain the cause." It was not until 1927 that even the point of impact of the meteorite was discovered, by an expedition that penetrated to the Tunguska River region in Siberia. An enormous area of devastation was found, almost twice that caused by Mount St. Helens, showing that a comparatively minor meteoritic collision can be far more destructive than the explosion of a volcano.

19 Once in every 5,000 to 10,000 years a meteoritic collision occurs which projects sufficient fine dust into the high atmosphere to make the Earth into a temporarily reflective planet. The resulting cutoff of sunlight robs the surface waters of the terrestrial ocean of their protective store of heat, and the air that blows over the land from the sea is then no longer warm enough to melt the snows of winter.

20 How long will the snow accumulate? Within two or three decades at most, all the fine dust will have settled to the Earth's surface under gravity and sunlight will no longer be reflected back into space. Warm summer air will blow again over the land, and within only a further year or two the accumulated snows will be melted into lakes, streams, and rivers. Admittedly, there would have been a number of very bad years, enough to throw human society into a crisis beside which the multitudinous troubles which now dog our daily lives would seem like pinpricks. But after a half a century things would be back to normal—seemingly.

21 This apparent loophole in what had seemed an inexorable line of reasoning troubled me for a long time until the day I chanced on a description of the following simple experiment: If air that has not been thoroughly dried, that contains a number of very small water drops, is cooled progressively in a chamber, the droplets do not

solidify into ice crystals as their temperature falls below the normal freezing point, but remain as a supercooled liquid down to a remarkably low temperature, close to −40°C, when at last the liquid water goes into ice.

22 If a beam of light passes through the chamber, and if one looks at it from a direction at right angles to the beam, the chamber appears dark so long as the droplets stay liquid. Their transition to ice is signaled by a sudden radiance from the interior of the chamber. This means that whereas liquid droplets transmit light beams, ice crystals scatter them.

23 Even in the driest desert regions of the Earth there is always more than sufficient water in the air, if it is condensed from vapor into fine crystals of ice, to produce an almost perfectly reflective blanket. Does this happen anywhere? It does, particularly in the polar regions. The ice crystals are known to polar explorers as "diamond dust," a name that illustrates their brilliant reflective properties. Diamond dust is responsible for a bewildering range of optical effects—halos, mock suns, arcs, coronas, and iridescent clouds.

24 Why does diamond dust not form everywhere? Because except in the polar regions, water droplets in the atmosphere are kept above the critical temperature, near −40°C, at which they would be transformed into ice. What prevents the temperature of water droplets from falling to −40°C throughout much of the high atmosphere is heat from the oceans. Reduce the heat supplied by the oceans to the air by about 25 per cent and diamond dust would form, not just in the polar regions but over much of the Earth.

25 But this is exactly what would happen in the situation I have described: fine particles thrown up into the high atmosphere, either by an enormous volcano or by the collision of a giant meteorite, would cool the surface of the ocean and the ability of the ocean to supply heat to the air would be significantly reduced. Diamond dust would create an additional particle blanket around the Earth that would stay long after the first particles had fallen to ground level under gravity, and the diamond dust would then take over the job of reflecting sunlight, and so keep the ocean cool indefinitely.

26 Clearly, there are two distinct self-maintaining cycles of the world climate. If the surface layer of the ocean is warm, as it is at present, enough heat passes from the ocean to the air to prevent

diamond dust forming, except in polar regions. Sunlight comes through to the ocean and keeps the surface warm. This is the first cycle.

27 The second goes exactly the opposite way. If the surface of the ocean is cool, insufficient heat goes into the air to prevent diamond dust forming. Significantly more sunlight is then reflected back into space and the surface of the ocean remains cool.

28 Both the first and second cycles are logically consistent. If the Earth happens to be in either of them it tends to stay in that cycle, unless a catastrophic incident causes a sudden jump from the one cycle to the other. Indeed, the two cycles are exactly those I have described as interglacial and ice ages, and the interlaced sequence of ice ages and the interglacials arises because of such catastrophic events as collisions of the Earth with giant meteorites or explosions of volcanoes.

29 Ice ages have exceedingly abrupt terminations. Something about the end of the last ice age took the mammoths by surprise. Along with the mastodon and woolly rhinoceros, they became extinct. Complete mammoths with surprisingly little degeneration have been recovered from present-day ice in Siberia. Either they died of hypothermia caused by freezing rain, or they blundered into bogs and pools of exceedingly cold water formed from melting permafrost.

30 When one considers the effect on mammoths of sudden heat from a brassy sky caused by the absorbent particles thrown up by an iron meteorite, all the evidence falls into place. The frozen ground would soften and the mammoths would flounder. Frozen pools and lakes would partially melt. In the conditions of poor visibility, the mammoths and other animals would be likely to blunder to their deaths in the icy bogs.

31 The progression of catastrophic events controls the sequence of ice ages and interglacial periods. The grim aspect of this is that because of the suddenness of the catastrophic events, switches back and forth between interglacial cycles and ice-age cycles occur swiftly, in timespans of a few decades at most.

32 One may derive some consolation from the possibility that the switch to the next ice age may still be several thousand years into the future. On the other hand, the switch could have occurred in 1908, if the giant meteorite whose light was seen by Miss K. Stephens had happened to be larger. The switch could occur tomorrow, and if it

were to do so there is no human being, young or old, who would escape its appalling consequences.

Additional Rhetorical Strategy

Comparison and Contrast (paragraphs 26–28).

Examining Words and Meaning

1. In what way does Hoyle set the stage for "the overwhelming threat . . . in store for mankind" (paragraph 4)? How does he dramatically use the fact that we are "apt to think that the ice age is over" (paragraph 4)? What resistance does he assume his audience will have toward his subject?
2. Look at Hoyle's terminology carefully. Circle words or phrases that you think are narrowly scientific or not part of ordinary use. On the basis of this examination, would you say that Hoyle's vocabulary is accessible or inaccessible to the general reader?

Focusing on Structures and Strategies

1. Because of its tightly constructed causal chain, Hoyle's essay may require more than one reading to get its full impact. Reread the essay with pen in hand and outline (as you read) the causal sequence Hoyle has assembled. Start by considering the sequence of events that leads to ice-free eras, then look at what happens in that chain to produce ice ages.
2. What natural event does the entire chain of events depend on? Why, for example, is it so important to Hoyle's case that the direct rays of the sun can't melt snow or ice?
3. What is the "apparent loophole" that Hoyle refers to in paragraph 21? How does it affect the causal sequence he had outlined? How, for example, would the loophole weaken his case if he hadn't noticed the effect of "diamond dust"? How does the diamond-dust effect strengthen the linkage of events?

Suggestions for Further Discussion and Writing

1. Suppose you were an important government official and Hoyle's catastrophic prediction was brought to your attention. How would you handle the situation? Write a brief essay in which you either (a) challenge Hoyle's catastrophic sequence of events by showing a few possible loopholes, or (b) soften the impact of Hoyle's catastrophic sequence of events by showing that the problems are not insurmountable.

2. What is the most speculative part of Hoyle's case? To what extent does his entire sequence depend on what he calls an "accident" in paragraph 15? Consider carefully Hoyle's reliance on "accidents" throughout his essay, and discuss how that reliance could weaken his inexorable chain.

4. CLARIFYING IDEAS

Definition

1 So fundamental is definition to the activities of thinking and writing that we too often take its procedures entirely for granted. As the vocabulary we slowly and sometimes painfully acquired in childhood and early adolescence becomes an almost unconscious part of our nature, we may begin to overlook the rock-bottom significance of many of our most common words. Worse, we may even begin to think their meanings so settled that we need never reconsider them at all. In fact, as our educations become more formalized we may tend to worry more about all the words we don't know than about all the words we do know. We bone up on vocabulary lists so we can pass tests that demonstrate our mastery of words like *lugubrious, acerbic, myopic,* and *obfuscate.* Yet what kind of test would examine our grasp of such familiar words as *friend, grief, honor, wrong, violence, courage, sex, community, time,* or *love*—words which form the emotional and intellectual contours of most of our conscious and even unconscious lives? In our writing, we should be able to perform well with both vocabularies—the common and the uncommon—but we need to remember that the most familiar words will probably require the most attention.

2 As we think and write, we should keep a close watch on the words we use most frequently. Such words make up the vital part of our vocabulary and are the ones we tend to be most careless about. Words like *time, love, right, male,* or *female* look and feel simple, but they can be tricky and elusive. We can't assume that people will always interpret such words—no matter how ordinary-sounding they

seem—exactly as we expect them to. An everyday word like *time,* for instance, may have radically different meanings and associations to a physicist, a terminally ill patient, a jazz musician, an Olympic runner, and a prisoner. (The second selection in this section shows two different imaginations dealing with the definition of a horse.) Legal cases, diplomatic negotiations, political movements, and even medical decisions (for example, that someone is, or is not, to be pronounced dead) can, as we well know, hang on the precise definition of a word. Even the way we define our own proper names—as the concluding essay, by Ralph Ellison, in this section suggests—can have a vital bearing on how we conduct our lives.

3 Definition is basic to communication. We don't really know what we are talking about unless we know what our words mean. This isn't to say that we must always have at hand a precise definition for every word we use, but we do need to know, especially when we write, just when our use of a word requires the support of a careful definition. At a rough football game in which there are injuries and fights, for example, we might think that college sports are getting pretty violent and not feel it necessary to ask ourselves what exactly we mean by "violent." But if we decided to make that observation the basis for a composition about college sports, we could not construct a convincing case for our idea unless we made our notion of violence sufficiently precise. Just when does rough play become violent play? What looks like violence to us may be exciting play to another spectator and well-executed play to the winning coach. Though at first it may seem obvious, the meaning of a common word like *violence* needs to be thought out carefully once we decide to make it one of the principal words of our composition. To do this, we need to understand some of the ways in which words are defined.

4 Ever since Socrates and Plato, philosophers who virtually invented definition as a conceptual and rhetorical instrument, thinkers have tried to explain precisely what definition is and how it works. There are probably as many types of definition as there are intellectual disciplines. For the practical purposes of composition, however, three types of definition are essential: lexical, stipulative, and extended.

LEXICAL DEFINITIONS

5 *Lexical definition*—the definition we find when we consult a dictionary—is the simplest and most commonly used type of defini-

tion. It can be the means by which we learn a new word or clarify a familiar one. When we use a word without really thinking about its use, it is because we are probably in agreement with its lexical definition. There is nothing at all wrong with this practice, since verbal communication would come to a grinding halt if we had to stop to define each word we used each time we used it. Lexical definitions are rarely cited in writing; when they are, it is to show that the writer believes there is a need to call attention to the way a word is commonly used. In "The Holocaust," for example, Bruno Bettelheim quotes a dictionary definition of the word *martyr* (see p. 285) to show how inappropriate the term is as a description of the Nazi victims.

6 When working with lexical definitions it is important to remember one thing: a lexical definition does not give us the complete meaning of a word. Instead, it gives us the word's accepted usage along with other basic information about the term's practical management. A good dictionary, for example, will generally supply us with the following: first, the range of a term's commonly accepted usages (for example, that *prejudice* can mean "any preconceived opinion or feeling, either favorable or unfavorable," not just unfavorable); second, the range of terms close in meaning to the word we are looking up (for example, that *rustic* can sometimes be synonymous with the terms *simple, artless, uncouth, rude,* or *boorish*); third, a brief notation on the word's roots (that *camera* derives from the Latin word for *vaulted room* or *vault*); and, fourth, the general class and distinguishing characteristics of a term (that a *whale* is "any of the larger marine mammals of the order Cetacea"). Such information about past and present usage, synonyms, etymology, and classification may, at times, be valuable knowledge, but it seldom gives us insight into the complete meaning of a word. If we look up, for example, a fairly complex everyday word like *adult,* we find that its primary definition is "having attained maturity," a phrase that, unless we know how to define the equally complex word *mature,* tells us very little. To understand a word fully we need to think beyond its dictionary synonyms. Looking up words like *oil* and *water* in a dictionary will yield little vital knowledge concerning the powerful political or cultural dimensions of those terms. And without a consideration of a word's wider context, its meaning cannot be fully understood. This is one reason why we should cite dictionary definitions rarely and why we should never begin essays with "Webster defines *X* as . . ." when we intend our discussion to be a serious exploration into the meaning of *X*.

STIPULATIVE DEFINITIONS

7 We use *stipulative definitions* when we deliberately want to alter in some way the customary lexical sense of a word. We may want to give a word a new shading or a sharper interpretation. We may find ourselves disagreeing with accepted usage and wanting to stipulate a new denotation; for example, we may decide that *adult* as defined by most dictionaries is too vague for our purposes, and so we make clear that in our essay we will use it in a more specific sense: "anyone regardless of sex or mental competence who is eighteen or over." We are also stipulating a definition when we want to focus on only one aspect of the lexical definition and not another; for example, in a paper we may want the term *classic* to refer only to the style or thought of ancient Greece and Rome, and not to the notion of lasting significance or recognized worth.

8 When using stipulative definitions in our writing we should always be sure to announce clearly the first time we use a word what our special definition of it is. We should then remain consistent in our use of the word and not drift back to its lexical definition. For example, here is how the noted social critic Ivan Illich begins a discussion of the wasteful use of energy in modern transportation:

> The discussion of how energy is used to move people requires a formal distinction between transport and transit as the two components of traffic. By *traffic* I mean any movement of people from one place to another when they are outside their homes. By *transit* I mean those movements that put human metabolic energy to use, and by *transport,* that mode of movement which relies on other sources of energy. These energy sources will henceforth be mostly motors, since animals compete fiercely with men for their food in an overpopulated world, unless they are thistle eaters like donkeys and camels.

Note that the writer's definitions are not precisely those we'd find in a dictionary. But neither are they so different from their normal dictionary entries as to cause us undue trouble as readers. Stipulative definitions, as this brief excerpt clearly shows, can be extremely useful in our writing when we need to make careful distinctions between words that our readers have little reason to regard as essentially different. For example, if in a paper we wanted to make a distinction between *maturity* and *adulthood,* we would have to develop stipulative definitions for these closely related words. Given the similar dictionary usages of these terms, we could not as writers expect our readers to be alert to any important shades of meaning we may find between them without the extra help of one or more stipulative definitions.

9 Clearly formed stipulative definitions can play a crucial role in accurate and forceful writing, but they do present dangers. By letting our special sense of a word stray too far from accepted usage—if we define *maturity,* say, as "the ability to read and write"—we risk confusing or losing readers who will naturally find it hard to shake off the weight of the word's ordinary lexical sense. It is a good idea when stipulating a definition to retain enough of a word's customary lexical usage to ensure comprehensibility. Try to avoid the communication impasse Humpty Dumpty gets himself into with Alice when he belligerently declares that words can mean whatever he chooses them to mean, "neither more nor less."

EXTENDED DEFINITIONS

10 Lexical and stipulative definitions are usually concise, tending toward specification and clarification rather than elaboration. *Extended definition,* on the other hand, is a method of defining in greater detail. We usually reserve extended definition for words that are complex because of their evaluative, abstract, or emotional dimensions. It allows us to put a key term or concept on exhibit, to look at it in a network of relations and through a variety of perspectives. Complex words like *equality, fear,* or *anxiety* can be defined penetratingly and comprehensively by tying in the defining process to other rhetorical strategies, such as controlling metaphor or comparison and contrast. Extended definitions may run for a paragraph or two, or, as is often the case, constitute the main topic of a composition (see, for example, Peter Homans's "The Western: The Legend and the Cardboard Hero," on p. 291). In one sense, extended definition resembles stipulative definition: it is advisable when constructing an extended definition not to set our sense of the word at odds with its accepted usage. An effective extended definition expands and improves the common usage rather than contradicts it.

11 As some of the following selections show, extended definition is a common feature of expository writing. It is the type of definition we will use most frequently in our writing. We may, as Peter Homans does with the word *western,* explore the essential meaning of a word

in order to learn more about some aspect of our culture; or we may, as Karen Horney does with the terms *fear* and *anxiety* (see p. 288), need to sharpen accepted definitions as a foundation for other concepts. To return to our earlier example, our observations on "violence" at a football game could lead to a carefully formulated essay on what violence means in our culture or to a few sentences or paragraphs on what violence means in college football. In either case, we'd need to take the word beyond the minimal definition provided by our dictionaries and discuss it within the wider context of our information and experience.

12 In addition to its practical compositional use, definition can play a central role in the formation of concepts. As we have seen, definition involves more than merely looking up the established meanings of words. It can be in itself a rewarding intellectual activity, a process indispensable to every area of human inquiry: as the economist Karl Marx searched for an accurate definition of *commodity,* he developed an entirely new way of thinking about the value of human labor; attempting to construct a precise definition of *hysteria,* Sigmund Freud found himself confronted with a radically new conception of the mind. As we think through our compositions, we should try to remain particularly sensitive to the definitions of the words we are working with, their margins of accuracy, their opportunities for refinement or expansion. It is one of the best ways to transform old knowledge into new.

Alchemy

Lewis Thomas

If Lewis Thomas had simply looked up the word alchemy *in a dictionary, he would have found a definition similar to the following: "a medieval form of chemistry, aiming chiefly at discovering methods for transmuting base metals into gold and finding a universal solvent and an elixer of life." But for the purposes of this essay, Thomas wanted to explore the term beyond its lexical definition. His goal in the essay was to show how the roots of modern science can be found in the old-fashioned assumptions and techniques of alchemy. To accomplish this, he needed to look at the word's range of connotations, its historical dimensions, and its relation to scientific method. Not once in his essay, from* Late Night Thoughts on Listening to Mahler's Ninth Symphony, *does Thomas refer directly to the word's lexical definition, though you will notice how the key terms of that definition are introduced and their significance enlarged.*

For biographical information on Lewis Thomas, see page 109.

1 Alchemy began long ago as an expression of the deepest and oldest of human wishes: to discover that the world makes sense. The working assumption—that everything on earth must be made up from a single, primal sort of matter—led to centuries of hard work aimed at isolating the original stuff and rearranging it to the alchemists' liking. If it could be found, nothing would lie beyond human grasp. The transmutation of base metals to gold was only a modest part of the prospect. If you knew about the fundamental substance, you could do much more than make simple money: you could boil up a cure-all for every disease affecting humankind, you could rid the world of evil, and, while doing this, you could make a universal solvent capable of dissolving anything you might want to dissolve. These were heady ideas, and generations of alchemists worked all their lives trying to reduce matter to its ultimate origin.

terms of lexical definition

2 To be an alchemist was to be a serious professional, requiring long periods of apprenticeship and a great deal of late-night study. From the earliest years of the profession, there was a lot to read. The documents can be traced back to Arabic, Latin, and Greek scholars of the ancient world, and beyond them to Indian Vedic texts as far back as the tenth century B.C. All the old papers contain a formidable array of information, mostly expressed in incantations, which were required learning for every young alchemist and, by design, incomprehensible to everyone else. The word "gibberish" is thought by some to refer back to Jabir ibn Hayyan, an eighth-century alchemist,

who lived in fear of being executed for black magic and worded his doctrines so obscurely that almost no one knew what he was talking about.

3 Indeed, black magic was what most people thought the alchemists were up to in their laboratories, filled with the fumes of arsenic, mercury, and sulphur and the bubbling infusions of all sorts of obscure plants. We tend to look back at them from today's pinnacle of science as figures of fun, eccentric solitary men wearing comical conical hats, engaged in meaningless explorations down one blind alley after another. It was not necessarily so: the work they were doing was hard and frustrating, but it was the start-up of experimental chemistry and physics. The central idea they were obsessed with—that there is a fundamental, elementary particle out of which everything in the universe is made—continues to obsess today's physicists.

references to lexical definition

4 They never succeeded in making gold from base metals, nor did they find a universal elixir in their plant extracts; they certainly didn't rid the world of evil. What they did accomplish, however, was no small thing: they got the work going. They fiddled around in their laboratories, talked at one another incessantly, set up one crazy experiment after another, wrote endless reams of notes, which were then translated from Arabic to Greek to Latin and back again, and the work got under way. More workers became interested and then involved in the work, and, as has been happening ever since in science, one thing led to another. As time went on and the work progressed, error after error, new and accurate things began to turn up. Hard facts were learned about the behavior of metals and their alloys, the properties of acids, bases, and salts were recognized, the mathematics of thermodynamics were worked out, and, with just a few jumps through the centuries, the helical molecule of DNA was revealed in all its mystery.

5 The current anxieties over what science may be doing to human society, including the worries about technology, are no new thing. The third-century Roman emperor Diocletian decreed that all manuscripts dealing with

alchemy were to be destroyed, on grounds that such enterprises were against nature. The work went on in secrecy, and, although some of the material was lost, a great deal was translated into other languages, passed around, and preserved.

connotations of word

6 The association of alchemy with black magic has persisted in the public mind throughout the long history of the endeavor, partly because the objective—the transmutation of one sort of substance to another—seemed magical by definition. Partly also because of the hybrid term: *al* was simply the Arabic article, but *chemy* came from a word meaning "the black land," *Khemia,* the Greek name for Egypt. Another, similar-sounding word, *khumeia,* meant an infusion or elixir, and this was incorporated as part of the meaning. The Egyptian origin is very old, extending back to Thoth, the god of magic (who later reappeared as Hermes Trismegistus, master of the hermetic seal required by alchemists for the vacuums they believed were needed in their work). The notion of alchemy may be as old as language, and the idea that language and magic are somehow related is also old. "Grammar," after all, was a word used in the Middle Ages to denote high learning, but it also implied a practicing familiarity with alchemy. *Gramarye,* an older term for grammar, signified occult learning and necromancy. "Glamour," of all words, was the Scottish word for grammar, and it meant, precisely, a spell, casting enchantment.

etymology of word

extends etymology to broaden range of connotations

broadens range of connotations further

7 Medicine, from its dark origins in old shamanism millennia ago, became closely linked in the Middle Ages with alchemy. The preoccupation of alchemists with metals and their properties led to experiments—mostly feckless ones, looking back—with the therapeutic use of all sorts of metals. Paracelsus, a prominent physician of the sixteenth century, achieved fame from his enthusiastic use of mercury and arsenic, based on what now seems a wholly mystical commitment to alchemical philosophy as the key to understanding the universe and the human body simultaneously. Under his influence, three centuries of patients with all varieties of illness were treated with

strong potions of metals, chiefly mercury, and vigorous purgation became standard medical practice.

8 Physics and chemistry have grown to scientific maturity, medicine is on its way to growing up, and it is hard to find traces anywhere of the earlier fumblings toward a genuine scientific method. Alchemy exists only as a museum piece, an intellectual fossil, so antique that we no longer need be embarrassed by the memory, but the memory is there. Science began by fumbling. It works because the people involved in it work, and *work together.* They become excited and exasperated, they exchange their bits of information at a full shout, and, the most wonderful thing of all, they keep *at* one another.

Relation of "alchemy" to present-day sciences

9 Something rather like this may be going on now, without realizing it, in the latest and grandest of all fields of science. People in my field, and some of my colleagues in the real "hard" sciences such as physics and chemistry, have a tendency to take lightly and often disparagingly the efforts of workers in the so-called social sciences. We like to refer to their data as soft. We do not acknowledge as we should the differences between the various disciplines within behavioral research—we speak of analytical psychiatry, sociology, linguistics, economics, and computer intelligence as though these inquiries were all of a piece, with all parties wearing the same old comical conical hats. It is of course not so. The principal feature that the social sciences share these days is the attraction they exert on considerable numbers of students, who see the prospect of exploring human behavior as irresistible and hope fervently that a powerful scientific method for doing the exploring can be worked out. All of the matters on the social-science agenda seem more urgent to these young people than they did at any other time in human memory. It may turn out, years hence, that a solid discipline of human science will have come into existence, hard as quantum physics, filled with deep insights, plagued as physics still is by ambiguities but with new rules and new ways of getting things done. Like, for instance, getting rid of thermonuclear weapons, patriotic rhetoric, and nationalism all at once. If anything like this does turn up we will be looking back at today's social scientists, and their close

colleagues the humanists, as having launched the new science in a way not all that different from the accomplishment of the old alchemists, by simply working on the problem—this time, the fundamental, primal universality of the human mind.

return to terms of lexical definition

Reading for Rhetorical Strategy

Note in paragraph 1 how Lewis Thomas introduces the key terms of the dictionary definition without ever clumsily saying "the dictionary defines alchemy as. . . ." Though the dictionary definition does not state it, in paragraphs 2–3 Thomas indicates that one of the word's principle connotations involves "black magic" and this connotation is important to our full understanding of the word. In paragraph 6 Thomas's breakdown of the word's etymology reinforces the magical connotations and helps deepen our understanding not only of the term but of the *concept* of alchemy. Thomas's examination of the word's connotations has prepared the reader for the main point of the essay, presented in paragraphs 7–9—the vital connection between alchemy and modern science. Note how Thomas ends his essay by returning to the dictionary terms. But note, too, how the meaning of those terms is now enhanced by the connotations and concepts that he explored throughout his extended definition.

What Is a Horse?

Charles Dickens

The most popular and by many accounts the greatest English novelist, Charles Dickens (1812–1870) created a host of memorable characters in more than a dozen monumental novels from Pickwick Papers *(1837) to his most finely crafted exploration of English life,* Our Mutual Friend *(1865).*

The Gradgrind School, scene of the opening chapters of Hard Times *(1854), is less a satirical exaggeration than an accurate report of the schools for the poor run according to the "new mechanical system of education" developed by Joseph Lancaster early in the Industrial Revolution. The Victorian fascination with encyclopedias, compendiums, and statistics of all sorts is clearly embodied in Thomas Gradgrind, for whom "facts alone are wanted in life." He will allow only the lexical definition of words, only the enumeration of attributes like those rattled off by Bitzer in the following selection.*

1 Thomas Gradgrind, sir. A man of realities. A man of fact and calculations. A man who proceeds upon the principle that two and two are four, and nothing over, and who is not to be talked into allowing for anything over. Thomas Gradgrind, sir—peremptorily Thomas—Thomas Gradgrind. With a rule and a pair of scales, and the multiplication table always in his pocket, sir, ready to weigh and measure any parcel of human nature, and tell you exactly what it comes to. It is a mere question of figures, a case of simple arithmetic. You might hope to get some other nonsensical belief into the head of George Gradgrind, or Augustus Gradgrind, or John Gradgrind, or Joseph Gradgrind (all suppositious, nonexistent persons), but into the head of Thomas Gradgrind—no, sir!

2 In such terms Mr Gradgrind always mentally introduced himself, whether to his private circle of acquaintance, or to the public in general. In such terms, no doubt, substituting the words 'boys and girls', for 'sir', Thomas Gradgrind now presented Thomas Gradgrind to the little pitchers before him, who were to be filled so full of facts.

3 Indeed, as he eagerly sparkled at them from the cellarage before mentioned, he seemed a kind of cannon loaded to the muzzle with facts, and prepared to blow them clean out of the regions of childhood at one discharge. He seemed a galvanizing apparatus, too, charged with a grim mechanical substitute for the tender young imaginations that were to be stormed away.

4 'Girl number twenty,' said Mr Gradgrind, squarely pointing with his square forefinger, 'I don't know that girl. Who is that girl?'

5 'Sissy Jupe, sir,' explained number twenty, blushing, standing up, and curtseying.

6 'Sissy is not a name,' said Mr Gradgrind. 'Don't call yourself Sissy. Call yourself Cecilia.'

7 'It's father as calls me Sissy, sir,' returned the young girl in a trembling voice, and with another curtsey.

8 'Then he has no business to do it,' said Mr Gradgrind. 'Tell him he mustn't. Cecilia Jupe. Let me see. What is your father?'

9 'He belongs to the horse-riding, if you please, sir.'

10 Mr Gradgrind frowned, and waved off the objectionable calling with his hand.

11 'We don't want to know anything about that, here. You mustn't tell us about that, here. Your father breaks horses, don't he?'

12 'If you please, sir, when they can get any to break, they do break horses in the ring, sir.'

13 'You mustn't tell us about the ring, here. Very well, then. Describe your father as a horsebreaker. He doctors sick horses, I dare say?'

14 'Oh yes, sir.'

15 'Very well, then. He is a veterinary surgeon, a farrier and horsebreaker. Give me your definition of a horse.'

16 (Sissy Jupe thrown into the greatest alarm by this demand.)

17 'Girl number twenty unable to define a horse!' said Mr Gradgrind, for the general behoof of all the little pitchers. 'Girl number twenty possessed of no facts, in reference to one of the commonest of animals! Some boy's definition of a horse. Bitzer, yours.'

18 The square finger, moving here and there, lighted suddenly on Bitzer, perhaps because he chanced to sit in the same ray of sunlight which, darting in at one of the bare windows of the intensely whitewashed room, irradiated Sissy. For, the boys and girls sat on the face of the inclined plane in two compact bodies, divided up the centre by a narrow interval; and Sissy, being at the corner of a row on the sunny side, came in for the beginning of a sunbeam, of which Bitzer, being at the corner of a row on the other side, a few rows in advance, caught the end. But, whereas the girl was so dark-eyed and dark-haired, that she seemed to receive a deeper and more lustrous colour from the sun when it shone upon her, the boy was so light-eyed and light-haired that the self-same rays appeared to draw out of him what little colour he ever possessed. His cold eyes would hardly have been eyes, but for the short ends of lashes which, by bringing them into immediate contrast with something paler than themselves, expressed their form. His short-cropped hair might have been a mere continuation of the sandy freckles on his forehead and face. His skin was so unwholesomely deficient in the natural tinge, that he looked as though, if he were cut, he would bleed white.

19 'Bitzer,' said Thomas Gradgrind. 'Your definition of a horse.'

20 'Quadruped. Graminivorous. Forty teeth, namely twenty-four grinders, four eye-teeth, and twelve incisive. Sheds coat in the spring; in marshy countries, sheds hoofs, too. Hoofs hard, but requiring to be shod with iron. Age known by marks in mouth.' Thus (and much more) Bitzer.

21 'Now girl number twenty,' said Mr Gradgrind. 'You know what a horse is.'

Additional Rhetorical Strategies

Description (paragraphs 1, 18); Comparison and Contrast (paragraphs 3, 18).

Examining Words and Meaning

1. What is the significance of Gradgrind's addressing Sissy as "girl number twenty" (paragraph 4)? And why does he think that "Sissy" is not a name?
2. Look up the following words in the dictionary: peremptorily (paragraph 1); suppositious (paragraph 1); galvanizing (paragraph 3); farrier (paragraph 15); lustrous (paragraph 18); tinge (paragraph 18); quadruped (paragraph 20); graminivorous (paragraph 20).

Focusing on Structures and Strategies

1. Suppose that the selection opened in this way: "My name is Thomas Gradgrind, sir, and I am a man of realities and of fact and calculations." Why would this opening be less effective than the one Dickens gives us? Where else in the selection do the lengths and rhythms of the sentences help to convey a clear sense of Gradgrind and the way his mind works?
2. Would you say that Gradgrind is obsessed with lexical, stipulative, or extended definition? What sort of definition does he seem to be incapable of making? Which kinds of definition does Dickens imply are most important?

Suggestions for Further Discussion and Writing

1. Dickens's passage raises the question of what an education should, and what it should not, be. Gradgrind's preferences are clear. Are

Dickens's similar? How can you tell? What are your own thoughts about what an education should be? Do you think that schools should emphasize facts more, or that they should allow more flexibility and creativity at the risk of not teaching some necessary facts?

2. Choose any relatively common word, such as *horse.* First, pretend that you are Bitzer, and write out his definition of it. Then define the word in the way you think it should be defined. Which definition is more difficult to write? Which tells your reader more?

We're Not Really "Equal"

Thomas Sowell

"The real issue is whether or not we are going to talk sense." And as the economist Thomas Sowell (1930–) points out in the following essay, talking sense is very much a matter of defining our terms systematically. Not only does Sowell's essay point out the necessity of systematic definition, it also conveniently demonstrates in its method two thinking processes by which we can arrive at systematic definitions in our writing. One process is to define a term by eliminating everything which it is not; the other is to describe something similar to the subject of our definition and then to delineate the differences between them.

The author of Ethnic America *(1981), from which this selection is taken, Thomas Sowell is a senior fellow at Stanford University's Hoover Institute and a member of the Economic Policy Advisory Board. A high-school dropout, Sowell attended Howard and Harvard universities on the G.I. Bill and then obtained a Ph.D. in economics from the University of Chicago. As a prominent black scholar in the largely white field of political economy, Sowell has had a long and personal concern with the term* equality. *Besides* Ethnic America, *he has written ten other books, among them* Pink and Brown People *(1981) and* Markets and Minorities *(1981), plus numerous essays, newspaper columns, and scholarly articles.*

1 As a teacher I have learned from sad experience that nothing so bores students as being asked to define their terms systematically

before discussing some exciting issue. They want to get on with it, without wasting time on petty verbal distinctions.

2 Much of our politics is conducted in the same spirit. We are for "equality" or "the environment," or against an "arms race," and there is no time to waste on definitions and other Mickey Mouse stuff. This attitude may be all right for those for whom political crusades are a matter of personal excitement, like rooting for your favorite team and jeering the opposition. But for those who are serious about the consequences of public policy, nothing can be built without a solid foundation.

3 "Equality" is one of the great undefined terms underlying much current controversy and antagonism. This one confused word might even become the rock on which our civilization is wrecked. It should be worth defining.

4 Equality is such an easily understood concept in mathematics that we may not realize it is a bottomless pit of complexities anywhere else. That is because in mathematics we have eliminated the concreteness and complexities of real things. When we say that two plus two equals four, we either don't say two *what* or we say the same what after each number. But if we said that two apples plus two apples equals four oranges, we would be in trouble.

SENSE

5 Yet that is what we are saying in our political reasoning. And we are in trouble. Nothing is more concrete or complex than a human being. Beethoven could not play center field like Willie Mays, and Willie never tried to write a symphony. In what sense are they equal—or unequal? The common mathematical symbol for inequality points to the smaller quantity. But which is the smaller quantity—and in whose eyes—when such completely different things are involved?

6 When women have children and men don't, how can they be either equal or unequal? Our passionate desire to reduce things to the simplicity of abstract concepts does not mean that it can be done. Those who want to cheer their team and boo the visitors may like to think that the issue is equality versus inequality. But the real issue is whether or not we are going to talk sense. Those who believe in inequality have the same confusion as those who believe in equality. The French make better champagne than the Japanese, but the Japanese make better cameras than the French. What sense does it make

to add champagne to cameras to a thousand other things and come up with a grand total showing who is "superior"?

7 When we speak of "equal justice under law," we simply mean applying the same rules to everybody. That has nothing whatsoever to do with whether everyone performs equally. A good umpire calls balls and strikes by the same rules for everyone, but one batter may get twice as many hits as another.

8 In recent years we have increasingly heard it argued that if outcomes are unequal, then the rules must have been applied unequally. It would destroy my last illusion to discover that Willie Mays didn't really play baseball any better than anybody else, but that the umpires and sportswriters just conspired to make it look that way. Pending the uncovering of intricate plots of this magnitude, we must accept the fact that performances are very unequal in different aspects of life. And there is no way to add up these apples, oranges and grapes to get one sum total of fruit.

9 Anyone with the slightest familiarity with history knows that rules have often been applied very unequally to different groups. (A few are ignorant or misguided enough to think that this is a peculiarity of American society.) The problem is not in seeing that unequal rules can lead to unequal outcomes. The problem is in trying to reason backward from unequal outcomes to unequal rules as the sole or main cause.

10 There are innumerable places around the world where those who have been the victims of unequal rules have nevertheless vastly outperformed those who are favored. Almost nowhere in Southeast Asia have the Chinese minority had equal rights with the native peoples, but the average Chinese income in these countries has almost invariably been much higher than that of the general population. A very similar story could be told from the history of the Jews in many countries of Europe, North Africa and the Middle East. To a greater or lesser extent, this has also been the history of the Ibos in Nigeria, the Italians in Argentina, the Armenians in Turkey, the Japanese in the United States—and on and on.

CONFUSED TERMS

11 It would be very convenient if we could infer discriminatory rules whenever we found unequal outcomes. But life does not always accommodate itself to our convenience.

12 Those who are determined to find villains but cannot find evi-

dence often resort to "society" as the cause of all our troubles. What do they mean by "society" or "environment"? They act as if these terms were self-evident. But environment and society are just new confused terms introduced to save the old confused term, equality.

13 The American environment or society cannot explain historical behavior patterns found among German-Americans if these same patterns can be found among Germans in Brazil, Australia, Ireland and elsewhere around the world. These patterns may be explained by the history of German society. But if the words "environment" or "society" refer to things that may go back a thousand years, we are no longer talking about either the causal or the moral responsibility of American society. If historic causes include such things as the peculiar geography of Africa or of southern Italy, then we are no longer talking about human responsibility at all.

14 This does not mean that there are no problems. There are very serious social problems. But that means that serious attention will be required to solve them—beginning with defining our terms.

Additional Rhetorical Strategies

Illustration (paragraphs 5, 6, 10); Cause and Effect (paragraphs 9–12).

Examining Words and Meaning

1. As a teacher, Sowell claims he has learned that the systematic definition of words bores his students. As a student, do you think he is correct? Why or why not?
2. How does Sowell himself define the "confused word" *equality?* Why doesn't he use a dictionary definition? Where in his essay can you find his definition?

Focusing on Structures and Strategies

1. What is the main issue that Sowell deals with in this essay? Is it the definition of *equality?* If not, how does equality fit into his discussion?

2. Why does Sowell bring up the question of human responsibility in paragraph 13? How does this concept relate to equality?

Suggestion for Further Discussion and Writing

1. Instead of considering all the things equality is not, think of all the things it is. Then write a brief essay challenging Sowell's negative definition with a positive one. A good way to tackle this assignment would be to devise an answer to Sowell's rhetorical question in paragraph 6: "When women have children and men don't, how can they be either equal or unequal?" How would you answer that?

The Holocaust

Bruno Bettelheim

One of the world's most distinguished child psychologists, Bruno Bettelheim was born in Vienna in 1903. He fled to America in 1939, after spending a year in the Buchenwald and Dachau concentration camps. He is currently a professor of education, psychology, and psychiatry at the University of Chicago. His most widely acclaimed books are The Uses of Enchantment: The Meaning and Importance of Fairy Tales *(1976),* Surviving and Other Essays *(1979), from which the following selection is drawn,* On Learning to Read: The Child's Fascination with Meaning *(1982),* Freud and Man's Soul *(1982), and* A Good Enough Parent *(1987).*

Early in the course of his essay "The Holocaust—One Generation After," Bettelheim pauses in his analysis to take a close look at the meaning of the word holocaust. *He traces the history of the term, argues its inadequacy to describe what happened to millions of Jews, and speculates about the reasons why we use a word that distances us from the events it is supposed to name.*

1 To begin with, it was not the hapless victims of the Nazis who named their incomprehensible and totally unmasterable fate the

"holocaust." It was the Americans who applied this artificial and highly technical term of the Nazi extermination of the European Jews. But while the event when named as mass murder most foul evokes the most immediate, most powerful revulsion, when it is designated by a rare technical term, we must first in our minds translate it back into emotionally meaningful language. Using technical or specially created terms instead of words from our common vocabulary is one of the best-known and most widely used distancing devices, separating the intellectual from the emotional experience. Talking about "the holocaust" permits us to manage it intellectually where the raw facts, when given their ordinary names, would overwhelm us emotionally—because it was catastrophe beyond comprehension, beyond the limits of our imagination, unless we force ourselves against our desire to extend it to encompass these terrible events.

2 This linguistic circumlocution began while it all was only in the planning stage. Even the Nazis—usually given to grossness in language and action—shied away from facing openly what they were up to and called this vile mass murder "the final solution of the Jewish problem." After all, solving a problem can be made to appear like an honorable enterprise, as long as we are not forced to recognize that the solution we are about to embark on consists of the completely unprovoked, vicious murder of millions of helpless men, women, and children. The Nuremberg judges of these Nazi criminals followed their example of circumlocution by coining a neologism out of one Greek and one Latin root: genocide. These artificially created technical terms fail to connect with our strongest feelings. The horror of murder is part of our most common human heritage. From earliest infancy on, it arouses violent abhorrence in us. Therefore in whatever form it appears we should give such an act its true designation and not hide it behind polite, erudite terms created out of classical words.

3 To call this vile mass murder "the holocaust" is not to give it a special name emphasizing its uniqueness which would permit, over time, the word becoming invested with feelings germane to the event it refers to. The correct definition of "holocaust" is "burnt offering." As such, it is part of the language of the psalmist, a meaningful word to all who have some acquaintance with the Bible, full of the richest emotional connotations. By using the term "holocaust," entirely false associations are established through conscious and unconscious connotations between the most vicious of mass murders and ancient rituals of a deeply religious nature.

4 Using a word with such strong unconscious religious connotations when speaking of the murder of millions of Jews robs the victims of this abominable mass murder of the only thing left to them: their uniqueness. Calling the most callous, most brutal, most horrid, most heinous mass murder a burnt offering is a sacrilege, a profanation of God and man.

5 Martyrdom is part of our religious heritage. A martyr, burned at the stake, is a burnt offering to his god. And it is true that after the Jews were asphyxiated, the victims' corpses were burned. But I believe we fool ourselves if we think we are honoring the victims of systematic murder by using this term, which has the highest moral connotations. By doing so, we connect for our own psychological reasons what happened in the extermination camps with historical events we deeply regret, but also greatly admire. We do so because this makes it easier for us to cope; only in doing so we cope with our distorted image of what happened, not with the events the way they did happen.

6 By calling the victims of the Nazis "martyrs," we falsify their fate. The true meaning of "martyr" is: "One who voluntarily undergoes the penalty of death for refusing to renounce his faith" *(Oxford English Dictionary).* The Nazis made sure that nobody could mistakenly think that their victims were murdered for their religious beliefs. Renouncing their faith would have saved none of them. Those who had converted to Christianity were gassed, as were those who were atheists, and those who were deeply religious Jews. They did not die for any conviction, and certainly not out of choice.

7 Millions of Jews were systematically slaughtered, as were untold other "undesirables," not for any convictions of theirs, but only because they stood in the way of the realization of an illusion. They neither died for their convictions, nor were they slaughtered because of their convictions, but only in consequence of the Nazis' delusional belief about what was required to protect the purity of their assumed superior racial endowment, and what they thought necessary to guarantee them the living space they believed they needed and were entitled to. Thus while these millions were slaughtered for an idea, they did not die for one.

8 Millions—men, women, and children—were processed after they had been utterly brutalized, their humanity destroyed, their clothes torn from their bodies. Naked, they were sorted into those who were destined to be murdered immediately, and those others who had a short-term usefulness as slave labor. But after a brief

interval they, too, were to be herded into the same gas chambers into which the others were immediately piled, there to be asphyxiated so that, in their last moments, they could not prevent themselves from fighting each other in vain for a last breath of air.

9 To call these most wretched victims of a murderous delusion, of destructive drives run rampant, martyrs or a burnt offering is a distortion invented for our comfort, small as it may be. It pretends that this most vicious of mass murders had some deeper meaning; that in some fashion the victims either offered themselves or at least became sacrifices to a higher cause. It robs them of the last recognition which could be theirs, denies them the last dignity we could accord them: to face and accept what their death was all about, not embellishing it for the small psychological relief this may give us.

10 We could feel so much better if the victims had acted out of choice. For our emotional relief, therefore, we dwell on the tiny minority who did exercise some choice: the resistance fighters of the Warsaw ghetto, for example, and others like them. We are ready to overlook the fact that these people fought back only at a time when everything was lost, when the overwhelming majority of those who had been forced into the ghettos had already been exterminated without resisting. Certainly those few who finally fought for their survival and their convictions, risking and losing their lives in doing so, deserve our admiration; their deeds give us a moral lift. But the more we dwell on these few, the more unfair are we to the memory of the millions who were slaughtered—who gave in, did not fight back—because we deny them the only thing which up to the very end remained uniquely their own: their fate.

Additional Rhetorical Strategies

Argument (throughout); Cause and Effect (paragraph 1).

Examining Words and Meaning

1. Look up *genocide* (paragraph 2) in a good dictionary. What are the Greek and Latin roots that Bettelheim speaks of? What other words

can you think of with these roots? Do you agree that this word shields us from the harshness of the action it describes?

2. What words and phrases does Bettelheim use in place of *holocaust, martyr, genocide,* and so forth? Do they have a greater impact on you than the terms he objects to?

Focusing on Structures and Strategies

1. In paragraph 2, what is the rhetorical effect of Bettelheim's comparing our circumlocution to that of the Nazis? In what ways does it make us re-examine words that we often use without thinking?
2. What sort of definition—lexical, stipulative, or extended—does Bettelheim develop for the major terms used in this selection? Does his using definition in this way help you to see its rhetorical potential? How so?

Suggestions for Further Discussion and Writing

1. Many of us have probably grown up not knowing the origin and historical connotations of words such as *holocaust* and *genocide.* What connotations do the words have for you? Is it possible that they affect you differently than they affect Bettelheim?
2. What other events, past or present, do we put at a distance by speaking of them with indirect, protective language? Write an essay in which you focus on the language with which we refer to one such event. You may choose something from your own experience—such as a death in the family—or something you read about in the newspaper, such as the plight of the homeless or the status of political hostages in an area of political oppression. In either case, look carefully at what language people use to describe the event. What do the words really mean? Are they used in this sense in the situation you are analyzing? Explain how people are trying to skirt the edges of reality by using this kind of language.

Fear and Anxiety

Karen Horney

Making careful, precise distinctions between words which are often used indistinguishably in everyday conversation is crucial to all areas of study. Words defined one way in one discipline are often defined in a different way in another discipline; for example, the term class *is used quite differently in mathematics and political science.In the following excerpt from her famous study,* The Neurotic Personality of Our Time *(1937), psychiatrist Karen Horney carefully examines the differences between two closely related words,* fear *and* anxiety, *words of special importance for her work with neurotic patients and for her study of neurosis.Born in Germany and trained as a Freudian psychoanalyst, Horney (1885–1952) grew critical of Freud's view of women and skeptical of his contention that sexual and aggressive instincts are the motivating forces in human beings. She became an outspoken doubter at a time when the Freudian faithful were particularly intolerant of heretics. At a meeting in New York City, Karen Horney was interrogated about her differences with Freud and judged unqualified to teach psychoanalysis. The following week she and twenty of her supporters founded a rival institute of psychological study, which continues to flourish.*

1 When a mother is afraid that her child will die when it has only a pimple or a slight cold we speak of anxiety; but if she is afraid when the child has a serious illness we call her reaction fear. If someone is afraid whenever he stands on a height or when he has to discuss a topic he knows well, we call his reaction anxiety; if someone is afraid when he loses his way high up in the mountains during a heavy thunderstorm we would speak of fear. Thus far we should have a simple and neat distinction: fear is a reaction that is proportionate to the danger one has to face, whereas anxiety is a disproportionate reaction to danger, or even a reaction to imaginary danger.

2 This distinction has one flaw, however, which is that the decision as to whether the reaction is proportionate depends on the average knowledge existing in the particular culture. But even if that knowledge proclaims a certain attitude to be unfounded, a neurotic

will find no difficulty in giving his action a rational foundation. In fact, one might get into hopeless arguments if one told a patient that his dread of being attacked by some raving lunatic is neurotic anxiety. He would point out that his fear is realistic and would refer to occurrences of the kind he fears. The primitive would be similarly stubborn if one considered certain of his fear reactions disproportionate to the actual danger. For instance, a primitive man in a tribe which has taboos on eating certain animals is mortally frightened if by any chance he has eaten the tabooed meat. As an outside observer you would call this a disproportionate reaction, in fact an entirely unwarranted one. But knowing the tribe's beliefs concerning forbidden meat you would have to realize that the situation represents a real danger to the man, danger that the hunting or fishing grounds may be spoiled or danger of contracting an illness.

3 There is a difference, however, between the anxiety we find in primitives and the anxiety we consider neurotic in our culture. The content of neurotic anxiety, unlike that of the primitive, does not conform with commonly held opinions. In both the impression of a disproportionate reaction vanishes once the meaning of the anxiety is understood. There are persons, for example, who have a perpetual anxiety about dying; on the other hand, because of their sufferings they have a secret wish to die. Their various fears of death, combined with their wishful thinking with regard to death, create a strong apprehension of imminent danger. If one knows all these factors one cannot help but call their anxiety about dying an adequate reaction. Another, simplified example is seen in persons who become terrified when they find themselves near a precipice or a high window or on a high bridge. Here again, from without, the fear reaction seems to be disproportionate. But such a situation may present to them, or stir up in them, a conflict between the wish to live and the temptation for some reason or another to jump down from the heights. It is this conflict that may result in anxiety.

4 All these considerations suggest a change in the definition. Fear and anxiety are both proportionate reactions to danger, but in the case of fear the danger is a transparent, objective one and in the case of anxiety it is hidden and subjective. That is, the intensity of the anxiety is proportionate to the meaning the situation has for the person concerned, and the reasons why he is thus anxious are essentially unknown to him.

5 The practical implication of the distinction between fear and anxiety is that the attempt to argue a neurotic out of his anxiety—the

method of persuasion—is useless. His anxiety concerns not the situation as it stands actually in reality, but the situation as it appears to him. The therapeutic task, therefore, can be only that of finding out the meaning certain situations have for him.

Additional Rhetorical Strategies

Comparison and Contrast (paragraphs 1, 3); Illustration (paragraphs 2, 3).

Examining Words and Meaning

1. What is the first distinction Horney offers between *fear* and *anxiety?* What does she think the flaw in this distinction is?

2. If necessary, look up these words in a dictionary: proportionate (paragraph 2); neurotic (paragraph 2); taboos (paragraph 2); imminent (paragraph 3). Which of these words have you seen or heard before? Do they seem to be technical jargon? What does this tell you about the audience Horney had in mind for her essay?

Focusing on Structures and Strategies

1. Since Horney later qualifies the clear distinction between *fear* and *anxiety* that she makes in paragraph 1, why does she offer the distinction in the first place? How is it necessary to her definition?

2. At what point in this selection does Horney offer what she considers a satisfactory distinction between *fear* and *anxiety*? What is the effect of her working up to this point so carefully? Why might her definition seem less thorough if she simply offered it without leading up to it?

Suggestions for Further Discussion and Writing

1. After rereading this selection, do you think some of your anxieties may actually be fears? Do you think some of what you thought

were fears are actually anxieties? Why? What conflicts might be behind some of your anxieties?

2. Write an essay of definition in which you distinguish two different but frequently related terms: *courage* and *bravery, cowardice* and *caution, love* and *lust, loyalty* and *servility.* Try to prepare for and lead up to a definition rather than simply delivering one. Use examples to make all distinctions clear and keep your reader aware of the complexities and difficulties of defining your two terms.

The Western: The Legend and the Cardboard Hero

Peter Homans

By analyzing the essential ingredients of the western, Peter Homans arrives at a definition that reveals its underlying mythic structure and significance. Born in New York in 1930, Homans earned degrees at Princeton, the Protestant Episcopal Theological Seminary in Virginia, and the University of Chicago. In addition to writing about popular culture, he has written Theology After Freud: An Interpretive Inquiry *(1970) and* Jung in Context: Modernity and the Making of a Psychology *(1979). In "The Western: The Legend and the Cardboard Hero," Homans reveals his sharp eye for relations of popular culture to the timeless pattern of myth.*

1 He is the Law West of Tombstone, he is The Virginian at High Noon. He is Frontier Marshal, Knight of the Range, Rider of the Purple Sage. He Has Gun, Will Travel, and his name is Matt Dillon, Destry, Shane.

2 He is the hero of every Western that ever thundered out of the movies or TV screen, this Galahad with a Colt .45 who stalks injustice on the dusty streets of Dodge. Or Carson City. Or Virginia City.

3 Once he accomplishes his mission, he vanishes into the mists, as do all true heroes of all true legends. But where Hercules goes to Olympus and King Arthur to Avalon, this galoot rides Old Paint into the sunset.

4 With few variations, the movies have been telling this story for more than half a century. There have, in fact, been Western movies as long as there have been movies; the first American narrative film was a Western, *The Great Train Robbery,* made in 1903. Without the Westerns, it would be hard to imagine television today. Far outstripping the rowdy little boys who were its first enraptured audience, the Western has gone round the globe to become the youngest of the world's mythologies.

5 For each of us, even the word "Western" brings to mind an ordered sequence of character, event and detail. There may, of course, be variations within the pattern—but the basic outline remains constant. Details often vary, especially between movie and television Westerns, because the latter are essentially continued stories. Nonetheless, from the endless number of Westerns we have all seen, a basic concept emerges.

6 The Western takes place in a desolate, abandoned land. The desert, as a place without life, is indispensable. The story would not be credible were it set in a jungle, a fertile lowland or an arctic wasteland. We are dealing with a form of existence deprived of vitality.

7 This desert effect is contradicted by the presence of a town. Among the slapped-together buildings with false fronts, lined awkwardly along a road forever thick with dust, only three stand out—the saloon, the bank and the marshal's office (the hero's dwelling).

8 The saloon is the most important building in the Western. It is the only place in the story where people can be seen together time after time. It thereby functions as a meetinghouse, social center, church. More important, it is the setting for the climax of the story, the gunfight. No matter where the fight ends, it starts in the saloon.

9 The bank is a hastily constructed, fragile affair. Its only protection consists of a sniveling, timid clerk, with a mustache and a green eyeshade, who is only too glad to hand over the loot. Has there ever been a Western in which a robber wondered whether he could pull off his robbery?

10 The marshal's office appears less regularly. Most noticeable is the absence of any evidence of domesticity. We rarely see a bed, a place for clothes or any indication that a person actually makes his home here. There is not even a mirror. The overall atmosphere is that of austerity, which, we are led to suspect, is in some way related to our hero's virtue, and not to his finances.

11 The town as a whole has no business or industry. People have

money, but we rarely see them make it. Homelife is conspicuous by its absence. There are no families, children, dogs. The closest thing to a home is a hotel, and this is rarely separated from the saloon.

12 One of the most interesting people in the town is the "derelict professional." He was originally trained in one of the usual Eastern professions (law, medicine, letters, ministry), but since his arrival in the West, he has become corrupted by drink, gambling, sex or violence. The point is that the traditional mentors of society (counselor, healer, teacher, shepherd) cannot exist in an uncorrupted state under the pressure of Western life. Somewhat similar is the "nonviolent Easterner." He often appears as a well-dressed business man, or as a very recent graduate of Harvard. In the course of the plot's development, this character is either humiliated or killed. The East, we soon note, is incapable of action when action is most needed.

13 The "good girl" is another supporting type in the cast of characters. Pale and without appetite, she, too, is from the East and is classically represented as the new schoolmarm. The "bad girl" is alone in the world and usually works for her living in the saloon as a waitress or dancer. Both girls have their eye on the hero.

14 The bartender observes the action, but rarely becomes involved in it. "The boys," those bearded, grimy people who are always "just there" drinking and gambling in the saloon, function as an audience. No hero ever shot it out with his adversary without these people watching.

15 Then we come to the principals. We meet the hero in the opening phase of the action. He is, above all, a transcendent figure, originating beyond the town. He rides into the town from nowhere; even if he is the marshal, his identity is disassociated from the people he must save. We know nothing of any past activities, relationships, future plans or ambitions. There are no friends, relatives, family, mistresses—not even a dog or cat—and even with his horse, he has a strangely formal relationship.

16 At first, the hero is lax to the point of laziness. Take his hat, for example. It sits exactly where it was placed—no effort has been made to align it. With feet propped up on the porch rail, frame balanced on a chair or stool tilted back on its rear legs, hat pushed slightly over the eyes, hands clasped over the buckle of his gun belt, he is a study in contrived indolence. Now he has time on his hands, but he knows his time is coming, and so do we.

17 The hero indicates no desire for women. He appears somewhat bored with the whole business. He never blushes, or betrays any

enthusiasm. His monosyllabic stammer and brevity of speech clearly indicate an intended indifference.

18 In the drinking scenes, we are likely to see the hero equipped with the traditional shot glass and bottle. We seldom see him pay for more than one drink. He gulps his drink, rarely enjoys it and is impatient to be off. In the gambling scenes, his poker face veils any inner feelings of greed, enthusiasm or apprehension. We note, however, that he always wins or refuses to play. Similarly, he is utterly unimpressed by and indifferent to money.

19 There are hundreds of variations of the villain, but each is unshaven, darkly clothed and from the West. Like the hero, he is from beyond the town. He is inclined to cheat at cards, get drunk, lust after women who do not return the compliment, rob banks and, finally, shoot people he does not care for, especially heroes.

20 The impact of this evil one on the town is electric, suddenly animating it with vitality and purpose. Indeed, it is evil, rather than good, that actually gives meaning to the lives of these people. Nevertheless, they all know (as we do) that they are of themselves ultimately powerless to meet this evil. What is required is the hero—a transcendent power originating from beyond the town.

21 Notice what has happened to this power. Gone are the hero's indolence and lack of intention. Now, he is infused with vitality, direction and seriousness, in order to confront this ultimate threat. Once the radical shift has been accomplished, the hero (like the audience) is ready for the final conflict.

22 While the fight can take many forms (fistfight, fight with knives or whips, even a scowling match in which the hero successfully glares down the evil one), the classic and most popular form is the encounter with six-guns. It is a built-up and drawn-out affair, always allowing enough time for an audience to gather. The two men must adhere to an elaborate and well-defined casuistry as to who draws first, when it is proper to draw, etc. Although the hero's presence makes the fight possible—i.e., he insists on obstructing the evil one in some way; it is the latter who invariably attacks first. Were the hero ever to draw first, the story would no longer be a Western. With the destruction of the evil one, the action phase is completed.

23 In the closing phase, the town and its hero return to their preaction ways. One more event must take place, however, before the story can conclude. The hero must renounce any further involvement with the town. Traditionally, the hero marries the heroine and settles down. The Western hero always refuses—at least on televi-

sion. He cannot identify himself with the situation he has influenced. When this has been made clear, the story is over.

24 The Western is, as most people by this time are willing to acknowledge, a popular myth that sets forth certain meanings about what is good and bad, right and wrong. Evil, according to the myth, is the failure to resist temptation. Temptation consists of five activities: drinking, gambling, moneymaking, sex and violence. In the drinking scenes, the hero is offered not one drink, but a whole bottle. He has at his disposal the opportunity for unlimited indulgence and its consequent loss of self-control. Gambling is a situation over which one has rather limited control—one loses, but the hero does not lose. He wins, thereby remaining in control. Wealth is not seized, although it is available to him through the unguarded bank. And both good girl and bad girl seek out the hero, to no avail—he remains a hero.

25 We perceive in the evil one a terrible power, which he has acquired at a great price; he has forfeited the control and resistance that sustain and make the hero what he is. The villain is the embodiment of the failure to resist temptation; he is the failure of denial. This is the real meaning of evil in the myth of the Western, and it is this that makes the evil one truly evil. He threatens the hero's resistance; each taunt and baiting gesture is a lure to the forfeiture of control and leads to the one temptation that the hero cannot afford to resist: the temptation to destroy temptation.

26 But why must the hero wait to be attacked? Why must he refrain from drawing first? The circumstances are contrived in order to make the violent destruction of the evil one appear just and virtuous. This process whereby desire is at once indulged and veiled is the "inner dynamic." It is the key to the Western, explaining not only the climax of the story, but everything else uniquely characteristic of it. What is required is that temptation be indulged while providing the appearance of having been resisted. Each of the minor-temptation episodes—drink, cards, moneymaking and sex—takes its unique shape from this need and is a climaxless Western in itself.

27 The derelict professional is derelict, and the nonviolent Easterner is weak, precisely because they have failed to resist temptation in the manner characteristic of the hero. Because these two types originate in the East, they have something in common with the good girl. Everything Eastern in the Western is weak, emotional, feminine. This covers family life, intellectual life, professional life. Only by becoming Westernized can the East be redeemed. The Western there-

fore is more a myth about the East than it is about the West; it is a secret and bitter parody of Eastern ways.

28 In summary, then, the Western is a myth in which evil appears as a series of temptations to be resisted by the hero. When faced with the embodiment of these temptations, he destroys the threat. But the story is so structured that the responsibility for the act falls upon the adversary, permitting the hero to destroy while appearing to save.

29 The Western bears a significant relationship to puritanism, in which it is the proper task of the will to rule and contain the spontaneous, vital aspects of life. Whenever vitality becomes too pressing, and the dominion of the will becomes threatened, the self must find some other mode of control. The puritan will seek a situation that allows him to express vitality while appearing to resist it. The Western provides just this opportunity, for the entire myth is shaped by the inner dynamic of apparent control and veiled expression. Indeed, in the gunfight, the hero's heightened gravity and dedicated exclusion of all other loyalties present a study in puritan virtue, while the evil one presents nothing more or less than the old New England Protestant devil—strangely costumed, to be sure—the traditional tempter whose horrid lures never allow the good puritan a moment's peace. In the gunfight, there are deliverance and redemption.

30 Here, then, is the real meaning of the Western: It is a puritan morality tale in which the savior-hero redeems the community from the temptations of the devil. Tall in the saddle, he rides straight from Plymouth Rock to a dusty frontier town, and though he be the fastest gun this side of Laramie, his Colt .45 is on the side of the angels.

Additional Rhetorical Strategies

Illustration (paragraphs 1, 26); Description (paragraphs 8–15); Cause and Effect (paragraphs 12, 27); Narration (paragraph 18); Comparison and Contrast (paragraphs 24, 27).

Examining Words and Meaning

1. According to Homans, what are the essential characteristics of a western? Does he emphasize the similarities or the differences between various westerns? Why do you think he does so?

2. Homans describes the villain as "the evil one" (paragraph 20). What associations does this phrase have? How is the hero described in this paragraph? What metaphor, then, is Homans establishing? What other words and phrases contribute to the metaphor?

3. If necessary, consult your dictionary for the meaning of the following words: galoot (paragraph 3); austerity (paragraph 10); mentors (paragraph 12); lax (paragraph 16); indolence (paragraph 16); casuistry (paragraph 22).

Focusing on Structures and Strategies

1. Notice the organization of Homans's essay. What is the topic of paragraphs 6–11? Of paragraphs 12–14? Of paragraphs 15–18? Of paragraphs 19–20? Why does Homans order his thoughts in this way? Suppose, for example, that paragraphs 6–11 followed paragraphs 19–20. How would this have affected the transition to the rest of the essay?

2. At what point in the essay does Homans start to state explicitly the significance of the western he describes? Why does he wait so long to do so? Does he suggest by his word choice in his description of the western what he will later state directly? Be specific.

Suggestions for Further Discussion and Writing

1. To what extent is the Puritan morality that Homans finds in the western still operating in our culture? Do we still act out the "inner dynamic"? Do we express our vitality by suppressing it? Or have things changed? Is it still a male virtue to be controlled and detached, for example? Do we consider virtue to be the resisting of temptation? Discuss the question as it applies to the culture around you: to movies, dancing, advertising, popular music, and so on.

2. Write an essay in which you do for another genre of movies or television shows what Homans has done for the western. Consider the typical police show, situation comedy, soap opera, or the like. Describe the similarities that all the shows in your chosen category have. Then analyze the significance of the show: What message does it give us? What cultural and social values does it reinforce?

Hidden Name and Complex Fate

Ralph Ellison

What's in a name? The two greatest nineteenth-century British neurophysicians were Lord Russell Brain and Sir Henry Head. One of the great twentieth-century British philosophers is J. T. Wisdom. In general, of course, people's names bear no relations to their vocations. Nevertheless, as Ralph (Waldo) Ellison demonstrates, a name is a crucial matter, bearing closely on identity and position.

Perhaps more so than the names for things and thoughts, our own personal names remind us of the arbitrary origin and the inevitable influence of all words. Beginning with a variation of the familiar "let x *equal* y*" formula of mathematical word problems, Ellison, in the course of the following selection, implicitly defines the "suggestive powers of names and of the magic involved in naming."*

Named by his father after the eminent American essayist and poet, Ralph Waldo Emerson, Ellison was born in Oklahoma in 1914. After studying music and sculpture and studiously avoiding the works of his namesake, Ellison moved to New York City during the depression and began to work for the Federal Writers Project. He has lectured widely on cultural matters and comparative literature and has taught writing at major colleges and universities. His first novel, The Invisible Man *(1952), which chronicles the development of a black youth from naive trust in others to his loss of social identity, is generally considered one of the most distinguished novels of our time. Ellison published a book of political writings,* Going to the Territory, *in 1986.*

1 Let Tar Baby, that enigmatic figure from Negro folklore, stand for the world. He leans, black and gleaming, against the wall of life utterly noncommittal under our scrutiny, our questioning, starkly unmoving before our naïve attempts at intimidation. Then we touch him playfully and before we can say *Sonny Liston!*[1] we find ourselves stuck. Our playful investigations become a labor, a fearful struggle, an *agon.* Slowly we perceive that our task is to learn the proper way of freeing ourselves to develop, in other words, technique.

[1]Charles (Sonny) Liston, a world heavyweight boxing champion, lost his title to Cassius Clay (now Muhammad Ali) in 1964. [Eds.]

2 Sensing this, we give him our sharpest attention, we question him carefully, we struggle with more subtlety; while he, in his silent way, holds on, demanding that we perceive the necessity of calling him by his true name as the price of our freedom. It is unfortunate that he has so many, many "true names"—all spelling chaos; and in order to discover even one of these we must first come into the possession of our own names. For it is through our names that we first place ourselves in the world. Our names, being the gift of others, must be made our own.

3 Once while listening to the play of a two-year-old girl who did not know she was under observation, I heard her saying over and over again, at first with questioning and then with sounds of growing satisfaction, "I am Mimi Livisay? . . . *I* am Mimi Livisay. I *am* Mimi Livisay . . . I am *Mimi* Li-vi-say! I am Mimi . . ."

4 And in deed and in fact she was—or became so soon thereafter, by working playfully to establish the unity between herself and her name.

5 For many of us this is far from easy. We must learn to wear our names within all the noise and confusion of the environment in which we find ourselves; make them the center of all of our associations with the world, with man and with nature. We must charge them with all our emotions, our hopes, hates, loves, aspirations. They must become our masks and our shields and the containers of all those values and traditions which we learn and/or imagine as being the meaning of our familial past.

6 And when we are reminded so constantly that we bear, as Negroes, names originally possessed by those who owned our enslaved grandparents, we are apt, especially if we are potential writers, to be more than ordinarily concerned with the veiled and mysterious events, the fusions of blood, the furtive couplings, the business transactions, the violations of faith and loyalty, the assaults; yes, and the unrecognized and unrecognizable loves through which our names were handed down unto us.

7 So charged with emotion does this concern become for some of us, that we have, earlier, the example of the followers of Father Divine and, now, the Black Muslims, discarding their original names in rejection of the bloodstained, the brutal, the sinful images of the past. Thus they would declare new identities, would clarify a new program of intention and destroy the verbal evidence of a willed and ritualized discontinuity of blood and human intercourse.

8 Not all of us, actually only a few, seek to deal with our names in this manner. We take what we have and make of them what we

can. And there are even those who know where the old broken connections lie, who recognize their relatives across the chasm of historical denial and the artificial barriers of society, and who see themselves as bearers of many of the qualities which were admirable in the original sources of their common line (Faulkner has made much of this); and I speak here not of mere forgiveness, nor of obsequious insensitivity to the outrages symbolized by the denial and the division, but of the conscious acceptance of the harsh realities of the human condition, of the ambiguities and hypocrisies of human history as they have played themselves out in the United States.

9 Perhaps, taken in aggregate, these European names which (sometimes with irony, sometimes with pride, but always with personal investment) represent a certain triumph of the spirit, speaking to us of those who rallied, reassembled and transformed themselves and who under dismembering pressures refused to die. "Brothers and sisters," I once heard a Negro preacher exhort, "let us make up our faces before the world, and our names shall sound throughout the land with honor! For we ourselves are our *true* names, not their epithets! So let us, I say, Make Up Our Faces and Our Minds!"

10 Perhaps my preacher had read T. S. Eliot, although I doubt it. And in actuality, it was unnecessary that he do so, for a concern with names and naming was very much a part of that special area of American culture from which I come, and it is precisely for this reason that this example should come to mind in a discussion of my own experience as a writer.

11 Undoubtedly, writers begin their *conditioning* as manipulators of words long before they become aware of literature—certain Freudians would say at the breast. Perhaps. But if so, that is far too early to be of use at this moment. Of this, though, I am certain: that despite the misconceptions of those educators who trace the reading difficulties experienced by large numbers of Negro children in Northern schools to their Southern background, these children are, in *their* familiar South, facile manipulators of words. I know, too, that the Negro community is deadly in its ability to create nicknames and to spot all that is ludicrous in an unlikely name or that which is incongruous in conduct. Names are not qualities; nor are words, in this particular sense, actions. To assume that they are could cost one his life many times a day. Language skills depend to a large extent upon a knowledge of the details, the manners, the objects, the folkways, the psychological patterns, of a given environment. Humor and wit

depend upon much the same awareness, and so does the suggestive power of names.

12 "A small brown bowlegged Negro with the name 'Franklin D. Roosevelt Jones' might sound like a clown to someone who looks at him from the outside," said my friend Albert Murray, "but on the other hand he just might turn out to be a hell of a fireside operator. He might just lie back in all of that comic juxtaposition of names and manipulate you deaf, dumb and blind—and you not even suspecting it, because you're thrown out of stance by his name! There you are, so dazzled by the F.D.R. image—which you *know* you can't see—and so delighted with your own superior position that you don't realize that it's *Jones* who must be confronted."

13 Well, as you must suspect, all of this speculation on the matter of names has a purpose, and now, because it is tied up so ironically with my own experience as a writer, I must turn to my own name.

14 For in the dim beginnings, before I ever thought consciously of writing, there was my own name, and there was, doubtless, a certain magic in it. From the start I was uncomfortable with it, and in my earliest years it caused me much puzzlement. Neither could I understand what a poet was, nor why, exactly, my father had chosen to name me after one. Perhaps I could have understood it perfectly well had he named me after his own father, but that name had been given to an older brother who died and thus was out of the question. But why hadn't he named me after a hero, such as Jack Johnson, or a soldier like Colonel Charles Young, or a great seaman like Admiral Dewey, or an educator like Booker T. Washington, or a great orator and abolitionist like Frederick Douglass? Or again, why hadn't he named me (as so many Negro parents had done) after President Teddy Roosevelt?

15 Instead, he named me after someone called Ralph Waldo Emerson, and then, when I was three, he died. It was too early for me to have understood his choice, although I'm sure he must have explained it many times, and it was also too soon for me to have made the connection between my name and my father's love for reading. Much later, after I began to write and work with words, I came to suspect that he was aware of the suggestive powers of names and of the magic involved in naming.

16 I recall an odd conversation with my mother during my early teens in which she mentioned their interest in, of all things, prenatal culture! But for a long time I actually knew only that my father read a lot, and that he admired this remote Mr. Emerson, who was some-

thing called a "poet and philosopher"—so much so that he named his second son after him.

17 I knew, also, that whatever his motives, the combination of names he'd given me caused me no end of trouble from the moment when I could talk well enough to respond to the ritualized question which grownups put to very young children. Emerson's name was quite familiar to Negroes in Oklahoma during those days when World War I was brewing, and adults, eager to show off their knowledge of literary figures, and obviously amused by the joke implicit in such a small brown nubbin of a boy carrying around such a heavy moniker, would invariably repeat my first two names and then to my great annoyance, they'd add "Emerson."

18 And I, in my confusion, would reply, "No, *no, I'm* not Emerson; he's the little boy who lives next door." Which only made them laugh all the louder. "Oh no," they'd say, "*you're* Ralph Waldo Emerson," while I had fantasies of blue murder.

19 For a while the presence next door of my little friend, Emerson, made it unnecessary for me to puzzle too often over this peculiar adult confusion. And since there were other Negro boys named Ralph in the city, I came to suspect that there was something about the combination of names which produced their laughter. Even today I know of only one other Ralph who had as much comedy made out of his name, a campus politician and deep-voiced orator whom I knew at Tuskegee, who was called in friendly ribbing, *Ralph Waldo Emerson Edgar Allan Poe,* spelled Powe. This must have been quite a trial for him, but I had been initiated much earlier.

20 During my early school years the name continued to puzzle me, for it constantly evoked in the faces of others some secret. It was as though I possessed some treasure or some defect, which was invisible to my own eyes and ears; something which I had but did not *possess,* like a piece of property in South Carolina, which was mine but which I could not have until some future time. I recall finding, about this time, while seeking adventure in back alleys—which possess for boys a superiority over playgrounds like that which kitchen utensils possess over toys designed for infants—a large photographic lens. I remember nothing of its optical qualities, of its speed or color correction, but it gleamed with crystal mystery and it was beautiful.

21 Mounted handsomely in a tube of shiny brass, it spoke to me of distant worlds of possibility. I played with it, looking through it with squinted eyes, holding it in shafts of sunlight, and tried to use it for a magic lantern. But most of this was as unrewarding as my

attempts to make the music come from a phonograph record by holding the needle in my fingers.

22 I could burn holes through newspapers with it, or I could pretend that it was a telescope, the barrel of a cannon, or the third eye of a monster—*I* being the monster—but I could do nothing at all about its proper function of making images; nothing to make it yield its secret. But I could not discard it.

23 Older boys sought to get it away from me by offering knives or tops, agate marbles or whole zoos of grass snakes and horned toads in trade, but I held on to it. No one, not even the white boys I knew, had such a lens, and it was my own good luck to have found it. Thus I would hold on to it until such time as I could acquire the parts needed to make it function. Finally I put it aside and it remained buried in my box of treasures, dusty and dull, to be lost and forgotten as I grew older and became interested in music.

24 I had reached by now the grades where it was necessary to learn something about Mr. Emerson and what he had written, such as the "Concord Hymn" and the essay "Self-Reliance," and in following his advice, I reduced the "Waldo" to a simple and, I hoped, mysterious "W," and in my own reading I avoided his works like the plague. I could no more deal with my name—I shall never really master it—than I could find a creative use for my lens. Fortunately there were other problems to occupy my mind. Not that I forgot my fascination with names, but more about that later. . . .

Additional Rhetorical Strategies

Analogy (paragraph 1); Illustration (paragraphs 3, 8, 12); Cause and Effect (paragraph 7); Narration (paragraphs 14–24).

Examining Words and Meaning

1. What do you think that Ellison means when he says that the world has "many 'true names'—all spelling chaos" (paragraph 2)? Why is it so important that we discover one of these names?

2. According to Ellison, what relationship should we have with our names? Why is this relationship particularly difficult to attain for

blacks? What are some of the ways in which blacks have responded to this situation? How is the black community that Ellison describes sensitive to the question of names?

3. Refer to a dictionary for the meanings of the following words: enigmatic (paragraph 1); agon (paragraph 1); furtive (paragraph 6); obsequious (paragraph 8); aggregate (paragraph 9); exhort (paragraph 9); incongruous (paragraph 11); prenatal (paragraph 16); nubbin (paragraph 17); moniker (paragraph 17).

Focusing on Structures and Strategies

1. At what point does Ellison turn to discussing himself? Why do you think that he waits so long to do so? What relevance does the material before this point have to his autobiographical reflections?
2. Exactly what is it that needs defining here? Of the three kinds of definition discussed in the introduction to this section—lexical, stipulative, and extended—which would you say that Ellison is using? Does the problem of definition here seem easy or difficult to you?

Suggestions for Further Discussion and Writing

1. Has Ellison's essay made you think about your name in new ways? We often take our names for granted: Ellison suggests that we may have to come to terms consciously with our names before we know who we are. How "unified" are you with your name? When people mistake or mispronounce it, do you flinch? Have you ever assumed, temporarily, another name? What did it feel like to do so?
2. Ellison says that it is an act of courage for a black to keep his name rather than change it. What do you think about changing one's name? Write an essay in which you consider the implications of doing so for marital, religious, or other reasons. Do you think it is better to keep or to change our names in such circumstances?

Classification

1 As a method of thinking in writing, classification helps us sort out information about a subject into logically related categories. Its uses in writing range from the simple division of a general subject for the sake of clarity and convenience (for example, contact versus noncontact sports) to the complex build-up or unraveling of complete systems of knowledge (as in zoology). Classification offers writers both procedures for identifying fully all the parts of a subject as well as structures for organizing our thoughts about that subject.

2 Classification is often closely connected with definition in our thinking and writing. Definition establishes, in a brief or intensive way, exactly what a particular term does and does not mean. Classification presupposes that writers and readers agree on a term's general meaning and are more interested in identifying and understanding completely the various specific parts that make up the whole term. Classification therefore operates in a much broader field than that of definition. Writers working with classification begin with a subject, analyze it carefully, divide it into categories, and then classify each of its components into one of these categories according to some specifically shared quality.

3 The principles of classification can be used to enrich our understanding of even the most familiar subjects. Consider for a moment the ways lips can meet:

> If one wants to classify the kiss, then one must consider several principles of classification. One may classify kissing with respect to sound. Here the language is not sufficiently elastic to record all my observations. I do not believe that all the languages in the world have an adequate supply of onomatopoeia to denote the different sounds I have heard at my uncle's house. Sometimes it was smacking, sometimes hissing, sometimes crackling, sometimes explosive, sometimes squeaky, and so on forever. One may also classify kissing with regard to contact, as in the close kiss, or the passing kiss, and the clinging kiss. One may classify them with reference to the time element, as the brief and the prolonged. With reference to time, there is still another classification, and this is the only one I really care about. There is an enormous difference between the first kiss and all the others. The first kiss is incommensurable with everything which is included in the other classifications; it is indifferent to sound, touch, time in general. The first kiss is, however, qualitatively different from all others. There are only a few people who consider this; it would really be a pity if there was but one who had thought about it.

4 This passage, drawn from *Either/Or* (1843), the first major work by the Danish philosopher Søren Kierkegaard, is part of a thorough analysis of the conflict between aesthetics (the sense of the beautiful) and ethics (the principles of right conduct). Kierkegaard demonstrates in the passage just how handy classification can be when writers are looking for an easy way into their subjects and trying to chart out a clear course for developing their thinking and writing. In effect, this passage reveals that the very process of classifying can give both shape and substance to our sentences. So too, as we can readily see here, classification works especially well when writers want to focus on refining related terms or ideas. By using classification simply and directly (signaled here by the repetition of "One may classify"), Kierkegaard also makes it easy for his audience to follow his train of thought. And along the way, the word choices he makes to classify the kiss reveal how onomatopoetic such distinctions can be. It is, in fact, the process of carefully thinking through the classification of the kiss that leads to his stating so ardent a conclusion: "There is an enormous difference between the first kiss and all the others."

5 We most often use classification when we deal with a subject that is extensive or complicated, or both. Scientists, for example, rely on classification to create order out of the enormous amount of information generated by their observations and analyses. Given the intri-

cacy of their subjects and the need to be exact in their thinking, scientists could hardly function without classification. On another level, it is standard procedure for government officials to classify, say, the documents they produce, the armed forces they employ, and the citizens they tax. Corporate executives also depend on classification: of sales, profits, personnel, stockholders, and inventories. In a similar manner, university administrators regularly classify students each semester by, among other factors, grades, credits carried, credits earned, and financial status.

6 Perhaps more so than we realize, classification is also a feature of our own daily academic and personal routines. Consider what it would be like to find the one book needed to finish our research paper if the library had not organized its holdings according to some readily understood principle of classification. Or take an activity as commonplace as shopping in a supermarket. Think of the mass confusion that would result on a crowded Saturday afternoon if the store manager hadn't grouped similar products and put signs up over each aisle, classifying its contents. We group together the courses we have enjoyed, the teachers we have admired. We also classify the foods we have eaten, the restaurants we have been to, and so on. (For an example of the classification of such an everyday activity as reading, see Donald Hall's essay on p. 321.) In all these instances, classification helps us analyze and control our experience and, thereby, serves as an invaluable aid to memory and a means of clarification. But ordinarily, we do not normally carry classification through to the minute, exhaustive stages expected of scientists and other professionals. Nonetheless, the fundamental operations of classification are governed by the same principles in all forms of thinking and writing.

7 The normal procedure to follow in classification begins with the writer's analyzing a subject carefully in order to divide it into all of its parts. This initial activity, called either *analysis* or *division,* arranges the subject into clear-cut and manageable categories. Once these parts have been identified, the writer then groups—classifies—each of the individual aspects of the subject into clusters around a shared quality. If, for example, the subject were modern transportation, a topic far too cumbersome to begin writing about immediately, we could make the subject easier to handle by breaking it down into its parts: land vehicles, sea vehicles, and aircraft. The goal of this analysis or division would be to identify all the subject's components. We would then classify—that is, group together—sleds, bicycles, motorcycles, automobiles, buses, trains, and monorails in the first category;

various sail and power boats in the second; and airplanes, helicopters, gliders, dirigibles, and any other machine capable of flight in the third. Depending on the writer's interests, each individual element in a subdivision could, in turn, be defined and classified further. Automobiles could be broken down into additional subclasses according to manufacturer, size, price, gas mileage, repair estimates, and the like. The writer's purpose would determine the nature and extent of the classification.

8 Effective classification depends on several related principles. In the initial stage, when we analyze the general subject in order to divide it into subclasses, we should take care that these divisions are distinct enough to prevent any overlap. If, for example, we were asked to classify automobiles based on their size, we might reasonably and accurately establish such subclasses as—to use the curious language of automotive advertising—subcompact, compact, intermediate, and full-sized. But it would be inaccurate to create such categories as front-wheel drive or disc brakes. These last two subdivisions are neither consistent with the prevailing factor of size nor mutually exclusive; that is, front-wheel drive and disc brakes could well be a feature of a car of any size, and many models are now promoted as having both front-wheel drive and disc brakes. Had we introduced such categories, we would have mistakenly shifted the basis for classification during the course of our thinking. At each level of classification, only one principle should be applied, and consistently, to all the elements being considered—in this case, size.

9 The automobile example also touches another essential point about using classification in thinking and writing. Since we have established that all subdivisions should be mutually exclusive, we might expect that significant differences would distinguish one category from another. But, in the case presented in the preceding paragraphs, it would be fair to question the distinction in size between a subcompact and a compact car. We would need to determine whether these categories are sufficiently different or are simply examples of advertisers' lapsing into the fallacy of classification known as *hairsplitting.* To prevent this in our own thinking and writing, we should base our subdivisions on a clearly articulated principle of classification.

10 In its simplest form, called *partition* or *binary,* classification divides a subject in two: one positive category, one negative. The assumption here is that *non-* can be prefixed to any term in the second category, as in *athletic–nonathletic.* This form of classification also re-

quires that all subsequent classes be split in two. For example, the athletic director of a college may want to identify likely candidates for a newly formed varsity volleyball team. The first step would be to classify the student body into athletes and nonathletes. Next, those athletes who have played the sport would be isolated from those who have not. This procedure would establish a suitable group of candidates for the team. Partition or binary classification is most appropriate for narrow, very limited purposes. It is most often simply a matter of convenience. It is obviously inexact; it tells us, for example, nothing more about the college's students than whether or not they have played volleyball. In this, as in all other instances when we classify, the thoroughness of the classification should be consistent with our purpose and with the complexity of the subject.

11 Classification also creates larger, far more intricate structures for thinking and writing. The chemist's periodic table of elements is, for example, the result of an elaborate, painstakingly precise system of classification. It is, in fact, a model of one of the great classificatory systems of modern thought. Each discipline has something analogous to it: an outline of essential components. That classification approximates the goal and work of an outline may be its chief value to us when we are thinking in writing. It can help organize our thoughts and conveniently group related words and ideas before we actually set out to write. Once we've begun writing, classification can help structure our thinking at the level of both the paragraph and the whole essay. As soon as we've identified the components in the classification, we can take each up fully, one at a time, with, say, a paragraph devoted to each. This may take the form of naming the subclass to be considered at the beginning of the paragraph and proceeding to describe each of its members in detail and to say something important about it. Progressing from one distinct subclass to the next helps readers to understand the subject being discussed and to follow the points being made about it. Classification also minimizes the risk of oversimplifying the subject and reducing it to little more than a stereotype. Because we are used to following through completely on our thinking, we are more alert to the potential complexity and divisions of a subject. But most important, with classification the general statements we make about a subject will be more solidly grounded in specific evidence and therefore more convincing.

12 Through classification, the most prominent aspects of a subject come more sharply into focus, and our dominant ideas about it be-

come easier for readers to understand. Classification is both a procedure and a structure for thinking and writing. It enables us to present our ideas about a subject clearly, thoroughly, and convincingly.

Notes on Punctuation

Lewis Thomas

Gertrude Stein once confessed to having led "a long and complicated life" with "the real question of punctuation, periods, commas, colons, semi-colons and capitals and small letters." In "Notes on Punctuation," from The Medusa and the Snail, *Lewis Thomas recounts his own affectionate and at times tangled relationship with all those marks that direct the syntactic traffic of our sentences. Arranging punctuation marks into "stops" and "indicators of tone," Thomas playfully reveals his preferences—his fondness for semicolons and his disfavor of colons—and describes their uses.*

For biographical information on Lewis Thomas, see page 109.

1 There are no precise rules about punctuation (Fowler lays out some general advice (as best he can under the complex circumstances of English prose (he points out, for example, that we possess only four stops (the comma, the semicolon, the colon and the period (the question mark and exclamation point are not, strictly speaking, stops; they are indicators of tone (oddly enough, the Greeks employed the semicolon for their question mark (it produces a strange sensation to read a Greek sentence which is a straightforward question: Why weepest thou; (instead of Why weepest thou? (and, of course, there are parentheses (which are surely a kind of punctuation making this whole matter much more complicated by having to count up the left-handed parentheses in order to be sure of closing with the right number (but if the parentheses were left out, with nothing to work with but the stops, we would have considerably more flexibility in the deploying of layers of meaning than if we tried to separate all the clauses by physical barriers (and in the latter case, while we might

have more precision and exactitude for our meaning, we would lose the essential flavor of language, which is its wonderful ambiguity))))))))))).

2 The commas are the most useful and usable of all the stops. It is highly important to put them in place as you go along. If you try to come back after doing a paragraph and stick them in the various spots that tempt you you will discover that they tend to swarm like minnows into all sorts of crevices whose existence you hadn't realized and before you know it the whole long sentence becomes immobilized and lashed up squirming in commas. Better to use them sparingly, and with affection, precisely when the need for each one arises, nicely, by itself.

3 I have grown fond of semicolons in recent years. The semicolon tells you that there is still some question about the preceding full sentence; something needs to be added; it reminds you sometimes of the Greek usage. It is almost always a greater pleasure to come across a semicolon than a period. The period tells you that that is that; if you didn't get all the meaning you wanted or expected, anyway you got all the writer intended to parcel out and now you have to move along. But with a semicolon there you get a pleasant little feeling of expectancy; there is more to come; read on; it will get clearer.

4 Colons are a lot less attractive, for several reasons: firstly, they give you the feeling of being rather ordered around, or at least having your nose pointed in a direction you might not be inclined to take if left to yourself, and, secondly, you suspect you're in for one of those sentences that will be labeling the points to be made: firstly, secondly and so forth, with the implication that you haven't sense enough to keep track of a sequence of notions without having them numbered. Also, many writers use this system loosely and incompletely, starting out with number one and number two as though counting off on their fingers but then going on and on without the succession of labels you've been led to expect, leaving you floundering about searching for the ninthly or seventeenthly that ought to be there but isn't.

5 Exclamation points are the most irritating of all. Look! they say, look at what I just said! How amazing is my thought! It is like being forced to watch someone else's small child jumping up and down crazily in the center of the living room shouting to attract attention. If a sentence really has something of importance to say, something

quite remarkable, it doesn't need a mark to point it out. And if it is really, after all, a banal sentence needing more zing, the exclamation point simply emphasizes its banality!

6 Quotation marks should be used honestly and sparingly, when there is a genuine quotation at hand, and it is necessary to be very rigorous about the words enclosed by the marks. If something is to be quoted, the *exact* words must be used. If part of it must be left out because of space limitations, it is good manners to insert three dots to indicate the omission, but it is unethical to do this if it means connecting two thoughts which the original author did not intend to have tied together. Above all, quotation marks should not be used for ideas that you'd like to disown, things in the air so to speak. Nor should they be put in place around clichés; if you want to use a cliché you must take full responsibility for it yourself and not try to job it off on anon., or on society. The most objectionable misuse of quotation marks, but one which illustrates the dangers of misuse in ordinary prose, is seen in advertising, especially in advertisements for small restaurants, for example "just around the corner," or "a good place to eat." No single, identifiable, citable person ever really said, for the record, "just around the corner," much less "a good place to eat," least likely of all for restaurants of the type that use this type of prose.

7 The dash is a handy device, informal and essentially playful, telling you that you're about to take off on a different tack but still in some way connected with the present course—only you have to remember that the dash is there, and either put a second dash at the end of the notion to let the reader know that he's back on course, or else end the sentence, as here, with a period.

8 The greatest danger in punctuation is for poetry. Here it is necessary to be as economical and parsimonious with commas and periods as with the words themselves, and any marks that seem to carry their own subtle meanings, like dashes and little rows of periods, even semicolons and question marks, should be left out altogether rather than inserted to clog up the thing with ambiguity. A single exclamation point in a poem, no matter what else the poem has to say, is enough to destroy the whole work.

9 The things I like best in T. S. Eliot's poetry, especially in the *Four Quartets,* are the semicolons. You cannot hear them, but they are there, laying out the connections between the images and the ideas. Sometimes you get a glimpse of a semicolon coming, a few lines farther on, and it is like climbing a steep path through woods and

seeing a wooden bench just at a bend in the road ahead, a place where you can expect to sit for a moment, catching your breath.

10 Commas can't do this sort of thing; they can only tell you how the different parts of a complicated thought are to be fitted together, but you can't sit, not even take a breath, just because of a comma,

Reading for Rhetorical Strategy

Writers classify material essentially in two ways, either (1) according to a classification system they invent for their own purposes, or (2) according to a familiar system that depends on well-known categories. In his essay on reading, for example, Donald Hall (see p. 321) made up his own system of classification based on his experiences with different types of readers. In "Notes on Punctuation," however, Lewis Thomas organizes his essay around the familiar forms of punctuation covered in any writer's handbook.

Though Thomas's purposes are personal and humorous—he is not attempting to write an exhaustive treatise on the subject—he nevertheless refers to most of the types of punctuation covered in Fowler's *Modern English Usage* under "stops." Note that in paragraph 1 Thomas divides punctuation into three categories: "stops," "indicators of tone," and "parentheses" (which includes the dash). He then proceeds to deal with each major type of punctuation in a paragraph-by-paragraph fashion, playfully illustrating his points as he goes along. In paragraph 8 Thomas considers the use of punctuation in poetry, reminding his readers that Fowler has dealt only with the "circumstances of English prose." If we broke "Notes on Punctuation" down into a formal outline, its main divisions would thus be I. Prose, and II. Poetry.

Drinking in Houston

Larry McMurtry

"The essay is a place one visits occasionally, when one is tired of home," wrote novelist (of best-selling novels like Lonesome Dove [*1985*],

The Last Picture Show [*1986*], *and* Texasville [*1987*] *) and screenwriter Larry McMurtry (1936–   ) in the preface to his first collection of essays,* In a Narrow Grave *(1968): "It offers the comforts of a fine hotel: one can stroll about in one's best clothes and ruminate upon those things one never has time to ruminate upon at home." In the following selection, McMurtry looks at the bars in Houston and lines them up behind the kinds of people who frequent them and the aspects of the city they exemplify.*

1 If one were forced to choose a single aspect of Houston and from that aspect infer or characterize the city I think I would choose its bars, or, to be fully accurate, its bars and clubs. The upper class, for the most part, inhabits the upper air. Their clubs are very posh, if in a somewhat River Okie way, and tend to be altitudinally remote. There is a club on top of almost every tall building in town; the elevation they provide is both physical and psychological. They help relieve the hunger for heights that can seize one in a city only forty-one feet above sea level; and they also put their members well above the masses who cannot afford such relief.

2 The hundreds of middle-class clubs are generally squat one-story affairs, converted restaurants with imitation Las Vegas furniture and deafening acoustics. They provide a certain relief from the neolithic Texas liquor laws and are rather rigidly divided as to clientele between "swinging singles" (their phrase) and uneasily-marrieds who have just noticed middle-age crooking his finger at them.

3 The poor have beer-bars, hundreds of them, seldom fancy but reliably dim and cool. Most of them are equipped with jukeboxes, shuffleboards, jars of pig's feet and talkative drunks. There are lots of bar burlesques, where from 3 P.M. on girls gyrate at one's elbow with varying degrees of grace. On the East side there are a fair number of open-air bars—those who like to watch the traffic can sit, drink Pearl, observe the wrecks, and listen to "Hello, Vietnam" on the jukebox. Louisiana is just down the road, and a lot of the men wear Cajun sideburns and leave their shirttails out. On the West side cowboys are common. Members of the cross-continental hitchhiking set congregate on Franklin Street, at places like The Break-ing Point Lounge. Symbolic *latinos* slip over to the Last Concert, on the North side; or, if they are especially bold, go all the way to McCarty Street, where one can view the most extraordinary example of Mexican saloon-and-whorehouse architecture north of the border.

Additional Rhetorical Strategy

Illustration (paragraphs 1–3).

Examining Words and Meaning

1. What is the principle upon which McMurtry bases his classification of Houston's bars? How many basic categories does he offer? Of these, which does he seem most interested in? What subdivisions of this category does he make?
2. Look up the following words in a dictionary: neolithic (paragraph 2); burlesques (paragraph 3); gyrate (paragraph 3); Cajun (paragraph 3).

Focusing on Structures and Strategies

1. What is McMurtry's stated purpose for talking about the bars and clubs of Houston? What is his attitude toward each of the groups of bars he describes?
2. McMurtry's classification is supported by a series of details. As you review his paragraphs, select one detail from each and explain how this detail helps make his classification more effective.

Suggestion for Further Discussion and Writing

1. What else, besides bars, might you use to give a picture of your town to a reader? Choose a set of public places—parks, theaters, playgrounds, restaurants, schools, and so on—that you can classify, as McMurtry classifies bars, and use them to describe your town. What sort of person frequents each school, playground, or restaurant? Do rich people gravitate to one place, the poor to another? If you wish, you may move beyond classification to make more general observations.

Cinematypes

Susan Allen Toth

Susan Allen Toth was born in Ames, Iowa, in 1940 and spent much of her earliest years in that rural stretch of the American Midwest. She attended Smith College and the University of California, Berkeley, before earning a Ph.D. in English literature at the University of Minnesota in 1969. She has taught English at San Francisco State University and, since 1969, at Macalester College in St. Paul, Minnesota. She has published numerous articles and stories in such diverse magazines as Cosmopolitan, Harper's, McCall's, Ms., *and the* Great River Review. *In 1981, Toth published the first volume of her autobiography,* Blooming: A Small-Town Girlhood, *to great acclaim. The second volume of her memoirs,* Ivy Days: Growing Up Back East, *appeared in 1984.*

"Cinematypes" was first printed in the May 1980 issue of Harper's *with the subtitle "Going to the Movies." In it, Toth creates a delightful classification of the men with whom she sees "films" and "movies," and expresses her own preference for viewing "old Technicolor musicals" and vintage Hollywood dramas, ones she is careful to note "will all end happily."*

1 Aaron takes me only to art films. That's what I call them, anyway: strange movies with vague poetic images I don't always understand, long dreamy movies about a distant Technicolor past, even longer black-and-white movies about the general meaninglessness of life. We do not go unless at least one reputable critic has found the cinematography superb. We went to *The Devil's Eye,* and Aaron turned to me in the middle and said, "My God, this is *funny.*" I do not think he was pleased.

2 When Aaron and I go to the movies, we drive our cars separately and meet by the box office. Inside the theater he sits tentatively in his seat, ready to move if he can't see well, poised to leave if the film is disappointing. He leans away from me, careful not to touch the bare flesh of his arm against the bare flesh of mine. Sometimes he leans so far I am afraid he may be touching the woman on his other

side. If the movie is very good, he leans forward, too, peering between the heads of the couple in front of us. The light from the screen bounces off his glasses; he gleams with intensity, sitting there on the edge of his seat, watching the screen. Once I tapped him on the arm so I could whisper a comment in his ear. He jumped.

3 After *Belle de Jour* Aaron said he wanted to ask me if he could stay overnight. "But I can't," he shook his head mournfully before I had a chance to answer, "because I know I never sleep well in strange beds." Then he apologized for asking. "It's just that after a film like that," he said, "I feel the need to assert myself."

4 Pete takes me only to movies that he thinks have redeeming social value. He doesn't call them "films." They tend to be about poverty, war, injustice, political corruption, struggling unions in the 1930s, and the military-industrial complex. Pete doesn't like propaganda movies, though, and he doesn't like to be too depressed, either. We stayed away from *The Sorrow and the Pity;* it would be, he said, just too much. Besides, he assured me, things are never that hopeless. So most of the movies we see are made in Hollywood. Because they are always topical, these movies offer what Pete calls "food for thought." When we saw *Coming Home,* Pete's jaw set so firmly with the first half-hour that I knew we would end up at Poppin' Fresh Pies afterward.

5 When Pete and I go to the movies, we take turns driving so no one owes anyone else anything. We leave the car far from the theater so we don't have to pay for a parking space. If it's raining or snowing, Pete offers to let me off at the door, but I can tell he'll feel better if I go with him while he finds a spot, so we share the walk too. Inside the theater Pete will hold my hand when I get scared if I ask him. He puts my hand firmly on his knee and covers it completely with his own hand. His knee never twitches. After a while, when the scary part is past, he loosens his hand slightly and I know that is a signal to take mine away. He sits companionably close, letting his jacket just touch my sweater, but he does not infringe. He thinks I ought to know he is there if I need him.

6 One night, after *The China Syndrome,* I asked Pete if he wouldn't like to stay for a second drink, even though it was past midnight. He thought a while about that, considering my offer from all possible angles, but finally he said no. Relationships today, he said, have a tendency to move too quickly.

7 Sam likes movies that are entertaining. By that he means movies that Will Jones in the *Minneapolis Tribune* loved and either *Time* or *Newsweek* rather liked; also movies that do not have sappy love stories, are not musicals, do not have subtitles, and will not force him to think. He does not go to movies to think. He liked *California Suite* and *The Seduction of Joe Tynan,* though the plots, he said, could have been zippier. He saw it all coming too far in advance, and that took the fun out. He doesn't like to know what is going to happen. "I just want my brain to be tickled," he says. It is very hard for me to pick out movies for Sam.

8 When Sam takes me to the movies, he pays for everything. He thinks that's what a man ought to do. But I buy my own popcorn, because he doesn't approve of it; the grease might smear his flannel slacks. Inside the theater, Sam makes himself comfortable. He takes off his jacket, puts one arm around me, and all during the movie he plays with my hand, stroking my palm, beating a small tattoo on my wrist. Although he watches the movie intently, his body operates on instinct. Once I inclined my head and kissed him lightly just behind his ear. He beat a faster tattoo on my wrist, quick and musical, but he didn't look away from the screen.

9 When Sam takes me home from the movies, he stands outside my door and kisses me long and hard. He would like to come in, he says regretfully, but his steady girlfriend in Duluth wouldn't like it. When the *Tribune* gives a movie four stars, he has to save it to see with her. Otherwise her feelings might be hurt.

10 I go to some movies by myself. On rainy Sunday afternoons I often sneak into a revival house or a college auditorium for old Technicolor musicals: *Kiss Me Kate, Seven Brides for Seven Brothers, Calamity Jane,* even once, *The Sound of Music.* Wearing sagging jeans so I can prop my feet on the seat in front, I sit toward the rear where no one can see me. I eat large handfuls of popcorn with double butter. Once the movie starts, I feel completely at home. Howard Keel and I are old friends; I grin back at him on the screen. I know the sound tracks by heart. Sometimes when I get really carried away I hum along with Kathryn Grayson, remembering how I once thought I would fill out a formal like that. I am rather glad now I never did. Skirts whirl, feet tap, acrobatic young men perform impossible feats, and then the camera dissolves into a dream sequence I know I can comfortably follow. It is not, thank God, Bergman.

11 If I can't find an old musical, I settle for Hepburn and Tracy,

vintage Grant or Gable, on adventurous days Claudette Colbert or James Stewart. Before I buy my ticket I make sure it will all end happily. If necessary, I ask the girl at the box office. I have never seen *Stella Dallas* or *Intermezzo.* Over the years I have developed other peccadilloes: I will, for example, see anything that is redeemed by Thelma Ritter. At the end of *Daddy Long Legs* I wait happily for the scene when Fred Clark, no longer angry, at last pours Thelma a convivial drink. They smile at each other, I smile at them, I feel they are smiling at me. In the movies I go to by myself, the men and women always like each other.

Additional Rhetorical Strategies

Definition (paragraphs 1, 7); Illustration (throughout); Narration (paragraphs 2, 5, 6, 8–11); Cause and Effect (paragraphs 3–4, 6, 8).

Examining Words and Meaning

1. This essay suggests that our movie choices reflect something of our personality. Identify each of the four movie "types" described in the essay. What are some of the personality traits, either physical characteristics or behavioral tendencies, which "fit" each type? How is each person's character related to his or her reasons for wanting to go to the movies? To what extent do you think the author's assumption is valid?
2. What distinction does Toth draw between the meaning of the words "films" and "movies"? What role does each of the following factors play in defining "films" and "movies": subject matter, treatment, geography? What other factors might you infer from Toth's account to distinguish between "films" and "movies"? Which does she prefer? Why?

Focusing on Structures and Strategies

1. What criteria does Toth establish as the basis for classifying the kinds of movies her male friends enjoy? In what ways does she use

the same criteria to discuss her own preferences? In what ways are her criteria different from theirs? Point to specific words and phrases to verify your contention.

2. This essay is not merely a "scientific" study of moviegoers; it also tells a story about how people relate to one another at the movies. Identify some of the differences among the three men in terms of their behavior toward the author. In what sense do they reflect a progression? What elements do they have in common? How is their behavior toward the narrator related to their desire to go to the movies in the first place? How does the author's account of going to the movies with these three men prepare us for her own movie preferences? How is her behavior at the movies different from all three of the other "types"? Why do you think this is the case?

3. How would you characterize Toth's tone in this selection? Does it remain consistent? If not, when and how does it change? With what effect? Look at the essay's sentence structure, its diction, its choice of detail. What are some of the characteristics of its style? How does the author's style allow her to discuss the relationships between men and women without becoming "sentimental"?

4. Reread Toth's final two paragraphs. How would you characterize the movies that she sees by herself? In what specific ways are these two final paragraphs a response to those that precede them?

Suggestions for Further Discussion and Writing

1. The success of Toth's efforts in this selection depends to a great extent on her readers' recognizing that the people described in "Cinematypes" are essentially stereotypes. How is this process of identifying people as "types" related to the movies?

2. Much of the appeal of this selection can be traced to Toth's prompting us to think about ordinary experiences from strikingly fresh perspectives. Write a paragraph of classification on a subject that is not only familiar but also seldom the subject of classification.

3. Keeping Toth's system of classification in mind, write an essay in which you classify a small group of friends according to their reactions to a commonplace, shared experience: the courses they register for, the music they listen to, the food they eat, and the like. In preparing your essay, be sure that the basis for your classification is evident to your readers.

Four Kinds of Reading

Donald Hall

Reading first-rate writers and attempting to write like them is one very useful way both to know and to express ourselves better. Even the most prolific writers learn a great deal from reading the work of others. Donald Hall (1928–)—a highly accomplished poet, playwright, editor, teacher, and a wide-ranging freelance writer—offers the following incisive view of the mutual dependence of reading and writing:

> *A good way to learn to write well is to read good prose. Gradually we acquire the manners that make the good writing we admire. It is like learning a foreign language by living with a family that speaks it, by shopping in it, and by listening to television shows with dialogue in it.*

The clarity and simplicity of Hall's advice mark all of his writing: to date seven books of poems, eight volumes of prose, and twelve edited collections of fiction and poetry, along with scores of essays in periodicals as different as Playboy *and* Country Journal. *Educated at Harvard, Oxford, and Stanford, Hall taught at the University of Michigan from 1957 to 1975, when he devoted himself exclusively to writing and tending the family farm in Durham, New Hampshire. He has also lectured on literature and read his poetry at more than 400 colleges.*

In the following essay, Hall divides reading into four basic categories, each distinguished by a characteristic manner and purpose and by the amount of reflection demanded.

1 Everywhere one meets the idea that reading is an activity desirable in itself. It is understandable that publishers and librarians—and even writers—should promote this assumption, but it is strange that the idea should have general currency. People surround the idea of reading with piety, and do not take into account the purpose of reading or the value of what is being read. Teachers and parents praise the child who reads, and praise themselves, whether the text be *The Reader's Digest* or *Moby Dick.* The advent of TV has increased the false values ascribed to reading, since TV provides a vulgar alter-

native. But this piety is silly; and most reading is no more cultural nor intellectual nor imaginative than shooting pool or watching *What's My Line.*

2 It is worth asking how the act of reading became something to value in itself, as opposed for instance to the act of conversation or the act of taking a walk. Mass literacy is a recent phenomenon, and I suggest that the aura which decorates reading is a relic of the importance of reading to our great-great-grandparents. Literacy used to be a mark of social distinction, separating a small portion of humanity from the rest. The farm laborer who was ambitious for his children did not daydream that they would become schoolteachers or doctors; he daydreamed that they would learn to read, and that a world would therefore open up to them in which they did not have to labor in the fields fourteen hours a day for six days a week in order to buy salt and cotton. On the next rank of society, ample time for reading meant that the reader was free from the necessity to spend most of his waking hours making a living of any kind. This sort of attitude shades into the contemporary man's boast of his wife's cultural activities. When he says that his wife is interested in books and music and pictures, he is not only enclosing the arts in a delicate female world; he is saying that he is rich enough to provide her with the leisure to do nothing. Reading is an inactivity, and therefore a badge of social class. Of course, these reasons for the piety attached to reading are never acknowledged. They show themselves in the shape of our attitudes toward books; reading gives off an air of gentility.

3 It seems to me possible to name four kinds of reading, each with a characteristic manner and purpose. The first is reading for information—reading to learn about a trade, or politics, or how to accomplish something. We read a newspaper this way, or most textbooks, or directions on how to assemble a bicycle. With most of this sort of material, the reader can learn to scan the page quickly, coming up with what he needs and ignoring what is irrelevant to him, like the rhythm of the sentence, or the play of metaphor. Courses in speed reading can help us read for this purpose, training the eye to jump quickly across the page. If we read *The New York Times* with the attention we should give a novel or a poem, we will have time for nothing else, and our mind will be cluttered with clichés and dead metaphors. Quick eye-reading is a necessity to anyone who wants to keep up with what's happening, or learn much of what has happened in the past. The amount of reflection, which interrupts and slows down the reading, depends on the material.

4 But it is not the same activity as reading literature. There ought to be another word. If we read a work of literature properly, we read slowly, and we hear all the words. If our lips do not actually move, it's only laziness. The muscles in our throats move, and come together when we see the word "squeeze." We hear the sounds so accurately that if a syllable is missing in a line of poetry we hear the lack, though we may not know what we are lacking. In prose we accept the rhythms, and hear the adjacent sounds. We also register a track of feeling through the metaphors and associations of words. Careless writing prevents this sort of attention, and becomes offensive. But the great writers reward this attention. Only by the full exercise of our powers to receive language can we absorb their intelligence and their imagination. This kind of reading goes through the ear—though the eye takes in the print, and decodes it into sound—to the throat and the understanding, and it can never be quick. It is slow and sensual, a deep pleasure that begins with touch and ends with the sort of comprehension that we associate with dream.

5 Too many intellectuals read in order to reduce images to abstractions. With a philosopher one reads slowly, as if it were literature, but much time must be spent with the eyes turned away from the pages, reflecting on the text. To read literature this way is to turn it into something it is not—to concepts clothed in character, or philosophy sugar-coated. I think that most literary intellectuals read this way, including the brighter Professors of English, with the result that they miss literature completely, and concern themselves with a minor discipline called the history of ideas. I remember a course in Chaucer at my University in which the final exam largely required the identification of a hundred or more fragments of Chaucer, none as long as a line. If you liked poetry, and read Chaucer through a couple of times slowly, you found yourself knowing them all. If you were a literary intellectual, well-informed about the great chain of being, chances are you had a difficult time. To read literature is to be intimately involved with the words on the page, and never to think of them as the embodiments of ideas which can be expressed in other terms. On the other hand, intellectual writing—closer to mathematics on a continuum that has at its opposite pole lyric poetry—requires intellectual reading, which is slow because it is reflective and because the reader must pause to evaluate concepts.

6 But most of the reading which is praised for itself is neither literary nor intellectual. It is narcotic. Novels, stories and biographies—historical sagas, monthly regurgitations of book clubs, four-

and five-thousand word daydreams of the magazines—these are the opium of the suburbs. The drug is not harmful except to the addict himself, and is no more injurious to him than Johnny Carson or a bridge club, but it is nothing to be proud of. This reading is the automated daydream, the mild trip of the housewife and the tired businessman, interested not in experience and feeling but in turning off the possibilities of experience and feeling. Great literature, if we read it well, opens us up to the world, and makes us more sensitive to it, as if we acquired eyes that could see through things and ears that could hear smaller sounds. But by narcotic reading, one can reduce great literature to the level of *The Valley of the Dolls.* One can read *Anna Karenina* passively and inattentively, and float down the river of lethargy as if one were reading a confession magazine: "I Spurned My Husband for a Count."

7 I think that everyone reads for narcosis occasionally, and perhaps most consistently in late adolescence, when great readers are born. I remember reading to shut the world out, away at a school where I did not want to be; I invented a word to name my disease: "bibliolepsy," on the analogy of narcolepsy. But after a while the books became a window on the world, and not a screen against it. This change doesn't always happen. I think that late adolescent narcotic reading accounts for some of the badness of English departments. As a college student, the boy loves reading and majors in English because he would be reading anyway. Deciding on a career, he takes up English teaching for the same reason. Then in graduate school he is trained to be a scholar, which is painful and irrelevant, and finds he must write papers and publish them to be a Professor—and at about this time he no longer requires reading for narcosis, and he is left with nothing but a Ph.D. and the prospect of fifty years of teaching literature; and he does not even like literature.

8 Narcotic reading survives the impact of television, because this type of reading has even less reality than melodrama; that is, the reader is in control: once the characters reach into the reader's feelings, he is able to stop reading, or glance away, or superimpose his own daydreams. The trouble with television is that it writes its own script. Literature is often valued precisely because of its distance from the tangible. Some readers prefer looking into the text of a play to seeing it performed. Reading a play, it is possible to stage it oneself by an imaginative act; but it is also possible to remove it from real people. Here is Virginia Woolf, who was lavish in her praise of the

act of reading, talking about reading a play rather than seeing it: "Certainly there is a good deal to be said for reading *Twelfth Night* in the book if the book can be read in a garden, with no sound but the thud of an apple falling to the earth, or of the wind ruffling the branches of the trees." She sets her own stage; the play is called *Virginia Woolf Reads Twelfth Night in a Garden.* Piety moves into narcissism, and the high metaphors of Shakespeare's lines dwindle into the flowers of an English garden; actors in ruffles wither, while the wind ruffles branches.

Additional Rhetorical Strategies

Illustration (paragraphs 2, 3, 8); Comparison and Contrast (paragraphs 3, 4, 8); Process Analysis (paragraphs 3–6); Cause and Effect (paragraph 7).

Examining Words and Meaning

1. In Hall's judgment, what was the original value of reading? What images did readers have of themselves in earlier generations? Is reading still associated with such identities today? Explain. How, in effect, are readers perceived in contemporary American society?
2. What distinctions does Hall draw among the various kinds of people who read literature and who teach it? How does Hall distinguish reading literature from speed reading?
3. If you are uncertain about the meaning of the following words, consult a dictionary: gentility (paragraph 2); regurgitations (paragraph 6); lethargy (paragraph 6); narcolepsy (paragraph 7); narcissism (paragraph 8).

Focusing on Structures and Strategies

1. How distinct are Hall's four categories of reading? Do they overlap in any way? Be specific. How thoroughly does Hall develop each category? Does he seem more interested in one than the other? Explain. In which category would you place his essay? Why?

2. Hall opens his essay on what seems like a rather argumentative note; he questions the widespread assumption that "reading is an activity desirable in itself." In the first two paragraphs, how does Hall encourage his readers to re-examine their attitudes toward the value of reading? What strategies does he use to convince his audience that as he notes in paragraph 2, "reading is an inactivity"? How does he make so disputable a contention seem reasonable?
3. Reread the final paragraph. What is the effect of Hall's quoting Virginia Woolf on reading Shakespeare? Is Hall claiming that Shakespeare should only be seen on stage and not read? What is the effect of the repetition of the word *ruffles* in the last sentence?

Suggestions for Further Discussion and Writing

1. In paragraph 8, Hall contrasts reading and watching television. Compare what he has to say here with the discussions of Joyce Maynard (p. 354), Marie Winn (p. 404), and Michael Arlen (p. 451) on the same subject. Whose discussion do you find more memorable? Why?
2. Consider some common activity—say, watching television, viewing films, or choosing clothes to wear. Write an essay in which you create categories for those activities. Remember, classify the activity rather than the subject. Make the mind's activity the focus of your essay.

The Need for Secrecy

Sissela Bok

Her purpose in writing on ethical issues, Sissela Bok has declared, is "to narrow the gap between the worlds of the moral philosopher and those confronting urgent practical moral choices." Born in Stockholm, Sweden, in 1934, Sissela Bok spent her early years there as well as in Switzerland, France, and the United States. She studied in Europe and the United States and earned B.A. and M.A. degrees at George

Washington University before taking a Ph.D. in philosophy at Harvard University in 1970. She has served on the Ethics Advisory Board to the Secretary of Health, Education, and Welfare and has taught ethics and philosophy at various colleges and universities, including Harvard. Sissela Bok's courses—and her publications—focus on the ethics of public and private behavior. She has published in numerous professional and popular journals, including Ethics *and* Scientific American. *In 1978, her first book-length study appeared, entitled* Lying: Moral Choice in Public and Private. *Her most recent book is* Secrets: On the Ethics of Concealment and Revelation *(1983), from which the following selection is drawn.*

In her essay Bok presents a convincing case for the need for secrecy as an expression of human autonomy. In summarizing the claims "in defense of some control over secrecy and openness," she classifies four elements of human autonomy and argues that "with no control over secrecy and openness, human beings could not remain either sane or free."

1 Secrecy is as indispensable to human beings as fire, and as greatly feared. Both enhance and protect life, yet both can stifle, lay waste, spread out of all control. Both may be used to guard intimacy or to invade it, to nurture or to consume. And each can be turned against itself; barriers of secrecy are set up to guard against secret plots and surreptitious prying, just as fire is used to fight fire.

2 We must keep in mind this conflicted, ambivalent experience of secrecy as we study it in its many guises, and seek standards for dealing with it. But because secrecy is so often negatively defined and viewed as primarily immature, guilty, conspiratorial, or downright pathological, I shall first discuss the need for the protection it affords.

3 Consider how, in George Orwell's *Nineteen Eighty-four,* Winston Smith tried to preserve one last expression of independence from the Thought-police. He had decided to begin a diary, even though he knew he thereby risked death or at least twenty-five years in a forced-labor camp. He placed himself in an alcove in his living room where the telescreen could not see him, and began to write. When he found himself writing DOWN WITH BIG BROTHER over and over, he panicked and was tempted to give up.

> He did not do so, however, because he knew that it was useless. Whether he wrote DOWN WITH BIG BROTHER, or whether he refrained from writing it, made no difference. Whether he went on with the diary, or whether he did not go on with it, made no difference. The Thought-police would get him just the same. He had committed—would still

> have committed, even if he had not set pen to paper—the essential crime that contained all others in itself. Thoughtcrime, they called it. Thoughtcrime was not a thing that could be concealed forever. You might dodge successfully for a while, even for years, but sooner or later they were bound to get to you.

Subjected to near-complete surveillance, Winston Smith was willing to risk death rather than to forgo the chance to set down his thoughts in secret. To the extent that he retained some secrecy for his views, he had a chance to elude the Thought-police. Though aware that "sooner or later they were bound to get to you," he did not know that he was under surreptitious observation even as he prepared to write—that his most secret undertaking was itself secretly spied upon.

4 Conflicts over secrecy—between state and citizen, as in this case, or parent and child, or in journalism or business or law—are conflicts over power: the power that comes through controlling the flow of information. To be able to hold back some information about oneself or to channel it and thus influence how one is seen by others gives power; so does the capacity to penetrate similar defenses and strategies when used by others. True, power requires not only knowledge but the capacity to put knowledge to use; but without the knowledge, there is no chance to exercise power. To have no capacity for secrecy is to be out of control over how others see one; it leaves one open to coercion. To have no insight into what others conceal is to lack power as well. Those who are unable or unwilling ever to look beneath the surface, to question motives, to doubt what is spoken, are condemned to live their lives in ignorance, just as those who are unable to keep secrets of their own must live theirs defenseless.

5 Control over secrecy provides a safety valve for individuals in the midst of communal life—some influence over transactions between the world of personal experience and the world shared with others. With no control over such exchanges, human beings would be unable to exercise choice about their lives. To restrain some secrets and to allow others freer play; to keep some hidden and to let others be known; to offer knowledge to some but not to all comers; to give and receive confidences and to guess at far more: these efforts at control permeate all human contact.

6 Those who lose all control over these relations cannot flourish in either the personal or the shared world, nor retain their sanity. If experience in the shared world becomes too overwhelming, the sense

of identity suffers. Psychosis has been described as the breaking down of the delineation between the self and the outside world: the person going mad "flows out onto the world as through a broken dam." Conversely, experience limited to the inside world stunts the individual: at best it may lead to the aching self-exploration evoked by Nietzsche. "I am solitude become man—That no word ever reached me forced me to reach myself. . . ."

7 The claims in defense of some control over secrecy and openness invoke four different, though in practice inseparable, elements of human autonomy: identity, plans, action, and property. They concern protection of what we are, what we intend, what we do, and what we own.

8 The first of these claims holds that some control over secrecy and openness is needed to order to protect identity: the sense of what we identify ourselves as, through, and with. Such control may be needed to guard solitude, privacy, intimacy, and friendship. It protects vulnerable beliefs or feelings, inwardness, and the sense of being set apart: of having or belonging to regions not fully penetrable to scrutiny, including those of memory and dream; of being someone who is more, has become more, has more possibilities for the future than can ever meet the eyes of observers. Secrecy guards, therefore, not merely isolated secrets about the self but access to the underlying experience *of* secrecy.

9 Human beings can be subjected to every scrutiny, and reveal much about themselves; but they can never be entirely understood, simultaneously exposed from every perspective, completely transparent either to themselves or to other persons. They are not only unique but unfathomable. The experience of such uniqueness and depth underlies self-respect and what social theorists have called the sense of "the sacredness of the self." This sense also draws on group, familial, and societal experience of intimacy and sacredness, and may attach to individual as well as to collective identity. The growing stress in the last centuries on human dignity and on rights such as the right to privacy echoes it in secular and individualized language.

10 Without perceiving some sacredness in human identity, individuals are out of touch with the depth they might feel in themselves and respond to in others. Given such a sense, however, certain intrusions are felt as violations—a few even as desecrations. It is in order to guard against such encroachments that we recoil from those who would tap our telephones, read our letters, bug our rooms: no

matter how little we have to hide, no matter how benevolent their intentions, we take such intrusions to be demeaning.

11 Not only does control over secrecy and openness preserve central aspects of identity; it also guards their *changes,* their growth or decay, their progress or backsliding, their sharing and transformation of every kind. Here as elsewhere, while secrecy can be destructive, some of it is indispensable in human lives. Birth, sexual intimacy, death, mourning, experiences of conversion or of efforts to transcend the purely personal are often surrounded by special protections, and with rituals that combine secrecy and openness in set proportions.

12 Consider, for example, the role of secrecy, probing, and revelation with respect to pregnancy. In most cultures its workings have been thought mysterious, miraculous, at times terrifying. Like other experiences in which human boundaries are uncertain or shifting, pregnancy often increases vulnerability and the need for secrecy. Merely conjectured at first and pondered in secret by women, then perhaps revealed to a few, it is destined to unfold and to become known to many more. It is a period of heightened inwardness, awe, and joy for many women, giving them a sense of mattering in part because they have a secret to keep or to reveal. At times these feelings are overwhelmed by fear and anxiety—concerning the future of the baby, perhaps, or of the pregnant mother herself once her condition becomes known.

13 A work that illuminates such conflicts over secrecy in pregnancy is *The Confessions of Lady Nijō,* written in fourteenth-century Japan. When still a child, Lady Nijō was forced to become the concubine of a retired emperor. She had several babies not fathered by him. Her book tells of the strategems required each time to conceal her pregnant state, and to give birth in secret to a baby she could never hope to rear but had to turn over to others; it recounts her despair over this fate, her fear lest the emperor should learn she was the mother of a baby not his own, and her repeated attempts to escape her life at court to travel and write poetry as a Buddhist nun. Like Lady Nijō, women in many other cultures have had to conceal their condition, fearful that it be noticed, and afraid of the gossip, the loss of face if they were unmarried, perhaps the dismissal from work once concealment was no longer possible.

14 The second and third claims to control over secrecy presuppose the first. Given the need to guard identity, they invoke, in addition, the need for such control in order to protect plans and actions.

15 Choice is future-oriented, and never fully expressed in present

action. It requires what is most distinctive about human reasoning: intention—the capacity to envisage and to compare future possibilities, to make estimates, sometimes to take indirect routes to a goal or to wait. What is fragile, unpopular, perhaps threatened, such as Winston Smith's plan to express his views freely in his diary, seeks additional layers of secrecy. To the extent that it is possible to strip people of their capacity for secrecy about their intentions and their actions, their lives become more transparent and predictable; they can then the more easily be subjected to pressure and defeated.

16 Secrecy for plans is needed, not only to protect their formulation but also to develop them, perhaps to change them, at times to execute them, even to give them up. Imagine, for example, the pointlessness of the game of chess without secrecy on the part of the players. Secrecy guards projects that require creativity and prolonged work: the tentative and the fragile, unfinished tasks, probes and bargaining of all kinds. An elopement or a peace initiative may be foiled if prematurely suspected; a symphony, a scientific experiment, or an invention falters if exposed too soon. In speaking of creativity, Carlyle stressed the need for silence and secrecy, calling them "the element in which great things fashion themselves together."

17 Joint undertakings as well as personal ones may require secrecy for the sharing and working out of certain plans and for cooperative action. Lack of secrecy would, for instance, thwart many negotiations, in which all plans cannot easily be revealed from the outset. Once projects are safely under way, however, large portions of secrecy are often given up voluntarily, or dispelled with a flourish. Surprises are sprung and jokes explained. The result of the jury trial can be announced, the statue unveiled, the secretly negotiated treaty submitted for ratification, the desire to marry proclaimed. Here again, what is at issue is not secrecy alone, but rather the control over secrecy and openness. Many projects need both gestation and emergence, both confinement and publicity. Still others, such as certain fantasies and daydreams and hopes, may be too ephemeral or intimate, at times too discreditable, ever to see the light of day.

18 Secrecy about plans and their execution, therefore, allows unpredictability and surprise. These are often feared; yet without them human existence would not only be unfree but also monotonous and stifling. Secrecy heightens the value of revelations; it is essential for arousing suspense, whether through stories told, surprises prepared, or waiting times imposed. It can lend the joy of concentration and solemnity to the smallest matters. Secrecy may also lower intensity

and provide relief, so that when a revelation is finally made—as after the death of those most intimately connected with events described in an author's private diaries—the anguish of exposure is lessened. In all these ways, secrecy is the carrier of texture and variety. Without it, and without the suspense and wit and unexpectedness it allows, communication would be oppressively dull—lifeless in its own right.

19 The fourth claim to control over secrecy concerns property. At its root, it is closely linked to identity, in that people take some secrets, such as hidden love letters, to *belong* to them more than to others, to be *proper to* them. We link such secrets with our identity, and resist intrusions into them. But the claim to own secrets about oneself is often far-fetched. Thus the school-bus driver who has a severe heart condition cannot rightfully claim to *own* this medical information, even though it concerns him intimately. Even when outsiders have less need to share the information than in such a case, the question who owns a secret may be hard to answer. Should one include only those "about whom" it is a secret, those who claim a right to decide whether or not to disclose it, or all who know it?

20 In addition to such questions of owning secrets, secrecy is invoked to protect what one owns. We take for granted the legitimacy of hiding silver from burglars and personal documents from snoopers and busybodies. Here, too, the link to identity is close, as is that to plans and their execution. For had we no belongings whatsoever, our identity and our capacity to plan would themselves be threatened, and in turn survival itself. As H. L. A. Hart points out, life depends on the respect for at least "some minimal form of the institution of property (though not necessarily individual property) and the distinctive kind of rule which requires respect for it." At the most basic level, if crops are to be grown, land must be secure from indiscriminate entry, and food must be safe from being taken by others.

21 The four claims to control over secrecy and openness to protect identity, plans, actions, and property are not always persuasive. They may be stretched much too far, or abused in many ways. No matter how often these claims fail to convince, however, I shall assume that they do hold for certain fundamental human needs. Some capacity for keeping secrets and for choosing when to reveal them, and some access to the underlying experience of secrecy and depth, are indispensable for an enduring sense of identity, for the ability to plan and to act, and for essential belongings. With no control over secrecy and openness, human beings could not remain either sane or free.

Additional Rhetorical Strategies

Comparison and Contrast (paragraph 1); Illustration (throughout); Narration (paragraphs 3, 6); Definition (paragraphs 4, 6, 9); Cause and Effect (paragraphs 4–6, 17); Argument (throughout).

Examining Words and Meaning

1. Identify the four kinds of secrecy discussed in this essay. How is each one defined? How are they related? Although Bok never explicitly defines "secrecy," how does her classification system help to identify what she regards as the essential characteristics of a secret? How does her classification scheme help to support her claim that secrets are necessary? Identify other ways in which secrets might be classified.
2. How does Bok define the difference between "secrecy" and "power"? What, in her view, are the consequences of a person's not having the capacity to establish secrecy? Of not having insight into secrecy? How do the points she makes about the relationship between "secrecy" and "power" contribute to her overall purpose?
3. What does Bok mean when she observes that human beings are "not only unique but unfathomable" (paragraph 9)? In this respect, what do social theorists mean when they talk about "the sacredness of the self"?

Focusing on Structures and Strategies

1. Based on Bok's explanations and examples, how does she distinguish between secrecy that is justified and unjustified? What "protections" does Bok assert that secrecy provides? What, in effect, is Bok's principal point about the need for some control over secrecy and openness in society?
2. Why, according to Bok, are secrets necessary? In what ways would life be less interesting without secrecy? Under what circumstances, both personal and social, are secrets necessary? How, according to Bok, does the ability to control secrets result in power? How do they help to protect independence?

3. Bok discusses two extended examples of the need for secrets: Winston Smith's need in *Nineteen Eighty-Four* to keep a diary, and Lady Nijō's need to keep her pregnancy a secret. How are these two situations similar? Why do these two figures need to keep secrets? How do these examples help to clarify what Bok means when she speaks of the need for secrecy? What aspects of her argument do they not help to illustrate? Think of situations which would help to illustrate these aspects.

4. Review the substance of her argument "in defense of some control over secrecy and openness." Does she argue as convincingly for the need for control over secrecy as she does for control over openness? Which of her four claims do you find most convincing? Why? Which do you find the least convincing? Explain why.

Suggestions for Further Discussion and Writing

1. Bok also suggests that, like fire, secrecy has the potential for misuse. Although she does not specifically discuss abuses of this power, under what conditions might keeping a secret prove harmful or dangerous? What kinds of guidelines might one establish for protecting the right to secrecy and for guarding against possible abuses?

2. In *Works and Days,* the ancient Greek poet Hesiod defines gossip in the following aphoristic terms: "Gossip is an evil thing by nature, she's a light weight to lift up, / oh very easy, but heavy to carry, and hard to put down again." Consider your own experience with this subject. How would you classify the different kinds of gossip you have encountered in your life? What criteria would enable you to classify different kinds of gossip? Write an essay in which you classify gossip, supporting each of the points you make with an example or anecdote. What conclusion do these points lead you to make about the functions of gossip in contemporary American society?

3. Consider this old French proverb: "Nothing is so burdensome as a secret." Review your own experience. Have you ever been asked to keep a confidence that soon proved especially difficult to respect? Write an essay in which you recount the circumstances that led to your having been told this secret. Then recount the consequences you suffered as a result of maintaining this confidence.

Illustration

1 Illustration is a process through which writers select specific examples to represent, clarify, and support either general or abstract statements. Illustration is such an indispensable feature of thinking and writing that it is difficult even to imagine a successful writer's doing without it. Yet illustration is also such an accustomed part of our thinking that we may well take it for granted and not fully appreciate how it can work to strengthen our writing. The primary functions of illustration in writing are to make abstractions concrete and to lend detail to generalization. But illustration also clarifies our ideas, helps readers to follow the course of our thinking, heightens their interest in our subject, and, generally, adds substance to our prose.

2 Of all the methods of thinking in writing presented in this book, illustration (also called exemplification) is undoubtedly the one with which we are most familiar. Our daily conversations are punctuated with such phrases as *for example, for instance,* and the like. When we use such phrases, we are using illustration: we are explaining through examples. An example may be thought of as a part, a model, or a pattern of something. *Example* is often used interchangeably with such terms as *instance, case, sample,* and *specimen.* Each term helps explain something larger. Dictionary definitions, for example, regularly use illustration. *The American Heritage Dictionary* defines *mixed metaphor* as a "succession of metaphors that produce an

incongruous and ludicrous effect." The dictionary proceeds immediately to illustrate—to exemplify—this abstract statement with a concrete instance: "for example: *His mounting ambition was soon bridled by a wave of opposition.*" The example is offered to ensure that the precise meaning of the phrase is clearly understood. Such an illustration highlights the standard way in which an example carries thinking from the abstract to the concrete.

3 For most writers, illustration is an instinctive process: we sense the need for an example each time we discuss a subject in abstract or general terms. If we decided to talk about America in the 1960s as a "rebellious decade," we would immediately be aware that we ought to supply examples to support our contention. While we might choose the women's-liberation, the civil-rights, and the anti-war movements as our major examples, we would also need to develop each in enough detail to make our point convincing. If we were writing about the recurrence of organized abuses of civil rights in this country, we might substantiate our thesis with such examples as the excesses of nineteenth-century vigilante groups or the violent activities of the Ku Klux Klan today. Illustration usually anticipates such questions as "Can you be more specific?" "What evidence can you provide to support this statement?" "What are some examples of the point you are making?" Examples offer concrete representations of general or abstract thinking. They make our ideas clearer.

4 Consider, for example, how the columnist and novelist William Safire draws on the principles of illustration to clarify and reinforce the controlling idea of his essay "On Keeping a Diary"—that each of us should keep a fairly regular written account of our personal observations:

> Diaries remind us of details that would otherwise fade from memory and make less vivid our recollection. Navy Secretary Gideon Welles, whose private journal is an invaluable source for Civil War historians, watched Abraham Lincoln die in a room across the street from Ford's Theater and later jotted down a detail that puts the reader in the room: "The giant sufferer lay extended diagonally across the bed, which was not long enough for him. . . ." . . .
>
> Diaries can be written in psychic desperation, intended to be burned, as a hold on sanity: "I won't give up the diary again," wrote novelist Franz Kafka. "I must hold on here, it is the only place I can." Or written in physical desperation, intended to be read, as in the last entry in Arctic explorer Robert Scott's diary: "For God's sake look after our people. . . ."

As this passage demonstrates, illustration adds a great deal of detail to our writing. Consider the alternative: Safire's point would not be nearly as convincing if he had simply given us reasons for keeping a diary without also illustrating each of those reasons. In effect, illustration adds texture to our sentences and paragraphs as well as substance to each of the points we want to make in our essays.

5 Illustration invariably adds detail to our writing. Particular examples may appear in individual sentences or paragraphs, or they may even constitute an entire essay. If we were to write an essay in which we developed the thesis that the image of black Americans in advertising has changed significantly during the past two decades, we would have to support this thesis with an analysis of several examples. A single example may not prove sufficient to support a generalization. So, too, each example requires an adequate number of details to be convincing. If we wanted to discuss, say, the most significant recent directions in American popular music, we might well choose Bob Dylan, Prince, Bruce Springsteen, and Deborah Harry as our examples. It would then be appropriate to move on to consider in some detail each of their latest albums. One example may well lead to a series of others. In this instance, perhaps we would want to go on to discuss the lyrics of their music or the nature of their performances in concert—depending, of course, on our announced purpose, audience, and space limitations.

6 The choice of examples depends on the demands of a clearly stated thesis. Our essays should include only those examples that have a direct bearing on the thesis. So, too, the examples to be included should, taken together, touch on all aspects of the thesis or the general points that we intend to make. If, for example, we were writing about the economic effects of a national health-care plan, we could draw on any number of examples, including the plan's consequences for patients, insurance companies, doctors, nurses, and other professionals in the health services and related fields. Yet in an essay dealing with, say, the effectiveness of the United Nations as a peacekeeping force in international crises, the gradual and detailed unfolding of one or two extended examples—the ongoing Arab-Israeli border disputes or the Soviet invasion of Afghanistan—may be the most appropriate way to assemble sufficient details to establish a clear and convincing thesis. We ought to remember, however, that as we reduce the number of examples to be discussed, we increase the need for treating each with greater specificity. It is not the number of examples that makes an essay successful but rather how well each

is integrated into the writer's presentation, how pertinent each is to the point being made.

7 Illustration may also take the form of an anecdote, fable, parable, or analogy that displays the general point being made. As in all other cases of illustration, care must be exercised to ensure that each example is finally precise enough to be entirely clear to all of our readers.

8 When we select an example, we choose a part to represent the whole. One important thing to remember when using illustration is that what can be said about one example can be said about any other in the group to which it belongs. When writing about, say, the second-class status of women in American professional sports, we would do well to cite as an example the discrepancies in tennis-tournament prize money. The point illustrated by this example could also be applied to other professional sports: basketball, golf, baseball, squash, and softball. In this case, tennis would be a fair and representative example for the proposed thesis: namely, that the material and psychological rewards of athletics remain fewer for women than men. Yet it would be unreasonable to compare the salaries of male and female professional football players, since the women's professional league is still in its formative stages. In sum, the examples we choose to support the points we make should be at once typical and striking: they must be vivid enough to attract and hold the reader's attention and yet representative enough to be taken seriously.

9 Considerable importance should be attached to the positioning and timing of illustration in our writing. Each point should be illustrated fully, one at a time. The confusion of mixing one example with another must be avoided. Perhaps the best way to eliminate such potential disorder in our writing is to place each example as near as possible to the point being made. But should a series of examples be called for, we ought to remember that the positions of greatest emphasis are at the beginning and the end.

10 Illustration is an integral part of nearly every method of thinking in writing. It appears frequently, as we will see in other sections of this book, in description and narration, and it enhances all other rhetorical techniques. Whether we use it within the confines of a single sentence or throughout an entire essay, illustration helps tighten loose generalizations and effectively prevents us from jumping to conclusions—that is, from basing generalizations on a single example. But most important, illustration makes abstract ideas concrete and, in doing so, makes our thinking in writing more lucid and persuasive.

Death in the Open

Lewis Thomas

In nearly all expository writing, we move back and forth between generalization and example. We observe a number of examples and form a generalization; or we begin with a generalization and support it with several examples. In this essay from The Lives of the Cell, *Lewis Thomas clearly moves through similar patterns. The peculiar shock of seeing dead animals on the road leads him to speculate about death in general, a generalization that he then supports with additional examples. As you read the essay, note the continuous interplay between Thomas's major generalizations ("everything in the world dies") and his highly particularized instances ("the fly struggling on the porch floor of the summer house in October"). For Thomas's essay, such examples are more than rhetorical devices; they represent the only way we have of truly confronting the "abstraction" of death.*

For biographical information on Lewis Thomas, see page 109.

1 Most of the dead animals you see on highways near the cities are dogs, a few cats. Out in the countryside, the forms and coloring of the dead are strange; these are the wild creatures. Seen from a car window they appear as fragments, evoking memories of woodchucks, badgers, skunks, voles, snakes, sometimes the mysterious wreckage of a deer.

2 It is always a queer shock, part a sudden upwelling of grief, part unaccountable amazement. It is simply astounding to see an animal dead on a highway. The outrage is more than just the location; it is the impropriety of such visible death, anywhere. You do not expect to see dead animals in the open. It is the nature of animals to die alone, off somewhere, hidden. It is wrong to see them lying out on the highway; it is wrong to see them anywhere.

3 Everything in the world dies, but we only know about it as a kind of abstraction. If you stand in a meadow, at the edge of a hillside, and look around carefully, almost everything you can catch sight of is in the process of dying, and most things will be dead long before you are. If it were not for the constant renewal and replacement going on before your eyes, the whole place would turn to stone and sand under your feet.

4 There are some creatures that do not seem to die at all; they simply vanish totally into their own progeny. Single cells do this. The cell becomes two, then four, and so on, and after a while the last trace is gone. It cannot be seen as death; barring mutation, the descendants are simply the first cell, living all over again. The cycles of the slime mold have episodes that seem as conclusive as death, but the withered slug, with its stalk and fruiting body, is plainly the transient tissue of a developing animal; the free-swimming amebocytes use this organ collectively in order to produce more of themselves.

5 There are said to be a billion billion insects on the earth at any moment, most of them with very short life expectancies by our standards. Someone has estimated that there are 25 million assorted insects hanging in the air over every temperate square mile, in a column extending upward for thousands of feet, drifting through the layers of the atmosphere like plankton. They are dying steadily, some by being eaten, some just dropping in their tracks, tons of them around the earth, disintegrating as they die, invisibly.

6 Who ever sees dead birds, in anything like the huge numbers stipulated by the certainty of the death of all birds? A dead bird is an incongruity, more startling than an unexpected live bird, sure evidence to the human mind that something has gone wrong. Birds do their dying off somewhere, behind things, under things, never on the wing.

7 Animals seem to have an instinct for performing death alone, hidden. Even the largest, most conspicuous ones find ways to conceal themselves in time. If an elephant missteps and dies in an open place, the herd will not leave him there; the others will pick him up and carry the body from place to place, finally putting it down in some inexplicably suitable location. When elephants encounter the skeleton of an elephant out in the open, they methodically take up each of the bones and distribute them, in a ponderous ceremony, over neighboring acres.

8 It is a natural marvel. All of the life of the earth dies, all of the time, in the same volume as the new life that dazzles us each morning, each spring. All we see of this is the odd stump, the fly struggling on the porch floor of the summer house in October, the fragment on the highway. I have lived all my life with an embarrassment of squirrels in my backyard, they are all over the place, all year long, and I have never seen, anywhere, a dead squirrel.

9 I suppose it is just as well. If the earth were otherwise, and all the dying were done in the open, with the dead there to be looked

at, we would never have it out of our minds. We can forget about it much of the time, or think of it as an accident to be avoided, somehow. But it does make the process of dying seem more exceptional than it really is, and harder to engage in at the times when we must ourselves engage.

10 In our way, we conform as best we can to the rest of nature. The obituary pages tell us of the news that we are dying away, while the birth announcements in finer print, off at the side of the page, inform us of our replacements, but we get no grasp from this of the enormity of scale. There are 3 billion of us on the earth, and all 3 billion must be dead, on a schedule, within this lifetime. The vast mortality, involving something over 50 million of us each year, takes place in relative secrecy. We can only really know of the deaths in our households, or among our friends. These, detached in our minds from all the rest, we take to be unnatural events, anomalies, outrages. We speak of our own dead in low voices; struck down, we say, as though visible death can only occur for cause, by disease or violence, avoidably. We send off for flowers, grieve, make ceremonies, scatter bones, unaware of the rest of the 3 billion on the same schedule. All of that immense mass of flesh and bone and consciousness will disappear by absorption into the earth, without recognition by the transient survivors.

11 Less than a half century from now, our replacements will have more than doubled the numbers. It is hard to see how we can continue to keep the secret, with such multitudes doing the dying. We will have to give up the notion that death is catastrophe, or detestable, or avoidable, or even strange. We will need to learn more about the cycling of life in the rest of the system, and about our connection to the process. Everything that comes alive seems to be in trade for something that dies, cell for cell. There might be some comfort in the recognition of synchrony, in the information that we all go down together, in the best of company.

Reading for Rhetorical Strategy

Lewis Thomas begins by briefly listing some of the dead animals commonly found on American roads. The shock of these concrete observations—a "shock" because we seldom see "death in the open"—leads him to a generalization: "Everything in the world dies, but we only know about it as a kind of abstraction" (paragraph 3). Thomas then offers numerous examples of creatures whose deaths usually remain hidden from view: single cells (paragraph 4), insects (paragraph 5), birds (paragraph 6), elephants (paragraph 7), squirrels in the backyard (paragraph 8). These examples lead him to another generalization: the absence of visible death makes "the process of dying seem more exceptional than it really is." For his final example, Thomas turns to the "relative secrecy" of human death (paragraph 10) and our peculiar detachment from the enormity of death on the planet. The incredible number of people dying leads him to his final generalization: we will not be able to keep death a hidden process much longer. We may finally be forced to bring death into the open. Note how the true meaning of his title changes as his essay moves to its conclusion.

One Hundred Per Cent American

Ralph Linton

An average day for an average American turns out to be made up of things that are far from being one hundred percent American. What we sleep on, what we wear, and even what we call ourselves have foreign origins.

Writing for the American Mercury *magazine in 1937, Ralph Linton illustrates his opening understatement that "some" foreign ideas have been imported into the American way of life with so many examples that the reader might well wonder whether it is valid to speak of "Americanism" or a purely American heritage.*

1 There can be no question about the average American's Americanism or his desire to preserve this precious heritage at all costs. Nevertheless, some insidious foreign ideas have already wormed their way into his civilization without his realizing what was going on. Thus dawn finds the unsuspecting patriot garbed in pajamas, a garment of East Indian origin; and lying in a bed built on a pattern

which originated in either Persia or Asia Minor. He is muffled to the ears in un-American materials: cotton, first domesticated in India; linen, domesticated in the Near East; wool from an animal native to Asia Minor; or silk whose uses were first discovered by the Chinese. All these substances have been transformed into cloth by methods invented in Southwestern Asia. If the weather is cold enough he may even be sleeping under an eiderdown quilt invented in Scandinavia.

2 On awakening he glances at the clock, a medieval European invention, uses one potent Latin word in abbreviated form, rises in haste, and goes to the bathroom. Here, if he stops to think about it, he must feel himself in the presence of a great American institution; he will have heard stories of both the quality and frequency of foreign plumbing and will know that in no other country does the average man perform his ablutions in the midst of such splendor. But the insidious foreign influence pursues him even here. Glass was invented by the ancient Egyptians, the use of glazed tiles for floors and walls in the Near East, porcelain in China, and the art of enameling on metal by Mediterranean artisans of the Bronze Age. Even his bathtub and toilet are but slightly modified copies of Roman originals. The only purely American contribution to the ensemble is the steam radiator, against which our patriot very briefly and unintentionally places his posterior.

3 In this bathroom the American washes with soap invented by the ancient Gauls. Next he cleans his teeth, a subversive European practice which did not invade America until the latter part of the eighteenth century. He then shaves, a masochistic rite first developed by the heathen priests of ancient Egypt and Sumer. The process is made less of a penance by the fact that his razor is of steel, an iron-carbon alloy discovered in either India or Turkestan. Lastly, he dries himself on a Turkish towel.

4 Returning to the bedroom, the unconscious victim of un-American practices removes his clothes from a chair, invented in the Near East, and proceeds to dress. He puts on close-fitting tailored garments whose form derives from the skin clothing of the ancient nomads of the Asiatic steppes and fastens them with buttons whose prototypes appeared in Europe at the close of the Stone Age. This costume is appropriate enough for outdoor exercise in a cold climate, but is quite unsuited to American summers, steam-heated houses, and Pullmans. Nevertheless, foreign ideas and habits hold the unfortunate man in thrall even when common sense tells him that the

authentically American costume of gee string and moccasins would be far more comfortable. He puts on his feet stiff coverings made from hide prepared by a process invented in ancient Egypt and cut to a pattern which can be traced back to ancient Greece, and makes sure that they are properly polished, also a Greek idea. Lastly, he ties about his neck a strip of bright-colored cloth which is a vestigial survival of the shoulder shawls worn by seventeenth-century Croats. He gives himself a final appraisal in the mirror, an old Mediterranean invention, and goes downstairs to breakfast.

5 Here a whole new series of foreign things confronts him. His food and drink are placed before him in pottery vessels, the popular name of which—china—is sufficient evidence of their origin. His fork is a medieval Italian invention and his spoon a copy of a Roman original. He will usually begin the meal with coffee, an Abyssinian plant first discovered by the Arabs. The American is quite likely to need it to dispel the morning-after effects of overindulgence in fermented drinks, invented in the Near East; or distilled ones, invented by the alchemists of medieval Europe. Whereas the Arabs took their coffee straight, he will probably sweeten it with sugar, discovered in India; and dilute it with cream, both the domestication of cattle and the technique of milking having originated in Asia Minor.

6 If our patriot is old-fashioned enough to adhere to the so-called American breakfast, his coffee will be accompanied by an orange, domesticated in the Mediterranean region, a cantaloupe domesticated in Persia, or grapes domesticated in Asia Minor. He will follow this with a bowl of cereal made from grain domesticated in the Near East and prepared by methods also invented there. From this he will go on to waffles, a Scandinavian invention, with plenty of butter, originally a Near-Eastern cosmetic. As a side dish he may have the egg of a bird domesticated in Southeastern Asia or strips of the flesh of an animal domesticated in the same region, which have been salted and smoked by a process invented in Northern Europe.

7 Breakfast over, he places upon his head a molded piece of felt, invented by the nomads of Eastern Asia, and, if it looks like rain, puts on outer shoes of rubber, discovered by the ancient Mexicans, and takes an umbrella, invented in India. He then sprints for his train—the train, not sprinting, being an English invention. At the station he pauses for a moment to buy a newspaper, paying for it with coins invented in ancient Lydia. Once on board he settles back to inhale the fumes of a cigarette invented in Mexico, or a cigar invented in

Brazil. Meanwhile, he reads the news of the day, imprinted in characters invented by the ancient Semites by a process invented in Germany upon a material invented in China. As he scans the latest editorial pointing out the dire results to our institutions of accepting foreign ideas, he will not fail to thank a Hebrew God in an Indo-European language that he is a one hundred per cent (decimal system invented by the Greeks) American (from Americus Vespucci, Italian geographer).

Additional Rhetorical Strategy

Narrative (throughout).

Examining Words and Meaning

1. What is Linton's attitude toward the "foreign influence" on American life? What, for example, is the tone of the phrase "insidious foreign ideas" (paragraph 1)? What leads you to your conclusion? What other words and phrases in the essay seem to convey a similar tone?

2. If necessary, check the dictionary for the meaning of the following words: insidious (paragraph 1); garbed (paragraph 1); eiderdown (paragraph 1); ablutions (paragraph 2); masochistic (paragraph 3); penance (paragraph 3); steppes (paragraph 4); prototypes (paragraph 4); thrall (paragraph 4).

Focusing on Structures and Strategies

1. How much of this essay would you describe as statement? How much is illustration? If the essay were reduced to nothing but statement, how long would it be? How effective?

2. Why do you think that Linton makes his case in the form of a narrative? How would the effect of the essay be different had he simply listed the origins of the items he mentions?

Suggestions for Further Discussion and Writing

1. What is Linton spoofing in this essay? After rereading it, what would you think was a popular political stance at the time he wrote (1937)? Can you point to any evidence that the attitude he was spoofing in 1937 is current today?

2. Write a narrative modeled after Linton's in which you select examples and then comment upon them to make a similar point. If, for example, you wanted to show how tedious a housewife's schedule can be, you could recount what she does each day, choosing the best examples to support your thesis. If you wanted to show that secretaries are as important to business as executives, you might construct a narrative in which the secretaries disappeared for a day and business came to a halt.

Winning: Why We Keep Score

Roy Blount, Jr.

His peers describe Roy Blount, Jr., as "The Number One magazine writer in the country" and as a versatile stylist whose humorous treatment of a broad range of subjects has earned him a reputation as a contemporary heir of Mark Twain. Blount, however, views his work in far more modest terms: "I am not the kind of person who feels right about calling himself a 'writer,' even. It sounds like something you would assert, falsely, in a singles bar." Blount is even more reluctant to call himself an "author." He describes the difference in the following characteristically droll terms: "A writer, as we know, writes; an author has written. What does an author do? Auth? Authorize? An author authors. But never in the present tense. No one says, when asked what he or she is doing, 'I'm authoring.'"

Blount's distinguished career as a "writer" began with a one-year stint as a reporter for Georgia's Decatur-DeKalb News *and with summer internships at New York's* Morning Telegraph *and at the* New Orleans Times-Picayune*—positions he held before completing his undergraduate studies at Vanderbilt University with honors in 1963. After taking an M.A. degree at Harvard in the following year, Blount* *returned to writing full-time and worked as a reporter, editorial writer, and columnist at the* Atlanta Journal *(1966–68) before joining* Sports Illustrated, *where he continued to write for the next eight years, including service in 1974–75 as Associate Editor. When asked to describe the shape of his career, Blount provided the following telegraphic summary: "raised in the South by Southern parents. Couldn't play third base well enough so became college journalist. Ridiculed cultural enemies. Boosted integration. Decided to write, teach. Went to Harvard Graduate School. Didn't like it. Went back to journalism. Liked it. Got a column. Ridiculed cultural enemies. Wrote limericks. Boosted integration. Wanted to write for magazines. Took writing job at* Sports Illustrated. *Have seen country, met all kinds of people, heard all different kinds of talk. Like it."*

In the years since he devoted himself to full-time writing, Blount has published scores of humorous articles and several noteworthy books, including Crackers *(1980),* One Fell Soup: or, I'm Just a Bug on the Windshield of Life *(1982), and more recently* Not Exactly What I Had in Mind *(1985). In "Winning," originally published in a special sports section in the* New York Times Magazine, *Blount presents a wry view of the fact that while triumph may be elusive in everyday life, sports gives contemporary Americans winners—and losers—with every tick of the clock. As Blount illustrates, winning isn't everything, but it is everywhere.*

1 I hoped that my researches into the matter of winning would verify something I had long suspected: that the word "triumph" derives from the Roman custom of requiring the vanquished to say "umph" three times. No such luck.

2 I have learned, however, that the roots of the word "win" go very deep, perhaps all the way back to a Hittite verb meaning "to copulate." "Win" is a branch of one immemorial tree whose diverse other sprouts include "Venus," "venerate," "venison" and "venom."

3 I have also at long last figured out, to my own satisfaction, why it is that advertisements for watches—watches with hands—almost invariably show the time to be somewhere between 10:08 and 10:12.

4 V for victory. Rocky frozen with his arms upraised. Actually, Rocky may have stood at something closer to 11:05, but it's the same principle. People eternally tend to take sides and to want their side to win. Watchmongers know this.

5 So do people in the sports business. Life, history and serious literature seldom provide examples of outright uncontestable victory, but sports does every day. In sports, what's won won't come unwon.

Sportspersons who win get to keep on making a living by playing games, or by managing those who play games, or by hiring and firing those who play or manage. Sportspersons who lose, don't. One way or the other, sportspersons tend to get pretty grim. So how come we call it "playing" and how come we call them "games"?

6 I promise this will not be another of those "Are we placing too much emphasis on winning and thereby losing track of the true purpose of sport?" ruminations. For one thing, I'm not sure what the true purpose of sports is, aside from moving the runner on second to third with less than two outs.

7 On the other hand, when was the last time you read one of those ruminations? Isn't it getting a bit thick lately, all the talk about winning, being a winner, in sports and out? Thicker even than usual? And is anybody even complaining about it anymore?

8 "Wanna be a winner?" asks a television commercial. "Buy a Chevy." What? Are people running home to their families these days and shouting, "I won! I won! I bought us a Chevrolet"? I wouldn't be surprised.

9 In this country today, 220 books are in print whose titles *begin* with the word "Winning." Only the One Great Scorer knows how many other available titles contain some form of the word "win." Here are just a few:

10 "A Winner's Notebook," "Be a Winner," "How to Win at Office Politics," "How to Unlock the Secrets of Winning & Good Luck," "Win the Happiness Game," "Act Like a Winner," "Dressing to Win," "It's Your Turn to Win at Work & at Home," "Why Winners Win," "Choose to Win!" and "Z-Cycle: Winning by a Force of a Fourth Type."

11 I don't know what a force of a fourth type is, but more and more it seems that Americans are being divided into two types. The business news is full of coups: the overtakers taking over the overtaken. A magazine ad for Puma sneakers shows George Brett of the Kansas City Royals poised to swing his bat with a vengeance, and the caption reads: "ATTACK. Because if you're not the predator, you're the prey." The Republicans—led by a man who once made a baseball movie called "The Winning Team" and a football movie in which he played the person referred to in the phrase "Win one for the Gipper"—seem to have a Dynasty going; whereas the Democrats are too abject at the moment to be identified with any television program, unless it be "One Day at a Time." The term for a social misfit in high school these days, I gather from my children, is "loser."

12 How can anybody in America relax and have a good time anymore, if every morning presents anew the question, "Am I going to win today?" Even the defense establishment seems to feel insecure. One bright A.M. this winter, *The New York Times* reported that, "The Reagan Administration, rejecting proposals for delay or compromise, began a high-level lobbying effort today to win a showdown on the MX missile." Fearful that Congress would "kill the new missile," the Administration was eager to win overwhelming Congressional support for it before the Easter recess, when Congressmen were seen likely, in the words of a Pentagon spokesman, to "get their brains beat out by every church group, every Mother for Peace." I didn't even know there still *were* any Mothers for Peace, and yet the military-industrial complex is afraid it can't lick them.

13 Can this prevailing state of mind be explained by the notion that we now live in a "zero-sum society," in which any one faction's gain is another's loss? Or is fallout from America's no-win situation in Vietnam (and now in the Middle East, if not Latin America) to blame? You can't win, trying to answer questions like that. I will attempt only to make a few points. About winning, its relativity, its limitations.

14 "Winning is the ethic of football," Don Shula, the head coach of the Miami Dolphins, once said. "You start with having to win, and you work back." It must be noted that the most insistent talk of winning in sports comes from coaches and managers. That's because a coach or manager's won-loss record is his only statistic. He must win to have coached well. But that doesn't mean Shula is out of line.

15 If all you care about a sports event is who wins, you can't appreciate it fully. But neither can you if you don't care at all. To get into a game wholeheartedly you have to root. And to play a game wholeheartedly, at its highest levels, you must go all out—not to look pretty or enjoy the way the playing surface feels under your kangaroo-skin shoes, but to win. Falling in love is solipsistic unless it involves winning another's heart.

16 But romance is not pretty if it aims to *squelch* another's heart. The most recent final National Basketball Association playoff series, between the Los Angeles Lakers and the Boston Celtics, should have been a beaut, but for me it was spoiled by Boston's constant harping on intimidation. The Celtics kept implying that the Lakers lacked character, would fold; to prove their point, the Celtics' big men tried to beat up the Lakers. As it happened, the Lakers called upon their own heavy bangers, Mitch Kupchak and Kurt Rambis, who busted

heads effectively enough that Los Angeles (thanks also to magnificence from the stately Kareem Abdul-Jabbar and the Celtics' forgetting how to make the ball go through the basket) wore Boston down. But only one of the six games was delightful. That was the fourth, won at the buzzer by the Celtics. "There is so much *spunk* in this game," exclaimed Tom Heinsohn, the telecaster, and he was right. But the kind of courage shown in the series generally had too much to do with pressure and not enough with grace.

17 Winning is the ethic of sports in the sense that, as a novelist once said, credibility is the ethic of fiction. When Donald Trump, the owner of the New Jersey Generals, says he'd rather see his team lose an exciting game than win a boring one, you wonder whether he wouldn't be better suited to the movie business. (Trump reportedly suggested to other owners that their teams go easy on his quarterback, Doug Flutie, because Flutie's entertainment value was so crucial to the United States Football League). When John McKay, in his last game as head coach of Tampa Bay in the National Football League, directed his defensive unit to lie down and give up a quick touchdown so that his running back, James Wilder, could get the ball back in time to try for an N.F.L. single-season record for yardage gained rushing and receiving, lovers of football cringed. The integrity of sports lies in trying to win, not to show off. Players must be determined to win if fans are to suspend their disbelief.

18 But nobody wants to read a novel whose narrator keeps crying out, "By God, this story is credible! No, damn it, now it's losing credibility! I'll see about that! These characters *better* be credible, or I'll kill them off!" That is, in effect, what George Steinbrenner—the most visible owner, unfortunately, in sports—keeps saying about his Yankees. When they lose, he apologizes for them publicly (though he is constitutionally unapologetic about himself). He accuses various Yankees of having "spit the bit." He takes it upon himself to assert that Dave Winfield, whom he acquired for the Yankees and who is one of baseball's best players, is "not a proven winner." He dismisses managers obsessively. He does not understand the game.

19 "Winning ugly" is a phrase that is gaining currency in sportswriting. As a description of inelegant fortitude, it is amiable enough. Perhaps Shakespeare's Henry IV had a point when he said, "For nothing can seem foul to those that win." But since he spoke of war we know he was overlooking a great deal. The lust for victory can

be ugly indeed, as we saw when 38 people died last May in a soccer riot in Brussels.

20 "Winning isn't everything," said the late Vince Lombardi, revered head coach of the Green Bay Packers, "it's the only thing." You have to give Lombardi credit. He produced great teams, and his players, at least in retrospect, said they loved him. The kind of drive he apotheosized is America's motor. If life were based on need, rather than hustle, then winning might be regarded as everything. The athlete's will to win is one of those primal amoral urges—like the businessman's to maximize profits and the journalist's to get the word out—that our system takes as a given. And competition is not an exclusively capitalistic tool. It was Marx who said: "The proletarians have nothing to lose but their chains. They have a world to win."

21 It is worth reminding ourselves, however, that Lombardi's famous saying is crazy. The only thing that is everything is everything itself, and not even sports can be boiled down any further than to the binary W/L. If winning were the only thing it would not be such a big deal. And we would not treasure the memory of Joe Don Looney, Bo Belinsky, Johnny Blood. There wouldn't even *be* any Chicago Cubs.

22 When I heard that Angelo Dundee, the trainer of Muhammad Ali and Sugar Ray Leonard, had a book out entitled "I Only Talk Winning," I was at first dismayed. Dundee is widely regarded as a decent, affable, hardly monomaniacal man. I felt better when I read the book's last paragraph:

23 "I've called this book 'I Only Talk Winning' for a reason. In life, there are positive and negative thoughts. And hey, it doesn't cost you a cent more to think positively. 'I Only Talk Winning' stands for 'Don't be afraid of losing.' Losing is nothing. There is no such thing as failure, only learning how."

24 Literally, I guess that, too, is crazy. It comes off a bit over-rosy compared with, say, these lines by William Blake:

> *They win who never near the goal;*
> *They run who halt on wounded feet;*
> *Art hath its martyrs like the soul,*
> *Its victors in defeat.*

25 But, hey, could Blake handle fighters? I like what Dundee says, because it rises above venom, aversion, totalitarianism.

26 Something else I like is a memory from the 1973 N.F.L. playoffs.

I had spent that season hanging around with the Pittsburgh Steelers to write a book. The Steelers had just been trounced by Oakland. Their campaign had been a failure, in pro football terms, because it had not ended in ultimate victory. I had stood with the players on the sidelines as Raider fans threw things at us, reviled us, cried out in the nastiest of tones, "You guys are *lewsers.*" The following season the Steelers would win the first of four Super Bowls, and I would celebrate that triumph, which was sweet, on the sidelines. But this was a losing locker room. And yet here's what Andy Russell, the Pittsburgh co-captain, told me, his eyes shining:

27 "I was into that game. There was no other world outside it. There was nothing. That's the thrill."

28 "Does that make it hard to lose?" I asked.

29 "No, easier. You know you gave it all you had. Some games you're distracted, by an injury or something, and you get down on yourself, question your character. This game I was away, into the *game.* We lost. But all I could think afterwards was, 'Damn, I had fun.' "

30 Another thing that 10:10 on a watch-face suggests is a big smile.

Additional Rhetorical Strategies

Definition (paragraphs 2, 19); Cause and Effect (paragraphs 5, 12); Classification (paragraph 11); Comparison and Contrast (paragraphs 11, 22).

Examining Words and Meaning

1. According to Blount, what makes the world of sports so appealing? How would you characterize his opinion of this world and its emphasis on winning? What does he mean when he ways that "winning is the ethic of sports in the sense that . . . credibility is the ethic of fiction"? What, finally, is Blount's attitude toward winning and losing? How does that attitude help clarify his purpose in writing this essay?

2. What exactly does Blount mean when he talks of "watchmongers" (paragraph 4) and "winning ugly" (paragraph 19)? What is the

relationship of these terms to the overall point of his essay? With respect to the effects of winning, how does Blount illustrate that the world of sports is essentially different from daily life? What examples does Blount provide to underscore this distinction?

Focusing on Structures and Strategies

1. Although most of Blount's examples are culled from athletics, his essay has more general implications as well. What are some other areas which make use of the language of winning and losing? How well does this language translate into these other areas? How might his attitude toward winning apply to these areas as well?

2. Blount's topic is essentially philosophical and potentially very serious. How does he manage to keep the subject from sounding too ponderous? Look particularly at the early paragraphs. How does Blount attempt to draw his readers into his topic? Where does he finally identify what the principal point of his essay is? Why does he wait so long to do this?

3. Blount uses a wide range of brief examples to illustrate each of his points about winning. Identify several of the most striking of these examples. From what areas of life, besides athletics, does Blount draw these examples? How do these examples help to prevent his sentences from sliding into abstraction?

4. Consider the diction Blount uses in this essay. How would you characterize his word choices? Are they primarily formal? informal? something else? At what points in his essay does Blount seem to rely on colloquial expressions? With what effect? When does he draw on clichés from the sportsworld? With what effect?

5. How would you characterize the sentence structure of Blount's essay? What structure seems to dominate his essay? What is the effect of Blount's repeating this particular structure? How would you describe the organization of his paragraphs? What principle of composition seems to underpin the structure of his paragraphs? What is the effect of this paragraph structure?

6. Blount occasionally introduces literary references to clarify and support the points he makes. (See, for example, his references to William Shakespeare in paragraph 19 and to William Blake in paragraph 24.) What is the effect of such references? What is the effect of his frequent references to advertising?

Suggestions for Further Discussion and Writing

1. Blount calls winning "one of those primal amoral urges . . . that our system takes as a given." What does this suggest about our need to win? Why is the need to win so important to human nature? How might this need relate to the desire of sports fans as well as of the participants? How might one attempt to reduce the tendency toward "winning ugly" in sports?
2. Consider the specific occasions in which the term "loser" can be used in contemporary American society. Choose one such instance and consider the ways in which you can illustrate the various meanings of the word with examples drawn from that occasion. Use Blount's essay as a model, and range freely, as he does, between humorous and serious examples of the points you are making.
3. Blount opens paragraph 12 with the following observation: "How can anybody in America relax and have a good time anymore, if every morning presents anew the question, 'Am I going to win today?' " Consider this statement carefully and write an essay in which you illustrate how his assertion can—or cannot—be applied with equal accuracy to American life in the 1970s and/or in the 1960s. What examples can you draw on to demonstrate that either—or both—of these decades were as preoccupied with "winning" as Blount claims Americans are in the 1980s?

I Remember . . .

Joyce Maynard

As an eighteen-year-old Yale freshman, Joyce Maynard created a literary sensation when she published a long, wry appraisal of the jaded youth of the 1960s in The New York Times. *In that essay—expanded into book-length form as* Looking Back *(1974)—as well as in her first novel,* Baby Love *(1981), Maynard sees television as a dominant force in the ordinary lives of contemporary Americans.* Domestic Affairs, *essays on "the pleasures of motherhood and family life," appeared in*

1987. In the following selection, written for TV Guide *magazine, she assesses the impact of television on her own adolescence and on the behavior and values of her generation.*

1 We got our TV set in 1959, when I was 5. So I can barely remember life without television. I have spent 20,000 hours of my life in front of the set. Not all of my contemporaries watched so much, but many did, and what's more, we watched the same programs, heard the same commercials, were exposed to the same end-of-show lessons. So there is, among this generation of television children, a shared history, a tremendous fund of common experience. These massive doses of TV have not affected all of us in an identical way, and it would be risky to draw broad conclusions. But if a sociologist were—rashly—to try to uncover some single most important influence on this generation, which has produced Patty Hearst and Alice Cooper and the Jesus movement and the peace movement; if he were searching for the roots of 1960's psychedelia and 1970's apathy, he would do well to look first at television.

2 My own motives are less ambitious. I know, simply, that a rerun of *I Love Lucy* or *Father Knows Best,* the theme music from *Dr. Kildare* or the sad, whistling refrain from *Lassie* can make me stand, frozen, before the set. It is as if I, and not Timmy Martin, had been stuck in an abandoned mine shaft during a thunderstorm, as if I, and not Lucy Ricardo, had dropped a diamond ring somewhere in the batter of a seven-layer cake. I didn't so much *watch* those shows when I was little; I let them wash over me. Now I study them like a psychiatrist on his own couch, looking hungrily for some clue inside the TV set to explain the person I have become.

3 I was not a dull or energyless child, or neglected by my parents. Our house was full of books and paints, and sometimes I did choose to draw or ride my bike. But the picture of my childhood that comes to mind is one of a dimly lit room in a small New Hampshire town and a girl listening, leaden-eyed, to some talk-show rendition of "I Left My Heart in San Francisco." It is a picture of myself at age 8, wise to the ways of "Vegas," the timing of standup comics, the marriages of Zsa Zsa Gabor, the advertising slogans of Bufferin and Fab.

4 And what did all this television watching teach me? Well, I rarely swallowed the little pellets of end-of-show morals presented in the television shows I watched (that crime does not pay, that one

must always obey one's parents). But I observed something of the way the world works: that life is easier if one fits in with the established conventions; that everything is easier if one has a pretty face.

5 And in the process of acquiring those melancholy truths I picked up an embarrassingly large fund of knowledge that is totally unusable (except, perhaps, ironically, on some television game show). I can hum Perry Mason's theme song or give the name of the actress who played Donna Reed's best friend. I would happily trade that knowledge for the facility with piano or ballet I might have had if I'd spent those television hours practicing music and dance instead. But something else I gained from television should be less lightly dismissed. I guess it is a sense of knowing America, not simply its vulgarities but its strengths as well: the rubber face of Lucille Ball, the lovableness of Americans on *Candid Camera,* an athlete's slow-motion grace in an instant replay on *Monday Night Football.*

6 So many hours of television I watched—hundreds of bank robberies, touch-and-go operations and barroom fights, millions of dollars' worth of refrigerators awarded to thousands of housewives who kissed dozens of game-show moderators—and yet the list of individual programs I remember is very short. One is the Beatles' appearance, the winter I was 10, on *The Ed Sullivan Show.* I remember the on-camera shooting of Lee Oswald, and the face of Jacqueline Kennedy at her husband's funeral. A few particularly marvelous episodes of the old *Dick Van Dyke Show* stand out: Laura Petrie getting her toe stuck in the bathroom faucet; Rob imagining that he's going bald. One or two *I Love Lucy* shows, *Andy Griffith* shows, a Miss America contestant who sang a number from "The Sound of Music"—dressed like a nun—and then whipped off her habit to reveal a spangled bathing suit. I remember a special five-part *Dr. Kildare* segment in which a team of doctors had to choose five patients for a lifesaving kidney machine out of eight candidates. I remember getting up at midnight to watch Neil Armstrong land on the moon—expecting to be awed, but falling asleep instead.

7 My strongest memories are of one series and one character. Not the best, but the one that formed me more than any other, that haunts me still, and left its mark on a good-sized part of a generation: *Leave It to Beaver.* I watched that show every day after school (fresh from my own failures) and studied it, like homework, because the Cleaver family was so steady and normal—and my own was not—and because the boys had so many friends, played basketball, drank sodas, *fit in.* Watching that series and other family situation comedies was almost like taking a course in how to be an American.

8 I loved my father, but I longed secretly for a "Dad" like Ward Cleaver, who puttered in a work shed, building bookcases and oiling hinges, one who spent his Saturday afternoons playing golf or mowing the lawn or dipping his finger into cake batter whipped up by a mother in a frilly apron who spent her time going to PTA meetings and playing bridge with "the girls." Wally Cleaver, the older brother, was one of those boys destined to be captain of every team he plays on. But Beaver had his problems—often he was uncoordinated, gullible, less than perfectly honest, tricked by his older brother's friends, made fun of. He lost library books and haircut money. Once he sent away for a "free" accordion and suddenly found himself wildly in debt. Of course he got caught—he always did. I remember him so clearly, as familiar to me as a brother.

9 Occasionally I go to college campuses. Some student in the audience always mentions Beaver Cleaver, and when the name is spoken, a satisfied murmur can be heard in the crowd. Somebody—a stranger, in his 20s now—wrote to say he watches *Beaver* reruns every morning. He just wanted to share memories of the show with me and recall favorite episodes. We were not readers, after all, this stranger and I. We have no great literary tradition behind us. Our heritage is television. Wally and Beaver Cleaver were our Tom Sawyer and Huck Finn.

10 There's something terribly sad about this need to reminisce, and the lack of real stories, true experiences, to reminisce about. Partly it is that we grew up in the '60s, when life was soft, and partly that we grew up with television, which made life softer. We had Vietnam, of course, and civil-rights battles, and a brief threat of nuclear attack that led neighbors, down the block, to talk of building a fallout shelter. But I remember the large events, like the Kennedy and King assassinations, the space launches and the war, as I experienced them through television. I watched it all from a goose-down-filled easy chair with a plate of oatmeal cookies on my lap—on television.

11 We grew up to be observers, not participants, to respond to action, not initiate it. And I think finally, it was this lack of real hardship (when we lacked for nothing else) that was our greatest hardship and that led so many among this television generation to seek out some kind of artificial pain. Some of us, for a time at least, gave up matching skirt-and-sweater sets for saffron-colored Hare Krishna robes; some gave up parents and clean-cut fiances for the romance of poverty and the excitement of crime. Rebellion like that is not so much inspired by television violence as it is brought about

by television banality: it is a response not to *The Man from U.N.C.L.E.* but to *Father Knows Best.* One hears it said that hatred of an idea is closer to love than to indifference. Large and angry rejections of the bourgeois, the conventional—the Beaver Cleaver life—aren't so surprising, coming from a generation that grew up admiring those things so much.

12 Television smartened us up, expanded our minds, and then proceeded to fill them with the only kinds of knowledge it had to offer: names of Las Vegas nightclubs, brands of detergent, players of bit parts. And knowledge—accurate or not—about life: marriage as we learned about it from Ozzie and Harriet. Justice as practiced by Matt Dillon. Politics as revealed to us on the 6 o'clock news.

13 Anguished, frustrated and enraged by a decade of war in Vietnam as we saw it on the news, we became part of the news ourselves—with peace marches, rallies in the streets. But only briefly; we were easily discouraged, quick to abandon hope for change and to lose interest. That, also, comes from a television-watching childhood, I think: a short attention span, and a limpness, an inertia, acquired from too many hours spent in the easy chair, never getting up except to change the channels.

Additional Rhetorical Strategy

Cause and Effect (throughout).

Examining Words and Meaning

1. What basic objections does Maynard raise about television? What does she see as the most serious consequences of watching so much television? How thoroughly does she illustrate the effect television has had on her generation? What does she say television has taught her about herself? What does she find in television that seems to be missing in her own life? What, finally, is her attitude toward television? Does she see it primarily as a pernicious influence on contemporary American life, as a means of knowing better the world around us, or as some more complex blend of these extremes? Explain, illustrating each point you make.

2. What, in Maynard's judgment, accounts for television's power to, as she says, "make me stand, frozen, before the set" (paragraph 2)? What exactly does she mean when she talks in the same paragraph of not so much watching television programs as letting them "wash over me"?
3. Which television programs mentioned do *you* think reinforce the "melancholy truths" that Maynard speaks of in paragraph 5? Why?

Focusing on Structures and Strategies

1. This selection originally appeared in *TV Guide* magazine. What is there in the essay that the editors of *TV Guide* would have found most appealing? Why?
2. What connections do you perceive between the first sentence in paragraph 4 and paragraph 10? Where else in the essay does she speak of memory? Show how her memories of television control the tone and diction of her writing.
3. Maynard consistently uses the first-person singular throughout the essay. When and how does she build her specific experience into general hypotheses about television?
4. In paragraph 11, Maynard mentions that "hatred of an idea is closer to love than to indifference." It is obvious that she has some affectionate memories of television, yet her essay ends on a highly critical note. Are you surprised by this shift or has she prepared you for it? Explain. Does her affection for the medium make her criticism of it more convincing? Compare Maynard's essay in this respect to Marie Winn's (p. 404) and Michael Arlen's (p. 451). Which essay makes you more cautious about watching television? Why?

Suggestions for Further Discussion and Writing

1. Some readers may find it difficult to imagine growing up in a world without television. If you were actually born into such a world, describe what substituted for television in your youth. If you were born into a world which television seemed to dominate, interview a few older relatives and friends to discover what it was like to grow

up without television. What, in effect, was the "shared history," the "fund of common experience" for such people?

2. One of Maynard's most provocative statements comes at the end of paragraph 7: "Watching that series [*Leave It to Beaver*] and other family situation comedies was almost like taking a course in how to be an American." Choose the family situation comedy you watch most often, study it carefully, and then write an essay in which you illustrate how it can teach someone "how to be an American."

3. Maynard talks of having spent "20,000 hours of my life in front of the set" (paragraph 1). Approximate the total number of hours you have spent watching television. Do you find yourself watching more or less now? Why? Do you find the influence of TV on your life to be increasing or decreasing? Write an essay in which you carefully illustrate the impact television has had on your self-perception as well as on your relations with others and your sense of yourself as an American.

Less Work for Mother?

Ruth Schwartz Cowan

Thomas A. Edison published an article entitled "The Woman of the Future" in a 1912 issue of Good Housekeeping *magazine in which he presented what he—and many other Americans—regarded as an inspirational vision of housewives transformed into "domestic engineers" and American homes turned into efficiently managed, self-enclosed technological units:*

> *The housewife of the future will be neither a slave to servants nor herself a drudge. She will give less attention to the home, because the home will need less; she will be rather a domestic engineer than a domestic laborer, with the greatest of all handmaidens, electricity, at her service. This and other mechanical forces will so revolutionize the woman's world that a large portion of the aggregate of woman's energy will be conserved for use in broader, more constructive fields.*

Edison reported that his greatest anxiety focused on what American women would do to prepare themselves to cope with all the "free" time he believed his, and other, inventions suddenly created for them. In the essay that follows, Ruth Schwartz Cowan addresses Edison's concern and illustrates just how far removed from reality his vision of American woman would stray by the end of the twentieth century.

Ruth Schwartz Cowan is a professor of history and Director of Women's Studies at the State University of New York at Stony Brook. She is the author of More Work for Mother: The Ironies of Household Technology from the Open Hearth to the Microwave *(1983). Cowan published "Less Work for Mother?" in the Spring 1987 issue of* Invention and Technology. *In the essay, she illustrates that modern technology enables the contemporary American housewife to do much more work in the house than ever before—with both positive and negative effects.*

1 Things are never what they seem. Skimmed milk masquerades as cream. And laborsaving household appliances often do not save labor. This is the surprising conclusion reached by a small army of historians, sociologists, and home economists who have undertaken, in recent years, to study the one form of work that has turned out to be most resistant to inquiry and analysis—namely, housework.

2 During the first half of the twentieth century, the average American household was transformed by the introduction of a group of machines that profoundly altered the daily lives of housewives; the forty years between 1920 and 1960 witnessed what might be aptly called the "industrial revolution in the home." Where once there had been a wood- or coal-burning stove there now was a gas or electric range. Clothes that had once been scrubbed on a metal washboard were now tossed into a tub and cleansed by an electrically driven agitator. The dryer replaced the clothesline; the vacuum cleaner replaced the broom; the refrigerator replaced the icebox and the root cellar; an automatic pump, some piping, and a tap replaced the hand pump, the bucket, and the well. No one had to chop and haul wood any more. No one had to shovel out ashes or beat rugs or carry water; no one even had to toss egg whites with a fork for an hour to make an angel food cake.

3 And yet American housewives in 1960, 1970, and even 1980 continued to log about the same number of hours at their work as their grandmothers and mothers had in 1910, 1920, and 1930. The

earliest time studies of housewives date from the very same period in which time studies of other workers were becoming popular—the first three decades of the twentieth century. The sample sizes of these studies were usually quite small, and they did not always define housework in precisely the same way (some counted an hour spent taking children to the playground as "work," while others called it "leisure"), but their results were more or less consistent: whether rural or urban, the average American housewife performed fifty to sixty hours of unpaid work in her home every week, and the only variable that significantly altered this was the number of small children.

4 A half century later not much had changed. Survey research had become much more sophisticated, and sample sizes had grown considerably, but the results of the time studies remained surprisingly consistent. The average American housewife, now armed with dozens of motors and thousands of electronic chips, still spends fifty to sixty hours a week doing housework. The only variable that significantly altered the size of that number was full time employment in the labor force; "working" housewives cut down the average number of hours that they spend cooking and cleaning, shopping and chauffeuring, to a not insignificant thirty-five—virtually the equivalent of another full-time job.

5 How can this be true? Surely even the most sophisticated advertising copywriter of all times could not fool almost the entire American population over the course of at least three generations. Laborsaving devices must be saving something, or Americans would not continue, year after year, to plunk down their hard-earned dollars for them.

6 And if laborsaving devices have not saved labor in the home, then what is it that has suddenly made it possible for more than 70 percent of the wives and mothers in the American population to enter the work force and stay there? A brief glance at the histories of some of the technologies that have transformed housework in the twentieth century will help us answer some of these questions.

7 The portable vacuum cleaner was one of the earliest electric appliances to make its appearance in American homes, and reasonably priced models appeared on the retail market as early as 1910. For decades prior to the turn of the century, inventors had been trying to create a carpet-cleaning system that would improve on the carpet sweeper with adjustable rotary brushes (patented by Melville Bissell in 1876), or the semiannual ritual of hauling rugs outside and beating

them, or the practice of regularly sweeping the dirt out of a rug that had been covered with dampened, torn newspapers. Early efforts to solve the problem had focused on the use of large steam, gasoline, or electric motors attached to piston-type pumps and lots of hoses. Many of these "stationary" vacuum-cleaning systems were installed in apartment houses or hotels, but some were hauled around the streets in horse-drawn carriages by entrepreneurs hoping to establish themselves as "professional house-cleaners."

8 In the first decade of the twentieth century, when fractional-horsepower electric motors became widely—and inexpensively—available, the portable vacuum cleaner intended for use in an individual household was born. One early model—invented by a woman, Corrine Dufour—consisted of a rotary brush, an electrically driven fan, and a wet sponge for absorbing the dust and dirt. Another, patented by David E. Kenney in 1907, had a twelve-inch nozzle, attached to a metal tube, attached to a flexible hose that led to a vacuum pump and separating devices. The Hoover, which was based on a brush, a fan, and a collecting bag, was on the market by 1908. The Electrolux, the first of the canister types of cleaner, which could vacuum something above the level of the floor, was brought over from Sweden in 1924 and met with immediate success.

9 These early vacuum cleaners were hardly a breeze to operate. All were heavy, and most were extremely cumbersome to boot. One early home economist mounted a basal metabolism machine on the back of one of her hapless students and proceeded to determine that more energy was expended in the effort to clean a sample carpet with a vacuum cleaner than when the same carpet was attacked with a hard broom. The difference, of course, was that the vacuum cleaner did a better job, at least on carpets, because a good deal of what the broom stirred up simply resettled a foot or two away from where it had first been lodged. Whatever the liabilities of the early vacuum cleaners may have been, Americans nonetheless appreciated their virtues; according to a market survey done in Zanesville, Ohio, in 1926, slightly more than half the households owned one. Eventually improvements in the design made these devices easier to operate. By 1960 vacuum cleaners could be found in 70 percent of the nation's homes.

10 When the vacuum cleaner is viewed in a historical context, however, it is easy to see why it did not save housewifely labor. Its introduction coincided almost precisely with the disappearance of the domestic servant. The number of persons engaged in household

service dropped from 1,851,000 in 1910 to 1,411,000 in 1920, while the number of households enumerated in the census rose from 20.3 million to 24.4 million. Moreover, between 1900 and 1920 the number of household servants per thousand persons dropped from 98.9 to 58.0, while during the 1920s the decline was even more precipitous as the restrictive immigration acts dried up what had once been the single most abundant source of domestic labor.

11 For the most economically comfortable segment of the population, this meant just one thing: the adult female head of the household was doing more housework than she had ever done before. What Maggie had once done with a broom, Mrs. Smith was now doing with a vacuum cleaner. Knowing that this was happening, several early copywriters for vacuum cleaner advertisements focused on its implications. The vacuum cleaner, General Electric announced in 1918, is better than a maid: it doesn't quit, get drunk, or demand higher wages. The switch from Maggie to Mrs. Smith shows up, in time-study statistics, as an increase in the time that Mrs. Smith is spending at her work.

12 For those—and they were the vast majority of the population—who were not economically comfortable, the vacuum cleaner implied something else again: not an increase in the time spent in housework but an increase in the standard of living. In many households across the country, acquisition of a vacuum cleaner was connected to an expansion of living space, the move from a small apartment to a small house, the purchase of wall-to-wall carpeting. If this did not happen during the difficult 1930s, it became more possible during the expansive 1950s. As living quarters grew larger, standards for their upkeep increased; rugs had to be vacuumed every week, in some households every day, rather than semiannually, as had been customary. The net result, of course, was that when armed with a vacuum cleaner, housewives whose parents had been poor could keep more space cleaner than their mothers and grandmothers would have ever believed possible. We might put this everyday phenomenon in language that economists can understand: The introduction of the vacuum cleaner led to improvements in productivity but not to any significant decrease in the amount of time expended by each worker.

13 The history of the washing machine illustrates a similar phenomenon. "Blue Monday" had traditionally been, as its name implies, the bane of a housewife's existence—especially when Monday turned out to be "Monday . . . and Tuesday to do the ironing."

Thousands of patents for "new and improved" washers were issued during the nineteenth century in an effort to cash in on the housewife's despair. Most of these early washing machines were wooden or metal tubs combined with some kind of hand-cranked mechanism that would rub or push or twirl laundry when the tub was filled with water and soap. At the end of the century, the Sears catalog offered four such washing machines, ranging in price from $2.50 to $4.25, all sold in combination with hand-cranked wringers.

14 These early machines may have saved time in the laundering process (four shirts could be washed at once instead of each having to be rubbed separately against a washboard), but they probably didn't save much energy. Lacking taps and drains, the tubs still had to be filled and emptied by hand, and each piece still had to be run through a wringer and hung up to dry.

15 Not long after the appearance of fractional-horsepower motors, several enterprising manufacturers had the idea of hooking them up to the crank mechanisms of washers and wringers—and the electric washer was born. By the 1920s, when mass production of such machines began, both the general structure of the machine (a central-shaft agitator rotating within a cylindrical tub, hooked up to the household water supply) and the general structure of the industry (oligopolistic—with a very few firms holding most of the patents and controlling most of the market) had achieved their final form. By 1926 just over a quarter of the families in Zanesville had an electric washer, but by 1941 fully 52 percent of all American households either owned or had interior access (which means that they could use coin-operated models installed in the basements of apartment houses) to such a machine. The automatic washer, which consisted of a vertically rotating washer cylinder that could also act as a centrifugal extractor, was introduced by the Bendix Home Appliance Corporation in 1938, but it remained expensive, and therefore inaccessible, until after World War II. This machine contained timing devices that allowed it to proceed through its various cycles automatically; by spinning the clothes around in the extractor phase of its cycle, it also eliminated the wringer. Although the Bendix subsequently disappeared from the retail market (versions of this sturdy machine may still be found in Laundromats), its design principles are replicated in the agitator washers that currently chug away in millions of American homes.

16 Both the early wringer washers and their more recent automatic

cousins have released American women from the burden of drudgery. No one who has ever tried to launder a sheet by hand, and without the benefits of hot running water, would want to return to the days of the scrubboard and tub. But "labor" is composed of both "energy expenditure" and "time expenditure," and the history of laundry work demonstrates that the one may be conserved while the other is not.

17 The reason for this is, as with the vacuum cleaner, twofold. In the early decades of the century, many households employed laundresses to do their wash; this was true, surprisingly enough, even for some very poor households when wives and mothers were disabled or employed full-time in field or factory. Other households—rich and poor—used commercial laundry services. Large, mechanized "steam" laundries were first constructed in this country in the 1860s, and by the 1920s they could be found in virtually every urban neighborhood and many rural ones as well.

18 But the advent of the electric home washer spelled doom both for the laundress and for the commercial laundry; since the housewife's labor was unpaid, and since the washer took so much of the drudgery out of washday, the one-time expenditure for a machine seemed, in many families, a more sensible arrangement than continuous expenditure for domestic services. In the process, of course, the time spent on laundry work by the individual housewife, who had previously employed either a laundress or a service, was bound to increase.

19 For those who had not previously enjoyed the benefits of relief from washday drudgery, the electric washer meant something quite different but equally significant: an upgrading of household cleanliness. Men stopped wearing removable collars and cuffs, which meant that the whole of their shirts had to be washed and then ironed. Housewives began changing two sheets every week, instead of moving the top sheet to the bottom and adding only one that was fresh. Teenagers began changing their underwear every day instead of every weekend. In the early 1960s, when synthetic no-iron fabrics were introduced, the size of the household laundry load increased again; shirts and skirts, sheets and blouses that had once been sent out to the dry cleaner or the corner laundry were now being tossed into the household wash basket. By the 1980s the average American housewife, armed now with an automatic washing machine and an automatic dryer, was processing roughly ten times (by weight) the

amount of laundry that her mother had been accustomed to. Drudgery had disappeared, but the laundry hadn't. The average time spent on this chore in 1925 had been 5.8 hours per week; in 1964 it was 6.2.

20 And then there is the automobile. We do not usually think of our cars as household appliances, but that is precisely what they are since housework, as currently understood, could not possibly be performed without them. The average American housewife is today more likely to be found behind a steering wheel than in front of a stove. While writing this article I interrupted myself five times: once to take a child to field-hockey practice, then a second time, to bring her back when practice was finished; once to pick up some groceries at the supermarket; once to retrieve my husband, who was stranded at the train station; once for a trip to a doctor's office. Each time I was doing housework, and each time I had to use my car.

21 Like the washing machine and the vacuum cleaner, the automobile started to transform the nature of housework in the 1920s. Until the introduction of the Model T in 1908, automobiles had been playthings for the idle rich, and although many wealthy women learned to drive early in the century (and several participated in well-publicized auto races), they were hardly the women who were likely to be using their cars to haul groceries.

22 But by 1920, and certainly by 1930, all this had changed. Helen and Robert Lynd, who conducted an intensive study of Muncie, Indiana, between 1923 and 1925 (reported in their famous book *Middletown*), estimated that in Muncie in the 1890s only 125 families, all members of the "elite," owned a horse and buggy, but by 1923 there were 6,222 passenger cars in the city, "roughly one for every 7.1 persons, or two for every three families." By 1930, according to national statistics, there were roughly 30 million households in the United States—and 26 million registered automobiles.

23 What did the automobile mean for the housewife? Unlike public transportation systems, it was convenient. Located right at her doorstep, it could deposit her at the doorstep that she wanted or needed to visit. And unlike the bicycle or her own two feet, the automobile could carry bulky packages as well as several additional people. Acquisition of an automobile therefore meant that a housewife, once she had learned how to drive, could become her own door-to-door delivery service. And as more housewives acquired automobiles, more businessmen discovered the joys of dispensing with delivery services—particularly during the Depression.

24 To make a long story short, the iceman does not cometh anymore. Neither does the milkman, the bakery truck, the butcher, the grocer, the knife sharpener, the seamstress, or the doctor. Like many other businessmen, doctors discovered that their earnings increased when they stayed in their offices and transferred the responsibility for transportation to their ambulatory patients.

25 Thus a new category was added to the housewife's traditional job description: chauffeur. The suburban station wagon is now "Mom's Taxi." Children who once walked to school now have to be transported by their mothers; husbands who once walked home from work now have to be picked up by their wives; groceries that once were dispensed from pushcarts or horse-drawn wagons now have to be packed into paper bags and hauled home in family cars. "Contemporary women," one time-study expert reported in 1974, "spend about one full working day per week on the road and in stores compared with less than two hours per week for women in the 1920s." If everything we needed to maintain our homes and sustain our families were delivered right to our doorsteps—and every member of the family had independent means for getting where she or he wanted to go—the hours spent on housework by American housewives would decrease dramatically.

26 The histories of the vacuum cleaner, the washing machine, and the automobile illustrate the varied reasons why the time spent in housework has not markedly decreased in the United States during the last half century despite the introduction of so many ostensibly laborsaving appliances. But these histories do not help us understand what has made it possible for so many American wives and mothers to enter the labor force full-time during those same years. Until recently, one of the explanations most often offered for the startling increase in the participation of married women in the work force (up from 24.8 percent in 1950 to 50.1 percent in 1980) was household technology. What with microwave ovens and frozen foods, washer and dryer combinations and paper diapers, the reasoning goes, housework can now be done in no time at all, and women have so much time on their hands that they find they must go out and look for a job for fear of going stark, raving mad.

27 As every "working" housewife knows, this pattern of reasoning is itself stark, raving mad. Most adult women are in the work force today quite simply because they need the money. Indeed, most "working" housewives today hold down not one but two jobs; they put in what has come to be called a "double day." Secre-

taries, lab technicians, janitors, sewing machine operators, teachers, nurses, or physicians for eight (or nine or ten) hours, they race home to become chief cook and bottle washer for another five, leaving the cleaning and the marketing for Saturday and Sunday. Housework, as we have seen, still takes a lot of time, modern technology notwithstanding.

28 Yet household technologies have played a major role in facilitating (as opposed to causing) what some observers believe to be the most significant social revolution of our time. They do it in two ways, the first of which we have already noted. By relieving housework of the drudgery that it once entailed, washing machines, vacuum cleaners, dishwashers, and water pumps have made it feasible for a woman to put in a double day without destroying her health, to work full-time and still sustain herself and her family at a reasonably comfortable level.

29 The second relationship between household technology and the participation of married women in the work force is considerably more subtle. It involves the history of some technologies that we rarely think of as technologies at all—and certainly not as household appliances. Instead of being sheathed in stainless steel or porcelain, these devices appear in our kitchens in little brown bottles and bags of flour; instead of using switches and buttons to turn them on, we use hypodermic needles and sugar cubes. They are various forms of medication, the products not only of modern medicine but also of modern industrial chemistry: polio vaccines and vitamin pills; tetanus toxins and ampicillin; enriched breads and tuberculin tests.

30 Before any of these technologies had made their appearance, nursing may well have been the most time-consuming and most essential aspect of housework. During the eighteenth and nineteenth centuries and even during the first five decades of the twentieth century, it was the woman of the house who was expected (and who had been trained, usually by *her* mother) to sit up all night cooling and calming a feverish child, to change bandages on suppurating wounds, to clean bed linens stained with excrement, to prepare easily digestible broths, to cradle colicky infants on her lap for hours on end, to prepare bodies for burial. An attack of the measles might mean the care of a bedridden child for a month. Pneumonia might require six months of bed rest. A small knife cut could become infected and produce a fever that would rage for days. Every summer brought the fear of polio epidemics, and every polio epidemic left some group of mothers with the perpetual problem of tending to the

needs of a handicapped child. Cholera, diphtheria, typhoid fever—if they weren't fatal—could mean weeks of sleepless nights and hard-pressed days. "Just as soon as the person is attacked," one experienced mother wrote to her worried daughter during a cholera epidemic in Oklahoma in 1885, "be it ever so slightly, he or she ought to go to bed immediately and stay there; put a mustard [plaster] over the bowels and if vomiting over the stomach. See that the feet are kept warm, either by warm iron or brick, or bottles of hot water. If the disease progresses the limbs will begin to cramp, which must be prevented by applying cloths wrung out of hot water and wrapping round them. When one is vomiting so terribly, of course, it is next to impossible to keep medicine down, but in cholera it must be done."

31 These were the routines to which American women were once accustomed, routines regarded as matters of life and death. To gain some sense of the way in which modern medicines have altered not only the routines of housework but also the emotional commitment that often accompanies such work, we need only read out a list of the diseases for which most American children are unlikely to succumb today, remembering how many of them once were fatal or terribly disabling: diphtheria, whooping cough, tetanus, pellagra, rickets, measles, mumps, tuberculosis, smallpox, cholera, malaria, and polio.

32 And many of today's ordinary childhood complaints, curable within a few days of the ingestion of antibiotics, once might have entailed weeks, or even months, of full-time attention: bronchitis; strep throat; scarlet fever; bacterial pneumonia; infections of the skin, or the eyes, or the ears, or the airways. In the days before the introduction of modern vaccines, antibiotics, and vitamin supplements, a mother who was employed full-time was a serious, sometimes life-endangering threat to the health of her family. This is part of the reason why life expectancy was always low and infant mortality high among the poorest segment of the population—those most likely to be dependent upon a mother's wages.

33 Thus modern technology, especially modern medical technology, has made it possible for married women to enter the work force by releasing housewives not just from drudgery but also from the dreaded emotional equation of female employment with poverty and disease. She may be exhausted at the end of her double day, but the modern "working" housewife can at least fall into bed knowing that her efforts have made it possible to sustain her family at a level of

health and comfort that not so long ago was reserved only for those who were very rich.

Additional Rhetorical Strategies

Cause and Effect (throughout); Comparison and Contrast (paragraphs 2–4, 26, 34); Description (paragraphs 2, 8); Definition (paragraphs 3, 17, 28); Process Analysis (paragraph 9); Classification (paragraphs 29–30).

Examining Words and Meaning

1. What are some of the ways in which Cowan accounts for the fact that the modern housewife spends as much time doing housework as her counterpart at the beginning of the century? How has the nature of that time changed for the American housewife?
2. In more general terms, how have modern appliances affected the quality of life? If people are not using machines to help them save time, for what purposes are they using them? What are some possible ways to account for the fact that, given laborsaving appliances, people tend to find ways to make more work for themselves?
3. According to Cowan, what changes have made it possible for women to work a "double day"? Cowan does not elaborate on the fact that although many contemporary American women are working two full-time jobs, they are also doing significantly less housework. How might you account for this?

Focusing on Structures and Strategies

1. What kinds of evidence does Cowan use to illustrate her points? What reasons might she have for this range of illustration? What does it suggest about her imagined relationship with the audience for whom she is writing?

2. What is the portrait of the woman suggested by this essay? How does the conclusion, for example, influence this portrait? Cowan does not consider whether or not the image of what it meant to be a housewife changed during this period. What inferences on this subject might be drawn from the information she includes? What is the significance of the fact that her portrait is based on average figures? How do you react to this characterization? What presence do men assume in these statistics? in Cowan's thinking?

3. Cowan provides a good deal of historical background about the manufacture of appliances, and especially about the vacuum cleaner and the washing machine. What characteristics do these inventions share? Why does Cowan include this information in her account of the changes in household practices? What seems to be her attitude toward these machines? What are some of the reasons Cowan suggests for why Americans are so attached to the latest inventions?

4. The success of this essay depends in part on Cowan's ability to establish a cause and effect relationship between historical developments and statistics regarding housework. Examine some of the passages in which she constructs these connections. How convincing are her arguments? What additional information might help to confirm her claims? What other explanations might account for the same facts?

Suggestions for Further Discussion and Writing

1. Choose an invention more recent than the vacuum cleaner, the washing machine, and the automobile. Trace the historical and cultural circumstances out of which this invention has emerged. What effect has the invention had on contemporary American gender identity, social behavior, and the culture at large? Write an essay, modeled on Cowan's, in which you assess the impact of this invention on contemporary American society.

2. Consider some aspect of Americans' behavior—their dating, drinking, eating, or smoking habits, for example. Go to the library and examine carefully the ways in which these activities are depicted in American advertisements during the first three decades of the twentieth century. Choose one such activity and then turn to the depiction of this activity in contemporary American advertising. Based on your observations, what general conclusions can you

present about the perceptible changes in the ways in which this activity was—and is—presented to the American public? Write an essay in which you support this general conclusion by illustrating it with abundant evidence from your research. Be sure both to present this general conclusion and to provide specific examples of these changes to verify your claim.

5. DISCOVERING RESEMBLANCES

Comparison and Contrast

1 We use comparison to explore the similarities that seem to link subjects. Many of our everyday decisions are actually simple instances of comparison: what clothes to wear, what to eat, which brands to buy, whether we should write a letter, read a book, make a call, or watch television. We repeatedly—however subtly or even unconsciously—rely on comparison to map out our options and to help us get through the choices we make each day. So, too, more consequential decisions—where to go to college, what to do after graduation, how best to raise a family—are most often the result of thinking comparatively.

2 As a method of thinking and writing, comparison establishes similarities between subjects drawn from the same class or general category. Comparison is inseparable from contrast. We use contrast to highlight differences. When considering how any two things are similar, we undoubtedly will also discover more exactly how they are different. For example, the decision to buy a stereo-cassette deck is based, for most of us, on a good deal of comparative shopping. We check the prices of the leading brands and examine the performance features of the models we can afford: all the ones we are considering offer "Dolby" noise reduction, and push-button controls for recording, playing, and ejecting a cassette. But one has "memory," the other does not; one shuts off automatically, the other does not; and so on. When we think or write in comparative terms, we invariably touch upon contrasts.

3 As an expression of thinking in writing, comparison is often

used in conjunction with other rhetorical strategies, particularly when writers want to establish underlying or supporting causes, narratives, or descriptions of points to be made later in the essay. But comparison can also be extremely effective when writers make it the principal mode of their exposition. It can help us to discover more salient points to make about a subject. For example, Tom Wolfe's comparison of the moon landing with Columbus's voyages (see p. 389) adds another dimension to the National Aeronautics and Space Administration's accomplishment at the same time that it extends the range of that event's significance. Comparison is also a useful method for making abstract or remote subjects more concrete and readily accessible. By comparing the everyday language that surrounds tuberculosis and cancer, Susan Sontag, in "A Rhetoric of Disease" (p. 419), analyzes the modern tendency to concoct psychological explanations of illness. And, perhaps most importantly, comparison helps us sort out experience. John Mack Faragher's comparison of pioneer diaries (see p. 412) makes it easier to understand the different roles of men and women in settling the American West. Training in discovering similarities and making distinctions—both qualitatively and quantitatively—better prepares us to express convincingly our understanding of complex subjects.

4 Comparison involves two basic operations: first, considering two categories of the same subject, and second, examining the common features of those two categories. A diagram of these relationships may be charted as follows:

A is like *B* with respect to *S*

S

A / *B*

A ________ (S_1) ________ B

A ________ (S_2) ________ B

A ________ (S_3) ________ B

A ________ (S_4) ________ B

Etc.

In this structure *A* is the first component in the comparison, *B* the second. *S* designates the subject about which an idea, a tentative conclusion, is developed. This controlling statement in turn determines the bases (S_1–S_4) for establishing similarities (and differences) between *A* and *B*.

5 Now let us look at the diagram in operation. Suppose that we want to write an essay about the relative merits of nuclear and solar energy. We've come to the conclusion that solar energy is the safest, most abundant, and least expensive source of energy for the future. We recognize that advocates of nuclear energy might disagree, so we decide to organize our essay by comparing the two. Within that framework, the structure of the comparison might look something like this:

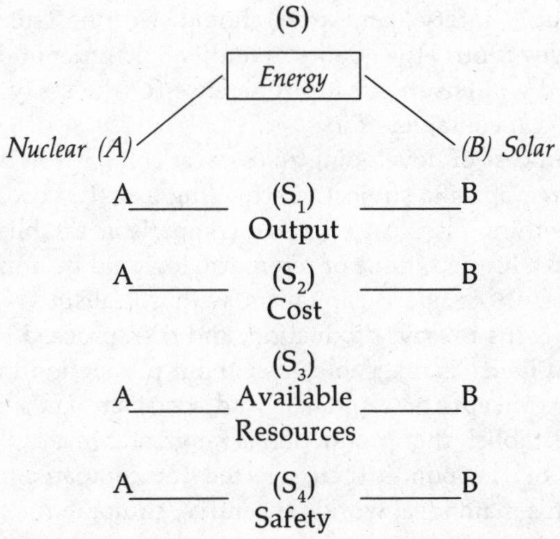

This diagram should make clear that the points to be compared must normally be stated in the same set of terms. They must be drawn from roughly similar categories of experience or levels of abstraction and share at least several characteristics. It would be appropriate to compare, for example, one city, restaurant, sport, college, or politician with another; but it would be inappropriate to compare, say, a dormitory room with a textbook. In the preceding diagram, nuclear and solar energy can be appropriately compared because they are both forms of energy. So too, "output," "cost," "available resources," and "safety" are suitable points to consider in nearly any proposed discussion of energy.

6 When writing essays of comparison, we ought to remember that the points of comparison are related to the subject but not necessarily to each other: each point can be thought of as a *discrete* factor in our comparison. In our diagram, for example, "output" has no necessary or logical connection to "cost," nor "available resources" to "safety."

Yet all of these points are related by virtue of their contribution to our main idea about energy. The diagram also suggests just how careful we must be when developing an essay of comparison. Determining the relative emphasis of comparison and contrast depends on what we want to say about our subject. In this instance, we would be more likely to spend most of our time contrasting nuclear and solar energy, trying to prove that solar energy offers a more promising alternative source of future energy. It is our idea about the subject—our tentative conclusion about it—to which all points in the comparison (in this case, "output," "safety," and so on) should be connected. Having this dominant idea control the quality, quantity, and order of the points to be compared will ensure greater coherence for the essay and keep it from being a meaningless *list.*

7 The process of developing an essay of comparison begins when we settle on a specific subject, discovering exactly how it is like or unlike something else. An effective comparison establishes a clear purpose and a limited frame of reference. It would be unmanageable, for example, to compare capitalism with socialism. We ought to narrow the focus to, say, production, and then proceed to develop a specific, and hence manageable, idea about production in relation to the general concepts of capitalism and socialism. Let's say that we wanted to establish that production is far greater in a capitalist economy. Each of the points then selected for comparison should be related to this main idea: worker incentive, equipment, organization, markets, and so on. These points, in turn, should be unfolded fully and given sufficient attention.

8 Comparison can be a particularly strong method for shaping expository essays, especially when writers are confident that they know both sides of their subject well enough to draw an accurate, detailed, and balanced account of each side. Comparison is even more effective when writers present differences in what are normally regarded as similar subjects or when they uncover similarities that were not previously apparent. Consider, for example, the following opening paragraph from "A Report on the New Feminism," an essay by Ellen Willis, a music and film critic and a leading figure in the women's movement in America:

> Like the early feminist movement, which grew out of the campaign to end slavery, the present-day women's movement has been inspired and influenced by the black liberation struggle. The situation of women and blacks is similar in many ways. Just as blacks live in a world defined by whites, women live in a world defined by males. (The

> generic term of human being is "man"; "woman" means "wife of man.") To be female or black is to be peculiar; whiteness and maleness are the norm. Newspapers do not have "men's pages," nor would anyone think of discussing the "man problem." Racial and sexual stereotypes also resemble each other: women, like blacks, are said to be childish, incapable of abstract reasoning, innately submissive, biologically suited for menial tasks, emotional, close to nature.

Willis's paragraph clearly highlights the principles of comparison and contrast. She quickly establishes a series of striking comparisons between the struggle for black liberation and the feminist movement. Notice, too, that Willis refines her comparison as she develops the paragraph: she first states that the situation of women and blacks is similar, defines that similarity by saying that both women and blacks are outsiders, then provides examples that prove her point. She also makes her paragraph much more interesting to read for her audience by varying her sentence structure. She presents background information, notes the norms against which women and blacks are regarded as "peculiar," and illustrates the sexual and racial stereotypes that have contributed to the second-class status of both groups. Willis manages to develop these comparisons within seven sentences and to organize them into a brief but effective paragraph. Her paragraph also demonstrates that a writer's focus should always be on developing perceptive comparisons, avoiding those that are obvious or little more than clever.

9 The organization of an essay of comparison depends on the complexity of the subject and the length needed to make a convincing presentation of both sides. There are three standard methods for organizing a comparison. The first, what we may call the *whole-subject-by-whole-subject* design, presents all of the features of one side *(A)* in relation to the subject *(S)* and then presents all of the features of the other side *(B)* in the same sequence. Aristotle's comparison of youth and old age (see p. 385) is a particularly vivid example of whole-subject-by-whole-subject comparison. Following this pattern, an outline of the essay comparing nuclear and solar energy would look like this:

Controlling Idea, or Thesis

I. Introduction

II. Nuclear Energy
   A. Output
   B. Cost

C. Available Resources
D. Safety

III. Solar Energy
A. Output
B. Cost
C. Available Resources
D. Safety

IV. Summary

This organization is best suited to relatively short essays, ones in which readers will have no difficulty remembering each of the points about nuclear energy until each is compared with solar power. In such instances, the writer is concerned more with the overall comparative effect than with any one of the details involved. This whole-subject-by-whole-subject design offers the writer a simple, easily handled structure for organizing points of comparison that are *limited in number and complexity.* One of the risks of the design, however, is that the writer will produce what are in effect separate essays—one on nuclear energy, the other on solar energy. Yet the writer may minimize this possibility by consistently focusing on the specific points of comparison (S_1–S_4) rather than on the general terms *nuclear* and *solar* (A and B).

10 For longer, more complex essays, writers normally adapt for their particular purpose the *point-by-point comparison.* Using the same example, the outline of a point-by-point comparison would look like this:

Controlling Idea, or Thesis

I. Introduction

II. Output
A. Nuclear Energy
B. Solar Energy

III. Cost
A. Nuclear Energy
B. Solar Energy

IV. Available Resources
A. Nuclear Energy
B. Solar Energy

V. Safety
   A. Nuclear Energy
   B. Solar Energy

VI. Summary

Depending on the complexity of the issues involved, each of the points of comparison could be unfolded in either a single paragraph or a series of paragraphs. And the amount of space given to each of the two sides within each point should be roughly the same. One advantage of this method is that it allows writers to make any number of finely drawn connections between subjects. (See, for example, Tom Wolfe's essay on p. 389.)

11 A third possible method of organization—the *sentence-by-sentence* comparison—occurs less frequently in writing. It usually appears in isolated paragraphs, very brief essays, or in the especially intense circumstances of an examination, when time restraints may demand that we restrict ourselves to a sentence-by-sentence comparison. This method of organizing a comparison adapts the basic procedures of a point-by-point comparison to the level of a limited series of sentences.

12 As we have seen, comparison and contrast can organize our thinking in writing—from single paragraphs to long expository essays. Long expository essays frequently draw on all three forms of comparison. (See, for example, Susan Sontag's essay on p. 419.) Whatever the length or the particular method of comparison we are working with, we should remember that our essay will have far greater potential for succeeding if we organize carefully the sequence of points to be compared. In essays of comparison, the final point commands the most emphasis.

13 Comparison helps us to write more imaginatively and authoritatively. Discovering and developing similarities or differences is one way, for example, to simplify complex thoughts and make them more accessible to ourselves and others. Yet, in addition to what it literally says, a well-formulated comparison reinforces the reader's sense that we are particularly knowledgeable and in command of both our subject and our idea about it. To develop a comparison is to demonstrate that we know and can write about *A;* that we know and can write about *B;* that we know and can write about the precise relationship that exists between *A* and *B;* and that we can marshal this knowledge in support of a distinctive idea

about the subject in question. In general, a comparison or contrast structure for an essay helps us establish and maintain control over a series of points throughout the process of composition—a control that increases the confidence of both writers and readers of expository prose.

The Tucson Zoo

Lewis Thomas

While visiting the Tucson Zoo, Lewis Thomas is momentarily transfixed by a powerful instinctive response to a family of otters and a neighboring family of beavers. He inexplicably begins to feel that he is somehow "coded" for these animals, that they release in him an extremely pleasurable sense of friendship and affection. The feeling is, he realizes, quite unscientific, yet it leads him to reflect on some of the major conflicts of modern biology—the contrasting issues of reductionism versus holism, autonomic versus conscious behavior, solitary versus social instincts. As you read this essay, from The Medusa and the Snail, *notice how these contrasting viewpoints form the basis of nearly every paragraph.*

For biographical information on Lewis Thomas, *see page 109.*

1 Science gets most of its information by the process of reductionism, exploring the details, then the details of the details, until all the smallest bits of the structure, or the smallest parts of the mechanism, are laid out for counting and scrutiny. Only when this is done can the investigation be extended to encompass the whole organism or the entire system. So we say.

2 Sometimes it seems that we take a loss, working this way. Much of today's public anxiety about science is the apprehension that we may forever be overlooking the whole by an endless, obsessive preoccupation with the parts. I had a brief, personal experience of this misgiving one afternoon in Tucson, where I had time on my hands and visited the zoo, just outside the city. The designers there have cut a deep pathway between two small artificial ponds, walled by clear glass, so when you stand in the center of the path you can look into the depths of each pool, and at the same time you can regard

the surface. In one pool, on the right side of the path, is a family of otters; on the other side, a family of beavers. Within just a few feet from your face, on either side, beavers and otters are at play, underwater and on the surface, swimming toward your face and then away, more filled with life than any creatures I have ever seen before, in all my days. Except for the glass, you could reach across and touch them.

3 I was transfixed. As I now recall it, there was only one sensation in my head: pure elation mixed with amazement at such perfection. Swept off my feet, I floated from one side to the other, swiveling my brain, staring astounded at the beavers, then at the otters. I could hear shouts across my corpus callosum, from one hemisphere to the other. I remember thinking, with what was left in charge of my consciousness, that I wanted no part of the science of beavers and otters; I wanted never to know how they performed their marvels; I wished for no news about the physiology of their breathing, the coordination of their muscles, their vision, their endocrine systems, their digestive tracts. I hoped never to have to think of them as collections of cells. All I asked for was the full hairy complexity, then in front of my eyes, of whole, intact beavers and otters in motion.

4 It lasted, I regret to say, for only a few minutes, and then I was back in the late twentieth century, reductionist as ever, wondering about the details by force of habit, but not, this time, the details of otters and beavers. Instead, me. Something worth remembering had happened in my mind, I was certain of that; I would have put it somewhere in the brain stem; maybe this was my limbic system at work. I became a behavioral scientist, an experimental psychologist, an ethologist, and in the instant I lost all the wonder and the sense of being overwhelmed. I was flattened.

5 But I came away from the zoo with something, a piece of news about myself: I am coded, somehow, for otters and beavers. I exhibit instinctive behavior in their presence, when they are displayed close at hand behind glass, simultaneously below water and at the surface. I have receptors for this display. Beavers and otters possess a "releaser" for me, in the terminology of ethology, and the releasing was my experience. What was released? Behavior. What behavior? Standing, swiveling flabbergasted, feeling exultation and a rush of friendship. I could not, as the result of the transaction, tell you anything more about beavers and otters than you already know. I learned nothing new about them. Only about me, and I suspect also about you, maybe about human beings at large: we are endowed with genes which code out our reaction to beavers and otters, maybe our reaction to each other as well. We are stamped with stereotyped,

unalterable patterns of response, ready to be released. And the behavior released in us, by such confrontations, is, essentially, a surprised affection. It is compulsory behavior and we can avoid it only by straining with the full power of our conscious minds, making up conscious excuses all the way. Left to ourselves, mechanistic and autonomic, we hanker for friends.

6 Everyone says, stay away from ants. They have no lessons for us; they are crazy little instruments, inhuman, incapable of controlling themselves, lacking manners, lacking souls. When they are massed together, all touching, exchanging bits of information held in their jaws like memoranda, they become a single animal. Look out for that. It is a debasement, a loss of individuality, a violation of human nature, an unnatural act.

7 Sometimes people argue this point of view seriously and with deep thought. Be individuals, solitary and selfish, is the message. Altruism, a jargon word for what used to be called love, is worse than weakness, it is sin, a violation of nature. Be separate. Do not be a social animal. But this is a hard argument to make convincingly when you have to depend on language to make it. You have to print up leaflets or publish books and get them bought and sent around, you have to turn up on television and catch the attention of millions of other human beings all at once, and then you have to say to all of them, all at once, all collected and paying attention: be solitary; do not depend on each other. You can't do this and keep a straight face.

8 Maybe altruism is our most primitive attribute, out of reach, beyond our control. Or perhaps it is immediately at hand, waiting to be released, disguised now, in our kind of civilization, as affection or friendship or attachment. I don't see why it should be unreasonable for all human beings to have strands of DNA coiled up in chromosomes, coding out instincts for usefulness and helpfulness. Usefulness may turn out to be the hardest test of fitness for survival, more important than aggression, more effective, in the long run, than grabbiness. If this is the sort of information biological science holds for the future, applying to us as well as to ants, then I am all for science.

9 One thing I'd like to know most of all: when those ants have made the Hill, and are all there, touching and exchanging, and the whole mass begins to behave like a single huge creature, and *thinks,* what on earth is that thought? And while you're at it, I'd like to know a second thing: when it happens, does any single ant know about it? Does his hair stand on end?

Reading for Rhetorical Strategy

In the first few sentences, Lewis Thomas points out two contrasting processes of modern biological science—its "obsessive preoccupation with the parts" and its need to "encompass the whole organism." The contrast is essentially one between reductionism and holism. Thomas then recounts "a brief, personal experience" that vividly dramatizes these larger, scientific viewpoints. In paragraph 3, Thomas experiences a totally unscientific view of "whole, intact beavers and otters in motion." But the moment is brief, and in paragraph 4 Thomas returns to reductionist thinking. The experience, however, produces a valuable insight—not into beavers and otters—but into some of the contrasting impulses of the human species. These impulses he examines by comparing human beings to ants in paragraph 6. In the remaining three paragraphs Thomas explores several additional contrasting views of human nature: are we basically isolated individuals or social animals? Are we motivated by selfish or altruistic goals? Are we intrinsically aggressive or cooperative creatures? Note how these contrasting views grow directly out of Thomas's opening comparison of reductionist and holistic scientific processes.

Youth and Old Age

Aristotle

Aristotle (384–322 B.C.) defines rhetoric as "the faculty of observing in any given case the available means of persuasion." His treatise on rhetoric, originally a kind of operator's manual for public speaking, is still regarded as one of the foremost treatments of verbal strategies and persuasive methods.

In the following passage, Aristotle first characterizes young men in detail and then proceeds from that description to point out the contrasting characteristics of elderly men.

1 Young men have strong passions, and tend to gratify them indiscriminately. Of the bodily desires, it is the sexual by which they are most swayed and in which they show absence of self-control. They are changeable and fickle in their desires, which are violent

while they last, but quickly over: their impulses are keen but not deep-rooted, and are like sick people's attacks of hunger and thirst. They are hot-tempered and quick-tempered, and apt to give way to their anger; bad temper often gets the better of them, for owing to their love of honor they cannot bear being slighted, and are indignant if they imagine themselves unfairly treated. While they love honor, they love victory still more; for youth is eager for superiority over others, and victory is one form of this. They love both more than they love money, which indeed they love very little, not having yet learnt what it means to be without it—this is the point of Pittacus' remark about Amphiaraus.[1] They look at the good side rather than the bad, not having yet witnessed many instances of wickedness. They trust others readily, because they have not yet often been cheated. They are sanguine; nature warms their blood as though with excess of wine; and besides that, they have as yet met with few disappointments. Their lives are mainly spent not in memory but in expectation; for expectation refers to the future, memory to the past, and youth has a long future before it and a short past behind it: on the first day of one's life one has nothing at all to remember, and can only look forward. They are easily cheated, owing to the sanguine disposition just mentioned. Their hot tempers and hopeful dispositions make them more courageous than older men are; the hot temper prevents fear, and the hopeful disposition creates confidence; we cannot feel fear so long as we are feeling angry, and any expectation of good makes us confident. They are shy, accepting the rules of society in which they have been trained, and not yet believing in any other standard of honor. They have exalted notions, because they have not yet been humbled by life or learnt its necessary limitations; moreover, their hopeful disposition makes them think themselves equal to great things—and that means having exalted notions. They would always rather do noble deeds than useful ones: their lives are regulated more by moral feeling than by reasoning; and whereas reasoning leads us to choose what is useful, moral goodness leads us to choose what is noble. They are fonder of their friends, intimates, and companions than older men are, because they like spending their days in the company of others, and have not yet come to value either their friends or anything else by their usefulness to themselves. All their mistakes are in the direction of doing things excessively and vehemently. They disobey Chilon's precept[2] by overdoing every-

[1]The actual remark is unknown. [Eds.]

[2]. . . "(do) nothing in excess." [Eds.]

thing; they love too much and hate too much, and the same with everything else. They think they know everything, and are always quite sure about it; this, in fact, is why they overdo everything. If they do wrong to others, it is because they mean to insult them, not to do them actual harm. They are ready to pity others, because they think every one an honest man, or anyhow better than he is: they judge their neighbor by their own harmless natures, and so cannot think he deserves to be treated in that way. They are fond of fun and therefore witty, wit being well-bred insolence.

2 Such, then, is the character of the Young. The character of Elderly Men—men who are past their prime—may be said to be formed for the most part of elements that are the contrary of all these. They have lived many years; they have often been taken in, and often made mistakes; and life on the whole is a bad business. The result is that they are sure about nothing and *under-do* everything. They 'think', but they never 'know'; and because of their hesitation they always add a 'possibly' or a 'perhaps,' putting everything this way and nothing positively. They are cynical; that is, they tend to put the worse construction on everything. Further, their experience makes them distrustful and therefore suspicious of evil. Consequently they neither love warmly nor hate bitterly, but following the hint of Bias they love as though they will some day hate and hate as though they will some day love.[3] They are small-minded, because they have been humbled by life: their desires are set upon nothing more exalted or unusual than what will help them to keep alive. They are not generous, because money is one of the things they must have, and at the same time their experience has taught them how hard it is to get and how easy to lose. They are cowardly, and are always anticipating danger; unlike that of the young, who are warm-blooded, their temperament is chilly; old age has paved the way for cowardice; fear is, in fact, a form of chill. They love life; and all the more when their last day has come, because the object of all desire is something we have not got, and also because we desire more strongly that which we need most urgently. They are too fond of themselves; this is one form that small-mindedness takes. Because of this, they guide their lives too much by considerations of what is useful and too little by what is noble—for the useful is what is good for oneself, and the noble what is good absolutely. They are not shy, but shameless rather; caring less for what is noble than for what is useful, they feel contempt for what

[3]Bias of Priene; "they treat friends as probable future enemies and their enemies as probable future friends." [Eds.]

people may think of them. They lack confidence in the future; partly through experience—for most things go wrong, or anyhow turn out worse than one expects; and partly because of their cowardice. They live by memory rather than by hope; for what is left to them of life is but little as compared with the long past; and hope is of the future, memory of the past. This, again, is the cause of their loquacity; they are continually talking of the past, because they enjoy remembering it. Their fits of anger are sudden but feeble. Their sensual passions have either altogether gone or have lost their vigor: consequently they do not feel their passions much, and their actions are inspired less by what they do feel than by the love of gain. Hence men at this time of life are often supposed to have a self-controlled character; the fact is that their passions have slackened, and they are slaves to the love of gain. They guide their lives by reasoning more than by moral feeling; reasoning being directed to utility and moral feeling to moral goodness. If they wrong others, they mean to injure them, not to insult them. Old men may feel pity, as well as young men, but not for the same reason. Young men feel it out of kindness; old men out of weakness, imagining that anything that befalls any one else might easily happen to them, which, as we saw, is a thought that excites pity. Hence they are querulous, and not disposed to jesting or laughter—the love of laughter being the very opposite of querulousness.

3 Such are the characters of Young Men and Elderly Men. People always think well of speeches adapted to, and reflecting, their own character; and we can now see how to compose our speeches so as to adapt both them and ourselves to our audiences.

Additional Rhetorical Strategy

Description (throughout).

Examining Words and Meaning

1. Do young men act more by reasoning or by moral feeling, according to Aristotle? Do they differ from old men in this respect? What do you think Aristotle means by the terms *reasoning* and *moral feeling?*

2. Look up in a dictionary any of these words that are unfamiliar to you: indiscriminately (paragraph 1); sanguine (paragraph 1); precept

(paragraph 1); cynical (paragraph 2); loquacity (paragraph 2); querulousness (paragraph 2).

Focusing on Structures and Strategies

1. Aristotle is using the first of the three methods outlined for comparison and contrast essays; he describes first the young men, then the old. Suppose that he had used the second method instead, giving a series of point-by-point contrasts. How would his doing so have affected the comparison? Which of the two methods do you think would give one a better sense of the *character* of a young or an old man, and which would give more emphasis to the *ways* in which they are different?

2. Does Aristotle follow more or less the same sequence in discussing the characteristics of old men as he does in describing young men? If you were rewriting this selection, would you order things differently?

Suggestions for Further Discussion and Writing

1. What are the reasons that Aristotle gives for the differences between the young and the old? Reviewing these reasons, does it seem to you that Aristotle takes a cheerful or a gloomy view of what life does to us?

2. Is Aristotle right in his judgments about youth and old age? Write your own version of "Youth and Old Age," giving your evaluation of the differences between old and young men or old and young women. Follow Aristotle's method if you wish, or use one of the two other methods outlined in the introduction to this section.

Columbus and the Moon

Tom Wolfe

When it seemed certain that Tom Wolfe would miss a deadline for an article to be published in Esquire *magazine, his editor told him to type up his notes so the staff could salvage something to follow the pictures already set for the article. Wolfe began as if he were writing a letter and continued to type through the night, finishing just before the office opened. Later that day, his editor called to say that he was removing the salutation and "running the rest as is." The article constitutes one of the first examples of the "new journalism," a form of reporting that uses many of the techniques of the novel and that Wolfe has not only practiced but also theorized about. Wolfe later developed that article into his first book,* The Kandy-Kolored, Tangerine-Flake Streamline Baby *(1965). Since then, Wolfe has written numerous articles on nearly every phase of American culture and published seven more books—ranging from a psychedelic memoir of a cross-country trip (*The Electric Kool-Aid Acid Test, *1968) to an exploration of the inner world of the early astronauts (*The Right Stuff, *1979). Among his latest books are* From Bauhaus to Our House *(1981), a study of modern architecture; and his first novel* Bonfire of the Vanities *(1987).*

In this 1979 essay comparing Columbus's expeditions to the New World with those of the National Aeronautics and Space Administration to the moon, Wolfe leads the reader to draw an inference about how history will regard NASA.

1 The National Aeronautics and Space Administration's moon landing 10 years ago today was a Government project, but then so was Columbus's voyage to America in 1492. The Government, in Columbus's case, was the Spanish Court of Ferdinand and Isabella. Spain was engaged in a sea race with Portugal in much the same way that the United States would be caught up in a space race with the Soviet Union four and a half centuries later.

2 The race in 1492 was to create the first shipping lane to Asia. The Portuguese expeditions had always sailed east, around the southern tip of Africa. Columbus decided to head due west, across open ocean, a scheme that was feasible only thanks to a recent invention—the magnetic ship's compass. Until then ships had stayed close to the great land masses even for the longest voyages. Likewise, it was only thanks to an invention of the 1940's and early 1950's, the high-speed electronic computer, that NASA would even consider propelling astronauts out of the Earth's orbit and toward the moon.

3 Both NASA and Columbus made not one but a series of voyages. NASA landed men on six different parts of the moon. Columbus made four voyages to different parts of what he remained convinced was the east coast of Asia. As a result both NASA and

Columbus had to keep coming back to the Government with their hands out, pleading for refinancing. In each case the reply of the Government became, after a few years: "This is all very impressive, but what earthly good is it to anyone back home?"

4 Columbus was reduced to making the most desperate claims. When he first reached land in 1492 at San Salvador, off Cuba, he expected to find gold, or at least spices. The Arawak Indians were awed by the strangers and their ships, which they believed had descended from the sky, and they presented them with their most prized possessions, live parrots and balls of cotton. Columbus soon set them digging for gold, which didn't exist. So he brought back reports of fabulous riches in the form of manpower; which is to say, slaves. He was not speaking of the Arawaks, however. With the exception of criminals and prisoners of war, he was supposed to civilize all natives and convert them to Christianity. He was talking about the Carib Indians, who were cannibals and therefore qualified as criminals. The Caribs would fight down to the last unbroken bone rather than endure captivity, and few ever survived the voyages back to Spain. By the end of Columbus's second voyage, in 1496, the Government was becoming testy. A great deal of wealth was going into voyages to Asia, and very little was coming back. Columbus made his men swear to return to Spain saying that they had not only reached the Asian mainland, they had heard Japanese spoken.

5 Likewise by the early 1970's, it was clear that the moon was in economic terms pretty much what it looked like from Earth, a gray rock. NASA, in the quest for appropriations, was reduced to publicizing the "spinoffs" of the space program. These included Teflon-coated frying pans, a ballpoint pen that would write in a weightless environment, and a computerized biosensor system that would enable doctors to treat heart patients without making house calls. On the whole, not a giant step for mankind.

6 In 1493, after his first voyage, Columbus had ridden through Barcelona at the side of King Ferdinand in the position once occupied by Ferdinand's late son, Juan. By 1500, the bad-mouthing of Columbus had reached the point where he was put in chains at the conclusion of his third voyage and returned to Spain in disgrace. NASA suffered no such ignominy, of course, but by July 20, 1974, the fifth anniversary of the landing of Apollo 11, things were grim enough. The public had become gloriously bored by space exploration. The fifth anniversary celebration consisted mainly of about 200 souls,

mostly NASA people, sitting on folding chairs underneath a camp meeting canopy on the marble prairie outside the old Smithsonian Air Museum in Washington listening to speeches by Neil Armstrong, Michael Collins, and Buzz Aldrin and watching the caloric waves ripple.

7 Extraordinary rumors had begun to circulate about the astronauts. The most lurid said that trips to the moon, and even into earth orbit, had so traumatized the men, they had fallen victim to religious and spiritualist manias or plain madness. (Of the total 73 astronauts chosen, one, Aldrin, is known to have suffered from depression, rooted, as his own memoir makes clear, in matters that had nothing to do with space flight. Two teamed up in an evangelical organization, and one set up a foundation for the scientific study of psychic phenomena—interests the three of them had developed long before they flew in space.) The NASA budget, meanwhile, had been reduced to the light-bill level.

8 Columbus died in 1509, nearly broke and stripped of most of his honors as Spain's Admiral of the Ocean, a title he preferred. It was only later that history began to look upon him not as an adventurer who had tried and failed to bring home gold—but as a man with a supernatural sense of destiny, whose true glory was his willingness to plunge into the unknown, including the remotest parts of the universe he could hope to reach.

9 NASA still lives, albeit in reduced circumstances, and whether or not history will treat NASA like the admiral is hard to say.

10 The idea that the exploration of the rest of the universe is its own reward is not very popular, and NASA is forced to keep talking about things such as bigger communications satellites that will enable live television transmission of European soccer games at a fraction of the current cost. Such notions as "building a bridge to the stars for mankind" do not light up the sky today—but may yet.

Additional Rhetorical Strategies

Cause and Effect (paragraph 2); Narration (paragraphs 4–6); Illustration (paragraphs 5, 7).

Examining Words and Meaning

1. What are some of the similarities that Wolfe finds between the voyages of Columbus and those of NASA? Why do you think he selects *these* similarities rather than others; that is, what do you think the point of his selection is?

2. What does Wolfe's use of such words and phrases as *testy* (paragraph 4), *bad-mouthing* (paragraph 6), *the light-bill level* (paragraph 7), and *broke* (paragraph 8) tell you about his tone? How does this influence your attitude toward his subject?

Focusing on Structures and Strategies

1. Which of the three methods outlined for writing comparison-and-contrast papers does Wolfe seem to be using here? Why do you think he chose this method rather than one of the other two? Beyond this, how else is the article organized: What moment in Columbus's career, for example, does Wolfe first mention, and what moment does he mention last? Suppose that Wolfe had arranged his material differently. How would this have changed the effect of his article?

2. Look back at Wolfe's first paragraph. Does it strike you as an abrupt or a leisurely introduction? What does it lead the reader to expect about the subject matter of the article? About the author's attitude toward his material?

Suggestions for Further Discussion and Writing

1. What do you know about Columbus and the moon project after reading Wolfe's piece that you did not know before? Does this new information lead you to regard these voyages of exploration in a new light? Take one of Wolfe's paragraphs that you found especially revealing, and explain how it altered your perceptions of Columbus, or the moon project, or both. What do you think Wolfe's purpose is in giving you this information?

2. Write an essay in which you discuss why, if we still seem to value Columbus for taking on the unknown, we seem to have lost this feeling for the Apollo astronauts.

Stallone vs. Springsteen

Jack Newfield

Over the course of more than twenty years as investigative reporter and columnist, Jack Newfield remains one of America's most widely read and admired journalists. "I'm writing to have an effect," he declares, and he has used his columns and reports to tackle virtually every major issue in contemporary American local and national affairs—from corruption in sports and politics to acts of violence against individuals and the culture.

Born and raised in Brooklyn, New York, Jack Newfield earned a B.A. at Hunter College in the City University of New York before beginning his career as a journalist with a job as a copyboy at the New York Mirror. *After serving as editor of a neighborhood weekly, the* West Side News, *Newfield moved in 1964 to New York City's most celebrated—and controversial—weekly newspaper, the* Village Voice. *In more than two decades of writing for the* Village Voice, *Newfield has served for many readers as the city's public conscience. His collected columns appeared as* The Education of Jack Newfield *(1984). He remains a frequent contributor to a wide range of cultural journals and critical quarterlies, including* The Nation *and* Partisan Review. *Among his book-length publications are* Robert Kennedy: A Memoir *(1969) and* The Permanent Government: Who Really Rules New York *(with Paul du Brul; revised and updated in 1981).*

In "Stallone vs. Springsteen," Newfield analyzes how America's two most popular working-class heroes project fundamentally different values and how their work is pulling this country in strikingly different directions. Published originally with the subtitle "Which Dream Do You Buy?" in the April 1986 issue of Playboy *magazine, Newfield's essay proposes at once that Sylvester Stallone's Rambo movies have added reality to the list of casualties of the Vietnam War and that Bruce Springsteen's songs, in contrast, appeal "to the best in all of us."*

1 Bruce Springsteen and Sylvester Stallone are the two great working-class heroes of American mass culture. Springsteen had the best-selling album of 1985 and Stallone had the second most successful movie. On the surface, they share stunning similarities of biceps, bandannas, American flags, Vietnam themes, praise from President Reagan and uplifting feelings of national pride. Bumper stickers proclaim, BRUCE—THE RAMBO OF ROCK.

2 But beneath the surface—and between the lines—these two American heroes of the Eighties are sending opposite messages. They are subtly pulling the 18-to-35-year-old generation toward two competing visions of the American future.

3 Stallone's *Rocky* and *Rambo* films—especially the latter—are about violence and revenge in a context of fantasy. Rambo never pays a price in body bags or pain or blood or doubt or remorse or fear. The enemy is stereotyped and therefore dehumanized. The emotions Stallone liberates are hostility and aggression: Audiences come out of the theater wanting to kick some Commie ass in Nicaragua.

4 By contrast, the essential human feeling Springsteen liberates is empathy—compassion for the common man trapped in the dead-end world of the hourly wage. The realistic words of Springsteen's best songs are about the hurt of unemployed workers; about reconciliation with estranged parents through understanding *their* lives; about staying hopeful even though experience falls short of the American dream.

5 In *Rambo,* Stallone depicts the Vietnam veteran as a killing machine, a deranged, rampaging executioner. In *Born in the U.S.A.,* Springsteen depicts the Vietnam veteran as neglected—wanting to be reintegrated into society as a normal person but getting the brush-off from a bureaucrat at the Veterans Administration. Recall the misunderstood and misheard words of the Springsteen anthem:

Got in a little hometown jam,
So they put a rifle in my hand.
Sent me off to a foreign land
To go and kill the yellow man. . . .
Come back home to the refinery.
Hiring man says, "Son, if it was up to me. . . ."
Went down to see my VA man;
He said, "Son, don't you understand now?"
I had a brother at Khé Sanh
Fighting off the Viet Cong.
They're still there; he's all gone.

He had a woman he loved in Saigon—
I got a picture of him in her arms now. . . .

6 The difference between Stallone and Springsteen is perhaps best illuminated by reading an essay George Orwell wrote in 1945, before either Stallone or Springsteen was born. In the essay, *Notes on Nationalism,* Orwell makes a distinction between nationalism and patriotism and then suggests that they are, in fact, opposites:

> By "nationalism," I mean first of all the habit of assuming that human beings can be classified like insects and that whole blocks of millions or tens of millions of people can confidently be labeled "good" or "bad." But secondly—and this is much more important—I mean the habit of identifying oneself with a single nation or other unit, placing it beyond good and evil and recognizing no other duty than that of advancing its interests. Nationalism is not to be confused with patriotism . . . since two different and even opposing ideas are involved. By "patriotism" I mean a devotion to a particular place and a particular way of life, which one believes to be the best in the world but has no wish to force upon other people. Patriotism is of its nature defensive, both militarily and culturally. Nationalism, on the other hand, is inseparable from the desire for power. . . .
>
> It can plausibly be argued, for instance—it is even probably true—that patriotism is an inoculation against nationalism.

7 Stallone as Rambo snarls, "Damn Russian bastards" and kills a few more. Springsteen introduces *This Land Is Your Land,* the first encore at all his concerts, as "the greatest song ever written about America," and then reminds his fans, "Remember, *nobody wins unless everybody wins."* That's one difference between nationalism and patriotism.

8 Stallone manipulates Americans' feelings of frustration over the lost Vietnam war and helps create a jingoistic climate of emotion in which a future war might be welcomed. Springsteen asks us to honor the neglected and rejected Vietnam veterans, so that we won't glide gleefully into the next war without remembering the real cost of the last one. That's a second difference between nationalism and patriotism.

9 "It's a right-wing fantasy," said Stallone, talking to *Time* about last summer's big hit. "What Rambo is saying is that if they could fight again, it would be different." He added that he was looking for another "open wound" as a site for a sequel, possibly Iran or Afghanistan.

10 Ron Kovic is a paraplegic author and Vietnam veteran. As an honored guest at Springsteen's opening-night concert last August at the Giants' stadium in New Jersey, Kovic told reporters, "I've been sitting in this wheelchair for the past 18 years. And I can only thank Bruce Springsteen for all he has done for Vietnam veterans. *Born in the U.S.A.* is a beautiful song that helped me personally to heal." The difference between looking for another open wound as a movie backdrop and creating music that is healing—that's a third distinction between nationalism and patriotism.

11 Congressman Lane Evans of Illinois is an ex-Marine. *"Rambo,"* he says, "is dangerous because it is dishonest about reality. It creates the myth of a superhuman, invincible *macho* man as the quick-fix solution to all our international problems. Stallone is saying to people that the answer is always to send in a rescue mission of former Green Berets and commandos. That is certainly *not* the remedy for complex situations like Nicaragua."

12 But what Stallone did with *Rambo* was brilliant in an opportunistic way. He replayed the war to give it a happy ending. In doing that, he raised false hopes among tormented M.I.A. and POW families that are destined to be crushed by real life.

13 "I came out of the movie angry," says Dr. Charlie Clements, an activist for Vietnam-veteran causes. "I came out of the movie feeling exploited as a veteran. I came out thinking that this movie exploits America."

14 Stallone himself escaped military service, though he was eligible for the draft during the bloodiest years of the Vietnam war. (Springsteen did not serve, either. He was 4-F because of a concussion caused by a motorcycle accident. But the issue is not the courage to serve; it is the hypocrisy of not serving but promoting wars for others to fight.) Like John Wayne, Stallone became a celluloid hero with the help of stunt men and special-effects experts. The undisputed facts are these: Stallone was a girls' athletic coach at an elite private school in Switzerland from 1965 to 1967. From 1967 to 1969, he was a student in the drama department of the University of Miami. While America was losing the Vietnam war during the early Seventies, Stallone was making the soft-core flick *A Party at Kitty and Studs.*

15 In the November 8, 1976, issue of *The Village Voice,* Pete Hamill published a favorable profile of Stallone. The piece contained several revealing quotes from "America's Hero" about his ethics and lifestyle during the years when 58,000 of his countrymen were dying in Viet-

nam. Of his tenure as an acting student, Stallone said, "I learned it is actually possible to function without brain waves for two years." Of his tour of duty at the school in Switzerland, he confided, "I didn't want to ski. I just wanted to get loaded and play pinball machines. Essentially, I was the imported American sheep dog for these little lambs, these girls. . . ."

16 Congressman Andrew Jacobs of Indiana was disabled as a Marine during the Korean War. When I asked him for his thoughts on *Rambo,* he deliberated for a moment and said, "The issue is hypocrisy, nothing else. I doubt if there are 20 of us in Congress who have ever faced a man with a rifle who was actually trying to kill you. Few of them here even have the slightest notion of the bone-chilling terror of war. It all reminds me of something the Twenties columnist 'Kin' Hubbard wrote: 'There is too much said about the glory of dying for your country by those who never tried it.' "

17 Nationalism, as defined by Orwell, is an intoxicating but essentially negative emotion, because it is, by its very nature, intolerant. It does not respect the rights of minorities or the dignity of neighbors. It is a will to power that negates complexity. Its most extreme avatars are monstrous lunatics such as Khomeini, Qaddafi, Botha, Farrakhan and Kahane.

18 The milder form of nationalism, as represented by Stallone, is less harmful. Stallone doesn't have Governmental power, and he doesn't push the issue; he usually retreats behind his movie character and tells most interviewers he is nonpolitical.

19 But the messages his images communicate to masses of impressionable young people sometimes do have damaging consequences. For example, the week *Rambo,* with its negative stereotypes of Asians, opened in Boston last spring, there were two incidents in which Southeast Asian refugees were badly beaten up by gangs of white youths.

20 In the more recent *Rocky IV*—which Stallone wrote, directed and starred in—the villainous foe is a Russian who fights dirty, takes illegal steroid injections and wears a black mouthpiece. Cleverly named Ivan Drago, he is depicted as a robotlike extension of the Evil Empire. Critics have written that it is the most simplistic and one-dimensional of all the *Rocky* movies. It lacks the interesting subplots and realistic blue-collar atmosphere of the original *Rocky,* with its loan shark and neighborhood gym; this time, Stallone literally and figuratively wraps himself in the American flag—proving that sequels are the last refuge of nationalists.

21 The worst features of Stallone's nationalism are the values it enshrines and reinforces: racism, violence, militarism and—possibly most subversive of all—simplicity. The convergence of these emotions can make war and foreign intervention seem like a sporting event. Or a movie.

22 Bruce Springsteen's patriotism is rooted in a different set of values, apparent in his songs: the old-fashioned virtues of work, family, community, loyalty, dignity, perseverance, love of country. His fundamental theme is the gap between America's promise and performance and his resilient faith in the eventual redemption of that promise. He sees America as it is, with all its jobless veterans, homeless people and urban ghettos. And he retains his idealism *in spite of everything,* because his patriotism has room for paradox. At a Springsteen concert, one song makes you want to cheer for America, the next makes you want to cry for America—and then change it.

23 Springsteen conveys compassion for the casualty, for the ordinary person who may not be articulate. His empathy is for men with "debts no honest man can pay." From his immense pride in his home town comes a homage to closed textile mills and "Main Street's whitewashed windows and vacant stores." Out of his populist patriotism comes his affection for people who feel "like a dog that's been beat too much" and his reconciling respect for his working-class father:

> *Daddy worked his whole life for nothing but the pain.*
> *Now he walks these empty rooms, looking for something to blame.*

24 These songs are social, not political. They don't offer platforms, slogans or rhetoric. They don't imply easy remedies and they don't endorse politicians. Springsteen himself says he has not voted since 1972, and he is enrolled in no political party.

25 But despite his stance of electoral alienation, Springsteen writes songs that make you want to be a better citizen, if you borrow your sense of citizenship from the Ten Commandments, the Sermon on the Mount and the Bill of Rights. And he lives those values. He sings, "And for my nineteenth birthday I got a union card"; he has also donated $20,000 to a Pittsburgh soup kitchen and food bank run by Local 1397 of the steelworkers' union. And he contributed $15,000 to a health clinic outside Tucson because it was giving free care to striking Phelps-Dodge mineworkers after the company cut off their medical

benefits. During 1985, Springsteen made donations of more than $1,000,000 to populist groups. The man has an instinctive purity.

26 Nor is his bonding with Vietnam veterans a calculated commercial alliance. In 1980, at a time when the vets were still shunned rejects from a war everyone wanted to forget, Springsteen began, without any publicity, to donate funds to Vietnam Veterans of America. In 1981, he gave a benefit concert that raised $100,000 and kept the organization alive. That August night, the stage was lined with vets in wheelchairs, and Springsteen talked to his audience more intimately than he had ever done before. And he sang unforgettable renditions of *Who'll Stop the Rain* and *Bye, Bye, Johnny* that had vets weeping and cheering at the same time.

27 "We would not exist if it were not for Bruce Springsteen," says Robert Muller, the president of Vietnam Veterans of America. "My hope is that ten years down the road, he'll run for President."

28 There are disturbing racial images in *Rambo*—and perhaps in the most recent *Rocky* sequels—but Springsteen's bands have always been integrated. And in an interview published in the December 6, 1984, issue of *Rolling Stone,* Springsteen spoke with intelligent candor about his own racial attitudes:

> 29 I think it's *difficult,* because we were all brought up with sexist attitudes and racist attitudes. But hopefully, as you grow older, you get some sort of insight into that and—I know it's corny—try to treat other people the way you would want them to treat you. . . .
>
> 30 What unites people very often is their fear. What unites white people in some places is their fear of black people. What unites guys is maybe a denigrating attitude toward women—or sometimes maybe women have an attitude toward men. And these things are then in turn exploited by politicians, which turns into fear—knee-jerk fear of the Russians or of whatever *ism* is out there. . . .
>
> 31 Like, some of our economic policies are a real indirect kind of racism, in which the people that get affected most are black people who are at the lower end of the economic spectrum. And I think somewhere inside, people know this—I really do. They don't fess up to it, but somewhere inside there is a real meanness in using things this way.

32 Springsteen and Stallone, two messiahs of American mass culture, two muscular men—tugging this country's flag in different directions.

33 Sylvester Stallone, at bottom, is a faker, feeding us fantasies as therapy for our national neuroses. He is appealing to the dark side

that exists in all of us, the part of us that wants to get even with everyone who has ever gotten the better of us, the part that finds it easier to understand a stereotype than an individual, the part that dreams of vengeance that never fails and never leaves an aftertaste of guilt.

34 Bruce Springsteen appeals to the best in all of us. His songs ask us to forgive the sinner but to remember the sin; to respect one another but to question authority; to refuse to compromise our ideals ("no retreat, no surrender"); to keep growing but to continue to love our parents and our home towns; to feel a responsibility for sharing with our countrymen who have less property and less power.

35 "I think what's happening now," Springsteen told one interviewer, "is people want to forget. There was Vietnam, there was Watergate, there was Iran—we were beaten, we were hustled and then we were humiliated. And I think people got a need to feel good about the country they live in. But what's happening, I think, is that need—which is a good thing—is gettin' manipulated and exploited. . . .

36 "One of the things that was always on my mind was to maintain connections with the people I'd grown up with and the sense of community where I came from. That's why I stayed in New Jersey. The danger of fame is in *forgetting.*"

Additional Rhetorical Strategies

Illustration (throughout); Argument (throughout); Definition (paragraphs 6, 18); Cause and Effect (paragraphs 11–13, 20, 22–23, 26); Narration (paragraph 15); Description (paragraph 21).

Examining Words and Meaning

1. A good deal of Newfield's comparison and contrast of Sylvester Stallone and Bruce Springsteen depends on invoking George Orwell's distinction between "nationalism" and "patriotism." List—and explain—the major differences between "nationalism" and "patriotism" as defined by George Orwell. In what specific ways does the life and work of these two heroes correspond to Orwell's

definitions? What, in effect, are the specific ways in which Newfield stresses Stallone's aggressiveness in contrast to Springsteen's defensiveness? Do you agree with Orwell's definitions? With Newfield's application of them?

2. Newfield characterizes Sylvester Stallone and Bruce Springsteen as "the two great working-class heroes of American mass culture." According to Newfield, what are the essential characteristics of the contemporary American hero? Which of these traits do Stallone and Springsteen share? What are the fundamental differences that Newfield emphasizes in order to contrast their roles in contemporary American popular culture?

Focusing on Structures and Strategies

1. This essay is organized as a comparison and contrast between two seemingly similar "American heroes." Which of the three methods outlined for writing comparison and contrast does Newfield use here? Show how he either applies this method consistently throughout the essay or note when he varies from it. What are the advantages/disadvantages of Newfield's having chosen this particular method of comparison and contrast?

2. What is Newfield's explicit goal in writing this essay? Does he also develop a larger, argumentative or persuasive purpose? If so, explain when and how this larger purpose is revealed. How does the essay's organization help to reinforce Newfield's purpose in writing the piece?

3. Why does each of these heroes appeal to the imaginations of working-class Americans? What values does each represent? What aspects of the *Rambo* movies do people react to negatively? What aspects of Springsteen's music are people especially drawn to? How balanced is Newfield's view of these two, very different, cultural heroes? Do you agree with the author's assessment of each? Why? Why not?

4. What kinds of evidence does the author present in order to support his characterization of Stallone and Springsteen? For example, describe the feelings Stallone evokes in his *Rambo* movies and Springsteen elicits in his songs. How are common people depicted by Stallone and Springsteen? How are Vietnam veterans presented?

5. What is the point of Newfield's summary of Stallone's biography during the 1960s (paragraphs 14–15)? What is the effect of *not* comparing and contrasting Stallone's life during the years of the Vietnam War with Springsteen's? How does Newfield extend his point about hypocrisy in the paragraphs that follow his criticism of Stallone? What is Newfield's reaction to Springsteen's report that he has not voted since 1972? What is your reaction to that same fact? In what way does Newfield suggest that Springsteen provides hope for contemporary America through his music? Through his personal actions?
6. This essay originally appeared in *Playboy* magazine. Consider the audience for this magazine. Do you think this an appropriate place to publish this article? Why or why not?

Suggestions for Further Discussion and Writing

1. Newfield quotes Springsteen as saying that "what unites people very often is their fear." Do you agree? How does this add to the characterization of Springsteen? How does it reflect on Stallone?
2. Consider Newfield's word choices. What words and phrases of the comparison bear connotations that reveal the author's stance? If you were Sylvester Stallone, how might you counter Newfield's criticism of your life and work?
3. Review George Orwell's definitions of "nationalism" and "patriotism." Consider the many other words that traditionally have had a great impact on America's collective consciousness. *Freedom, liberty, self-determination,* and *self-reliance* are but a few. Write an essay in which you choose two such seemingly similar words and compare and/or contrast their meanings and their importance in American history.
4. As you review Newfield's essay on Stallone and Springsteen, think of two other public figures who exemplify sharply contrasting views of American values. You might want to draw these public figures from the world of entertainment (for example, singer Joan Baez vs. movie actor John Wayne) or politics and public affairs (Lieutenant Colonel Oliver North vs. consumer advocate Ralph Nader). Write an essay in which you demonstrate how these public figures exemplify the traits Orwell associates with "nationalism" and "patriotism."

Television and Reading

Marie Winn

To read well is to be reasonably confident of meeting the challenges of any text. It is an invigorating exercise, one that requires a training similar to that of serious athletes. In the famous "Spring" chapter of Walden, *Henry David Thoreau states this comparison most succinctly:*

> *To read well, that is, to read books in a true spirit, is a noble exercise and one that will task the reader more than any exercise which the customs of the day esteem. It requires a training such as the athletes underwent, the steady intention almost of the whole life to this object. Books must be read as deliberately and reservedly as they were written.*

In the following essay, Marie Winn updates Thoreau's metaphor by contrasting the intellectual rigors of reading to the inactivity associated with watching the world roll by "in living color" on television. Drawn from her study The Plug-in Drug: Television, Children and the Family *(1977), the selection also considers the effects of watching television on how children perceive the world around them.*

A graduate of Radcliffe and Columbia University, Marie Winn has published numerous children's books and does freelance writing on contemporary media issues.

1 Until the television era a young child's access to symbolic representations of reality was limited. Unable to read, he entered the world of fantasy primarily by way of stories told to him or read to him from a book. But rarely did such "literary" experiences take up a significant proportion of a child's waking time; even when a willing reader or storyteller was available, an hour or so a day was more time than most children spent ensconced in the imagination of others. And when the pre-television child *did* enter those imaginary worlds, he always had a grown-up escort along to interpret, explain, and comfort, if need be. Before he learned to read, it was difficult for the child to enter the fantasy world alone.

2 For this reason the impact of television was undoubtedly greater on preschoolers and pre-readers than on any other group. By

means of television, very young children were able to enter and spend sizable portions of their waking time in a secondary world of incorporeal people and intangible things, unaccompanied, in too many cases, by an adult guide or comforter. School-age children fell into a different category. Because they could read, they had other opportunities to leave reality behind. For these children television was merely *another* imaginary world.

3 But since reading, once the school child's major imaginative experience, has now been virtually eclipsed by television, the television experience must be compared with the reading experience to try to discover whether they are, indeed, similar activities fulfilling similar needs in a child's life.

WHAT HAPPENS WHEN YOU READ

4 It is not enough to compare television watching and reading from the viewpoint of quality. Although the quality of the material available in each medium varies enormously, from junky books and shoddy programs to literary masterpieces and fine, thoughtful television shows, the *nature* of the two experiences is different and that difference significantly affects the impact of the material taken in.

5 Few people besides linguistics students and teachers of reading are aware of the complex mental manipulations involved in the reading process. Shortly after learning to read, a person assimilates the process into his life so completely that the words in books seem to acquire an existence almost equal to the objects or acts they represent. It requires a fresh look at a printed page to recognize that those symbols that we call letters of the alphabet are completely abstract shapes bearing no inherent "meaning" of their own. Look at an "o," for instance, or a "k." The "o" is a curved figure; the "k" is an intersection of three straight lines. Yet it is hard to divorce their familiar figures from their sounds, though there is nothing "o-ish" about an "o" or "k-ish" about a "k." A reader unfamiliar with the Russian alphabet will find it easy to look at the symbol "Ш" and see it as an abstract shape; a Russian reader will find it harder to detach that symbol from its sound, *shch.* And even when trying to consider "k" as an abstract symbol, we cannot see it without the feeling of a "k" sound somewhere between the throat and the ears, a silent pronunciation of "k" that occurs the instant we see the letter.

6 That is the beginning of reading: we learn to transform abstract figures into sounds, and groups of symbols into the combined sounds that make up the words of our language. As the mind transforms the abstract symbols into sounds and the sounds into words, it "hears" the words, as it were, and thereby invests them with meanings previously learned in the spoken language. Invariably, as the skill of reading develops, the meaning of each word begins to seem to dwell within those symbols that make up the word. The word "dog," for instance, comes to bear some relationship with the real animal. Indeed, the word "dog" seems to *be* a dog in a certain sense, to possess some of the qualities of a dog. But it is only as a result of a swift and complex series of mental activities that the word "dog" is transformed from a series of meaningless squiggles into an idea of something real. This process goes on smoothly and continuously as we read, and yet it becomes no less complex. The brain must carry out all the steps of decoding and investing with meaning each time we read; but it becomes more adept at it as the skill develops, so that we lose the sense of struggling with symbols and meanings that children have when they first learn to read.

7 But not merely does the mind *hear* words in the process of reading; it is important to remember that reading involves images as well. For when the reader sees the word "dog" and understands the idea of "dog," an image representing a dog is conjured up as well. The precise nature of this "reading image" is little understood, nor is there agreement about what relation it bears to visual images taken in directly by the eyes. Nevertheless images necessarily color our reading, else we would perceive no meaning, merely empty words. The great difference between these "reading images" and the images we take in when viewing television is this: we *create* our own images when reading, based upon our own life experiences and reflecting our own individual needs, while we must accept what we receive when watching television images. This aspect of reading, which might be called "creative" in the narrow sense of the word, is present during all reading experiences, regardless of *what* is being read. The reader "creates" his own images as he reads, almost as if he were creating his own, small, inner television program. The result is a nourishing experience for the imagination. As Bruno Bettelheim notes, "Television captures the imagination but does not liberate it. A good book at once stimulates and frees the mind."

8 Television images do not go through a complex symbolic transformation. The mind does not have to decode and manipulate during

the television experience. Perhaps this is a reason why the visual images received directly from a television set are strong, stronger, it appears, than the images conjured up mentally while reading. But ultimately they satisfy less. A ten-year-old child reports on the effects of seeing television dramatizations of books he has previously read: "The TV people leave a stronger impression. Once you've seen a character on TV, he'll always look like that in your mind, even if you made a different picture of him in your mind before, when you read the book yourself." And yet, as the same child reports, "the thing about a book is that you have so much freedom. You can make each character look exactly the way you want him to look. You're more in control of things when you read a book than when you see something on TV."

9 It may be that television-bred children's reduced opportunities to indulge in this "inner picture-making" accounts for the curious inability of so many children today to adjust to nonvisual experiences. This is commonly reported by experienced teachers who bridge the gap between the pretelevision and the television eras.

10 "When I read them a story without showing them pictures, the children always complain—'I can't see.' Their attention flags," reports a first-grade teacher. "They'll begin to talk or wander off. I have to really work to develop their visualizing skills. I tell them that there's nothing to see, that the story is coming out of my mouth, and that they can make their own pictures in their 'mind's eye.' They get better at visualizing, with practice. But children never needed to learn how to visualize before television, it seems to me."

VIEWING VS. READING: CONCENTRATION

11 Because reading demands complex mental manipulations, a reader is required to concentrate far more than a television viewer. An audio expert notes that "with the electronic media it is openness [that counts]. Openness permits auditory and visual stimuli more direct access to the brain . . . someone who is taught to concentrate will fail to perceive many patterns of information conveyed by the electronic stimuli."

12 It may be that a predisposition toward concentration, acquired, perhaps, through one's reading experiences, makes one an inadequate television watcher. But it seems far more likely that the reverse situation obtains: that a predisposition toward "openness" (which

may be understood to mean the opposite of focal concentration), acquired through years and years of television viewing, has influenced adversely viewers' ability to concentrate, to read, to write clearly—in short, to demonstrate any of the verbal skills a literate society requires.

PACE

13 A comparison between reading and viewing may be made in respect to the pace of each experience, and the relative control a person has over that pace, for the pace may influence the ways one uses the material received in each experience. In addition, the pace of each experience may determine how much it intrudes upon other aspects of one's life.

14 The pace of reading, clearly, depends entirely upon the reader. He may read as slowly or as rapidly as he can or wishes to read. If he does not understand something, he may stop and reread it, or go in search of elucidation before continuing. The reader can accelerate his pace when the material is easy or less than interesting, and slow down when it is difficult or enthralling. If what he reads is moving, he can put down the book for a few moments and cope with his emotions without fear of losing anything.

15 The pace of the television experience cannot be controlled by the viewer; only its beginning and end are within his control as he clicks the knob on and off. He cannot slow down a delightful program or speed up a dreary one. He cannot "turn back" if a word or phrase is not understood. The program moves inexorably forward, and what is lost or misunderstood remains so.

16 Nor can the television viewer readily transform the material he receives into a form that might suit his particular emotional needs, as he invariably does with material he reads. The images move too quickly. He cannot use his own imagination to invest the people and events portrayed on television with the personal meanings that would help him understand and resolve relationships and conflicts in his own life; he is under the power of the imagination of the show's creators. In the television experience the eyes and ears are overwhelmed with the immediacy of sights and sounds. They flash from the television set just fast enough for the eyes and ears to take them in before moving on quickly to the new pictures and sounds . . . so as *not to lose the thread.*

17 Not to lose the thread . . . it is this need, occasioned by the irreversible direction and relentless velocity of the television experience, that not only limits the workings of the viewer's imagination, but also causes television to intrude into human affairs far more than reading experiences can ever do. If someone enters the room while one is watching television—a friend, a relative, a child, someone, perhaps, one has not seen for some time—one must continue to watch or one will lose the thread. The greetings must wait, for the television program will not. A book, of course, can be set aside, with a pang of regret, perhaps, but with no sense of permanent loss.

18 A grandparent describes a situation that is, by all reports, not uncommon:

19 "Sometimes when I come to visit the girls, I'll walk into their room and they're watching a TV program. Well, I know they love me, but it makes me feel *bad* when I tell them hello, and they say, without even looking up, 'Wait a minute . . . we have to see the end of this program.' It hurts me to have them care more about that machine and those little pictures than about being glad to see me. I know that they probably can't help it, but still. . . ."

20 Can they help it? Ultimately the power of a television viewer to release himself from his viewing in order to attend to human demands arising in the course of his viewing is not altogether a function of the pace of the program. After all, the viewer might *choose* to operate according to human priorities rather than electronic dictatorship. He might quickly decide "to hell with this program" and simply stop watching when a friend entered the room or a child needed attention.

21 He might . . . but the hypnotic power of television makes it difficult to shift one's attention away, makes one desperate not to lose the thread of the program. . . .

THE BASIC BUILDING BLOCKS

22 There is another difference between reading and television viewing that must affect the response to each experience. This is the relative acquaintance of readers and viewers with the fundamental elements of each medium. While the reader is familiar with the basic building blocks of the reading medium, the television viewer has little acquaintance with those of the television medium.

23 As a person reads, he has his own writing experience to fall

back upon. His understanding of what he reads, and his feelings about it, are necessarily affected, and deepened, by his possession of writing as a means of communicating. As a child begins to learn reading, he begins to acquire the rudiments of writing. That these two skills are always acquired together is important and not coincidental. As the child learns to read words, he needs to understand that a word is something he can write himself, though his muscle control may temporarily prevent him from writing it clearly. That he wields such power over the words he is struggling to decipher makes the reading experience a satisfying one right from the start.

24 A young child watching television enters a realm of materials completely beyond his control—and understanding. Though the images that appear on the screen may be reflections of familiar people and things, they appear as if by magic. The child cannot create similar images, nor even begin to understand how those flickering, electronic shapes and forms come into being. He takes on a far more powerless and ignorant role in front of the television set than in front of a book.

25 There is no doubt that many young children have a confused relationship to the television medium. When a group of preschool children were asked, "How do kids get to be on your TV?" only 22 percent of them showed any real comprehension of the nature of the television images. When asked, "Where do the people and kids and things go when your TV is turned off?" only 20 percent of the three-year-olds showed the smallest glimmer of understanding. Although there was an increase in comprehension among the four-year-olds, the authors of the study note that "even among the older children the vast majority still did not grasp the nature of television pictures."

26 The child's feelings of power and competence are nourished by another feature of the reading experience that does not obtain for television: the nonmechanical, easily accessible, and easily transportable nature of reading matter. The child can always count on a book for pleasure, though the television set may break down at a crucial moment. The child may take a book with him wherever he goes, to his room, to the park, to his friend's house, to school to read under his desk: he can *control* his use of books and reading materials. The television set is stuck in a certain place; it cannot be moved easily. It certainly cannot be casually transported from place to place by a child. The child must not only watch television wherever the set is located, but he must watch certain programs at certain times, and is powerless to change what comes out of the set and when it comes out.

27 In this comparison of reading and television experiences a picture begins to emerge that quite confirms the commonly held notion that reading is somehow "better" than television viewing. Reading involves a complex form of mental activity, trains the mind in concentration skills, develops the powers of imagination and inner visualization; the flexibility of its pace lends itself to a better and deeper comprehension of the material communicated. Reading engrosses, but does not hypnotize or seduce the reader from his human responsibilities. Reading is a two-way process: the reader can also write; television viewing is a one-way street: the viewer cannot create television images. And books are ever available, ever controllable. Television controls.

Additional Rhetorical Strategies

Cause and Effect (paragraphs 1, 2, 7–9, 11, 12); Process Analysis (paragraphs 5–7); Definition (paragraph 7); Illustration (throughout).

Examining Words and Meaning

1. Summarize Winn's description of the stages of the reading process. How consistent are your own first reading experiences with her analysis?
2. What does Winn see as the most fundamental difference between reading and watching television? Do you think she has omitted potential points of comparison? Be as specific as possible.
3. Would you characterize Winn's diction in this essay as primarily abstract or concrete? Point to specific examples to support your response.

Focusing on Structures and Strategies

1. The introduction to this section says that there must be a controlling idea, or thesis, to a comparison if it is to be more than a list of points. What is the controlling idea in Winn's comparison?

2. Of the three possible methods for organizing an essay of comparison, which does she use? How effectively does she use it? Be as specific as possible.

Suggestions for Further Discussion and Writing

1. Michael Arlen (p. 451) also writes about the passive nature of television watching. Compare and/or contrast both Arlen's and Winn's arguments and their distinctive methods of presenting them. Which essay is more effective? Why?
2. What are your earliest recollections of reading? What were you reading? Why were you reading it? What were your attitudes toward that experience? Write an essay in which you compare and/or contrast your attitude toward reading as a child with your attitude now. Be sure to have a controlling idea for your essay and account for any significant changes between your attitude then and now. (An alternative exercise would be to focus on the changes in your attitudes toward watching television.)
3. Winn's argument in this essay is not against the quality of television but rather against the nature of the experience itself, which is perceived as fundamentally passive. Could her argument be mustered against other, more respected activities? Consider, for example, such activities as attending a lecture or a concert. Write an essay comparing and/or contrasting two such activities, ones that often seem in danger of lulling the spectator into some sort of passivity. Explain why each activity prompts passive behavior, and suggest possible ways to make such experiences more active.

Pioneer Diaries of Women and Men

John Mack Faragher

The long, dangerous trek of pioneers across the overland trail remains one of the great American adventure stories of the nineteenth century. But unlike most of the fictional adventure tales of that time, this was one experience that involved the arduous cooperation of both sexes. As one of the emigrant women put it: "They talk of the times that tried men's souls but this was the time [that tried] both men and women's souls."

In the following selection taken from Women and Men on the Overland Trail *(1980), John Mack Faragher, a professor of history at Mount Holyoke College, closely examines the diaries kept by pioneers during the seven-month trip. He finds in the different writing styles of men and women an accurate reflection of how separate social and cultural worlds can persist even in the thick of a common effort.*

1 Differences between the worlds of men and women are reflected in the emigrant diaries. Despite similarity in content, there was a notable difference in the style of men's and women's writing. Women usually wrote with a pervasive personal presence, most often using the first person. "I am now sitting on a hill side on a stone, a little distant from the camp," Rebecca Ketcham wrote in her diary late one afternoon. "After I commenced writing Mrs Dix called to me to come to her to see a beautiful bunch of verbena she had found. I went and looked about with her a little, then sat down again to my writing. Very soon Camela called to me to see how the wild peas grow." Even in less fluently written women's diaries, the subject "I" tended to be the ultimate standard of perception. "Met yesterday a very long and steep road coming out of Grande River bottom. I never saw as crooked a road in my life." Men, on the contrary, typically employed the more impersonal "we."[1] Sometimes the referent of this pronoun is hard to specify, shifting with the context. Usually the "we" most clearly referred to the men as a group.

> [May 4, 1851] We traveled 16 miles this day over very hilly road.
> [May 6] This day we left camp at 8 o'clock and traveled 12 miles, camped where we found but little wood and poor water.
> [May 7] This day we gathered up and started after traveling five or six miles it commenced blowing and raining very hard. We all got very wet.
> [May 8] This morning some of our women washed. We gathered up afternoon and traveled ten miles and camped on an open prairie, where we had no wood and but little grass.

[1]Sixty-three percent of the women diarists consistently used the *I,* but only 46 percent of the men.

The subject of these passages is not clear until the women are introduced; then the "we" seems to be masculine. Another man wrote, "We drove up and turned out our stock to grass while the girls got busy getting supper."

2 Women diarists typically located themselves in relation to space and time—often taking care to note where they were sitting, what they had been doing, and what was going on around them as they wrote. "The sun is shining bright and warm, and a cool breeze blowing makes it very nice indeed, and it seems very much like home. . . . Oh, they are starting, so I must stop for today. . . . Trying to write walking, but it won't do." Most women did not go into quite the detail Agnes Stewart included in this passage, but men, by contrast, were likely not to bother with any of these, content to assume that the fact of writing itself established a sufficient identifying framework.[2]

3 Men's writing was usually plain, unadorned, and terse.

> Fri 10 made this day 14 and encamped at the Willow Springs good water but little grass 3 Buffaloes killed the Main Spring 1-½ miles above
> Sat 11 Made this day 20 Miles to Independence Rock Camped below the Rock good water ½ way
> Sun 12 Lay by this day.

Women, on the other hand, frequently employed a range of stylistic elaborations. They took care to identify names of people and places and specify dates and times, while men regularly left names out, neglected to record dates, and abbreviated their words and phrases, sometimes beyond recognition.[3] Most women used extended description: colorful adjectives, qualifying phrases, long passages of explanation and summary. Elizabeth Dixon Smith, who often wrote long passages, commented that "I would have written a great deal more if I had the opportunity. Sometimes I would not get the chance to write for two or three days, and then would have to rise in the night when my babe and all hands were asleep, light a candle and write." It was a rare man, however, who regularly employed elaborating devices in his diary writing.[4]

[2]Ninety-four percent of the women diarists and 44 percent of the men explicitly placed themselves in relation to time and space at least once in their accounts.

[3]Seventy-five percent of women and 39 percent of men used exact names, dates, and places in their accounts.

[4]Seventy-nine percent of women and 22 percent of men used one or more forms of extended description at least once.

4 In general, men and women were concerned with different orders of meaning. There was an almost inverse relationship in the way most men wrote about objects and things, most women about people.[5] The following two passages—both written somewhat more elaborately than the mode for either sex—illustrate the differences:

> [September 23, 1843] We went up to the ford & fastened our waggons to gether as we did at the upper crossing & drove over. This ford is better than the upper one, tho it is a bout 8 or 10 inches deeper than the upper one. Tho we went strate a craws, & in camped on the bank. Grazing indifferent.
> [September 24] We struck through the hill & struck a creek & in camped Grazing indifferent. Dist 12.
> [September 25] We continued through the hills & struck a smawl spring in nine miles Grazing indifferent. Then we struck a nonther one in 5 or 6 miles. Tolerable incampement Then we struck a smaller branch at nite. Grazing indifferent. Distance 19.

> [June 16, 1853] Frank and a number of young friends are amusing themselves with the "Mansions of Happiness" and judging from their merry laugh, I should think they were enjoying it very much indeed. Father has taken his pillow under the wagon and is having his daily siesta. Willie is watching the horses and I am in the wagon, spending an hour with you, my dear children.

5 These differences in writing style conform to the differences between the social and cultural worlds of men and women. Speech patterns, it is known, can reflect such cultural differences. "Different social structures may generate different speech systems or linguistic codes. The latter entail for the individual specific principles of choice which regulate the selections he makes from the totality of options represented by a given language."[6] In other words, groups enjoying different social and cultural relations but sharing the same language will make use of different syntactic and lexical selections for every-

[5]Twenty-nine percent of men diarists wrote primarily about people, versus 64 percent of women diarists.

[6]Basil Bernstein, "Elaborated and Restricted Codes: Their Social Origins and Consequences," in Alfred G. Smith, ed., *Communication and Culture* (New York: Holt, Rinehart, and Winston, 1966), p. 429.

day communication in a given social situation; these language choices in use are known as codes.

6 The connections between speech and written language are complicated, the latter mediated by formal conventions that do not apply to everyday speech. But as Arthur Ponsonby notes in his study of diaries, diary writing may be the closest of all written forms to speech. The effort to conform to a stylistic convention requires too much of a person making daily entries. "You have no time to think, you do not want to think, you want to remember, you cannot consciously adopt any particular artifice; you jot down the day's doings either briefly or burst out impulsively here and there into detail; and without being conscious of it, you yourself emerge and appear out of the sum total of those jottings, however, brief they may be."[7] The overland diaries fit Ponsonby's characterization precisely; lacking in formalities, they are probably good, though limited, representations of the speech codes employed by men and women.

7 Basil Bernstein has distinguished between two general types of language codes in contemporary English speech that correspond remarkably well to the contrasting styles in the diary writings of these mid-nineteenth-century men and women. Men's diaries may be characterized by their use of a "restrictive" code, that is, a code drawn from a narrow range of choices: unelaborated prose, written in apparent haste, emphasizing the how rather than the why, with implicit as distinguished from explicit meanings. Such a code typically appears among people in close behavioral connection, sharing common assumptions and expectations. In this context group members can assume that their fellows understand without having everything stated explicitly. The "we" dominates the "I," because people assume a common identity. Restrictive codes are part of a communal situation; the communication of gesture, motion, and physical interaction often substitutes for language and discourages the development of expressive skills.

8 Women's writing best fits the contrasting designation of "elaborated" code: the use of extended description, modifying words and phrases, and explicit statement. Elaborated codes are required in situations where social connections are weak or lacking and language is employed to bridge the gap between individuals. In these circumstances people cannot assume a common understanding but must use

[7] Arthur Ponsonby, *English Diaries,* 2nd ed. (London: Methuen, 1923), p. 5.

language quite explicitly to inquire and inform. Consequently rather less is taken for granted; clarification, elucidation, and discovery are the primary tasks of verbal communication. This code, then, takes as its subject not a group but individuals (the "I" and the other), places a premium upon empathy, and is in general most often associated with a people-oriented content.

9 The analysis of the diary writing suggests again that essentially different social situations of men and women were associated with different cultural phenomena. The men's world was made of the stuff of action, a world of closely shared identifications, expectations, and assumptions. In the standardized and even ritualized behavior of men lay the ability to communicate without verbal expression. "The men generally," William Oliver reported, "are not very talkative." For women, however, articulation was at the very heart of their world, for verbal expression could achieve an interpersonal closeness that was socially denied by the exclusion of women from the public world and their isolation at home. In contradistinction to his silent men, Oliver remarked that he had overheard women "unfasten the sluices of their eloquence, and fairly maintain the character of their sex." A large part of women's rich cultural heritage was verbal—women's voluminous lore. And women were required to learn the cultural art of conversation and communication, including letter and diary writing, to make up for the social isolation of the farm.

10 Psychologically this analysis further suggests that the meek feminine character assumed that she needed to explain and elaborate her feelings in order to make herself understood. Women's empathy for others was the other side of women's concern that their true selves be truly communicated by taking time and care with language. Masculine characters, on the other hand, assumed that they were understood and saw no need to articulate things that seemed perfectly obvious to them. The face men presented to the world, however, was held rigid; no tears were allowed to soften the harsh exterior to reveal the emotional essence within. Men assumed that their public faces, silent and brooding, represented their true selves, but they were fooling themselves. Men hid their feelings from themselves, understood themselves in an incomplete way, but found comfort in the company of their similarly repressed brothers. These were men, in Avery Craven's well-chosen words, "with homely vices and virtues and with more than their share of half-starved emotions."

Additional Rhetorical Strategies

Illustration (throughout); Classification (paragraphs 7, 8); Definition (paragraphs 7, 8); Cause and Effect (paragraphs 9, 10).

Examining Words and Meaning

1. In what ways did the point of view in the emigrant diaries of women differ from that of men? What evidence does Faragher give to illustrate this difference?
2. Why do you think Faragher starts by referring to the "differences between the worlds" of men and women diarists? How would the effect of the opening have been different had he said "different experience" or "different styles"?
3. Check the following words in the dictionary, if necessary: syntactic (paragraph 5); lexical (paragraph 5); elucidation (paragraph 8); empathy (paragraph 8); contradistinction (paragraph 9).

Focusing on Structures and Strategies

1. Which of the three methods outlined for writing essays of comparison and contrast does Faragher use here? Suppose he had chosen a different method. How would this have changed the effect and the emphasis of the passage?
2. Why does Faragher go to such lengths in paragraph 6 to establish that diaries are closer than most other forms of writing to everyday speech? What objection is Faragher anticipating, and how might his argument be less convincing had he not anticipated it?

Suggestions for Further Discussion and Writing

1. Along with other members of your class, keep a journal for a few days or weeks, trying as much as possible to write as though you

were speaking. At the end of the period, read aloud or distribute some sample journal entries in class. Is it possible to make any general distinctions between the writing of the women in the class and that of the men?

2. After listening carefully to and observing the behavior of some of the people you know, write an essay in which you compare and contrast the speech and behavior of contemporary men and women. What, for example, do they talk about in informal social situations—people or things? Do women seem to need language more, as Faragher says the emigrant diarists did? Can you find evidence of restrictive or elaborated codes?

A Rhetoric of Disease

Susan Sontag

Susan Sontag has been a teacher of English, philosophy, and religion, a writer-in-residence at Rutgers University, a novelist, short-story writer, critic, screen writer, and director of motion pictures. She has received awards from the American Association of University Women, the Rockefeller Foundation, the Guggenheim Memorial Foundation, and was a recipient of the George Polk Memorial Award for contributions toward the better appreciation of theater, motion pictures, and literature. "Writing," she once remarked, "is a mysterious activity. One has to be, at different stages of conception and execution, in a state of extreme alertness and consciousness and in a state of great naivete and ignorance. Although this is probably true of the practice of any art, it may be more true of writing because the writer—unlike the painter or composer—works in a medium that one employs all the time, throughout one's waking life."

The following selection is from Illness As Metaphor *(1978), a study of how deeply rooted figurative language has interfered with our ability to come to terms with two of the most lethal diseases of the last two centuries. Susan Sontag compares the figurative significance of tuberculosis in the past with the figurative significance of cancer today, while contrasting their physical effects.*

1

1 Two diseases have been spectacularly, and similarly, encumbered by the trappings of metaphor: tuberculosis and cancer.

2 The fantasies inspired by TB in the last century, by cancer now, are responses to a disease thought to be intractable and capricious—that is, a disease not understood—in an era in which medicine's central premise is that all diseases can be cured. Such a disease is, by definition, mysterious. For as long as its cause was not understood and the ministrations of doctors remained so ineffective, TB was thought to be an insidious, implacable theft of a life. Now it is cancer's turn to be the disease that doesn't knock before it enters, cancer that fills the role of an illness experienced as a ruthless, secret invasion—a role it will keep until, one day, its etiology becomes as clear and its treatment as effective as those of TB have become.

3 Although the way in which disease mystifies is set against a backdrop of new expectations, the disease itself (once TB, cancer today) arouses thoroughly old-fashioned kinds of dread. Any disease that is treated as a mystery and acutely enough feared will be felt to be morally, if not literally, contagious. Thus, a surprisingly large number of people with cancer find themselves being shunned by relatives and friends and are the object of practices of decontamination by members of their household, as if cancer, like TB, were an infectious disease. Contact with someone afflicted with a disease regarded as a mysterious malevolency inevitably feels like a trespass; worse, like the violation of a taboo. The very names of such diseases are felt to have a magic power. In Stendhal's *Armance* (1827), the hero's mother refuses to say "tuberculosis," for fear that pronouncing the word will hasten the course of her son's malady. And Karl Menninger has observed (in *The Vital Balance*) that "the very word 'cancer' is said to kill some patients who would not have succumbed (so quickly) to the malignancy from which they suffer." This observation is offered in support of anti-intellectual pieties and a facile compassion all too triumphant in contemporary medicine and psychiatry. "Patients who consult us because of their suffering and their distress and their disability," he continues, "have every right to resent being plastered with a damning index tab." Dr. Menninger recommends that physicians generally abandon "names" and "labels" ("our function is to help these people, not to further afflict them")—which would mean, in effect, increasing secretiveness and medical paternalism. It is not naming as such that is pejorative or

damning, but the name "cancer." As long as a particular disease is treated as an evil, invincible predator, not just a disease, most people with cancer will indeed be demoralized by learning what disease they have. The solution is hardly to stop telling cancer patients the truth, but to rectify the conception of the disease, to de-mythicize it.

4 When, not so many decades ago, learning that one had TB was tantamount to hearing a sentence of death—as today, in the popular imagination, cancer equals death—it was common to conceal the identity of their disease from tuberculars and, after they died, from their children. Even with patients informed about their disease, doctors and family were reluctant to talk freely. "Verbally I don't learn anything definite," Kafka wrote to a friend in April 1924 from the sanatorium where he died two months later, "since in discussing tuberculosis . . . everybody drops into a shy, evasive, glassy-eyed manner of speech." Conventions of concealment with cancer are even more strenuous. In France and Italy it is still the rule for doctors to communicate a cancer diagnosis to the patient's family but not to the patient; doctors consider that the truth will be intolerable to all but exceptionally mature and intelligent patients. (A leading French oncologist has told me that fewer than a tenth of his patients know they have cancer.) In America—in part because of the doctors' fear of malpractice suits—there is now much more candor with patients, but the country's largest cancer hospital mails routine communications and bills to outpatients in envelopes that do not reveal the sender, on the assumption that the illness may be a secret from their families. Since getting cancer can be a scandal that jeopardizes one's love life, one's chance of promotion, even one's job, patients who know what they have tend to be extremely prudish, if not outright secretive, about their disease. And a federal law, the 1966 Freedom of Information Act, cites "treatment for cancer" in a clause exempting from disclosure matters whose disclosure "would be an unwarranted invasion of personal privacy." It is the only disease mentioned.

5 All this lying to and by cancer patients is a measure of how much harder it has become in advanced industrial societies to come to terms with death. As death is now an offensively meaningless event, so that disease widely considered a synonym for death is experienced as something to hide. The policy of equivocating about the nature of their disease with cancer patients reflects the conviction that dying people are best spared the news that they are dying, and that the good death is the sudden one, best of all if it happens while

we're unconscious or asleep. Yet the modern denial of death does not explain the extent of the lying and the wish to be lied to; it does not touch the deepest dread. Someone who has had a coronary is at least as likely to die of another one within a few years as someone with cancer is likely to die soon from cancer. But no one thinks of concealing the truth from a cardiac patient: there is nothing shameful about a heart attack. Cancer patients are lied to, not just because the disease is (or is thought to be) a death sentence, but because it is felt to be obscene—in the original meaning of that word: ill-omened, abominable, repugnant to the senses. Cardiac disease implies a weakness, trouble, failure that is mechanical; there is no disgrace, nothing of the taboo that once surrounded people afflicted with TB and still surrounds those who have cancer. The metaphors attached to TB and to cancer imply living processes of a particularly resonant and horrid kind.

2

6 Throughout most of their history, the metaphoric uses of TB and cancer crisscross and overlap. The *Oxford English Dictionary* records "consumption" in use as a synonym for pulmonary tuberculosis as early as 1398. (John of Trevisa: "Whan the blode is made thynne, soo folowyth consumpcyon and wastyng.") But the pre-modern understanding of cancer also invokes the notion of consumption. The OED gives as the early figurative definition of cancer: "Anything that frets, corrodes, corrupts, or consumes slowly and secretly." (Thomas Paynell in 1528: "A canker is a melancolye impostume, eatynge partes of the bodye.") The earliest literal definition of cancer is a growth, lump, or protuberance, and the disease's name—from the Greek *karkinos* and the Latin *cancer,* both meaning crab—was inspired, according to Galen, by the resemblance of an external tumor's swollen veins to a crab's legs; not, as many people think, because a metastatic disease crawls or creeps like a crab. But etymology indicates that tuberculosis was also once considered a type of abnormal extrusion: the word tuberculosis—from the Latin *tūberculum,* the diminutive of *tūber,* bump, swelling—means a morbid swelling, protuberance, projection, or growth. Rudolf Virchow, who founded the science of cellular pathology in the 1850s, thought of the tubercle as a tumor.

7 Thus, from late antiquity until quite recently, tuberculosis was—typologically—cancer. And cancer was described, like TB, as a

process in which the body was consumed. The modern conceptions of the two diseases could not be set until the advent of cellular pathology. Only with the microscope was it possible to grasp the distinctiveness of cancer, as a type of cellular activity, and to understand that the disease did not always take the form of an external or even palpable tumor. (Before the mid-nineteenth century, nobody could have identified leukemia as a form of cancer.) And it was not possible definitively to separate cancer from TB until after 1882, when tuberculosis was discovered to be a bacterial infection. Such advances in medical thinking enabled the leading metaphors of the two diseases to become truly distinct and, for the most part, contrasting. The modern fantasy about cancer could then begin to take shape—a fantasy which from the 1920s on would inherit most of the problems dramatized by the fantasies about TB, but with the two diseases and their symptoms conceived in quite different, almost opposing, ways.

8 TB is understood as a disease of one organ, the lungs, while cancer is understood as a disease that can turn up in any organ and whose outreach is the whole body.

9 TB is understood as a disease of extreme contrasts: white pallor and red flush, hyperactivity alternating with languidness. The spasmodic course of the disease is illustrated by what is thought of as the prototypical TB symptom, coughing. The sufferer is wracked by coughs, then sinks back, recovers breath, breathes normally; then coughs again. Cancer is a disease of growth (sometimes visible; more characteristically, inside), of abnormal, ultimately lethal growth that is measured, incessant, steady. Although there may be periods in which tumor growth is arrested (remissions), cancer produces no contrasts like the oxymorons of behavior—febrile activity, passionate resignation—thought to be typical of TB. The tubercular is pallid some of the time; the pallor of the cancer patient is unchanging.

10 TB makes the body transparent. The X-rays which are the standard diagnostic tool permit one, often for the first time, to see one's insides—to become transparent to oneself. While TB is understood to be, from early on, rich in visible symptoms (progressive emaciation, coughing, languidness, fever), and can be suddenly and dramatically revealed (the blood on the handkerchief), in cancer the main symptoms are thought to be, characteristically, invisible—until the last stage, when it is too late. The disease, often discovered by chance or through a routine medical checkup, can be far advanced

without exhibiting any appreciable symptoms. One has an opaque body that must be taken to a specialist to find out if it contains cancer. What the patient cannot perceive, the specialist will determine by analyzing tissues taken from the body. TB patients may see their X-rays or even possess them: the patients at the sanatorium in *The Magic Mountain* carry theirs around in their breast pockets. Cancer patients don't look at their biopsies.

11 TB was—still is—thought to produce spells of euphoria, increased appetite, exacerbated sexual desire. Part of the regimen for patients in *The Magic Mountain* is a second breakfast, eaten with gusto. Cancer is thought to cripple vitality, make eating an ordeal, deaden desire. Having TB was imagined to be an aphrodisiac, and to confer extraordinary powers of seduction. Cancer is considered to be desexualizing. But it is characteristic of TB that many of its symptoms are deceptive—liveliness that comes from enervation, rosy cheeks that look like a sign of health but come from fever—and an upsurge of vitality may be a sign of approaching death. (Such gushes of energy will generally be self-destructive, and may be destructive of others: recall the Old West legend of Doc Holliday, the tubercular gunfighter released from moral restraints by the ravages of his disease.) Cancer has only true symptoms.

12 TB is disintegration, febrilization, dematerialization; it is a disease of liquids—the body turning to phlegm and mucus and sputum and, finally, blood—and of air, of the need for better air. Cancer is degeneration, the body tissues turning to something hard. Alice James, writing in her journal a year before she died from cancer in 1892, speaks of "this unholy granite substance in my breast." But this lump is alive, a fetus with its own will. Novalis, in an entry written around 1798 for his encyclopedia project, defines cancer, along with gangrene, as "full-fledged *parasites*—they grow, are engendered, engender, have their structure, secrete, eat." Cancer is a demonic pregnancy. St. Jerome must have been thinking of a cancer when he wrote: "The one there with his swollen belly is pregnant with his own death" *("Alius tumenti aqualiculo mortem parturit").* Though the course of both diseases is emaciating, losing weight from TB is understood very differently from losing weight from cancer. In TB, the person is "consumed," burned up. In cancer, the patient is "invaded" by alien cells, which multiply, causing an atrophy or blockage of bodily functions. The cancer patient "shrivels" (Alice James's word) or "shrinks" (Wilhelm Reich's word).

13 TB is a disease of time; it speeds up life, highlights it, spiritual-

izes it. In both England and France, consumption "gallops." Cancer has stages rather than gaits; it is (eventually) "terminal." Cancer works slowly, insidiously: the standard euphemism in obituaries is that someone has "died after a long illness." Every characterization of cancer describes it as slow, and so it was first used metaphorically. "The word of hem crepith as a kankir," Wyclif wrote in 1382 (translating a phrase in II Timothy 2:17); and among the earliest figurative uses of cancer are as a metaphor for "idleness" and "sloth."[1] Metaphorically, cancer is not so much a disease of time as a disease or pathology of space. Its principal metaphors refer to topography (cancer "spreads" or "proliferates" or is "diffused"; tumors are surgically "excised"), and its most dreaded consequence, short of death, is the mutilation or amputation of part of the body.

14 TB is often imagined as a disease of poverty and deprivation—of thin garments, thin bodies, unheated rooms, poor hygiene, inadequate food. The poverty may not be as literal as Mimi's garret in *La Bohème;* the tubercular Marguerite Gautier in *La Dame aux Camélias* lives in luxury, but inside she is a waif. In contrast, cancer is a disease of middle-class life, a disease associated with affluence, with excess. Rich countries have the highest cancer rates, and the rising incidence of the disease is seen as resulting, in part, from a diet rich in fat and proteins and from the toxic effluvia of the industrial economy that creates affluence. The treatment of TB is identified with the stimulation of appetite, cancer treatment with nausea and the loss of appetite. The undernourished nourishing themselves—alas, to no avail. The overnourished, unable to eat.

15 The TB patient was thought to be helped, even cured, by a change in environment. There was a notion that TB was a wet disease, a disease of humid and dank cities. The inside of the body became damp ("moisture in the lungs" was a favored locution) and had to be dried out. Doctors advised travel to high, dry places—the mountains, the desert. But no change of surroundings is thought to help the cancer patient. The fight is all inside one's own body. It may be, is increasingly thought to be, something in the environment that has caused the cancer. But once cancer is present, it cannot be reversed or diminished by a move to a better (that is, less carcinogenic) environment.

[1]As cited in the OED, which gives as an early figurative use of "canker": "that pestilent and most infectious canker, idlenesse"—T. Palfreyman, 1564. And of "cancer" (which replaced "canker" around 1700): "Sloth is a Cancer, eating up that Time Princes should cultivate for Things sublime"—Edmund Ken, 1711.

16 TB is thought to be relatively painless. Cancer is thought to be, invariably, excruciatingly painful. TB is thought to provide an easy death, while cancer is the spectacularly wretched one. For over a hundred years TB remained the preferred way of giving death a meaning—an edifying, refined disease. Nineteenth-century literature is stocked with descriptions of almost symptomless, unfrightened, beatific deaths from TB, particularly of young people, such as Little Eva in *Uncle Tom's Cabin* and Dombey's son Paul in *Dombey and Son* and Smike in *Nicholas Nickleby,* where Dickens described TB as the "dread disease" which "refines" death

> of its grosser aspect . . . in which the struggle between soul and body is so gradual, quiet, and solemn, and the result so sure, that day by day, and grain by grain, the mortal part wastes and withers away, so that the spirit grows light and sanguine with its lightening load. . . .

Contrast these ennobling, placid TB deaths with the ignoble, agonizing cancer deaths of Eugene Gant's father in Thomas Wolfe's *Of Time and the River* and of the sister in Bergman's film *Cries and Whispers.* The dying tubercular is pictured as made more beautiful and more soulful; the person dying of cancer is portrayed as robbed of all capacities of self-transcendence, humiliated by fear and agony.

Additional Rhetorical Strategies

Definition (paragraphs 2, 6, 12, 13); Illustration (throughout); Cause and Effect (throughout); Narration (paragraphs 7, 9).

Examining Words and Meaning

1. How does Sontag characterize the attitude of modern industrial societies toward death? What differences does she see between our feelings about dying from cardiac disease and our feelings about cancer? Why does she focus on the latter?
2. When, according to Sontag, were people first able to distinguish between tuberculosis and cancer? What do the ways in which the words for the two diseases were used in centuries past tell us about the differences between past and present perceptions of them? And

what are the major differences that have arisen between our perceptions of cancer and our perceptions of tuberculosis, now that we can distinguish the two?

3. Check in the dictionary, as needed, for the meanings of these words: trappings (paragraph 1); pejorative (paragraph 3); tantamount (paragraph 4); equivocating (paragraph 5); etymology (paragraph 6); euphemism (paragraph 13); carcinogenic (paragraph 15).

Focusing on Structures and Strategies

1. In what part of the essay does Sontag stress the similarities between conceptions of tuberculosis and conceptions of cancer? In what part does she stress the differences? How does she lead up to the turning point between these two sections?

2. What seems to be the principle of organization for paragraphs 8 through 16? Look, for example, at the way each of these paragraphs opens. What are the advantages of this sort of approach? What might some of the possible disadvantages be?

Suggestions for Further Discussion and Writing

1. Sontag's writing makes us think about one thing we would probably rather avoid thinking about—dying. Does what she says in paragraph 5 seem to you to be an accurate evaluation of our society's—and our—attitude toward death and dying? Is she correct, for example, in saying that cancer touches off greater fears, greater feelings of repugnance, than a heart attack?

2. Sontag says that tuberculosis, in generations past, and cancer, in the present, have been regarded with fascination as taboo diseases. Apparently, then, taboos change over time. What are some other taboos—sexual, religious, medical, and the like—that you suspect have been altered during the past generation or two? Choose one such taboo and find someone of a different generation (your grandparents or your parents) and ask the person to talk about how that taboo was regarded ten, twenty, thirty, or forty years ago. Write an essay comparing the attitude of your generation toward the subject with the attitude of the earlier generation. What differences are there? Which attitude do you prefer?

Analogy

1 When we find a number of point-by-point resemblances between the features of two different things—like the heart and a pump or the human brain and a computer—we are thinking with the help of analogy. In expository writing, analogy is particularly useful for making abstract or hard-to-follow subjects easier to visualize and understand. Analogy also plays an important organizing role in such narrative forms as fables and allegories. In descriptive writing it can help make our observations more vivid and concrete. In argument, analogy is a method of reasoning in which we infer *possible* similarities between two things on the basis of *established* similarities. In general, analogy works in our writing and thinking in two ways: first, as a means of illustration by which we make difficult topics easier to understand; and, second, as a means of reasoning by which we can draw conclusions for an argument.

2 Analogy often is loosely used to describe many types of comparison. For clear thinking and writing, however, it seems best to stay close to the term's original mathematical sense of *proportion:* one thing is to another as a third thing is to a fourth. This form of analogy shows up frequently on aptitude tests. A simple illustration would be:

Head : Hat :: Foot : *X*
X is

(A) Book	(C) Shoe
(B) Sweater	(D) Ankle

We should have no trouble coming up with "(C) Shoe" as our answer. Quite clearly, a shoe bears the same relationship to a foot that a hat does to a head. To supply the missing part of the analogy, we first determined the relationship between the two given parts of our equation, then found the term that made the relationship between the second pair equivalent to the first.

3 The key word here is *relationship.* The above analogy (admittedly, a simple one) works as all analogies do—by establishing an equivalency of relationships. Shoes and hats are similar here not because they are both objects of clothing but because as objects of clothing they bear similar relations to corresponding parts of the body, a relation that a sweater—also an article of clothing—does not bear to foot. We can keep our root analogy going quite easily in this case by extending the equation so that it eventually covers all body parts and their corresponding articles of clothing.

4 One reason that the hat–shoe analogy looks so simple is that it draws all of its comparisons from the same class of objects. But not all analogies work in such an elementary fashion. In fact, the kinds of analogies that require the most thought (and that we can learn the most from) work by demonstrating similar relations between different classes of phenomena. Analogies of this type are often used in scientific explanation—for example, the customary comparisons of the heart to a pump or the brain to a computer. Consider the brain–computer resemblance. The brain is said to be like a computer because some of the parts and functions of the brain are related to the brain in ways that certain parts and functions of a computer are related to the computer. Unlike our earlier example, the similarity is one of relations within two objects belonging to two entirely different classes (one a part of the body, the other a human invention).

5 We can obtain a clearer notion of how analogies are constructed by diagramming the example of the brain–computer comparison. The basic analogical equation $A : B :: C : D$ might be restated as follows:

A: B (Brain) $::$ $C : D$ (Computer)
A_1 (Memory) : $B :: C_1$ (Storage System) : D
A_2 (Information) : $B :: C_2$ (Input data) : D
A_3 (Synapses) : $B :: C_3$ (Circuitry) : D
A_4 (Neuron) : $B :: C_4$ (Bit) : D

Note that the analogy proceeds by establishing a series of point-by-point correspondences that are linked both horizontally (A_1 is like C_1) and vertically ($A_1 \ldots A_2 \ldots A_3$ are all parts of the same object). In the physical and social sciences an effective analogy will usually contain a high degree of such point-by-point correspondences. The more characteristics B and D possess in common, the more probable any additional characteristic of D will be shared by B, and the more legitimate the overall comparison becomes. If the pattern of correspondences between both parts of the analogy (the analogates) is convincingly extensive, scientists can then make fairly reliable predictions about the similarity of additional features. Particularly strong analogies—for example, models—can provide the ground for forceful inductive arguments.

6 Yet, despite the intellectual attraction of analogies and the working models they can lead to, we should approach argument by analogy with a good deal of caution. No matter how legitimately constructed, analogies frequently suppress as many dissimilarities as they express similarities. A computer, for example, bears a resemblance only to the cognitive areas of the brain. Vast resources of the brain affecting emotions, perceptions, sensations, balance, and spatial orientation are overlooked by the analogy. And even with respect to cognition it is potentially troublesome to compare a completely input-dependent machine to an organism which still gives every indication of being at least partially "self-programming." No psychiatrist has yet had to analyze a computer's dreams.

7 These limitations should not discourage us from using analogy in our thinking and writing. Carefully worked-out analogies can be of enormous value in helping us organize and express our ideas. Subjects especially abstract or difficult to grasp can be more readily comprehended or more easily visualized when referred analogically to more familiar or more easily understood structures. Speaking of the brain *as if* it were a computer or the heart *as if* it were a pump helps us to grasp concretely some of the functions of those complex organs in ways we might not be able to do if we thought about them directly. In "The Salmon Instinct" (p. 447), William Humphrey shows that analogy can also be an effective means of explaining human behavior that might otherwise be inexplicable.

8 Though analogies can be enormously useful in helping us construct forceful arguments and explain complicated matters clearly, they also can give our writing pictorial vitality and emphasis. For example, here is a passage in which Henry David Thoreau uses an analogy for visual impact:

> Cape Cod is the bared and bended arm of Massachusetts! the shoulder is at Buzzard's Bay; the elbow, or crazy-bone, at Cape Mallebarre; the wrist at Truro; and the sandy fist at Provincetown,—behind which the State stands on her guard, with her back to the Green Mountains, and her feet planted on the floor of the ocean, like an athlete protecting her Bay,—boxing with northeast storms, and, ever and anon, heaving up her Atlantic adversary from the lap of earth,—ready to thrust forward her other fist, which keeps guard the while upon her breast at Cape Ann.

Note that Thoreau doesn't merely state that his native Massachusetts is a rugged land; he makes us *see* that ruggedness by means of an effective analogy.

9 Since all analogies can be diagrammed according to the ratio formula shown above, let's break down Thoreau's analogy into its point-by-point resemblances to observe how it works. The central resemblance—the root comparison from which the parallel relationships originate—depends upon Thoreau's connection between the state of Massachusetts and the human body. The diagram looks as follows:

A (Part of the State) : B (Massachusetts) :: C (Part of the Body) : D (The Body)
A_1 (Cape Cod) : B (Massachusetts) :: C_1 (The Arm) : D (The Body)
A_2 (Buzzard's Bay) : B :: C_2 (The Shoulder) : D
A_3 (Cape Mallebarre) : B :: C_3 (The Elbow) : D
A_4 (Truro) : B :: C_4 (The Wrist) : D
A_5 (Provincetown) : B :: C_5 (The Fist) : D
A_6 (Cape Ann) : B :: C_6 (The Breast) : D

Notice, too, how Thoreau enhances the visual power of his analogy by comparing Massachusetts not just to the human body but to the human body in a fighter's stance.

10 When used imaginatively, analogy can be far more than a rhetorical strategy for simplification or emphasis: it can be a stimulus to creative thinking. By linking together two separate conceptual or physical entities, we may begin to perceive new implications and new connections that may lead to an entirely altered understanding of our subject. An analogy between the relation of God the Father to the Trinity and the relation of the sun to the solar system led the German astronomer Johannes Kepler (1571–1630) to a radically new conception of planetary motion. The English physician William Harvey (1578–1657) reported that the notion of the circulation of blood in the body first occurred to him when he noticed that the "flaps" inside the

veins behaved as valves and that the heart was essentially a pump. Other kinds of analogies have left an indelible mark on human consciousness. We see the passage of human life as a pilgrimage or voyage, the world as a stage, time as a river, largely because of deep-rooted analogies sustained by myth and literature throughout the ages.

11 In all analogies, we should expect to find some nonanalogical elements, areas that do not correspond exactly. Consequently, a potentially vital analogy will always involve a conflict between its logical limitations and its rhetorical usefulness. When we work with an analogy, we should try beforehand to sketch out the full range of its relational correspondences. Our "blueprint" will then help us discover precisely how much strain our comparison will bear. It will also help us decide how many points of similarity our composition actually requires. The "extendibility" of an analogy will play a key part in determining the range and organization of our ideas, but the effect of a potentially rich analogy can be virtually negated if we drag out resemblances to the point of triviality.

12 In the selections that follow, we will see how various writers have put analogy to work effectively, making the abstract concrete, the unobservable observable, the remote near, the strange familiar.

The Attic of the Brain

Lewis Thomas

A powerful method of reasoning, analogy can also be used as an effective method of explanation. Writers will often turn to analogy when they want to make abstract ideas clear and vivid, when they want their readers to be able to picture concepts not easily pictured—such as how the mind works. In this essay from Late Night Thoughts on Listening to Mahler's Ninth Symphony, *Lewis Thomas, a writer whose essays are embedded with vivid analogies, attempts to make us aware of the close resemblances between human memory and the dusty attics of old houses. To accomplish this, Thomas constructs the following core analogy: the brain is like a house. This comparison then allows him to understand the function of memory in the brain as similar to the way attics function in houses. It also allows him to consider some of the ways that changes in architecture resemble fashionable changes in life-style.*

1 My parents' house had an attic, the darkest and strangest part of the building, reachable only by placing a stepladder beneath the trapdoor and filled with unidentifiable articles too important to be thrown out with the trash but no longer suitable to have at hand. This mysterious space was the memory of the place. After many years all the things deposited in it became, one by one, lost to consciousness. But they were still there, we knew, safely and comfortably stored in the tissues of the house.

2 These days most of us live in smaller, more modern houses or in apartments, and attics have vanished. Even the deep closets in which we used to pile things up for temporary forgetting are rarely designed into new homes.

3 Everything now is out in the open, openly acknowledged and displayed, and whenever we grow tired of a memory, an old chair, a trunkful of old letters, they are carted off to the dump for burning.

4 This has seemed a healthier way to live, except maybe for the smoke—everything out to be looked at, nothing strange hidden under the roof, nothing forgotten because of no place left in impenetrable darkness to forget. Openness is the new life-style, no undisclosed belongings, no private secrets. Candor is the rule in architecture. The house is a machine for living, and what kind of a machine would hide away its worn-out, obsolescent parts?

5 But it is in our nature as human beings to clutter, and we hanker for places set aside, reserved for storage. We tend to accumulate and outgrow possessions at the same time, and it is an endlessly discomforting mental task to keep sorting out the ones to get rid of. We might, we think, remember them later and find a use for them, and if they are gone for good, off to the dump, this is a source of nervousness. I think it may be one of the reasons we drum our fingers so much these days.

6 We might take a lesson here from what has been learned about our brains in this century. We thought we discovered, first off, the attic, although its existence has been mentioned from time to time by all the people we used to call great writers. What we really found was the trapdoor and a stepladder, and off we clambered, shining flashlights into the corners, vacuuming the dust out of bureau drawers,

puzzling over the names of objects, tossing them down to the floor below, and finally paying around fifty dollars an hour to have them carted off for burning.

7 After several generations of this new way of doing things we took up openness and candor with the febrile intensity of a new religion, everything laid out in full view, and as in the design of our new houses it seemed a healthier way to live, except maybe again for smoke.

8 And now, I think, we have a new kind of worry. There is no place for functionless, untidy, inexplicable notions, no dark comfortable parts of the mind to hide away the things we'd like to keep but at the same time forget. The attic is still there, but with the trapdoor always open and the stepladder in place we are always in and out of it, flashing lights around, naming everything, unmystified.

9 I have an earnest proposal for psychiatry, a novel set of therapeutic rules, although I know it means waiting in line.

10 Bring back the old attic. Give new instructions to the patients who are made nervous by our times, including me, to make a conscious effort to hide a reasonable proportion of thought. It would have to be a gradual process, considering how far we have come in the other direction talking, talking all the way. Perhaps only one or two thoughts should be repressed each day, at the outset. The easiest, gentlest way might be to start with dreams, first by forbidding the patient to mention any dream, much less to recount its details, then encouraging the outright forgetting that there was a dream at all, remembering nothing beyond the vague sense that during sleep there had been the familiar sound of something shifting and sliding, up under the roof.

11 We might, in this way, regain the kind of spontaneity and zest for ideas, things popping into the mind, uncontrollable and ungovernable thoughts, the feel that this notion is somehow connected unaccountably with that one. We could come again into possession of real memory, the kind of memory that can come only from jumbled forgotten furniture, old photographs, fragments of music.

12 It has been one of the great errors of our time to think that by thinking about thinking, and then talking about it, we could possibly straighten out and tidy up our minds. There is no delusion more damaging than to get the idea in your head that you understand the functioning of your own brain. Once you acquire such a notion, you run the danger of moving in to take charge, guiding your thoughts, shepherding your mind from place to place, *controlling* it, making lists

of regulations. The human mind is not meant to be governed, certainly not by any book of rules yet written; it is supposed to run itself, and we are obliged to follow it along, trying to keep up with it as best we can. It is all very well to be aware of your awareness, even proud of it, but never try to operate it. You are not up to the job.

13 I leave it to the analysts to work out the techniques for doing what now needs doing. They are presumably the professionals most familiar with the route, and all they have to do is turn back and go the other way, session by session, step by step. It takes a certain amount of hard swallowing and a lot of revised jargon, and I have great sympathy for their plight, but it is time to reverse course.

14 If after all, as seems to be true, we are endowed with unconscious minds in our brains, these should be regarded as normal structures, installed wherever they are for a purpose. I am not sure what they are built to contain, but as a biologist, impressed by the usefulness of everything alive, I would take it for granted that they are useful, probably indispensable organs of thought. It cannot be a bad thing to own one, but I would no more think of meddling with it than trying to exorcise my liver, an equally mysterious apparatus. Until we know a lot more, it would be wise, as we have learned from other fields in medicine, to let them be, above all not to interfere. Maybe, even—and this is the notion I wish to suggest to my psychiatric friends—to stock them up, put more things into them, make *use* of them. Forget whatever you feel like forgetting. From time to time, practice *not* being open, discover new things *not* to talk about, learn reserve, hold the tongue. But above all, develop the human talent for forgetting words, phrases, whole unwelcome sentences, all experiences involving wincing. If we should ever lose the loss of memory, we might lose as well that most attractive of signals ever flashed from the human face, the blush. If we should give away the capacity for embarrassment, the touch of fingertips might be the next to go, and then the suddenness of laughter, the unaccountable sure sense of something gone wrong, and, finally, the marvelous conviction that being human is the best thing to be.

15 Attempting to operate one's own mind, powered by such a magical instrument as the human brain, strikes me as rather like using the world's biggest computer to add columns of figures, or towing a Rolls-Royce with a nylon rope.

16 I have tried to think of a name for the new professional activity, but each time I think of a good one I forget it before I can get it

written down. Psychorepression is the only one I've hung on to, but I can't guess at the fee schedule.

Reading for Rhetorical Strategy

Lewis Thomas suggests his central analogy in the title of his essay. To describe the brain as possessing an attic is to picture the brain in terms of a house, with memory being to the brain what the attic is to a house. Thomas brings these connections directly together in his opening paragraph, referring to a house as though it were a living organism. The expository point of the analogy, however, becomes clear in paragraph 2, when we realize that Thomas has extended the architectural resemblance to make a point about contemporary life. Just as houses have become more "open," so too has the "new life-style." Thomas then sees the growing popularity of candor and psychotherapy in terms of the vanishing attic and proposes a return to some degree of repression. Notice how throughout the essay Thomas finds connections between the language of architecture and the language of psychology. In paragraph 14, for example, he recommends that our unconscious minds "be regarded as normal structures, installed wherever they are for a purpose." So rich is Thomas's analogy that throughout his essay the concrete details related to attics—the trapdoors, the clutter, the mysterious articles—suggest corresponding images for the mind.

The Allegory of the Cave

Socrates, Glaucon

Plato

The writings of Plato (ca. 429–347 B.C.) have bequeathed a rich intellectual vision which has remained the foundation for much of subsequent philosophical inquiry in Western civilization. Born of aristocratic Athenian parents, Plato traveled widely in Egypt, Italy, and Sicily after the death of his mentor, Socrates, in 399 B.C. Sometime after

387 B.C., Plato founded his Academy, in which he taught until his death. The most famous student at the Academy was Aristotle, who studied with Plato for twenty years.

The following selection from Plato's Republic dramatizes his belief in a hierarchy of knowledge. As is evident in his recounting of our plight in the allegory of the cave, Plato believes that we are trapped by the deception of our senses. He envisions us as prisoners in a cave, able to see only the shadows of reality. Philosophical education, expressed in the dialectical form of argument (what he calls "dialogue"), can best free us from the constraints of our limited view of the world and enable us to know the most profound meaning of good, beauty, truth.

1 And now, I said, let me show in a figure how far our nature is enlightened or unenlightened: Behold! human beings living in an underground den, which has a mouth open toward the light and reaching all along the den; here they have been from their childhood, and have their legs and necks chained so that they cannot move, and can only see before them, being prevented by the chains from turning round their heads. Above and behind them a fire is blazing at a distance, and between the fire and the prisoners there is a raised way; and you will see, if you look, a low wall built along the way, like the screen which marionette-players have in front of them, over which they show the puppets.

2 I see.

3 And do you see, I said, men passing along the wall carrying all sorts of vessels, and statues and figures of animals made of wood and stone and various materials, which appear over the wall? Some of them are talking, others silent.

4 You have shown me a strange image, and they are strange prisoners.

5 Like ourselves, I replied; and they see only their own shadows, or the shadows of one another, which the fire throws on the opposite wall of the cave?

6 True, he said; how could they see anything but the shadows if they were never allowed to move their heads?

7 And of the objects which are being carried in like manner they would only see the shadows?

8 Yes, he said.

9 And if they were able to converse with one another, would they not suppose that they were naming what was actually before them?

10 Very true.

11 And suppose further that the prison had an echo which came from the other side, would they not be sure to fancy when one of the passers-by spoke that the voice which they heard came from the passing shadow?

12 No question, he replied.

13 To them, I said, the truth would be literally nothing but the shadows of the images.

14 That is certain.

15 And now look again, and see what will naturally follow if the prisoners are released and disabused of their error. At first, when any of them is liberated and compelled suddenly to stand up and turn his neck round and walk and look toward the light, he will suffer sharp pains; the glare will distress him, and he will be unable to see the realities of which in his former state he had seen the shadows; and then conceive someone saying to him, that what he saw before was an illusion, but that now, when he is approaching nearer to being and his eye is turned toward more real existence, he has a clearer vision—what will be his reply? And you may further imagine that his instructor is pointing to the objects as they pass and requiring him to name them—will he not be perplexed? Will he not fancy that the shadows which he formerly saw are truer than the objects which are now shown to him?

16 Far truer.

17 And if he is compelled to look straight at the light, will he not have a pain in his eyes which will make him turn away to take refuge in the objects of vision which he can see, and which he will conceive to be in reality clearer than the things which are now being shown to him?

18 True, he said.

19 And suppose once more, that he is reluctantly dragged up a steep and rugged ascent, and held fast until he is forced into the presence of the sun himself, is he not likely to be pained and irritated? When he approaches the light his eyes will be dazzled, and he will not be able to see anything at all of what are now called realities.

20 Not all in a moment, he said.

21 He will require to grow accustomed to the sight of the upper world. And first he will see the shadows best, next the reflections of men and other objects in the water, and then the objects themselves; then he will gaze upon the light of the moon and the stars and the

spangled heaven; and he will see the sky and the stars by night better than the sun or the light of the sun by day?

22 Certainly.

23 Last of all he will be able to see the sun, and not mere reflections of him in the water, but he will see him in his own proper place, and not in another; and he will contemplate him as he is.

24 Certainly.

25 He will then proceed to argue that this is he who gives the season and the years, and is the guardian of all that is in the visible world, and in a certain way the cause of all things which he and his fellows have been accustomed to behold?

26 Clearly, he said, he would first see the sun and then reason about him.

27 And when he remembered his old habitation, and the wisdom of the den and his fellow-prisoners, do you not suppose that he would felicitate himself on the change, and pity them?

28 Certainly, he would.

29 And if they were in the habit of conferring honors among themselves on those who were quickest to observe the passing shadows and to remark which of them went before, and which followed after, and which were together; and who were therefore best able to draw conclusions as to the future, do you think that he would care for such honors and glories, or envy the possessors of them? Would he not say with Homer,

> "Better to be the poor servant of a poor master,"

and to endure anything, rather than think as they do and live after their manner?

30 Yes, he said, I think that he would rather suffer anything than entertain these false notions and live in this miserable manner.

31 Imagine once more, I said, such a one coming suddenly out of the sun to be replaced in his old situation; would he not be certain to have his eyes full of darkness?

32 To be sure, he said.

33 And if there were a contest, and he had to compete in measuring the shadows with the prisoners who had never moved out of the den, while his sight was still weak, and before his eyes had become steady (and the time which would be needed to acquire this new habit of sight might be very considerable), would he not be ridiculous? Men would say of him that up he went and down he came

without his eyes; and that it was better not even to think of ascending; and if anyone tried to loose another and lead him up to the light, let them only catch the offender, and they would put him to death.

34 No question, he said.

35 This entire allegory, I said, you may now append, dear Glaucon, to the previous argument; the prison-house is the world of sight, the light of the fire is the sun, and you will not misapprehend me if you interpret the journey upward to be the ascent of the soul into the intellectual world according to my poor belief, which, at your desire, I have expressed—whether rightly or wrongly, God knows. But, whether true or false, my opinion is that in the world of knowledge the idea of good appears last of all, and is seen only with an effort; and, when seen, is also inferred to be the universal author of all things beautiful and right, parent of light and of the lord of light in this visible world, and the immediate source of reason and truth in the intellectual; and that this is the power upon which he who would act rationally either in public or private life must have his eye fixed.

36 I agree, he said, as far as I am able to understand you.

37 Moreover, I said, you must not wonder that those who attain to this beatific vision are unwilling to descend to human affairs; for their souls are ever hastening into the upper world where they desire to dwell; which desire of theirs is very natural, if our allegory may be trusted.

38 Yes, very natural.

39 And is there anything surprising in one who passes from divine contemplations to the evil state of man, misbehaving himself in a ridiculous manner; if, while his eyes are blinking and before he has become accustomed to the surrounding darkness, he is compelled to fight in courts of law, or in other places, about the images or the shadows of images of justice, and is endeavoring to meet the conceptions of those who have never yet seen absolute justice?

40 Anything but surprising, he replied.

41 Anyone who has common-sense will remember that the bewilderments of the eyes are of two kinds, and arise from two causes, either from coming out of the light or from going into the light, which is true of the mind's eye, quite as much as of the bodily eye; and he who remembers this when he sees anyone whose vision is perplexed and weak, will not be too ready to laugh; he will first ask whether that soul of man has come out of the brighter life, and is unable to see because unaccustomed to the dark, or having turned from dark-

ness to the day is dazzled by excess of light. And he will count the one happy in his condition and state of being, and he will pity the other; or, if he have a mind to laugh at the soul which comes from below into the light, there will be more reason in this than in the laugh which greets him who returns from above out of the light into the den.

42 That, he said, is a very just distinction.

Additional Rhetorical Strategies

Description (paragraph 1); Cause and Effect (throughout); Classification (paragraph 40); Argument (throughout).

Examining Words and Meaning

1. Identify the important elements of the allegory of the cave. What is each of these elements meant to represent about the human condition? In what ways is the journey out of the cave intended as an allegory of the search for knowledge? What is the end of that search?
2. How does the newly released prisoner of the cave respond if he is forced into the light? How can he come to see the light? What does this suggest about Plato's views about the nature of learning?

Focusing on Structures and Strategies

1. Analogy works by establishing a series of part-by-part resemblances between two different things. Outline the series of point-by-point resemblances that Plato creates in this selection from the *Republic.* At what point does he explicitly introduce the analogy? How does he develop this analogy?
2. What is the effect of presenting his "lesson" in the form of a dialogue? What principles of argument underpin the structure of this dialogue? Support your response by pointing to specific passages.

3. What happens to the liberated prisoner who then returns to the cave? How does he regard the actions of the other prisoners? To what do the contests and honors conferred among the prisoners correspond allegorically? Why, in effect, do you suppose that Plato, in terms of the allegory he is creating, does not simply conclude when the person has "seen the light"?

4. This excerpt from Plato's *Republic* not only provides an allegory for the search for knowledge, it also dramatizes the enlightenment of a student by means of a dialogue with his teacher. Given Plato's view of the coming into knowledge, why do you think he communicated his "lesson" by means of an allegory—rather than using some more straightforward method?

Suggestions for Further Discussion and Writing

1. Try writing an essay in which you create an analogy to illustrate how "enlightened or unenlightened" contemporary Americans are. Set your analogy within a description of some portion of a landscape—a mountain, a lake, a river, a valley. Extend the analogy as far as you can, but do not let it become far-fetched.

2. This selection from Plato's *Republic* is one of the most famous stories in Western civilization. Write an essay in which you develop an analogy between a well-known story and some contemporary issue that interests you. If you started, for example, with the story of Cinderella, what in the contemporary world might she represent? What would the prince stand for? The fairy godmother? Be sure that the details you emphasize in your narration will fit easily into the analogy you have in mind.

3. In addition to its instructional purposes, analogy is often used in satire and parody: the reader is surprised to discover that the author's subject is actually something other than what it seems. Write an essay in which you use an analogy to satirize or parody an established institution or group of people. Suppose, for example, that you want to poke fun at politicians and decide to do so by using radio disk jockies as your subject. How would you find a set of resemblances that would permit you to discuss one group in terms of another? Once you have constructed a set of point-by-point resemblances, work these into an essay that satirizes the behavior of politicians without directly mentioning politicians. Have fun with the language. What "record," for example, would a D.J. run on?

Reading the River

Mark Twain

One of America's outstanding novelists and humorists, Samuel Langhorne Clemens (Mark Twain) was born near the Mississippi River, in the town of Florida, Missouri, in 1835. Widely read and admired in his own time, Twain's classic novels, The Adventures of Tom Sawyer *(1876) and* The Adventures of Huckleberry Finn *(1885), have secured him a prominent place in American literary history.*

Twain was also a prolific journalist, essayist, and writer of nonfiction. He published a series of articles on his years as an apprentice pilot on the Mississippi River in The Atlantic *in 1875. In 1882, Twain's publisher suggested that he use these essays as the basis for a book and urged Twain to revisit the scenes of his earlier exploits. But times—and life on the Mississippi—had changed greatly since his years as a cub pilot; the river had lost much of its antebellum "romance and beauty." Twain published his youthful and seasoned views of life on the river in a book-length autobiographical narrative,* Life on the Mississippi *(1883). In the following selection, Twain creates a series of striking analogies to express a vivid sense of the wisdom he acquired while learning his trade.*

1 . . . The face of the water, in time, became a wonderful book—a book that was a dead language to the uneducated passenger but which told its mind to me without reserve, delivering its most cherished secrets as clearly as if it uttered them with a voice. And it was not a book to be read once and thrown aside, for it had a new story to tell every day. Throughout the long twelve hundred miles there was never a page that was void of interest, never one that you could leave unread without loss, never one that you would want to skip, thinking you could find higher enjoyment in some other thing. There never was so wonderful a book written by man, never one whose interest was so absorbing, so unflagging, so sparklingly renewed with every reperusal. The passenger who could not read it was charmed with a peculiar sort of faint dimple on its surface (on the rare occa-

sions when he did not overlook it altogether) but to the pilot that was an *italicized* passage; indeed it was more than that, it was a legend of the largest capitals with a string of shouting exclamation-points at the end of it, for it meant that a wreck or a rock was buried there that could tear the life out of the strongest vessel that ever floated. It is the faintest and simplest expression the water ever makes, and the most hideous to a pilot's eye. In truth, the passenger who could not read this book saw nothing but all manner of pretty pictures in it, painted by the sun and shaded by the clouds, whereas to the trained eye these were not pictures at all, but the grimmest and most dead-earnest of reading matter.

2 Now when I had mastered the language of this water, and had come to know every trifling feature that bordered the great river as familiarly as I knew the letters of the alphabet, I had made a valuable acquisition. But I had lost something, too. I had lost something which could never be restored to me while I lived. All the grace, the beauty, the poetry, had gone out of the majestic river! I still kept in mind a certain wonderful sunset which I witnessed when steamboating was new to me. A broad expanse of the river was turned to blood; in the middle distance the red hue brightened into gold, through which a solitary log came floating, black and conspicuous; in one place a long, slanting mark lay sparkling upon the water; in another the surface was broken by boiling, tumbling rings, that were as many-tinted as an opal; where the ruddy flush was faintest, was a smooth spot that was covered with graceful circles and radiating lines, ever so delicately traced; the shore on our left was densely wooded, and the somber shadow that fell from this forest was broken in one place by a long, ruffled trail that shone like silver; and high above the forest wall a clean-stemmed dead tree waved a single leafy bough that glowed like a flame in the unobstructed splendor that was flowing from the sun. There were graceful curves, reflected images, woody heights, soft distances; and over the whole scene, far and near, the dissolving lights drifted steadily, enriching it every passing moment with new marvels of coloring.

3 I stood like one bewitched. I drank it in, in a speechless rapture. The world was new to me, and I had never seen anything like this at home. But as I have said, a day came when I began to cease from noting the glories and the charms which the moon and the sun and the twilight wrought upon the river's face; another day came when I ceased altogether to note them. Then, if that sunset scene had been

repeated, I should have looked upon it without rapture, and should have commented upon it, inwardly, after this fashion: "This sun means that we are going to have wind to-morrow; that floating log means that the river is rising, small thanks to it; that slanting mark on the water refers to a bluff reef which is going to kill somebody's steamboat one of these nights, if it keeps on stretching out like that; those tumbling 'boils' show a dissolving bar and a changing channel there; the lines and circles in the slick water over yonder are a warning that that troublesome place is shoaling up dangerously; that silver streak in the shadow of the forest is the 'break' from a new snag, and he has located himself in the very best place he could have found to fish for steamboats; that tall dead tree, with a single living branch, is not going to last long, and then how is a body ever going to get through this blind place at night without the friendly old landmark?"

4 No, the romance and beauty were all gone from the river. All the value any feature of it had for me now was the amount of usefulness it could furnish toward compassing the safe piloting of a steamboat. Since those days, I have pitied doctors from my heart. What does the lovely flush in a beauty's cheek mean to a doctor but a "break" that ripples above some deadly disease? Are not all her visible charms sown thick with what are to him the signs and symbols of hidden decay? Does he ever see her beauty at all, or doesn't he simply view her professionally and comment upon her unwholesome condition all to himself? And doesn't he sometimes wonder whether he has gained most or lost most by learning his trade?

Additional Rhetorical Strategies

Comparison and Contrast (paragraph 1); Description (paragraph 2); Cause and Effect (paragraph 3).

Examining Words and Meaning

1. According to Twain, in what sense is the river like a book? How does this relate to Twain's ability to see signs of what lies beneath the surface of the river? What is gained by being able to read that

book? What is lost? What, in effect, is the purpose of Twain's using an analogy to describe the Mississippi?

2. Review the Introduction to this section, where analogy is defined as the writer's effort to establish a point-by-point resemblance between two fundamentally different things. How thoroughly does Twain develop the resemblance between reading a river and reading a book? Point to specific words and phrases to support your response. Why, for example, does Twain italicize the word *italicized* (paragraph 1)? How does this word relate to Twain's analogy?

3. In his first paragraph Twain says that the knowledge gained by the ability to read the book provides unending enjoyment, but he later indicates that this knowledge is also a burden. What in particular is the nature of the knowledge gleaned from the river? How can it be both a pleasure and a problem? Is this characteristic of the river still part of the analogy to reading or not? Explain your response with detailed references to the text.

Focusing on Structures and Strategies

1. Compare Twain's two descriptions of the same river scene. How would you characterize the differences between them? What attitude toward the river and the surrounding scenery is communicated by each? How do Twain's diction and style change in order to communicate these different impressions?

2. How does the ability to "read the river" diminish the romance and beauty of the river? What is the analogy that Twain creates in paragraph 3? How does the analogy in paragraph 3 prepare for the one created in paragraph 4? How do the analogies created in paragraphs 3 and 4 relate to the phrase "romance and beauty"?

3. At the end of the essay, Twain introduces a new analogy: between the river pilot and the doctor. How does Twain see them as similar? To what does he compare the river in this analogy? How is the doctor's knowledge like that of the pilot? Why does he pity the doctor?

4. Consider paragraph 4. How does Twain underline the sense of loss that accompanied the acquisition of a new "language"? Are the questions he poses in this paragraph meant to be answered? Why or why not?

Suggestions for Further Discussion and Writing

1. What is the function of Twain's describing the sunset in paragraph 2? What does this paragraph contribute to the overall effect of the passage?
2. Create an inventory of your own skills and knowledge. Choose one aspect of your skill and/or knowledge and write an essay in which you create an analogy to express the significance of the skill or knowledge you possess. How has this skill or knowledge changed your life?
3. Write an essay in which you explain how being an expert at something has changed your attitude toward that subject. Use an analogy to help illustrate your point.

The Salmon Instinct

William Humphrey

William Humphrey was born in Clarksville, Texas, in 1924. In his short stories, novels, and essays, he has consistently recorded—with a keen sensitivity for evocative detail—the importance of place in the development of the American character. His first novel, Home from the Hill *(1958), won awards for its irresistible portrayal of the rituals and routines that mark the distinctive character of a small east Texas town. In the following passage from his autobiography,* Farther Off from Heaven *(1977), Humphrey attempts through means of analogy to describe the powerful instinctual drive that finally brought him back to the place of his birth after an absence of thirty-two years.*

1 When James I, King of England, was asked why he was going back, after a long absence, to visit his native Scotland, he replied, "The salmon instinct."

2 The salmon is in his early adolescence when he leaves his native stream, impelled by an irresistible urge for something he has never known, the salt, salt sea. There he stays for the rest of his life, until he feels another prompting equally irresistible, the urge to reproduce

himself. This the salmon can do only in that same stream in which he was born. And so, from distances as great as fifteen hundred miles, the old salmon heads for home.

3 Many things can, and do, kill the salmon on his long voyage home, but nothing can deter or detour him. Not the diseases and parasites he is prone to, not fishermen, commercial or sporting, not the highest falls. He endures them, he eludes them, he leaps them, impelled by his ardent homesickness. Though long an expatriate, he knows his nationality as a naturalized American knows his, and back to the country of his birth he goes, as though throughout all the years away he has kept his first passport. Through the pathless sea he finds his way unerringly to the river down which he came on his voyage out long ago, and past each of its tributaries, each more temptingly like the one he is seeking the nearer he gets to that special one, as towns in the same county are similar but not the same. When he gets to his, he knows it—as I, for instance, know Clarksville, and would know it even if, like the salmon, I had but one sense to lead me to it. The name given the salmon in Latin is *Salmo salar:* the fish that will leap waterfalls to get back home. Some later Linnaeus of the human orders must have classed me at birth among the Humphreys: in Welsh the name means "One who loves his hearth and home."

4 But I began to doubt my homing instincts, to think I had wandered too far away, stayed gone too long, when, after crossing the ocean, I went back those thirty-two years later.

5 I had spent a few days in Dallas first, as the homecoming salmon spends a few days in the estuary to reaccustom himself to sweet water after all his years at sea before ascending to his native stream; for although that is what he now longs for, those uterine waters of his, too sudden a change from the salt is a shock to him. Dallas had always been brackish to me.

6 The nearer I got to Clarksville the farther from it I seemed to be. This was not where I was spawned. Strange places had usurped the names of towns I used to know. It was like what the British during World War II, fearing an invasion, had done, setting real but wrong place-names and roadsigns around the countryside so that the enemy in, say, Kent would find himself in villages belonging to Lancashire.

7 Gone were the spreading cottonfields I remembered, though this was the season when they should have been beginning to

whiten. The few patches that remained were small and sparse, like the patches of snow lingering on in sunless spots in New England in March and April. The prairie grass that had been there before the fields were broken for cotton had reclaimed them. The woods were gone—even Sulphur Bottom, that wilderness into which my father had gone in pursuit of the fugitive gunman: grazing land now, nearly all of it. For in a move that reverses Texas history, a move totally opposite to what I knew in my childhood, one which all but turns the world upside down, which makes the sun set in the East, Red River Country has ceased to be Old South and become Far West. I who for years had had to set my Northern friends straight by pointing out that I was a Southerner, not a Westerner, and that I had never seen a cowboy or for that matter a beefcow any more than they had, found myself now in that Texas of legend and the popular image which when I was a child had seemed more romantic to me than to a boy of New England precisely because it was closer to me than to him and yet still worlds away. Gone from the square were the bib overalls of my childhood when the farmers came to town on Saturday. Ranchers now, they came in high-heeled boots and rolled-brim hats, a costume that would have provoked as much surprise, and even more derision, there, in my time, as it would on Manhattan's Madison Avenue.

8 You can never ascend the same river twice, an early philosopher tells us. Its course, its composition are ever changing. Even so, one of its natives knows it, even one, like the salmon, who has spent most of his life away. I had been away from Clarksville since my father's death, and although ever since then I had been surprised each day to find myself alive, I was now an older man than he had lived to be. In that time much had changed in Clarksville; still, it was where I belonged.

9 Just as the salmon must leave home when the time comes, so he must return to round out his life. There where he was born, he dies.

Additional Rhetorical Strategies

Narration (paragraphs 2, 3); Definition (paragraph 3); Comparison and Contrast (paragraph 6); Description (paragraph 7).

Examining Words and Meaning

1. What is the salmon instinct? Why does Humphrey use it as an analogy for his desire to go home, rather than simply saying "I wanted to go home"?
2. Why does Humphrey say that "this was not where I was spawned" (paragraph 6)? Explain his word choice. What is its effect?

Focusing on Structures and Strategies

1. Where in this selection does Humphrey first *explicitly* compare himself to the salmon? At this point, which is emphasized, the life of the salmon or the life of the author? Do you think the effect of the passage would be different if Humphrey had introduced the analogy *after* saying he returned to Clarksville?
2. What does the last paragraph suggest about Humphrey's feelings toward his own life? Why does he imply these feelings through the analogy, rather than stating them directly?
3. What is the distinction between farmers and ranchers in paragraph 7, and why does it matter so much to the writer?

Suggestions for Further Discussion and Writing

1. Have you ever returned to a place you used to live—an old hometown, a house, an apartment? Did visiting it touch off feelings similar to Humphrey's? If not, can you imagine someday feeling about a place as strongly as Humphrey does here? Why or why not?
2. Humphrey's analogy suggests that we are sometimes driven by forces that are not unique to human beings—the homing instinct, in this case. How is this true for you? After thinking carefully about yourself—your habits, your feelings about the place you live, the ways that you deal with people, and so forth—write an essay in which you explain some part of your behavior by comparing yourself to an animal. How do you see yourself differently after doing so?

Prufrock Aloft; Prufrock Before the Television Set

Michael Arlen

Michael Arlen has written extensively on the subject of television, finding the cathode tube itself more ominous than the sex and violence most critics of the medium condemn. His fear is that rather than inciting us to violence, television may be telling us to do nothing at all—nothing, that is, but continue to sit before it.

Through his odd but apt analogy between the act of watching television and the enforced passivity of an airline passenger strapped into a seat, Arlen questions the need in us that would find satisfaction in such a "programmed" existence. We are analogous as well, Arlen suggests, to Prufrock, the anxious narrator of T. S. Eliot's famous poem, whose timid and passive behavior in many ways typifies the modern personality.

Arlen is the author of three collections of essays on television, The Living Room Wars *(1969),* The View from Highway 1 *(1976), and* The Camera Age *(1981). A graduate of Harvard University, Arlen has written for* Life *magazine,* The New Yorker, Esquire, Harper's, *and many other periodicals. He is also the author of* Exiles *(1970),* An American Verdict *(1973),* Passage to Ararat *(1975), and* Thirty Seconds *(1980).*

1 A few days ago, while seated snugly in an airplane seat on my way back to New York from Chicago, with a drink in front of me, last week's copy of *Sports Illustrated* on my lap, the soothing hum of the engines washing over my ears, and with the memory of the hectic taxi ride to the airport and wretched traffic jams and ticket-counter chaos already receding in my brain, it occurred to me that a rather striking similarity existed between the situation I found myself in then, flying in a modern airliner, and what I've often felt as I watch television. To begin with, both experiences are largely passive experiences. But this shared passivity is itself more complicated than it seems, for though it produces in both cases an obvious condition of quiet and inactivity, it also demands from the passen-

ger or viewer a very definite emotional commitment. One might call it a commitment to specifically nonaggressive and uninvolved behavior.

2 Consider the airplane journey, for example. In many ways, the level of ordinary comfort for passengers has been decreasing since the days of the old Pan American Clippers, with their well-appointed dining rooms and sleeping quarters. Even so, there is undoubted pleasure of a sort to be had in a routine jetliner trip of reasonable length, at least without squalling babies or hyperactive grandparents in one's vicinity. As an extreme instance of this, I mention the experience of a friend who, being harried to exhaustion by a project in New York, determined suddenly to fly to California for a few days by the sea. No sooner was he airborne on the way out than he began to relax. Five hours later in California, however, once on the ground and dealing with baggage and car rentals and freeways and his overcrowded motel-by-the-sea, he began again to unravel. The same evening, he drove back to the airport, took a return flight to New York, and, after five more hours of airplane massage, was in a suitable condition for resuming work.

3 People still talk of the romance of travel, and perhaps it is still romance for cruise-ship passengers or fashionable visitors to Ethiopian ruins. But where travel was formerly an active and difficult undertaking, with the pleasure to be gained from it consisting largely in the mastery of the event (or of the unexpected sequence of events), nowadays the point is not so much in surmounting the chance encounter as in never having one. The goal of modern travel, in fact, is to have "experience" (as on a photo-safari to Kenya), but without experiences: without involvement. Indeed, involvement and aggressive behavior are actively discouraged, as anyone has discovered, for example, who ever tried to open a dialogue with an airline employee as to *what* the maintenance crew were doing to an certain engine (and *why*) that required a departure delay of three and a half hours.

4 Once aboard the shiny, experienceless airplane, however, our passenger lumpishly settles into his narrow seat, usually disheveled in mind or spirit from the hurly-burly of the outside world, often still quivering from the hazards of actually getting to the airplane. If he is a business traveler, flying first-class at company expense, the stewardess has already relieved him of his coat and briefcase: his downtown symbols. Wifelike, too, she will give him an initial reward for having reached her: a Bloody Mary. Perhaps also a smile, a bit of chat,

depending on how severe the pressures of the airplane-household have been. Prufrock, in effect, has arrived home: to *his* seat, with a number on it that matches the number on his boarding pass so that no one may take it from him. Now he need do nothing more, except buckle himself into it, and follow modest instructions "for his own safety and comfort," and continue to act unaggressively. For doing so, he will be rewarded throughout the voyage: by forward progress through the air; by the loan of a magazine; by the outright gift of the airline's own magazine ("Yours to keep after deplaning"); by more drinks; by the larger hospitality of a meal; by preselected music for his ears; even by the appurtenances of an overnight guest: a pillow and a blanket. Indeed, a veritable shower of benefits is rained upon the passenger by the authorities of the airplane (including periodic descriptions of the unseen ground being traversed, which are delivered over loudspeaker by the unseen captain), who ask in return only that the passenger continue to do nothing, stay quiet, keep still. Bathroom privileges are formally tendered, but can be suddenly revoked. Primary addictive substances, such as cigarettes, are permitted the passengers more rapidly after takeoff than secondary substances, such as alcohol, which (except in first class) might cause unrest or even spill. When all the right conditions are met, determined by the chief authority in the cockpit, moderate mobility is allowed, but since there is usually no place to walk to, except the bathroom, it is a pleasure seldom accepted. Besides, as the captain announces, even when the seat-belt sign has been turned off one would do well to keep buckled and stay put.

5 Passivity, in short, holds sway in the modern airliner. And when aggression reappears, it is sternly chastised. Right after the plane has landed, for example, but before it has arrived at the gate, several passengers—doubtless summoned once more to their former aggressive ways by the imminence of the outside world—will leap to their feet and begin reaching for coats and bags like children who have been held too long in school. At this point, the formerly benign stewardess becomes severe and quickly reprimands the unruly passengers for their aggression. If these passengers, she suggests, do not abandon their aggressive behavior and return to the domicile of their seats, they will be deprived of the one thing they still lack: further forward motion toward the gate. Thereupon, the misbehaving passengers feign nonaggressive behavior, making the pretense of returning to their seats, though rarely quite doing so, until the second the

plane has docked at the gate and they have been released from the spell of docility. Immediately, aggression floods back into the veins, and now all the passengers crowd the aisle, then push past each other down the airport corridor, and once again resume their conflicts over baggage, taxis, buses, or parking space.

6 It seems to me that the experience of watching most commercial television involves a similar passivity, and even a similar sense of the experienceless voyage. Here, of course, the seat belts are figurative rather than actual, though there appears to be a variety of television lounge chairs on the market whose chief function seems to be to safely enclose the viewer during his nightly journey as if he were on a space flight. Also, it is probably no more than a coincidence that the TV dinner and the standard airline meal are made the same way, with the same technology, often the same ingredients, and generally the same results. Of course, with television, the forward motion is through time, not space, but the effect is somewhat the same, since in today's world final destinations rarely exist. That is to say: the end of each day's program schedule, like O'Hare Airport, is as much a beginning as a terminus.

7 In any case, rewards for good (i.e., uninvolving, nonaggressive) behavior flow similarly throughout the TV voyage as on the airplane trip. First, there is the vague sense of progress or forward motion induced by the seemingly linear progression of the evening's programs. We have seen Show A and are now starting on Show B, which is a step forward, at least in time. But where are we then? Show C, and then Show D and E, and then bed. And then the new day's shows. Thus, the present program contains the next one, and so forth; each new satisfaction breeds another. Second, there are the messages of the commercial sponsors, which act on the viewer in two different ways, both of them "beneficial." On a symbolic level, as is well known, they sing to him of a better, finer life: of a new car to make him feel rich; of a new hair spray to make him feel virile; of a laxative to make him feel "regular." But on a more immediate, less dreamlike level, the commercial interruption is also a release: permission, as it were, from the authority of the network or station to make a trip to the bathroom or to get another bottle of beer from the refrigerator. The instant gratification that comes from the beer or the bathroom (while the commercials are supposedly being ignored) is in fact a stand-in for the larger, more abstract rewards they promise. And throughout this period of time travel via television, aggressive or involving behavior is once again discouraged, though not so much by

steely Clairol stewardesses as by the form and content of the programs themselves.

8 These nightly, factory-made entertainments are sometimes dismissed as soporific, and sometimes extolled as fascinating, gripping, *fun,* but the fact is that though they are sometimes each of these things, for the most part they are none of them. They are, instead, permeable: constructed in such a way that life can seep through them. A book, for example, is not permeable; even a trashy book is hard to read with any enjoyment while one is paying bills or talking on the telephone. And plays and movies are just as opaque in this way, though increasingly the TV-trained audience tries to engage in casual domestic chitchat while seated in darkened theaters, staring at the actors on the stage or giant screen. But television programs not only coexist with routine household transactions; they seem to present a kind of porous substance to the audience that almost invites an uninvolved, quiescent response. Who has not, for example, observed a family living room (one's own!) where somebody's "favorite program" is on the air, while the somebody in question carries on a desultory conversation with another party, and somebody else (also watching) gossips on the telephone with Clara, and somebody else (naturally also watching) doodles with her history homework? Do the TV programs create our uninvolved response to them? Or does the uninvolved nature of the modern family somehow evoke the TV programs? Whatever the answer, there seems to be a kind of subliminal understanding in effect, a new form of social compact. In any case, if fear of flying has played some part in creating the ceremonial ritual of the seat belt and the stewardess, then fear of another kind has presumably helped to shape the quite unusually uninvolving nature of our television entertainments. Is it fear of the future or of impersonal, uncontrolled technology, as is periodically suggested? Or, once again, just fear of ourselves? At any rate, one can know this much: that the passengers who angrily jam the airplane aisles and rush pell-mell down airport corridors for taxis are the same people who, moments before, sat meekly buckled in by seat belts. As it is, the TV viewers who chat and read and pay the bills and even have sex while looking at and through their "favorite programs" could probably only engage in one activity that doesn't blend easily with the soft messages of the TV set: they could really *notice* one another. One imagines that most of them would do so if they could.

Additional Rhetorical Strategies

Illustration (paragraph 2); Process Analysis (paragraph 4).

Examining Words and Meaning

1. What word in the opening paragraph summarizes the "striking similarity" between watching television and flying? Trace this term throughout the essay by circling each instance of the word and its synonyms.
2. What does Arlen mean by an "experienceless voyage" in paragraph 6? Do you think of traveling in these terms? Would someone flying for the first time feel this way? Explain how Arlen's assumptions about his audience's previous experiences affect the way he views the experience of flying in general.

Focusing on Structures and Strategies

1. Where does Arlen introduce his central resemblance? How does he extend the resemblance into an analogy? Reread the essay in order to chart out Arlen's point-by-point similarities. List as many as you can.
2. Using your list of point-by-point similarities, try to extend his principal resemblance even further. Comment on the strength of the analogy: Do you think it is a fertile or a fragile one?
3. Trace the ideas of passivity and lack of experience throughout the essay. How have these concepts helped Arlen extend his main observation (flying is like watching television) into a complete essay?

Suggestions for Further Discussion and Writing

1. Do you essentially agree or disagree with Arlen's attitude toward flying and watching television? Do you feel passive in a plane? In

front of a television set? (If you've never flown, think how that would serve as a counter to Arlen's point.)

2. Most literature collections contain T. S. Eliot's poem "The Love Song of J. Alfred Prufrock." Track it down and read it. Discuss the idea of human passivity as it appears in the poem and Arlen's essay. Do you think Prufrock was a good model for Arlen to use in his essay? Explain your response.

6. MAKING CLAIMS

Argument

1 In one form or another, arguments take up a sizable portion of our everyday lives. We quarrel with a friend over a broken appointment, dispute a call in a close game, try to change our roommate's mind about dropping a course, disagree with a police officer about a parking ticket, argue with a salesperson about the correct price of a product. Argument is even an ongoing process of our consciousness. We frequently carry on debates inside our heads: "If she says that, then I'll just point out. . . ." We also conduct arguments with ourselves as a necessary aid to decision-making and problem-solving. Though our everyday arguments can range from highly abstract debates with a friend about the existence of God to such practical disputes as who gets to use the shower first, most of our arguments arise spontaneously and are usually worked out only to the degree necessary to win or to resolve the conflict.

2 When it comes to expressing arguments on paper, however, our everyday types of argument will not always stand up. They tend to be far too informally presented, loosely constructed, and undeveloped. In rhetoric, argument is a special form of discourse, one that attempts to convince an audience that a specific claim or proposition is true wholly because a supporting body of logically related statements is also true. In a well-constructed argument, once we establish the truth of statements *A, B,* and *C,* and so forth, then we can reasonably be expected to assent to the principal claim or assertion. In other words, the truth of a statement is

entirely dependent on the previously acknowledged truth of other statements.

3 For example, suppose we want to argue that standardized admission tests represent an unfair criterion by which to evaluate college applicants. To win our audience's assent to that claim, we must present *reasons* for believing the tests to be inadequate. We might construct our argument around such relevant points as:

1. The tests are culturally biased against minorities and disadvantaged students.
2. They focus on isolated bits of knowledge.
3. They ignore taste and judgment.
4. They give insufficient attention to creativity.
5. They tend to reward quicker and more competitive students while penalizing those who prefer to take their time and consider problems thoroughly.
6. They fail to give proper attention to writing ability.

Our reasons should be relevant to the main point of the argument (to complain about the early-morning hour of some of the tests would not be convincing); they should also be supported by facts (we need to research such things as reliability of scores, which subject areas are tested, and how writing ability is evaluated). Once we had systematically demonstrated that our set of reasons—or other reasons like these—was true, or very likely true, then we could feel confident that our main proposition should also be accepted as true.

4 The main business of an argument is to convince an audience by means of careful reasoning that a certain claim is true. As such, argument is ordinarily distinguished from another rhetorical means of convincing audiences—persuasion. Though no firm line can be drawn to mark off the boundaries between these two age-old rhetorical methods, critics customarily see argument largely as a rational appeal to the understanding and persuasion largely as an emotional appeal to the will. Argument attempts to convince an audience of a truth; persuasion, of a course of action. Argument also relies less heavily on stylistic features than does persuasion and builds its case upon a tight network of logical connections rather than upon powerful oratorical techniques. Clear-cut distinctions may hold in some extreme cases, but in most thinking and writing we should expect to

find argument mixed with some degree of persuasion and persuasion tinged with some elements of argument. As a working distinction, however, we could say that the overall purpose of argument is to obtain an audience's *assent* (that is, its acceptance of a statement or abstract proposition), whereas the overall purpose of persuasion is to obtain an audience's *consent* (that is, its voluntary agreement to or acquiescence in a plan or desire). The elements of persuasion will be more fully examined in the next chapter.

5 The ability to make claims confidently and support them with well-constructed arguments is one of the best indications of cognitive and verbal achievement. In many professions—especially in law, journalism, education, science, and business—the formulation of convincing arguments is a skill few can afford to do without. In order to learn the enormously useful and intellectually satisfying art of arguing well, we need to know the various components of a solidly designed argument. For practical purposes, we can divide an argument into three components: first, its *claim,* which may also be referred to as its assertion, statement, proposition, or thesis-statement; second, its *reasoning pattern,* which is the logical relation of premises—that is, the statements forming the basis of an argument—and conclusions; and third, its *organization,* which includes the positioning of evidence, the order of points or reasons, and the interrelation of additional rhetorical strategies. In this section, we will examine the main characteristics of these three elements and some of the ways they function in our thinking and writing.

CLAIMS

6 The first important element to consider in an argument is its claim or proposition—the point of the argument. Though this sounds obvious, we need only recall how often we have listened to or read arguments and wondered, "What's the point?" We should make sure when constructing an argument that it is built around what can reasonably be called an arguable point. In our everyday lives we argue loosely about many topics that would not be considered legitimate subjects for an extended, formal argument. For example, in an essay, we cannot seriously present an argument about commands such as "Pass the mashed potatoes" or "Turn down the music," though we might get into heated arguments about such imperatives in our daily lives. Assertions of taste, such as "Tea tastes better than

coffee," also don't constitute a legitimate basis for argument (but if we changed the assertion to "Tea is better for one's health than coffee," we would have an arguable point, one that might be supported with appropriate medical documentation). Likewise, matters of fact constitute another area of nonarguable propositions. There is no point in constructing arguments in order to demonstrate information that is "findable"—the distance from the earth to the moon or Mickey Mantle's 1955 batting average.

7 Arguable claims generally fall into four categories:

1. *Claims about meaning:* "What is X?" These are propositions that center on how we define or interpret something. What do we mean by "pornography"? Is a defendant "sane" enough to stand trial?

2. *Claims about value:* "Is X good or bad, right or wrong, useful or useless?" Though propositions about the value of something can rarely be argued conclusively, they do constitute a large and vital part of what intelligent people argue about: "Is capital punishment morally wrong?" "Who is funnier, Woody Allen or Eddie Murphy?" "Is *War and Peace* a better novel than *Anna Karenina?*" When we make ethical and aesthetic evaluations, we need to base our judgments on clear and consistent criteria.

3. *Claims about consequences:* "What will happen as a result of X?" "What is the upshot of our believing X?" We argue over consequences whenever we examine the causal patterns involved in certain ideas and actions. Such arguments usually take an "if X, then Y" form: "If an international law is passed that apportions the solar system to different nations, then space will become a theater of war." "If America were suddenly plunged into another great depression, then there would be a vast resettlement of rural areas."

4. *Claims about policy:* "What should be done about X?" In arguments having to do with policy, the proposition is usually stated in the form of a proposal and the operative words are *ought* and *should.* "Gun control ought to be mandatory in every state." "Utility companies should be nationalized." "Advertising on children's television programs ought to be better regulated."

8 Though an argument may focus entirely on any one of these four types of claims, many extended arguments depend upon a mixture of all of them. We may decide, say, to draw up an argument defending the right of women to have abortions (a claim about value), and in the course of the argument define what we mean by

abortion (a claim about meaning), discuss the social benefits of abortion (a claim about consequences), and recommend that abortions be covered by health insurance (a claim about policy).

REASONING

9 An arguable claim may make a compelling assertion, but it is nothing without a sound argument to back it up. That is where the second component of argument—the reasoning process—comes in. Put simply, reasoning is a special kind of thinking in which pieces of information are used in such a way as to yield new pieces of information. There are basically two types of reasoning: deductive and inductive. Roughly speaking, *deductive* arguments proceed from the general to the particular; *inductive* arguments proceed from the particular to the general. Thus, "All dogs are carnivorous; Fido is a dog; therefore Fido is carnivorous" is a deductive argument in that it proceeds from a general truth about a class (all dogs) to a truth about a particular member of that class (Fido). An inductive argument would proceed like this: "Spot is carnivorous, Fido is carnivorous, Lassie is carnivorous; they are all dogs; therefore all dogs are carnivorous." From an enumeration of truths about particular members of a class (Spot, Fido, and Lassie), we move to a truth about the class as a whole (all dogs).

10 There are many exceptions to the simple inductive–deductive dichotomy outlined above. For a more precise distinction between the two types of reasoning we need to consider the relationship between premises and conclusions. A deductive argument leads to a *necessary* conclusion—that is, the conclusion is logically entailed by the premises. Once we accept the premises as true and the connection between the premises and conclusions as *valid,* [1] then we must accept the truth of the conclusion. If all dogs are carnivorous and Fido is a dog, then it must follow that "Fido is carnivorous." In such deductive arguments the conclusions are said to be logically necessary.

11 This particular structure of deductive reasoning—two premises and a conclusion—makes up what is known in logic as a *syllogism.* A typical syllogism may be outlined and illustrated as follows:

[1] *Validity* refers not to whether a statement expresses a true fact but to whether it is consistent with logic.

Major premise: All *P* is *Q*	All dogs are carnivorous
Minor premise: *R* is *P*	Fido is a dog
Conclusion: *R* is *Q*	Therefore, Fido is carnivorous

Syllogisms can take many different forms, however, and some of them can be quite tricky. We might, for example, argue that because two things are alike in some respects they are therefore identical. Such reasoning would lead to incorrectly constructed syllogisms, though both premises are true:

All dogs are carnivorous	true premise	
All cats are carnivorous	true premise	invalid
Therefore all cats are dogs	false conclusion	form

Or, a syllogism can contain two true premises, be invalidly drawn, but lead to a true conclusion:

All dogs are carnivorous	true premise	
Fido is carnivorous	true premise	
Therefore Fido is a dog (Fido		invalid
might have been a carnivorous cat)	true conclusion	form

Or, a syllogism can be correctly drawn from a false premise and thus lead to a false conclusion

All dogs have five legs	false premise	
Fido is a dog	true premise	invalid
Therefore Fido has five legs	false conclusion	form

Syllogisms that are correctly formed but false are, it is important to remember, still accepted as *valid.* The validity of deductive reasoning is wholly a matter of correct syllogistic construction and is not related to the truth or falsity of the premises. Only true premises and a valid construction will yield a conclusion that is both true and logically necessary. In our thinking and writing, we should always make sure that our premises are true, or at least probably true, and our conclusions are validly drawn.

12 If we find ourselves devising an argument to counter the argument of another, we must be concerned not only with the soundness of our own reasoning but with the *un*soundness of our opponent's. In logic, the term *fallacy* denotes any form of invalid, deceptive, or

unfair reasoning. In the glossary of this book, under "ARGUMENT, Fallacies of," we have presented brief explanations of the most frequently occurring fallacies. A familiarity with them, and others, is necessary for anyone who hopes to attain competence in the art of argumentation.

13 Unlike deductive reasoning, inductive reasoning does not yield logically necessary conclusions. Inductive premises may give us excellent reasons for believing that our conclusion is true, but they can never logically entail the truth. To return to our example: we observe that Fido is carnivorous, Lassie is carnivorous, Spot is carnivorous, and these observations may well incline us to the conclusion that all dogs are carnivorous. In other words, we reach our conclusion entirely by means of a generalization based on a limited number of instances. Induction is the process of reasoning by which we move from evidence about *some* members of a particular class to a proposition about *all* members of that class. The strength of that movement—the "inductive leap" as it is sometimes called—from particular examples to general statement depends wholly on the unstated assumption that future instances will confirm our generalization: that the fifteenth, hundredth, thousandth, and millionth dog we observe will also be carnivorous. But no matter how many dogs in our sample, the conclusion will still be an inductive one. At no point will the sheer number of observations change the inductive argument into a deductive one—that is to say, one in which the conclusion is necessary.

14 This is not meant to discredit inductive reasoning. Induction is not a less useful form of reasoning than deduction; in many cases, it is the only kind possible. We need to rely on inductive arguments continually in our everyday lives. Scientific knowledge could not exist were it not for the reliability of solid inductive reasoning. In fact, the premises of deductive syllogisms are often formed out of the conclusions obtained from inductive processes. Certain premises, such as "Dogs are carnivorous" or "Human beings are mortal," are considered true not because of definition but because of the overwhelming number of confirmative instances. Using an inductive conclusion as the premise of a deductive argument, however, does not mean we have magically transformed induction into deduction. The main difference, we should recall, between the two types of reasoning has to do with the way conclusions are drawn from premises and not at all with the truth-value of the premises alone.

15 In the argumentative prose of capable writers, inductive enumerations and deductive syllogisms rarely appear in the skeletal forms shown above. Even Aristotle, who considered the discovery of the syllogism his greatest achievement, realized that interesting, engaging prose could not easily incorporate syllogistic reasoning in its naked forms. For one thing, syllogisms quickly become tiresome to read; for another, it is not always necessary to provide a logically complete account of how we get from one point to another. Aristotle recognized that the language people actually use relies not on fully developed syllogisms but on abbreviated syllogisms, which he called "enthymemes." An *enthymeme* is a syllogism in which a premise or a conclusion is unexpressed: "Fido eats meat because he is a dog" is a compressed way of stating the syllogistic conclusion without spelling out the entire deductive process. Sometimes an argument can be expressed more emphatically if the conclusion is left out: "To win a pennant you need strong pitching, but strong pitching is just what the Angels don't have." Though the logical conclusion is obvious, it is all the more forceful for having the audience supply it itself.

16 Though enthymemes can help make argument less verbose and the reasoning process less tediously diagrammatic, they can also be the cause of ambiguity and inconsistency. The meaning of a missing premise or conclusion may not always be as clear to an audience as we think it is. Furthermore, the missing portion of the syllogism—the dropped premise or conclusion—is no less a part of the argument merely because it is left unstated. The person constructing the argument is equally responsible for the sense and consistency of its implicit as well as its explicit parts. In an extended argument which depends on many suppressed syllogisms, we can easily get ourselves tangled up in an invisible network of implied assumptions and conclusions that may not hang together logically if worked out point by point. In the next chapter, we will see how some types of persuasion strategically use enthymemes as a way of by-passing certain premises and conclusions that the speaker does not want the audience to consider. In reading and listening to arguments, it is always a good idea to make the implied assumptions—the unstated premises and conclusions—as explicit as we can. This is one of the best means of finding holes in arguments and discovering points for rebuttal. We need not make our assumptions always explicit in our writing, but we should carefully keep track of

the implied portions of our argument so that our own claims can stand up to the same tough-minded logical criticism we should be bringing to the arguments of others.

ORGANIZATION

17 The reasoning process is, of course, the heart of the argument. As the philosopher Monroe Beardsley says, argument is "reasoning's verbal record." Regardless of the truth of our claim, however, an argument stands or falls on the strength of the organizational framework that ties together the reasons we assemble to support our claim. For the most part, reasons can be assembled in one of two ways: we can structure our argument upon a series of independent reasons or upon a closely linked chain of interdependent reasons. Whether linked or separate, the reasons we assemble must be related carefully to our claim. How they are related to each other often determines our principle of organization.

18 In our earlier case concerning the inadequacy of standardized examinations, for example, six points were raised to show why the tests do not provide fair criteria for admissions decisions. These six reasons, though generally related by subject, were not dependent on each other; each answered our claim with a separate instance of educational inadequacy. Given the nature of the reasons, the overall organization of our argument would most likely be the arrangement of reasons we thought would provide the most effective argumentative order (usually strongest reason first, followed by weaker reasons, and ending with a strong summarizing reason to conclude our argument pointedly). Another important part of our organization would be the connection of each reason to our central claim in such a way that our proposition would be continually reinforced in the course of our argument. This reinforcement can usually be done through such logical signal words and phrases as *therefore, hence, it follows that, proves that, allows us to conclude that, consequently, thus, so, indicates that,* and so on.

19 The other method of organizing our argument—the chain structure—can be used only when we have a set of interdependent points. Suppose we decided to argue that the standardized admission tests were especially unfair because they scored results against a norm that was no longer applicable. We could then demonstrate

through a succession of closely linked reasons that test scores are based on past standards; that recent data indicate that the scores have dropped dramatically on a national basis; that this drop is best explained by decreased learning ability; that the statistical decrease in learning ability based on the test-score data correlates closely with environmental increases of atomic waste due to nuclear testing; that since this environmental change constitutes a drastic historical change, contemporary students should not be rated according to the older standards of a cleaner environment; that therefore, since the test norms are based on these older standards, the admission tests are especially unfair to today's applicants. As we can see from this example, the strength of the argument depends on the strength of our *chain* of reasons, the conclusions of one point becoming the premises of the next. The organization of chain-structured arguments depends less upon an arrangement of points according to their relative importance than it does upon an arrangement of points according to their logical sequence.

20 Of all the structures and strategies for thinking in writing examined in this book, argumentation probably relies on a greater variety of rhetorical features than any other. In order to formulate arguable claims, we need to sharpen our definitions, make accurate classifications, and be alert to causal connections. But these are just a few considerations. Well-constructed arguments also make ample use of relevant illustration, work in process analysis, and frequently rely on narration, description, and comparison to support their claims. Carefully reasoned, tightly constructed argumentative essays prove that rhetoric not only is the art of writing well, but is vitally and instrumentally related to the art of thinking straight and true.

The Hazards of Science

Lewis Thomas

In classical literature, "hubris" referred to a state of excessive pride or arrogant self-confidence that invariably led to a tragic hero's downfall. Today, as Lewis Thomas points out in the following essay from The

Medusa and the Snail, *the word has been revived as a pejorative term for scientific enterprise. To critics of contemporary science, many scientists are perceived as arrogant in their research aims, insolently pursuing goals that will lead the human race to a tragic end. Yet, the key issues in this topic are not always as clear-cut as the critics of science maintain. Before stating his own position, Thomas must first come to terms with a problem that arises in all serious controversy: he must make sure we know "what the argument is really about."*

1 The code word for criticism of science and scientists these days is "hubris." Once you've said that word, you've said it all; it sums up, in a word, all of today's apprehensions and misgivings in the public mind—not just about what is perceived as the insufferable attitude of the scientists themselves but, enclosed in the same word, what science and technology are perceived to be doing to make this century, this near to its ending, turn out so wrong.

2 "Hubris" is a powerful word, containing layers of powerful meaning, derived from a very old word, but with a new life of its own, growing way beyond the limits of its original meaning. Today, it is strong enough to carry the full weight of disapproval for the cast of mind that thought up atomic fusion and fission as ways of first blowing up and later heating cities as well as the attitudes which led to strip-mining, offshore oil wells, Kepone, food additives, SSTs, and the tiny spherical particles of plastic recently discovered clogging the waters of the Sargasso Sea.

3 The biomedical sciences are now caught up with physical science and technology in the same kind of critical judgment, with the same perjorative word. Hubris is responsible, it is said, for the whole biological revolution. It is hubris that has given us the prospects of behavior control, psychosurgery, fetal research, heart transplants, the cloning of prominent politicans from bits of their own eminent tissue, iatrogenic disease, overpopulation, and recombinant DNA. This last, the new technology that permits the stitching of one creature's genes into the DNA of another, to make hybrids, is currently cited as the ultimate example of hubris. It is hubris for man to manufacture a hybrid on his own.

4 So now we are back to the first word again, from "hybrid" to "hubris," and the hidden meaning of two beings joined unnaturally together by man is somehow retained. Today's joining is straight out of Greek mythology: it is the combining of man's capacity with the special prerogative of the gods, and it is really in this sense of outrage

that the word "hubris" is being used today. This is what the word has grown into, a warning, a code word, a shorthand signal from the language itself: if man starts doing things reserved for the gods, deifying himself, the outcome will be something worse for him, symbolically, than the litters of wild boars and domestic sows were for the ancient Romans.

5 To be charged with hubris is therefore an extremely serious matter, and not to be dealt with by murmuring things about anti-science and anti-intellectualism, which is what many of us engaged in science tend to do these days. The doubts about our enterprise have their origin in the most profound kind of human anxiety. If we are right and the critics are wrong, then it has to be that the word "hubris" is being mistakenly employed, that this is not what we are up to, that there is, for the time being anyway, a fundamental misunderstanding of science.

6 I suppose there is one central question to be dealt with, and I am not at all sure how to deal with it, although I am quite certain about my own answer to it. It is this: are there some kinds of information leading to some sorts of knowledge that human beings are really better off not having? Is there a limit to scientific inquiry not set by what is knowable but by what we *ought* to be knowing? Should we stop short of learning about some things, for fear of what we, or someone, will do with the knowledge? My own answer is a flat no, but I must confess that this is an intuitive response and I am neither inclined nor trained to reason my way through it.

7 There has been some effort, in and out of scientific quarters, to make recombinant DNA into the issue on which to settle this argument. Proponents of this line of research are accused of pure hubris, of assuming the rights of gods, of arrogance and outrage; what is more, they confess themselves to be in the business of making live hybrids with their own hands. The mayor of Cambridge and the attorney general of New York have both been advised to put a stop to it, forthwith.

8 It is not quite the same sort of argument, however, as the one about limiting knowledge, although this is surely part of it. The knowledge is already here, and the rage of the argument is about its application in technology. Should DNA for making certain useful or interesting proteins be incorporated into *E. coli* plasmids or not? Is there a risk of inserting the wrong sort of toxins or hazardous viruses, and then having the new hybrid organisms spread beyond the laboratory? Is this a technology for creating new varieties of pathogens, and should it be stopped because of this?

9 If the argument is held to this level, I can see no reason why it cannot be settled, by reasonable people. We have learned a great deal about the handling of dangerous microbes in the last century, although I must say that the opponents of recombinant-DNA research tend to downgrade this huge body of information. At one time or another, agents as hazardous as those of rabies, psittacosis, plague, and typhus have been dealt with by investigators in secure laboratories, with only rare instances of self-infection of the investigators themselves, and no instances at all of epidemics. It takes some high imagining to postulate the creation of brand-new pathogens so wild and voracious as to spread from equally secure laboratories to endanger human life at large, as some of the arguers are now maintaining.

10 But this is precisely the trouble with the recombinant-DNA problem: it has become an emotional issue, with too many irretrievably lost tempers on both sides. It has lost the sound of a discussion of technological safety, and begins now to sound like something else, almost like a religious controversy, and here it is moving toward the central issue: are there some things in science we should not be learning about?

11 There is an inevitably long list of hard questions to follow this one, beginning with the one which asks whether the mayor of Cambridge should be the one to decide, first off.

12 Maybe we'd be wiser, all of us, to back off before the recombinant-DNA issue becomes too large to cope with. If we're going to have a fight about it, let it be confined to the immediate issue of safety and security, of the recombinants now under consideration, and let us by all means have regulations and guidelines to assure the public safety wherever these are indicated or even suggested. But if it is possible let us stay off that question about limiting human knowledge. It is too loaded, and we'll simply not be able to cope with it.

13 By this time it will have become clear that I have already taken sides in the matter, and my point of view is entirely prejudiced. This is true, but with a qualification. I am not so much in favor of recombinant-DNA research as I am opposed to the opposition to this line of inquiry. As a longtime student of infectious-disease agents I do not take kindly the declarations that we do not know how to keep from catching things in laboratories, much less how to keep them from spreading beyond the laboratory walls. I believe we learned a lot about this sort of thing, long ago. Moreover, I regard it as a form of hubris-in-reverse to claim that man can make deadly pathogenic microorganisms so easily. In my view, it takes a long time and a great

deal of interliving before a microbe can become a successful pathogen. Pathogenicity is, in a sense, a highly skilled trade, and only a tiny minority of all the numberless tons of microbes on the earth has ever been involved itself in it [sic]; most bacteria are busy with their own business, browsing and recycling the rest of life. Indeed, pathogenicity often seems to me a sort of biological accident in which signals are misdirected by the microbe or misinterpreted by the host, as in the case of endotoxin, or in which the intimacy between host and microbe is of such long standing that a form of molecular mimicry becomes possible, as in the case of diptheria toxin. I do not believe that by simply putting together new combinations of genes one can create creatures as highly skilled and adapted for dependence as a pathogen must be, any more than I have ever believed that microbial life from the moon or Mars could possibly make a living on this planet.

14 But, as I said, I'm not at all sure this is what the argument is really about. Behind it is that other discussion, which I wish we would not have to become enmeshed in.

15 I cannot speak for the physical sciences, which have moved an immense distance in this century by any standard, but it does seem to me that in the biological and medical sciences we are still far too ignorant to begin making judgments about what sorts of things we should be learning or not learning. To the contrary, we ought to be grateful for whatever snatches we can get hold of, and we ought to be out there on a much larger scale than today's, looking for more.

16 We should be very careful with that word "hubris," and make sure it is not used when not warranted. There is a great danger in applying it to the search for knowledge. The application of knowledge is another matter, and there is hubris in plenty of our technology, but I do not believe that looking for new information about nature, at whatever level, can possibly be called unnatural. Indeed, if there is any single attribute of human beings, apart from language, which distinguishes them from all other creatures on earth, it is their insatiable, uncontrollable drive to learn things and then to exchange the information with others of the species. Learning is what we do, when you think about it. I cannot think of a human impulse more difficult to govern.

17 But I can imagine lots of reasons for trying to govern it. New information about nature is very likely, at the outset, to be upsetting to someone or other. The recombinant-DNA line of research is already upsetting, not because of the dangers now being argued about but because it is disturbing, in a fundamental way, to face the fact

that the genetic machinery in control of the planet's life can be fooled around with so easily. We do not like the idea that anything so fixed and stable as a species line can be changed. The notion that genes can be taken out of one genome and inserted in another is unnerving. Classical mythology is peopled with mixed beings—part man, part animal or plant—and most of them are associated with tragic stories. Recombinant DNA is a reminder of bad dreams.

18 The easiest decision for society to make in matters of this kind is to appoint an agency, or a commission, or a subcommittee within an agency to look into the problem and provide advice. And the easiest course for a committee to take, when confronted by any process that appears to be disturbing people or making them uncomfortable, is to recommend that it be stopped, at least for the time being.

19 I can easily imagine such a committee, composed of unimpeachable public figures, arriving at the decision that the time is not quite ripe for further exploration of the transplantation of genes, that we should put this off for a while, maybe until next century, and get on with other affairs that make us less discomfited. Why not do science on something more popular, say, how to get solar energy more cheaply? Or mental health?

20 The trouble is, it would be very hard to stop once this line was begun. There are, after all, all sorts of scientific inquiry that are not much liked by one constituency or another, and we might soon find ourselves with crowded rosters, panels, standing committees, set up in Washington for the appraisal, and then the regulation, of research. Not on grounds of the possible value and usefulness of the new knowledge, mind you, but for guarding society against scientific hubris, against the kinds of knowledge we're better off without.

21 It would be absolutely irresistible as a way of spending time, and people would form long queues for membership. Almost anything would be fair game, certainly anything to do with genetics, anything relating to population control, or, on the other side, research on aging. Very few fields would get by, except perhaps for some, like mental health, in which nobody really expects anything much to happen, surely nothing new or disturbing.

22 The research areas in the greatest trouble would be those already containing a sense of bewilderment and surprise, with discernible prospects of upheaving present dogmas.

23 It is hard to predict how science is going to turn out, and if it is really good science it is impossible to predict. This is in the nature of the enterprise. If the things to be found are actually new, they are

by definition unknown in advance, and there is no way of telling in advance where a really new line of inquiry will lead. You cannot make choices in this matter, selecting things you think you're going to like and shutting off the lines that make for discomfort. You either have science or you don't, and if you have it you are obliged to accept the surprising and disturbing pieces of information, even the overwhelming and upheaving ones, along with the neat and promptly useful bits. It is like that.

24 The only solid piece of scientific truth about which I feel totally confident is that we are profoundly ignorant about nature. Indeed, I regard this as the major discovery of the past hundred years of biology. It is, in its way, an illuminating piece of news. It would have amazed the brightest minds of the eighteenth-century Enlightenment to be told by any of us how little we know, and how bewildering seems the way ahead. It is this sudden confrontation with the depth and scope of ignorance that represents the most significant contribution of twentieth-century science to the human intellect. We are, at last, facing up to it. In earlier times, we either pretended to understand how things worked or ignored the problem, or simply made up stories to fill the gaps. Now that we have begun exploring in earnest, doing serious science, we are getting glimpses of how huge the questions are, and how far from being answered. Because of this, these are hard times for the human intellect, and it is no wonder that we are depressed. It is not so bad being ignorant if you are totally ignorant; the hard thing is knowing in some detail the reality of ignorance, the worst spots and here and there the not-so-bad spots, but no true light at the end of any tunnel nor even any tunnels that can yet be trusted. Hard times, indeed.

25 But we are making a beginning, and there ought to be some satisfaction, even exhilaration, in that. The method works. There are probably no questions we can think up that can't be answered, sooner or later, including even the matter of consciousness. To be sure, there may well be questions we can't think up, ever, and therefore limits to the reach of human intellect which we will never know about, but that is another matter. Within our limits, we should be able to work our way through to all our answers, if we keep at it long enough, and pay attention.

26 I am putting it this way, with all the presumption and confidence that I can summon, in order to raise another, last question. Is this hubris? Is there something fundamentally unnatural, or intrinsi-

cally wrong, or hazardous for the species in the ambition that drives us all to reach a comprehensive understanding of nature, including ourselves? I cannot believe it. It would seem to me a more unnatural thing, and more of an offense against nature, for us to come on the same scene endowed as we are with curiosity, filled to overbrimming as we are with questions, and naturally talented as we are for the asking of clear questions, and then for us to do nothing about it or, worse, to try to suppress the questions. This is the greater danger for our species, to try to pretend that we are another kind of animal, that we do not need to satisfy our curiosity, that we can get along somehow without inquiry and exploration and experimentation, and that the human mind can rise above its ignorance by simply asserting that there are things it has no need to know. This, to my way of thinking, is the real hubris, and it carries danger for us all.

Reading for Rhetorical Strategy

Lewis Thomas begins by setting out in the first four paragraphs the position of critics who believe that advanced research, especially in the biomedical sciences, is an example of "hubris." Thomas identifies himself as one of those engaged in such research and notes that the charge is one to be taken seriously. In paragraph 6, he reduces the argument to a central question: Should there be limits set to scientific inquiry? Thomas deals with the issues of this question throughout the remainder of the essay. In paragraph 7, he raises one of the main hazards in biomedical science—recombinant-DNA research. Though he notes some of the risks, he believes (mainly on the basis of personal experience) that the dangers are exaggerated and, furthermore, that the argument is essentially over the application of knowledge, not scientific inquiry in itself. In paragraph 13, Thomas goes to the heart of the central issue and in paragraph 17, he sets out the reasons that people would want to limit inquiry in certain areas. In paragraphs 18–21, he anticipates how they might go about doing so. From paragraph 23 on, Thomas outlines the reasons for his position—that we should not set limits to scientific inquiry. His reasons ultimately depend on his view of human nature, that we have an "insatiable, uncontrollable drive to learn things and then to exchange the information. . . ." Thomas concludes by turning his opponent's argument on its head. The real "hubris" does not come from science, but from the critics of science who would arrogantly suppress our fundamental human curiosity.

The Idiocy of Rural Life

What Jessica Lange didn't say about the perils of farming

Jeffrey L. Pasley

Jeffrey Pasley currently works as a reporter/researcher for The New Republic, *for which he has written several articles, including an examination of college newspapers, entitled "Paper Pushers," as well as "Inside Dope," on Jimmy Carter's recent public "comeback," and "Postmodern Hustle," about the big business of TV political advertising.*

Jeffrey Pasley was born and raised in Topeka, Kansas, where he attended a rural high school. He earned a degree in history at Carleton College in Minnesota and helped found a student political magazine, The Carleton Observer. *These settings provided him with an opportunity to experience rural life firsthand, experiences which serve as the backdrop for his essay on "The Idiocy of Rural Life."*

In a recent interview, he reported that he wrote "The Idiocy of Rural Life" mainly to "dispel the 'myth' which enlightened and well-meaning people have about commercial farming," a myth, he added, which many farmers and politicians are in no hurry to contradict because it serves their interests. The research he did while preparing to write "The Idiocy of Rural Life" convinced him that medium-size family farms are indeed in trouble, but he also observed that current attempts at legislation do the farmers a disservice by making them more dependent on the government. Though he does not favor the idea, he believes that the only way to deal with the plight of the medium-size family farmers is to allow them to grapple with their own finances, a course which he envisions as leading to an increasing number of supercorporation farms.

The bourgeoisie has subjected the country to the rule of the towns. It has created enormous cities, has greatly increased the urban population as compared with the rural, and has thus rescued a considerable part of the population from the idiocy of rural life.

—Marx and Engels, *The Manifesto of the Communist Party*

If we let Republican farm policies drive our family farmers off the land, then your food won't be grown by farmers whose names are

Jones or Smith or Anderson. No, your food will be raised by Tenneco Corporation, or Chevron, or ITT.

—Senator Tom Harkin, Democrat of Iowa

1 The idea that people still farm for a living in 1986 is an alien and yet somehow romantic one, redolent of grandparents and "Little House on the Prairie." A 1986 *New York Times* poll reported that 58 percent of Americans believe that "farm life is more honest and moral than elsewhere," and 67 percent think that "farmers have closer ties to their families than elsewhere." Images of rural life dominate the "Americana" that passes for tradition in the United States. At a holiday like Thanksgiving, when we are supposed to give thanks to our Pilgrim ancestors and the "bounty" before us, we pay homage to the values embodied in the idea of the "family farm."

2 At one time, this reverence for farm life made sense. The United States began as an agricultural nation. In 1790, 93 percent of the American population worked on farms. Agricultural products made up 80 percent of exports. The Founders, knowing which side their breadbasket was buttered on, heaped extravagant praise on the nation's farmers. "Cultivators of the earth are the most valuable citizens," wrote Thomas Jefferson. "They are the most vigorous, the most independent, the most virtuous, & they are tied to the country & wedded to its liberty and interests by the most lasting bonds."

3 The "family farm" remained a powerful myth long after it ceased to be a political fact. "The great cities rest upon our broad and fertile prairies. Burn down your cities and leave our farms, and your cities will spring up again as if by magic; but destroy our farms and the grass will grow in the streets of every city in the country," thundered Populist leader William Jennings Bryan. Yet as the myth gained strength, Americans were actually leaving the farm by the millions. Though the number of farmers continued to grow until 1920, the cities grew much faster, and the percentage of the American population working in agriculture declined with every census after 1790. The figure dropped to 30 percent by 1910, and to three percent in 1985. As the country grew, it exposed its citizens to creature comforts and other opportunities to prosper more easily, which made it hard to keep the farmers down on the farm. As farmers sold out or quit, those who remained bought up their land. Average farm size increased from 152 acres in 1930 to 441 acres in 1985.

4 I grew up outside Topeka, Kansas, attended a rural high school that had an Ag-Science building but no auditorium, and graduated from a college in the Minnesota farm country. In my experience, the

standard image of the farmer has more to do with urban romanticism than with reality. Yet when the most recent farm crisis hit the nation's front pages and movie screens in 1985, the "family farm" captured the national imagination. Journalists suddenly found the stuff of Greek tragedy in Ames, Iowa. "Beauty is a cruel mask," wrote Paul Hendrickson of the *Washington Post,* "when the earth rolls right up to the edge of the interstate, freshly turned. When the rosebud trees are bleeding into pinks and magentas. When the evening rain is soft as lanolin." And so on.

5 With the papers full of stories about farmers going out of business, committing suicide, or shooting their bankers, farm-state politicians and activists began to campaign for a program specifically to help "family" farms, a proposal that evolved into the "Save the Family Farm Act." Introduced in October by Harkin and Representative Richard Gephardt of Missouri, the bill would impose mandatory controls on the amount farmers could produce and the extent of land they could farm, and would force larger farmers to set aside a larger percentage of their acreage. The bill would roughly double commodity prices (followed by additional yearly increases), sharply increasing the cost of raw food products. A small price to pay, its proponents say, so that family farmers can afford to maintain their traditional way of life. For supporters of the bill, the question is not primarily economic. On humanitarian grounds, they want to preserve the family farm as a way of life. On social grounds, they want a Jeffersonian countryside of small, independent landowners. Yet when I asked Charles O. Frazier of the National Farmers Organization, which supports the Harkin bill, whether the measure might hurt farmers in the long run, he replied, "To hell with the long run, we're talking about running a business."

6 Farmers are just like everyone else. They want to make money and live better than their parents did—and better than their neighbors, if possible. Urbanites often confuse the folksy ways of some farmers with an indifference to material wealth and the refinements that it brings. The difference between farmers and city-dwellers lies not in a different attitude toward money, but in different choices about what to spend it on. Washington lawyers want to make money to buy a BMW and a vacation in Paris. The average farmer may prefer a big pick-up truck with floodlights on top and a motor home he can take to Florida for the winter. Indeed, the young farmers who are in the most trouble today got that way by expanding their operations too quickly in the 1970s. Farmers aren't uniquely greedy, just ambitious like any other businesspeople.

7 In any case, family ownership of farms is not in danger. Non-family corporations operate only 0.3 percent of the nation's farms, own only 1.6 percent of the farmland, and account for only 6.5 percent of total sales of farm products. Agriculture simply doesn't offer a big enough return to attract many large corporations. Though farmland has become concentrated in the hands of fewer landowners, more than half of the large farms are owned by families, in many cases organized as partnerships or family corporations. "The family farm today is grandpa, two sons, and some grandsons who all help manage the place. The family farm of the future is a family farm corporation. These are stronger operations than the old-style family farms," said Jim Diggins, vice president of Farmer's National Company, an Omaha farm management firm.

8 The USDA divides farms into five classes: rural residences ("hobby farmers"), small family, family, large family, and very large farms. The farm crisis has left the large and very large family farms relatively untouched. Because of their economies of scale, even when prices drop they can still make a profit. Large family farmers operate an average of 1,807 acres, hold an average of $1.6 million in assets, and clear an average income of around $78,000 a year; and they are located in areas where living costs are low. Families on very large farms hold an average of 3,727 acres and net an average annual family income in 1983 of almost $600,000.

9 What the Pa Ingalls fans have in mind are rural residences and small family farms, which usually occupy 300 acres or less. Although these small farmers make up two-thirds of the total, however, they do not depend on agriculture for their living. According to the USDA, their "off-farm income" has exceeded their "on-farm income" ever since 1967. The yeomen of 1986 till the soil only as a sideline, and make 90 percent to 100 percent of their income from jobs or businesses off the farm. So the "farm crisis" isn't impoverishing them.

10 In fact, just about the only ones really endangered by the current crisis are medium-sized family farmers. It is this group, which amounts to one-fourth of all farmers, whom the Save the Family Farm Act proposes to save. They are hardly what Jefferson had in mind. On average, they own about 800 acres with assets approaching $1 million. Despite their size, they are far from self-sufficient. These are the farmers, by and large, who depend on government subsidies. Their troubles lie in the basic economic facts of the institution. Unlike small farmers, who have other sources of income, or large farmers, who have diversified multimillion-dollar operations, the family farmer gets paid only when he sells his crops. In between harvests,

he must borrow money if he is to stay in business and feed his family. In no other industry does a worker need to take out loans in order to keep his job. The farmer is at the mercy of the interest rate, as well as the weather and the grain markets. They have the vulnerabilities of workers and businessmen with few of the benefits—neither employment security and benefits on the one hand, nor freedom and the possibility of lavish income on the other.

11 These family farmers occupy a precarious center between the larger and smaller operations. Their farms are big enough to require full-time work but not big enough to lower costs or allow them to take full advantage of new technology. In order to compete with the large farms, the family farmer has to invest in the same expensive machinery and chemicals. Because he has fewer assets, his debts are proportionately much higher. He often has to sell his crop when he needs to make a payment, rather than when the price is highest. His high costs relative to his size make his profit margin razor-thin when it exists at all.

12 Thus medium-sized family farmers rely heavily on the increasing value of their land to help them pay their debts and get new loans. While inflation plagued the rest of the country in the 1970s, family farmers experienced a boom, as food prices and especially land values climbed to unprecedented heights. When inflation slowed down in the 1980s, so did the farm economy, sending land values through the floor. The farmers who invested heavily in new land on the wave of rising values found themselves hopelessly trapped when the values fell. The moral of this tale cannot be missed: those family farmers' fortunes depended not on their farming abilities, but on land values, a factor out of their control. Their ownership of land made them only more dependent. According to the USDA, farmers that leased more land weathered the crisis better, since they had fewer debts to pay at inflated interest rates. The family farmer has always walked this economic treadmill. The United States had its first farm crisis, Shays' Rebellion in 1786, before it had a Constitution.

13 How, then, did American family farmers become, in Harkin's words, "the most efficient and productive in the world"? Family farmers can keep labor costs very low because the family provides the bulk of the labor. Family farms operate under vastly different labor standards than the rest of American industry. "Child labor laws do not apply to family farms because family farms must have child labor to survive," wrote Minnesota politician and family farm alumnus

Darrell McKigney. "Twenty or thirty years ago farm families commonly had ten or more children. [With automation] today five or six is a more common size." From a very early age, family farm children participate in every phase of the operation, from work with dangerous heavy equipment to close contact with carcinogenic chemicals and disease-carrying animals. In numerous farm areas, so many children are taken out of school at harvest time that the schools officially close until the harvest is finished. Practices that would be outrageous at a textile mill suddenly become all warm and cuddly when they appear on the family farm.

14 Family farmers also achieve efficiency through a draconian work schedule that no self-respecting union would allow. "The farm family does physically demanding and highly stressful work at least 14 hours a day (often at least 18 hours a day during harvest season), seven days a week, 365 days a year without a scheduled vacation or weekends off," wrote McKigney. "The farmer must endure all of this without the benefit of a health plan, safety regulations, a retirement plan, workmen's compensation, or any of the benefits that most U.S. labor unions demand." Psychologist Peter Keller, past president of the Association for Rural Mental Health, pointed out that many farmers are permanently tied to their farms. A dairy farmer, for instance, cannot just take off for a two-week vacation and not milk his cows. "Farmers lose perspective on the other things in life," said Keller. "The farm literally consumes them."

15 And the family farm physically consumes those who work on it, too. According to the National Safety Council, farming is the nation's most dangerous job—more dangerous even than working in a mine. In 1983 farming clocked in at 55 job-related deaths per 100,000 workers, or five times the rate for all major industries combined. In 1984 Tom Knudson of the *Des Moines Register* published a Pulitzer Prize-winning series that cataloged the myriad health and safety risks run by farmers. Farmers working with powerful farm machinery face death or maiming by crushing, chopping, asphyxiation, or electrocution. ("As he reached for a stalk of corn dangling from the corn picker, Vern Tigges of Dexter felt a jolt. In the next moments in a fierce and frantic struggle with the machine, three fingers were ripped from his hand.") They may be poisoned by the nitrogen dioxide gas that accumulates in grain silos, or have their lungs permanently damaged from breathing the air in enclosed hog pens. They may be crippled by "farmer's lung disease," caused by moldy grain dust. They may develop leukemia from contact with

herbicides used on corn. (Iowa farmers contract leukemia 24 percent more frequently than the average American.) Knudson wrote that recent health findings exploded "the myth of farming as the good life of fresh air and sunshine."

16 But what about the benefits of good-old-fashioned-lemonade values and the supportive friendliness of a rural community? Though hard data is difficult to come by, many small towns appear to suffer from teenage pregnancy, alcoholism, and other social maladies at rates that are higher than average. One New England study showed relatively high suicide rates among farmers during a period antedating the farm crisis. And rural communities haven't always stood by their financially troubled members. Sociologist Paul Lasley's Iowa Farm and Rural Life Poll reported that a majority of Iowa farmers felt they received little or no support from their churches, neighbors, schools, or local voluntary organizations. At a "town meeting" with Representative Tim Penny, Democrat of Minnesota, in New Market, Minnesota, I heard farmers ridicule the idea of slightly higher property taxes to improve the area's meager school system practically in the same breath that they demanded higher subsidies for themselves. These things never happened on "The Waltons."

17 The usual lesson gleaned from the facts of farm life is that there is nothing wrong with the family farm that higher commodity prices won't solve. Yet farm programs have come and farm programs have gone, and still farmers (and especially farmer's children) have left, for the simple reason that life is usually better off the farm. "It is a way of life, but so was the village blacksmith," says economist William H. Peterson. The urban "wage-slave" worker, for all his lack of "independence" and supposed alienation from his work, has some decided advantages over the rural yeoman. He has the security of a regular income, and definite hours set aside for his leisure. More often than not, the law guarantees the non-farmer a safe place to work, and protects him from the whims of his employer. The urban wage-earner has daily contact with a wide variety of other people, and access to cultural events and decent public services.

18 Proponents of Harkin-Gephardt and similar measures worry about where farmers will go once they leave the land. Yet former farmers do not just fade away. They have skills and work habits that many employers find attractive. (If they sell their farms, they will also have several hundred thousand dollars.) Growing farm manage-

ment companies hire experienced farmers to manage large rented operations, under much more favorable terms and conditions than they could get on their own. Farmers working for others would demand better working conditions. Many states now have retraining programs for those who give up farming and want to learn a new trade or profession.

19 I saw the movie *Country* on a rainy Monday night in Topeka. Two farmers and their wives and a group of teenage girls were the only other people in the theater. The farmers complained loudly throughout the first hour of the film, and then left, shaking their heads in disgust. The girls sat through the final credits, sniffling at the plight of Sam Shepard and Jessica Lange. At a farm protest rally in Minnesota, I heard a song that went like this:

> *Now some folks say*
> *There ain't no hell*
> *But they don't farm*
> *So they can't tell.*

20 We should take the singer at his word. Tyrants from Stalin to Mao to Pol Pot have subjugated their populations by forcing them to "stay on the land." Given the conditions of life on the family farm, if ITT or Chevron or Tenneco really does try to force some family farmers off their land, they might well be doing them a favor.

Additional Rhetorical Strategies

Illustration (throughout); Comparison and Contrast (paragraphs 2–3, 6–7); Cause and Effect (paragraphs 5, 10–11, 13, 15, 18); Definition (paragraphs 7–8); Classification (paragraph 8).

Examining Words and Meaning

1. What does Pasley mean when he observes that "the standard image of the farmer has more to do with urban romanticism than with reality" (paragraph 4)? What is this "romantic" view of farmers and farming which Pasley attributes to city dwellers? In what ways has this view influenced the "national imagination"? According to Pasley,

how has this view influenced political attempts to save the family farm? What larger purpose do legislators seem to have in mind when proposing such legislation as "Save the Family Farm Act"?

2. Pasley spends a good deal of time in his opening paragraphs recounting the myths of the traditional "family farm." As he develops his essay, however, he shifts the focus of his readers' attention to contemporary definitions and examples of the "family farm." In what specific ways has it changed? What does Pasley see as the advantages/disadvantages of this new definition? Do you agree? Explain your response.

Focusing on Structures and Strategies

1. Consider the organization of Pasley's essay. How does he structure the sequence of points he makes in opposition to what he calls "this reverence for farm life"? On what sort of evidence does Pasley seem to rely on most in formulating his argument? How well does he anticipate the points his opponents on this issue might make? How well does he counter their arguments?

2. How does Pasley characterize the life of the farmer and the typical family farm? What makes Pasley feel he is qualified to say what farm life is "really" like? How does he counter the sense of the farmer as self-sufficient and independent? Why is it important both to his debunking and to his economic argument to show that farmers are "just like everyone else," that is, ambitious?

3. Pasley's dispelling of the family farm myth serves as the basis for his political and economic attitudes. Why, according to Pasley, is the medium-size family farm the only type of farm endangered by the current farm crisis? On what contingencies does the success of such farmers depend? In what ways does Pasley see the urban "wage-slave" as holding a more desirable position?

4. How does Pasley's attempt to show the "idiocies" of rural life relate to his suggestions that farmers who leave farming will not necessarily suffer? Pasley devotes a great deal of time to demonstrating the dangers and difficulties of farming in order to conclude that farmers leave because "life is usually better off the farm." Given the evidence Pasley supplies, how else might you account for the fact that so many farmers leave their careers? What additional evidence might you collect either to strengthen Pasley's claim or your own? Although Pasley never specifically states what he

thinks should be done about the farm crisis, how would you characterize his attitudes?

Suggestions for Further Discussion and Writing

1. What is the effect of Pasley's invoking a passage from *The Manifesto of the Communist Party* for his title? In what other ways is—or isn't—this passage an appropriate source for arguing his case against farm life?
2. Comment on the role children play in maintaining the "family farm." What is your view of the fact that few child labor laws do not apply to farming? Write an essay in which you argue for—or against—exempting the children of farmers from the protection of child labor laws.
3. Several other aspects of contemporary American rural life might well also be characterized as having "more to do with romanticism than with reality." Consider, for example, the modern-day image of the cowboy most "urbanites" cultivate. So too, how far from reality have American urban dwellers strayed in their collective image of, say, Native Americans, forest rangers, and lumberjacks? Write an essay in which you argue that the "romantic" image of one of these groups is sadly out of touch with the reality of their day-to-day lives. Conclude your essay by documenting the damage done to these groups by the urban public's maintaining such distorted, "romantic" images.

The Idiocy of Urban Life

or, The Cow's Revenge

Henry Fairlie

Henry Fairlie is a British-born political and social commentator and contributing editor to The New Republic. *Educated at Corpus Christi College in Oxford University, he began his career as a feature writer for*

The Observer *in London before serving from 1950 to 1954 as a political editorial writer on the* London Times. *Since coming to the United States, Fairlie has shifted his focus to contemporary American politics. He is the author of such critical studies of the American political scene as* The Life of Politics *(1969),* The Kennedy Promise *(1973),* The Spoiled Child of the Western World *(1976),* The Miscarriage of the American Idea of Our Time *(1976), and acerbic profiles of the Democratic and Republican parties in the twentieth century. More recently, he has published* The Seven Deadly Sins Today. *His work is consistently distinguished by his incisive and witty analysis of American Life.*

Henry Fairlie published "The Idiocy of Urban Life" in a January 1987 issue of The New Republic *as a response to Jeffrey Pasley's essay, "The Idiocy of Rural Life" published one month earlier in* The New Republic. *Pasley's essay (the title was derived from a famous passage in* The Communist Manifesto) *appears on page 476.*

Fairlie draws on his apparently abundant reserves of irony to challenge—and delightfully invert—Pasley's contention that the prevailing public image of rural life in contemporary America, like the "standard image of the farmer," has "more to do with urban romanticism than with reality."

1 Between about 3 a.m. and 6 a.m. the life of the city is civil. Occasionally the lone footsteps of someone walking to or from work echo along the sidewalk. All work that has to be done at those hours is useful—in bakeries, for example. Even the newspaper presses stop turning forests into lies. Now and then a car comes out of the silence and cruises easily through the blinking traffic lights. The natural inhabitants of the city come out from damp basements and cellars. With their pink ears and paws, sleek, well-groomed, their whiskers combed, rats are true city dwellers. Urban life, during the hours when they reign, is urbane.

2 These rats are social creatures, as you can tell if you look out on the city street during an insomniac night. But after 6 a.m., the two-legged, daytime creatures of the city begin to stir; and it is they, not the rats, who bring the rat race. You might think that human beings congregate in large cities because they are gregarious. The opposite is true. Urban life today is aggressively individualistic and atomized. Cities are not social places.

3 The lunacy of modern city life lies first in the fact that most city dwellers who can do so try to live outside the city boundaries. So the

two-legged creatures have created suburbs, exurbs, and finally rururbs (rurbs to some). Disdaining rural life, they try to create simulations of it. No effort is spared to let city dwellers imagine they are living anywhere but in a city: patches of grass in the more modest suburbs, broader spreads in the richer ones further out; prim new trees planted along the streets; at the foot of the larger back yards, a pretense to bosky woodlands. Black & Decker thrives partly on this basic do-it-yourself rural impulse in urban life; and with the declining demand for the great brutes of farm tractors, John Deere has turned to the undignified business of making dinky toy tractors for the suburbanites to ride like Roman charioteers as they mow their lawns.

4 In the city itself gentrification means two tubs of geraniums outside the front door of a town house that has been prettified to look like a country cottage. The homes, restaurants, and even offices of city dwellers are planted thick with vegetation. Some executives have window boxes inside their high-rise offices; secretaries, among their other chores, must now be horticulturists. Commercials on television, aimed primarily at city dwellers, have more themes of the countryside than of urban life. Cars are never seen in a traffic jam, but whiz through bucolic scenery. Lovers are never in tenements, but drift through sylvan glades. Cigarettes come from Marlboro Country. Merrill Lynch is a bull. Coors is not manufactured in a computerized brewery, but taken from mountain streams.

5 The professional people buy second homes in the country as soon as they can afford them, and as early as possible on Friday head out of the city they have created. The New York intellectuals and artists quaintly say they are "going to the country" for the weekend or summer, but in fact they have created a little Manhattan-by-the-Sea around the Hamptons, spreading over the Long Island potato fields whose earlier solitude was presumably the reason why they first went there. City dwellers take the city with them to the country, for they will not live without its pamperings. The main streets of America's small towns, which used to have hardware and dry goods stores, are now strips of boutiques. Old-fashioned barbers become unisex hairdressing salons. The brown rats stay in the cities because of the filth the humans leave during the day. The rats clean it up at night. Soon the countryside will be just as nourishing to them, as the city dwellers take their filth with them.

6 The recent dispersal of the urban middle-class population is

only the latest development in this now established lunatic pattern. People who work in Cleveland live as far out as lovely Geauga and Ashtabula counties in northeast Ohio, perhaps 30 or 50 miles away. A bank manager in Chardon, which used to be a gracious market town in Geauga, once explained to me how the city people who come to live there want about five acres of land. "But they want the five acres for themselves alone, and not for others who come to follow their example, though no one is going to supply the services—electricity, gas, sewerage, water—for a few people living on their five acres. So the place fills up, and soon they've rebuilt the urban life they said they were escaping. What is more, they don't like paying for those services, since the rich come out to escape the high city taxes." They also force up the price of land and old houses, so that real estate is put beyond the reach of farmers and others who must work there.

7 In the old industrial cities, people lived near their places of work. The mill hands lived around the cotton mill, and the mill owner lived close at hand, in the big house on the hill, looking down on the chimney stacks belching out the smoke that was the evidence they were producing and giving employment. The steelworkers and the steel magnate lived close to the steel mill. The German brewer Miller lived next to his brewery in Milwaukee. The city churches had congregations that were representative of both the resident population and the local working population. It wasn't so much that work gave meaning to life as that it created a community that extended into and enriched the residential community, and sustained a solidarity among the workers. It was the automakers, especially the ever revolutionary Henry Ford, who realized that their own product enabled them to build factories far from the dispersed homes of the workers, and not unconsciously they appreciated that a dispersed work force would be docile.

8 Work still gives meaning to rural life, the family, and churches. But in the city today work and home, family and church, are separated. What the office workers do for a living is not part of their home life. At the same time they maintain the pointless frenzy of their work hours in their hours off. They rush from the office to jog, to the gym or the YMCA pool, to work at their play with the same joylessness. In the suburbs there is only an artificial community life—look at the notice board of community activities in a new satellite town like Reston, outside Washington. They breathlessly exhort the resident to a variety of boring activities—amateur theatricals, earnest

lectures by officers of the United Nations Association, sing-songs—a Tupperware community culture as artificial as the "lake" in the supposed center of the town. These upright citizens of Reston were amazed one day when they found that their bored children were as hooked on drugs as those in any ghetto.

9 Even though the offices of today's businesses in the city are themselves moving out to the suburbs, this does not necessarily bring the workers back closer to their workplace. It merely means that to the rush-hour traffic into the city there is now added a rush-hour traffic out to the suburbs in the morning, and back around and across the city in the evening. As the farmer walks down to his farm in the morning, the city dweller is dressing for the first idiocy of his day, which he not only accepts but even seeks—the journey to work.

10 This takes two forms: solitary confinement in one's own car, or the discomfort of extreme overcrowding on public transport. Both produce angst. There are no more grim faces than those of the single drivers we pedestrians can glimpse at the stoplights during the rush hour. It is hard to know why they are so impatient in the morning to get to their useless and wearisome employments; but then in the evening, when one would have thought they would be relaxed, they are even more frenetic. Prisoners in boxes on wheels, they do not dare wonder why they do it. If they take to public transit, there may still be the ritual of the wife driving the breadwinner to the subway station, and meeting him in the evening. Life in the suburbs and exurbs has become a bondage to the hours of journeying.

11 The car, of course, is not a vehicle suitable to the city. The problems of traffic in the city, over which urban planners have wracked their brains for years, could be simply eliminated if private cars were banned, or if a swinging tax were levied on those who drive into the city alone. The dollar toll in New York should be raised to five dollars—each way. There should be a toll on all the bridges crossing the Potomac from Virginia, and at every point where the rush hour drivers cross the District line from Maryland. The urban dwellers in Virginia and Maryland make sure that their jurisdictions obstruct any legitimate way the District might force the suburban daytime users of the city to pay for its manifold services. But ten dollars a day to cross into Washington, in addition to parking fees, would soon cut down the urban idiocy of bringing a small room to work and parking it in precious space for eight hours.

12 On the bus or subway each morning and evening other urban

dwellers endure the indignity of being crushed into unwelcome proximity with strangers whom they have no wish to communicate with except in terms of abuse, rancor, and sometimes violent hostility. The wonder is not that there is an occasional shooting on public transit, but that shootings are not daily occurrences. The crushing of people together on the subway can have unintended results. One of my memories is of being on a London tube at rush hour in my younger days, pressed against a young woman who was with her boyfriend. To my surprise, though not unwelcome, her hand slipped into mine. It squeezed. Mine squeezed back. Her expression when they got out at Leicester Square, and she found she'd been holding my hand, and even had begun pulling me off the train, has not been easy to forget in 35 years. But generally even eye contact on public transport is treated as an act of aggression or at least harassment.

13 This primary urban activity of getting to and from work has other curious features. As every Englishman visiting America for the first time remarks, the smell of deodorants on a crowded bus or subway in the morning is overpowering. Even the stale smell of the human body would be preferable. It must account for the glazed looks—perhaps all deodorants contain a gas introduced by the employers to numb the urban office workers to the fatuity of their labors.

14 But whether they have come by car or public transit, the urban office workers must continue their journey even after they have gotten to the city. They then must travel in one of the banks of elevators that often run the height of three city blocks or more. Once again they are herded into confined spaces. City people are so used to moving in herds that they even fight to cram themselves into the elevators, as they do into buses or subway cars, as if it mattered that they might get to their pointless occupations a minute later. The odd thing about the elevators themselves is that there are no fares for distances often longer than those between two bus stops. Office elevators are public transit, free to anyone who needs to use them—but there's no such thing as a free elevator ride, as the president will tell you. Banks of elevators occupy large areas of valuable city land on every floor. This and the cost of running and maintaining them is written into the rents paid by the employers. If the urban workers had not been reduced to a docile herd, they would demand that the employers who expect them to get to work subsidize all the public transport into the city, while leaving those who bring their rooms on wheels to pay for themselves.

15 In the modern office building in the city there are windows that don't open. This is perhaps the most symbolic lunacy of all. Outdoors is something you can look at through glass but not touch or hear. These windows are a scandal because they endanger the lives of office workers in case of fire. But no less grievous, even on the fairest spring or fall day the workers cannot put their heads outside. The employers do not mind this, may have even conspired with the developers to dream up such an infliction, because the call of spring or fall would distract their employees. Thus it's not surprising that the urban worker has no knowledge of the seasons. He is aware simply that in some months there is air conditioning, and in others through the same vents comes fetid central heating. Even outside at home in their suburbs the city dwellers may know that sometimes it's hot, and sometimes cold, but no true sense of the rhythms of the seasons is to be had from a lawn in the back yard and a few spindly trees struggling to survive.

16 City dwellers can now eat the vegetables of their choice at almost any time of the year—always with the proviso that they will never taste a fresh vegetable, even though the best supermarkets have various ways to touch them up. Anyone who has not eaten peas picked that morning has never tasted a pea. The simple fact is that some frozen vegetables (frozen within hours of being picked) are fresher than the alleged fresh vegetables on the produce counter of the supermarkets. The suburbanite again struggles to simulate the blessings of rural life by maintaining a vegetable patch in the back yard. The main consequence of this melancholy pursuit comes in high summer, when office workers bring in their homegrown tomatoes to share with their colleagues, ill-colored, lump-faced objects with scars all over them, since they have not been staked correctly.

17 The city dweller reels from unreality to unreality through each day, always trying to recover the rural life that has been surrendered for the city lights. (City life, it is worth noticing, has produced almost no proverbs. How could it when proverbs—a rolling stone gathers no moss, and so on—are a distillation from a sane existence?) No city dweller, even in the suburbs, knows the wonder of a pitch-dark country lane at night. Nor does he naturally get any exercise from his work. When jogging and other childish pursuits began to exercise the unused bodies of city dwellers, two sensible doctors (a breed that has almost died with the general practitioner) said that city workers could get their exercise better in more natural ways. They could begin by walking upstairs to their office floors instead of using the elevators.

18 Every European points out that Americans are the most round-shouldered people in the world. Few of them carry themselves with an upright stance, although a correct stance and gait is the first precondition of letting your lungs breathe naturally and deeply. Electric typewriters cut down the amount of physical exertion needed to hit the keys; the buttons on a word processor need even less effort, as you can tell from the posture of those who use them. They might as well be in armchairs. They rush out to jog or otherwise Fonda-ize their leisure to try to repair the damage done during the day.

19 Dieting is an urban obsession. Country dwellers eat what they please, and work it off in useful physical employments, and in the open air, cold or hot, rainy or sunny. Mailmen are the healthiest city workers. When was your mailman last ill for a day? If one reads the huge menus that formed a normal diet in the 19th century, you realize that even the city dwellers could dispatch these gargantuan repasts because they still shared many of the benefits of rural life. (Disraeli records a meal at the house of one lordly figure that was composed of nine meat or game entrées. The butler asked after the eighth, "Snipe or pheasant, my lord?") They rode horseback to work or to Parliament even in the coldest weather, and nothing jolts and enlivens the liver more than riding. Homes were cold in the winter, except in the immediate vicinity of the hearth or stove. Cold has a way of eating up excess fat. No wonder dieting is necessary in a cossetted life in which the body is forced to do no natural heavy work.

20 Everything in urban life is an effort either to simulate rural life or to compensate for its loss by artificial means. The greatest robbery from the country in recent years has of course been Levi's, which any self-respecting farmer or farm worker is almost ashamed to wear nowadays. It was when Saks Fifth Avenue began advocating designer jeans years ago that the ultimate urban parody of rural life was reached. The chic foods of the city have to be called health foods, which would seem a tautology in the country. And insofar as there used to be entertainments in the city that enticed, these can now be enjoyed more than sufficiently on VCRs and stereos.

21 It is from this day-to-day existence of unreality, pretense, and idiocy that the city people, slumping along their streets even when scurrying, never looking up at their buildings, far less the sky, have the insolence to disdain and mock the useful and rewarding life of the country people who support them. Now go out and carry home

a Douglas Fir, call it a Christmas tree, and enjoy 12 days of contact with nature. Of course city dwellers don't know it once had roots.

Additional Rhetorical Strategies

Illustration (throughout); Definition (paragraph 4); Cause and Effect (paragraphs 4, 7, 10, 12, 15, 16, 18, 19); Comparison and Contrast (implied throughout).

Examining Words and Meaning

1. What does Fairlie mean when he speaks of the "rural impulse in urban life"? What examples of this impulse does Fairlie present as his essay proceeds? What attitude does he express toward each of these impulses? What, for example, is his attitude toward suburbanites?
2. Consider the fun Fairlie has playing with familiar words, phrases, and expressions. Here is one example: "Office elevators are public transit, free to anyone who needs to use them—but there's no such thing as a free elevator ride . . ." (paragraph 14). Locate additional examples of similar plays on words. What is the effect of such efforts? Do they increase or decrease the overall effectiveness of his essay? Explain why.

Focusing on Structures and Strategies

1. In what specific ways does Fairlie's essay constitute a rebuttal to Jeffrey Pasley's essay, "The Idiocy of Rural Life," published one month before in *The New Republic* (see p. 476)? Outline each of Pasley's points and show how Fairlie responds to it. Whom do you find more convincing on each point? Why?
2. In his final paragraph, Fairlie announces: "It is from this day-to-day existence of unreality, pretense, and idiocy that the city people . . . have the insolence to disdain and mock the useful and rewarding life of the country people who support them." What are the implications

of this remark? What does it assume about the relation between city and country dwellers? In what sense does this conclusion "respond" to the Pasley article? What aspects of the Pasley essay does Fairlie ignore? In what ways does Fairlie's essay merely illustrate the romanticization of country life which Pasley attempts to expose?

3. This essay might well have been called "The *Ironies* of Urban Life." Identify the major ironies Fairlie discusses in connection with city living. How do these ironies relate to Fairlie's characterization of the "unreality" and "artificiality" of city life? Identify as many examples of this artificiality as possible in Fairlie's article. How do these ironies contribute to the sense of "angst" which Fairlie associates with city living?

4. With these ironies in mind, look again at the opening paragraphs of the essay. How is Fairlie's portrait of the city between 3 A.M. and 6 A.M. ironic? What are the effects, for example, of such sentences as "Even the newspaper presses stop turning forests into lies" and "The natural inhabitants of the city come out from damp basements and cellars"? Explain how the force of the first paragraph hinges on the word "rats." How does Fairlie exemplify and develop this image—and the associated metaphor of the "rat race"—as the essay proceeds? Point to specific words and phrases to verify your response.

5. Fairlie speaks of city life as "parodying" country life. How does he use this as evidence of the desirability and superiority of country life? How else might this aspect of city life be construed? What specific examples does Fairlie include as contrasts to the artificiality of city life? What do these examples have in common? How would you describe Fairlie's concept of an ideal, "natural" life? Consider particularly his vision of community, work, and health.

Suggestions for Further Discussion and Writing

1. Fairlie spends approximately one-third of his essay describing the idiocy of "the journey to work." How does he characterize the people who participate in this daily ritual? How does the journey to work emphasize the city dweller's "bondage"? How are Fairlie's descriptions of space in the city used to stress this sense of confinement and isolation?

2. Irony often can be an effective ingredient in successful arguments. Using Fairlie's essay as a model, write a similarly ironic attack on

some controversial aspect of modern American life. The pernicious influence of advertising on daily behavior might well be one such widely held and controversial public belief. The American need to fix blame for public embarrassments or calamities is another. The list is long. After you have settled on a topic, develop a proposition about that topic and argue convincingly—and ironically—in support of your claim. Be sure to build in, as Fairlie does here, generous attention to ironic effects.

3. The conflict between "the idiocy of" rural and urban life is grounded in fundamentally opposing assumptions about, among other matters, the relative values of time and space in urban and rural experience. Consider other examples of conflicting assumptions about experience. The differing assumptions that many people still hold about what men and women can—and cannot—do is but one convenient example. Consider the consequences of such a view of male/female inequality—military registration. What do you think the "orthodox" view is concerning this controversial subject? Write an essay in which you summarize the orthodox view as succinctly as you can. Then try to refute it by using the same strategies of argument that Fairlie uses in his essay. You'll need to examine—and challenge—the assumptions that underpin the orthodox view of such an issue.

Fifty Million Handguns

Adam Smith

"Adam Smith" is the pseudonym of George Goodman, a Harvard graduate, Rhodes Scholar, financial reporter, columnist, lecturer, screenwriter, and co-founder of New York *magazine. One of America's most widely read and accomplished financial analysts, Goodman began his career in journalism as a reporter for* Collier's *and* Barron's. *In 1958, he moved to* Time *and* Fortune, *where he served as an associate editor until 1960. After several years as the vice president of the Lincoln Fund and as a screenwriter in Los Angeles, Goodman returned to reporting on the financial world. During the period when he edited* Institutional Investor, *he also helped put* New York

magazine into print. The recipient of many honors and awards (including the G. M. Loeb Award for Distinguished Achievement in Writing about Business and Finance), Goodman is also the author of several novels and screenplays, among them The Wheeler Dealers *(1963) and* The Americanization of Emily *(1964). Under the pseudonym "Adam Smith," Goodman has also published a great deal of nonfiction—most notably* The Money Game *(1968),* Supermoney *(1972),* Powers of Mind *(1975), and* Paper Money *(1981).*

For the past several years, Goodman has also been a contributing editor of Esquire. *In the following essay, which first appeared in* Esquire *in 1981, Goodman dispassionately balances the pros and cons of gun control and concludes that some form of regulation is needed to reduce America's penchant for violence.*

1 "You people," said my Texas host, "do not understand guns or gun people." By "you people" he meant not just me, whom he happened to be addressing, but anyone from a large eastern or midwestern city. My Texas host is a very successful businessman, an intelligent man. "There are two cultures," he said, "and the nongun culture looks down on the gun culture."

2 My Texas host had assumed—correctly—that I do not spend a lot of time with guns. The last one I knew intimately was a semiautomatic M-14, and, as any veteran knows, the Army bids you call it a weapon, not a gun. I once had to take that weapon apart and reassemble it blindfolded, and I liked it better than the heavy old M-1. We were also given a passing introduction to the Russian Kalashnikov and the AK-47, the Chinese copy of that automatic weapon, presumably so we could use these products of our Russian and Chinese enemies if the need arose. I remember that you could drop a Kalashnikov in the mud and pick it up and it would still fire. I also remember blowing up a section of railroad track using only an alarm clock, a primer cord, and a plastic called C-4. The day our little class blew up the track at Fort Bragg was rather fun. These experiences give me some credibility with friends from the "gun culture." (Otherwise, they have no lasting social utility whatsoever.) And I do not share the fear of guns—at least of "long guns," rifles and shotguns—that some of my college-educated city-dweller friends have, perhaps because of my onetime intimacy with that Army rifle, whose serial number I still know.

3 In the gun culture, said my Texas host, a boy is given a .22 rifle around the age of twelve, a shotgun at fourteen, and a .30-caliber rifle at sixteen. The young man is taught to use and respect these instruments. My Texas host showed me a paragraph in a book by Herman Kahn in which Kahn describes the presentation of the .22 as a rite of passage, like a confirmation or a bar mitzvah. "Young persons who are given guns," he wrote, "go through an immediate maturing experience because they are thereby given a genuine and significant responsibility." Any adult from the gun culture, whether or not he is a relative, can admonish any young person who appears to be careless with his weapon. Thus, says Kahn, the gun-culture children take on "enlarging and maturing responsibilities" that their coddled upper-middle-class counterparts from the nongun culture do not share. The children of my Texas host said "sir" to their father and "ma'am" to their mother.

4 I do not mean to argue with the rite-of-passage theory. I am quite willing to grant it. I bring it up because the subjects of guns and gun control are very emotional ones, and if we are to solve the problems associated with them, we need to arrive at a consensus within and between gun and nongun cultures in our country.

5 Please note that the rite-of-passage gifts are shotguns and rifles. Long guns have sporting uses. Nobody gives a child a handgun, and nobody shoots a flying duck with a .38 revolver. Handguns have only one purpose.

6 Some months ago, a college friend of mine surprised a burglar in his home in Washington, D.C. Michael Halberstam was a cardiologist, a writer, and a contributor to this magazine. The burglar shot Halberstam, but Halberstam ran him down with his car on the street outside before he died, and the case received widespread press. I began to work on this column, in high anger, right after his death. A few days later, John Lennon was killed in New York. These two dreadful murders produced an outpouring of grief, followed immediately by intense anger and the demand that something be done, that Congress pass a gun-control law. The National Rifle Association was quick to point out that a gun-control law would not have prevented either death; Halberstam's killer had already violated a whole slew of existing laws, and Lennon's was clearly sufficiently deranged or determined to kill him under any gun law. The National Rifle Association claims a million members, and it is a highly organized lobby. Its Political Victory Fund "works for the defeat of antigun candidates and for the support and election of progun office seekers." Let us

grant the National Rifle Association position that the accused killers in these two recent spectacular shootings might not have been deterred even by severe gun restrictions.

7 In the course of researching this column, I talked to representatives of both the progun and the antigun lobbies. Anomalies abound. Sam Fields, a spokesman for the National Coalition to Ban Handguns, is an expert rifleman who was given a gun at age thirteen by his father, a New York City policeman. The progun banner is frequently carried by Don Kates Jr., who describes himself as a liberal, a former civil rights worker, and a professor of constitutional law. Fields and Kates have debated each other frequently. Given their backgrounds, one might expect their positions to be reversed.

8 Some of the progun arguments run as follows:

9 Guns don't kill people, people kill people. Gun laws do not deter criminals. (A 1976 University of Wisconsin study of gun laws concluded that "gun-control laws have no individual or collective effect in reducing the rate of violent crime.") A mandatory sentence for carrying an unlicensed gun, says Kates, would punish the "ordinary decent citizens in high-crime areas who carry guns illegally because police protection is inadequate and they don't have the special influence necessary to get a 'carry' permit." There are fifty million handguns out there in the United States already; unless you were to use a giant magnet, there is no way to retrieve them. The majority of people do not want guns banned. A ban on handguns would be like Prohibition—widely disregarded, unenforceable, and corrosive to the nation's sense of moral order. Federal registration is the beginning of federal tyranny; we might someday need to use those guns against the government.

10 Some of the antigun arguments go as follows:

11 People kill people, but handguns make it easier. When other weapons (knives, for instance) are used, the consequences are not so often deadly. Strangling or stabbing someone takes a different degree of energy and intent than pulling a trigger. Registration will not interfere with hunting and other rifle sports but will simply exercise control over who can carry handguns. Ordinary people do not carry handguns. If a burglar has a gun in his hand, it is quite insane for you to shoot it out with him, as if you were in a quick-draw contest in the Wild West. Half of all the guns used in crimes are stolen; 70 percent of the stolen guns are handguns. In other words, the supply of handguns used by criminals already comes to a great extent from the households these guns were supposed to protect.

12 "I'll tell you one thing," said a lieutenant on the local police force in my town. "You should never put that decal in your window, the one that says THIS HOUSE IS PROTECTED BY AN ARMED CITIZEN. The gun owners love them, but that sign is just an invitation that says 'Come and rob my guns.' Television sets and stereos are fenced at a discount; guns can actually be fenced at a premium. The burglar doesn't want to meet you. I have had a burglar tell me, 'If I wanted to meet people, I would have been a mugger.' "

13 After a recent wave of burglaries, the weekly newspaper in my town published a front-page story. "Do not buy a gun—you're more likely to shoot yourself than a burglar," it said. At first the police agreed with that sentiment. Later, they took a slightly different line. "There is more danger from people having accidents or their kids getting hold of those guns than any service in defending their houses; but there was a flap when the paper printed that, so now we don't say anything," said my local police lieutenant. "If you want to own a gun legally, okay. Just be careful and know the laws."

14 What police departments tell inquiring citizens seems to depend not only on the local laws but also on whether or not that particular police department belongs to the gun culture.

15 Some of the crime statistics underlying the gun arguments are surprising. Is crime-ridden New York City the toughest place in the country? No: your chances of being murdered are higher in Columbus, Georgia, in Pine Bluff, Arkansas, and in Houston, Texas, among others. Some of the statistics are merely appalling: we had roughly ten thousand handgun deaths last year. The British had forty. In 1978, there were 18,714 Americans murdered. Sixty-four percent were killed with handguns. In that same year, *we had more killings with handguns by children ten years old and younger than the British had by killers of all ages.* The Canadians had 579 homicides last year; we had more than twenty thousand.

16 H. Rap Brown, the Sixties activist, once said, "Violence is as American as apple pie." I guess it is. We think fondly of Butch Cassidy and the Sundance Kid; we do not remember the names of the trainmen and the bank clerks they shot. Four of our Presidents have died violently; the British have never had a prime minister assassinated. *Life* magazine paid $8,000 to Halberstam's accused killer for photos of his boyhood. Now he will be famous, like Son of Sam. The list could go on and on.

17 I am willing to grant to the gunners a shotgun in every closet. Shotguns are not used much in armed robberies, or even by citizens in arguments with each other. A shotgun is a better home-defense

item anyway, say my police friends, if only because you have to be very accurate with a handgun to knock a man down with one. But the arguments over which kinds of guns are best only demonstrate how dangerously bankrupt our whole society is in ideas on personal safety.

18 Our First Lady has a handgun.

19 Would registry of handguns stop the criminal from carrying the unregistered gun? No, and it might afflict the householder with some extra red tape. However, there is a valid argument for registry. Such a law might have no immediate effect, but we have to begin somewhere. We license automobiles and drivers. That does not stop automobile deaths, but surely the highways would be even more dangerous if populated with unlicensed drivers and uninspected cars. The fifty million handguns outstanding have not caused the crime rate to go down. Another two million handguns will be sold this year, and I will bet that the crime rate still does not go down.

20 Our national behavior is considered close to insane by some of the other advanced industrial nations. We have gotten so accustomed to crime and violence that we have begun to take them for granted; thus we are surprised to learn that the taxi drivers in Tokyo carry far more than five dollars in cash, that you can walk safely around the streets of Japan's largest cities, and that Japan's crime rate is going *down.* I know there are cultural differences; I am told that in Japan the criminal is expected to turn himself in so as not to shame his parents. Can we imagine that as a solution to crime here?

21 In a way, the tragic killings of Michael Halberstam and John Lennon have distracted us from a larger and more complex problem. There is a wave of grief, a wave of anger—and then things go right on as they did before. We become inured to the violence and dulled to the outrage. Perhaps, indeed, no legislation could stop murders like these, and perhaps national gun legislation would not produce overnight change. The hard work is not just to get the gunners to join in; the hard work is to do something about our ragged system of criminal justice, to shore up our declining faith in the institutions that are supposed to protect us, and to promote the notion that people should take responsibility for their own actions.

22 What makes us so different from the Japanese and the British and the Canadians? They are not armed, as we are, yet their streets and houses are far safer. Should we not be asking ourselves some sober questons about whether we are living the way we want to?

Additional Rhetorical Strategies

Definition (paragraph 1); Cause and Effect (paragraphs 3, 6, 19); Narration (paragraphs 2, 6); Illustration (paragraphs 6, 9, 15); Comparison and Contrast (paragraphs 15, 20, 22).

Examining Words and Meaning

1. In what sense do members of what Smith calls "the gun culture" equate owning a gun with "a rite of passage, like a confirmation or a bar mitzvah"? Consider the nature of the simile Smith cites here. In what specific ways does—or doesn't—the reference to "confirmation or a bar mitzvah" strike you as appropriate? When—and how—does Smith acknowledge the validity of this "rite of passage theory"? With what effect?

2. What is the point of Smith's distinguishing between "long guns" and "handguns"? How does this distinction help Smith to express his own position on gun control? In this respect, how does he anticipate opposing points of view on this issue and work toward establishing a "consensus" between the "gun culture" and the nongun culture?

Focusing on Structures and Strategies

1. Smith begins his essay by quoting a member of the "gun culture," ostensibly Smith's opposition. Why does he include the particular comment that "you people . . . do not understand guns or gun people"? How does this anticipate Smith's later emphasis on the need to reach a "consensus"? How does it characterize Smith himself? Similarly, why does Smith call his opponent "my Texas host"? Why does he stress this man's use of "you people"? Indicate other ways in which Smith attempts to problematize the typical divisions between gun and nongun cultures.

2. Why does Smith emphasize his personal experience with guns and his personal interest in gun control legislation? How does he use these personal issues to convince his readers to agree with him? In his account of his war experiences and the death of his friend Michael Halberstam, Smith focuses on description rather than on

moral judgment. Yet how does he communicate his attitude toward these events? How does this strategy strengthen or weaken his argument?

3. Explain the "rite of passage" theory of gun ownership. Why does Smith devote so much space to describing it? Why does he express his willingness to "grant" it? How does he use it to lead into his focus on the danger of handguns?

4. Examine carefully the section in which Smith reviews "some . . . arguments" both for and against gun control. Once again Smith seems quite willing to present both sides of the argument equitably. How does he organize this section in order to give more credence to the pro–gun arguments? How do the arguments "against" differ in nature from the arguments "for"? How does he use these impersonal arguments to introduce his own views which follow?

5. Smith grants that registry of handguns would not prevent criminals from carrying illegal weapons, nor would it have prevented the deaths of Halberstam and Lennon. Why, then, does he still consider it an important measure?

6. Ultimately, Smith is concerned with a "larger and more complex problem" than specific violent crimes. How does he define that problem? How does he use this problem to support his argument in favor of handgun registration?

Suggestions for Further Discussion and Writing

1. Review Smith's efforts to summarize as accurately as possible opposing points of view on gun control. What additional assertions, if any, can you think of that Smith might have made in support of either side on this issue?

2. Consider two prominent slogans representing opposing views of gun control: "Guns don't kill people—people do"; "Guns don't die—people do." Write an essay in which you examine carefully the assumptions—and the implications—that attend these two slogans.

3. Smith makes a determined effort to distinguish between the need to register handguns and what he calls "long guns." How defensible is Smith's position with respect to this distinction? How feasible is it for Smith to argue that one but not the other kind of gun be registered? Write a brief essay (approximately 500 words) in which you defend—or attack—the wisdom of Smith's drawing such a distinction.

The Case Against More Laws

Henry A. Selib

The national debate over the benefits and liabilities of gun control continues unabated. Advocates on both sides of the issue marshal alarming statistics to strengthen their claims. A recent study, published in a 1986 issue of the New England Journal of Medicine, *examined the police files of gun-related deaths in King County, Washington—an area that includes Seattle and neighboring communities. Of the 743 gun-related deaths that occurred between 1978 and 1983, 398 took place in a home where a gun was located. Of that 398, 333 were classified as suicides, 41 as criminal homicides, 12 as accidental deaths, 9 were listed under "self-protection," and 3 as "self-inflicted" but unclassified. Arthur Kellerman and Donald Reay, authors of the study, used these figures to argue that having a gun at home is more likely to kill than to protect people. But the National Rifle Association's Paul Blackman wrote a brief rejoinder in which he noted that Kellerman and Reay's study listed only deaths and not the number of instances when intruders were wounded or repelled by a weapon. And so the debate continues.*

Henry A. Selib is a member of both the National Rifle Association and the Massachusetts State Rifle and Pistol Association. The following essay, which appeared in the Boston Globe *on April 3, 1973, at the invitation of the newspaper's editors, offers at once an impassioned defense of why guns ought not to be outlawed and a systematic attack on the use of statistics by what Selib calls "the anti-gun crowd."*

1 Not long ago, Detroit enacted severely restricting anti-gun laws. Within a year, anti-gun forces all over the country were trumpeting that crimes of violence in which guns had been used showed a marked reduction in that city.

2 Unfortunately, the anti-gun crowd conveniently forgot to tell us that at the time the new laws were enacted, the Detroit police force was augmented by about 14 percent with most of the added officers assigned to the city's high crime areas. It was the police, of course, that lowered the crime rate, not the new laws, for all kinds of crime in Detroit showed reduction.

3 The fact is that the growing incidence of crime—especially violent crime—in our country cannot be traced to so simple a cause as the number of guns in private hands or the lack of various gun laws.

4 The evidence that one can connect gun ownership with crimes of violence simply doesn't exist, and this forces the anti-gun crowd to manufacture evidence or to distort and misinterpret whatever can be used to their advantage.

5 They indicate, for example, that in states with strong gun laws, the crime rate is lower than in states with little restrictive legislation. Like many half truths, this too is terribly misleading. In states like New Hampshire, Iowa, Vermont, and many others where gun laws are "weaker," or non-existent (i.e., Vermont), the per capita homicide rate is actually much lower than it is in many states where the laws are tough. Thus, we might just as well argue that the stronger the gun laws, the higher the homicide rate.

6 The facts are that homicide rates are high in the south (weak laws); moderately high in the big industrial states (stronger laws); and low through the north, northwest and upper New England (weak laws). There simply is no connection between a community's gun laws or lack thereof and the incidence of gun crimes.

7 Or take this oft-quoted canard: "Since 1900, 750,000 Americans have been killed by privately owned guns." This assertion, taken from Carl Bakal's *The Right to Bear Arms,* is based upon incomplete records and estimates, and its obvious implication is [that all of these killings are] homicides. But Bakal's figures include at least 140,000 accidents and 340,000 suicides.

8 The long-standing controversy between the advocates of strict gun controls and those opposed has proven only that a mass of "facts" and statistics are easily available to those on both sides to use selectively. Indeed, sometimes the same facts are used to support both sides.

9 Let me show you how this can be. The anti-gun group asks us to note that in England, where severe, restrictive legislation against pistol ownership has existed since the turn of the century, there is little gun homicide and little crime committed with guns. This is supposed to be a compelling argument in favor of stricter gun controls here.

10 But in the decade from 1960 to 1970, gun crimes in England increased some 750 percent—this in a country where there aren't

supposed to be any pistols in private hands. What is demonstrated forcefully in England is that in a place where guns are outlawed, only outlaws have guns.

11 There is a terrible irony here. Whenever some community succeeds in enacting tough gun laws, the happiest people are the criminals. They know that the law-abiding citizen will obey the new law, however much he may believe it ineffective. The criminal, of course, doesn't give up or register his guns and he knows that he can now rob or steal with the likelihood that no one will have the means to resist him.

12 Ample and powerful evidence demonstrates that criminals operate more effectively in areas where firearms laws do not properly address the problem of community crime.

13 In Oak Park, a suburb of Chicago, Illinois, a law was enacted several years ago banning the ownership of firearms in that city by those who do not require them in their occupation.

14 Oak Park did not have a crime problem when the law was passed, but as the criminal element discovered that the community had been disarmed the city rapidly became a haven for them and the crime rate there has soared.

15 At about the same time that Oak Park passed its law banning guns, the citizens of Kennesaw, a suburb of Atlanta, Georgia, dismayed by a particularly high and rising crime rate, enacted legislation *requiring* every household to have a weapon and ammunition.

16 Although Kennesaw's population has approximately doubled in the intervening years, crime there has virtually disappeared. The criminals have no wish to rob and plague a place where the means to resist them is ever present.

17 The gun owner, the sportsman, the competition shooter, the firearms collector would be willing, even anxious, to give up his hobby if someone, somewhere, could demonstrate that his community would be safer, and sharp inroads would be made in the fight against crime. Gun owners have as much respect and reverence for life as the antigunners and are just as appalled at the rate at which violent crime seems to be growing in some parts of our country.

18 There is no question but that some people should not—must not—have guns. Because of this, some sort of regulation is obviously necessary. Most everyone would agree that felons, addicts, morons, juveniles, alcoholics, the mentally incompetent and others in whose

hands even an icepick or baseball bat becomes a deadly weapon, should be denied guns.

19 But unless it can be demonstrated that an individual should not have a gun, he should be issued a license and should be counseled in the proper and safe use of the weapon. Punishment for crimes committed with guns must be specially severe, but let not the average gun owner suffer because a few people cannot be trusted.

20 If we want to eliminate violence in our society, whether guns are involved or not, let us attack the problem as the socio-economic problem that it is.

21 The nuts and the misguided will continue to kill one way or another, and the criminal will continue his nefarious ways. But these are all reflections that violence and crime are abroad in the land, not that guns are the cause. Indeed, magazines like *The American Rifleman,* official publication of the National Rifle Association (NRA), often devote considerable space to stories of crimes that never happened because somebody had a gun to prevent them. The NRA has, for more than 100 years, been in the forefront of advocating strict penalties for wrongdoers who use guns; for educating citizens young and old in the proper use of guns.

22 Crime and violence are immense problems, and their elimination should be a major concern for all of us.

23 Let's not hamstring our police, and let's allocate the necessary state funds to do the job.

24 But don't make the gun owner a patsy for a problem he didn't create and can't control alone.

25 That's like reducing traffic deaths by enacting laws prohibiting drinking.

Additional Rhetorical Strategies

Cause and Effect (paragraphs 1–3, 11); Illustration (paragraphs 5, 21).

Examining Words and Meaning

1. To what extent does Selib feel that gun ownership should be regulated? What basic characteristics distinguish the "gun owner" from "the nuts and the misguided"? How might gun ownership

regulations distinguish between them? What would be the strengths and weaknesses of such regulations?

2. What does Selib mean when he refers to the "half truths" of the opponents of gun control? What evidence does he offer to validate this claim?

3. What does Selib mean when he says that violence is a "socio-economic problem" (paragraph 20)? Why is it important to his argument that he relocate the problem? How does it help to equate his position as a gun owner with his audience's desire to reduce crime?

Focusing on Structures and Strategies

1. The first half of Selib's essay concentrates on refuting the case for gun control. What is his central claim in this section? How does he characterize the position of those who favor gun control? How does this characterization strengthen or weaken his own stance? How successful is his refutation?

2. Selib asserts that statistics can be used to defend either pro– or anti–gun control claims. How does he organize the first half of his essay in order to demonstrate this? How does he use his argument and its organization to reinforce his position against gun control? Once he has dismissed statistics as an unreliable basis for argumentation, what method(s) does he use to support his position?

3. Selib is careful to keep from stating his personal position on gun control, speaking instead for "gun owners" or the National Rifle Association. What other techniques does Selib use to suggest his impartial examination of the issue? How do you respond to his statement of facts such as "in a place where guns are outlawed, only outlaws have guns"? Suggest in what ways such statements are effective or ineffective? How does he use language to indicate his personal opinion without directly stating it?

4. Consider the nature of Selib's argument in paragraph 5. How convincing do you find his explanation here? Do the same for paragraph 6. What is the logical extension of Selib's position in this paragraph? Is it that *any* form of gun control is not needed? Explain your answer.

5. Reread the four, brief, single-sentence paragraphs that close Selib's essay. At first glance, they seem to violate the conventions of composition calling for fully developed paragraphs. Yet, given the

fact that they appeared in a newspaper and were positioned at the very end of the essay, how might they be regarded as effective paragraphs? What would be the effect, for example, had they been grouped together to form a single, closing paragraph? How does the strength of their assertions depend to a large extent on this particular format?

Suggestions for Further Discussion and Writing

1. Selib concentrates on those who own guns for sport or hobby rather than for defense. How might it have affected his argument had he included this reason for wanting to own a gun?
2. Consider another widely debated public issue. Restrictions on smoking in public spaces, in offices, and on airplanes is one such issue. Advertising prophylactics on television to combat the spread of the AIDS virus is another. You need not restrict yourself to these possible issues. After you have settled on an issue to address, write an essay in which you argue in favor of—or in opposition to—such restriction. Be sure to account for the major points of the opposing view and to refute each convincingly.

Persuasion

1 Nearly all of us spend a good deal of time each day trying to deal with various kinds of appeals—personal, professional, and commercial attempts to influence our thinking and direct our behavior. We are repeatedly encouraged, flattered, seduced, badgered, warned, and even threatened to consider this, to believe that, to do this, to buy that. But just as we are the targets of such requests, we also make quite a few ourselves: we may, for example, try to induce the manager of the local stereo shop to repair our receiver today rather than tomorrow, to encourage our friends to register for a particular biology course, to convince civic officials to lower our town's minimum age for drinking, to prevail upon our parents to let us share an apartment off-campus. Such appeals, whether they concern our everyday routines or our most intricate decisions, invariably involve some element of persuasion.

2 Persuasion is written or oral discourse aimed at disposing an audience to think and act in accordance with a speaker's[1] will. To persuade is to resolve, change, or re-form an individual's or a group's feelings, opinions, beliefs, and actions in any effective manner. For many of us, the word *persuasion* calls to mind the manipulative tricks of twentieth-century advertising, politics, and propaganda. The alluring promises of corporations, religious sects, and political factions,

[1]For the sake of convenience, the term *speaker* will be used in reference to all types of verbal presentation, both oral and written.

as well as the strident pleas of an increasing number of special-interest groups, have helped create an atmosphere in which a term like *persuasion* has come to be associated with deception and exploitation, as well as with more subtle forms of mass seduction and indoctrination. Yet, though persuasion can be a more emotional form of writing and speaking than exposition and argument, there is also no reason why persuasion cannot serve the equally sensible and honorable end of encouraging, as Aristotle maintains it did, some virtuous behavior. It is this more positive sense—persuasion without a dubious ulterior motive—that is worth exploring in detail as a procedure for structuring our thinking and writing.

3 Aristotle divides persuasion into rational, emotional, and ethical appeals. *Rational appeals* rely on the speaker's ability to summon logic and good sense to move an audience to a specific action. *Emotional appeals* aim at an audience's feelings, at arousing a nonintellectual response as a means to secure some determined course of action. *Ethical appeals* are based on the speaker's personal presence, character, and reputation. Aristotle maintains that the most persuasive writing blends all three. Determining what should be the most effective mixture of such appeals depends on several interrelated factors: the subject, the desired action, the audience addressed, and the speaker's relationship with that audience. The proposed action may be clear-cut and well within sight—as in political addresses, lobbying, and sermons. Yet, on such ceremonial occasions as inaugurations, commencements, and holidays, the action called for may be less specific, perhaps a resolution rather than an immediate action. Persuasion in such cases amounts to inspirational statements which people are expected to apply to their own individual circumstances. There may be occasions, however, when the need for action is apparent but the possibilities of doing something are restricted for the audience. (See, for example, Mike Royko's "A Faceless Man's Plea," p. 523.)

4 A rational appeal must conform to the basic principles of argument, including accurate information, logical development, and convincing evidence. (For a discussion of argument, see pp. 459–468.) Persuasion, when it employs the principles of logic to promote an action, takes an audience beyond the conventional boundaries of argument. Both seek to earn an audience's *assent* to a particular belief. Argument, in fact, closes when the speaker is sure of such assent. But persuasion continues to work with the evidence of an argument,

using it as the motive for doing something. In this respect, persuasion appeals both to intelligence and will; it aims at not only conviction but also action. It seeks an audience's *consent.*

5 Suppose, for example, that we are asked to write an essay in which we argue on behalf of the claim that drug abuse has contributed substantially to the increase in urban crime. We will have written a successful argument when we have gathered sufficient evidence and carefully built it into a convincing case. But such an essay could be made persuasive by using the same evidence for a different purpose—to propose a specific course of action. In this instance, we might urge our city's legislators to mandate a two-pronged attack on drugs and crime—say, to order stiffer penalties for pushers and wider availability of detoxification and counseling services for users. As this example suggests, argument and persuasion are often closely allied. An essay dominated by one usually will also include elements of the other, the precise combination being determined by the anticipated response of the audience.

6 Composing a successful persuasive essay depends to a great extent on knowing our audience and how receptive it will be to what we have to say. We need to discover as much as possible about people's beliefs, prejudices, and interests before we can persuade them to follow a desired course of action. Persuasion is addressed, then, to a specific audience; whereas an argumentative essay is addressed to a general audience, which includes anyone interested in discovering the facts of an issue. Persuasive writing attempts to solidify the speaker's relationship with an audience, by frequently acknowledging the audience's presence. (See Sojourner Truth's speech on p. 546.) Political speeches, for example, nearly always include specific references to the audience present. There is a prevailing sense of intimacy in persuasive writing, of speaking directly to a specific audience, of guiding it toward belief and action. In this respect, the more an audience is brought into an essay—that is, acknowledged by having its special characteristics highlighted—the more likely the writing will be persuasive.

7 Persuasion begins when we establish a common ground of belief with our audience. By identifying ourselves with a particular group and focusing on areas of agreement, we are more likely to persuade each member to follow our recommended course of action. One of the surest ways to dispose an audience favorably to our ideas is to start with what they already know, with what they would

readily assent to. Thus persuasion first concentrates on reaffirmation, on reminding an audience of what it already believes. While argument must respond directly to anticipated objections, persuasion glosses over resistance. If, for example, we are writing a persuasive essay on the plight of migrant workers, we might not want to refer to their status as illegal aliens. Persuasion is also less rigorous when it comes to dealing with implied assumptions. The key terms in a persuasive essay are rarely as carefully defined as in argument, and we need not be concerned about complete conformity to the technical requirements of logic. (For a discussion of some of the technical requirements of logic, see pp. 463–467.) Whereas the conclusions drawn in argument are necessary (the evidence points insistently toward one conclusion), in persuasion they are important to the extent that they move the audience to a desired action. The crucial issue in persuasion remains just how far we can move our readers *beyond* the point to which they would readily agree.

8 For example, we are asked to write an essay designed to persuade our college's administrators that the physically handicapped deserve equal access to each floor in every building on campus. We would not need to spend a great deal of time arguing on behalf of the validity of such a principle. But we would need to gather convincing evidence that some students do not now enjoy easy access. We could then propose specific ways to remedy the problem—say, by installing additional ramps and elevators and by providing adequate reserved parking for the handicapped near the entrance to each building. Persuasion, in effect, fuses an argument and an agenda. It leads an audience, to quote St. Augustine on persuasion, "not merely to know what should be done, but to do what they know should be done." In this sense, persuasion, unlike argument, gradually turns into subtle forms of command.

9 The persuasive writing we most often encounter is based on appeals to an audience's emotions: anger, fear, frustration, contentment, desires, and the like. In deciding which emotion to appeal to, we should take into account the appropriateness of such an appeal to both the subject and the proposed action as well as the knowledge we have of the audience's temperament. In an appeal to the emotions, we must establish a substantive connection between the course of action being urged and the particular emotion being aroused. Appeals to the emotions of an audience are usually put at the end of an essay.

10 The standard procedure for structuring a persuasive essay is to

interest people through their intellectual curiosity and then to move them to action through an emotional appeal. Reversing the order weakens the likelihood of action. Starting with an appeal to reason also shows greater respect for the audience and its collective intelligence. Yet, finally, nothing is more important to the success of an emotional appeal than the speaker who makes the presentation. In the end, an audience is often persuaded nearly as much by the personality of the speaker as by the substance of what is said.

11 The ethical appeal in persuasion is based on the sense of character the speaker projects: usually a combination of personal qualities and credibility. The speaker establishes the ethical appeal of an essay—what Aristotle called its *ethos*—by conveying an impression of himself or herself as someone with good sense and good will. The importance of an ethical appeal may be seen by contrasting the different roles the speaker plays in argument and persuasion. In argument, an intelligent, clear-headed person's assent to the facts and truth of a matter normally has very little, if anything, to do with his or her response to the speaker's character and personality. In persuasion, however, our *consent* to follow a particular course of action has a great deal to do with our feelings about the speaker. The ethical appeal in persuasion works rather simply: the audience identifies with the speaker and consequently considers seriously whatever that person has to say. And, if the speaker projects the image of being not only decent and well-meaning but also perceptive, well-informed, and sympathetic to the needs and desires of the audience, its members will all the more readily agree to the speaker's proposed course of action.

12 The writer of effective, reputable persuasion—unlike the speaker in much advertising and propaganda—sounds modest, reasonable, and candid. He or she takes into account the points of view of others, has a practical grasp of complex problems, and offers commonsense solutions. This is a person we have confidence in—someone we can trust and perhaps even emulate. For example, in response to as volatile a subject as the escalating tensions among ethnic groups in a community, such a person would resist both oversimplifying the issues involved and urging some precipitous action. Instead, such a person would demonstrate sensitivity to the perspectives and interests of each contending party and offer prudent measures to seal the rift and restore friendly relations. Such a person thinks, speaks, writes, and acts on the strength of personal conviction. Consider, for

example, Adrienne Rich's speech to the entering class at Douglass College (see p. 551). Rich's identification with her all-female audience, her plea that these students take responsibility for the substance and direction of their lives, and her ability to convey the impression that she herself measures up to the standards of what she requests of her audience—all contribute to making her remarks especially persuasive to the specific group she is addressing.

13 Persuasive writing should be as imaginative and memorable as it is reasonable. Adrienne Rich's address offers ample evidence of these qualities and also highlights several other standard stylistic features of effective persuasive writing. Her remarks feature a great deal of *repetition.* What is repeated in this instance *reaffirms* fundamental feminist beliefs and *reinforces* noble personal, social, educational, and political values. The repetition of phrases and words, such as "Responsibility to yourself means," "It means," "active," and "passive," binds her presentation into a powerful, convincing whole and prompts her audience to endorse what she says: women should *"claim* a woman-directed education." The writing is persuasive not only because certain phrases are repeated but also because the general style of the presentation is so direct and serious. The *tone* is appropriate to the subject, occasion, and audience. Rich's address also demonstrates that word *choices* and *phrasing* in persuasive writing need to be especially vivid and clearly memorable. Each point in the essay is strengthened by evocative details and convincing illustrations.

14 Our efforts to write persuasively ought to be guided by a few reminders. We should:

1. Hone down our subject so that we have a manageable idea with a clearly stated proposed course of action
2. Introduce the issue in a way that enhances our credibility and disposes our audience both intellectually and emotionally to hear what we have to say
3. State vigorously and develop fully the claim, the proposition itself
4. Be certain that the proofs we summon to support the recommended action are tied directly to our announced purpose
5. Make sure that the rational, emotional, and ethical appeals are evident throughout the essay
6. Use the conclusion of the essay to recapitulate the important points and to reaffirm the necessity of the proposed action.

15 Following these procedures for structuring a persuasive essay will increase the likelihood that our audience will understand our claim, assent to its merit, and consent to a particular course of action.
16 The formal writing requirements of many academic disciplines call for less frequent practice in persuasion than in other forms of writing. This does not hold equally true, however, outside of college, where the ability to speak and write persuasively can make a decided difference in our careers and our communities.

Late Night Thoughts on Listening to Mahler's Ninth Symphony

Lewis Thomas

Among the most persuasive essays are those that make a powerful impact on an audience's emotions. Such emotional appeals are especially effective when the writer convincingly displays the very emotions he or she wants an audience to feel. Often, writers will attempt to establish an empathetic writer–reader bond, thus identifying themselves directly with their audience. Observe in the following essay how Lewis Thomas identifies himself both with members of his generation and with those of a younger generation as he constructs an angry, frustrated indictment against those who support the nuclear arms race. Observe, too, how he skillfully weaves together the close associations of music and emotion to reinforce his persuasive appeal.

1 I cannot listen to Mahler's Ninth Symphony with anything like the old melancholy mixed with the high pleasure I used to take from this music. There was a time, not long ago, when what I heard, especially in the final movement, was an open acknowledgment of death and at the same time a quiet celebration of the tranquillity connected to the process. I took this music as a metaphor for reassurance, confirming my own strong hunch that the dying of every living creature, the most natural of all experiences, has to be

a peaceful experience. I rely on nature. The long passages on all the strings at the end, as close as music can come to expressing silence itself, I used to hear as Mahler's idea of leave-taking at its best. But always, I have heard this music as a solitary, private listener, thinking about death.

2 Now I hear it differently. I cannot listen to the last movement of the Mahler Ninth without the door-smashing intrusion of a huge new thought: death everywhere, the dying of everything, the end of humanity. The easy sadness expressed with such gentleness and delicacy by that repeated phrase on faded strings, over and over again, no longer comes to me as old, familiar news of the cycle of living and dying. All through the last notes my mind swarms with images of a world in which the thermonuclear bombs have begun to explode, in New York and San Francisco, in Moscow and Leningrad, in Paris, in Paris, in Paris. In Oxford and Cambridge, in Edinburgh. I cannot push away the thought of a cloud of radioactivity drifting along the Engadin, from the Moloja Pass to Ftan, killing off the part of the earth I love more than any other part.

3 I am old enough by this time to be used to the notion of dying, saddened by the glimpse when it has occurred but only transiently knocked down, able to regain my feet quickly at the thought of continuity, any day. I have acquired and held in affection until very recently another sideline of an idea which serves me well at dark times: the life of the earth is the same as the life of an organism: the great round being possesses a mind: the mind contains an infinite number of thoughts and memories: when I reach my time I may find myself still hanging around in some sort of midair, one of those small thoughts, drawn back into the memory of the earth: in that peculiar sense I will be alive.

4 Now all that has changed. I cannot think that way anymore. Not while those things are still in place, aimed everywhere, ready for launching.

5 This is a bad enough thing for the people in my generation. We can put up with it, I suppose, since we must. We are moving along anyway, like it or not. I can even set aside my private fancy about hanging around, in midair.

6 What I cannot imagine, what I cannot put up with, the thought that keeps grinding its way into my mind, making the Mahler into a hideous noise close to killing me, is what it would be like to be young. How do the young stand it? How can they keep their sanity?

If I were very young, sixteen or seventeen years old, I think I would begin, perhaps very slowly and imperceptibly, to go crazy.

7 There is a short passage near the very end of the Mahler in which the almost vanishing violins, all engaged in a sustained backward glance, are edged aside for a few bars by the cellos. Those lower notes pick up fragments from the first movement, as though prepared to begin everything all over again, and then the cellos subside and disappear, like an exhalation. I used to hear this as a wonderful few seconds of encouragement: we'll be back, we're still here, keep going, keep going.

8 Now, with a pamphlet in front of me on a corner of my desk, published by the Congressional Office of Technology Assessment, entitled *MX Basing,* an analysis of all the alternative strategies for placement and protection of hundreds of these missiles, each capable of creating artificial suns to vaporize a hundred Hiroshimas, collectively capable of destroying the life of any continent, I cannot hear the same Mahler. Now, those cellos sound in my mind like the opening of all the hatches and the instant before ignition.

9 If I were sixteen or seventeen years old, I would not feel the cracking of my own brain, but I would know for sure that the whole world was coming unhinged. I can remember with some clarity what it was like to be sixteen. I had discovered the Brahms symphonies. I knew that there was something going on in the late Beethoven quartets that I would have to figure out, and I knew that there was plenty of time ahead for all the figuring I would ever have to do. I had never heard of Mahler. I was in no hurry. I was a college sophomore and had decided that Wallace Stevens and I possessed a comprehensive understanding of everything needed for a life. The years stretched away forever ahead, forever. My great-great grandfather had come from Wales, leaving his signature in the family Bible on the same page that carried, a century later, my father's signature. It never crossed my mind to wonder about the twenty-first century; it was just there, given, somewhere in the sure distance.

10 The man on television, Sunday midday, middle-aged and solid, nice-looking chap, all the facts at his fingertips, more dependable looking than most high-school principals, is talking about civilian defense, his responsibility in Washington. It can make an enormous difference, he is saying. Instead of the outright death of eighty million American citizens in twenty minutes, he says, we can, by careful planning and practice, get that number down to only forty million,

maybe even twenty. The thing to do, he says, is to evacuate the cities quickly and have everyone get under shelter in the countryside. That way we can recover, and meanwhile we will have retaliated, incinerating all of Soviet society, he says. What about radioactive fallout? he is asked. Well, he says. Anyway, he says, if the Russians know they can only destroy forty million of us instead of eighty million, this will deter them. Of course, he adds, they have the capacity to kill all two hundred and twenty million of us if they were to try real hard, but they know we can do the same to them. If the figure is only forty million this will deter them, not worth the trouble, not worth the risk. Eighty million would be another matter, we should guard ourselves against losing that many all at once, he says.

11 If I were sixteen or seventeen years old and had to listen to that, or read things like that, I would want to give up listening and reading. I would begin thinking up new kinds of sounds, different from any music heard before, and I would be twisting and turning to rid myself of human language.

Reading for Rhetorical Strategy

Lewis Thomas opens his brief essay by describing in paragraphs 1 and 2 how the nuclear threat to all of humanity has seriously affected his response to one of his favorite classical symphonies. In paragraph 5, he identifies himself with his own generation, and in the next paragraph he introduces his main theme (the effect the nuclear arms race must be having on young people) by establishing an emotional connection between himself and sixteen- or seventeen-year-olds. Note how he repeats variations of the phrase "If I were sixteen or seventeen years old . . ." in paragraphs 6, 9, and 11, in a way that suggests musical repetition. (Such verbal repetition, as we all know from advertising, plays a large role in persuasive writing.) In paragraph 10, Thomas reveals the horror of the arms race by embodying it in a single spokesman, whom he never directly attacks: he mimics the man's style, believing that the official language itself is a convincing argument against the pro-MX position. In paragraph 11, Thomas returns to his emotional identification with young people, describing how he would feel if he "were sixteen or seventeen years old and had to listen to that." Note that through this identification he effectively appeals not only to young people but to the feelings of his own generation.

"Stop Handguns Before They Stop You"

(See advertisement on p. 520.)

Examining Words and Meaning

1. What is the meaning of the phrase "The pen is mightier than the gun"? What is its effect in this ad? Is there any irony—either intended or unintended—evident in the use of this phrase? Explain your answer.

Focusing on Structures and Strategies

1. What is the effect of painting the handgun so as to resemble the United States flag? How does this decision add to or detract from the impact of the advertisement?
2. How is the audience for this advertisement expected to read the phrase "GOD BLESS AMERICA"? What tone of voice do you hear the speaker of this ad using in this line?

Suggestions for Further Discussion and Writing

1. Draft the text of an advertisement that advocates a specific course of public action in response to an issue of national importance. You may choose any issue and take any stand you wish, but be sure to keep the focus on the need for action clear throughout the advertisement.
2. What special interest do you represent—students? laborers? farmers? political refugees? Write an essay in which you call for some action to be taken on behalf of that special interest. Relate an incident in which you can demonstrate the need for public action on the issue. Begin your essay by discussing the general issue of which your case is an example. Appeal to feelings that you know your audience already has.

(Text continues on p. 522.)

"Stop Handguns Before They Stop You"

As special interest groups lobbied to win public support to encourage—or discourage—federal, state, and local legislators on gun control, such national organizations as the Washington, D.C., -based National Rifle Association and Handgun Control, Inc., sponsored a series of advertisements to call public attention to the respective merits of their cases. The two advertisements that follow suggest just how closely one special interest group monitors—and seeks to refute—the logic of the opposition.

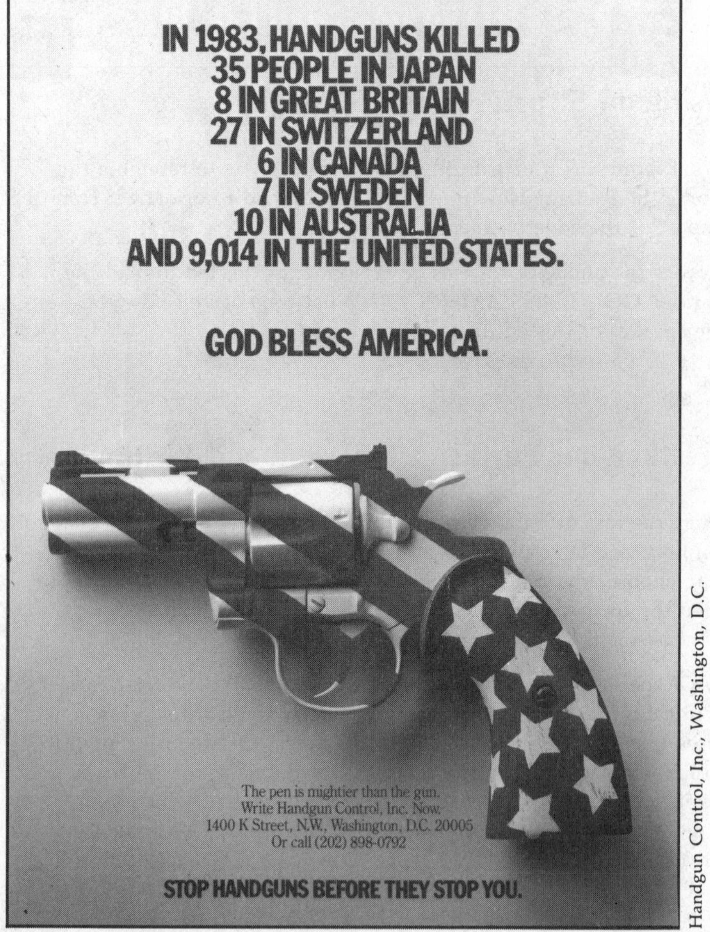

IN 1983, HANDGUNS KILLED
35 PEOPLE IN JAPAN
8 IN GREAT BRITAIN
27 IN SWITZERLAND
6 IN CANADA
7 IN SWEDEN
10 IN AUSTRALIA
AND 9,014 IN THE UNITED STATES.
GOD BLESS AMERICA.
The pen is mightier than the gun.
Write Handgun Control, Inc. Now.
1400 K Street, N.W., Washington, D.C. 20005
Or call (202) 898-0792
STOP HANDGUNS BEFORE THEY STOP YOU.

Handgun Control, Inc., Washington, D.C.

"In the U.S., Crime Pays Because Criminals Don't!"

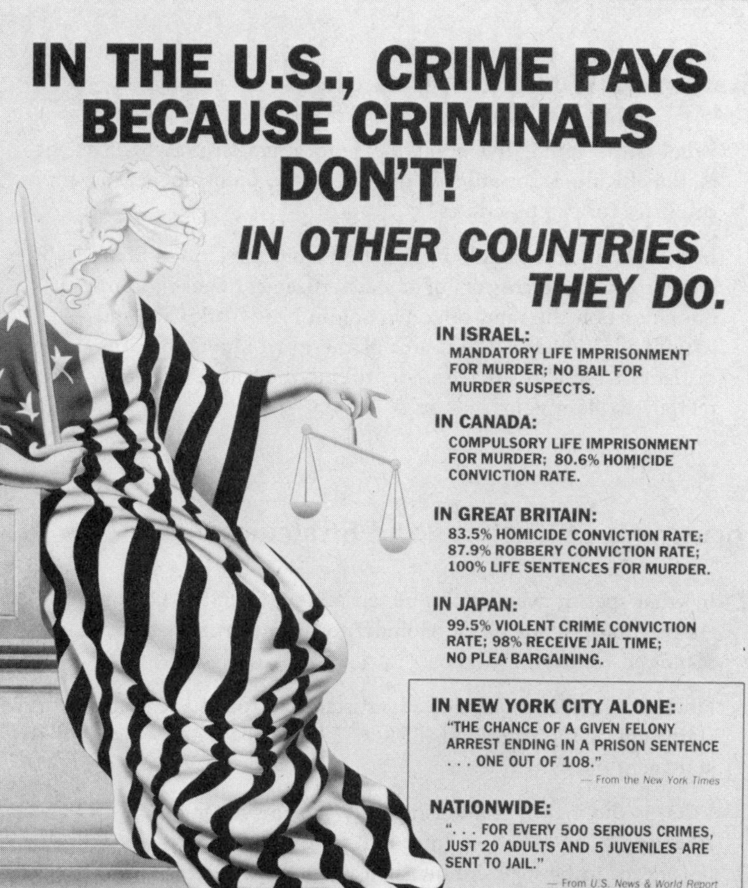

© National Rifle Association.

"In the U.S., Crime Pays Because Criminals Don't!"

(Text continued from p. 519.)

Examining Words and Meaning

1. What is the cumulative effect of the information presented by the National Rifle Association in this list of the punishments in various countries for capital crimes?
2. In presenting comparable information from the United States, why do you think the creators of the advertisement chose to present quotations on the rates of conviction in New York City and nationwide? What is the source of these two quotations? of the statistics from abroad? Does identifying the source of these statistics matter? Explain your answer.

Focusing on Structures and Strategies

1. In what specific ways is this advertisement from the National Rifle Association intended as a rejoinder to the advertisement from Handgun Control, Inc.?
2. How are the readers of this advertisement expected to respond to the statement "GOD HELP AMERICA"? In what tone of voice is that statement presented?
3. What is the logical relationship between the statement "GOD HELP AMERICA" and the two lines that follow it? If the relationship is not meant to be logical, how then would you describe it? What are the effects of these three lines?

Suggestion for Further Discussion and Writing

1. Look carefully through recent issues of such nationally distributed magazines as *Time, Newsweek,* and *Sports Illustrated,* as well as popular hunting magazines. Find an advertisement for the National Rifle Association. Do the same for a group advocating gun control.

Compare and contrast the strategies in the presentation of the language and graphics of these advertisements to the strategies used by the N.R.A. and Handgun Control, Inc., in the advertisements reprinted on the preceding pages. Write an essay in which you summarize the changes in the arguments used to win public support for the positions of pro– and anti–gun control groups. Which group has presented a more persuasive case for its position? Why?

A Faceless Man's Plea

Mike Royko

Sometimes there is no other way to express outrage and indignation than to holler. But when one of those hollering times comes to a writer like Mike Royko, the rage is captured and hurled at the insensible antagonist through his column in the Chicago Daily News. *He knows his audience, and he knows how they will respond to what he has to tell them. But because he is an experienced writer, he also knows how to present the plea of an injured man so it will be most affecting, so it will stir others to the outrage he feels.*

1 Leroy Bailey just turned 26. He was one of seven kids from a broken family in Connecticut. He had been in the infantry in Vietnam only one month.

2 Then the rocket tore through the roof of his tent while he was sleeping and exploded in his face.

3. He was alive when the medics pulled him out. But he was blind. And his face was gone. It's the simplest way to describe it: He no longer had a face.

4 That was in the spring of 1968. He went to an Army hospital, was discharged and shipped to Hines VA Hospital, west of Chicago.

5 After three years and much surgery, they told him there was little more they could do for him. He still had no face.

6 Now Bailey spends most of his life in the basement of his brother's home in La Grange. The brother moved here from the East to be near him while he was hospitalized.

7 He knits wool hats, which a friend sells for him. He listens to the radio or to a tape player.

8 Because of his terrible wound, most of the goals and pleasures of men his age will always be denied him.

9 But there is one thing he would like to be able to do some day. It isn't much, because most of us take it for granted.

10 He would like to eat solid foods.

11 Since 1968, he has eaten nothing but liquids. He uses a large syringe to squirt liquid foods down his throat.

12 Last year, through some friends of his brother, Bailey met a doctor who specializes in facial surgery.

13 The doctor, Charles Janda of Oak Brook, said he believed he could reconstruct Bailey's face so that he could eat solid foods.

14 But it would require a series of at least six separate operations, possibly more.

15 Bailey eagerly agreed, and the first operation was performed at Mercy Hospital.

16 Then Dr. Janda and the hospital sent their bills to the Veterans Administration.

17 They did this because Bailey and his brother were under the impression that the VA would pay for any treatment he needed that wasn't available in the VA.

18 The VA refuses to pay the bills. The reason was explained in a remarkable letter sent to Bailey by a VA official. (The italics are mine.)

19 "Dear Mr. Bailey:

20 "Reference is made to the enclosed invoice for services given to you for selective plastic surgery done on Sept. 22, 1972.

21 *"It is regretted that payment on the above cannot be approved, since the treatment was for a condition other than that of your service-connected disability.*

22 "Outpatient treatment and/or medication may only be authorized for the treatment of a disability which has been adjudicated by the Veterans Administration as incurred in or aggravated by military service.

23 "Any expense involved for this condition must be a personal transaction between you and the doctor."

24 It is astonishing, I know, but the VA actually told him that he was being treated for something "other than that of your service-connected disability."

25 I can't even begin to comprehend what they can be talking about. Until he was hit by a rocket, he had teeth. Now he has none. He had eyes. Now he has none. He had a nose. Now he has none. People could look at him. Now most of them turn away.

26 So how can this surgery be for anything else but his "service-connected disability"?

27 I read through his medical records. He could have received a 100-per cent disability rating for any of four separate reasons. He could have received an 80-per cent disability rating for another reason, and a 30-per cent rating for still another.

28 The medical report uses such language as "scars, disfiguring . . . exceptional repugnant deformity . . . entire midface is missing . . . massive facial injury."

29 Bailey believes that the VA thinks he wants the surgery just to look better, that it is "cosmetic" surgery.

30 Even if that were so, then why in the hell not? If we can afford $5 million to make the San Clemente property prettier, we can do whatever is humanly possible for this man's face.

31 But Bailey insists it isn't his appearance that concerns him. He knows it will never be normal.

32 He explains his feelings in an appeal he filed months ago with the VA:

33 "The only thing I am asking for is the ability to chew and swallow my food.

34 "This was the purpose for the whole series of painful and unsuccessful operations I underwent in Hines Hospital between the day of my injury on May 6, 1968, and my eventual discharge from the hospital in 1971.

35 "At the time, I was told the very depressing news that nothing further could be done.

36 "I will never be able to accept this decision . . ."

37 In some bureaucrat's file cabinet is Bailey's appeal. It has been there for many months.

38 Every day that it sits there, Bailey takes his syringe and squirts liquid nourishment down his throat.

39 If his appeal is turned down, he will spend the rest of his life

doing that. Not even once will he be able to sit down and eat at the dinner table with his brother's family, before going back down to the basement to knit hats.

Additional Rhetorical Strategies

Narration (paragraphs 1–8); Cause and Effect (paragraphs 15–23, 25); Illustration (paragraphs 19–24, 33–36).

Examining Words and Meaning

1. Why does Leroy Bailey want plastic surgery? On what grounds does the Veterans Administration refuse to pay for it? What is wrong with the VA's case?
2. Why is saying "he no longer had a face" (paragraph 3) "the simplest way to describe it"? How might a detailed description of Bailey's injuries be less effective than Royko's simple statement?
3. In paragraph 28, why does Royko select the words that he does from Bailey's medical report? What sort of language do we usually expect medical reports to contain? In what ways is the language here exceptional?

Focusing on Structures and Strategies

1. Consider the bureaucrat's phrases "reference is made" (paragraph 20) and "it is regretted" (paragraph 21). Why doesn't the official say "I refer" and "I regret"? What does his language tell us about the degree of responsibility he wants to accept for his actions? Where else in the bureaucrat's letter does the passive voice have a similar effect?
2. How does Royko use paragraph 24 to demolish completely the VA's case? Why does the way he arranges his sentences here have such a

powerful impact on us? Is the appeal in this paragraph primarily emotional, rational, or ethical? Does Royko seem to rely entirely on this sort of appeal throughout his essay? If not, what other passage in the text do you think constitutes a different sort of appeal?

3. Why is Royko's last paragraph so persuasive? How does he appeal to our everyday experience to make us sympathetic to Bailey's plight? How does his selection of details earlier in the account make his last sentence so effective?

Suggestions for Further Discussion and Writing

1. What differences do you find between the way Royko writes and the way the VA official writes? What can we learn about how *not* to write from the bureaucrat's letter?

2. Write an essay in which you rely to a large extent on narration to be persuasive. For example, you might give an account of an exceptionally bright friend who was denied admission to a prestigious university because his or her grades in science were poor. How might such a story be used to persuade college officials to establish more flexible admissions policies? Or, to persuade your town's legislators to allocate more funds for the police force, you might recount the story of a neighbor who was robbed and beaten while waiting for a bus. If you wish, include your own reactions to the story, as Royko does here, but try to make the narration strong enough to be persuasive.

Why Nobody Loves a Politician

H. L. Mencken

At the age of nine, equipped with his first library card, H. L. Mencken (1880–1956) began, as he reports in his autobiography, "to inhabit a world that was two-thirds letterpress and only one-third trees, fields, streets, and people. I acquired round shoulders, spindly shanks, and a despondent view of humanity. I read everything that I could find in

English. . . . To this day [at age sixty] I am still what might be called a reader, and have a high regard for authors." At the time he wrote these words, H. L. Mencken had become one of the most astute readers—and critics—of American life and institutions as well as one of our most prolific and controversial authors.

A journalist, magazine editor, essayist, and philologist, Mencken wrote on virtually every important issue in early twentieth-century America. The list of his books, articles, reviews, poems, and newspaper reports and columns runs well over 300 pages. Intellectually, Mencken was into everything, and everything he wrote was marked by a distinctive imaginative intelligence: impertinent and acerbic, but also always clear-headed and often quite humorous. He made no claims to be a scholar, yet his study, The American Language *(1936), remains a landmark in the field of linguistics. As a cultural and political commentator, Mencken had few peers. His relentless attacks on declining standards of literacy and what he called the "unwarranted pretensions" of public officials galvanized several generations of discontented Americans.*

As a writer, Mencken always remembered to be entertaining. He never forgot his readers. In fact, he cultivated audiences and repeatedly encouraged them to regard themselves as the "truly civilized minority." Yet almost paradoxically, he repeatedly took the offensive in what he wrote, with humor and ridicule as his chief weapons. Mencken characterized his own style in the final lines of his last book, aptly titled Minority Report *(1956): "The imbeciles who have printed acres of comments on my books have seldom noticed the chief character of my style. It is that I write with almost scientific precision—that my meaning is never obscure." Yet, as the following passage suggests, if Mencken used a pen with all of the precision of a brain surgeon, he also relied on the emotive power of language. Rarely did he unfold a colorless rational argument. As a master of the art of rhetoric, Mencken worked his words for all they were worth—in this case to propose a provocative plan for American political reform.*

1 Next to kidnappers, politicians seem to be the most unpopular men in this great Republic. Nobody ever really trusts them. Whatever they do is commonly ascribed to ignoble motives. The country is always glad to see them humiliated, as when Congress is forced to dance as the White House whistles.

2 I fear I must add, as a moral theologian of 30 years' practice, that this ill fame is pretty well supported by the known facts. It may not be deserved in all cases, but it is surely deserved in most. Politicians as a class radiate a powerful odor. Their business is almost as firmly grounded on false pretenses as that of the quack doctor or shyster lawyer. What really concerns them first, last, and all the time

is simply their own jobs. Get close to them, and they will admit this frankly.

3 Imagine a professional politician in a very tight place, with 100 votes standing between him and his job, and then imagine him getting news that 110 voters on the other side have suddenly turned cannibal, and are full of enthusiasm for their new fad. What will he do? He will begin to see cannibalism in a new light, and to find a lot of good in it. I do not say that he will take the stump for it—at least not so long as it polls only 110 votes—but certainly he will not take the stump against it. And neither will his opponent.

4 The American people learned a great deal about politicians during the Prohibition Reign of Terror. To be sure, there were some dry politicians who were actually dry; but the votes that maintained the Anti-Saloon League in power at both ends of Pennsylvania Avenue came largely from men who cheated at every chance, and some of them ranked among the most assiduous lushes ever seen in Washington, a town always eminent for a hundred years for its passionate guzzling.

5 These babies, as every one will recall, turned a series of magnificent flipflops when the wet cyclone hit them. Their rubber knees and shockproof backbones worked perfectly, and they landed squarely on their feet, panting and lathering for repeal. I could give you a list of them, with statistics of their speed and tankage. They were mainly so stupid or so far gone in liquor that they didn't see the cyclone coming, and when it struck them suddenly at Chicago, where they had gathered for the national conventions, they were thrown into such a panic that some of them actually sobered up. They came to town hiccuping for law enforcement and they left 10 days later hiccuping for repeal.

6 Such dizzy somersaults are all in the day's work of a politician. The Democratic professionals at Washington, not to mention many of the Republicans, got converted to the New Deal overnight, and they will be unconverted with the same expedition when it blows up.

7 One hears sometimes of politicians who claim to have lost something by "entering the public service." Usually they say they could have made more money outside and led happier lives. But this is true once or twice in a blue moon. The typical politician does far better in politics than he could have done at anything else.

8 Now and then, of course, a man of genuine ability and integrity blunders into a governor's chair, or into Congress, or into some other political place, but he seldom lasts very long. The average American Congressman is about on a level, intellectually and morally, with a

bartender in a second-rate saloon or a head barber in a third-rate shop. As for the governors, they are so low-down that two or three of the 48 are always being impeached for grave crimes and misdemeanors and there is always at least one who is on his way to the hoosegow. During the past 15 years no less than 20 governors have been charged with downright felonies, and four or five have actually gone to prison. The rest, though maybe honest enough, are mainly only demagogues and mountebanks. It would be hard to find any other class of presumably reputable men who show so high an average of rogues and charlatans.

9 The most nearly decent fellows in politics, in all probability, are the fanatics—at least at the start of their careers. But even the fanatics, if they last long enough, usually turn into professional politicians.

10 The picture that I draw is a dark one, and there may be some who will protest that it is too sad. If so, then I can only reply that they do not know politicians. Everyone who has actually lived with politicians, including all those members of the fraternity who have reformed and are trying to lead honest lives, will tell you substantially what I tell you. It is precisely such men as I have described who make and execute the laws of this imperial nation and are the lords of us all. No one in his sober senses would trust them in any other place of responsibility calling for sound skill and common decency. A doctor who was so plainly a suspicious character would lose all his patients, and a lawyer on the same level would have only thieves for clients. Yet we not only hand over our lives and property to their keeping; we also pay them handsomely for robbing and betraying us, and give them higher honor than we give to any other class of men.

11 What ails them? Why are they so ornery? Plainly enough most of them are recruited from a somewhat inferior stratum of the population. The typical newcomer at the trade is a young man of cloudy background and equivocal standards, whose yearning to live easily far outruns his ability to earn an honorable living.

12 This young man tries politics because it offers him a good job quickly. The talents that push him ahead are not those of a diligent and able man; they are those of a cheap-jack. The tricks that he has to master are the tricks most useful to a corn doctor at a county fair. The most dangerous thing he can do is to tell the truth.

13 I haven't the slightest doubt that many a youngster makes his first venture into politics full of laudable resolve to avoid all this buncombe and skullduggery. But if he has as much as a single electron of cerebral tissue in his head, he discovers very quickly that all the virtues he dreams of practicing are handicaps to him, and that he

must either purge himself of them or give up all thought of a political career.

14 In brief, the rules and hazards of the game run implacably against indulgence in any such rectitude. It is a luxury for rich men's sons who crave only a term in the legislature between Harvard and despair—not a diet fit to nourish professionals. The beginner who really wants to get on must grasp the bitter fact that votes are never won in any substantial numbers by the devices taught in Sunday schools. They are won by far more realistic artifices, of which two are salient. The first is to go out into the highways and byways and there flatter and enchant the boobs with blah. The second is to come to terms with the herdsmen who keep droves of boobs in corrals ready to be knocked down to the highest bidder.

15 What is to be remembered is that virtually all the politicians in the United States have wallowed in their time in those two mud holes; if they hadn't they wouldn't be where they are today. They have all talked balderdash from the stump, they have all throbbed to the huzzas of morons, they have all promised what they knew they couldn't deliver, and they have all connived at more or less open corruption. If there is an exception in all this broad land, then I apologize to him most humbly. But I never met him and never heard of him.

16 Try to imagine what would happen to a doctor who had to get his patients by scratching their backs, and kissing their babies, and attending all their raffles and birthday parties, and marching in all their parades. Certainly the effect upon his professional integrity would hardly be salubrious. Now imagine him obliged to go to the saloon keeper at the corner for permission to practice at all, and giving the saloon keeper, in return for his permit, the right to dictate his prescriptions. Surely it would be asking too much of human nature to expect him to remember his Hippocratic oath. If he kept out of jail he'd be doing enough.

17 Well, every politician, whether large or small, is in that boat, or has been in it in the past. Even the mightiest of them, frowning down on the world from his glittering balloon, has yielded his neck to some boss in his day, whether openly or behind the door, and done his share of fawning over idiots, and discharged his five million words of hooey. In so far as he is a man of any sense whatever, he has got on by flattering and fooling his inferiors. A suspicious character from the start, by virtue of his trade, he has gradually bent himself this way and that to fit every suspicion, and so he emerges at last as a kind of chartered public enemy, safe from the

police so long as he is reasonably careful, and living on the troubles of the people.

18 How are we to improve him—or get rid of him? The first, I believe is a sheer impossibility. So long as we want to enjoy the excitement of democracy we must be prepared to endure its curses, and one of them is the fact that when two men stand up before a mob, the one honest and the other a fraud, the mob always prefers the fraud. He is always longer on promises and readier with soothing and hence can be more charming to persons incapable of thought. Years ago I proposed a way out that got no attention at the time but maybe had some merit. It was based on a question: Why should there be any politicians at all? Why should we hand over our affairs to men so palpably dubious and chosen so ridiculously? Why should we assume that the capacity to enchant and hoodwink ignorant and credulous people is the capacity to serve the whole community? Why not get rid of the difficulty by abolishing politics altogether and choosing our rulers by lot? Why not take away all the rewards of public office and make the holding of it not a privilege but a duty?

19 The scheme may sound crazy at first sight; but if we are content to choose men at random and against their will to go into a jury box and decide the gravest matters of life and death, then why shouldn't we be willing to trust the same men with other matters? If they are fit to execute the laws, then why aren't they fit to make them? That making laws requires any special knowledge is surely not a fact, for it is done today mainly by amateurs, and the professionals intermingled with them are more often than not incompetent or dishonest. The only real difference between the amateurs in a jury box and those in a legislature is that the former have no private interest in the case before them.

20 I offer my plan to the Brain Trust.[1] If it is adopted before Congress meets in January the professors will have a much easier time than they now seem likely to have.

Additional Rhetorical Strategies

Illustration (throughout); Cause and Effect (paragraphs 1, 11, 12); Comparison and Contrast (paragraph 10); Analogy (paragraph 16); Argument (throughout).

[1]A popular name at the time for Franklin D. Roosevelt's policy advisers, who were largely drawn from academic life. [Eds.]

Examining Words and Meaning

1. What is the effect of Mencken's title? What relationship does the title establish between Mencken and his readers? How, specifically, is this relationship strengthened in the first paragraph of the essay?

2. How does Mencken verify his contention that the business of politicians is "almost as firmly grounded on false pretenses as that of the quack doctor or shyster lawyer" (paragraph 2)? What effect does he intend here? Does he follow up on this claim as the essay proceeds?

3. Look up these words in a dictionary, if necessary: ignoble (paragraph 1); mountebanks (paragraph 8); charlatans (paragraph 8); cheap-jack (paragraph 12); buncombe (paragraph 13); implacably (paragraph 14); salubrious (paragraph 16).

Focusing on Structures and Strategies

1. Consider why Mencken calls himself "a moral theologian of 30 years' practice" in paragraph 2. What response does he intend to elicit from his readers by using this phrase? Can you point to specific moments later in the essay when he thinks or sounds like a moral theologian?

2. Is the analogy Mencken creates between doctors and politicians in paragraph 16 a fair one? Mencken is often as witty as he is vituperative. Point to specific examples of his wit, and discuss how he uses them to persuade his readers to adopt his plan for political reform. When and how does he anticipate the objections of his readers to his proposal?

3. Mencken claimed that he wrote with "almost scientific precision." Can you point to specific passages here where his self-appraisal seems to be accurate? Can you also point to specific moments when his appeal is basically emotional or ethical?

Suggestions for Further Discussion and Writing

1. In what specific ways does Mencken appeal to his readers' prejudices toward politicians? When and how does he create the sense that he

is a man of good sense and good will? When, for example, does Mencken sound conciliatory? Why are these moments so effective?

2. Mencken wrote this essay nearly fifty years ago. From what you know of politicians since then, do his perceptions seem as applicable in the 1970s and 1980s as he would claim they were in the 1920s and 1930s? Be as specific as possible in your response.

3. Imagine a world in which Mencken has had his way, a world in which politics has been abolished and we regularly choose our rulers by lot. Write a persuasive essay aimed at winning your audience's consent to your proposal to return to the world of politics.

The Passing Wisdom of Birds

Barry Lopez

With the publication of his best-selling nonfiction work, Of Wolves and Men *(1978), Barry Lopez emerged as one of the most popular and articulate voices on the subject of nature and the environment. One reviewer has characterized his writing as "some of the most thoughtful and knowledgeable prose around. He is a 'naturalist' without any of the adolescent awe or back-to-nature self-righteousness that flaws so much recent nature writing."*

Born in Port Chester, New York, in 1945, Barry Lopez turned to full-time writing after earning an undergraduate degree at Notre Dame University and a master's degree at the University of Oregon. He has contributed articles, essays, and short fiction to numerous periodicals, ranging from Audubon, Country Journal, Geo, *and* Sierra *to* Parabola, Rocky Mountain, Smithsonian, *and* Travel and Leisure. *In addition, he has served as a contributing editor to* North American Review *and* Harper's, *as well as a guest editor of a special section on "The American Indian Mind" in a 1978 issue of* Quest *magazine.*

Among Lopez's book-length publications are collections of fictional narratives, Desert Notes: Reflections in the Eye of a Raven *(1976) and* The Dance of Herons *(1979), and Native American trickster tales and short stories,* Winter Count *(1981). In addition to* Of Wolves and Men, *Lopez is best known for* Arctic Dreams

(1986), a richly detailed account of his travels in the Arctic Circle over a four-year period, for which he received the American Book Award for Nonfiction in 1986.

Asked to explain his interest in both writing and nature, Lopez responded: "I care about language and landscape, both separately and for the connection between them, which is what writing is to me. I think a great deal about the therapeutic value of story and language, and about the ethical issues in writing. I once said I wrote because of a hatred of lies. And that I went into the natural world because you could examine the nature of your prejudices there without fear of reprisal." In the following selection, published originally in the Autumn 1985 Orion Nature Quarterly, *Lopez offers a persuasive account of the ways in which we can transcend the ignorance and brutality that have characterized the Western relationship to wild nature.*

1 On the eighth of November, 1519, Hernando Cortés and four hundred Spanish soldiers marched self-consciously out of the city of Iztapalapa, Mexico, and started across the great Iztapalapan Causeway separating the lakes of Xochimilco and Chalco. They had been received the afternoon before in Iztapalapa as demigods; but they stared now in disbelief at what lay before them. Reflecting brilliantly on the vast plain of dark water like a landscape of sunlit chalk, its lines sharp as cut stone in the dustless air at 7200 feet, was the Aztec Byzantium—Tenochtitlán. Mexico City.

2 It is impossible to know what was in the facile, highly charged mind of Cortés that morning, anticipating his first meeting with the reluctant Montezuma; but Bernal Díaz, who was present, tells us what was on the minds of the soldiers. They asked each other was it *real*—gleaming Iztapalapa behind them, the smooth causeway beneath their feet, imposing Tenochtitlán ahead? The Spanish had been in the New World for twenty-seven years, but what they discovered in the Valley of Mexico that fall "had never been heard of or seen before, nor even dreamed about" in their world. What astounded them was not, solely, the extent and sophistication of the engineering that divided and encompassed the lakes surrounding Tenochtitlán; nor the evidence that a separate culture, utterly different from their own, pursued a complex life in this huge city. It was the depth and pervasiveness of the natural beauty before their senses.

3 The day before, they had strolled the spotless streets of Iztapalapa through plots of full-blossomed flowers, arranged in pat-

terns and in colors pleasing to the eye; through irrigated fruit orchards; and into still groves of aromatic trees like cedar. They sat in the shade of bright cotton awnings in quiet stone patios and marveled at the robustness and the well-tended orderliness of the vegetable gardens around them. Roses glowed against the lime-washed walls of the houses like garnets and alexandrites. In the hour before sunset, the cool, fragrant air was filled with the whirr and flutter of birds, and lit with bird song.

4 That had been Iztapalapa. Mexico City, they thought, even as their leader dismounted that morning with solemn deliberation from that magical creature, the horse, to meet an advancing Montezuma ornately caparisoned in gold and silver and bird feathers—Mexico City, they thought as they approached, could only outdo Iztapalapa. And it did. With Montezuma's tentative welcome they were free to wander in its various precincts. Mexico City confirmed the image of a people gardening with meticulous care and with exquisite attention to line and detail at the edge of nature.

5 It is clear from Díaz's historical account that the soldiers were stunned by the physical beauty of Tenochtitlán. Venice came to their minds in comparison, because of its canals; but Venice was not as intensely fresh, as well lit as Mexico City. And there was not to be found in Venice, or in Salamanca or Paris for that matter, anything like the great aviaries where thousands of birds—white egrets, energetic wrens and thrushes, fierce accipiters, brilliantly colored parrots—were housed and tended. They were as captivating, as fabulous, as the displays of flowers: vermilion flycatchers, copper-tailed trogons, green jays, blue-throated hummingbirds, and summer tanagers. Great blue herons, brooding condors. And, throughout the city, wild birds nested.

6 Even Cortés, intensely preoccupied with politics, with guiding a diplomacy of conquest in the region, noticed the birds. He was struck, too, by the affinity of the Mexican people for their gardens and for the measured and intricate flow of water through their city. He took time to write Charles V in Spain, describing it all.

7 Cortés's men, says Díaz, never seemed to tire of the arboretums, gardens, and aviaries in the months following their entry into the city. By June, 1520, however, Cortés's psychological manipulation of Montezuma and a concomitant arrogance, greed, and disrespect on the part of the Spanish military force had become too much for the Mexicans, and they drove them out. Cortés, relentless and vengeful, returned to the Valley of Mexico eleven months later with a larger

army and laid siege to the city. Canal by canal, garden by garden, home by home, he destroyed what he had described to Charles V as "the most beautiful city in the world." On June 16, in a move calculated to humiliate and frighten the Mexican people, Cortés set fire to the aviaries.

8 The grotesqueness and unmitigated violence of Cortés's act has come back to me repeatedly in reading of early European encounters with the landscapes of the New World, like a kind of darkness. The siege of Mexico City was fought barbarously on both sides; and the breathtaking parks and beautiful gardens of Mexico City, of course, stood hard by temples in which human life was regularly offered up to Aztec gods, by priests whose hair was matted with human gore and blood. No human culture has ever existed apart from its dark side. But what Cortés did, even under conditions of war, flies wildly in the face of a desire to find a dignified and honorable relationship with nature. It is an ambitious and vague longing, but one that has been with us for centuries, I think, and which today is a voice heard clearly from many different quarters—political science, anthropology, biology, philosophy. The desire is that, our colonial conquests of the human and natural world finally at an end, we will find our way back to a more equitable set of relationships with all we have subjugated. I say back because the early cultures from which Western civilization evolved, such as the Magdalenian phase of Cro-Magnon culture in Europe, apparently had a less contentious arrangement with nature before the development of agriculture in northern Mesopotamia, and the rise of cities.

9 The image of Cortés burning the aviaries is not simply for me an image of a kind of destructive madness that lies at the heart of imperialistic conquest; it is also a symbol of a long-term failure of Western civilization to recognize the intrinsic worth of the American landscape, and its potential value to human societies that have since come to be at odds with the natural world. While English, French, and Spanish explorers were cruising the eastern shores of America, dreaming of feudal fiefdoms, gold, and political advantage, the continent itself was, already, occupied in a complex way by more than five hundred different cultures, each of which regarded itself as living in some kind of enlightened intimacy with the land. A chance to rediscover the original wisdom inherent in the myriad sorts of human relationships possible with the nonhuman world, of course, was not of concern to us in the sixteenth century, as it is now, particularly to

geographers, philosophers, historians and ecologists. It would not in fact become clear for centuries that the metaphysics we had thrown out thousands of years before was still intact in tribal America. America offered us the opportunity to deliberate with historical perspective, to see if we wished to reclaim that metaphysics.

10 The need to reexamine our experience in the New World is, increasingly, a practical need. Contemporary American culture, founded on the original material wealth of the continent, on its timber, ores, and furs, has become a culture that devours the earth. Minerals, fresh water, darkness, tribal peoples, everything the land produces we now consume in prodigious amounts. There are at least two schools of thought on how to rectify this high rate of consumption, which most Western thinkers agree is unsustainable and likely wrongheaded if not disastrous. First, there are technical approaches. No matter how sophisticated or innovative these may be, however, they finally seem only clever or artful adjustments, not solutions. Secondly, we can consider a change in attitude toward nature, adopting a fundamentally different way of thinking about it than we have previously had, perhaps ever had as human beings. The insights of aboriginal peoples are of inestimable value here in rethinking our relationships with the natural world (i.e., in figuring out how to get ourselves back *into* it); but the solution to our plight, I think, is likely to be something no other culture has ever thought of, something over which !Kung, Inuit, Navajo, Walbiri, and the other traditions we have turned to for wisdom in the twentieth century will marvel at as well.

11 The question before us is how do we find a viable natural philosophy, one that places us again within the elements of our natural history. The answer, I believe, lies with wild animals.

II

12 Over the past ten years it has been my privilege to spend time in the field in North America with biologists studying several different kinds of animals, including wolves, polar bears, mountain lions, seals, and whales. Of all that could be said about this exercise, about people watching animals, I would like to restrict myself to but one or two things. First, although such studies are scientific they are conducted by human beings, whose individual speculations may take them out beyond the bounds of scientific inquiry. The animals they scrutinize can draw them back into an older, more intimate and less

rational association with the local landscape. In this frame of mind they may privately begin to question the methodology of Western science, especially its purported objectivity and its troublesome lack of heart. It may seem incapable of addressing questions the scientist intuits are crucial. Even as they perceive its flaws, however, scientists continue to offer such studies as a highly dependable source of reliable information—and it is. Science's flaws as a tool of inquiry are relatively minor and it is further saved by its strengths.

13 Science's strength lies with its rigor and objectivity and it is undoubtedly as rigorous as any system available to us. Even with its flaws (its failure, for example, to address disorderly or idiosyncratic behavior) field biology is as strong and reliable in its way as the collective wisdom of a hunting people actively involved with the land. The highest order of field work being done in biology today, then, from an elucidation of the way polar bears hunt ringed seals to working out the ecology of night-flying moths pollinating agaves in the Mojave Desert, forms part of the foundation for a modern realignment with the natural world. (The other parts of the foundation would include work done by anthropologists among hunter-gatherer people and studies by natural geographers; philosophical work in the tradition of Aldo Leopold and Rachel Carson; and the nearly indispensable element of personal experience.)

14 I often search out scientific reports to read; many are based on years of research and have been patiently thought through. Despite my regard, however, I read with caution, for I cannot rid myself of the thought that, even though it is the best theoretical approach we have, the process is not perfect. I have participated in some of this type of work and know that innocent mistakes are occasionally made in the data. I understand how influential a misleading coincidence can become in the overall collection of data; how unconsciously the human mind can follow a teasing parallel. I am cautious, too, for even more fundamental reasons. It is hard to say exactly what any animal is *doing.* It is impossible to know when or where an event in an animal's life begins or ends. And our human senses confine us to realms that may contain only a small part of the information produced in an event. Something critical could be missing and we would not know. And as far as the experiments themselves are concerned, although we can design and carry out thousands of them, no animal can ever be described as the sum of these experiments. And, finally, though it is possible to write precisely about something, this does not automatically mean one is accurate.

15 The scientific approach is flawed, therefore, by its imposition of a subjective framework around animal behavior; but it only fails, really, because it is incomplete. We would be rash, using this approach exclusively, to claim to understand any one animal, let alone the environment in which that animal is evolving. Two remedies to this dilemma of the partially-perceived animal suggest themselves. One, obviously, is to turn to the long-term field observations of non-Western cultural traditions. These non-Aristotelian, non-Cartesian, non-Baconian views of wild animals are stimulating, challenging, and, like a good bibliography, heuristic, pointing one toward discovery. (They are also problematic in that, for example, they do not take sufficiently into account the full range of behavior of migratory animals and they have a highly non-linear (though ultimately, possibly, more correct) understanding of population biology.)

16 A second, much less practiced remedy is to cultivate within ourselves a sense of mystery—to see that the possibilities for an expression of life in any environment, or in any single animal, are larger than we can predict or understand, and that this is all right. Biology should borrow here from quantum physics, which accepts the premise that, under certain circumstances, the observer can be deceived. Quantum physics, with its ambiguous particles and ten-dimensional universes, is a branch of science that has in fact returned us to a state of awe with nature, without threatening our intellectual capacity to analyze complex events.

17 If it is true that modern people desire a new relationship with the natural world, one that is not condescending, manipulative, and purely utilitarian; and if the foundation upon which the relationship is to be built is as I suggest—a natural history growing largely out of science and the insights of native peoples—then a staggering task lies before us.

18 The initial steps to be taken seem obvious. First, we must identify and protect those regions where landscapes largely undisturbed by human technology remain intact. Within these ecosystems lie blueprints for the different patterns of life that have matured outside the pervasive influence of myriad Western technologies (though no place on earth has escaped their influence entirely). We can contemplate and study endlessly the natural associations here, and draw from these smaller universes a sophisticated wisdom about process and event, and about evolution. Second, we need to subscribe a great public support to the discipline of field biology, that not invalid inquiry into the lives of wild animals. Third, we need to seek

an introduction to the reservoirs of intelligence that native cultures have preserved in both oral tradition and in their personal experience with the land, the highly complex detail of a way of life not yet torn entirely from the fabric of nature.

19 We must, too, look out after the repositories of our own long-term cultural wisdom more keenly. Our libraries, which preserve the best of what we have to say about ourselves and nature, are under siege in an age of cost-benefit analysis. We need to immerse ourselves thoughtfully, too, in what is being written and produced on tape and film, so that we become able to distinguish again between truthful expression and mere entertainment. We need to do this not only for our own sake but so that our children, who too often have only the half-eclipsed lives of zoo animals or the contrived dramas of television wildlife adventure before them, will know that this heritage is disappearing and what we are apt to lose with it.

20 What disappears with a debasement of wild landscapes is more than genetic diversity, more than a homeland for Henry Beston's "other nations," more, to be perfectly selfish, than a source of future medical cures for human illness or a chance for personal revitalization on a wilderness trip. We stand to lose the focus of our ideals. We stand to lose our sense of dignity, of compassion, even our sense of what we call God. The philosophy of nature we set aside 8,000 years ago in the Fertile Crescent we can, I think, locate again and greatly refine in North America. The New World is a landscape still overwhelming in the vigor of its animals and plants, resonant with mystery. It encourages, still, an enlightened response toward indigenous cultures that differ from our own, whether Aztecan, Lakotan, lupine, avian, or invertebrate. By broadening our sense of the intrinsic worth of life and by cultivating respect for other ways of moving toward perfection, we may find a sense of resolution we have been looking for, I think, for centuries.

21 Two practical steps occur to me. Each by itself is so small I hate to set it forth; but to say nothing would be cowardly, and both appear to me to be reasonable, a beginning. They also acknowledge an obvious impediment; to bridge the chasm between a colonial attitude toward the land and a more filial relationship with it takes time. The task has always been, and must be, carried into the next generation.

22 The first thought I would offer is that each university and college in the country establish the position of university naturalist, a position to be held by a student in his or her senior year and passed on at the end of the year to another student. The university naturalist

would be responsible for establishing and maintaining a natural history of the campus, would confer with architects and groundskeepers, escort guests, and otherwise look out after the nonhuman elements of the campus, their relationships to human beings, and the preservation of this knowledge. Though the position itself might be honorary and unsalaried, the student would receive substantial academic credit for his or her work and would be provided with a budget to conduct research, maintain a library, and produce an occasional paper. Depending on his or her gifts and personality, the university naturalist might elect to teach a course or to speak at some point during the academic year. In concert with the university archivist and university historian, the university naturalist would seek to protect the relationships-in-time that define a culture's growth and ideals.

23 A second suggestion is more difficult to implement, but no less important than a system of university naturalists. In recent years several American and British publishers, have developed plans to reprint in an extended series classic works of natural history. These plans should be pursued; the list of books should include not only works of contemporary natural history but early works by such people as Thomas Nuttall and William Bartram, so that the project has historical depth. It should also include books by nonscientists who have immersed themselves "beyond reason" in the world occupied by animals and who have emerged with stunning reports, such as J. A. Baker's *The Peregrine.* And books that offer us a resounding and affecting vision of the landscape, such as John Van Dyke's *The Desert.* It should also include the work of anthropologists who have worked, or are working, with the native peoples of North America to define an indigenous natural history, such as Richard Nelson's *Make Prayers to the Raven.* And a special effort should be made to unearth those voices that once spoke eloquently for parts of the country the natural history of which is now too often overlooked, or overshadowed, by a focus on western or northern North American ecosystems: the pine barrens of New Jersey, the Connecticut River Valley, the White Mountains of New Hampshire, the remnant hardwood forests of Indiana and Ohio, the Outer Banks, the relictual prairies of Texas, and the mangrove swamps and piney woods of Georgia.

24 Such a collection, it seems to me, should be assembled with several thoughts in mind. It should be inexpensive so that the books can fall easily into the hands of young people. It should document the extraordinary variety of natural ecosystems in North America, and reflect the great range of dignified and legitimate human response

to them. And it should make clear that human beings belong in these landscapes, that they, too, are a part of the earth's natural history.

III

25 The image I carry of Cortés setting fire to the aviaries in Mexico City that June day in 1521 is an image I cannot rid myself of. It stands, in my mind, for a fundamental lapse of wisdom in the European conquest of America, an underlying trouble in which political conquest, personal greed, revenge, and national pride outweigh what is innocent, beautiful, serene, and defenseless—the birds. The incineration of these creatures 450 years ago is not something that can be rectified today. Indeed, one could argue, the same oblivious irreverence is still with us, among those who would ravage and poison the earth to sustain the economic growth of Western societies. But Cortés's act can be transcended. It is possible to fix in the mind that heedless violence, the hysterical cries of the birds, the stench of death, to look it square in the face and say that there is more to us than this, this will not forever distinguish us among the other cultures. It is possible to imagine that on the far side of the Renaissance and the Enlightenment we can recover the threads of an earlier wisdom.

26 Again I think of the animals, because of the myriad ways in which they have helped us since we first regarded each other differently. They offered us early models of rectitude and determination in adversity, which we put into stories. The grace of a moving animal, in some ineluctable way, kindles still in us a sense of imitation. They continue to produce for us a sense of the Other: to encounter a truly wild animal on its own ground is to know the defeat of thought, to feel reason overpowered. The animals have fed us; and the cultures of the great hunters particularly—the bears, the dogs, and the cats—have provided the central metaphors by which we have taken satisfaction in our ways and explained ourselves to strangers.

27 Cortés's soldiers, on their walks through the gleaming gardens of Tenochtitlán, would have been as struck by the flight paths of song birds as we are today. In neither a horizontal nor a vertical dimension do these pathways match the line and scale of human creation, within which the birds dwell. The corridors they travel are curved around some other universe. When the birds passed over them, moving across the grain of sunlight, the soldiers must have stopped occasionally to watch, as we do. It is the birds' independence

from predictable patterns of human design that draws us to them. In the birds' separate but related universe we are able to sense hope for ourselves. Against a background of the familiar, we recognize with astonishment a new pattern.

28 In such a moment, pausing to take in the flight of a flock of birds passing through sunshine and banking gracefully into a grove of trees, it is possible to move beyond a moment in the Valley of Mexico when we behaved as though we were insane.

Additional Rhetorical Strategies

Narration (paragraphs 1, 7); Description (paragraph 3); Comparison and Contrast (paragraph 5); Cause and Effect (paragraphs 7, 9, 10, 14, 20); Classification (paragraph 10).

Examining Words and Meaning

1. Toward what persuasive end has Lopez written this essay? Summarize briefly the major steps that Lopez proposes we take in order to preserve the ecological integrity of the natural world. What general role, for example, does he envision for educational institutions to play in the realignment of humankind and the natural world? What more particular role does he imagine that students might play?

2. Lopez opens his essay with an extended account of the Spanish conquest of Tenochtitlán. In what ways does he see this event as relating to his overall purpose in writing this essay? Consider, for example, how the behavior of the Spaniards might be likened to people in modern Western culture. What other inferences might you draw from Lopez's attention to the Spanish conquest of Mexico?

3. What does Lopez mean when he says, "What disappears with a debasement of wild landscapes is more than genetic diversity" (paragraph 20)? What are the specific steps Lopez proposes that we take in order to create a "foundation for a modern realignment with the natural world" (paragraph 13)? Comment on Lopez's assertion that personal experience will be "a nearly indispensable element" in such a potential realignment.

Focusing on Structures and Strategies

1. What is the thesis upon which Lopez builds his persuasive essay? Characterize the organization of his essay. Outline the movement from one paragraph to another. What is the effect of framing his essay with the account of the destruction of Mexico City and his personal reactions to those events? What does he gain/lose by this use of a first-person reaction to a remote historical incident?
2. Why is Lopez's use of the story of the conquest of Mexico, and his emphasis on the destruction of the aviaries, so persuasive? Why does his selection of details in this section of his essay function so effectively?
3. How does Lopez account for the fact that the Spaniards both admired and then destroyed the great city? How does the city itself represent the ideal that Lopez wishes to strive for? Why do you think Lopez uses this scene from the past as an example of the destruction of nature rather than a more recent example?
4. What is Lopez's attitude toward scientific research in nature? What does he see as its limitations? What is the source of these limitations? How does he think these limitations can be overcome? What general and specific recommendations does Lopez offer in order to work toward his goal of living with nature? How do these suggestions reflect his attitude toward the sciences, history, and academics in general?
5. What is the dramatic function of the birds in this essay? What larger concerns do they represent, both at the beginning of the essay and at the end? What does Lopez suggest we can learn by watching them? In this respect, what is "the passing wisdom of birds"? In what specific ways does Lopez's title contribute to the overall purpose of his essay?

Suggestions for Further Discussion and Writing

1. How would you describe the model of society that Lopez envisions? What are his models and sources for that vision? How would the culture he envisions differ from its models? How feasible do you think his goal is? How would you add to it or qualify it?
2. Implicit in Lopez's essay is the notion that Americans are rather casual in their response to the destruction of North America's

ecosystem. Continued neglect of our need to establish a more mutually beneficial "realignment with the natural world" poses the gravest dangers to both humankind and nature in the years ahead. What other events and issues with potentially enormously serious consequences can you think of that are being ignored or taken lightly by the general public in America? Write a persuasive essay addressed to the American public, pointing out the importance of the issue and urging people to regard the issue more responsibly. For example, you might take American corporations to task for continuing to pollute the environment rather than safeguarding the public against toxic wastes. Or you might point out what you consider to be the inexcusable waste of human resources as expressed in the serious deficiencies in our educational system. In this respect, you could not only discuss the possible consequences of such deficiencies but also propose specific ways for the American public to revise its attitudes toward education and to strengthen our schools. Remember, your goal in this essay is to persuade, to lead your readers to consent to some new behavior.

3. Write an essay in which you rely on some incident of historical importance to create a frame of reference for your own efforts to persuade your readers to adopt some new form of behavior. For example, consider the several, quite different historical incidents you might draw on in order to persuade your congressional representative to vote either in favor of or against the United States's increasing funding for military operations in Central America or Afghanistan. If you wish, include your own reactions to this historical incident, as Lopez does, but be sure that you choose an incident that will prove to be persuasive.

Sojourner Truth: And A'n't I a Woman?

Frances D. Gage

As the feminist movement of the 1970s grew out of the civil rights movement of the 1960s, so in the nineteenth century did woman's suffrage evolve from abolitionism. Neither of these associations proved totally supportive of the other. But if the women in the following passage seem to have been overly concerned with separating themselves from the abolitionists, the abolitionists were not above dissociation for expediency's sake, either. In the 1850s, some women may have worried that cooperation with the abolitionists would hurt their cause. In the 1860s, however, suffragists argued for a connection and complained that the newly signed Emancipation Proclamation freed only black men and left the question of women's rights by the wayside. But when Frederick Douglass heard their complaints, he told the women with whom he had marched that they should stand back, for this was "the Negro's hour."

"The Negro man's *hour," Sojourner Truth would have answered. An American abolitionist and suffragist born in New York State, Sojourner Truth (c. 1797–1883) left her domestic position in 1843, prompted by a "heavenly voice," and traveled throughout the North preaching emancipation and women's rights. Effectively interweaving economic-social reality and Biblical allusion, she argued persuasively for the fullest extension of equal rights to all colors and to both sexes. The following account is recorded in the reminiscences of Frances D. Gage, American abolitionist and author. In the selection, Sojourner Truth's oratorical powers are at their height as she challenges illusions with her question "And a'n't I a woman?"*

1 The leaders of the movement trembled on seeing a tall, gaunt black woman in a gray dress and white turban, surmounted with an uncouth sun-bonnet, march deliberately into the church, walk with the air of a queen up the aisle, and take her seat upon the pulpit steps. A buzz of disapprobation was heard all over the house, and there fell on the listening ear, "An abolition affair!" "Woman's rights and niggers!" "I told you so!" . . .

2 I chanced on that occasion to wear my first laurels in public life as president of the meeting. At my request order was restored, and the business of the Convention went on. Morning, afternoon, and evening exercises came and went. Through all these sessions old Sojourner, quiet and reticent as the "Lybian Statue," sat crouched against the wall on the corner of the pulpit stairs, her sun-bonnet shading her eyes, her elbows on her knees, her chin resting upon her broad, hard palms. At intermission she was busy selling the "Life of Sojourner Truth," a narrative of her own strange and adventurous life. Again and again, timorous and trembling ones came to me and said, with earnestness, "Don't let her speak, Mrs. Gage, it will ruin us. Every newspaper in the land will have our cause mixed up with

abolition and niggers, and we shall be utterly denounced." My only answer was, "We shall see when the time comes."

3 The second day the work waxed warm. Methodist, Baptist, Episcopal, Presbyterian, and Universalist ministers came in to hear and discuss the resolutions presented. One claimed superior rights and privileges for man, on the ground of "superior intellect"; another, because of the "manhood of Christ; if God had desired the equality of woman, He would have given some token of His will through the birth, life, and death of the Saviour." Another gave us a theological view of the "sin of our first mother."

4 There were very few women in those days who dared to "speak in meeting"; and the august teachers of the people were seemingly getting the better of us, while the boys in the galleries, and the sneerers among the pews, were hugely enjoying the discomfiture, as they supposed, of the "strong-minded." Some of the tender-skinned friends were on the point of losing dignity, and the atmosphere betokened a storm. When, slowly from her seat in the corner rose Sojourner Truth, who, till now, had scarcely lifted her head. "Don't let her speak!" gasped half a dozen in my ear. She moved slowly and solemnly to the front, laid her old bonnet at her feet, and turned her great speaking eyes to me. There was a hissing sound of disapprobation above and below. I rose and announced "Sojourner Truth," and begged the audience to keep silence for a few moments.

5 The tumult subsided at once, and every eye was fixed on this almost Amazon form, which stood nearly six feet high, head erect, and eyes piercing the upper air like one in a dream. At her first word there was a profound hush. She spoke in deep tones, which, though not loud, reached every ear in the house, and away through the throng at the doors and windows.

6 "Wall, chilern, whar dar is so much racket dar must be somethin' out o' kilter. I tink dat 'twixt de niggers of de Souf and de womin at de Norf, all talkin' 'bout rights, de white men will be in a fix pretty soon. But what's all dis here talkin' 'bout?

7 "Dat man ober dar say dat womin needs to be helped into carriages, and lifted ober ditches, and to hab de best place everywhar. Nobody eber helps me into carriages, or ober mud-puddles, or gibs me any best place!" And raising herself to her full height, and her voice to a pitch like rolling thunder, she asked, "And a'n't I a woman? Look at me! Look at my arm! (and she bared her right arm to the shoulder, showing her tremendous muscular power). I have

ploughed, and planted, and gathered into barns, and no man could head me! And a'n't I a woman? I could work as much and eat as much as a man—when I could get it—and bear de lash as well! And a'n't I a woman? I have borne thirteen chilern, and seen 'em mos' all sold off to slavery, and when I cried out with my mother's grief, none but Jesus heard me! And a'n't I a woman?

8 "Den dey talks 'bout dis ting in de head; what dis dey call it?" ("Intellect," whispered some one near.) "Dat's it, honey. What's dat got to do wid womin's rights or nigger's rights? If my cup won't hold but a pint, and yourn holds a quart, wouldn't ye be mean not to let me have my little half-measure full?" And she pointed her significant finger, and sent a keen glance at the minister who had made the argument. The cheering was long and loud.

9 "Den dat little man in black dar, he say women can't have as much rights as men, 'cause Christ wan't a woman! Whar did your Christ come from?" Rolling thunder couldn't have stilled that crowd, as did those deep, wonderful tones, as she stood there with outstretched arms and eyes of fire. Raising her voice still louder, she repeated, "Whar did your Christ come from? From God and a woman! Man had nothin' to do wid Him." Oh, what a rebuke that was to that little man.

10 Turning again to another objector, she took up the defense of Mother Eve. I can not follow her through it all. It was pointed, and witty, and solemn; eliciting at almost every sentence deafening applause; and she ended by asserting: "If de fust woman God ever made was strong enough to turn de world upside down all alone, dese woman togedder (and she glanced her eye over the platform) ought to be able to turn it back, and get it right side up again! And now dey is asking to do it, de men better let 'em." Long-continued cheering greeted this. " 'Bleeged to ye for hearin' on me, and now ole Sojourner han't got nothin' more to say."

11 Amid roars of applause, she returned to her corner, leaving more than one of us with streaming eyes, and hearts beating with gratitude. She had taken us up in her strong arms and carried us safely over the slough of difficulty turning the whole tide in our favor. I have never in my life seen anything like the magical influence that subdued the mobbish spirit of the day, and turned the sneers and jeers of an excited crowd into notes of respect and admiration. Hundreds rushed up to shake hands with her, and congratulate the glorious old mother, and bid her God-speed on her mission of "testifyin' agin concerning the wickedness of this 'ere people."

Additional Rhetorical Strategies

Description (paragraphs 1–5); Narration (throughout); Illustration (paragraphs 7–11).

Examining Words and Meaning

1. What does Sojourner Truth find that Southern blacks and Northern women have in common? How does she use herself as an example to help the women refute the men's arguments?
2. Suppose that the writer of this account had regularized the spelling and compensated for the speaker's dialect in setting down the speech. Would Sojourner Truth's oration be more or less effective? Why?
3. Look up these words in a dictionary, if they are unfamiliar to you: gaunt (paragraph 1); laurels (paragraph 2); reticent (paragraph 2); timorous (paragraph 2); august (paragraph 4); discomfiture (paragraph 4); betokened (paragraph 4); disapprobation (paragraph 4); Amazon (paragraph 5); slough (paragraph 11).

Focusing on Structures and Strategies

1. How does Sojourner Truth show that she recognizes the potential hostility of the crowd? How does she turn this recognition to her own advantage? Would you call her doing so a rational, an emotional, or an ethical appeal?
2. Why does Sojourner pause before her first "And a'n't I a woman"? How do her gestures reinforce her point? What is the effect of her repeating the question so often during her speech? What sort of appeal does the repetition constitute? How does it affirm a kind of womanhood that men tend not to see?

Suggestions for Further Discussion and Writing

1. Compare this selection to Adrienne Rich's commencement address (below). What are the problems facing women that each speaker

perceives? How much progress do you think there has been between Sojourner's time and our own? Is some of the progress illusory? How might the differences between the situations in which Sojourner Truth and Adrienne Rich speak account for the different rhetorical strategies they adopt?

2. Write an essay in which you answer charges made against you or a group you represent. You might disagree, for example, with the idea that seventeen-year-olds are too immature to buy a drink in your state. Try, if you can, to use repetition as Sojourner Truth does to emphasize your point. Don't avoid clear thinking, but concentrate on being persuasive, as opposed to logically thorough, in your composition.

Claiming an Education

Adrienne Rich

"For writers, and at the moment particularly for women writers," wrote Adrienne Rich in 1971, "there is the challenge and promise of a whole new psychic geography to be explored. But there is also a difficult and dangerous walking on the ice, as we try to find language and images for a consciousness we are just coming into, and with little in the past to support us." As one of America's major contemporary poets, Adrienne Rich has made a courageous journey into that "new psychic geography" and has mapped out its terrain in close to a dozen volumes of poetry.

Born in Baltimore in 1929, Rich won the 1974 National Book Award in poetry for Diving into the Wreck. *Her study of motherhood,* Of Woman Born: Motherhood as Experience and Institution *(1976), has been compared in importance to Simone de Beauvoir's classic,* The Second Sex. *A selection of poems from the body of her work appeared in* The Fact of a Doorframe: Poems Selected & Now, 1950–1984 *(1984) and a selection of prose writings in* Blood, Bread & Poetry: Selected Prose 1979–1985 *(1986). While poet in residence at Douglass College in New Jersey, Rich delivered the following speech to the incoming students of that school on September 6, 1977.*

1 For this convocation, I planned to separate my remarks into two parts: some thoughts about you, the women students here, and some thoughts about us who teach in a women's college. But ultimately, those two parts are indivisible. If university education means anything beyond the processing of human beings into expected roles, through credit hours, tests, and grades (and I believe that in a women's college especially it *might* mean much more), it implies an ethical and intellectual contract between teacher and student. This contract must remain intuitive, dynamic, unwritten; but we must turn to it again and again if learning is to be reclaimed from the depersonalizing and cheapening pressures of the present-day academic scene.

2 The first thing I want to say to you who are students, is that you cannot afford to think of being here to *receive* an education; you will do much better to think of yourselves as being here to *claim* one. One of the dictionary definitions of the verb "to claim" is: *to take as the rightful owner; to assert in the face of possible contradiction.* "To receive" is *to come into possession of; to act as receptacle or container for; to accept as authoritative or true.* The difference is that between acting and being acted-upon, and for women it can literally mean the difference between life and death.

3 One of the devastating weaknesses of university learning, of the store of knowledge and opinion that has been handed down through academic training, has been its almost total erasure of women's experience and thought from the curriculum, and its exclusion of women as members of the academic community. Today, with increasing numbers of women students in nearly every branch of higher learning, we still see very few women in the upper levels of faculty and administration in most institutions. Douglass College itself is a women's college in a university administered overwhelmingly by men, who in turn are answerable to the state legislature, again composed predominantly of men. But the most significant fact for you is that what you learn here, the very texts you read, the lectures you hear, the way your studies are divided into categories and fragmented one from the other—all this reflects, to a very large degree, neither objective reality, nor an accurate picture of the past, nor a group of rigorously tested observations about human behavior. What you can learn here (and I mean not only at Douglass but any college in any university) is how *men* have perceived and organized their experience, their history, their ideas of social relationships, good and evil, sickness and health, etc. When you read or hear about "great

issues," "major texts," "the mainstream of Western thought," you are hearing about what men, above all white men, in their male subjectivity, have decided is important.

4 Black and other minority peoples have for some time recognized that their racial and ethnic experience was not accounted for in the studies broadly labeled human; and that even the sciences can be racist. For many reasons, it has been more difficult for women to comprehend our exclusion, and to realize that even the sciences can be sexist. For one thing, it is only within the last hundred years that higher education has grudgingly been opened up to women at all, even to white, middle-class women. And many of us have found ourselves poring eagerly over books with titles like: *The Descent of Man; Man and His Symbols; Irrational Man; The Phenomenon of Man; The Future of Man; Man and the Machine; From Man to Man; May Man Prevail?; Man, Science and Society;* or *One-Dimensional Man*—books pretending to describe a "human" reality that does not include over one-half the human species.

5 Less than a decade ago, with the rebirth of a feminist movement in this country, women students and teachers in a number of universities began to demand and set up women's studies courses—to *claim* a woman-directed education. And, despite the inevitable accusations of "unscholarly," "group therapy," "fadism," etc., despite backlash and budget cuts, women's studies are still growing, offering to more and more women a new intellectual grasp on their lives, new understanding of our history, a fresh vision of the human experience, and also a critical basis for evaluating what they hear and read in other courses, and in the society at large.

6 But my talk is not really about women's studies, much as I believe in their scholarly, scientific, and human necessity. While I think that any Douglass student has everything to gain by investigating and enrolling in women's studies courses, I want to suggest that there is a more essential experience that you owe yourselves, one which courses in women's studies can greatly enrich, but which finally depends on you, in all your interactions with yourself and your world. This is the experience of *taking responsibility toward yourselves.* Our upbringing as women has so often told us that this should come second to our relationships and responsibilities to other people. We have been offered ethical models of the self-denying wife and mother; intellectual models of the brilliant but slapdash dilettante who never commits herself to anything the whole way, or the intelligent woman who denies her intelligence in order to seem more "fem-

inine," or who sits in passive silence even when she disagrees inwardly with everything that is being said around her.

7 Responsibility to yourself means refusing to let others do your thinking, talking, and naming for you; it means learning to respect and use your own brains and instincts; hence, grappling with hard work. It means that you do not treat your body as a commodity with which to purchase superficial intimacy or economic security; for our bodies and minds are inseparable in this life, and when we allow our bodies to be treated as objects, our minds are in mortal danger. It means insisting that those to whom you give your friendship and love are able to respect your mind. It means being able to say, with Charlotte Brontë's *Jane Eyre:* "I have an inward treasure born with me, which can keep me alive if all the extraneous delights should be withheld or offered only at a price I cannot afford to give."

8 Responsibility to yourself means that you don't fall for shallow and easy solutions—predigested books and ideas, weekend encounters guaranteed to change your life, taking "gut" courses instead of ones you know will challenge you, bluffing at school and life instead of doing solid work, marrying early as an escape from real decisions, getting pregnant as an evasion of already existing problems. It means that you refuse to sell your talents and aspirations short, simply to avoid conflict and confrontation. And this, in turn, means resisting the forces in society which say that women should be nice, play safe, have low professional expectations, drown in love and forget about work, live through others, and stay in the places assigned to us. It means that we insist on a life of meaningful work, insist that work be as meaningful as love and friendship in our lives. It means, therefore, the courage to be "different"; not to be continuously available to others when we need time for ourselves and our work; to be able to demand of others—parents, friends, roommates, teachers, lovers, husbands, children—that they respect our sense of purpose and our integrity as persons. Women everywhere are finding the courage to do this, more and more, and we are finding that courage both in our study of women in the past who possessed it, and in each other as we look to other women for comradeship, community, and challenge. The difference between a life lived actively, and a life of passive drifting and dispersal of energies, is an immense difference. Once we begin to feel committed to our lives, responsible to ourselves, we can never again be satisfied with the old, passive way.

9 Now comes the second part of the contract. I believe that in a women's college you have the right to expect your faculty to take you

seriously. The education of women has been a matter of debate for centuries, and old, negative attitudes about women's role, women's ability to think and take leadership, are still rife both in and outside the university. Many male professors (and I don't mean only at Douglass) still feel that teaching in a women's college is a second-rate career. Many tend to eroticize their women students—to treat them as sexual objects—instead of demanding the best of their minds. (At Yale a legal suit [*Alexander* v. *Yale*] has been brought against the university by a group of women students demanding a stated policy against sexual advances toward female students by male professors.) Many teachers, both men and women, trained in the male-centered tradition, are still handing the ideas and texts of that tradition on to students without teaching them to criticize its antiwoman attitudes, its omission of women as part of the species. Too often, all of us fail to teach the most important thing, which is that clear thinking, active discussion, and excellent writing are all necessary for intellectual freedom, and that these require *hard work.* Sometimes, perhaps in discouragement with a culture which is both antiintellectual and antiwoman, we may resign ourselves to low expectations for our students before we have given them half a chance to become more thoughtful, expressive human beings. We need to take to heart the words of Elizabeth Barrett Browning, a poet, a thinking woman, and a feminist, who wrote in 1845 of her impatience with studies which cultivate a "passive recipiency" in the mind, and asserted that "women want to be made to *think actively:* their apprehension is quicker than that of men, but their defect lies for the most part in the logical faculty and in the higher mental activities." Note that she implies a defect which can be remedied by intellectual training; *not* an inborn lack of ability.

10 I have said that the contract on the student's part involves that you demand to be taken seriously so that you can also go on taking yourself seriously. This means seeking out criticism, recognizing that the most affirming thing anyone can do for you is demand that you push yourself further, show you the range of what you *can* do. It means rejecting attitudes of "take-it-easy," "why-be-so-serious," "why-worry-you'll-probably-get-married-anyway." It means assuming your share of responsibility for what happens in the classroom, because that affects the quality of your daily life here. It means that the student sees herself engaged *with* her teachers in an active, ongoing struggle for a real education. But for her to do this, her teachers must be committed to the belief that women's minds and

experience are intrinsically valuable and indispensable to any civilization worthy the name; that there is no more exhilarating and intellectually fertile place in the academic world today than a women's college—*if* both students and teachers in large enough numbers are trying to fulfill this contract. The contract is really a pledge of mutual seriousness about women, about language, ideas, methods, and values. It is our shared commitment toward a world in which the inborn potentialities of so many women's minds will no longer be wasted, raveled-away, paralyzed, or denied.

Additional Rhetorical Strategies

Definition (paragraphs 2, 7); Illustration (paragraph 4).

Examining Words and Meaning

1. What are the two parts of the contract that Rich mentions here? What challenges does this contract present to the women she addresses? What challenges does it present to the educational institution? What attitudes toward women must both parties to the contract overcome?
2. According to Rich, what is the difference between receiving and claiming an education (paragraph 2)? How does she extend and amplify this distinction through the rest of her address?
3. Look up these words in a dictionary if they are unfamiliar to you: convocation (paragraph 1); poring (paragraph 4); dilettante (paragraph 6); dispersal (paragraph 8); rife (paragraph 9); raveled (paragraph 10).

Focusing on Structures and Strategies

1. Point to passages in Rich's speech where you think her appeal is primarily rational, where it is primarily emotional, and where it is primarily ethical. Which sort of appeal seems to you to predominate? To what extent might the circumstances in which Rich gave this speech influence the sort of appeal she makes?

2. What phrase does Rich repeat in paragraphs 7 and 8 to extend her definition of responsibility? How does she use this repetition to build to a rhetorical climax in paragraph 8? How might her argument be less effective without the repetition?

3. In what ways is the concluding paragraph of this address a summary of what Rich has said? How does she avoid having it sound too much like a conclusion, like a dull rehashing of what has already been established? In other words, how does Rich effectively *restate* her main points without *repeating* them?

Suggestions for Further Discussion and Writing

1. Discuss the implications of Rich's statement in paragraph 3 that our education reflects "neither objective reality, nor an accurate picture of the past, nor a group of rigorously tested observations about human behavior." How might her statement be true to your experience? How do the courses offered, the texts required, the relationships established in our education affect our perception of the way things are? What changes would you suggest to remedy the situation?

2. Imagine that you have been called upon to address a gathering of people sympathetic to what you are going to say. Choose any situation you wish: a group of friends about to enlist in the Navy, friends and relatives at your best friend's wedding party, a group of students about to protest a tuition raise. Write an address to such a group in which you explore the significance of what it is doing and challenge it to extend that behavior to new areas. Your address should affirm what the group is doing, but it should provoke new action as well.

Glossary

ALLITERATION: repetition of a consonant or vowel sound at the beginning or in the middle of words that are near enough to each other for the sound to draw attention: "through bogs and briers, barefooted and bareheaded" (Frederick Douglass, p. 176).

ALLUSION: an indirect or casual reference to an event, person, place, and so on, that is generally familiar or expected to be known by the intended audience of the work in which it appears. Useful for its economy, for its ability to suggest much in few words, an allusion must be carefully chosen to fit its context and its audience. Peter Homans, for example, refers to the hero of Westerns as "this Galahad with a Colt .45 who stalks injustice on the dusty streets of Dodge" (p. 29, paragraph 2) and thereby calls to mind the knight of Authurian legend.

AMBIGUITY: the result of expressing an idea in words that have two or more possible meanings. Ambiguity is sometimes unintentional, as when a pronoun is used without a clear referent. Ambiguity can be intentionally used as a means of enhancing the meaning of a passage. When it adds to the meaning, ambiguity is effective. When it obscures the meaning, it is an error.

ANALOGY: a set of point-by-point resemblances between members of the same class or between different classes. See the introduction to "Analogy," p. 428.

ANAPHORA: a device of repetition in which the same word or phrase occurs at the beginning of successive sentences or clauses. Anaphora is one of the more obvious schemes of repetition. It occurs most frequently at the end of an essay or when an attempt is being made to stir the emotions. (See Nikki Giovanni's "Knoxville Revisited," p. 84, paragraph 2.)

ANTICLIMAX: the arrangement of details so that the least important or incongruous follow the most important or appropriate. When used intentionally and with skill, anticlimax can have a humorous effect: "He has seen the ravages of war, he has known natural catastrophes, he has been to singles bars" (Woody Allen).

ANTITHESIS: a device in which contrasting ideas are juxtaposed, often in parallel structure. The balancing of unlike ideas in this way makes each more emphatic: "You have seen how a man was made a slave; you shall see how a slave was made a man" (Frederick Douglass, p. 174, paragraph 1).

ARGUMENT: a form of discourse which attempts to convince an audience that a specific claim or proposition is true wholly because a supporting body of logically related statements is also true. See the introduction to "Argument," p. 459.

ARGUMENT, Fallacies of: *Ad hominem,* a Latin phrase meaning "to the man," referring to arguments which turn away from the main issue in order to disparage individuals. Ad hominem arguments rely on intimidation and ignorance. Political campaign speeches often make use of this common but unethical tactic.

Ad populum, a Latin phrase for "to the people"; used when an argument appeals to prejudices and unfounded fears in an effort to distract the audience from the issues at hand. The use of emotionally charged language in an attempt to predispose one's audience to accept what is asserted without proof is an important part of ad populum argumentation.

Bandwagon, an appeal that tries to get its audience to adopt an opinion that "everyone else" is said to hold. Popular with advertisers and political candidates, attempts to get us to jump on a bandwagon rely on our eagerness to be on the winning side. The candidate "everyone is voting for" and the jeans "everyone will be wearing" are promoted with bandwagon appeals.

Begging the question, a form of reasoning which asserts an unsupported premise and later restates that premise as a conclusion. We argue that the Bible is the Word of God because God says so in the Bible. Begging the question is sometimes referred to as arguing in a circle.

Red herring, a device used to avoid the central issue of an argument. The term comes from the old hunting practice of dragging a herring across the trail of an animal to confuse the dogs. Attempts to change the subject during the course of an argument introduce a "red herring" to sidetrack one's opponent.

CAUSE AND EFFECT: a pervasive aspect of daily thought which assumes that every action or state of being is the result of another action or state of being. The usefulness of cause-and-effect reasoning has been largely discredited in many areas of physics, philosophy, and psychology. See the introduction to "Cause and Effect."

CLASSIFICATION: a procedure for identifying all of the parts of a subject as well as a structure for organizing our thoughts about the subject. See the introduction to "Classification."

CLICHÉ: an expression used more often because it comes readily to mind than because it really suits the purpose. A cliché is an expression so weakened by repetition as not to be able to bear the weight of meaning: "hold your horses"; "don't put the cart before the horse." For a discussion of clichéd metaphors, see pp. 28–29.

CLIMACTIC ORDER: the arrangement of words, phrases, sentences, scenes, or episodes that proceeds from the least important to the most important.

COHERENCE: the quality of effective relations between all parts of a written work. When writing is coherent, there is a logical and expressive connection recognizable between sentences, paragraphs, and parts of a work. Cohesive writing presents a subject consistently, through a clear sequence of ideas.

COMPARISON AND CONTRAST: comparison establishes similarities between subjects drawn from the same class or general category; contrast highlights the differences between them. See the introduction to "Comparison and Contrast," p. 375

CONNOTATION: a word's range of associations and tonal qualities acquired through usage. See the introduction to "Exploring Key Words."

CONTROLLING OR STRUCTURAL METAPHOR: a form of comparison in which key resemblances between the principal subject and a subsidiary subject or image are used to organize a composition. See pp. 25–27.

DEDUCTION: a strictly controlled form of reasoning which moves according to certain invariable rules from a premise to a logical conclusion. Deductive reasoning can produce valid arguments that are not necessarily true. See the introduction to "Argument," p. 463.

DEFINITION: an explanation of the meaning of a term accomplished in one of the following ways: *lexical definition,* a dictionary definition of accepted usage; *stipulative definition,* an announced description of the limits of a term's meaning that either extends or limits the lexical definition; *extended definition,* an expanded discussion of the meaning of a word. See the introduction to "Definition."

DENOTATION: the direct and explicit meaning of a particular word, as recorded in a dictionary. See the introduction to "Exploring Key Words," p. 2.

DESCRIPTION: a detailed verbal picture of a person, place, object, or state of mind. *Objective* description is primarily factual and excludes mention of the writer's personal evaluation or response. *Subjective* description includes attention to both the subject described and the writer's response to it. See the introduction to "Description."

DICTION: the choice of words. Good diction is the result of choosing the most appropriate words for the purpose. Words are chosen from various levels of usage: slang, colloquial, technical, informal, and formal. Drawing words from one of these levels more frequently than from the others determines the level of diction in a piece of writing. The way the chosen words are combined is, however, a matter of style and not of diction.

DIGRESSION: a turning aside from the main subject to interrupt the development of an idea with unrelated or vaguely related material. In an informal essay an interesting digression is not a fault. In a work with a strong plot or in a formal essay, a digression is usually considered a flaw.

EMPHASIS: stress or attention given to particular words or ideas. Emphasis ought to be controlled so that the most important and least important points in an essay are given respectively the most and least emphasis. Repetition emphasizes a point, as does placing it at the end of a sentence, paragraph, or essay. There are also mechanical devices which add emphasis: italics (underlining), exclamation points, capital letters. Because mechanical devices are too often used in attempts to compensate a lack of real significance, readers tend to dismiss such ploys to gain their attention. Making what must be remembered most memorable is best done through repetition, proportion, and position.

ENTHYMEME: the rhetorical equivalent of the syllogism. An enthymeme states one premise, implies another, and contains a conclusion derived from both. A syllogism leads to a logically necessary conclusion; an enthymeme leads to a tentative conclusion. The formal syllogism is constructed of universally valid propositions, whereas the enthymeme is built upon probable premises; for example, "That car will fail inspection because its brakes are worn out." A conclusion is stated: "That car will fail inspection." One premise is stated: "Its brakes are worn out." And one premise is implied: "Any car with worn-out brakes will fail inspection." (See the introduction to "Argument," p. 466.)

EUPHEMISM: use of a word or phrase less direct and considered less offensive than another word or phrase: as a military officer told a reporter, "You always write it's bombing, bombing, bombing. It's *not* bombing! It's *air support.*"

EXPOSITION: in nonfiction prose, the form of discourse that "puts forth" facts and ideas. Expository writing explains an idea about an object or abstraction. Most of the selections in this book make use of exposition.

HYPERBOLE: derived from the Greek meaning "to throw beyond." Hyperbole is an exaggeration used to increase the effect or emphasis of a statement. A characteristic of American speech, hyperbole is particularly pervasive in advertising. In expository prose, it is found more frequently in informal than in formal essays.

HYPOTHESIS: an unproved theory that is tentatively accepted as true in order to provide a basis for further investigation or argument. In an essay we often first state our idea about a subject as a hypothesis, and then examine, develop, support, and restate it as a conclusion.

ILLUSTRATION: a process in which writers select specific examples to represent, clarify, and support either general or abstract statements and principles. See the introduction to "Illustration."

IMAGE: an image can be a verbal representation of *any* type (not just visual) of sensory experience. The creation of images is one of the ways writing, particularly poetry, is made more immediate and effective. In an essay, an appropriate image can do much to communicate the depth of one's idea about a subject.

INDUCTION: the process of reasoning by which we move from evidence about *some* members of a particular class to a proposition about *all* members of that class. The conclusions reached by induction are never logically conclusive. See the introduction to "Argument," p. 465–466.

INFERENCE: a statement about what is still uncertain made on the basis of what is certain. See the introduction to "Observation and Inference."

IRONY: a kind of antithesis in which words or actions are seen as conveying the opposite of their surface significance. Of the many types of irony, verbal irony is most suited to the essay. In verbal irony, one's intended meaning is expressed in words which suggest an opposite literal meaning. The success of verbal irony depends upon the audience's ability to detect a difference between expression and intention.

METAPHOR: derived from the Greek word meaning *transfer,* it is the basic mental process by which we find resemblances between different kinds of things or ideas. See the introduction to "Making Metaphors."

METONOMY: derived from the Greek words meaning "other name." Metonomy substitutes some attribute or association of a thing in place of its name: the "White House" for the President, "cup" for the drink it holds, "paper" for the composition written on it. *Synecdoche,* a type of metonomy, substitutes the part for the whole, or the whole for the part: "strings" for violins, "wheels" for car; the "team" or "franchise" for the leading player.

NARRATION: a way of telling what happened by linking a succession of events together into a meaningful sequence. See the introduction to "Narration."

OBSERVATION: a deliberate mental activity in which we probe a subject in order to discover as much as possible about it. See the introduction to "Observation and Inference."

ONOMATOPOEIA: the use of words to echo the natural sound associated with the thing described or the formation of a single word, like *buzz* or *slap,* to represent the sound named. Although found more frequently in poetry, onomatopoeia occurs in expository prose on occasion: note the sound of kisses in Kierkegaard's classification (p. 306).

OXYMORON: a kind of compressed paradox which usually consists of a noun and its modifier. The modifier, however, seems to attribute to the noun a quality contradictory to its usual associations: *sweet sadness, deafening silence.* Used judiciously, an oxymoron can rise above its etymological meaning of "pointed foolishness" to focus attention sharply and convey a great deal in a few words. When used excessively, an oxymoron loses its point and appears only to be capricious word play.

PARADOX: a statement which seems contradictory but proves valid upon close inspection: "When my love swears that she is made of truth/I do believe her, though I know she lies" (Shakespeare, sonnet 138). Paradox creates temporary confusion in order to produce lasting clarity: "The single most important factor accounting for the doctrinal revival of ethnicity is the behavioral decline of ethnicity."

PARALLELISM: the arrangement of words, phrases, sentences, paragraphs, and sections of a composition so that elements of equal importance and function are given equal emphasis and form. Parallelism is one of the basic grammatical and rhetorical principles.

PERSONIFICATION: the attribution of human abilities or qualities to objects, animals, or abstractions. Helen Keller personifies imagination when she writes: "The silent worker is imagination which decrees reality out of chaos" (p. 86, paragraph 7). Fables usually portray animals as if they were human; Aesop's Fables are classic examples of this type of personification.

PERSUASION: written or oral discourse aimed at disposing an audience to think and act in accordance with the speaker's will. See the introduction to "Persuasion."

POINT OF VIEW: the vantage point from which writing is presented. In expository prose, the author's point of view may be compared to a light illuminating an object: the strength, color, and position of that light determine what aspect of the object we see, and affect what kind of response we have to it. See the introduction to "Narration."

PREMISE: either of the two propositions in a syllogism from which a conclusion is drawn. Etymologically, "to go before," premises are the assumptions (either believed or entertained) from which deductive reasoning proceeds. In a more general sense, premises are the assumptions an author bases an argument upon.

PURPOSE: the controlling intention of a composition. In an expository essay the general purpose might be to explain, convince, or describe, but the specific purpose would be, say, to convince the editors of the local newspaper that they had chosen to support the wrong candidate for mayor, or to explain to the readers of the college paper why the proposed tuition increase was passed without student opposition. When the purpose of an essay is stated directly, it is often called the thesis statement. Although the thesis statement expresses what you are trying to say, it does not fully explain your reason for saying it.

RHETORICAL QUESTION: a question posed not to provoke an answer but to assert or deny something indirectly. Rhetorical questions frequently occur in essays when the author is trying to disarm anticipated objections.

SIMILE: an explicit comparison of two things normally not considered alike, usually brought together by the words *like* or *as.* Thoreau compared grass to a ribbon: "The grass-blade, like a long green ribbon, streams from the sod into the summer." Dickens drew a simile between Thomas Gradgrind and a cannon: "He seemed a kind of cannon loaded to the muzzle with facts, and prepared to blow them clean out of the regions of childhood at one discharge" (p. 276, paragraph 3). See also the introduction to "Making Metaphors."

STYLE: in classical rhetoric, the choice of words and their arrangement. In contemporary usage, style generally refers to the relation between ideas and language. Robert Frost said that style is "the mind skating circles round itself as it moves forward." Diction, syntax, point of view, emphasis, figurative language all contribute to style. More difficult to define than to perceive, an author's style produces the recognizable individuality of a composition.

SYLLOGISM: a formal deductive argument composed of a major premise (All men are mortal), a minor premise (Socrates is a man), and a conclusion (therefore, Socrates is mortal). See the introduction to "Argument."

UNDERSTATEMENT: a form of irony in which something is said to be less than it is in order to emphasize its full meaning and significance. Understatement leaves it to the readers to build up what has been played down and therefore prompts them to engage actively in imagining the importance of what has been understated: "To say that he is ugly is nothing: to add that his figure is grotesque is to convey no adequate impression" (Edward Dicey on President Lincoln, p. 115, paragraph 1). When an offensive idea is understated, the result is a kind of euphemism. *Litotes* is a form of understatement in which the opposite of what is intended is denied: "This is no small matter."

AN ALTERNATE TABLE OF CONTENTS

Elements of Composition: Some Practical Writing Skills

1. Creating a Presence

Audience

Thomas Sowell, *We're Not Really "Equal"* (279); **Sissela Bok,** *The Need for Secrecy* (326); **Jeffrey L. Pasley,** *The Idiocy of Rural Life* (476); **Adam Smith,** *Fifty Million Handguns* (495); **Henry A. Selib,** *The Case Against More Laws* (503); **Mike Royko,** *A Faceless Man's Plea* (523); **Frances D. Gage,** *Sojourner Truth: And A'n't I a Woman?* (546); **Adrienne Rich,** *Claiming an Education* (551)

Purpose

To Inform

Betty Edwards, *Left and Right* (15); **Mary Gordon,** *More than Just a Shrine: Paying Homage to the Ghosts of Ellis Island* (55); **Mary Leakey,** *Footprints in the Ashes of Time* (62); **Helen Keller,** *A World of Impressions* (86); **Gretel Ehrlich,** *The Solace of Open Spaces* (135); **Rachel Carson,** *The Grey Beginnings* (220); **Barry Commoner,** *Three Mile Island* (241); **Ralph Ellison,** *Hidden Name and Complex Fate* (298); **Larry McMurtry,** *Drinking in Houston*

(313); **Lewis Thomas,** *Notes on Punctuation* (310); **Marie Winn,** *Television and Reading* (404); **Adam Smith,** *Fifty Million Handguns* (495)

To Instruct

George Lakoff and Mark Johnson, *Metaphors We Live By* (24); **Kurt Vonnegut,** *How to Write with Style* (197); **Ernest Hemingway,** *When You Camp Out, Do It Right* (202); **Donald Hall,** *Four Kinds of Reading* (321); **Aristotle,** *Youth and Old Age* (385); **Plato,** *Allegory of the Cave* (436)

To Reflect

Michael Anania, *Starting* (43); **Virginia Woolf,** *The Death of the Moth* (125); **E. B. White,** *The Ring of Time* (129); **Gretel Ehrlich,** *The Solace of Open Spaces* (135); **Lewis Thomas,** *Amity Street* (156); **Joyce Maynard,** *I Remember . . .* (354); **Mark Twain,** *Reading the River* (443); **William Humphrey,** *The Salmon Instinct* (447); **Michael Arlen,** *Prufrock Aloft; Prufrock Before the Television Set* (451)

To Entertain

Calvin Trillin, *Rural Literalism* (36); **Lewis Thomas,** *Notes on Punctuation* (310); **Susan Allen Toth,** *Cinematypes* (316); **Joyce Maynard,** *I Remember . . .* (354)

To Satirize

Russell Baker, *Life Can Be Hard* (11); **Charles Dickens,** *What Is a Horse?* (275); **Ralph Linton,** *One Hundred Per Cent American* (342)

To Persuade

see *Persuasion*

To Convince

Frederick Douglass, *How a Slave Was Made a Man* (174); **Sir Frederick Hoyle,** *The Next Ice Age* (256); **Bruno Bettelheim,** *The Holocaust* (283); **Sissela Bok,** *The Need for Secrecy* (326); **John Mack Faragher,** *Pioneer Diaries of Women and Men* (412); **Plato,** *Allegory of the Cave* (436); see also *Argument*

To Reform

Langston Hughes, *That Word* Black (8); **Sheila Tobias,** *Who's Afraid of Math, and Why?* (249); **Susan Sontag,** *A Rhetoric of*

Disease (419); **Jeffrey L. Pasley,** *The Idiocy of Rural Life* (476); **Adam Smith,** *Fifty Million Handguns* (495); **Henry A. Selib,** *The Case Against More Laws* (503); **Advertisement/***"Stop Handguns Before They Stop You"* (520)

2. Maintaining a Voice

Tone

Personal

Calvin Trillin, *Rural Literalism* (36); **Mary Gordon,** *More than Just a Shrine: Paying Homage to the Ghosts of Ellis Island* (55); **Joan Didion,** *On Morality* (80); **Nikki Giovanni,** *Knoxville Revisited* (83); **Helen Keller,** *A World of Impressions* (86); **Irene Oppenheim,** *On Waitressing* (93); **Nathaniel Hawthorne/Edward Dicey,** *On Abraham Lincoln* (113); **Gretel Ehrlich,** *The Solace of Open Spaces* (135); **Lewis Thomas,** *Amity Street* (156); **Marsha Rabe,** *Passages* (167); **Frederick Douglass,** *How a Slave Was Made a Man* (174); **Susan Allen Toth,** *Cinematypes* (316); **Joyce Maynard,** *I Remember . . .* (354); **Lewis Thomas,** *The Tucson Zoo* (382); **Mark Twain,** *Reading the River* (443); **William Humphrey,** *The Salmon Instinct* (447); **Jeffrey L. Pasley,** *The Idiocy of Rural Life* (476)

Impersonal

Betty Edwards, *Left and Right* (15); **Sir Frederick Treves,** *The Elephant Man* (118); **Rachel Carson,** *The Grey Beginnings* (220); **Barry Commoner,** *Three Mile Island* (241); **Sir Frederick Hoyle,** *The Next Ice Age* (256); **Sissela Bok,** *The Need for Secrecy* (326); **Aristotle,** *Youth and Old Age* (385); **John Mack Faragher,** *Pioneer Diaries of Women and Men* (412); **Susan Sontag,** *A Rhetoric of Disease* (419)

Humorous

Russell Baker, *Life Can Be Hard* (11); **Calvin Trillin,** *Rural Literalism* (36); **Michael Anania,** *Starting* (43); **Lewis Thomas,** *Notes on Punctuation* (310); **Susan Allen Toth,** *Cinematypes* (316)

Ironical

Simone de Beauvoir, *Woman* (6); **Russell Baker,** *Life Can Be Hard* (11); **Lewis Thomas,** *On Transcendental Metaworry* (193); **Ralph Linton,** *One Hundred Per Cent American*

(342); **Michael Arlen,** *Prufrock Aloft; Prufrock Before the Television Set* (451); **Henry Fairlie,** *The Idiocy of Urban Life* (485); **H. L. Mencken,** *Why Nobody Loves a Politician* (527)

Impassioned

Bruno Bettelheim, *The Holocaust* (283); **Advertisement/***"Stop Handguns Before They Stop You"* (520); **Advertisement/***"In the U.S., Crime Pays Because Criminals Don't"* (521); **Mike Royko,** *A Faceless Man's Plea* (523); **Frances D. Gage,** *Sojourner Truth: And A'n't I a Woman?* (546); **Adrienne Rich,** *Claiming an Education* (551)

Diction

Technical

Ernest Hemingway, *When You Camp Out, Do It Right* (202); **John McPhee,** *The Birch-Bark Canoe* (208); **Rachel Carson,** *The Grey Beginnings* (220); **Barry Commoner,** *Three Mile Island* (241); **Charles Dickens,** *What Is a Horse?* (275); **Mark Twain,** *Reading the River* (443)

Formal

Gretel Ehrlich, *The Solace of Open Spaces* (135); **Frederick Douglass,** *How a Slave Was Made a Man* (174); **Bruno Bettelheim,** *The Holocaust* (283); **Sissela Bok,** *The Need for Secrecy* (326); **Aristotle,** *Youth and Old Age* (385); **John Mack Faragher,** *Pioneer Diaries of Women and Men* (412); **Susan Sontag,** *A Rhetoric of Disease* (419); **Michael Arlen,** *Prufrock Aloft; Prufrock Before the Television Set* (451)

Informal

Russell Baker, *Life Can Be Hard* (11); **Nikki Giovanni,** *Knoxville Revisited* (83); **Lewis Thomas,** *Ponds* (109); **Marsha Rabe,** *Passages* (167); **Kurt Vonnegut,** *How to Write with Style* (197); **Ernest Hemingway,** *When You Camp Out, Do It Right* (202); **Lewis Thomas,** *Alchemy* (270); **Lewis Thomas,** *Notes on Punctuation* (310); **Susan Allen Toth,** *Cinematypes* (316); **Joyce Maynard,** *I Remember . . .* (354); **Tom Wolfe,** *Columbus and the Moon* (389); **Jack Newfield,** *Stallone vs. Springsteen* (394); **William Humphrey,** *The Salmon Instinct* (447)

Dialect

Langston Hughes, *That Word* Black (8); **Gretel Ehrlich,** *The Solace of Open Spaces* (135); **Ernest Hemingway,** *When You Camp*

Out, Do It Right (202); **Frances D. Gage,** *Sojourner Truth: And A'n't I a Woman?* (546)

Dialogue

George Orwell, *A Hanging* (181); **Charles Dickens,** *What Is a Horse?* (275); **Plato,** *Allegory of the Cave* (436)

3. Building Paragraphs

Topic Sentence

Terence McLaughlin, *Dirt* (17); **John Canaday,** *The Bellelli Family* (68); **Lewis Thomas,** *Ponds* (109); **Nathaniel Hawthorne,** *On Abraham Lincoln* (113); **Anne Hollander,** *Why It's Fashionable to Be Thin* (245); **Bruno Bettelheim,** *The Holocaust* (283); **Peter Homans,** *The Western: The Legend and the Cardboard Hero* (291); **Larry McMurtry,** *Drinking in Houston* (313); **Susan Allen Toth,** *Cinematypes* (316); **Aristotle,** *Youth and Old Age* (385); **Tom Wolfe,** *Columbus and the Moon* (389); **Jack Newfield,** *Stallone vs. Springsteen* (394); **John Mack Faragher,** *Pioneer Diaries of Women and Men* (412); **Mark Twain,** *Reading the River* (443); **H. L. Mencken,** *Why Nobody Loves a Politician* (527)

Support

Betty Edwards, *Left and Right* (15); **Sheila Tobias,** *Who's Afraid of Math, and Why?* (249); **Sir Frederick Hoyle,** *The Next Ice Age* (256); **Karen Horney,** *Fear and Anxiety* (288); **Lewis Thomas,** *Notes on Punctuation* (310); **Larry McMurtry,** *Drinking in Houston* (313); **Ralph Linton,** *One Hundred Per Cent American* (342); **John Mack Faragher,** *Pioneer Diaries of Women and Men* (412); **Susan Sontag,** *A Rhetoric of Disease* (419); **Advertisement**/*"In the U.S., Crime Pays Because Criminals Don't"* (521)

Coherence

Lewis Thomas, *Ponds* (109); **Sir Frederick Treves,** *The Elephant Man* (118); **Gretel Ehrlich,** *The Solace of Open Spaces* (135); **Lewis Thomas,** *On Transcendental Metaworry* (193); **Ernest Hemingway,** *When You Camp Out, Do It Right* (202); **Barry Commoner,** *Three Mile Island* (241); **Sir Frederick**

Hoyle, *The Next Ice Age* (256); **Bruno Bettelheim,** *The Holocaust* (283); **Karen Horney,** *Fear and Anxiety* (288); **Joyce Maynard,** *I Remember . . .* (354); **Susan Sontag,** *A Rhetoric of Disease* (419); **Adam Smith,** *Fifty Million Handguns* (495); **Henry A. Selib,** *The Case Against More Laws* (503); **H. L. Mencken,** *Why Nobody Loves a Politician* (527)

Order

General to Particular

Terence McLaughlin, *Dirt* (17); **Joan Didion,** *On Morality* (80); **Nikki Giovanni,** *Knoxville Revisited* (83); **Helen Keller,** *A World of Impressions* (86); **John Muir,** *Yosemite Falls* (122); **Lewis Thomas,** *Death in the Open* (339); **Jack Newfield,** *Stallone vs. Springsteen* (394)

Particular to General

Calvin Trillin, *Rural Literalism* (36); **Michael Anania,** *Starting* (43); **Lewis Thomas,** *The Tucson Zoo* (382); **Adam Smith,** *Fifty Million Handguns* (495)

Question/Answer

Sheila Tobias, *Who's Afraid of Math, and Why?* (249); **Sir Frederick Hoyle,** *The Next Ice Age* (256); **Thomas Sowell,** *We're Not Really "Equal"* (279); **Sissela Bok,** *The Need for Secrecy* (326); **Ruth Schwartz Cowan,** *Less Work for Mother?* (360); **Frances D. Gage,** *Sojourner Truth: And A'n't I a Woman?* (546)

Enumeration

George Lakoff and Mark Johnson, *Metaphors We Live By* (29); **John Canaday,** *The Bellelli Family* (68); **Sir Frederick Treves,** *The Elephant Man* (118); **Lewis Thomas,** *On Magic in Medicine* (236); **Lewis Thomas,** *Notes on Punctuation* (310); **Sissela Bok,** *The Need for Secrecy* (326); **Ralph Linton,** *One Hundred Per Cent American* (342); **Joyce Maynard,** *I Remember . . .* (354); **Ruth Schwartz Cowan,** *Less Work for Mother?* (360); **John Mack Faragher,** *Pioneer Diaries of Women and Men* (412); **William Humphrey,** *The Salmon Instinct* (447)

Transitions

Gretel Ehrlich, *The Solace of Open Spaces* (135); **Lewis Thomas,** *On Transcendental Metaworry* (193); **Alan Devoe,** *The*

Hibernation of the Woodchuck (217); **Sir Frederick Hoyle,** *The Next Ice Age* (256); **Bruno Bettelheim,** *The Holocaust* (283); **Karen Horney,** *Fear and Anxiety* (288); **Peter Homans,** *The Western: The Legend and the Cardboard Hero* (291); **Ralph Ellison,** *Hidden Name and Complex Fate* (298); **Sissela Bok,** *The Need for Secrecy* (326); **Barry Lopez,** *The Passing Wisdom of Birds* (534)

4. Framing an Essay

Effective Beginnings

Establishing the Importance of the Subject

Michael Anania, *Starting* (43); **Lewis Thomas,** *Death in the Open* (339); **Joyce Maynard,** *I Remember . . .* (354); **Ruth Schwartz Cowan,** *Less Work for Mother?* (360)

Anecdote

Mary Leakey, *Footprints in the Ashes of Time* (62); **Joan Didion,** *On Morality* (80); **Ellen Goodman,** *The "Sixties Kid"* (89); **Kurt Vonnegut,** *How to Write with Style* (197); **Mike Royko,** *A Faceless Man's Plea* (523)

Quotation

Calvin Trillin, *Rural Literalism* (36); **Gretel Ehrlich,** *The Solace of Open Spaces* (135); **John McPhee,** *The Birch-Bark Canoe* (208); **William Humphrey,** *The Salmon Instinct* (447)

Surprising Statement

Kurt Vonnegut, *How to Write with Style* (197); **Tom Wolfe,** *Columbus and the Moon* (389); **Jeffrey L. Pasley,** *The Idiocy of Rural Life* (476); **Henry A. Fairlie,** *The Idiocy of Urban Life* (485)

Posing a Central Problem or Question

Simone de Beauvoir, *Woman* (6); **Langston Hughes,** *That Word* Black (8); **Thomas Sowell,** *We're Not Really "Equal"* (279); **Donald Hall,** *Four Kinds of Reading* (321); **Sissela Bok,** *The Need for Secrecy* (326); **Lewis Thomas,** *The Hazards of Science* (468); **Adam Smith,** *Fifty Million Handguns* (495); **Henry A. Selib,** *The Case Against More Laws* (503); **Frances D. Gage,** *Sojourner Truth: And A'n't I a Woman?* (546)

Effective Conclusions

Summarizing Essential Points

John Canaday, *The Bellelli Family* (68); **Bruno Bettelheim,** *The Holocaust* (283); **Peter Homans,** *The Western: The Legend and the Cardboard Hero* (291); **Jack Newfield,** *Stallone vs. Springsteen* (394); **Barry Lopez,** *The Passing Wisdom of Birds* (534)

Stimulating Further Discussion

Simone de Beauvoir, *Woman* (6); **Lewis Thomas,** *Amity Street* (156); **Lewis Thomas,** *On Magic in Medicine* (236); **Thomas Sowell,** *We're Not Really "Equal"* (279); **Sissela Bok,** *The Need for Secrecy* (326); **Lewis Thomas,** *Death in the Open* (339); **Joyce Maynard,** *I Remember . . .* (354); **Tom Wolfe,** *Columbus and the Moon* (389); **John Mack Faragher,** *Pioneer Diaries of Women and Men* (412); **Lewis Thomas,** *The Attic of the Brain* (432); **H. L. Mencken,** *Why Nobody Loves a Politician* (529)

Suggesting Additional Applications

Lewis Thomas, *On Magic in Medicine* (236); **Aristotle,** *Youth and Old Age* (385)

Offering Recommendations, Solutions, or Answers

Barry Commoner, *Three Mile Island* (241); **Adam Smith,** *Fifty Million Handguns* (495); **Henry A. Selib,** *The Case Against More Laws* (503); **H. L. Mencken,** *Why Nobody Loves a Politician* (527); **Frances D. Gage,** *Sojourner Truth: And A'n't I a Woman?* (546); **Adrienne Rich,** *Claiming an Education* (551)

Selecting a Dramatic Example or Anecdote

Edward Hoagland, *Gramercy Gym* (40); **Michael Anania,** *Starting* (43); **Ellen Goodman,** *The "Sixties Kid"* (89); **Virginia Woolf,** *The Death of the Moth* (125); **Maxine Hong Kingston,** *The Wild Man of the Green Swamp* (164); **Neil Bell,** *In the Dark* (170); **George Orwell,** *A Hanging* (181); **Allen Toth,** *Cinematypes* (316); **Plato,** *Allegory of the Cave* (436); **Mike Royko,** *A Faceless Man's Plea* (523)

5. Using Information

Quotation

Joan Didion, *On Morality* (80); **Jack Newfield,** *Stallone vs. Springsteen* (394); **John Mack Faragher,** *Pioneer Diaries of Women and Men* (412); **Susan Sontag,** *A Rhetoric of Disease* (419); **Jeffrey L. Pasley,** *The Idiocy of Rural Life* (476)

Paraphrase

Marie Winn, *Television and Reading* (404)

Data/Evidence

Betty Edwards, *Left and Right* (15); **Mary Gordon,** *More than Just a Shrine: Paying Homage to the Ghosts of Ellis Island* (55); **Mary Leakey,** *Footprints in the Ashes of Time* (62); **Ernest Hemingway,** *When You Camp Out, Do It Right* (202); **Alan Devoe,** *The Hibernation of the Woodchuck* (217); **Rachel Carson,** *The Grey Beginnings* (220); **Lewis Thomas,** *On Magic in Medicine* (236); **Sheila Tobias,** *Who's Afraid of Math, and Why?* (249); **Sir Frederick Hoyle,** *The Next Ice Age* (256); **Larry McMurtry,** *Drinking in Houston* (313); **Jack Newfield,** *Stallone vs. Springsteen* (394); **Tom Wolfe,** *Columbus and the Moon* (389); **John Mack Faragher,** *Pioneer Diaries of Women and Men* (412); **Jeffrey L. Pasley,** *The Idiocy of Rural Life* (476); **Adam Smith,** *Fifty Million Handguns* (495); **Henry A. Selib,** *The Case Against More Laws* (503); **Barry Lopez,** *The Passing Wisdom of Birds* (534)

Contents, Alphabetical by Author

Michael Anania *Starting* 43
Aristotle *Youth and Old Age* 385
Michael Arlen *Prufrock Aloft; Prufrock Before the Television Set* 451

Russell Baker *Life Can Be Hard* 11
Simone de Beauvoir *Woman* 6
Neil Bell *In the Dark* 170
Bruno Bettelheim *The Holocaust* 283
Roy Blount, Jr. *Winning: Why We Keep Score* 346
Sissela Bok *The Need for Secrecy* 326

John Canaday *The Bellelli Family* 68
Rachel Carson *The Grey Beginnings* 220
Barry Commoner *Three Mile Island* 241
Ruth Schwartz Cowan *Less Work for Mother?* 360

Alan Devoe *The Hibernation of the Woodchuck* 217
Charles Dickens *What Is a Horse?* 275
Joan Didion *On Morality* 80
Annie Dillard *Dumbstruck* 52
Frederick Douglass *How a Slave Was Made a Man* 174

Betty Edwards *Left and Right* 15
Gretel Ehrlich *The Solace of Open Spaces* 135
Ralph Ellison *Hidden Name and Complex Fate* 298

Henry Fairlie *The Idiocy of Urban Life* 485
John Mack Faragher *Pioneer Diaries of Women and Men* 412

Frances D. Gage *Sojourner Truth: And A'n't I a Woman?* 546
Nikki Giovanni *Knoxville Revisited* 83
Ellen Goodman *The "Sixties Kid"* 89
Mary Gordon *More than Just a Shrine: Paying Homage to the Ghosts of Ellis Island* 55

Donald Hall *Four Kinds of Reading* 321
Nathaniel Hawthorne and Edward Dicey *On Abraham Lincoln* 113
Ernest Hemingway *When You Camp Out, Do It Right* 202
Edward Hoagland *Gramercy Gym* 40
Anne Hollander *Why It's Fashionable to be Thin* 245
Peter Homans *The Western: The Legend and the Cardboard Hero* 291
Karen Horney *Fear and Anxiety* 288
Sir Frederick Hoyle *The Next Ice Age* 256
Langston Hughes *That Word* Black 8
William Humphrey *The Salmon Instinct* 447

Helen Keller *A World of Impressions* 86
Maxine Hong Kingston *The Wild Man of the Green Swamp* 164

George Lakoff and Mark Johnson *Metaphors We Live By* 29
D. H. Lawrence *The Emotional Mind* 35
Mary Leakey *Footprints in the Ashes of Time* 62
Ralph Linton *One Hundred Per Cent American* 342
Barry Lopez *The Passing Wisdom of Birds* 534

Terence McLaughlin *Dirt* 17
Larry McMurtry *Drinking in Houston* 313
John McPhee *The Birch-Bark Canoe* 208
Joyce Maynard *I Remember . . .* 354
H.L. Mencken *Why Nobody Loves a Politician* 527

Jack Newfield *Stallone vs. Springsteen* 394

Irene Oppenheim *On Waitressing* 93
George Orwell *A Hanging* 181

Jeffrey L. Pasley *The Idiocy of Rural Life* 476
Plato *Allegory of the Cave* 436

Marsha Rabe *Passages* 167
Adrienne Rich *Claiming an Education* 551
Mike Royko *A Faceless Man's Plea* 523

Henry A. Selib *The Case Against More Laws* 503
Adam Smith *Fifty Million Handguns* 495
Susan Sontag *A Rhetoric of Disease* 419
Thomas Sowell *We're Not Really "Equal"* 279

Lewis Thomas *Alchemy* 270
________ *Amity Street* 156
________ *Death in the Open* 339
________ *Late Night Thoughts on Listening to Mahler's Ninth Symphony* 515
________ *Notes on Punctuation* 310
________ *On Magic in Medicine* 236
________ *On Transcendental Metaworry* 193
________ *Ponds* 109
________ *The Attic of the Brain* 432
________ *The Hazards of Science* 468
________ *The Tucson Zoo* 382
Sheila Tobias *Who's Afraid of Math, and Why?* 249
Susan Allen Toth *Cinematypes* 316
Sir Frederick Treves *The Elephant Man* 118
Calvin Trillin *Rural Literalism* 36
Mark Twain *Reading the River* 443

Kurt Vonnegut *How to Write with Style* 197

E.B. White *The Ring of Time* 129
Marie Winn *Television and Reading* 404
Tom Wolfe *Columbus and the Moon* 389
Virginia Woolf *The Death of the Moth* 125

Copyright Acknowledgments

P. 6, Simone de Beauvoir, "Woman," excerpted from *The Second Sex,* p. 1, by Simone de Beauvoir. Copyright © 1952 by Alfred A. Knopf, Inc. Reprinted by permission of the publisher.

P. 8, Langston Hughes, "That Word *Black,*" from *Simple Takes a Wife,* by Langston Hughes. Reprinted by permission of Harold Ober Associates, Incorporated. Copyright © 1953 by Langston Hughes. Copyright © 1981 by George Houston Bass.

P. 11, Russell Baker, "Life Can Be Hard," from *The New York Times Magazine,* July 13, 1986. Copyright © 1986 by The New York Times Company. Reprinted by permission.

P. 15, Betty Edwards, "Left and Right," from *Drawing on the Right Side of the Brain,* by Betty Edwards. Copyright © 1979 by Betty Edwards. Reprinted by permission of J. P. Tarcher, Inc.

P. 17, Terence McLaughlin, "Dirt," from *A Social History as Seen Through the Uses and Abuses of Dirt,* by Terence McLaughlin. Copyright © 1971 by Terence McLaughlin. Reprinted with permission of Stein and Day, Publishers.

P. 29, George Lakoff and Mark Johnson, "Metaphors We Live By," from *Metaphors We Live By,* by George Lakoff and Mark Johnson. Copyright © 1980 by The University of Chicago. All rights reserved. Reprinted by permission of The University of Chicago Press and the authors.

P. 35, D.H. Lawrence, "The Emotional Mind," from *Phoenix: The Posthumous Papers of D. H. Lawrence.* Copyright © 1936 by Frieda Lawrence; copyright renewed © 1964 by the estate of Frieda Lawrence Ravagli. Reprinted by permission of Viking-Penguin, Inc.

P. 36, Calvin Trillin, "Rural Literalism," from *The Nation,* September 12, 1981. Copyright © 1981 by *The Nation,* The Nation Company, Inc. Reprinted by permission of the publisher.

P. 40, Edward Hoagland, "Gramercy Gym," from *Walking the Dead Diamond River,* by Edward Hoagland. Copyright © 1972 by Edward Hoagland. Reprinted by permission of Random House, Inc.

P. 43, Michael Anania, "Starting," from *Chicago,* December 1985, p. 228. Copyright © 1985 by Michael Anania.

P. 52, Annie Dillard, "Dumbstruck," from pp. 5–6 of *Pilgrim at Tinker Creek,* by Annie Dillard. Copyright © 1974 by Annie Dillard. Reprinted by permission of Harper & Row Publishers, Inc.

P. 55, Mary Gordon, "More Than Just a Shrine: Paying Homage to the Ghosts of Ellis Island," from *The New York Times Magazine,* November 3, 1985. Copyright © 1985 by The New York Times Company. Reprinted by permission.

P. 62, Mary Leakey, "Footprints in the Ashes of Time," from *National Geographic Magazine,* April 1979. Reprinted by permission of the author and publisher.

P. 68, John Canaday, "The Bellelli Family," from *What Is Art?* by John Canaday. Copyright © 1980 by John Canaday. Reprinted by permission of Alfred A. Knopf, Inc.

P. 80, Joan Didion, "On Morality," from *Slouching Towards Bethlehem,* by Joan Didion. Copyright © 1965, 1968 by Joan Didion. Reprinted by permission of Farrar, Straus and Giroux, Inc.

P. 83, Nikki Giovanni, "Knoxville Revisited," from *Gemini,* by Nikki Giovanni. Copyright © 1971 by Nikki Giovanni. Reprinted by permission of Macmillan Publishing Company.

P. 89, Ellen Goodman, "The 'Sixties Kid,'" from *Close to Home,* by Ellen Goodman. Copyright © 1979 by The Boston Globe Newspaper Company/-Washington Post Writers Group. Reprinted by permission of the publisher.

P. 93, Irene Oppenheim, "On Waitressing," from *The Threepenny Review,* Summer 1986, pp. 14–15. Copyright © 1986 by *The Threepenny Review.* Reprinted by permission of the publisher.

P. 109, Lewis Thomas, "Ponds," from *The Medusa and the Snail,* by Lewis Thomas. Copyright © 1979 by Lewis Thomas. Reprinted by permission of Viking-Penguin, Inc.

P. 125, Virginia Woolf, "The Death of the Moth," from *The Death of the Moth and Other Essays,* by Virginia Woolf. Copyright © 1942 by Harcourt Brace Jovanovich, Inc.; copyright © 1970 by Marjorie T. Parsons, Executrix. Reprinted by permission of the publisher.

P. 129, E. B. White, "The Ring of Time," originally "The Ring of Time—Fiddler Bayou, March 22, 1956," from *Essays of E. B. White,* by E. B. White. Copyright © 1956 by E. B. White. Originally appeared in *The New Yorker.* Reprinted by permission of Harper & Row, Publishers, Inc.

P. 135, Gretel Ehrlich, "The Solace of Open Spaces," from *The Solace of Open Spaces* by Gretel Ehrlich. Copyright © 1985 by Gretel Ehrlich. Reprinted by permission of Viking-Penguin, Inc.

P. 156, Lewis Thomas, "Amity Street," from *The Youngest Science: Notes of a Medicine-*

Watcher by Lewis Thomas. Copyright © 1983 by Lewis Thomas. Reprinted by permission of Viking-Penguin, Inc.

P. 164, Maxine Hong Kingston, "The Wild Man of the Green Swamp," from *China Men,* by Maxine Hong Kingston. Copyright © 1980 by Maxine Hong Kingston. Reprinted by permission of the publisher.

P. 167, Marsha Rabe, "Passages," from *The New York Times,* July 26, 1979. Copyright © 1979 by The New York Times Company. Reprinted by permission of the publisher.

P. 170, Neil Bell, "In the Dark," from *Story Magazine.* Copyright © 1938 by Story Magazine. Reprinted by permission of Scholastic, Inc.

P. 181, George Orwell, "A Hanging," from *Shooting an Elephant and Other Essays,* by George Orwell. Copyright © 1950 by Sonia Brownell Orwell; renewed 1978 by Sonia Pitt-Rivers. Reprinted by permission of Harcourt Brace Jovanovich, Inc.

P. 193, Lewis Thomas, "On Transcendental Metaworry," from *The Medusa and the Snail* by Lewis Thomas. Copyright © 1979 by Lewis Thomas. Reprinted by permission of Viking-Penguin, Inc.

P. 197, Kurt Vonnegut, "How to Write with Style." Copyright © 1980 by International Paper Company. Reprinted by permission of International Paper Company.

P. 202, Ernest Hemingway, "When You Camp Out, Do It Right," from *Dateline: Toronto.* Copyright © 1985 Mary Hemingway, John Hemingway, Patrick Hemingway & Gregory Hemingway. Originally appeared in the Toronto Star, 1920. Reprinted by permission of Charles Scribner Sons.

P. 208, John McPhee, "The Birch-Bark Canoe," from *The Survival of the Birch-Bark Canoe,* by John McPhee. Copyright © 1975 by John McPhee. Reprinted by permission of Farrar, Straus and Giroux, Inc.

P. 217, Alan Devoe, "The Hibernation of the Woodchuck," from *Lives Around Us,* by Alan Devoe. Copyright © 1942 by Alan Devoe. Copyright renewed © 1970 by Mary Devoe Guinn. Reprinted by permission of Farrar, Straus and Giroux.

P. 220, Rachel Carson, "The Grey Beginnings," from *The Sea Around Us,* Revised Edition, by Rachel L. Carson. Copyright © 1950, 1951, 1961 by Rachel L. Carson; renewed 1979 by Roger Christie. Reprinted by permission of Oxford University Press, Inc.

P. 236, Lewis Thomas, "On Magic in Medicine," from *The Medusa and the Snail* by Lewis Thomas. Copyright © 1979 by Lewis Thomas. Reprinted by permission of Viking-Penguin, Inc.

P. 241, Barry Commoner, "Three Mile Island," excerpted from "Solar Versus Nuclear Energy: The Politics of Choice," in *The Politics of Energy,* by Barry Commoner. Copyright © 1979 by Barry Commoner. Reprinted by permission of Alfred A. Knopf, Inc.

P. 245, Anne Hollander, "Why It's Fashionable to Be Thin," from *Seeing Through Clothes,* by Anne Hollander. Copyright © 1975, 1976, 1978 by Anne L. Hollander. Reprinted by permission of Viking-Penguin, Inc.

P. 249, Sheila Tobias, "Who's Afraid of Math, and Why?" from *Overcoming Math*

Anxiety, by Sheila Tobias. Copyright © 1978 by Sheila Tobias. Reprinted by permission of W. W. Norton & Company, Inc.

P. 256, Sir Frederick Hoyle, "The Next Ice Age," from *World Press Review,* September 1981. Copyright © 1981 by Sir Fred Hoyle. Reprinted by permission of the author.

P. 270, Lewis Thomas, "Alchemy," from *Late Night Thoughts on Listening to Mahler's Ninth Symphony* by Lewis Thomas. Copyright © 1982 by Lewis Thomas. Reprinted by permission of Viking-Penguin, Inc.

P. 279, Thomas Sowell, "We're Not Really 'Equal,' " from *Newsweek,* September 7, 1981. Copyright © 1981 by Newsweek, Inc. All Rights Reserved. Reprinted by permission of the publisher and author.

P. 283, Bruno Bettelheim, "The Holocaust," from *Surviving and Other Essays,"* by Bruno Bettelheim. Copyright 1952, © 1960, 1962, 1969 by Bruno and Trude Bettelheim, as trustees. Reprinted by permission of Alfred A. Knopf, Inc.

P. 288, Karen Horney, "Fear and Anxiety," from the *Neurotic Personality of Our Time,* by Karen Horney, M.D. Copyright © 1937 by W. W. Norton & Company, Inc. Copyright renewed © 1964 by Renate Mintz, Brigitte Swarzenski, and Marianne von Eckardt. Reprinted by permission of W. W. Norton & Company, Inc.

P. 291, Peter Homans, "The Western: The Legend and the Cardboard Hero," from *Look* Magazine, March 13, 1962. Copyright © 1962 by Peter Homans. Reprinted by permission of the author.

P. 298, Ralph Ellison, "Hidden Name and Complex Fate," from *Shadow and Act,* by Ralph Ellison. Copyright © 1969 by Ralph Ellison. Reprinted by permission of Random House, Inc.

P. 310, Lewis Thomas, "Notes on Punctuation," from *Medusa and the Snail,* by Lewis Thomas. Copyright © 1979 by Lewis Thomas. Reprinted by permission of Viking-Penguin, Inc.

P. 313, Larry McMurtry, "Drinking in Houston," excerpted from "A Handful of Roses," in *In a Narrow Grave: Essays on Texas,* by Larry McMurtry, originally published by Encino Press. Copyright © 1968 by Larry McMurtry. Reprinted by permission of JCA Literary Agency Inc., as agents for the author.

P. 316, Susan Allen Toth, "Cinematypes," from *Harper's Magazine,* May 1980. Reprinted by permission of the author.

P. 321, Donald Hall, "Four Kinds of Reading," from *The New York Times,* January 26, 1969. Copyright ©1969 by The New York Times Company. Reprinted by permission.

P. 326, Sissela Bok, "The Need for Secrecy," from *Secrets: On the Ethics of Concealment and Revelation* by Sissela Bok. Copyright © 1982 by Sissela Bok. Reprinted by permission of Pantheon Books, a Division of Random House, Inc.

P. 339, Lewis Thomas, "Death in the Open," from *The Lives of a Cell,* by Lewis Thomas. Copyright © 1974 by Lewis Thomas. Reprinted by permission of Viking-Penguin, Inc.

P. 342, Ralph Linton, "One Hundred Per Cent American," from *The American Mercury* 40 (1937): 427–429.

P. 346, Roy Blount, Jr., "Winning: Why We Keep Score," from *The New York Times Magazine* (Sports Issue), September 29, 1985. Copyright © 1985 by The New York Times Company. Reprinted by permission.

P. 354, Joyce Maynard, "I Remember . . .," from *TV Guide*® *Magazine,* July 5, 1975. Copyright © 1975 by Joyce Maynard. Reprinted by permission of the author.

P. 360, Ruth Schwartz Cowan, "Less Work for Mother?" from *American Heritage of Science and Technology,* Spring 1987, pp. 57–63. Copyright © American Heritage, a division of Forbes Inc. Reprinted with permission of American Heritage of Invention and Technology, Spring 1987.

P. 382, Lewis Thomas, "The Tucson Zoo," from *The Medusa and the Snail,* by Lewis Thomas. Copyright © 1979 by Lewis Thomas. Reprinted by permission of Viking-Penguin, Inc.

P. 389, Tom Wolfe, "Columbus and the Moon," from *The New York Times,* July 20, 1979. Copyright © 1979 by The New York Times Company. Reprinted by permission of the publisher.

P. 394, Jack Newfield, "Stallone vs. Springsteen: Which Dream Do You Buy?" from *Playboy,* April 1986. Reprinted by permission of the author.

P. 404, Marie Winn, "Television and Reading," from *The Plug-in Drug: Television, Children, and the Family,* by Marie Winn. Copyright © 1977 by Marie Winn. Reprinted by permission of Viking-Penguin, Inc.

P. 412, John Mack Faragher, "Pioneer Diaries of Women and Men," from *Women and Men on the Overland Trail,* by John Mack Faragher. Copyright © 1979 by Yale University. Reprinted by permission of Yale University Press.

P. 419, Susan Sontag, "A Rhetoric of Disease," from *Illness as Metaphor,* pp. 5–17. Copyright © 1977, 1978 by Susan Sontag. Reprinted by permission of Farrar, Straus and Giroux, Inc.

P. 432, Lewis Thomas, "The Attic of the Brain," from *Late Night Thoughts on Listening to Mahler's Ninth Symphony,* by Lewis Thomas. Copyright © 1982 by Lewis Thomas. Reprinted by permission of Viking-Penguin, Inc.

P. 447, William Humphrey, "The Salmon Instinct," from *Farther Off from Heaven,* by William Humphrey. Copyright © 1976, 1977 by William Humphrey. Reprinted by permission of Delacorte Press.

P. 451, Michael Arlen, "Prufrock Aloft; Prufrock Before the Television Set," from *The Camera Age,* by Michael J. Arlen. Originally published in *The New Yorker.* Copyright © 1976, 1981 by Michael J. Arlen. Reprinted by permission of Farrar, Straus and Giroux, Inc.

P. 468, Lewis Thomas, "The Hazards of Science," from *The Medusa and the Snail,* by Lewis Thomas. Copyright © 1979 by Lewis Thomas. Reprinted by permission of Viking-Penguin, Inc.

P. 476, Jeffrey L. Pasley, "The Idiocy of Rural Life," from *The New Republic,* December 8, 1986. Copyright © 1986 by The New Republic, Inc. Reprinted by permission of *The New Republic.*

P. 485, Henry Fairlie, "The Idiocy of Urban Life," from *The New Republic,* January 5 and 12, 1987. Copyright © 1987 by The New Republic, Inc. Reprinted by permission of *The New Republic.*

P. 495, Adam Smith, "Fifty Million Handguns," from *Esquire,* April 1981. Copyright © 1981 by Adam Smith. Reprinted by permission of *Esquire.*

P. 503, Henry A. Selib, "The Case Against More Laws," from *The Boston Globe,* April 3, 1973. Reprinted by permission of the author.

P. 515, Lewis Thomas, "Late Night Thoughts on Listening to Mahler's Ninth Symphony," from *Late Night Thoughts on Listening to Mahler's Ninth Symphony,* by Lewis Thomas. Copyright © 1982 by Lewis Thomas. Reprinted by permission of Viking-Penguin, Inc.

P. 519, "Stop Handguns Before They Stop You" Advertisement courtesy of Handgun Control Inc. Reprinted by permission.

P. 519, "In the U.S., Crime Pays Because Criminals Don't!" Advertisement courtesy of National Rifle Association. Reprinted by permission.

P. 523, Mike Royko, "A Faceless Man's Plea," from *Chicago Daily News,* December 10, 1973. Reprinted by permission of the Chicago Sun-Times, Inc., 1987.

P. 527, H. L. Mencken, "Why Nobody Loves a Politician," from *Liberty Magazine.* Copyright © 1934 Liberty Publishing Corp. Reprinted by permission of Liberty Library Corporation.

P. 534, Barry Lopez, "The Passing Wisdom of Birds," from *Orion Nature Quarterly,* Autumn 1985. Copyright © Barry Lopez. Reprinted by permission of Sterling Lord Literistic, Inc.

P. 546, Adrienne Rich, "Claiming an Education," from *On Lies, Secrets, and Silence, Selected Prose 1966–1978,* by Adrienne Rich. First published in *the common woman,* vol. 1, no. 2 (Autumn 1977). Copyright © 1979 by W. W. Norton & Company, Inc. Reprinted by permission of W. W. Norton & Company, Inc.

About the Editors

Donald McQuade is Professor of English and Chancellor's Fellow at the University of California, Berkeley, where he coordinates the Writing Program as well as teaches American literature and American Studies. He is the former Director of the Writing Program at Queens College in the City University of New York, where he also served as Director of the American Studies Program. He has written, edited, and co-edited many essays and books on composition, including *Popular Writing in America, The Territory of Language: Linguistics, Stylistics, and the Teaching of Composition,* and *Student Writers at Work.* He has been elected to the Executive Committee of the Conference on College Composition and Communication as well as to the Council of Writing Program Administrators. Professor McQuade has also published extensively on American literature and culture. He serves as both the general and a contributing editor to *The Harper American Literature* and as general editor of the Modern Library College Editions series, for which he has prepared an edition of the writings of Ralph Waldo Emerson. He recently served as the guest curator of an exhibition entitled "Advertising America" at the Smithsonian Institution's Cooper-Hewitt Museum in New York.

Robert Atwan has coedited many college books, including *Popular Writing in America, The Harper American Literature, Why We Write, Writing Day by Day,*

One Hundred Major Modern Writers, Effective Writing for the College Curriculum, and *American Mass Media: Industries & Issues.* He has also prepared the *Random House Diagnostic Tests of English Composition.* His essays and reviews on fiction, poetry, psychology, and the popular arts have appeared in *The New York Times, The Los Angeles Times, The National Review, The Atlantic Monthly,* and professional literary and psychiatric journals. He has served as a consultant to educational television, several national testing programs, the Library of America, and the National Endowment for the Humanities. He is the series editor of the annual *Best American Essays* and teaches a writing workshop at Seton Hall University.

A Note on the Type

The text of this book was set by means of modern photocomposition in a text type called PALATINO. PALATINO is a contemporary creation of the German type designer Hermann Zapf. PALATINO is distinguished by broad letters and vigorous, inclined serifs typical of the work of a sixteenth-century Italian master of writing and reflects the early Venetian scripts influencing Zapf's creations.

This book was composed by ComCom, a division of Haddon Craftsmen. It was printed and bound by R. R. Donnelley & Sons Company in Harrisonburg, Va.

OBSERVING AMERICA

The following paintings, photographs, and advertisement explore the changing conception of American experience from the Civil War to the present. What insights does each offer into aspects of America's social, economic, political, and cultural history?

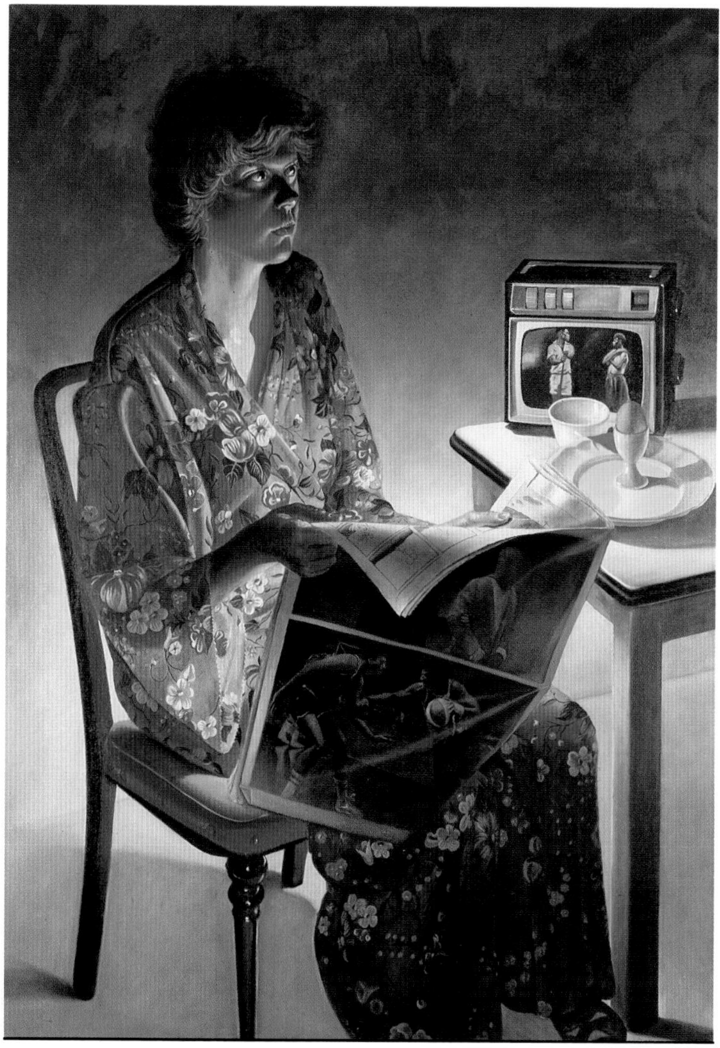

Alfred Leslie, "7 A.M. News," 1976–1978. Oil on canvas, 84 × 60 inches. *(Courtesy Allan Frumkin Gallery, New York; photo by eeva-inkeri.)*

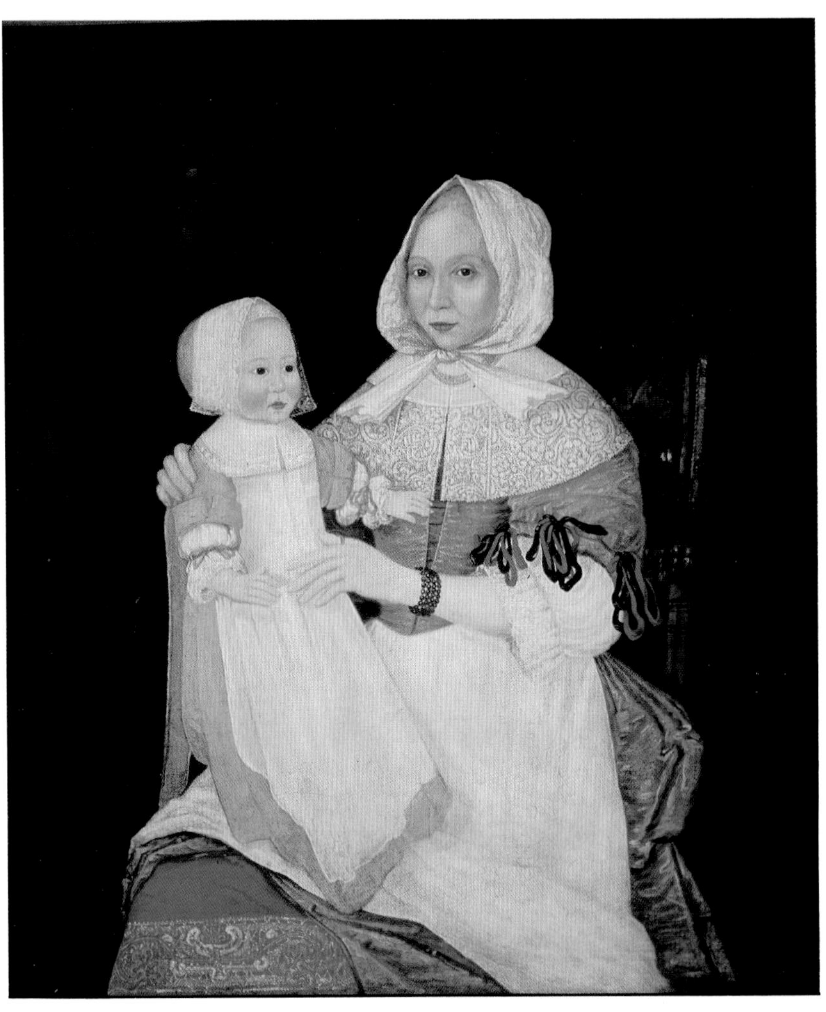

Unknown American artist, "Mrs. Elizabeth Freake and Baby Mary," ca. 1671–1674. Oil on canvas, 42½ × 36¾ inches. *(Worcester Art Museum, Worcester, Massachusetts, 1963.134, gift of Mr. and Mrs. Albert W. Rice.)*

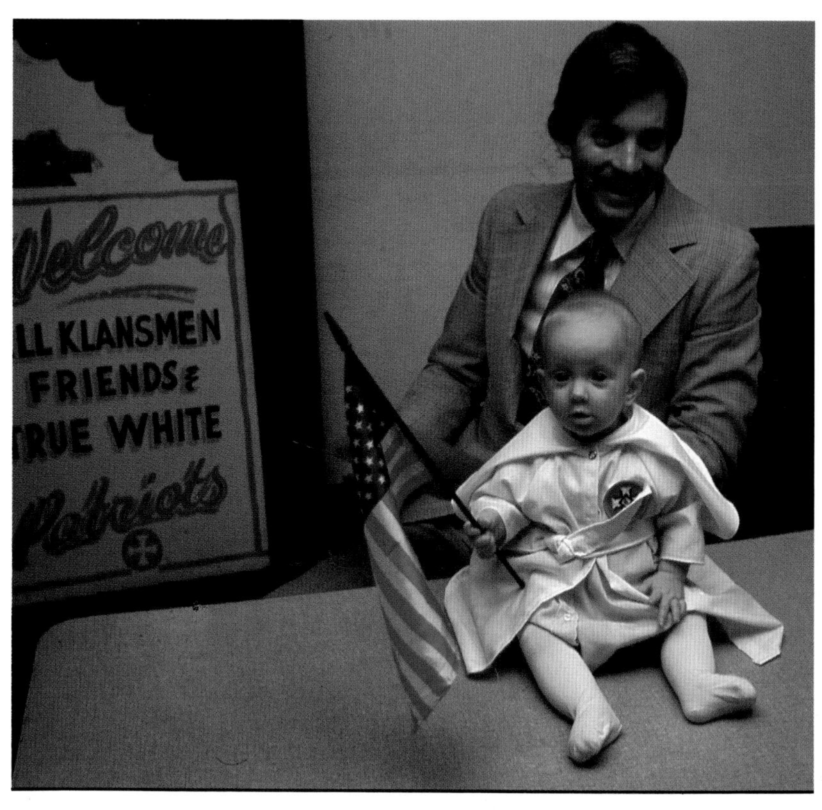

Ku Klux Klansman with child. *(Elliott Erwitt/Magnum.)*

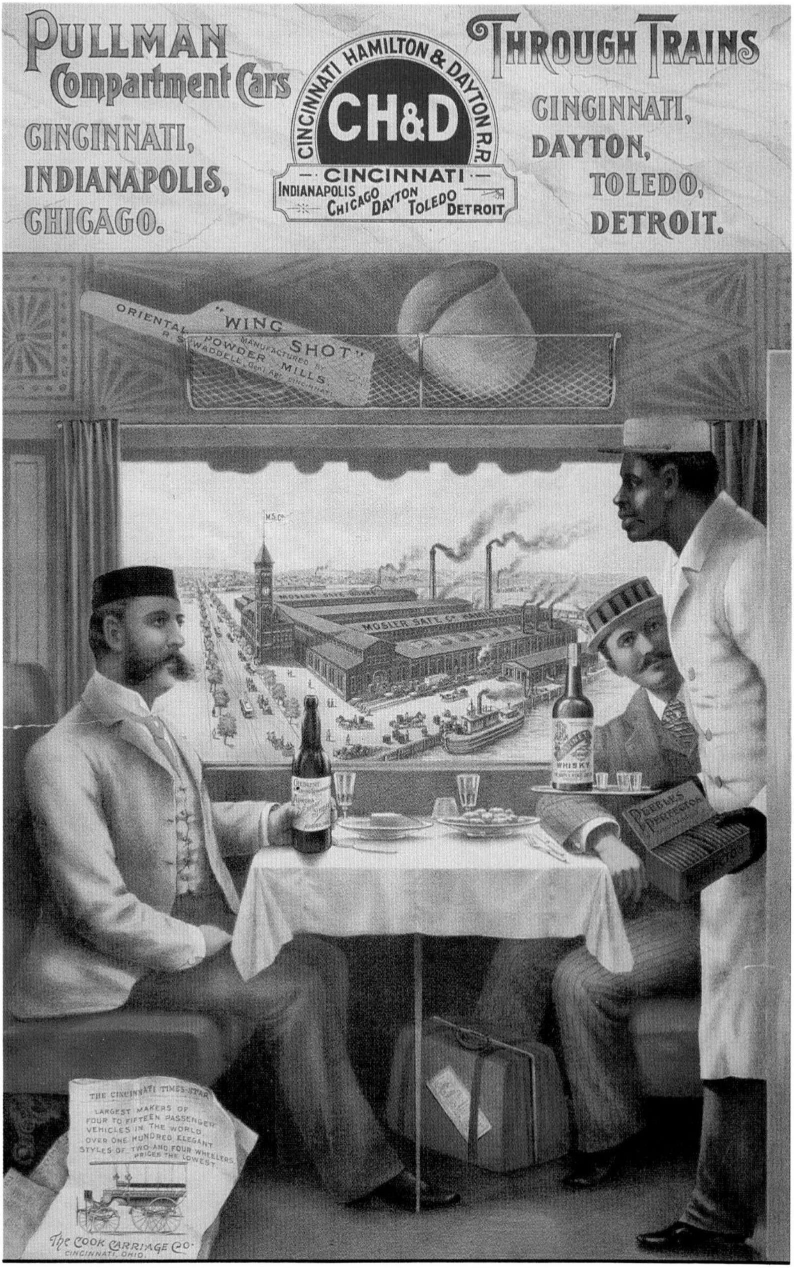

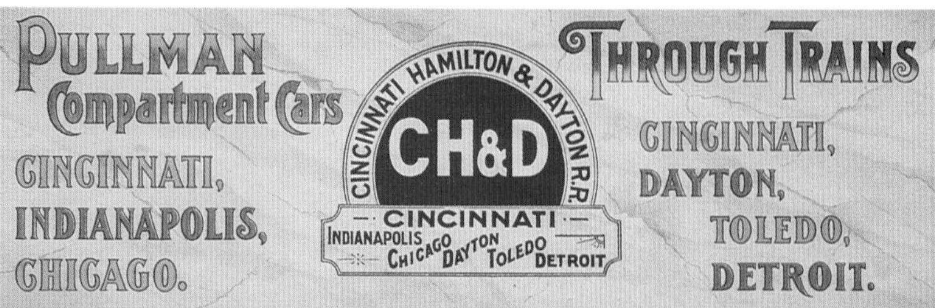

PULLMAN
Compartment Cars
CINCINNATI,
INDIANAPOLIS,
CHICAGO.
CINCINNATI HAMILTON & DAYTON R.R.
CH&D
CINCINNATI
INDIANAPOLIS CHICAGO DAYTON TOLEDO DETROIT
THROUGH TRAINS
CINCINNATI,
DAYTON,
TOLEDO,
DETROIT.
"WING SHOT"
ORIENTAL POWDER MILLS
MOSLER SAFE CO. HAMILTON
WHISKY
THE CINCINNATI TIMES-STAR
LARGEST MAKERS OF
FOUR TO FIFTEEN PASSENGER
VEHICLES IN THE WORLD.
OVER ONE HUNDRED ELEGANT
STYLES OF TWO AND FOUR WHEELERS.
PRICES THE LOWEST.
The COOK CARRIAGE CO.
CINCINNATI, OHIO.

Grant Wood, "Stone City, Iowa," 1930. Oil on composition board, 30¼ × 40 inches. *(Joslyn Art Museum, Omaha, Nebraska.)*

Cincinnati Hamilton & Dayton R.R. Pullman Compartment Cars—Interior Dining Car. Bella C. Landauer Collection Poster. *(Courtesy of The New-York Historical Society.)*

Amish buggy, Ohio. *(Eric Albrecht, Gahanna, Ohio.)*

Hostage parade, New York. *(Jake Rajs/The Image Bank.)*

Edward Hopper, "Nighthawks," 1942. Oil on canvas, 30 × 56½ inches. *(Courtesy of The Art Institute of Chicago, Friends of American Art Collection, 1942.51.)*

Richard Estes, "Central Savings," 1975. Oil on canvas, 36 × 48 inches. (*The Nelson-Atkins Museum of Art, Kansas City, Missouri, gift of the Friends of Art.*)